THE MYTH OF

ISLAMIC TOLERANCE

HOW ISLAMIC LAW TREATS NON-MUSLIMS

THE MYTH OF
ISLAMIC
TOLERANCE

HOW ISLAMIC LAW
TREATS NON-MUSLIMS

EDITED BY ROBERT SPENCER

Prometheus Books

59 John Glenn Drive
Amherst, New York 14228-2197

Published 2005 by Prometheus Books

Inquiries should be addressed to
Prometheus Books
59 John Glenn Drive
Amherst, New York 14228–2197
VOICE: 716–691–0133, ext. 207
FAX: 716–564–2711
WWW.PROMETHEUSBOOKS.COM

09 08 07 06 05   5 4 3 2

Library of Congress Cataloging-in-Publication Data

The myth of Islamic tolerance : how Islamic law treats non-Muslims / edited by Robert Spencer.
    p. cm.
  Includes bibliographical references.
  ISBN 1–59102–249–5 (hardcover : alk. paper)
  1. Dhimmis. 2. Religious minorities—Legal status, laws, etc.—Islamic countries.
I. Spencer, Robert, 1962–

KBP2449.M98 2004
297.2'8—dc22

                                                            2004016022

Printed in the United States of America on acid-free paper

CONTENTS

FOREWORD
THE GENESIS OF A MYTH

Ibn Warraq

ISLAM AND MINORITIES

I slam is a totalitarian ideology that aims to control the religious, social, and political life of mankind in all its aspects; the life of its followers without qualification; and the life of those who follow the so-called tolerated religions to a degree that prevents their activities from getting in the way of Islam in any way. And I mean Islam, I do not accept some spurious distinction between Islam and "Islamic fundamentalism" or "Islamic terrorism." The terrorists who planted bombs in Madrid; those responsible for the deaths of more than two thousand people on September 11, 2001, in New York and Washington, DC; and the ayatollahs of Iran were and are all acting canonically; their actions reflect the teachings of Islam, whether found in the Qur'an, in the acts and sayings of the Prophet, or Islamic law based on them.

Islamic law, the Sharia, is the total collection of theoretical laws that apply in an ideal Muslim community, one that has surrendered to the will of God. It is based, according to Muslims, on divine authority that must be accepted without criticism, without doubts and questions. It is an all-embracing system of duties to God, and it controls the entire life of the believer and the Islamic community. Islamic law intrudes into every nook and cranny of the life of an individual, who is not free to think for himself.

Given the totalitarian nature of Islamic law, Islam does not value the individual, who has to be sacrificed for the sake of the Islamic community. Collectivity has a special sanctity under Islam. Under these conditions, minorities are not tolerated. Expressing one's opinion or changing one's religion—the act of apostasy—is punishable by death.

Under Muslim law, the male apostate must be put to death, as long as he is an adult and in full possession of his faculties. If a pubescent boy apostatizes, he is imprisoned until he comes of age, when, if he persists in rejecting Islam, he must be put to death. Drunkards and the mentally disturbed are not held responsible for their apostasy. If a person has acted under compulsion he is not considered an apostate, his wife is not divorced, and his lands are not forfeited. According to Hanafis and Shia, a woman is imprisoned until she repents and adopts Islam once more, but according to the influential Ibn Hanbal, and the Malikis and Shafiites, she is also put to death. In general, execution must be by the sword, though there are examples of apostates tortured to death, strangled, burned, drowned, impaled, or flayed. The caliph Umar used to tie them to a post and had lances thrust into their hearts, and the Sultan Baybars II (1308–1309) made torture legal.

And the absence of any mention of apostasy in the penal codes of some contemporary Islamic countries in no way implies that a Muslim is free to leave his religion. In reality, the lacunae in the penal codes are filled by Islamic law, as in the case of Muhammad Taha, executed for apostasy in the Sudan in 1985, and hundreds of others have been executed for apostasy in Iran in recent years: for example, in 1998 Ruhollah Rowhani, fifty-two years old, was hanged for converting to the Bahai faith.

All Islamic human rights schemes, such as the 1981 Universal Islamic Declaration of Human Rights, the Cairo Declaration of Human Rights in Islam, and so on, severely restrict and qualify the rights of women as well as minorities such as non-Muslims and apostates, unbelievers, and heretics, who do not accept Islamic religious orthodoxy.

As for religious minorities, the relations of Muslims and non-Muslims are set in a context of a war: jihad. The totalitarian nature of Islam is nowhere more apparent than in the concept of jihad, the holy war, whose ultimate aim is to conquer the entire world and submit it to the one true faith, to the law of Allah. To Islam alone has been granted the truth—there is no possibility of salvation outside it. It is the sacred duty—an incumbent religious duty established in the Qur'an and the Traditions—of all Muslims to bring it to all humanity. Jihad is a divine institution, enjoined specially for the purpose of advancing Islam. Muslims must strive, fight, and kill in the name of God:

Q. 9.5–6: "Kill those who join other gods with God wherever you may find them."

Q. 4.76: "Those who believe fight in the cause of God."

Q. 8.12: "I will instill terror into the hearts of the Infidels, strike off their heads then, and strike off from them every fingertip."

Mankind is divided into two groups: Muslims and non-Muslims. The Muslims are members of the Islamic community, the *umma*, who possess territories in the *dar al-Islam*, the Land of Islam, where the edicts of Islam are fully promulgated. The non-Muslims are the *Harbi*, people of the *dar al-Harb*, the Land of Warfare—any country belonging to the infidels that has not been subdued by Islam but that, nonetheless, is destined to pass into Islamic jurisdiction either by conversion or by war (*jarb*). All acts of war are permitted in the *dar al-Harb*. Once the *dar al-Harb* has been subjugated, the *Harbi* become prisoners of war. The imam can do what he likes to them, depending on the circumstances.

In other cases, they are sold into slavery, exiled, or treated as dhimmis, who are tolerated as second-class subjects as long as they pay the *kharaj*, a kind of land tax, and the *jizya*, the poll tax, which has to be paid individually at a humiliating public ceremony to remind the non-Muslim minorities that they are inferior to the believers, the Muslims. In all litigation between a Muslim and a dhimmi, the validity of the oath or testimony of the dhimmi is not recognized. In other words, since a dhimmi is not allowed to give evidence against a Muslim, his Muslim opponent always gets off scot-free. No Muslim can be executed for having committed any crime against a dhimmi. Accusations of blasphemy against dhimmis are quite frequent, and the penalty is capital punishment. A non-Muslim man may not marry a Muslim woman. I should emphasize that all these principles are not merely of historical interest but are indeed still applied against non-Muslims in modern Iran, Pakistan, and Saudi Arabia, to name but a few countries.

Muslims are certain that Islam is not only the whole of God's truth, but also its final expression. Hence Muslims fear and persecute such post-Islamic religious movements as the Bahais and the Ahmadis. Here is Amnesty International on the plight of the Ahmadis: "Ahmadis consider themselves to be Muslims but they are regarded by orthodox Muslims as heretical because they call the founder of their movement al-Masih [the Messiah]: this is taken to imply that Muhammad is not the final seal of the prophets as orthodox Islam holds, i.e., the Prophet who carried the final message from God to humanity. . . . As a result of these divergences, Ahmadis have been subjected to discrimination and persecution in some Islamic countries. In the mid-1970s, the Saudi Arabia based World Muslim League called on Muslim governments worldwide to take action against Ahmadis. Ahmadis are since then banned in Saudi Arabia."[1]

But what of putative Islamic tolerance? Those apologists who continue to perpetuate the myth of Islamic tolerance should contemplate the massacre and extermination of the Zoroastrians in Iran; the million Armenians in Turkey; the Buddhists and Hindus in India; the more than six thousand Jews in Fez, Morocco, in 1033; hundreds of Jews killed in Cordoba between 1010 and 1013; the entire Jewish community of four thousand in Granada in 1066; the Jews in Marrakesh in 1232; the Jews of Tetuan, Morocco in 1790; the Jews of Baghdad in 1828; and so on ad nauseam.

THE GENESIS OF A MYTH

But how did the myth of Islamic tolerance arise?

The uncritical attitude toward Islam and the genesis of the myth of Islamic tolerance must be seen against the more general intellectual background of Europe's first encounter with non-European civilizations, especially in the sixteenth century—the age of exploration—when the notion of the "noble savage" was first fully developed. Of course, well before the discovery of the Americas, the Greeks and the Romans had had the corresponding myth of a golden age and the virtues of the barbarians. Even the expulsion of Adam and Eve from the Garden of Eden is but a variation of the idea of a golden age of simplicity and natural virtue that our ancestors putatively enjoyed in an unspoiled, ecologically sound wilderness.

In his *Germania*, written in 98 CE, Roman historian Tacitus contrasts the virtues of the Germans with the vices of contemporary Rome, the noble simplicity with the corruption and pretentiousness of Roman civilization. Significantly, as an "ethnological treatise it was singularly incoherent,"[2] but it worked well as a morality tale. Michel de Montaigne, Jean-Jacques Rousseau, and Edward Gibbon were all influenced by it.

Perhaps the real founder of the sixteenth-century doctrine of the noble savage was Peter Martyr Anglerius (1459–1525), contrasting the Spaniards with the Indians, whom he considered to be happier, being free of the anxieties of contemporary Spaniards.[3]

But it was left to Montaigne (1533–1592), under the influence of Peter Martyr, to develop the first full-length portrait of the noble savage in his celebrated essay "On Cannibals" (c. 1580), which is also the source of the idea of cultural relativism. Deriving his rather shaky information from a plain, simple fellow, Montaigne describes some of the more gruesome customs of the Brazilian Indians and concludes: "I am not so anxious that we should note the horrible savagery of these acts as concerned that, whilst judging their faults so correctly, we should be so blind to our own. I consider it more barbarous to eat a man alive than to eat him dead; to tear by rack and torture a body still full of feeling, to roast it by degrees, and then give it to be trampled and eaten by dogs and swine—a practice which we have not only read about but seen within recent memory, not between ancient enemies, but between neighbours and fellow-citizens and, what is worse, under the cloak of piety and religion—than to roast and eat a man after he is dead."[4]

Elsewhere in the essay, Montaigne emphazises their inevitable simplicity, state of purity, and freedom from corruption. Even their "fighting is entirely noble." Like Tacitus and Peter Martyr, Montaigne's rather dubious secondhand knowledge of these noble savages does not prevent him from criticizing and morally condemning his own culture and civilization: "[We] surpass them in every kind of barbarity."[5]

The sevententh century saw the first truly sympathetic accounts of Islam, but the most influential of these, those of Pierre Jurieu and Pierre Bayle, served the same purpose as those of Tacitus, Peter Martyr, and Montaigne. Let us hear Jurieu:

> It may be truly said that there is no comparison between the cruelty of the Saracens against the Christians, and that of Popery against the true believers. In the war against the Vaudois, or in the massacres alone on St. Bartholomew's Day, there was more blood spilt upon account of religion, than was spilt by the Saracens in all their persecutions of the Christians. It is expedient to cure men of this prejudice; that Mahometanism is cruel sect [*sic*], which was propagated by putting men to their choice of death, or the abjuration of Christianity. This is in no wise true; and the conduct of the Saracens was an evangelical meekness in comparison to that of Popery, which exceeded the cruelty of the cannibals.[6]

The whole import of Jurieu's *Lettres Pastorales* (1686–89) only becomes clear when we realize that Jurieu was a Huguenot pastor, the sworn enemy of Bossuet, and he was writing from Holland after the Revocation of the Edict of Nantes. He is using the apparent tolerance of the Muslims to criticise Roman Catholicism—for him the Saracen's "evangelical meekness" is a way of contrasting Catholicism's own barbarity as on St. Bartholomew's Day.

Bayle (1647–1706) was much influenced by Jurieu and continued the myth of Islamic tolerance, which persists to this day. He contrasts the tolerance of the Turks to the persecutions of Brahmans in India by the Portuguese, and the barbarities exercised by the Spaniards in America. "[The Muslims] have always had more humanity for other religions than the Christians."[7]

Bayle was a champion of toleration—was he not himself the victim of intolerance and forced to flee to Holland?

For Jurieu and Bayle in the seventeenth century, *Turk* was synonymous with *Muslim*; thus Turkish tolerance turned into Muslim tolerance in general. Between them, they showed no knowledge whatsoever of the early persecutions of Christians and Jews, the massacres of Hindus and Buddhists in the early conquest of the Indian province of Sind, the intolerance of the Almohads, and the persecution of the Zoroastrians, especially in the province of Khurasan. Even in their beloved Turkey, they seem unaware of the slaughter of Christians in the fall of Constantinople, when the streets literally ran with blood—there was not much evangelical meekness in evidence then. Nor do they refer to the inhumane system of the Devshirme in operation in contemporary Turkey. Many religious minorities sought and found refuge in Turkey to escape Catholic or Orthodox persecution: Jewish refugees from Spain after their expulsion in 1492 and 1496, known as the Marranos; Calvinists of Hungary; and others from Russia and Silesia. But they were there on sufferance, tolerated as second-class citizens. It was quite illegitimate of Jurieu and Bayle to talk of Muslim tolerance in general on the basis of their scanty knowledge of Islamic history, since the situation varied enormously from century to century, country to country, ruler to ruler. One thing is certain—there never was an interfaith utopia.

Even in seventeenth-century Turkey, so admired by Bayle and Jurieu, the situation was far from rosy. Here is how the English ambassador at Constantinople described the scene in 1662:

> This present Vizier degenerates nothing from the tyranie, & severitie of his father, but rather exceeds him in a naturall abhorrencie of Christians & their religion. For those churches, that were 2 yeares past burnt down in Galata & Const:ple, the ground was purchased at a deare rate from the Grand Sig:r by the Greekes, Armenians, & Romanists; but not with licence to build in the forme of Churches; or therein use any more rites, or services of religion. But these religions being too forward in their zeale, not only reedifyed them in the fashion of Churches, but resorted theither publickly to their divine service; wch the vizier hath made use of, as a wellcome opportunitie to demolish, & levell their Churches with the ground, wch hee doth with much passion, & malice, & comitted those who had the chiefe hand in the building to a severe imprisonment, excepting only my chiefe Druggerman, or interpreter who yet escapes free from any molestation by that security hee enioyes under my protection.[8]

Here is how scholar Bat Ye'or sums up the situation in the "tolerant" Turkish empire: "For strategic reasons the Turks forced the populations of the frontier region of Macedonia and the north of Bulgaria to convert, notably in the XVI and XVII centuries. Those who refused were executed or burnt alive."[9]

Letters Written by a Turkish Spy, published at the end of the seventeenth century, inaugurated the eighteenth-century vogue for the pseudo-foreign letter, such as Montesquieu's *Lettres Persanes* (1721), Madame de Grafigny's *Lettres d'une Peruvienne* (c. 1747), D' Argens' *Lettres Chinoises* (1750), Voltaire's Asiatic in the *Philosophical Dictionary* (1752), Horace Walpole's *Letter from Xo Ho*, a Chinese philosopher in London, to his friend Lien-Chi, at Peking (1757), and Oliver Goldsmith's *Citizen of the World* (1762), in which Lien Chi Altangi passes philosophical and satirical comments on the manners of the English.

Thus, by the eighteenth century, the noble savage was simply a device to criticize and comment on the follies of one's own civilization. The noble savage is no longer the simpleton from the jungle but a sophisticated and superior observer of the contemporary scene in Europe. By emphasising the corruption, vice, and degradation of the Europeans, eighteenth-century writers exaggerated the putative superiority of the alien culture, the wisdom of the Chinese or Persian or Peruvian moralist and commentator. They were not really interested in other cultures for their own sake; in fact, they had very little knowledge of these civilizations.

Against this intellectual background, we can understand why the eighteenth century so readily adopted the myth of Muhammad as a wise and tolerant ruler and lawgiver, when it was presented to them by Count Henri de Boulainvilliers (1658–1722). Boulainvilliers' apologetic biography of Muhammad appeared posthumously in London in 1730. It is impossible to exaggerate the importance of this book in shaping Europe's view of Islam and its founder, Muhammad; it certainly much influenced Voltaire and Gibbon. Boulainvilliers had no knowledge of Arabic and had to rely on secondary sources; thus his work is by no means a work of serious scholarship— on the contrary it contains many errors and "much embroidery."[10] Nonetheless, Boulainvilliers was able to use Muhammad and the origins of Islam as "a vehicle of his own theological prejudices" and as a weapon against Christianity in general and the clergy in particular. He found Islam reasonable; it did not require one to believe in impossibilities—no mysteries, no miracles. Muhammad, though not divine, was an incomparable statesman and a greater legislator than any one produced by ancient Greece. Jeffery has rightly called this work "a bombastic laudation of Mohammad in the interests of belittling Christianity. Hurgronje calls it 'an anti-clerical romance, the material of which was supplied by a superficial knowledge of Islamdrawn from secondary sources.' A little of the tar from Boulainvilliers' brush can be detected in Gibbon's. . . . *Decline and Fall*."[11]

George Sale's translation of the Qur'an (1734) is the first accurate one in English. Like Boulainvilliers, whose biography of Muhammad he had carefully read, Sale firmly believed that the Arabs "seem to have been raised up on purpose by God, to be a scourge to the Christian church, for not living answerably to that most holy religion which they had received."[12]

The attitude of Voltaire can be seen as typical of the entire century. Voltaire seems to have regretted what he had written of Muhammad in his scurrilous, and to a Muslim blasphemous, play *Mahomet* (1742), where the Prophet is presented as an impostor who enslaved men's souls: "Assuredly, I have made him out to be more evil than he was."[13] But his *Essai sur les Moeurs* (1756) and various entries in the *Philosophical Dictionary* show him to be prejudiced in Islam's favor at the expense of Christianity in general, and Catholicism in particular. Like Boulainvilliers and Sale, both of whom he had read, Voltaire uses Islam as a pretext to attack Christianity, which for him remained the "most ridiculous, the most absurd, and bloody religion that has ever infected the world."[14] Like many eighteenth-century intellectuals, Voltaire was a deist, that is to say, "he believed in the existence of God while opposing revealed religion—miracles, dogmas, and any kind of priesthood."[15]

In his *Sermon of the Fifty* (1762), Voltaire "attacks Christian mysteries like transubstantiation as absurd; Christian miracles as incredible; the Bible as full of contradictions." The God of Christianity was a cruel and hateful tyrant. "The true God, the sermon continues, 'surely cannot have been born of a girl, nor died on the gibbet, nor be eaten in a piece of dough.' Nor could he have inspired 'books, filled with contradictions, madness, and horror.'"[16]

By contrast, Voltaire finds the dogmas of Islam simplicity itself: there is but one God, and Muhammad is his Prophet. For all deists, the superficial rationality of Islam was appealing: no priests, no miracles, no mysteries. To this was added other false beliefs such as the absolute tolerance of Islam of other religions, in contrast to Christian intolerance.

Gibbon was much influenced by Boulainvilliers in particular but also by the eighteenth-century weltanschauung with its myths and preoccupations— in short, what we have been examining throughout this chapter. By the time Gibbon came around to writing his *History of the Decline and Fall of the*

Roman Empire (the first volume came out in 1776), there was, as Bernard Lewis puts it, "a vacancy for an Oriental myth." But what happened to the Chinese mentioned earlier? Here is how Lewis sums up the situation in the latter half of the eighteenth century:

> Europe has always needed a myth for purposes of comparison and castiga- tion. . . . The eighteenth-century Enlightenment had two ideal prototypes, the noble savage and the wise and urbane Oriental. There was some com- petition for the latter role. For a while the Chinese, held up as a model of moral virtue by the Jesuits and of secular tolerance by the philosophers, filled it to perfection in the Western intellectual shadowplay. Then disillu- sionment set in, and was worsened by the reports of returning travellers whose perceptions of China were shaped by neither Jesuitry nor philosophy, but by experience. By the time Gibbon began to write, there was a vacancy for an Oriental myth. Islam was in many ways suitable.[17]

What Lewis tells us about Gibbon is applicable to almost all the writers on Islam in the seventeenth and eighteenth centuries: "[Gibbon's] own imperfect knowledge and the defective state of European scholarship at the time hampered his work and sometimes blunted the skepticism which he usually brought to the sources and subjects of his historical inquiries. . . . The Muslim religious myths enshrined in the traditional biographical litera- ture on which all his sources ultimately rest were more difficult for him to detect, and there are failures of perception and analysis excusable in a his- torian of the time."[18]

Gibbon, like Voltaire, painted Islam in as favorable a light as possible in order to better contrast it with Christianity. He emphazised Muhammad's humanity as a means of indirectly criticizing the Christian doctrine of the divinity of Christ. His anticlericalism led Gibbon to underline Islam's sup- posed freedom from that accursed class, the priesthood. Indeed, the familiar pattern is reemerging—Islam used as a weapon against Christianity.

Gibbon's deistic view of Islam as a rational, priest-free religion, with Muhammad as a wise and tolerant lawgiver, enormously influenced the way all Europeans perceived a sister religion for years to come. Indeed, it established myths that are still accepted totally uncritically by scholars and laymen alike.

Both Voltaire and Gibbon subscribed to the myth of Muslim tolerance, which to them meant Turkish tolerance. But eighteenth-century Turkey was also far from being a land of interfaith utopia. Jews were treated contemptu- ously, recalled the traveler Carsten Niebuhr. And here is how another British ambassador describes the situation in Constantinople in 1758:

[T]he Grand Seignor [Sultan Mustafa III] himself affords us he is deter-
min'd to keep his laws, and to have them executed, that concerning dress
has been repeated and with uncommon solemnity. . . . [A] Jew on his sabbath was the first victim, the Grand Seignor going the rounds incognito, met
him, and not having the Executioner with him, without sending him [the
Jew] to the Vizir, had him executed, and his throat cut that moment, the day
after an Armenian follow'd, he was sent to the Vizir, who attempted to save
him, and condemn'd him to the Galleys, but the Capigilar Cheaia [head of
the guards] came to the Porte at night, attended with the executioner, to
know what was become of the delinquent, that first Minister had him
brought directly from the Galleys and his head struck off, that he might
inform his Master he had anticipated his Orders. A general terror has struck
all the people.[19]

Another ambassador in 1770, in Constantinople, writes that a law was
passed whereby any Greeks, Armenians, and Jews seen outside their homes
after nightfall were to be hanged without exception. A third ambassador,
writing in 1785, describes how any Christian churches secretly repaired by
the Christians were dismantled by the Turkish authorities because of protests
by Muslim mobs.[20]

Thomas Carlyle's account of Muhammad in his *On Heroes, Hero-wor-
ship, and the Heroic in History* (1841) is often considered the first truly sympathetic portrait by a Western intellectual. According to Prof. W. Montgomery Watt, Carlyle "laughed out of court the idea of an impostor being the
founder of one of the world's great religions."[21] Laughter is no substitute for
argument, and valid arguments are singularly lacking in Carlyle's essay.
Instead, we are presented "violent exclamatory rhetoric,"[22] wild mumblings
about "mysteries of nature." What "arguments" there are are fallacious.
Muhammad cannot have been an impostor. Why not? It is inconceivable that
so many people could have been taken in by a mere trickster and insincere
fraud. His genuineness lies in the success of his religion. Truth by numbers.
Carlyle parades the total number of Muslims, which he takes to be 180 million, in front of our eyes in order to impress us and falsely imply that
Muhammad cannot have persuaded so many of a false religion. But
Muhammad only persuaded a few thousand—the rest have simply followed
and copied one another; a large number of Muslims blindly follow the religion of their fathers, as something given. It is absurd to suggest that the vast
majority have examined the arguments for and against the sincerity of
Muhammad.

Second, to assess the truth of a doctrine by the number of people who believe it is also totally ridiculous. The number of people who believe in Scientology is increasing yearly; is its truth also growing year by year? There are more Christians worldwide than Muslims; is Christianity more true? When a book titled *100 Authors against Einstein* was published, Einstein remarked, "If I were wrong, then one would have been enough!" The converse is also true.

"But at least an insincere man could not have been so successful; leaving aside the truth of what he preached." Again, an obviously fallacious argument. How do we know Muhammad was sincere? "Because otherwise he would not have been so successful." Why was he so successful? Because he was sincere? A patently circular argument! It is said that L. Ron Hubbard bet Arthur C. Clarke that he could start a new religion and went out and founded the religion of Scientology. It is especially difficult to know how much of their own mumbo jumbo charlatans believe—televangelists, mediums, gurus, the Rev. Sun Myung Moon, the founders of religions, cults, and movements—there is a bit of Elmer Gantry in all of them.

Like his predecessors, Carlyle had a superficial knowledge of Islam—we can safely say that as a piece of scholarship, his essay on Muhammad is totally worthless—but, unlike them, he used Islam as a weapon against materialism and Benthamite utilitarianism. Deeply perturbed by the mechanical world that was emerging due to the Industrial Revolution, he had to resort to the comforting myth of the wisdom of the East. Like Gustave Flaubert's Bouvard, he longed for and expected regeneration from the Orient, which would wake the West from its spiritual paralysis. Carlyle adumbrated certain ideas that were to reappear throughout the nineteenth and twentieth century. First, Carlyle saw Islam as a confused form of Christianity, a bastard kind of Christianity, shorn of its absurd details. Whereas Dante and his contemporaries had seen Islam as a Christian heresy, and as something inferior, Carlyle saw it more positively: "Mahomet's Creed we called a kind of Christianity; . . . I should say a better kind than that of those miserable Syrian Sects, with their vain janglings about Homoiousion and Homoousion, the head full of worthless noise, the heart empty and dead!"[23]

As to Carlyle's actual portrait of Muhammad, it is but a reformulation of the noble savage but in a relgious garb, as someone in direct touch with the mysteries of existence, life, and nature; full of mystical intuition of the real nature of things denied to us in the skeptical, civilized West. "A spontaneous, passionate, yet just, true-meaning man! Full of wild faculty, fire and light: of wild worth, all uncultured; working out his life-task in the depths of the Desert there. . . . The word of such a man is a Voice direct from Nature's own heart." Elsewhere, Muhammad is descibed as "an uncultured semi-barbarous Son of Nature, much of the Bedouin still clinging to him."[24] The Arabs in general are seen as active but also meditative, with wild strong feelings, and they possess that supreme quality, "religiosity." Their religion is heartily believed. What is most important is sincerity, not truth—it hardly matters what is believed as long as it is believed with a fierceness that goes beyond mere reason. "The very falsehoods of Mahomet are truer than the truths of [of an insincere man]."[25]

Bertrand Russell and others have seen in Carlyle's ideas the intellectual ancestry of fascism. Carlyle's fascism can be seen in his uncritical adulation of the strong leader but also in his sentimental glorification of violence, cruelty, extremism, and irrationalism in his contempt for reason. "A candid ferocity . . . is in him; he does not mince matters."[26] It is astonishing that anyone took any of Carlyle's drivel seriously. But it is equally sad that Muslims peddle this nonsense as a separate pamphlet as a kind of seal of approval to show that a European takes their Prophet seriously. It is also surprising, since a careful reading of the chapter shows Muhammad in a less-than-flattering light: he is not always sincere, his moral precepts are not of the superfinest, he is by no means the truest of prophets, and so on. Above all, this chapter contains the famous insult to the Qur'an: "A wearisome confused jumble, crude, incondite; endless iterations, longwindedness, entanglement; most crude incondite;—insupportable stupidity, in short! Nothing but a sense of duty could carry any European through the Qur'an."[27] Or us through Carlyle!

Many of the European apologists of Islam of the seventeenth and eighteenth century had no proper acquaintance with the Arabic sources; most had only a superficial knowledge. They used Islam as a weapon against intolerance, cruelty, dogma, clergy, and Christianity.

Many European apologists of Islam of the nineteenth and twentieth centuries had a far greater knowledge of Islam and were, by contrast, devout Christians—priests, missionaries, and curates, who realized that, to be consistent, they had to accord Islam a large measure of religious equality, to concede Muhammad religious insight. They realized that Islam was a sister relgion, heavily influenced by Judeo-Christian ideas, and that Christianity and Islam stood or fell together; they knew that if they started criticizing the dogmas, doctrines, and absurdities of Islam, their own fantastic structure would start to crumble and eventually crash around them. They perceived a common danger in certain economic, philosophical, and social developments in the West—the rise of rationalism, skepticism, atheism, and secularism; the Industrial Revolution; and the Russian Revolution and the rise of Communism and materialism. Sir Hamilton Gibb writes of Islam as a Christian "engaged in a common spiritual enterprise."[28] But let us beware of skepticism: "Both Christianity and Islam suffer under the weight of worldly pressure, and the attack of scientific atheists and their like," laments Norman Daniel.[29]

Hence the tendency amongst Christian scholars to be rather uncritical—a tendency not to wish to offend Muslim friends and Muslim colleagues. Thus, by the end of the twentieth century, Christian scholars of Islam had become the unwitting guardians and perpetuators of the myth of Islamic tolerance.

NOTES

1. Amnesty International, ASA .33/15.91.

2. "Tacitus," in *Oxford Classical Dictionary*, ed. N. G. L. Hammond and H. H. Scullard (Oxford: Oxford University Press, 1978), p. 1034.

3. See, for example, Stelio Cro, *The Noble Savage: Allegory of Freedom* (Waterloo, ON: Wilfrid Laurier University Press, 1990).

4. Michel de Montaigne, "On Cannibals," in *Essays* trans. J. M. Cohen (Harmondsworth, UK: Penguin, 1978), p. 113.

5. Ibid., p. 114.

6. Quoted in Pierre Bayle, "Mahomet and Nestorius," in *Dictionary Historical and Critical*, trans. John Peter Bernard, Thomas Birch, and John Lockman, 10 vols. (London, 1740).

7. Ibid.

8. Quoted in Bat Ye'or, *The Decline of Eastern Christianity under Islam: From Jihad to Dhimmitude: Seventh–Twentieth Century*, trans. Miriam Kochan and David Littman (Madison, NJ: Fairleigh Dickinson University Press, 1996), p. 384.

9. Ibid., p. 90.

10. P. M. Holt, "The Treatment of Arab History by Prideaux, Ockley, and Sale," in *Historians of the Middle East*, ed. Bernard Lewis and P. M. Holt (London: Oxford University Press, 1962), p. 300.

11. Arthur Jeffery, "The Quest of the Historical Mohammed," *Muslim World* 16, no. 4 (October 1926): 32.

12. Quoted in Holt, "The Treatment of Arab History," p. 302.

13. Quoted in G. H. Bousquet, "Loi musulmane et droit européen," *Revue Psychologie des Peuples* (le Havre, France) 3 (1950): 110, n. 2.

14. Qutoed in Paul Edwards, "Voltaire," in *The Encyclopedia of Unbelief*, ed. Gordon Stein, vol. 2 (Amherst, NY: Prometheus Books, 1985), p. 715.

15. Edwards, "Voltaire," p. 718.

16. Ibid., p. 715.

17. Bernard Lewis, *Islam and the West* (New York: Oxford University Press, 1993), p. 95.

18. Ibid.

19. Quoted in Ye'or, *Decline of Eastern Christianity*, p. 385.

20. Ibid., pp. 386–89.

21. W. Montgomery Watt, in *Bell's Introduction to the Qur'an*, by Richard Bell, revised and enlarged by W. Mongomery Watt (Edinburgh: Edinburgh University Press, 1977), p. 17.

22. "Carlyle, Thomas," in *Oxford Companion to Literature*, ed. Margaret Drabble (Oxford: Oxford University Press, 1985), p. 171.

23. Thomas Carlyle, *Sartor Resartus: On Heroes and Hero Worship* (London: J. M. Dent & Sons, 1973), p. 297.

24. Ibid., pp. 288–301.

25. Ibid., p. 307.

26. Ibid., p. 306.

27. Ibid., p. 299.

28. Quoted in Norman Daniel, *Islam and the West* (New York: Columbia University Press, 1989), p. 306.

29. Daniel, *Islam*, p. 307.

PART 1.
ISLAMIC TOLERANCE: MYTH AMD REALITY

1. THE MYTH OF ISLAMIC TOLERANCE

Robert Spencer

THE MYTH OF ISLAMIC TOLERANCE

Like Christians, Muslims respect and revere Jesus. Islam teaches that Jesus is one of the greatest of God's prophets and messengers to humankind.

Like Christians, every day, over 1.3 billion Muslims strive to live by his teachings of love, peace, and forgiveness. Those teachings, which have become universal values, remind us that all of us, Christians, Muslims, Jews, and all others have more in common than we think.

So read an advertisement that the Council on American Islamic Relations (CAIR) placed in California newspapers in March 2004. For such ostensible attempts to promote harmony and cooperation between Christians and Muslims, CAIR has, despite the arrests of three of its officials on terror-related charges in 2002 and 2003,[1] maintained a reputation as a neutral civil rights organization dedicated to helping Muslims find a place within American secular society.

This ad campaign was just one part of larger efforts by Muslims, particularly in Western countries, to present a vision of Islam that is different from Osama bin Laden's—benign where his is lethal, open and accepting where his is fanatical and intransigent. The council and its allies have succeeded in virtually ruling out of polite society any idea of Islam except one that insists it is a religion that Western non-Muslims need not fear and must not despise. Their presentation of Islam as another of the world's great religions, closely akin to Judaism and Christianity and, like them, liable to be "hijacked" through no fault of its own by "extremists" who commit violence in its name, is one that is accepted as axiomatic by most Americans—to do otherwise would be regarded in many circles as tantamount to committing the cardinal American sin of "racism," despite the fact that Islam is not a race and most Muslims in the world today are not members of the ethnic group with which they are most often identified, the Arabs.

As a result, in America today millions of people, including many in influential sectors of the government and media, believe in Islam. Not that they believe in Allah and his prophet Muhammad, but they nonetheless have something akin to religious faith in an idea of Islam itself. This faith consists of various assumptions that have emanated from academia, the media, the State Department, groups like CAIR, and even the president of the United States and that have by now become unquestioned assumptions held by millions.

A cornerstone of this secular faith in Islam is that Islam is a tolerant faith. Jews and Christians, we are told, lived in harmony with Muslims during the era of the great Islamic empires of the past. When radical Muslims bombed Madrid on March 11, 2004, commentators reminded us that when Muslims ruled Spain, it was a beacon of tolerance and the envy of Europe. When radicals bombed synagogues in Istanbul on November 15, 2003, we were told that such bombings were particularly heartbreaking in a city that for so long had known peace and harmony between Muslims, Jews, and Christians.

The dogma of Islamic tolerance has important political implications. Sclerotic European states eyeing the rapid growth of their Muslim populations console themselves with tales of old al-Andalus, reassuring one another that Islamic hegemony not only wasn't all that bad—it was a veritable golden age. Investigators in Europe and America are discouraged from monitoring activity in mosques. After all, goes the dogma, terrorism isn't an Islamic problem. Islam is a supremely tolerant faith. No, terrorism is a problem of political grievances or socioeconomic imbalances. If Islam has anything at all to do with it, it is only as a tool of unscrupulous religious leaders, who probably don't even really believe in Islam at all, who use religious language to excite and manipulate the uneducated masses. European and American politicians and religious leaders make careful overtures to growing Islamic communities, which they assume will—with a few exceptions—assimilate at least to the extent of becoming peaceful and active participants in the political process. Why not? Islam is a tolerant faith.

In the face of its general acceptance and the opprobrium that awaits those who decline to toe the line, it seems churlish at best (if not a manifestation of more sinister intent) to challenge the idea of Islamic tolerance. But it is precisely because of these and other political uses to which the idea is put that the challenge must be made. The dogma of Islamic tolerance has become a potent political and cultural weapon; accordingly, it cannot and must not be out of bounds to examine the truth of this dogma.

If this dogma is false, its destructive power will be very great. Europeans and Americans will find themselves in the position of having encouraged millions of Muslims to come to their shores to live as equals, only to find that Islam doesn't accept a position as just one among a community of disparate religions but must struggle to make itself supreme. As Bat Ye'or, the great historian of dhimmitude, the institutionalized oppression of non-Muslims (dhimmis: "protected" or "guilty" people) under Islam, puts it:

> The civilization of dhimmitude does not develop all at once. It is a long process that involves many elements and a specific mental conditioning. It happens when peoples replace history by myths, when they fight to uphold these destructive myths, more than their own values because they are confused by having transformed lies into truth. They hold to those myths as if they were the only guarantee for their survival, when, in fact, they are the path to destruction. Terrorized by the evidence and teaching of history, those peoples prefer to destroy it rather than to face it. They replace history with childish tales, thus living in amnesia, inventing moral justification for their own self-destruction.[2]

If that is indeed the case, the political implications will be as manifold and complex as those that follow from the assumption that Islam is tolerant. Either way, the investigation is of the utmost urgency.

In this book are gathered a good number of the groundbreaking historical investigations of Bat Ye'or, who pioneered the study of dhimmitude as a distinct phenomenon of Islamic history, theology, and law.[3] Other essays delve into attendant matters: the fearless and erudite former Muslim Ibn Warraq examines the real legacy of enormously influential academic Edward Said. Said, of course, was a pioneer in his own right, tarring generations of careful scholars of the Islamic world as racists and imperialists (or, as Said would have had it, "Orientalists") and elevating the myth of Islamic tolerance to the dogmatic level in American and European universities. Mark Durie explores the teachings of Islam on issues of tolerance and peaceful coexistence as well as a number of related matters in his witness statement from the trial of two Christian preachers in Australia. The preachers were sued, rather intolerantly, by a Muslim group for allegedly defaming Islam and thereby violating Australia's newly minted hate crime laws. Their daring and creative defense was to have recourse to the Islamic writings themselves, which Durie surveys brilliantly here.

Other, smaller pieces bring to light various ways in which the myth of

Islamic tolerance wields influence today among policy makers, academics, and opinion makers. Each of these in its own way reveals the power and uses of the myth and demonstrates why it is so important to investigate the historical claims, as well as the assertions about Islamic law and theology, that are being made.

Another section of the book brings together some extremely revealing material from the UN Commission on Human Rights. Since these are documents delivered to address particular problems and issues before the United Nations, some of this material is overlapping, appearing in one document and again in another. I ask the reader's patience and understanding: these records reveal the stark realities of Islam's human rights record; some repetition was necessary in order to preserve their character. These documents show conclusively that the source of the conflict that the Islamic world has with the non-Muslim world is not Israel; Israel acts only as the canary in the mineshaft, as this material about rising antisemitism and Judeophobia makes clear. But the human rights records of Iran, Sudan, Pakistan, and elsewhere, and the enormous obstacles that Muslim freethinkers and apostates face, have nothing to do with Israel: they illuminate a deeper problem of ingrained Islamic intolerance. These documents illuminate many attempts to use the myth, as well as many outright contradictions of the myth, made by Islamic states at the United Nations—as well as the cognitive dissonance created for and by these states by the disagreements between UN human rights declarations and various provisions of Islamic law, the Sharia.

These UN statements and other documents indicate that the historical and jurisprudential issues discussed in the other essays are very much alive today—as alive as the myth of Islamic tolerance.

HISTORY AS POLITICS: THE USES OF THE MYTH OF ISLAMIC TOLERANCE

The myth of Islamic tolerance was from its inception a political creation. Ibn Warraq surveys its origins with magnificent precision and directness in the foreword to this volume. And according to Bat Ye'or, it gained great currency because of nineteenth-century European political machinations in the Balkans: "Curiously, this myth started in Bosnia-Herzegovina in the 19th century. It alleges that Turkish rule over Christians in its European provinces was just and lawful. That the Ottoman regime, being Islamic, was naturally 'tolerant' and well disposed toward its Christian subjects; that its justice was fair, and that safety for life and goods was guaranteed to Christians by Islamic laws. Ottoman rule was brandished as the most suitable regime to rule Christians of the Balkans."[4]

The European politicians' interest in propagating the myth of Islamic tolerance stemmed from the geopolitical realities of the day. "This theory," Bat Ye'or continues, "was advanced by European politicians in order to safeguard the balance of power in Europe, and in order to block the Russian advance towards the Mediterranean. To justify the maintenance of the Turkish yoke on the Slavs, this yoke had to be presented to the public opinion as a just government. The Ottoman Empire was painted by Turkophiles as a model for a multi-[ethnic], multi-religious empire."[5]

Of course, reality was considerably different. Non-Muslims in the Ottoman Balkan regions were subject to substantially the same regulations for dhimmis that prevailed elsewhere in the Islamic world and were dictated by the Sharia. These laws are outlined by Samuel Shahid and Bat Ye'or in several essays later in this book. Exceptions to the harsh inequalities mandated by these laws only proved the rule, for they generally resulted from periods of laxity. These were all too often followed by Islamic revivals that featured a reassertion of harsh Sharia strictures, boding ill for non-Muslim populations. For instance, in 1758 the British ambassador to the Sublime Porte noted that laws mandating that dhimmis must dress in a manner distinct from the dress of Muslims, and in a way that demonstrated their inferior status, were being enforced with a new rigor—a rigor that sprang from the deep religious convictions of Sultan Mustafa III: "The order against Christians & Jews Dress, except in modest Cloaths, browns blacks ... & as to caps & boots is most rigorously executed in a Manner unknown before, which alarms most all those who are not Mahometans, & makes them apprehend the utmost Rigour; it seems however but natural, when it is considered, that it comes from a self-denying religious Prince."[6]

The imposition of a dress code may seem to be a small matter in those days before Hitler-imposed Star of David badges on German Jews, but, as Shahid and Bat Ye'or demonstrate in their essays in this volume, the dress requirements were just the most visible element of a detailed system of regulations designed to ensure that dhimmi Jews and Christians would "feel themselves subdued," as commanded in the Qur'an (sura 9:29). By no stretch of the imagination does all this bespeak the atmosphere of openness, mutuality, and tolerance that is suggested by modern purveyors of the myth. This is especially true in light of the penalties: the same British official wrote that a Jew had been beheaded after being caught in clothes that violated the orders.

In 1860 Consul James Zohrab wrote a report from Sarajevo to the British ambassador to the Porte, Henry Bulwer, that sounds as if it could have been filed in the last ten years. "The hatred of the Christians toward the Bosniak Mussulmans," he tells Bulwer, "is intense." Some might imagine today that this hatred was a consequence of Christian intransigence and fundamentalism and a refusal to respond with any generosity to the proffered hand of Islamic tolerance. But that was not actually the case. "During a period of nearly 300 years," Zohrab explains, the Christians "were subjected to much oppression and cruelty. For them no other law but the caprice of their masters existed."[7]

Testimony like this made it difficult for the myth of Islamic tolerance to gain acceptance among any who cared to consult the historical record. During the nineteenth and twentieth centuries, indefatigable scholars of Islam such as Sir William Muir, David S. Margoliouth, Thomas Patrick Hughes, Arthur Jeffrey, and many others, while not specifically investigating the plight of the dhimmis, had made available to English readers a wealth of material that abundantly established Islam's attitude toward non-Muslims as hardly one of tolerance.

Consequently, for the mythmakers history itself had to be made over. This wasn't accomplished definitively until a considerable time after the birth of the myth; but it was ultimately accomplished in a most spectacular manner. In 1978, a Christian Arab professor, Edward Said, published *Orientalism*, which quickly became the defining text for academic study of Islam in the West. Said didn't so much establish that Islam had a genuine tradition of tolerance as make it racist to suggest otherwise. The great scholars of Islam such as Muir and Margoliouth were, in Said's view, simply tools of Western imperialism, whose visions of the Orient were not objective scholarship but politically motivated tracts designed only to portray the Muslim world as needing the guiding hand of Christian colonial masters.

Any criticism of Islam, including any questioning of the myth of Islamic tolerance, was thereafter deemed ipso facto imperialist and racist by an academic establishment that quickly fell in thrall to Saidism as an integral element of its overall program of hostility to the Western civilization and heritage. The myth of Islamic tolerance reigned supreme not because it was borne out by the facts, but because to challenge it was to identify oneself with a despised and discredited political program. So Said and his followers were actually guilty of the very thing for which they excoriated the Orientalists: they set out to force the facts to give way to overriding political realities.

Saidists are now in virtually complete control of American academic study of Islam. Their baneful influence is superbly illustrated by Daniel Pipes in "Jihad and the Professors," which shows just how divorced from reality their analyses of this key Islamic concept have become.

And since words like *jihad* have been introduced by Yasir Arafat, Osama bin Laden, Saddam Hussein, and others into international geopolitics, the rapid and total victory that the Saidists won in the academic sphere has also exerted a harmful influence on public policy. *Orientalism* appeared just as the multiculturalist ethic was taking root in the United States and Western Europe. Saidism was simultaneously a manifestation of that ethic and a further legitimization of it. Even to point out that Islamic societies had been less than tolerant toward their non-Muslim populations, and that this intolerance was mandated and reinforced by quite specific provisions of Islamic law, was to engage in an unacceptable ethnocentrism. This was the genesis of the attitude that prevented American officials (including the president of the United States) from using anything but the vaguest of generalities ("evildoers") to describe their Islamic terrorist foes after the World Trade Center and Pentagon attacks of September 11, 2001. To take notice of the Islamic motivations and goals of the jihadist attackers, except to deny their significance, would have made the Bush administration vulnerable to charges of racism: the kiss of death in American politics. So while Bush occasionally spoke of jihadists in reference to particular situations, he much more often energetically avoided any public linkage of Islam with the global jihad network that he began to confront in the war on terror.

This avoidance on many occasions made public statements by officials become something of a theater of the absurd. When American National Guard Spc. Ryan Anderson, a convert to Islam, was arrested after allegedly trying to contact and join up with al Qaeda, reporters asked a Guard spokesman, Lt. Col. Stephen Barger, about Anderson's religion. Barger replied: "Religious preferences are an individual right and responsibility, and I really can't get into it."[8] As if a devout Methodist or Zen Buddhist would have any interest in joining al Qaeda.

Ironically enough, even as Barger declined to consider the possibility that Islam might somehow be implicated in Anderson's behavior, he did so by means of a statement could only have been made by a Westerner. Islam, with its strong sense of the *umma,* the worldwide community of Muslim believers that transcends nationality, race, and political boundaries, as well as its detailed rules for virtually every aspect of human behavior, does not consider religion a private matter. But the possibility that a religious belief could have political implications, even if that belief involves so avowedly worldly and political a religion as Islam, has been ruled by the Saidists and their allies to be beyond the bounds of civilized discourse. That Islam cannot give rise except in "hijacked" form to extremism and violence, and that it is in its true form broadminded, tolerant, noble, and magnanimous—more so in many ways than Christianity—must be accepted as axiomatic by people like Lieutenant Colonel Barger. Otherwise, they risk losing their jobs and worse: being stigmatized as the spiritual and intellectual kin of people like David Duke and Bull Connor.

The myth of Islamic tolerance and its attendant dogmas are guarded jealously—sometimes in quite intolerant ways. When a French publisher undertook a translation of my book *Islam Unveiled* in 2003, he and the translator quickly began to receive death threats. Translator Guy Milliere explains: "I sent him [the publisher] the translation of the first thirty pages. A couple of weeks later I started to receive death threats by e-mail: 'You must be an enemy of Islam; you will die for what you do'; 'You must be a Jew; I hope somebody will slit your throat, you dirty Jew pig,' etc. . . . I asked the police to act; I have received no answer."[9]

In other words, you must say that Islam is peaceful and tolerant, or we will kill you.

THE CURRENT MYTH AND THE CURRENT REALITY

The almost universal prevalence of the myth of Islamic tolerance today has led to a strange phenomenon: non-Muslims hastening to assure the public that the Islam of the terrorists is not the "true Islam," which is, they maintain, a benign and tolerant thing. The former archbishop of canterbury, George Carey, after drawing the ire of the Muslim community in Britain by critical remarks about Islamic extremism, attempted to make amends in May 2004 by explaining, "Our world is in great peril. I am talking rather about a sharp ideological tension that separates the West from another world, that we call Islamic and yet does not reflect the true values of Islam."[10]

Carey didn't explain what qualified him to declare what are the "true values of Islam" and what aren't, or to dismiss the claims by Islamic radicals themselves to represent "true" or "pure Islam." Yet in Carey's England, Islamic radicals such as Sheikh Omar Bakri of the al-Muhajiroun group (which held a pro-Osama celebration on the first anniversary of the September 11 attacks) and Abu Hamza al-Masri (former imam of the Finsbury Park Mosque, where several jihadists including shoe bomber Richard Reid once worshiped) continue to teach young Muslims that their version of Islam is the "pure" (Salafi) form of the religion—and, according to the BBC, "moderate Muslims leaders have remained largely silent and have yet to provide a credible alternative."[11]

Around the same time that Carey was opining about "true Islam," the Army News Service published an opinion piece by a staff sergeant named Russell Bassett, drawing a sharp distinction between the terrorism of Osama bin Laden and Islam. Bassett quotes an American Muslim soldier, Spc. David Burgos: "I have read the Koran several times and there Islam teaches its followers to be peaceful. Islam is all about giving life, not taking it."[12] Bassett accepts this at face value and dismisses Islamic terrorists as motivated by politics, not religion; he makes no attempt, of course, to examine the Islamic justifications put forward by Osama and others for terrorism.

Bassett, to be sure, is not engaging in academic discourse, but his commentary is more than just the opinion of one American sergeant. It is a manifestation of the United States government's official position on these matters, and its publication by the Army News Service is clearly intended to advance Bassett's opinions among American troops.

Even stranger are instances when Western non-Muslims have taken it upon themselves to lecture radical Muslims about their supposed misuse of their faith. In November 2003, two American converts to Islam, Jeffrey Leon Battle and Patrice Lumumba Ford, were sentenced to eighteen years in prison for trying to join the Taliban and wage jihad against their fellow Americans. At the sentencing, US district judge Robert Jones scolded Ford: "You do not represent the Muslim faith. Muslims do not engage in the activities you engaged in. You are an insult to that faith."[13]

Such assumptions, of course, mesh perfectly with the image that many Muslims try to create for themselves in the eyes of the West. The Saudi English-language publication *Arab News* blamed Westerners' negative impressions of Islam on those Westerners' own prejudices. After quoting "blasphemous rhetoric that is the cause of Muslim rage today" from Christian fundamentalist preachers Franklin Graham, Pat Robertson, Jerry Falwell, and others, the columnist declares: "The practice of anti-Islam in the US needs to be addressed. The Muslim is not plotting to kill the infidel. The Arabs and Muslims are not all secretly plotting to take over the world in order to establish an Islamic caliphate."[14]

But Graham, Falwell, and Robertson didn't invent the idea that Muslims want to reestablish the caliphate, with all its intolerant provisions for non-Muslims. The *Arab News*'s reassurances ring hollow in the face of the statements and activities of radical Muslim groups around the world. Al Qaeda's online magazine, *Voice of Jihad*, exhorted jihad warriors in fall 2003: "We draw the attention of the *Mujahideen* to the strategy adopted by the Sheikh of the *Mujahideen*, Abu Abdallah Osama bin Laden, and Sheikh Dr. Ayman al-Zawahiri, and agreed to by many of the great *Mujahideen*, regarding combat against the enemy: Our number one enemy is the Jews and the Christians, and we must free ourselves to invest all our efforts until we annihilate them—and we are able do this if Allah allows us to do it—because they are the main obstacle to establishing the Islamic state."[15]

This goal of establishing the Islamic state—ruled by a caliph—is not al Qaeda's alone. The Muslim group Hizb-ut-Tahrir, which is active principally in Central Asia but also has members in Yemen, Egypt, and other Middle Eastern countries, as well as a presence among Muslim emigrants in the West, has openly declared its intention to "restore a worldwide Caliphate, uniting the world under Islamic rule."[16] The Indonesian Jemaah Islamiyah group that was responsible for the Bali bombing of October 2002 has also stated its intention to establish an Islamic state ruled by a caliph in Southeast Asia.[17]

In England, Sheikh Omar Bakri's Al-Muhajiroun group declared on its Web site: "Today the burden of working to establish the Khilafah and implement the Shari'ah is on the neck of all Muslims, it is an obligation [Fard] of the highest order that requires utmost effort and sacrifice. If we neglect this collective Fard then we are calling out to the wrath and anger of Allah [swt]. Muhammad [saw] and his Sahabah [ra] had the great honour of establishing the first Islamic State in Madinah by a bloodless coup de tat [*sic*]. Today we have the privilege of following the same footsteps and working for this righteous and honourable cause."[18]

Even the Islamic Affairs Department of the Saudi embassy in Washington, DC, called for the restoration of the caliphate, despite the *Arab News*'s ascribing of this idea to the "blasphemous rhetoric" of so-called Islamophobes: "Today's false idols, which dominate over the entire world, are Democracy, Capitalism, Socialism and Communism. Islam instead calls for a Khilafa [Caliphate] based on consultation, and a just economic system based on Zakat and a prohibition of usury."[19] Ultimately, an outcry brought about the removal of this material from the embassy Web site but no retraction from Saudi officials.

Yet no amount of evidence seems to shake the power of the myth of Islamic tolerance in Western public discourse. There seems to be no shortage of non-Muslim Westerners ready to assume that the myth is true and to behave accordingly, despite the potentially lethal consequences that could result from ignoring the words of the mujahedin themselves. A typical example came when Bill Graham, Canada's minister of foreign affairs, called for building bridges of understanding to Muslims as a response to terrorists' "exploiting Islam as a pretext for violence." Graham praised Canada's "diverse and flourishing Muslim communities," showing no awareness of the possibility that some within those communities subscribed to the radical Muslim caliphate/Sharia program. All this despite evidence to the contrary afforded by Canada's much-publicized Khadr family, which was deeply involved with Osama bin Laden and jihad in several ways—which so offended Canadian prime minister Jean Chrétien that he personally intervened to help secure the release of one Khadr family member, Ahmed Said Khadr, after he was jailed in Pakistan on suspicion of involvement in the bombing of the Egyptian embassy in 1995.[20]

Graham's statement reflected a Canadian government policy that has been torpid in implementing antiterrorism measures, did not support the Iraq war, and has not been a particular friend of Israel. Nonetheless, the day after his column appeared, an associate of Osama bin Laden named Khalid Khawaja told Canada's *National Post* that Western civilization was "selfish" and warned Canadians that the country could become the site of suicide bombing attacks. He praised death in an Islamic jihad as the best way to die and asked Canadians, "So how can you fight with us?"[21]

Despite the strong Islamic character of Khawaja's remarks, Graham made no statement revising his views. He seems certain that Khawaja and others like him represent a discredited radical fringe within a tolerant and benevolent religious tradition; statements and activities by that fringe group, even though conducted on a global scale, do not seem to shake his faith in the myth.

NON-MUSLIMS IN THE QUR'AN

The attitudes of modern Muslims toward non-Muslims are rooted, of course, in the Qur'an, which Muslims believe to be the eternal words of Allah dictated to the prophet Muhammad through the angel Gabriel. The Qur'an occupies an influence in the Islamic world that is far greater than that of the Bible in the West, even during the heyday of Christendom; it exerts a dominant and formative influence on the Muslim mind and culture.

Proponents of the myth of Islamic tolerance point to verses such as this one: "Those who believe [in the Qur'an], and those who follow the Jewish [scriptures], and the Christians and the Sabians, any who believe in Allah and the Last Day, and work righteousness, shall have their reward with their Lord; on them shall be no fear, nor shall they grieve" (sura 2:62; cf. 5:69 and 22:17). Muslim spokesmen in the West like to quote such verses and to stress, as in the Council on American Islamic Relations ad, the commonality between Islam and Christianity—and sometimes even between Islam and Judaism.

However, the preponderance of Qur'anic testimony favors not tolerance and harmony between Muslims and non-Muslims, but just the opposite. A fundamental component of the Qur'an's view of non-Muslims is the often repeated and implacable belief in its own superiority: "The Religion before Allah is Islam" (sura 3:19), or, as another translation has it, "The only true faith in God's sight is Islam." Muslims, accordingly, are also superior to others: "Ye are the best of peoples, evolved for mankind, enjoining what is right, forbidding what is wrong, and believing in Allah." By contrast, most Jews and Christians ("People of the Book") are wrongdoers: "If only the People of the Book had faith, it were best for them: among them are some who have faith, but most of them are perverted transgressors" (sura 3:110).

According to orthodox Muslim belief, the Qur'an is the final and perfect revelation from Allah, the one true God. It confirms earlier revelations—a fact of which Muhammad was evidently so sure that in the Qur'an he has Allah telling him that if he is harboring any doubts about the veracity of his experiences with Gabriel, he need only check with those who received scriptures before Muhammad's time—that is, Jews and Christians: "And if thou (Muhammad) art in doubt concerning that which We reveal unto thee, then question those who read the Scripture (that was) before thee. Verily the Truth from thy Lord hath come unto thee. So be not thou of the waverers" (sura 10:94).

Yet the testimony that the earlier scriptures were supposed to bear to the coming of Muhammad has been obscured by Jews and Christians. In a lengthy passage in a late sura (chapter) of the Qur'an, "al-Baqara" (the Cow), Allah castigates the Jews and Christians for rejecting Muhammad when they know better:

> We gave Moses the Book and followed him up with a succession of messengers; We gave Jesus the son of Mary Clear (Signs) and strengthened him with the holy spirit. Is it that whenever there comes to you a messenger with what ye yourselves desire not, ye are puffed up with pride? Some ye called impostors, and others ye slay! They say, "Our hearts are the wrappings (which preserve Allah's Word: we need no more)."
>
> Nay, Allah's curse is on them for their blasphemy: Little is it they

believe. And when there comes to them a Book from Allah, confirming what is with them, although from of old they had prayedfor victory against those without Faith, when there comes to them thatwhich they (should) have recognised, they refuse to believe in it but the curse of Allah is on those without Faith. Miserable is the price for which they have sold their souls, in that they deny (the revelation) which Allah has sent down, in insolent envy that Allah of His Grace should send it to any of His servants He pleases: Thus have they drawn on themselves Wrath upon Wrath. And humiliating is the punishment of those who reject Faith.

When it is said to them, "Believe in what Allah Hath sent down," they say, "We believe in what was sent down to us": yet they reject all besides, even if it be Truth confirming what is with them. Say: "Why then have ye slain the prophets of Allah in times gone by, if ye did indeed believe?"

There came to you Moses with clear (Signs); yet ye worshipped the calf (even) after that, and ye did behave wrongfully. And remember We took your covenant and We raised above you (the towering height) of Mount (Sinai), (saying): "Hold firmly to what We have given you, and hearken (to the Law)." They said: "We hear, and we disobey." And they had to drink into their hearts (of the taint) of the calf because of their Faithlessness. Say: "Vile indeed are the behests of your Faith if ye have any faith!". . .

Say: Whoever is an enemy to Gabriel—for he brings down the (revelation) to thy heart by Allah's will, a confirmation of what went before, and guidance and glad tidings for those who believe—whoever is an enemy to Allah and His angels and messengers, to Gabriel and Michael, lo! Allah is an enemy to those who reject Faith. We have sent down to thee Manifest Signs (ayat); and none reject them but those who are perverse. Is it not (the case) that every time they make a covenant, some party among them throw it aside? Nay, Most of them are faithless. And when there came to them a messenger from Allah, confirming what was with them, a party of the people of the Book threw away the Book of Allah behind their backs, as if (it had been something) they did not know! . . . If they had kept their Faith and guarded themselves from evil, far better had been the reward from their Lord, if they but knew! (sura 2:88–103)

By the evidence of this passage and others in the Qur'an, the Jews and Christians who remain in the world after the time of Muhammad are renegades who have rejected this final revelation out of corruption and malice and who have exchanged truth for falsehood: "The Jews call 'Uzair [Ezra] a son of Allah, and the Christians call Christ the son of Allah. That is a saying from their mouth; (in this) they but imitate what the unbelievers of old used to say" (sura 9:30). Nor is that remotely all. The Jews "have incurred divine displeasure): in that they broke their covenant; that they rejected the signs of Allah;

that they slew the Messengers in defiance of right; that they said, 'Our hearts are the wrappings (which preserve Allah's Word; We need no more)'; nay, Allah hath set the seal on their hearts for their blasphemy, and little is it they believe . . ." (sura 4:155). They even misrepresent the scriptures: "There is among them a section who distort the Book with their tongues: (As they read) you would think it is a part of the Book, but it is no part of the Book; and they say, 'That is from Allah,' but it is not from Allah. It is they who tell a lie against Allah, and (well) they know it!" (sura 3:78). They blasphemously doubt Allah's power: "The Jews say: 'Allah's hand is tied up.' Be their hands tied up and be they accursed for the (blasphemy) they utter" (sura 5:64).

The Qur'an also frequently censures Christians for believing in false doctrines—including beliefs that are central to the faith as it had been understood and practiced for as long as six centuries before Muhammad began preaching. Apparently misunderstanding the nature of the Christian Trinity, one verse has Allah quizzing Jesus: "O Jesus the son of Mary! Didst thou say unto men, worship me and my mother as gods in derogation of Allah?" Jesus answers: "Glory to Thee! Never could I say what I had no right (to say)" (sura 5:116).

In the book Allah frequently insists that he has no son—a fact Muslims believe to be an essential component of true monotheism. "Say: 'Praise be to Allah, who begets no son, and has no partner in (His) dominion: Nor (needs) He any to protect Him from humiliation: yea, magnify Him for His greatness and glory!'" (sura 17:111).

Finally Muhammad weaves his charges against Jews and Christians together by condemning Christians for believing that Jesus was crucified, and Jews for believing that they crucified him: "They said (in boast), 'We killed Christ Jesus the son of Mary, the Messenger of Allah'; but they killed him not, nor crucified him, but so it was made to appear to them, and those who differ therein are full of doubts, with no (certain) knowledge, but only conjecture to follow, for of a surety they killed him not" (sura 4:157).

Because of the cavalier, self-serving, and underhanded ways in which they have treated Allah's message, both Jews and Christians live under the curse of Allah: "Allah's curse be on them: how they are deluded away from the Truth!" (sura 9:30).

The idea that Jews and Christians are accursed recurs several times in the Qur'an. Both have rejected Allah and his messenger Muhammad:

Allah did aforetime take a covenant from the Children of Israel, and we appointed twelve captains among them. And Allah said: "I am with you: if ye (but) establish regular prayers, practice regular charity, believe in my messengers, honor and assist them, and loan to Allah a beautiful loan, verily I will wipe out from you your evils, and admit you to gardens with rivers flowing beneath; but if any of you, after this, resisteth faith, he hath truly wandered from the path of rectitude."

But because of their breach of their covenant, We cursed them, and made their hearts grow hard; they change the words from their (right) places and forget a good part of the message that was sent them, nor wilt thou cease to find them—barring a few—ever bent on (new) deceits: but forgive them, and overlook (their misdeeds): for Allah loveth those who are kind.

From those, too, who call themselves Christians, We did take a covenant, but they forgot a good part of the message that was sent them: so we estranged them, with enmity and hatred between the one and the other, to the day of judgment. And soon will Allah show them what it is they have done.

O People of the Book! There hath come to you our Messenger, revealing to you much that ye used to hide in the Book, and passing over much (that is now unnecessary): There hath come to you from Allah a (new) light and a perspicuous Book, wherewith Allah guideth all who seek His good pleasure to ways of peace and safety, and leadeth them out of darkness, by His will, unto the light, guideth them to a path that is straight. (sura 5:12–16)

All this leads directly to the Qur'an's notorious verses of jihad, such as this one from later in the same sura: "And slay them wherever ye catch them, and turn them out from where they have turned you out; for tumult and oppression are worse than slaughter; but fight them not at the Sacred Mosque, unless they (first) fight you there; but if they fight you, slay them. Such is the reward of those who suppress faith" (sura 2:190). Many Western Muslim spokesmen today deny that this verse applies to Jews and Christians of this age or any other, as they are in the Qur'an "People of the Book" and not idolaters. However, it is clear from the long passage above that Jews and Christians are indeed counted in the Qur'an among those who "suppress faith" and thus must be met by Muslims not with talk of tolerance and peaceful coexistence but with jihad warfare: "And fight them until persecution is no more, and religion is all for Allah. But if they cease, then lo! Allah is Seer of what they do" (sura 8:39).

Indeed, the sura that most Muslim scholars believe to have been the last one revealed—and hence the portion of the Qur'an that takes precedence over any contradictory passage revealed earlier—is sura 9, at-Tauba ("Repentance"). It explicitly enjoins Muslims to wage war against the People of the Book until they either convert to Islam or are subdued as second-class dhimmis: "Fight those who believe not in Allah nor the Last Day, nor hold that forbidden which hath been forbidden by Allah and His Messenger, nor acknowledge the religion of Truth, (even if they are) of the People of the Book, until they pay the Jizya [a special tax on non-Muslims] with willing submission, and feel themselves subdued" (sura 9:29).

In the end it is the will of Allah that Islam will triumph over all other religions: "He it is Who hath sent His messenger with the guidance and the Religion of Truth, that He may cause it to prevail over all religion, however much the idolaters may be averse" (sura 9:33).

This is tantamount to a declaration of war, and its spirit pervades the entire Muslim holy book. So far is the Qur'an from modern notions of tolerance and peaceful coexistence that it even warns Muslims not to befriend Jews and Christians—apparently including those who "feel themselves subdued" and are paying the *jiyza*: "O ye who believe! Take not the Jews and the Christians for your friends and protectors. They are but friends and protectors to each other. And he amongst you that turns to them (for friendship) is of them. Verily Allah guideth not a people unjust" (sura 5:51).

It is ironic in light of all this that the Qur'an also criticizes Jews and Christians for being *intolerant*. Allah warns Muhammad that "never will the Jews or the Christians be satisfied with thee unless thou follow their form of religion. Say: 'The Guidance of Allah, that is the (only) Guidance.' Wert thou to follow their desires after the knowledge which hath reached thee, then wouldst thou find neither Protector nor helper against Allah" (sura 2:120; cf. 2:135).

This is the Qur'an that pious Muslims cherish and memorize in its entirety; it is for them their primary guide to understanding how they should make their way in the world and deal with other people. It is nothing short of staggering that the myth of Islamic tolerance could have gained such currency in the teeth of the Qur'an's open contempt and hatred for Jews and Christians and incitements of violence against them—and a testimony to the ease with which one can convince himself of the truth of something in which one wants to believe, regardless of evidence to the contrary.

Non-Muslims in the Hadith

The Hadith, the traditions of the sayings and doings of the prophet Muhammad, are second in authority only to the Qur'an for most Muslims. In fact, Sunni Islam, the sect of 85 to 90 percent of Muslims worldwide, takes its name from the Sunnah, the Traditions, which Sunnis follow in contradistinction to Shi'ite Islam, which from the days of its great imams and in a different way thereafter invested more authority than do Sunnis in religious leaders. Sunnis rely instead, at least according to the theory, on the teachings of Muhammad as recorded in the Hadith and explicated by Islamic jurists.

The Hadith is voluminous, and much is of doubtful authenticity. But in the early centuries of Islam six collections were identified by Muslims as being substantially authentic and therefore trustworthy: those known today as *Sahih Sittah* ("reliable collections"): *Sahih Bukhari, Sahih Muslim,* the *Sunan of Abu Dawud,* the *Sunan of Ibn Majah,* the *Sunan of an-Nasai,* and the *Jami of at-Tirmidhi.* These, as applied and interpreted by jurists from the four principal Sunni *madhhabs,* or schools of jurisprudence (Hanafi, Hanbali, Maliki, and Shafi'i) form the primary source for the innumerable regulations of Islamic law, which governs virtually every aspect of life—from personal hygiene to macroeconomics. Although it is likely—and Western scholars have established in many cases—that many of these traditions that are revered as reliable are just as tenuous and inauthentic as many of those that are universally rejected, this fact has had little impact thus far in the Islamic world. Many of them enjoy normative status as principal sources for religious beliefs and practices. Critical analysis of both the Qur'an and Hadith has been slight and furtive among Muslims—largely owing to the fact that Islamic tolerance, both in history and today, does not generally extend to a willingness to allow the words of Allah to be examined and prodded. To allow this would be tantamount to admitting that the Qur'an is a human book, which few pious Muslims have been prepared to do ever since the comparatively rationalist Mutazilite sect was vanquished centuries ago and the idea that the Qur'an was uncreated was raised to the level of an unquestionable dogma. In any case, since these traditions are regarded as authentic by orthodox Muslims, they play a key role in the elaboration of Islamic intolerance and were accordingly muted in the era of the imposition of the myth of tolerance.

The Traditions' message regarding non-Muslims consists primarily of an amplification of that of the Qur'an. The Qur'an's inconsistent statements about whether or not Jews and Christians will enter paradise are resolved: "It is narrated on the authority of Abu Huraira that the Messenger of Allah (may peace be upon him) observed: By Him in Whose hand is the life of Muhammad, he who amongst the community of Jews or Christians hears about me, but does not affirm his belief in that with which I have been sent and dies in this state (of disbelief), he shall be but one of the denizens of Hell-Fire."[22] So once again we see that if there is any tolerance in Islam at all, it is only provisional, in anticipation of the great Day on which Allah will make it manifest to all that "the Religion before Allah is Islam" (sura 3:19). Another Hadith has Muhammad saying:

On the Day of Resurrection, a call-maker will announce, "Let every nation follow that which they used to worship." Then none of those who used to worship anything other than Allah like idols and other deities but will fall in Hell (Fire), till there will remain none but those who used to worship Allah, both those who were obedient (i.e., good) and those who were disobedient (i.e., bad) and the remaining party of the people of the Scripture. Then the Jews will be called upon and it will be said to them, "Who do you use to worship?" They will say, "We used to worship Ezra, the son of Allah." It will be said to them, "You are liars, for Allah has never taken anyone as a wife or a son. What do you want now?" They will say, "O our Lord! We are thirsty, so give us something to drink." They will be directed and addressed thus, "Will you drink," whereupon they will be gathered unto Hell (Fire) which will look like a mirage whose different sides will be destroying each other. Then they will fall into the Fire. Afterwards the Christians will be called upon and it will be said to them, "Who do you use to worship?" "They will say, 'We used to worship Jesus, the son of Allah.'" It will be said to them, "You are liars, for Allah has never taken anyone as a wife or a son," Then it will be said to them, "What do you want?" They will say what the former people have said. Then, when there remain (in the gathering) none but those who used to worship Allah (Alone, the real Lord of the Worlds) whether they were obedient or disobedient.[23]

Of course, consigning other groups to hellfire doesn't necessarily mean that one will not consent to live in peace as equals with them on earth. But Islam in its totality attempts an audacious recasting and, in a real sense, appropriation of Judaism and Christianity—a kind of theological imperialism that can serve as a useful analogy and paradigm for the true nature of the tolerance that Islamic jurists envision for this world.

For Muhammad did not hesitate to appropriate the central figures of Judaism and Christianity and to claim that they were Muslim. Noah, Abraham, Moses, and Jesus appear in the Qur'an and Hadith as Muslim prophets (see suras 2:87, 2:136, 3:84, 33:7, 42:13, etc.). Their religion was Islam—until it was corrupted by their wicked followers (who were, of course, the ancestors of the Jews and Christians, who remained outside the fold of Islam). In the Christians' case, Jesus will set this right in the latter days, returning to end the dhimmi status of non-Muslims in Islamic societies—not by initiating a new era of equality and harmony, but by abolishing Christianity and imposing Islam upon everyone:

Allah's Apostle said, "By Him in Whose Hands my soul is, surely (Jesus,) the son of Mary will soon descend amongst you and will judge mankind justly (as a Just Ruler); he will break the Cross and kill the pigs and there will be no Jizya (i.e., taxation taken from non Muslims). Money will be in abundance so that nobody will accept it, and a single prostration to Allah (in prayer) will be better than the whole world and whatever is in it." Abu Huraira added, "If you wish, you can recite (this verse of the Holy Book): 'And there is none of the people of the Scriptures (Jews and Christians) But must believe in him (i.e., Jesus as an Apostle of Allah and a human being) before his death. And on the Day of Judgment He will be a witness against them'" (4.159).[24]

To drive the point home, another tradition adds that Muhammad said: "How will you be when the son of Mary (i.e., Jesus) descends amongst you and he will judge people by the Law of the Qur'an and not by the law of Gospel?"[25]

Still, while all this and similar material is useful to refute the pseudo-multicultural posturing of contemporary Muslim advocacy groups (particularly in the United States), it doesn't add up in itself to anything particularly intolerant. Theological absolutism of a similar kind can be found in virtually all sects of Christianity, as well as in other religious traditions. But although sura 109 of the Qur'an—often quoted today—envisions a live-and-let-live attitude between Muslims and non-Muslims, that is far from the last word on the subject in either the Qur'an (as we have seen) or the Hadith. The Hadith expand upon verses 9:5 and 9:29 of the Qur'an with accounts of Muhammad's battles against unbelievers. One of the most notable of these records not a battle but an epistolary encounter between the Prophet of the new religion and the leader of the old empire, Heraclius of Byzantium. The account in Sahih Bukhari is full of unlikely details, including the assertion that Heraclius was mightily impressed by Muhammad and all but acknowledged his prophethood. To the dismay of courageous Muslim apostates through the centuries, the Heraclius of this hadith burbles to one of Muhammad's men: "I asked you whether there was anybody who, after embracing [Muhammad's] religion, became displeased and discarded his religion; your reply was in the negative. In fact, this is the sign of True Faith, for when its cheerfulness enters and mixes in the hearts completely, nobody will be displeased with it."

But most noteworthy is the brief, easy-to-overlook threat lobbed into the letter from the holy man: "Embrace Islam," he exhorted Heraclius, "and you will be safe."[26] No guarantee of safety or offer of truce is made in the event that Heraclius declines to accept Islam.

The imperative was to invite non-Muslims to become Muslim—as

Muhammad did Heraclius and Osama bin Laden did the United States in the late 1990s—and then fight those who refuse. This hadith delineates these choices, in accord with sura 9:29's mandate to fight Jews and Christians until they pay the non-Muslim poll tax (*jizya*)—or, of course, convert to Islam. Says Muhammad:

> Fight in the name of Allah and in the way of Allah. Fight against those who disbelieve in Allah. Make a holy war; do not embezzle the spoils; do not break your pledge; and do not mutilate (the dead) bodies; do not kill the children. When you meet your enemies who are polytheists, invite them to three courses of action. If they respond to any one of these you also accept it and withhold yourself from doing them any harm. Invite them to (accept) Islam; if they respond to you, accept it from them and desist from fighting against them. . . . If they refuse to accept Islam, demand from them theJizya. If they agree to pay, accept it from them and hold off your hands. If they refuse to pay the tax, seek Allah's help and fight them.[27]

When speaking of non-Muslim dhimmis, the *sahih ahadith* are primarily concerned with the collection of the *jizya*—which constituted the "source of the livelihood" of the Muslims.[28] The traditions say little about the way in which Islamic societies are soon going to ensure that non-Muslims "feel themselves subdued," in accordance with sura 9:29. But Muslims from the earliest ages seem to have been intent to fulfill this command and devised numerous ingenious ways to do so. This resulted in an elaborate system of regulation for the treatment of dhimmis that enforced their humiliation and inferiority on a daily basis—and that remained constant in the Islamic world, although they were enforced with varying degrees of ferocity in different regions over the ages. These regulations, as intolerant as they are, remain part of the Sharia to this day. Radical Islamic terror organizations around the world have repeatedly declared their intention to impose the Sharia wherever and whenever they can. This stands as an enduring threat to non-Muslims in nations with Muslim majorities and elsewhere.

NON-MUSLIMS IN ISLAMIC JURISPRUDENCE

As the schools of Islamic jurisprudence developed, they constructed upon these hadiths and passages of the Qur'an a legal structure for the treatment of non-Muslims. The features of this remained remarkably consistent across the centuries, and among all the legal schools. Take, for example, contemporary Saudi sheikh Marzouq Salem al-Ghamdi, who explained in a sermon the terms in which an Islamic society should tolerate the presence of non-Muslims in its midst:

> If the infidels live among the Muslims, in accordance with the conditions set out by the Prophet—there is nothing wrong with it provided they pay *Jizya* to the Islamic treasury. Other conditions are . . . that they do not renovate a church or a monastery, do not rebuild ones that were destroyed, that they feed for three days any Muslim who passes by their homes . . . that they rise when a Muslim wishes to sit, that they do not imitate Muslims in dress and speech, nor ride horses, nor own swords, nor arm themselves with any kind of weapon; that they do not sell wine, do not show the cross, do not ring church bells, do not raise their voices during prayer, that they shave their hair in front so as to make them easily identifiable, do not incite anyone against the Muslims, and do not strike a Muslim. . . . If they violate these conditions, they have no protection.[29]

Ghamdi's list of conditions was taken practically verbatim from traditional sources of Islamic law regarding non-Muslims. Nor was Ghamdi the only modern-day Muslim spokesman interested in reviving these ancient strictures. In 2001 Sheikh Ibrahim Madhi preached a quite similar sermon on Palestinian Authority television:

> We welcome, as we did in the past, any Jew who wants to live in this land as a Dhimmi, just as the Jews have lived in our countries, as Dhimmis, and have earned appreciation, and some of them have even reached the positions of counselor or minister here and there. We welcome the Jews to live as Dhimmis, but the rule in this land and in all the Muslim countries must be the rule of Allah. . . . Those from amongst the Jews and from amongst those who are not Jews who came to this land as plunderers, must return humiliated and disrespected to their countries.[30]

Responding to a similar statement made in 1999 about Palestinian Christians by Sheikh Yussef Salameh, the undersecretary for religious endowment for the Palestinian Authority, the Catholic archbishop of the Galilee, Butrus al-Mu'alem, thundered: "It is strange to me that there remains such backwardness in our society. . . . there are still those who amuse themselves with fossilized notions."[31]

Fossilized these notions may be, but abrogated or repudiated they are not. And unfortunately, those amusing themselves with them are not a small or insignificant group. In 1991 there appeared a new English translation of

'Umdat al-Salik (Reliance of the Traveller), a Shafi'i manual of Islamic law compiled by fourteenth-century jurist Ahmad ibn Naqib al-Misri (d. 1368). Someone who didn't know that virtually every other Islamic legal document contained much the same material might assume that this was the one to which Ghamdi and Madhi to reacquaint themselves with the particulars of dhimmi status. "The subject peoples," it declares, must "pay the non-Muslim poll tax (*jizya*)" and "are distinguished from Muslims in dress, wearing a wide cloth belt (*zunnar*); are not greeted with '*as-Salamu 'alaykum*' [the traditional Muslim greeting, "Peace be with you"]; must keep to the side of the street; may not build higher than or as high as the Muslims' buildings, though if they acquire a tall house, it is not razed; are forbidden to openly display wine or pork, . . . recite the Torah or Evangel aloud, or make public display of their funerals or feastdays; and are forbidden to build new churches."[32]

'Umdat al-Salik itself is not solely of interest to historians. The translator, an American convert to Islam named Nuh Ha Mim Keller, explains in an introduction that "not a single omission has been made" from Ibn Naqib's Arabic text, "though rulings about matters now rare or nonexistent have been left untranslated unless interesting for some other reason."[33] Underscoring its relevance for modern Muslims (and wary non-Muslims) is an endorsement from Cairo's venerable Al-Azhar University. Fath Allah Ya Sin Jazar, the general director of research, writing, and translation at Al-Azhar's Islamic Research Academy, gave the translation, and the manual itself, a resounding endorsement: "We certify that the . . . translation corresponds to the Arabic original and conforms to the practice and faith of the orthodox Sunni Community."[34]

Joseph Schacht, the great Columbia University professor of Arabic and Islamics in the days before Edward Said and his followers politicized the field, sums up the general position of all the schools of Islamic law in terms that illustrate just how far the legal superstructure of dhimmitude is from the myth of Islamic tolerance: "The basis of the Islamic attitude towards unbelievers is the law of war; they must be either converted or subjugated or killed (excepting women, children, and slaves); the third alternative, in general, occurs only if the first two are refused."[35]

This is, of course, in complete accord with the choices for unbelievers explained by the prophet Muhammad in the hadith quoted above: "When you meet your enemies who are polytheists, invite them to three courses of action." So also does Schacht's summary of the schools' restrictions on dhimmis contain no surprises for anyone familiar with Ghamdi's statement or the dictates of *'Umdat al-Salik*: "The treaty necessarily provides for the surrender of the non-Muslims with all duties deriving from it, in particular the payment of tribute, i.e., the fixed poll tax (*jizya*) and the land-tax (*kharaj*), the amount of which is determined from case to case.[36]

That may be, but another Islamic legal manual, the *Hedaya*, stipulates that "it is lawful to require twice as much"[37] from dhimmis as from Muslims—so while the rate may vary from dhimmi to dhimmi, it must never become a light or easy burden. Bat Ye'or illustrates in her exhaustive and illuminating historical works that this was seldom a temptation that Muslim rulers found difficult to overcome.

Schacht continues: "The non-Muslims must wear distinctive clothing and must mark their houses, which must not be built higher than those of Muslims, by distinctive signs; they must not ride horses or bear arms, and they must yield the way to Muslims; they must not scandalize the Muslims by openly performing their worship or their distinctive customs, such as drinking wine; they must not build new churches, synagogues, and hermitages; they must pay the poll tax under humiliating conditions."[38]

These laws are not strictly enforced today in most Islamic states. In Saudi Arabia they aren't because of that nation's status as the Muslim holy land. Non-Muslims aren't allowed to practice their religion at all in Saudi Arabia. Muhammad directed his followers to "turn out all *Al-Mushrikun* [unbelievers] from the Arabian Peninsula";[39] any non-Muslims who go to Saudi Arabia to work must strictly avoid any religious expression—those who dare violate this restriction have been imprisoned, expelled from the country, and sometimes even tortured.[40] Elsewhere the laws of dhimmitude gave way in the nineteenth and early twentieth centuries to pressure from the European colonial powers and were not components of the secular constitutions adopted by many Muslim states in the postcolonial period.

Nonetheless, centuries of enforcement of these laws have produced lingering cultural attitudes. That the Christian population of the Middle East, historically a significant presence, has plummeted during roughly the same period as the rise of radical Islam is no accident. While the ancestors of today's Middle Eastern Christians had no choice but to accept dhimmitude and lived within its restrictions for centuries without knowing or having the possibility of any other life, their contemporary descendants have grown up in a much freer environment, emancipated by secularism. Instead of reverting to the dhimmi subjugation that increasing numbers of their Muslim neighbors wish to impose on them, they are simply opting out of the region altogether—to its immense personal and cultural loss.

Nonetheless, this is understandable in light of the fact that Christians and other non-Muslims still face widespread discrimination and harassment all across the Islamic world. One notorious example was the case of Robert Hussein Qambar Ali, a Kuwaiti national who converted from Islam to Christianity in the 1990s. Hussein was arrested and tried for apostasy, even though the Kuwaiti constitution guarantees the freedom of religion and says nothing about the traditional Islamic prohibition on conversion to another faith. Mohammad al-Jadai, one of Hussein's prosecutors, explained: "Legislators did not regulate the question of apostasy in the Constitution because they never thought this kind of thing could happen here. The freedom of belief in the Constitution applies only to the religion of birth."[41]

This is a perspective that could only be informed by the Sharia provisions of dhimmitude. Such deeply ingrained attitudes informed the proceedings against Hussein. When he asked during a court hearing to see a memorandum from the prosecution, the prosecutor told the judge, "His blood is immoral! This document contains verses from the Holy Qur'an and should not be touched by this infidel!" Then he began quoting a passage from the memorandum that made abundantly clear the relationship between Kuwait's ostensibly tolerant secular law and the Sharia: "With grief I have to say that our criminal law does not include a penalty for apostasy. The fact is that the legislature, in our humble opinion, cannot enforce a penalty for apostasy any more or less than what our Allah and his messenger have decreed. The ones who will make the decision about his apostasy are: our Book, the Sunna, the agreement of the prophets and their legislation given by Allah."[42]

Later, when his home was burglarized, Hussein knew that he would get no satisfaction if he told Kuwaiti authorities about the crime. "I could tell them, but it is not a crime to steal or vandalize the property of an apostate. The police wouldn't even acknowledge that a burglary took place."[43]

Even in places where it is not fully enforced, the Sharia retains the status of a kind of metalaw, overriding and superseding the laws of the land whenever necessary. Consequently, the environment for non-Muslims in Islamic societies is not positive, and as radicalism increases, Muslims grow increasingly less tolerant toward their non-Muslim neighbors.

RADICAL MUSLIM THEORISTS ON NON-MUSLIMS

That intolerance is fueled also by the writings of some of the most popular and influential radical Muslim theorists of modern times. In the Egyptian Muslim Brotherhood theorist Sayyid Qutb's multivolume commentary on the Qur'an, *Fi Zilal al-Qur'an* (In the Shade of the Qur'an), Qutb writes venomously of Jews and Christians. In his exegesis of the verse mandating warfare against the People of the Book (sura 9:29), Qutb recites a litany of Islam's supposed historical grievances against the Jews, concluding: "In modern history, the Jews have been behind every calamity that has befallen the Muslim communities everywhere. They give active support to every attempt to crush the modern Islamic revival and extend their protection to every regime that suppresses such a revival. The other people of earlier revelations, the Christians, has been no less hostile."[44]

For Qutb, this hostility is not the result of various historical circumstances that could change for the better, or be overcome through dialogue and attempts at mutual understanding. On the contrary, Qutb explains that

> the Qur'anic statements concerning both groups are expressed as if they are stating established facts. God says to the unbelievers: "They shall not cease to fight you until they force you to renounce your faith, if they can." (2:217) He also says about the people of earlier revelations: "Never will the Jews nor yet the Christians be pleased with you unless you follow their faith." (2:120) This method of expression suggests that these are definitive statements describing permanent attitudes not individual or temporary cases. When we cast a quick glance at the history of these relations, on the basis of the attitudes adopted by the Jews and the Christians toward Islam and the Muslims in all periods of history, we will appreciate the full import of these true statements by God Himself. We also realize that such hostile attitudes are the rule, not the exception.[45]

What then is to be done with these renegades, these untrustworthy, dishonest, and hateful individuals? The Qur'an, of course, gives the answer: they must be "utterly subdued," in line with sura 9:29. Qutb explains: "As the only religion of truth that exists on earth today, Islam takes appropriate action to remove all physical and material obstacles that try to impede its efforts to liberate mankind from submission to anyone other than God. . . . The practical way to ensure the removal of these physical obstacles while not forcing anyone to adopt Islam[46] is to smash the power of those authorities based on false beliefs until they declare their submission and demonstrate this by paying the submission tax."[47]

Similarly, Indian radical theorist Sayyid Abdul Ala Maududi says that Muslims must fight against Jews, Christians, and others "not as one might think to compel the unbelievers into embracing Islam. Rather, their purpose is to put an end to the sovereignty and supremacy of the unbelievers so that the latter are unable to rule over men. The authority to rule should only be vested in those who follow the true faith; unbelievers who do not follow this true faith should live in a state of subordination. . . . 'To pay *jizyah* of their hands humbled' refers to payment in a state of submission."[48]

These men and other influential radicals were deeply traditionalist. Where socialism and Arab nationalism had introduced ideas of tolerance and equality for non-Muslims in the Muslim world, these theorists strenuously dissented on Islamic grounds. Qutb explicitly rejected democracy, socialism, communism, and all other ideologies as non-Islamic, and pitched his Islamic supremacism and intolerance precisely as the Islamic alternative.

That is the view that has swept the world in recent decades, with the rise of Islamic radical groups, global in extent, that look to Qutb as a forefather and intellectual mentor. It is ironic that the same period has seen the most intense growth of the myth of Islamic tolerance.

NOTES

1. United States District Court, Eastern District of Virginia, *United States of America v. Randall Todd Royer, Ibrahim Ahmed Al-Hamdi, Masoud Ahmad Khan, Yong Ki Kwon, Mohammed Aatique, Seifullah Chapman, Hammad Abdur-Raheem, Donald Thomas Surratt, Caliph Basha Ibn Abdur-Raheem, Khwaja Mahmood Hasan, Sabri Benkhala*, June 2003, http://news.findlaw.com/hdocs/docs/terrorism/usroyer603ind.pdf (accessed August 23, 2004). See also Terry Frieden, "'Jihad Network' Suspects Plead Not Guilty," CNN.com, July 3, 2003, http://www.cnn.com/2003/LAW/07/03/terror.arraignment; Nicholas K. Geranios, "Second Man with Ties to University of Idaho Arrested," Associated Press, March 14, 2003. For Khafagi's position with CAIR, which CAIR reportedly denies, see Carol Eisenberg, "A Troubling Year for Muslims in America," *Newsday*, September 2, 2002. For Ghassan Elashi, the third CAIR official arrested, and other illuminating information about the group, see Joe Kaufman, "The CAIR-Terror Connection," *FrontPageMagazine.com*, April 29, 2004, http://www.frontpagemag.com/Articles/ReadArticle.asp?ID=13175 (accessed August 23, 2004).

2. Bat Ye'or, "Myths and Politics: The Tolerant Pluralistic Islamic Society: Origin of a Myth," paper presented at the Lord Byron Foundation for Balkan Studies and International Strategic Studies Association Symposium on the Balkan War, August 31, 1995, http://www.dhimmitude.org/archive/LectureE1.html (accessed August 22, 2004).

3. Many of these have been collected at Bat Ye'or's Web site, "Dhimmis and Dhimmitude: The Status of Minorities under Islamic Rule," an outstanding resource: www.dhimmitude.org. The spelling of words, when not in a quotation, has generally been Americanized throughout, even in articles originally published in the United Kingdom.

4. Bat Ye'or, "Myths and Politics."

5. Ibid.

6. Quoted in Bat Ye'or, *The Decline of Eastern Christianity under Islam: From Jihad to Dhimmitude: Seventh–Twentieth Century*, trans. Miriam Kochan and David Littman (Madison, NJ: Fairleigh Dickinson University Press, 1996), p. 384.

7. Ibid., p. 423.

8. "Soldier Held on Suspicion of Espionage," CNN.com, February 13, 2004, http://www.cnn.com/2004/US/02/12/natl.guard.espionage/ (accessed August 23, 2004).

9. Stephen Brown, "France's Rushdie Affair," FrontPageMagazine.com, November 21, 2003, http://www.frontpagemag.com/Articles/ReadArticle.asp?ID= 10931 (accessed August 23, 2004).

10. "Carey Makes Fresh Islam Speech," BBC News online, May 12, 2004, http://news.bbc.co.uk/1/hi/uk/3708859.stm (accessed August 23, 2004).

11. "Fears as Young Muslims 'Opt Out,'" BBC News online, March 7, 2004, http://news.bbc.co.uk/1/hi/uk/3539535.stm (accessed August 23, 2004).

12. Russell Bassett, "Commentary: Islam—Respect the Faith, Not the Fanatics," Army News Service, May 14, 2004.

13. "Two Sentenced for Trying to Join Taliban," Associated Press, November 24, 2003.

14. Samar Fatany, "Stop the Attack against Islam," *Arab News*, May 12, 2004.

15. "2nd Issue of 'Voice of Jihad' Al-Qa'ida Online Magazine: Strategy to Avoid Clashes with Saudi Security Forces, Convert the World's Countries to Islam," Middle East Media Research Institute, October 31, 2003.

16. Igor Rotar, "Central Asia: Hizb-ut-Tahrir wants worldwide Sharia law," Forum 18 News Service, October 29, 2003.

17. David Isenberg, "Jemaah Islamiya 'Damaged but Dangerous,'" *Asia Times*, September 4, 2003.

18. "Obligatory to Implement the Shari'ah," www.muhajiroun.com.

19. Quoted in Steven Stalinsky, "The 'Islamic Affairs Department' of the Saudi Embassy in Washington, D.C.," Middle East Media Research Institute, November 26, 2003.

20. Bill Graham, "Now Is the Time to Reach Out to the Muslim World," *Globe and Mail*, May 14, 2004. For the Khadrs, see "Khadr Mother and Son Return to Canada," *Globe and Mail*, April 20, 2004. For Chrétien, see "Married to the Jihad: The Lonely World of al-Qa'ida's Wives," *Independent*, May 16, 2004.

21. Stewart Bell, "Al-Qaeda Says Canada Deserves Bombing: Jihad Spokesman Says Canadians Were Mean to Khadrs," *National Post*, May 15, 2004.

22. Imam Muslim, *Sahih Muslim*, trans. Abdul Hamid Siddiqi, rev. ed. (New Delhi: Kitab Bhavan, 2000), bk. 1, no. 284.

23. *The Translation of the Meanings of Sahih Bukhari*, trans. Muhammad Muhsin Khan, vol. 6 (Riyadh: Darussalam, 1997), bk. 65, no. 4581.

24. Ibid., vol. 4, bk. 60, no. 3448.

25. Ibid., vol. 4, bk. 60, no. 3449.

26. Ibid., vol. 4, bk. 56, no. 2941.

27. *Sahih Muslim*, bk. 19, no. 4294.

28. *Sahih Bukhari*, vol. 4, bk. 58, no. 3162.

29. Middle East Media Research Institute (MEMRI), "Friday Sermons in Saudi Mosques: Review and Analysis," MEMRI Special Report 10, September 26, 2002, http://www.memri.org/bin/articles.cgi?Page=archives&Area=sr&ID=SR01002 (accessed August 23, 2004). This undated sermon appeared on the Saudi Web site www.alminbar.net shortly before the MEMRI translation was published.

30. Middle East Media Research Institute, "A Friday Sermon on PA TV: . . . We Must Educate Our Children on the Love of Jihad . . . ," MEMRI Special Dispatch 240, July 11, 2001, http://www.memri.org/bin/articles.cgi?Page=archives&Area=sd &ID=SP24001 (accessed August 23, 2004).

31. Ibid.

32. Ahmed ibn Naqib al-Misri, *Reliance of the Traveller: A Classic Manual of Islamic Sacred Law*, trans. Nuh Ha Mim Keller (Beltsville, MD: Amana, 1999), secs. 011.3, 5.

33. Ibid., p. ix.

34. Ibid., p. xx.

35. Joseph Schacht, *An Introduction to Islamic Law* (Oxford: Clarendon Press, 1982), p. 130.

36. Ibid., p. 131.

37. Charles Hamilton, trans., *The Hedaya* (1870; reprint, Kitab Bhavan, 1994), p. 18.

38. Schacht, *Introduction to Islamic Law*, p. 131.

39. *Sahih Bukhari*, vol. 4, bk. 58, no. 3168.

40. See "Saudi Police Torture Indian Catholic for His Faith," ZENIT News Agency, June 2, 2004.

41. Quoted in Robert Hussein, *Apostate Son* (Colorado Springs, CO: Najiba, 1998), p. 120.

42. Ibid., p. 161.

43. Ibid., p. 193.

44. Sayyid Qutb, *In the Shade of the Qur'an*, trans. Adil Salahi, vol. 8 (Leicester, UK: Islamic Foundation and Islamonline.net, 2003), p. 115.

45. Ibid., p. 112.

46. In line with sura 2:256: "There is no compulsion in religion."

47. Ibid., p. 123.

48. Sayyid Abdul A'la Maududi, *Toward Understanding the Qur'an*, trans. Zafar Ishaq Ansari, vol. 3 (Leicester, UK: Islamic Foundation, 1990), p. 202.

PART 2.
ISLAMIC LAW REGARDING NON-MUSLIMS

Introduction

Robert Spencer

The two documents in this second section detail the particulars of Islamic law regarding the treatment of non-Muslims, with a particular focus on the aspect of that treatment that revolves around payment of the *jizya*, the special tax on non-Muslims. This payment has always been the centerpiece of the Islamic legal system regarding non-Muslims, as it is explicitly mentioned in the Qur'an (sura 9:29), while other elements of the treatment and status of the dhimmis are elaborations of this verse's command to make sure that the dhimmis "feel themselves subdued."

Both of these essays show conclusively, with extracts from all the schools of Islamic law, that there is no equality of dignity or rights for non-Muslims under Islamic law. The idea that Islamic states of the Middle Ages were somehow prototypes for today's Western, secular, multicultural societies founders upon these facts, utterly destroying any credibility of the myth of Islamic tolerance. Mythmakers must also confront the extraordinary unanimity of Islamic law on these points—not only from different schools but across the centuries and in all areas of the Islamic world. It is a truly remarkable example of the power of *ijma*—consensus. After all, as Muhammad is supposed to have said, "My community will never agree upon an error."[1] This consensus thus bears witness to the fact that the great majority of Muslims throughout history, and many even after the emancipation of the dhimmis in the nineteenth century (brought about by Western pressure), have accepted these principles as reasonable and right.

NOTE

1. See Abu Dawud, *Sunan Abu Dawud,* trans. Ahmad Hasan, (New Delhi: Kitab Bhavan, 1990), bk. 35, no. 4240.

RIGHTS OF NON-MUSLIMS IN AN ISLAMIC STATE

2.

Samuel Shahid

Recently a few books have been written about the rights of non-Muslims who are subjugated to the rule of Islamic law. Most of these books presented the Islamic view in a favorable fashion, without unveiling the negative aspect inherent in these laws. This brief study attempts to examine these laws as they are stated by the four schools of the *Fiqh* (jurisprudence). It aims at revealing to the reader the negative implications of these laws without ignoring the more tolerant views of modern reformers. It is our ardent hope that this study will reveal to our readers the bare truth in both its positive and its negative aspects.

THE CONCEPT OF "ISLAMIC STATE"

"An Islamic state is essentially an ideological state, and is thus radically different from a national state." This statement made by Maududi, a prominent Pakistani Muslim scholar, lays the basic foundation for the political, economic, social, and religious system of all Islamic countries that impose Islamic law. This ideological system intentionally discriminates among people according to their religious affiliations. Maududi summarizes the basic differences between Islamic and secular states as follows:

- An Islamic state is ideological. People who reside in it are divided into Muslims, who believe in its ideology, and non-Muslims, who do not believe.

Reprinted from the Answering Islam Web site, http://www.answering-Islam.org/NonMuslims/rights .htm. Used with permission.

- Responsibility for policy and administration of such a state "should rest primarily with those who believe in the Islamic ideology." Non-Muslims, therefore, cannot be asked to undertake or be entrusted with the responsibility of policymaking.
- An Islamic state is bound to distinguish (i.e., discriminates) between Muslims and non-Muslims. However the Islamic law, the "Sharia" guarantees to non-Muslims "certain specifically stated rights beyond which they are not permitted to meddle in the affairs of the state because they do not subscribe to its ideology." Once they embrace the Islamic faith, they "become equal participants in all matters concerning the state and the government."[1]

The above view is the representative of the *Hanifites*, one of the four Islamic schools of jurisprudence. The other three schools are the *Malikites*, the *Hanbilites* (the strictest and the most fundamentalist of all), and the *Shafiites*. All four schools agree dogmatically on the basic creeds of Islam but differ in their interpretations of Islamic law, which is derived from four sources:

- *Qur'an* (read or recite): The sacred book of the Muslim community, containing direct quotes from Allah as allegedly dictated by Gabriel.
- *Hadith* (narrative): The collections of Islamic traditions, including sayings and deeds of Muhammad as heard by his contemporaries, first-, second-, and third-hand.
- *Al-Qiyas* (analogy or comparison): The legal decision drawn by Islamic jurists based on precedent cases.
- *Ijma* (consensus): The interpretations of Islamic laws handed down by the consensus of reputed Muslim scholars in a certain country.

Textual laws prescribed in the Qur'an are few. The door is left wide open for prominent scholars versed in the Qur'an, the Hadith, and other Islamic disciplines to present their *fatwa* (legal opinion), as we shall see later.

Classification of Non-Muslims

In his article "The Ordinances of the People of the Covenant and the Minorities in an Islamic State," Sheikh Najih Ibrahim Ibn Abdullah remarks that legists classify non-Muslims or infidels into two categories: *dar al-Harb*, or the Household of War, which refers to non-Muslims who are not bound by a peace treaty or covenant and whose blood and property are not protected by the law of vendetta or retaliation; and *Dar es Salam*, or the Household of Peace, which refers to those who fall into three classifications:

- *Zimmis* (those in custody; also called dhimmis) are non-Muslim subjects who live in Muslim countries and agree to pay the *jizya* (tribute) in exchange for protection and safety, and to be subject to Islamic law. They enjoy a permanent covenant.
- People of the *hudna* (truce) are those who sign a peace treaty with Muslims after being defeated in war. They agree to reside in their own land, yet to be subject to the legal jurisprudence of Islam like dhimmis, provided they do not wage war against Muslims.
- A *Musta'min* (protected one) is a person who comes to an Islamic country as a messenger, merchant, visitor, or student wanting to learn about Islam. A *Musta'min* should not wage war against Muslims, and he is not obliged to pay the *jizya*, but he would be urged to embrace Islam. If a *Musta'min* does not accept Islam, he is allowed to return safely to his own country. Muslims are forbidden to hurt him in any way. When he is back in his own homeland, he is treated as one who belongs to the Household of War.[2]

This study will focus on the laws pertaining to dhimmis.

ISLAMIC LAW AND DHIMMIS

Muslim muftis (legal authorities) agree that the contract of the dhimmis should be offered primarily to the People of the Book, that is, Christians and Jews, then to the Magi and Zoroastrians. However, they disagree on whether any contract should be signed with other groups such as communists or atheists. The Hanbalites and the Shafiites believe that no contract should be made with the ungodly or those who do not believe in the supreme God. Hanifites and Malikites affirm that the *jizya* may be accepted from all infidels, regardless of their beliefs and faith in God. Abu Hanifa, however, did not want pagan Arabs to have this option because they are the people of the Prophet. They must be given only two options: accept Islam or be killed.

THE *JIZYA*

Jizya literally means "penalty." It is a protection tax levied on non-Muslims living under Islamic regimes, confirming their legal status. Maududi states that "the acceptance of the *jizya* establishes the sanctity of their lives and property, and thereafter neither the Islamic state nor the Muslim public has any right to violate their property, honor, or liberty." Paying the *jizya* is a symbol of humiliation and submission, because dhimmis are not regarded as citizens of the Islamic state, although they are, in most cases, natives to the country.

Such an attitude alienates the dhimmis from being an essential part of the community. How can a dhimmi feel at home in his own land, among his own people, and with his own government, when he knows that the *jizya* he pays is a symbol of humiliation and submission? In his book *The Islamic Law Pertaining to non-Muslims*, Sheikh 'Abdulla Mustafa al-Muraghi indicates that the *jizya* can only be exempted from dhimmi who become Muslim's or who die. The *Shafiites* reiterate that the *jizya* is not automatically put aside when a dhimmi embraces Islam. Exemption from the *jizya* has become an incentive to encourage dhimmis to relinquish their faith and embrace Islam.[3]

Sheik Najih Ibrahim Ibn Abdullah summarizes the purpose of the *jizya*. He says, quoting Ibn Qayyim al-Jawziyya, that the *jizya* is enacted "to spare the blood (of the dhimmis), to be a symbol of humiliation of the infidels and as an insult and punishment to them, and as the Shafiites indicate, the *jizya* is offered in exchange for residing in an Islamic country." Thus Ibn Qayyim adds, "Since the entire religion belongs to God, it aims at humiliating ungodliness and its followers, and insulting them. Imposing the *jizya* on the followers of ungodliness and oppressing them is required by God's religion. The Qur'anic text hints at this meaning when it says: 'until they give the tribute by force with humiliation' (Qur'an 9:29). What contradicts this is leaving the infidels to enjoy their might and practice their religion as they wish so that they would have power and authority."[4]

DHIMMIS AND RELIGIOUS PRACTICES

Muslims believe that the dhimmis are *mushrikun* (polytheists), for they see the belief in the Trinity of Christianity as belief in three gods. Islam is the only true religion, they claim. Therefore, to protect Muslims from corruption, especially against the unforgivable sin of *shirk* (polytheism), its practice is forbidden among Muslims, because it is considered the greatest abomination. When

Christians practice it publicly, it becomes an enticement and exhortation to apostasy. It is significant here to notice that according to Muraghi, dhimmis and infidels are polytheists and therefore, must have the same treatment.

According to Muslim jurists, the following legal ordinances must be enforced on dhimmis (Christians and Jews alike) who reside among Muslims:

- Dhimmis are not allowed to build new churches, temples, or synagogues. They are allowed to renovate old churches or houses of worship, provided they do not allow to add any new construction. "Old churches" are those that existed prior to Islamic conquest and are included in a peace accord by Muslims. Construction of any church, temple, or synagogue on the Arabian Peninsula (Saudi Arabia) is prohibited. It is the land of the Prophet, and only Islam should prevail there. Yet Muslims, if they wish, are permitted to demolish all non-Muslim houses of worship in any land they conquer.
- Dhimmis are not allowed to pray or read their sacred books out loud at home or in churches, lest Muslims hear their prayers.
- Dhimmis are not allowed to print their religious books or sell them in public places and markets. They are allowed to publish and sell them among their own people, in their churches and temples.
- Dhimmis are not allowed to install the cross on their houses or churches, since it is a symbol of infidelity.
- Dhimmis are not permitted to broadcast or display their ceremonial religious rituals on radio or television or to use the media or to publish any picture of their religious ceremonies in newspapers and magazines.
- Dhimmis are not allowed to congregate in the streets during their religious festivals; rather, each must quietly make his way to his church or temple.
- Dhimmis are not allowed to join the army unless there is indispensable need for them in which case they are not allowed to assume leadership positions but are considered mercenaries.

Maududi, who is a Hanifite, expresses a more generous opinion toward Christians. He says: "In their own towns and cities they are allowed to do so [i.e., practice their religion] with the fullest freedom. In purely Muslim areas, however, an Islamic government has full discretion to put such restrictions on their practices as it deems necessary."[5]

APOSTASY IN ISLAM

Apostasy means rejection of the religion of Islam either by action or the word of the mouth. "The act of apostasy, thus, put an end to one's adherence to Islam."[6] When one rejects the fundamental creeds of Islam, he rejects the faith, and this is an act of apostasy—such an act is a grave sin in Islam. The Qur'an comments, "How shall Allah guide those who reject faith after they accepted it and bore witness that the Apostle was true and the clear sign had come unto them? But Allah guides not the people of unjust. Of such the reward is that on them rests the curse of Allah, of His angels and of all mankind in that will they dwell; nor will their penalty be lightened, nor respite be their lot, except for those that repent after that and make amends; for verily Allah is Oft-forgiving, Most Merciful" (sura 3:86–89).

Officially, Islamic law requires Muslims not to force dhimmis to embrace Islam. It is the duty of every Muslim, they hold, to manifest the virtues of Islam so that those who are non-Muslims will convert willingly after discovering its greatness and truth. Once a person becomes a Muslim, he cannot recant. If he does, he will be warned first, then he will be given three days to reconsider and repent. If he persists in his apostasy, his wife is required to divorce him, his property is confiscated, and his children are taken away from him. He is not allowed to remarry. Instead, he should be taken to court and sentenced to death. If he repents, he may return to his wife and children or remarry. According to the Hanifites an apostate female is not allowed to get married. She must spend time in meditation in order to return to Islam. If she does not repent or recant, she will not be sentenced to death, but she is to be persecuted, beaten, and jailed until she dies. Other schools of Sharia demand her death. The above punishment is prescribed in a Hadith recorded by the Bukhari: "It is reported by 'Abaas . . . that the messenger of Allah . . . said, 'Whosoever changes his religion (from Islam to any other faith), kill him.'"[7] In his book *Shari'ah: The Islamic Law*, Doi remarks, "The punishment by death in the case of Apostasy has been unanimously agreed upon by all the four schools of Islamic jurisprudence."[8]

A non-Muslim wishing to become a Muslim is encouraged to do so, and anyone, even a father or a mother, who attempts to stop him may be punished. However, anyone who makes an effort to proselytize a Muslim to any other faith may face punishment.

CIVIC LAWS

Dhimmis and Muslims are subject to the same civic laws. They are to be treated alike in matters of honor, theft, adultery, murder, and damaging property. They have to be punished in accordance with Islamic law regardless of their religious affiliation. Dhimmis and Muslims alike are subject to Islamic laws in matters of civic business, financial transactions such as sales, leases, firms, establishment of companies, farms, securities, mortgages, and contracts. For instance, theft is punishable by cutting off the thief's hand whether he is a Muslim or a Christian. But when it comes to privileges, the dhimmis do not enjoy the same treatment. For instance, dhimmis are not issued licenses to carry weapons.

MARRIAGE AND CHILDREN

A Muslim male can marry a dhimmi girl, but a dhimmi man is not allowed to marry a Muslim girl. If a woman embraces Islam and wants to get married, her non-Muslim father does not have the authority to give her away to her bridegroom. She must be given away by a Muslim guardian.

　　If one parent is a Muslim, children must be raised as Muslims. If the father is a dhimmi and his wife converts to Islam, she must get a divorce; then she will have the right of custody of her child. Some fundamentalist schools indicate that a Muslim husband has the right to confine his dhimmi wife to her home and restrain her from going to her own house of worship.

CAPITAL PUNISHMENT

The Hanifites believe that both dhimmis and Muslims must suffer the same penalty for similar crimes. If a Muslim kills a dhimmi intentionally, he must be killed in return. The same applies to a Christian who kills a Muslim. But other schools of law have different interpretations of Islamic law. The Shafiites declare that a Muslim who kills a dhimmi must not be killed, because it is not reasonable to equate a Muslim with a polytheist (*mushrik*). In such a case, blood price must be paid. The penalty depends on the school of law adopted by the particular Islamic country where the crime or offense is committed. This illustrates the implication of different interpretations of the Islamic law based on the Hadith.

Each school attempts to document its legal opinion by referring to the Hadith or to an incident experienced by the Prophet or the "rightly guided" caliphs.

THE WITNESS OF DHIMMIS

Dhimmis cannot testify against Muslims. They can only testify against other dhimmi*s* or *Musta'min*. Their oaths are not considered valid in an Islamic court. According to the Sharia, a dhimmi is not even qualified to be under oath. Muraghi states bluntly, "The testimony of a Dhimmi is not accepted because Allah—may He be exalted—said: 'God will not let the infidels (*kafir*) have an upper hand over the believers.'"9 A dhimmi, regarded as an infidel, cannot testify against any Muslim, regardless of his moral credibility. If a dhimmi has falsely accused another dhimmi and was once punished, his credibility and integrity is tarnished, and his testimony is no longer acceptable. One serious implication of this is that if one Muslim has committed a serious offense against another, witnessed by dhimmis only, the court will have difficulty deciding the case, since the testimony of dhimmis is not acceptable. Yet this same dhimmi whose integrity is blemished, if he converts to Islam, will have his testimony accepted against the dhimmis and Muslims alike, because according to the Sharia, "By embracing Islam he has gained a new credibility which would enable him to witness." All he has to do is to utter the Islamic confession of faith before witnesses, and that will elevate him from being an outcast to being a respected Muslim enjoying all the privileges of a devout believer.

PERSONAL LAW

On personal matters of marriage, divorce, and inheritance, dhimmis are allowed to appeal to their own religious courts. Each Christian denomination has the right and authority to determine the outcome of each case. Dhimmis are free to practice their own social and religious rites at home and in church without interference from the state, even in such matters as drinking wine, rearing pigs, and eating pork, as long as they do not sell them to Muslims. Dhimmis are generally denied the right to appeal to an Islamic court in family matters, marriage, divorce, and inheritance. However, in the event a Muslim judge agrees to take such a case, the court must apply Islamic law.

POLITICAL RIGHTS AND DUTIES

The Islamic state is an ideological state; thus the head of the state inevitably must be a Muslim, because he is bound by the Sharia to conduct and administer the state in accordance with the Qur'an and the Sunna. The function of his advisory council is to assist him in implementing the Islamic principles and adhering to them. Anyone who does not embrace Islamic ideology cannot be the head of state or a member of the council.

Maududi, aware of the requirements of modern society, seems to be more tolerant toward dhimmis: "In regard to a parliament or a legislature of the modern type, which is considerably different from the advisory council in its traditional sense, this rule could be relaxed to allow non-Muslims to be members, provided that it has been fully ensured in the constitution that no law which is repugnant to the Qur'an and the Sunna should be enacted, that the Qur'an and the Sunna should be the chief source of public law, and that the head of the state should necessarily be a Muslim."[10]

Under these circumstances, the sphere of influence of non-Muslim minorities would be limited to matters relating to general problems of the country or to the interest of the minorities. Their participation should not damage the fundamental requirement of Islam. Maududi adds, "It is possible to form a separate representative assembly for all non-Muslim groups in the capacity of a central agency. The membership and the voting rights of such an assembly will be confined to non-Muslims and they would be given the fullest freedom within its frame-work."[11]

These views do not receive the approval of most other schools of the Sharia, which hold that non-Muslims are not allowed to assume any position that might bestow on them any authority over any Muslim. A position of sovereignty demands the implementation of Islamic ideology. It is alleged that a non-Muslim (regardless of his ability, sincerity, and loyalty to his country) cannot and would not work faithfully to achieve the ideological and political goals of Islam.

BUSINESS WORLD

The political arena and the official public sectors are not the only areas in which non-Muslims are not allowed to assume a position of authority. A Muslim employee who works in a company inquires in a letter "if it is permissible for a Muslim owner [of a company] to confer authority on a Christian over other Muslims."[12]

In response to this inquiry three eminent Muslim scholars issued their legal opinions. Sheikh Manna' K. al-Qubtan, professor of higher studies at the School of Islamic Law in Riyadh, indicates, "Basically, the command of non-Muslims over Muslims in not admissible, because God Almighty said: 'Allah will not give access to the infidels [i.e., Christians] to have authority over believers [Muslims]' (Qur'an 4:141). For God—Glory be to Him—has elevated Muslims to the highest rank (over all men) and foreordained to them the might, by virtue of the Qur'anic text in which God the Almighty said: 'Might and strength be to Allah, the Prophet [Muhammad] and the believers [Muslims]' (Qur'an 63:8)."

Thus the authority of non-Muslim over a Muslim is incompatible with these two verses, since the Muslim has to submit to and obey whoever is in charge over him. The Muslim therefore becomes inferior to him, and this should not be the case with the Muslim.

Dr. Salih al-Sadlan, professor of Sharia at the School of Islamic Law, Riyadh, cites the same verses and asserts that it is not permissible for a infidel (in this case, a Christian) to be in charge over Muslims whether in the private or public sector. Such an act

> entails the humiliaton of the Muslim and the exaltation of the infidel [Christian]. This infidel may exploit his position to humiliate and insult the Muslims who work under his administration. It is advisable to the company owner to fear God Almighty and to authorize only a Muslim over the Muslims. Also, the injunctions issued by the ruler, provides that an infidel should not be in charge when there is a Muslim available to assume the command. Our advice to the company owner is to remove this infidel and to replace him with a Muslim.

Dr. Fahd al-'Usaymi, professor of Islamic studies at the Teachers' College in Riyadh, remarks that the Muslim owner of the company should seek a Muslim employee who is better than the Christian manager, or equal to him or even less qualified but has the ability to be trained to obtain the same skill enjoyed by the Christian. It is not permissible for a Christian to be in charge of Muslims by the virtue of the general evidences that denote the superiority of the Muslim over others. Then he quotes sura 63:8 of the Qur'an and also cites verse 22 of sura 58: "Thou wilt not find any people who believe in Allah and the Last Day, loving those who resist Allah and His Apostle, even though they were their fathers or their sons, or their brothers, or their kindred." 'Usaymi claims that being under the authority of a Christian may force Muslims to flatter him and humiliate themselves to this infidel on the hope to obtain some of what he has. This is against the confirmed evidences. Then he alludes to the story of Umar Ibn al-Khattab, the second caliph, who was displeased with one of his governors, who appointed a dhimmi as a treasurer, and remarked, "Have the wombs of women become sterile that they gave birth only to this man?" Then 'Usaymi adds, "Muslims should fear God in their Muslim brothers and train them. . . . For honesty and fear of God are, originally, in the Muslim, contrary to the infidel [the Christian] who, originally, is dishonest and does not fear God."

Does this mean that a Christian who owns a business cannot employ a Muslim to work for him? Even worse, does this mean that a dhimmi, regardless of his unequal qualification, cannot be appointed to the position where he would serve his country best? This question demands an answer.

FREEDOM OF EXPRESSION

Maududi, who is more lenient than most Muslim scholars, presents a revolutionary opinion when he emphasizes that in an Islamic state, "all non-Muslims will have the freedom of conscience, opinion, expression, and association as the one enjoyed by Muslims themselves, subject to the same limitations as are imposed by law on Muslims."[13] Maududi's views are not accepted by most Islamic schools of law, especially in regard to freedom of expression involving criticism of Islam and the government. Even in a country like Pakistan, the homeland of Maududi, it is illegal to criticize the government or the head of state. Many political prisoners are confined to jails in Pakistan and most other Islamic countries. Through the course of history, except in rare cases, not even Muslims have been given freedom to criticize Islam without being persecuted or sentenced to death. It is far less likely for a dhimmi to get away with criticizing Islam.

In Maududi's statement, the term *limitations* is vaguely defined. If it were explicitly defined, one would find, in the final analysis, that it curbs any type of criticism against the Islamic faith and government.

Moreover, how can the dhimmis express the positive aspects of their religion when they are not allowed to use the media or advertise them on radio or television? Perhaps Maududi meant by his proposals to allow such freedom to dhimmis only among themselves. Otherwise, they would be subject to penalty. Yet Muslims are allowed, according to the Sharia to propagate their faith among all religious sects without any limitations.

MUSLIMS AND DHIMMIS

Relationships between Muslims and dhimmis are classified in two categories: what is forbidden and what is allowable.

The Forbidden

A Muslim is not allowed to

- emulate the dhimmis in their dress or behavior;
- attend dhimmi festivals or support them in any way which may give them any power over Muslims;
- lease his house or sell his land for the construction of a church, temple, liquor store, or anything that may benefit the dhimmi's faith;
- work for dhimmis in any job that might promote their faith, such as constructing a church;
- make any endowment to churches or temples;
- carry any vessel that contains wine, work in wine production, or transport pigs;
- address dhimmis with any title such as "my master" or "my lord."

The Allowable

A Muslim is allowed to

- financially assist the dhimmis, provided the money is not used in violation of Islamic law like buying wine or pork;
- give the right of preemption (priority in buying property) to his dhimmi neighbor (the hanbilites disapprove of this);
- eat food prepared by the People of the Book;
- console the dhimmis in an illness or in the loss of a loved one; it is also permissible for a Muslim to escort a funeral to the cemetery, but he has to walk in front of the coffin, not behind it, and he must depart before the deceased is buried;
- congratulate the dhimmis for a wedding, birth of a child, return from a long trip, or recovery from illness; however, Muslims are warned not to utter any word that may suggest approval of the dhimmis' faith, such as "May Allah exalt you," "May Allah honor you," or "May Allah give your religion victory."

CONCLUSION

This study shows us that non-Muslims are not regarded as citizens by any Islamic state, even if they are original natives of the land. To say otherwise is to conceal the truth. Justice and equality require that any Christian Pakistani, Melanesian, Turk, or Arab be treated as any other citizen of his own country. He deserves to enjoy the same privileges of citizenship regardless of religious affiliation. To claim that Islam is the true religion and to accuse other religions of infidelity is a social, religious, and legal offense against the People of the Book.

Christians believe that their religion is the true religion of God and Islam is not. Does that mean that Great Britain, which is headed by a queen, the head of the Church of England, should treat its Muslim subjects as a second class? Moreover, why do Muslims in the West enjoy all freedoms allotted to all citizens of these lands, while Muslim countries do not allow native Christians the same freedom? Muslims in the West build mosques, schools, and educational centers and have access to the media without any restriction. They publicly advertise their activities and are allowed to distribute their Islamic materials freely, while native Christians of any Islamic country are not allowed to do so. Why are Christians in the West allowed to embrace any religion they wish without persecution while a person who chooses to convert to another religion in any Islamic country is considered an apostate and must be killed if he persists in his apostasy? These questions and others are left for readers to ponder.

NOTES

1. S. Abul Ala Maududi, *The Rights of Non-Muslims in the Islamic State* (Lahore, Pakistan: Islamic Publications, 1982).

2. Najih Ibrahim bin Abdullah, "The Ordinances of the People of the Covenant and the Minorities in an Islamic State," *Balagh* (Cairo), May 29, 1988, and June 5, 1988.

3. Abdullah Mustapha Muraghi, *Islamic Law Pertaining to Non-Muslims* (Egypt: Library of Letters, n.d.).

4. Adbullah, "The Ordinances of the People of the Covenant and the Minorities in an Islamic State."

5. Maududi, *The Rights of Non-Muslims in the Islamic State.*

6. Ibid.

7. *The Translation of the Meanings of Sahih Bukhari*, trans. Muhammad Musin Khan, vol. 9 (Riyadh: Darussalam, 1997), bk. 88, no. 6922.

8. 'Abdur Rahman I. Doi, *Shari'a: The Islamic Law* (London: Taha, 1984).

9. Muraghi, *Islamic Law Pertaining to Non-Muslims*.

10. Maududi, *The Rights of Non-Muslims in the Islamic State*.

11. Ibid.

12. *Al-Muslim Weekly*, May 2, 1993.

13. Maududi, *The Rights of Non-Muslims in the Islamic State*.

THE JIZYA TAX

3. Equality and Dignity under Islamic Law?

Walter Short

INTRODUCTION

It is an oft-repeated assertion of Muslims that other faith communities have always been treated with respect and dignity by in a genuine Islamic state. Indeed, as one peruses Islamic literature, this claim is noticeable for the frequency of its presence. For example, Muslim author Suzanne Haneef states about Islam's attitude to other religious communities, "Islam does not permit discrimination in the treatment of other human beings on the basis of religion or any other criteria. . . . It emphasises neighborliness and respect for the ties of relationships with non-Muslims. . . . Within this human family, Jews and Christians, who share many beliefs and values with Muslims, constitute what Islam terms Ahl al-Kitab, that is, People of the Scripture, and hence Muslims have a special relationship to them as fellow 'Scriptuaries.'"[1]

Similarly, German convert Ahmed von Denffer, examining the position of Christians in Islam, states that "It is thus clear that, seen from the legal perspective, Christians are entitled to have their own prescriptions."[2] From what he terms the "Societal Perspective," he tackles the problem of sura 5:51, which warns against taking Jews and Christians as "friends": "On the other hand, Christians, being *ahl al-kitab*, may not be harassed or molested for being non-Muslims. It is true that the Qur'an warns against taking Jews and Christians as friends, but that does not mean they should be molested or harmed because of their being non-Muslims."[3]

So far, all very positive, but both Haneef and von Denffer are Muslims residing in the West, thus interacting with Christians and addressing a

Reprinted from http://debate.org.uk/topics/history/xstnc-5.html.

Western audience. Thus their approach will be conditioned by that reality. A somewhat different attitude is exhibited by a Muslim writer based in Saudi Arabia, a state, governed largely by Islamic law, that forbids all expressions of religious liberty: "In a country ruled by Muslim authorities, a non-Muslim is guaranteed his freedom of faith. . . . Muslims are forbidden from obliging a non-Muslim to embrace Islam, *but he should pay the tribute to Muslims readily and submissively*, surrender to Islamic laws, *and should not practice his polytheistic rituals openly*" (emphasis added).[4]

In this paper I will examine aspects of Islam's attitude to non-Muslims, especially the *jizya* tax, to consider whether Haneef's claim in particular is valid. My emphasis will be on Islamic law, since that practically regulates everyday relations. Since Muslims in the West, as much as in the Muslim world, uphold the divine character of the Sharia, based as it is primarily on the Qur'an and the Sunnah, and uphold the Islamic state with Islamic law as the ideal society, it is important to see what this would mean in practice for non-Muslims, if the caliphate were ever restored and applied to the West.

THE VALUE OF HUMAN LIFE

In the West, at least in constitutional terms, however inadequately worked out in practice in some places, the equality of human beings is a fundamental assumption—"all men are equal before the law." For this reason, justice is often depicted in statues as blindfolded; the class, religion, and race are irrelevant—the law, at least in terms of its goal, applies equally to everyone and safeguards everyone equally.

In Islamic law, however, this is simply not the case. The life of a Muslim is considered superior to that of a non-Muslim, so much so that although a non-Muslim killing a Muslim would be executed, the reverse would not occur.[5] This is despite the fact that murder is normally considered a capital offense in Islam, with regular executions in most Muslim states. This inequity is also demonstrable in the blood rate paid to non-Muslims where murder or injury has occurred, which is half that of a Muslim.[6] Effectively, this ruling means that a Muslim need not fear the usual retribution for murder if he kills a non-Muslim. The law deliberately and consciously does not protect non-Muslims as it does Muslims. The position of Islamic law is not that human life is sacred but that *Muslim* life is so.

The Value of Evidence

What we have just stated about justice becomes very pertinent when considering evidence in a court. Haneef's assertions can be immediately questioned by pointing to the fact that in Islam, the court testimony of a non-Muslim is considered inferior to that of a Muslim, a practice given official sanction in countries like Pakistan.[7] This means in practice that if a Muslim offends in some way against a Christian, whether by stealing from the latter, inflicting injury, or even committing rape, the Christian must gain at least another Christian witness even to match the testimony of the Muslim, and even then in practice the assumption is that the latter is a more credible witness. This rule also carries the insulting presumption that non-Muslims are intrinsically dishonest and unreliable witnesses per se.

Obviously, this considerably disadvantages non-Muslims and becomes of practical import when we consider the frequent charges of blasphemy used by Muslims against Christians in places like Pakistan, which usually have an ulterior motive (often personal or land disputes). Legal conditions such as these give unscrupulous Muslims the idea that it is "open season" on minorities. A similar ruling endangers the inheritance rights of Christian wives of Muslims.[8] Again, this gives opportunity to dishonest Muslim relatives of a widow.

The Value of Human Dignity

What we have just examined becomes very important when we consider the issue of human dignity. It almost naturally follows that if the life of a non-Muslim is considered inferior to that of a Muslim, the dignity of the former will be held in the same lack of esteem. Rape in most Muslim countries usually results in execution for the offender where the victim is a Muslim. Where the victim is a non-Muslim and the perpetrator is a Muslim, this is not the case.[9] Thus, the honor of a Christian woman is not considered equal to that of a Muslim woman. This ruling is quite chilling.

A particularly objectionable ruling concerns the Christian wife of a Muslim man. Their difference in religion precludes the possibility of having a common burial place. Moreover, if she is pregnant at the time of death, the fetus, being considered Muslim, cannot be buried in a Christian cemetery; thus the woman may not be buried there, either, and so must be buried in a "neutral" place.[10] Even in death, Christians are sometimes denied dignity.

THE VALUE OF HUMAN PROPERTY

The right to the defense of personal property is usually considered a fundamental liberty, and its violation by theft is punishable in all societies, again, irrespective of the religious identity of the thief or his victim. This is *not* the case in all circumstances in Islamic law. The situation is somewhat ambiguous at times, especially if items *haram* (forbidden) to Muslims are concerned.[11]

Another ruling, however, suggests that if a Muslim steals an item from a Christian, such as a gold crucifix, and then states that he did so in order to destroy this "infidel" object, he may escape prosecution.[12] Hence, there is nothing clear-cut in Islamic law that protects the property of Christian subjects, as would be the case in most Western systems, which protect all property, whatever people's race or faith.

RELIGIOUS LIBERTY

Most Western constitutions today guarantee complete religious liberty, in opinion, practice, and propagation. A person is perfectly free to hold or change his opinions or even to hold no religious opinions whatsoever. Under Islamic law, however, this is not the case. Although a person may be free to be a Muslim, Jew, Christian, or Zoroastrian, he may not hold other religious opinions, as the ban on paganism illustrates.[13]

Moreover, although a non-Muslim may change his religion to Islam or one other "Scriptuary" faith, a Muslim who converts from Islam faces execution.[14] It follows from this that Christians are forbidden to proselytize to Muslims, though no such reciprocal ban exists on Muslims. This also affects marriages, since if a Muslim apostatizes, the marriage is dissolved, and there is at least one recent example of this in Egypt, where a liberal Muslim was declared apostate by a court and his marriage dissolved, necessitating the couple's removal to the West; this illustrates that the ruling is not merely theoretical.[15]

Most blatantly, while the postwar era, especially since the 1970s, has seen an energetic upsurge of mosque construction in the West, there has been no corresponding development in Christian religious buildings in the Muslim world, since Islamic law permits only the repair of existing buildings, forbidding the construction of new ones.[16] The same ruling forbids any Christian presence whatsoever on the Arabian Peninsula; thus, whereas the Saudis recently constructed a giant mosque in Rome, there is no possibility of reciprocity for the Roman Catholics (or anyone else) to build even the smallest chapel in Saudi Arabia. The issue is not simply one of reciprocity; national Christians in the Muslim world are denied this right as well, whereas Muslims may freely construct mosques.

THE *JIZYA* TAX

The American Revolution was fought on the principle of "no taxation without representation," the idea being that constitutional equality was a precondition of the sovereign exercise of levying taxes. The only basis for different levels of taxation is socioeconomic distinction, but even here the tax is identical in character and is levied without regard for one's communal origins. The principle of distinction in progressive taxation is ability to pay. The tax imposed does not punish a businessman for his success. Refusal to pay will result in fines or imprisonment but never execution. Furthermore, the tax he pays grants him entitlement to the full protection of the state and thus full and equal citizenship. The goal of the tax is the same with everyone—the ability of the state to provide for the security and well-being of all its citizens.

This is not the case with the *jizya*, which is a tax that the dhimmis uniquely had to pay. It has its origins in sura 9:29, where it is explicitly revealed as a sign of the subjugation of conquered non-Muslims.[17] Hence, the tax is clearly a tribute and a sign of subjection, in no way equivalent to the alms tax, *zakat*. Yusuf Ali's comment on the *jizya* clarifies this:

> 1281 Jizya: the root meaning is compensation. The derived meaning, which became the technical meaning, was a poll tax levied from those who did not accept Islam, but were willing to live under the protection of Islam, and were thus tacitly willing to submit to its ideals being enforced in the Muslim State. There was no amount permanently fixed for it. It was in acknowledgment that those whose religion was tolerated would in their turn not interfere with the preaching and progress of Islam. Imam Shafi'i suggests one dinar per year, which would be the Arabian gold dinar of the Muslim States. The tax varied in amount, and there were exemptions for the poor, for females and children (according to Abu Hanifa), for slaves, and for monks and hermits. Being a tax on able-bodied males of military age, it was in a sense a commutation for military service. But see the next note. (9.29)

> 1282 'An Yadin (literally, from the hand) has been variously interpreted. The hand being the symbol of power and authority. I accept the interpreta-

tion "in token of willing submission." The Jizya was thus partly symbolic and partly a commutation for military service, but as the amount was insignificant and the exemptions numerous, its symbolic character predominated. See the last note. (9.29)

Sayyid Abul Ala Maududi, Quranic exegete and founder of the Islamist Pakistani group Jamaat-i-Islami was quite unapologetic about *jizya*: "The Muslims should feel proud of such a humane law as that of *Jizya*. For it is obvious that a maximum freedom that can be allowed to those who do not adopt the way of Allah but choose to tread the ways of error is that they should be tolerated to lead the life they like."[18] He interprets the Quranic imperative to jihad as having the aim of subjugating non-Muslims, to force them to pay the *jizya* as the defining symbol of their subjection: "Jews and the Christians . . . should be forced to pay *jizya* in order to put an end to their independence and supremacy so that they should not remain rulers and sovereigns in the land. These powers should be wrested from them by the followers of the true Faith, who should assume the sovereignty and lead others towards the Right Way."[19] The consequence of this is that in an Islamic state—specifically the *khilafah* (caliphate)—non-Muslims should be denied government posts, since the state exists for the Muslims, who alone are true citizens, whereas the non-Muslims are merely conquered residents, which the *jizya* signifies: "That is why the Islamic state offers them protection, if they agree to live as Zimmis [i.e., dhimmis] by paying *Jizya*, but it can not allow that they should remain supreme rulers in any place and establish wrong ways and establish them on others. As this state of things inevitably produces chaos and disorder, it is the duty of the true Muslims to exert their utmost to bring an end to their wicked rule and bring them under a righteous order."[20]

Differences of taxation demonstrate distinctions in citizenship. As a symbol of subjection, it signifies that the state is not really the common property of all its permanent residents, but only the Muslims. The non-Muslims are conquered outsiders. It demonstrates their inferior condition; it also punishes them for their disbelief in Islam. Islamic law makes it very clear that the *jizya* is punitive in character.[21] Further, it is to be levied with humiliation.[22] Hence, it is in no way comparable to Western tax systems. Even progressive taxation is not a "punishment" for economic success, nor is any tax specifically humiliating in character.

This illustrates that essentially, in an Islamic state, non-Muslims are in a similar but worse situation than prisoners out on parole, since they are still being punished—they are not considered "good, law-abiding citizens," however exemplary their conduct, but rather criminals given day leave. Their crime is their faith.[23] Moreover, their crime is capital in nature—they deserve death.[24] This demonstrates the unique character of the *jizya* tax: unlike Western taxes, payment does not grant equality and liberty to the payee but rather merely permission for another tax period *to live*; failure to pay it results in death. Again, it is rather analogous to a convict on parole, regularly visiting the police station or parole officer to register. This is different from the case of someone in the West who refuses to pay his tax for whatever reason; he is punished, though it must be stated not by execution, for breaking the law. The reverse is true with the *jizya*—the tax itself is punishment, and the payee lives in the permanent condition of being punished for his faith until he converts. Essentially, non-Muslims live under a permanent death threat.

CONCLUSION

Only by the wildest stretch of the imagination could the situation of non-Muslims under Islamic law be seen as one conferring equal citizenship, whatever Muslim apologists claim. Similarly, only a leap of fantasy could ever believe that such a situation is one that non-Muslims would welcome. The honor, dignity, equality, and even the lives of non-Muslims are by no means guaranteed under Islamic law. The *jizya* tax in particular demonstrates the constitutional inferiority and humiliation such a legal arrangement confers. For non-Muslims, it is rather like perpetually walking under the sword of Damocles, ready to fall at any moment. If Muslims wish Christians and others to regard an Islamic political order as something attractive, their scholars had best engage in a some heavy work of *ijtihad* to revise those elements of Islamic jurisprudence and legislation that are particularly offensive to non-Muslims.

NOTES

1. Suzanne Haneef, *What Everyone Should Know about Islam and Muslims* (Lahore, Pakistan: Kazi, 1979), p. 173.

2. Ahmed von Denffer, *Christians in the Qur'an and the Sunna* (Leicester, UK: Islamic Foundation, 1979), p. 38.

3. Ibid., p. 41.

4. Abdul Rahman Ben Hammad al-Omar, *The Religion of Truth* (Riyadh: General Presidency of Islamic Researches, 1991), p. 86.

5. *Sahih Bukhari* hadith 9.50, narrated by Abu Juhaifa: "I asked 'Ali 'Do you have anything Divine literature besides what is in the Qur'an?' Or, as Uyaina once said, 'Apart from what the people have?' 'Ali said, 'By Him Who made the grain split (germinate) and created the soul, we have nothing except what is in the Qur'an and the ability (gift) of understanding Allah's Book which He may endow a man with, and what is written in this sheet of paper.' I asked, 'What is on this paper?' He replied, 'The legal regulations of Diya (Blood-money) and the (ransom for) releasing of the captives, and the judgment that no Muslim should be killed in Qisas (equality in punishment) for killing a Kafir (disbeliever).' *Sunan of Abu Dawud* hadith 2745, narrated by Abdullah ibn Amr ibn al-As: "The Apostle of Allah (peace be upon him) said: . . . A believer shall not be killed for an unbeliever, nor a confederate within the term of confederation with him."

6. 7498 *Al-Risala* (Maliki manual), 37.04: "Blood Rate to Other Than Muslim Men": "The blood-wit for a woman shall be half that of a man. Similarly the blood-wit for a male Christian or Jew is half that of a male Muslim, and the blood-wit for their women is half that of their men. As for a Magian, his blood-wit is eight hundred dirhams. The blood-wit for their women is half that of their men. Similarly, in respect of wounds, compensation given to non-Muslims is half what is given to their Muslim counterparts."

7. 4833 *Al-Hedaya*, vol. 2 (Hanafi manual), "Christians and Jews May Testify Concerning Each Other":

The testimony of Zimmees with respect to each other is admissible, notwithstanding they be of different religions. Malik and Shafe'i have said that their evidence is absolutely inadmissible, because, as infidels are unjust, it is requisite to be slow in believing any thing they may advance, God having said (in the Koran) "When an unjust person tells you any thing, be slow in believing him"; whence it is that the evidence of an infidel is not admitted concerning a Muslim; and consequently, that an infidel stands (in this particular) in the same predicament with an apostate. The arguments of our doctors upon this point are twofold. First, it is related of the prophet, that he permitted and held lawful the testimony of some Christians concerning others of their sect. Secondly, an infidel having power over himself, and his minor children, is on that account qualified to be a witness with regard to his faith is not destructive of this qualification, because he is supposed to abstain from every thing prohibited in his own religion, and falsehood is prohibited in every religion. It is otherwise with respect to an apostate, as he possesses no power, either over his own person, or over that of another; and it is also otherwise with respect to a Zimmee in relation to a Muslim, because a Zimmee has no power over the person of a Muslim. Besides, a Zimmee may be suspected of inventing falsehoods against a Muslim, from the hatred he bears to him on account of the superiority of the Muslims over him.

3197 *Al-Hedaya*, vol. 1 (Hanafi manual) [qualification of a witness]: "It is necessary that the witnesses be . . . Muslims; the evidence of infidels not being legal with respect to Muslims."

8. 4781 *Al-Hedaya*, vol. 2 (Hanafi manual), chap. 4, "Of the Decrees of a Qazi Relative to Inheritance" [case of the widow of a Christian claiming her inheritance after having embraced the faith]:

If a Christian die, and his widow appear before the Qazi as a Muslima, and declare that "she had become so since the death of her husband," and the heirs declare that she had become so before his death, their declaration must be credited. Ziffer is of opinion that the declaration of the widow must be credited; because the change of her religion, as being a supervenient circumstance, must be referred to the nearest possible period. The arguments of our doctors are, that as the cause of her exclusion from inheritance, founded on difference of faith, exists in the present, it must therefore be considered as extant in the preterite, from the argument of the present;—in the same manner as an argument is derived from the present, in a case relative to the running of the water course of a mill;—that is to say, if a dispute arise between the lessor and lessee of a water-mill, the former asserting that the stream had run from the period of the lease till the present without interruption, and the latter denying this case, if the stream be running at the period of contention, the assertion of the lesser must be credited, but if otherwise, it follows that the argument in question suffices, on behalf of the heirs, to desert the plea of the widow. With respect to what Ziffer objects, it is to be observed that he has regard to the argument of apparent circumstances, for establishing the claim of the wife upon her husband's estate, and an argument of this nature does not suffice as proof to establish a right although it would suffice to annul one.

4782 *Al-Hedaya*, vol. 2 (Hanafi manual) [case of the Christian, widow of a Muslim, claiming under the same circumstances]:

If a Muslim, whose wife was once a Christian, should die, and the widow appear before the Qazi as a Muslima, and declare that she had embraced the faith prior to the death of her husband, and the heirs assert the contrary,— in this case also the assertion of the heirs must be credited, for no regard is paid, in this instance, to any argument derived from present circumstances, since such an argument is not capable of establishing a claim, and the widow is here the claimant of her husband's property. With respect to the heirs, on the contrary, they are repellents of the claim; and probability is an argument in their favour, the widow is supervenient, and is therefore an argument against her.

9. 7520 *Al-Risala* (Maliki manual), 37.27, "A Christian Rapist": "If a Christian rapes a Muslim woman he is to be killed immediately by any Muslim. But a Muslim cannot be executed on account of a non-believer."

10. *Fiqh-us-Sunnah*, Fiqh 4.75a, "A Non-Muslim Woman Who Dies While Carrying a Child by a Muslim Is to Be Buried in a Separate Grave": "Al-Baihaqi reported from Wathilah bin al-Asqa' that he buried a Christian woman bearing the child of a Muslim in a cemetery that belonged to neither Muslims nor Christians. Ahmad supports this opinion because he says that the woman, being a disbeliever, cannot be buried in a cemetery of Muslims, for they would suffer because of her punishment, nor can she be buried in a Christian cemetery because her fetus, which is a Muslim, would suffer by their punishment."

11. 5556 *Al-Hedaya*, vol. 3 (Hanafi manual), "Of the Usurpation of Things Which Are of No Value":

A Mussulman is responsible for destroying the wine or pork of a Zimmee—

If a Mussulman destroy wine or pork belonging to a Zimmee, he must compensate for the value of the same; whereas, if he destroy wine or pork belonging to a Mussulman, no compensation is due.—Shafei maintains that in the former case also no compensation is due. A similar disagreement subsists with respect to the case of a Zimmee destroying wine or pork belonging to a Zimmee; or of one Zimmee selling either of these articles to another; for such sale is lawful, according to our doctors,—in opposition to the opinion of Shafei. The argument of Shafei is that wine and pork are not articles of value with respect to Mussulmans,—nor with respect to Zimmees, as those are dependant of the Mussulmans with regard to the precepts of the Law. A compensation of property, therefore, for the destruction of these articles is not due. The arguments of our doctors are that wine and pork are valuable property with respect to Zimmees: for with them wine is the same as vinegar with the Mussulmans, and pork the same as mutton; and we, who are Mussulmans, being commanded to leave them in the practice of their religion, have consequently no right to impose a rule upon them.—As, therefore, wine and pork are with them property of value, it follows that whoever destroys these articles belonging to them does, in fact, destroy their property of value: in opposition to the case of carrion or blood, because these are not considered as property according to any religion, or with any sect.

5557 *Al-Hedaya*, vol. 3 (Hanafi manual):

And must compensate for it by a payment of the value.

Hence it appears that if a Mussulman destroy the wine or pork of a Zimmee, he must compensate for the value or the pork,—and also of the wine, notwithstanding that it be of the class of similars; because it is not lawful for Mussulmans to transfer the property of wine, as that would be to honour and respect it. It is otherwise where a Zimmee sells wine to a Zimmee, or destroys the wine of a Zimmee; for in these cases it is incumbent upon the seller to deliver over the wine to the purchase, and also upon the destroyer to give as a compensation a similar quantity of wine to the proprietor, since the transfer of the property of wine is not prohibited to Zimmees:—contrary to usury, as that is excepted from the contracts of Zimmees;—or to the case of the slave of a Zimmee, who having been a Mussulman becomes an apostate; for if any Mussulman kill this slave, he is not in that case responsible to the Zimmee, notwithstanding the Zimmee consider the slave as valuable property, since we Mussulmans are commanded to show our abhorrence of apostates. It is also otherwise with respect to the wilful omission of the Tasmeea, or invocation in the slaying of an animal, where the proprietor considers such omission as lawful, being for instance, of the sect of Shafei;—in other words, if a person of the sect of Haneefa destroy the flesh of an animal so alin [*sic*] by a person of the sect of Shafei, the Haneefite is not in that case responsible to the Shafeyite, notwithstanding the latter did, according to his tenets, believe the slain animal to have been valuable property; because the authority to convince the Shafeyite of the illegality of his practice is vested in the Haneefite, inasmuch as it is permitted to him to establish the illegality of it by reason and argument.

5561 *Al-Hedaya*, vol. 3 (Hanafi manual):

And must compensate for them by paying their intrinsic value.

Proceeding upon the doctrine of Haneefa, the destroyer, in the case here considered, is responsible for the value the articles bear in themselves, independent of the particular amusement to which they contribute. Thus if a female singer be destroyed, she must be valued merely as a slave girl; and the same of fighting rams, tumbling pigeons, game cocks, or eunuch slaves; in the other words, if any of these be destroyed, they must be valid and accounted for at the rate they would have borne if unfit for the light and evil purposes to which such articles are commonly applied; and other musical instruments. It is to be observed that, in the case of spilling Sikker or Monissaf, the destroyer is responsible for the value of the article, and not for a similar, because it does not become a Mussulman to be proprietor of such articles. If, on the contrary, a person destroy a crucifix belonging to a Christian, he is responsible for the value it bears as a crucifix; because Christians are left to the practice of their own religious worship.

12. 3915 *Al-Hedaya*, vol. 2 (Hanafi manual) [of a crucifix or chessboard]:

Amputation is not incurred by stealing a crucifix, although it be of gold,— nor by stealing a chess-board or chess pieces of gold, as it is in the thief's power to excuse himself, by saying "I took them with a view to break and destroy them, as things prohibited." It is otherwise with respect to coin bearing the impression of an idol, by the theft of which amputation is incurred; because the money is not the object of worship, so as to allow of it destruction, and thus leave it in the thief's power to excuse himself. It is recorded, as an opinion of Abu Yusuf, that if a crucifix be stolen out of a Christian place of worship, amputation is not incurred; but if it be taken from a house, the hand of the thief is to be struck off, for in such a situation it is lawful property, and the object of custody.

13. sura 9:28: "O ye who believe! Truly the pagans are unclean; so let them not after this year of theirs approach the Sacred Mosque."
Sahih Bukhari hadith 4.393, narrated by Said bin Jubair:

That he heard Ibn 'Abbas saying, "Thursday! And you know not what Thursday is? After that Ibn 'Abbas wept till the stones on the ground were soaked with his tears. On that I asked Ibn 'Abbas, "What is (about) Thursday?" He said, "When the condition (i.e. health) of Allah's Apostle deteriorated, he said, 'Bring me a bone of scapula, so that I may write something for you after which you will never go astray. The people differed in their opinions although it was improper to differ in front of a prophet. They said, 'What is wrong with him? Do you think he is delirious? Ask him (to understand).' The Prophet replied, 'Leave me as I am in a better state than what you are asking me to do.' Then the Prophet ordered them to do three things saying, 'Turn out all the pagans from the Arabian Peninsula, show respect to all foreign delegates by giving them gifts as I used to do.'" The sub-narrator added, "The third order was something beneficial which either Ibn 'Abbas did not mention or he mentioned but I forgot."

14. *Al-Hedaya*, vol. 2 (Hanafi manual), chap. 9, "Of the Laws Concerning Apostates":

An exposition of the faith is to be laid before an apostate;
    When a Muslim apostatises from the faith, an exposition thereof is to be laid before him, in such a manner that if his apostasy should have arisen from any religious doubts or scruples, those may be removed. The reason for laying an exposition of the faith before him is that it is possible some doubts or errors may have arisen in his mind, which may be removed by such exposition; and as there are only two modes of repelling the sin of apostasy, namely, destruction or Islam, and Islam is preferable to destruction, the evil is rather to be removed by means of an exposition of the faith;—but yet this exposition of the faith is not incumbent,* (according to what the learned have remarked upon his head,) since a call to the faith has already reached the apostate.

* That is, it is lawful to kill an apostate without making any attempt to recover him from his apostasy.

4131 *Al-Hedaya*, vol. 2 (Hanafi manual) [who, if he does not repent within three days, is put to death, whether he be a freeman or a slave]:

An apostate is to be imprisoned for three days, within which time if he return to the faith, it is well: but if not, he must be slain.

It is recorded in the Jama Sagheer that "an exposition of the faith is to be laid before an apostate, and if he refuse the faith, he must be slain":— and with respect to what is above stated, that "he is to be imprisoned for three days," it only implies that if he require a delay, three days may be granted him, as such is the term generally admitted and allowed for the purpose of consideration. It is recorded from Haneefa and Abu Yusuf that the granting of a delay of three days in laudable, whether the apostate require it or not: and it is recorded from Shafe'i that it is incumbent on the Imam to delay for three days, and that it is not lawful for him to put the apostate to death before the lapse of that time; since it is most probable that a Muslim will not apostatise but from some doubt or error arising in his mind; wherefore some time is necessary for consideration; and this is fixed at three days. The arguments of our doctors upon this is fixed at three days. The arguments of our doctors upon this point are twofold.—First, God, says, in the Koran, "Slay the Unbelievers," without any reserve of a delay of three days being granted to them; and the prophet has also said "Slay the man who changes his religion," without mentioning any thing concerning a delay: Secondly, an apostate is an infidel enemy, who has received a call to the faith, wherefore he may be slain upon the instant, without any delay. An apostate is termed on this occasion an infidel enemy, because he is undoubtedly such; and he is not protected, since he has not required a protection; neither is he a Zimmee, because capitation-tax has not been accepted from him; hence it is proved that he is an infidel enemy.* It is to be observed that, in these rules, there is no difference made between an apostate who is a freeman, and one who is a slave, as the arguments upon which they are established apply equally to both descriptions.

* Arab. Hirbee; a term which the translator has generally rendered alien, and which applies to any infidel not being a subject of the Muslim government.

7512 *Al-Risala* (Maliki manual), 37.19, "Crimes against Islam":

A freethinker (zindiq) must be put to death and his repentance is rejected. A freethinker is one who conceals his unbelief and pretends to follow Islam. A magician also is to be put to death, and his repentance also is to be rejected. An apostate is also killed unless he repents. He is allowed three days grace; if he fails to utilise the chance to repent, the execution takes place. This same also applies to women apostates.

If a person who is not an apostate admits that prayer is obligatory but will not perform it, then such a person is given an opportunity to recant by the time of the next prayer; if he does not utilise the opportunity to repent and resume worship, he is then executed. If a Muslim refuses to perform the pilgrimage, he should be left alone and God himself shall decide this case. If a Muslim should abandon the performance of prayer because he disputes its being obligatory, then such a person shall be treated as an apostate—he should be given three days within which to repent. If the three days lapse without his repenting, he is then executed.

Whoever abuses the Messenger of God—peace and blessing of God be upon him—is to be executed, and his repentance is not accepted.

If any dhimmi (by 'dhimmi' is meant a non-Muslim subject living in a Muslim country) curses the Prophet—peace be upon him—or abuses him by saying something other than what already makes him an unbeliever, or abuses God Most High by saying something other than what already makes him an unbeliever, he is to be executed unless at that juncture he accepts Islam.

The property of an apostate after his execution is to be shared by the Muslim community.

15. 7410 *Al-Risala* (Maliki manual), 32.11, "Effects of Change of Religion": "If either of a couple apostatises, according to the view of other jurists, such a marriage is to be dissolved without a divorce."

16. 4120 *Al-Hedaya*, vol. 2 (Hanafi manual) [The construction of infidel places of worship in a Muslim territory is unlawful; but those already founded there may be repaired]:

The construction of churches or synagogues in the Muslim territory is unlawful, this being forbidden in the traditions:—but if places of worship originally belonging to Jews or Christians be destroyed, or fall to decay,* they are at liberty to repair them,—because buildings cannot endure for ever, and as the Imam has left these people to the exercise of their own religion, it is a necessary inference that he has engaged not to prevent them from rebuilding or repairing their churches and synagogues. If, however, they attempt to remove these, and to build them in a place different from their former situation, the Imam must prevent them, since this is an actual construction: and the places which they use as hermitages are held in the same light as their churches, wherefore the construction of those also is unlawful. It is otherwise with respect to such places of prayer as are within their dwellings, which they are not prohibited from constructing, because these are an appurtenance to the habitation. What is here said is the rule with respect to cities; but not with respect to villages or hamlets; because as the tokens of Islam (such as public prayer, festivals, and so forth) appear in cities, Zimmees should not be permitted to celebrate the token of infidelity there, in the face of them; but as the tokens of Islam do not appear in villages or hamlets, there is no occasion to prevent the construction of synagogues or churches there. Some allege that in our country Zimmees are to be prohibited from constructing churches or synagogues, not only in cities, but also in villages and hamlets; because in the villages of our country various tokens of Islam appear; and what is recorded from Haneefa, (that the prohibition against building churches and synagogues is confined to cities, and does not extend to villages and hamlets) relates solely to the villages of Koofa; because the greater part of the inhabitants of these villages are Zimmees, there being few Muslims among them, wherefore the tokens of Islam do not there appear: moreover, in the territory of Arabia, Zimmees are prohibited from constructing churches of synagogues either in cities or villages, because the prophet has said "Two religions cannot be professed together in the peninsula of Arabia."

17. sura 29: "Fight those who believe not in Allah nor the Last Day nor hold that forbidden which hath been forbidden by Allah and His apostle nor acknowledge the religion of truth (even if they are) of the People of the Book until they pay the Jizya with willing submission and feel themselves subdued."

18. Sayyid Abul Ala Maududi, *The Meaning of the Qur'an*, vol. 2 (Lahore, Pakistan: Islamic Publications, 1993), p. 183.

19. Ibid.

20. Ibid., 2:186.

21. *Al-Hedaya*, vol. 2 (Hanafi manual):

[The] capitation-tax is a sort of punishment inflicted upon infidels for their obstinacy in infidelity, (as was before stated;) whence it is that it cannot be accepted of the infidel if he send it by the hands of a messenger, but must be exacted in a mortifying and humiliating manner, by the collector sitting and receiving it from him in a standing posture: (according to one tradition, the collector is to seize him by the throat, and shake him, saying, "Pay your tax, Zimmee!")—It is therefore evident that capitation-tax is a punishment; and where two punishments come together, they are compounded, in the same manner as in Hidd, or stated punishment. Secondly, capitation-tax is a substitute for destruction in respect to the infidels, and a substitute for personal aid in respect to the Muslims, (as was before observed;)—but it is a substitute for destruction with regard to the future, not with regard to the past, because infidels are liable to be put to death only in future, in consequence of future war, and not in the past. In the same manner, it is also a substitute and in the past.

Al-Hedaya, vol. 2 (Hanafi manual) [arrear of capitation-tax is remitted upon the subject's death or conversion to the faith]:

> If a person become a Muslim, who is indebted for any arrear of capitation-tax, such arrear is remitted: and in the same manner, the arrear of capitation-tax due from a Zimmee is remitted upon his dying in a state of infidelity. . . . Capitation-tax is a species of punishment inflicted upon infidels on account of their infidelity, whence it is termed Jizyat, which is derived from Jizya, meaning retribution; now the temporal punishment of infidelity is remitted in consequence of conversion to the faith; and after death it cannot be inflicted, because temporal punishments are instituted solely for the purpose of removing evil, which is removed by either death or Islam. Thirdly, capitation-tax is a substitute for aid to the Muslims, and as the infidel in question, upon embracing the faith, becomes enabled to aid them in his own person, capitation-tax consequently drops upon his Islam.

22. 4118 *Al-Hedaya*, vol. 2 (Hanafi manual) [in a case of arrear for two years, only one year's tax is levied]:

> If a Zimmee owe capitation-tax for two years, it is compounded,—that is, the tax for one year only is exacted of him:—and it is recorded, in the Jama-Sagheer, that if capitation-tax be not exacted of a Zimmee until such time as the year has elapsed, and another year arrived, the tax for the past year cannot be levied. This is the doctrine of Haneefa. The two disciples maintain that the tax for the past year may be levied. If, however, a Zimmee were to die near the close of the year, in this case the tax for that year cannot be exacted, according to all our doctors: and so likewise, if he die in the middle of the year, (which instance has been already treated of.) Some assert that the above difference of opinion obtains also with respect to tribute upon land: whilst others maintain that there is no difference of opinion whatever respecting it, but that it is not compounded, according to all our doctors.— The argument of the two disciples (where they dissent) is that capitation-tax is a consideration, (as was before said,) and if the considerations be numerous, and the exaction practicable, they are all to be exacted; and in the case in question the exaction of capitation-tax for the two years is practicable: contrary to where the Zimmee becomes a Muslim, for in this case the exaction is impracticable. The arguments of Haneefa upon this point are twofold. First, capitation-tax is a sort of punishment inflicted upon infidels for their obstinacy in infidelity, (as was before stated;) whence it is that it cannot be accepted of the infidel if he send it by the hands of a messenger, but must be exacted in a mortifying and humiliating manner, by the collector sitting and receiving it from him in a standing posture: (according to one tradition, the collector is to seize him by the throat, and shake him,

saying, "Pay your tax, Zimmee!")—It is therefore evident that capitation-tax is a punishment; and where two punishments come together, they are compounded, in the same manner as in Hidd, or stated punishment. Secondly, capitation-tax is a substitute for destruction in respect to the infidels, and a substitute for personal aid in respect to the Muslims, (as was before observed;)—but it is a substitute for destruction with regard to the future, not with regard to the past, because infidels are liable to be put to death only in future, in consequence of future war, and not in the past. In the same manner, it is also a substitute and in the past. With respect to what is quoted from the Jama Sagheer—"and another year also pass," so as to make two years,—for it is there mentioned that capitation-tax is due at the end of the year, wherefore it is requisite that another year be elapsed, so as to admit of an accumulation of two years' tax, after which the two year's taxes are compounded:—Others, again, allege that the passage is to be taken in its literal sense; and as capitation-tax is held by Haneefa to be due upon the commencement of the year, it follows that by one year passing, and another arriving, an accumulation of the tax for two years takes place.

23. 3989 *Al-Hedaya*, vol. 2 (Hanafi manual) [infidels may be attacked without provocation]: "The destruction of the sword is incurred by infidels, although they be not the first aggressors, as appears from various passages in the sacred writings which are generally received to this effect."

24. *Al-Hedaya*, vol. 2 (Hanafi manual): "[The] capitation-tax is due only in lieu of destruction. . . . That is to say, is imposed as a return from the mercy and forbearance shown by the Muslims, and as a substitute for that destruction which is due upon infidels."

3997 *Al-Hedaya*, vol. 2 (Hanafi manual), states that infidels refusing either to embrace the faith or to pay tribute may be attacked.

PART 3.
ISLAMIC PRACTICE REGARDING NON-MUSLIMS

Introduction

Robert Spencer

The articles in this section are closely intertwined with those in part 2, as much of this material also details the legal status of non-Muslims in Islamic law. This collection of Bat Ye'or articles and supplemental material—the first authored by David G. Littman and Bat Ye'or thirty years ago—elucidates the reality of this legal superstructure by detailing how these laws were applied and their close relation to the legal and theological Islamic doctrine of jihad (see "Historical Amnesia")—a concept that has been given a renewed martial emphasis by today's radical Muslim theorists.

In the course of Bat Ye'or's historical explorations, she clarifies many common modern misconceptions, including one idea that often goes hand in hand with the idea of Islamic tolerance: the notion that the behavior, or indeed the very existence, of the modern state of Israel is the root cause of the friction between the Islamic world and the West, and that if Israel were to disappear, so would any impediments to a new flowering of the tolerant, humane, and generous Islamic spirit (see "Dhimmi Peoples: Oppressed Nations"). In fact, unfortunately, Israel is just one arena of the global jihad, and antisemitism but one manifestation of the intolerant spirit of contempt and disdain that generally has marked Islamic relations with members of the Qur'an's "People of the Book."

Another misconception exploded here by Bat Ye'or ("Islam and the Dhimmis") is the idea that the historical record of Islamic intolerance is somehow mitigated by worse behavior on the part of medieval Christian Europe toward its Jewish populations. Such comparisons, she notes, are virtually impossible to make and ultimately pointless.

For our purposes, it is sufficient to note that whatever may have been the sins of Christendom, they are in the past, but the dhimmi system of intolerance is still very much part of Islamic Sharia.

PROTECTED PEOPLES
4. UNDER ISLAM

David G. Littman and Bat Ye'or

J ews and Christians had been living throughout the Orient, Egypt, and North Africa for centuries before they were overrun in the seventh and subsequent centuries by successive waves of Bedouin invaders from Arabia, who, under the banner of Islam, subjugated peoples and territories from India to Spain. Many of the more important indigenous Jewish centers from Mesopotamia to the Atlantic could lay claim, at that time, to a continuous community existence dating back one thousand years, and those in their ancient homeland, the "Land of Israel," to as long as two millennia.

The initial administrative tolerance of the conquerors was dictated by expediency and realpolitik, but as Arab colonization took root, the social and economic conditions of the local, colonized populations worsened. During the long centuries of Arab-Muslim domination, the surviving remnants of once-flourishing Jewish and Christian communities—who had neither fled nor been killed nor converted to Islam—were juridically and socially relegated to an inferior condition of subjection and humiliation difficult to comprehend today.

Their status was that of *ahl al-dhimma*[1]—protected peoples, i.e., peoples tolerated in the Muslim lands: *dar al-Islam* (House of Islam)—which subjected them to the disabilities and humiliations laid down in specific regulations commonly known as the Covenant of Umar, which degraded both the individual and the community.[2]

Up to the last decades of the nineteenth century, and even into the twentieth, the Jews in most of North Africa (until European domination: i.e.,

First published in 1976 by the Centre d'Information et de Documentation sur le Moyen-Orient, Geneva, Switzerland.

Algeria [1830], Tunisia [1881], Egypt [1882], Libya [1911], and Morocco [1912]), Yemen, and other Muslim lands of the Orient were still obliged to live in isolated groups amid the general population. They resided in special quarters and were constrained to wear distinctive clothing; the carrying of arms was forbidden to them, and their sworn testimony was not accepted under Muslim jurisdiction.

The indigenous Christian populations fared no better. Throughout the Islamic lands they had, like the Jews, been reduced to the inferior status of dhimmis[3] and had been virtually eliminated from North Africa by the twelfth century, during the Almohad persecutions.

For twelve hundred years, the dhimmis were *tolerated* in Muslim lands on the terms laid down in the Covenant of Umar, the refusal or infringement of which could incur the death penalty.

The dhimmi status was referred to by Egyptian Abu Zahra, at an important conference of theologians (1968) held at the Islamic University of Al-Azhar in Cairo under the patronage of President Gamal Abdul Nasser: "But we say to those who patronize the Jews that the latter are dhimmis, people of obligation, who have betrayed the covenant in conformity with which they have been accorded protection."[4]

President Anwar el-Sadat's declaration on the feast of Muhammad's birth (April 25, 1972) also relates to this basic Islamic dhimmi concept: "They [the Jews] shall return and be as the Koran said of them: 'condemned to humiliation and misery.' . . . We shall send them back to their former status."[5] This highly evocative expression is based on a verse from the Qur'an (sura 9:29) and on its traditional theological exegesis; it is strangely reminiscent of a passage from a poem composed in the "golden age" of Arab-Muslim tolerance nine centuries ago. In a bitter anti-Jewish ode against Joseph Ibn Nagrella (the Jewish minister of the Muslim ruler of Grenada in Spain), Abu Ishaq, a well-known eleventh-century Arab jurist and poet, is unambiguous: "Put them back where they belong and reduce them to the lowest of the low. . . . Turn your eyes to other [Muslim] countries and you will find the Jews there are outcast dogs. . . . Do not consider it a breach of faith to kill them. . . . They have violated our covenant with them so how can you be held guilty against the violators?"[6] Nagrella and an estimated five thousand Jews of Grenada were subsequently slaughtered on December 30, 1066. This figure is more than the number of Jews reported to have been killed by the pillaging Crusaders throughout the Rhineland thirty years later, at the time of the First Crusade.

Antoine Fattal, in his authoritative study on the legal status of non-Muslims in Muslim lands, has written:

> The dhimmi is a second-class citizen. If he is tolerated, it is for reasons of a spiritual nature, since there is always the hope that he might be converted; or of a material nature, since he bears almost the whole tax burden. He has his place in society, but he is constantly reminded of his inferiority. . . . In no way is the dhimmi the equal of the Muslim. He is marked out for social inequality and belongs to a despised caste; unequal in regard to individual rights; unequal as regards taxes; unequal in the law courts, as his evidence is not admitted by any Muslim tribunal, and for the same crime his punishment is greater than that imposed on Muslims. No social relationship, no fellowship is possible between Muslims and dhimmis. . . . Even today, the study of the jihad is part of the curriculum of all the Islamic institutes. In the universities of al-Azhar, Najaf, and Zaitouné, students are still taught that the holy war is a binding prescriptive decree, pronounced against the infidels, which will only be revoked with the end of the world.[7]

Likewise Louis Gardet, a Catholic theologian and a respected orientalist, one of the leaders of the contemporary "dialogue" between Islam and Christianity, has stressed,

> The dhimmi should always behave as an inferior; he should adapt a humble and contrite attitude. For example, in the payment of the *jizya*, or poll tax, the qadi, on receiving the money, must make as if to give the dhimmi a light slap in the face so as to remind him of his place.[8] The dhimmi should everywhere give way to the Muslim. . . . If Islam did not invent the ghettos, it can be said that it was the first to institutionalize them. (The rules established by medieval Christian princes, in particular those of the popes for the ghetto of Rome, are often copies of Muslim prescriptions relating to dhimmis.) The Reverend Father Bonsirven provided a brief but evocative summing-up of the civil and political situation of the Jews in the Middle Ages in his lecture at the Catholic Institute in Paris, later published with the title "Au Ghetto" in the January 1940 issue of *La Question d'Israël*. In fact, and without the R. F. Bonsirven having realized it, most of the rules, prescriptions and measures that he described repeat the regulations concerning the dhimmis attributed to Umar I.[9]

The historian of the Hafsides, Robert Brunschwig, also remarked that "Islam subjected the dhimmis to special fiscal and vestimentary obligations." He noted that, toward the end of the twelfth century, in the Almohad empire (North Africa and Spain), the Jews were compelled to wear a distinctive mark, besides ridiculous clothes. "Would it not be strange if it were the Almohad example which made Christendom decide to adopt the same sort of measure? The Jews were first compelled to wear a distinctive badge in Christian lands at the beginning of the thirteenth century (first officially promulgated at the Fourth Lateran Council of 1216)."[10]

The late renowned orientalist Gustave von Grunebaum wrote in 1971, "It would not be difficult to put together the names of a very sizeable number of Jewish subjects or citizens of the Islamic area who have attained to high rank, to power, to great financial influence, to significant and recognized intellectual attainment; and the same could be done for Christians. But it would not be difficult to compile a lengthy list of persecutions, arbitrary confiscations, attempted forced conversions, or pogroms." He referred in detail to the well-known letter, written to the suffering Yemenite Jews toward the end of the twelfth century by Jewish philosopher Maimonides, who had found refuge in Fatimid Egypt after fleeing twice (from Spain and Morocco) from the intolerant Almohads: "and it is known to you that no nation stood against Israel more hostile than they [meaning the Muslims], that no nation did evil to perfection in order to weaken us and belittle us and degrade us like them."[11]

Bernard Lewis, the much respected historian and coeditor of the *Encyclopaedia of Islam*, emphasized in a 1968 article,

> The golden age of equal rights was a myth, and belief in it was a result, more than a cause, of Jewish sympathy for Islam. The myth was invented in 19th-century Europe as a reproach to Christians—and taken up by Muslims in our own time as a reproach to Jews. . . . European travellers to the East in the age of liberalism and emancipation are almost unanimous in deploring the degraded and precarious position of Jews in Muslim countries, and the dangers and humiliations to which they were subject. Jewish scholars, acquainted with the history of Islam and with the current situation in Islamic lands, can have had no illusions on this score. Vambéry [1904] is unambiguous: "I do not know any more miserable, helpless, and pitiful individual on God's earth than the Jahudi in those countries."[12]

One could provide scores of similar testimonies from earlier and later travelers to the Orient and North Africa. Here are but three general comments from the 1850s. A few other documents are included as well.

The Abbé Godard, who had travelled to North Africa, Egypt, and Palestine, noted in 1858, "It is said that in Rome the Jews never pass under Titus's Arch, but if they also keep such long memories and grudges in Muslim lands, I do not see where they could walk."[13]

A Romanian Jew, "Benjamin II," who traveled extensively during five years in the Orient and the Maghreb, drew a revealing comparison: "How happy I would be if [by my book of travels] I could interest them [the Jews of Europe] in the plight of their coreligionists who are the victims of oriental barbarism and fanaticism. Our strong and free brethren, who have the good fortune to live under liberal regimes, where they are governed by wise laws and are treated humanely, will understand how deplorable and urgent is the abnormal situation of their brethren in the Orient. Religion demands it; humanity requires it. May the Almighty One lessen the burden of so many tribulations; may he reward their heroism after centuries of slavery and their indomitable faith under such cruel persecutions."[14]

Jacob Saphir was born in Poland and taken to Safed in Galilee when he was ten; he fled to Jerusalem after the Safed pogroms of 1836 and later traveled widely in the Yemen and the East in 1858–59. On the conditions of the Jews of the Yemen, whose situation was pitiful, he had this to say: "In short, the suffering of the Jews in Yemen [1858–59] baffle all description. Even in the Holy Land things did not look rosy before 1830, as I know from my own experience. But in comparison with the Yemen, even Palestine could then be regarded as the land of freedom, and in the former country the Jew is regarded as a hated prey."[15]

The detailed report (1910) of Yomtob Sémach showed that fifty years later nothing had basically changed in the deplorable condition of the Jews of the Yemen.[16]

Numerous unpublished nineteenth-century documents, as well as reports by European travelers,[17] confirm that the discriminatory status applied to the Jews under Islam continued under one form or another in most Arab lands until the early years of the twentieth century. Thousands of Jews were assassinated singly, and collectively, *as Jews*, in Islamic lands from the Atlantic to the Persian Gulf during the half century before World War I. Forced conversions were not infrequent, often after girls and boys had been abducted.

It was only after the establishment of European protectorates in all of North Africa, Egypt, and the Orient (with the exception of the Yemen, where the Jews had to wait till 1949–50, when they were airlifted to Israel in "Operation Magic Carpet") that the remaining oppressed non-Muslim minorities gained de jure equal rights with Muslims, and not always even then—for example, the Jews of Morocco and the majority of those of Tunisia remained under the protection of their monarchs until the middle of the twentieth century, and as dhimmis their sworn testimony was never legally recognized under Muslim jurisprudence.

Under European rule, Christians and Jews enjoyed physical security—and some even a certain affluence—that lasted for two or three generations.

As each Arab country won its national independence, the situation of the minorities worsened, often becoming intolerable. More than one thousand Jews were killed in anti-Jewish rioting from 1938 to 1949 in Baghdad (1941/46/48), Tripoli (1945/48), Aden (1947), Aleppo (1945/47/48), Damascus (1938/45/49), Oudja and Djerade (Morocco), Cairo (1948), and so on. Similar tragedies happened during the same period to many indigenous Christian groups throughout the Arab world.

One can hardly blame, anachronistically, the Zionist Congress (1897), the Balfour Declaration (1917), or the declaration of Israel's independence (1948) for past centuries of Arab-Muslim oppression.

A Moroccan Muslim, Saïd Ghallab, provided an authoritative testimony in an article published in 1965 in Jean-Paul Sartre's periodical *Les Temps Modernes*:

> The worst insult one Moroccan can make to another is to call him a Jew. . . . My childhood friends have remained anti-Jewish. They mask their virulent antisemitism by maintaining that the state of Israel was the creation of Western imperialism. My Communist comrades have fallen into this trap themselves. Not a single issue of the communist press denounces either the antisemitism of the Moroccans or that of their government. . . . And the integral Hitlerite myth is cultivated among the popular class. Hitler's massacre of the Jews was acclaimed with delight. It is even believed that Hitler is not dead, but very much alive. And his arrival is awaited (like that of the Imam el Mahdi) to free the Arabs from Israel.[18]

The general Arab opposition to the existence of an independent sovereign state of Israel in its ancient homeland has its roots in traditional Islamic attitudes and dhimmi concepts.[19] The contemporary hostile Arab attitudes toward Jews (nearly one million have fled from a dozen Arab countries since World War II, three-quarters of them to Israel)[20] and other minorities is not something unusual in the Arab world; what was unusual, for the dhimmis, was the relative calm of the preceding two or three generations, during the period of European domination.

The root of the present Lebanese tragedy is religious, whatever the political and social aspects. In 1860, the brutal massacre of several thousand Christians in Syria and Lebanon occurred soon after the passing of the Hatti Hümayun edict (1856), which had granted equal rights with Muslims to Christians and Jews. The French intervened militarily, and combined European pressure obliged the Sultan to accept an autonomous Christian-Lebanese province, albeit still under Ottoman suzerainty. The determination of the indigenous Maronites (and other oriental Christian ethnic groups) to survive in their ancient homeland is a millenary phenomenon that should be recognized for what it is: an age-old resistance against foreign imperialist domination. Today, whether or not the Palestinians and other groups are participating willingly or are being used by fanatical leaders to achieve the ultimate aims of jihad does not change the essence of the historical pattern—simply because the slogans and catchwords used may lead to popular confusion.

A deeper knowledge of the past history of the non-Muslim minorities of these regions may help the student or observer to better understand the real aims behind some of the present-day slogans of Arab propagandists—for example, the PLO's plans for a *secular* Arab-Palestine state that is to replace Israel. One should bear in mind that this "politicidal" goal is fully supported by all Arab leaders, including Col. Muammar al-Gadhafi, who is a fervent believer in the fundamental, unchangeable truths of Islam and the Qur'an.

It is worth considering, as a conclusion, the profound observation made in 1968 by Georges Vajda, the eminent orientalist of the French Centre National de Recherches Scientifique:

> In the light of the foregoing facts [illustrated in his article], it seems clear that, unless it changes its principles, goes against the deepest feelings of its coreligionists and calls in question its own raison d'être, no Muslim power, however "liberal" it may like to think itself (we say "it may like to think itself" and not "it claims itself to be"), could depart from the line of conduct followed in the past and continued de facto in the present, in conferring on the Jews anything but the historic status of "protection," patched up with ill-digested and unassimilated Western phraseology. The same applies to the Christian minority, however it may attempt to secure its position by increasingly anti-Jewish attitudes (one should not forget the recent Vatican Council), inspired by political necessity but also on account of the *odium theologicum* that is even more firmly rooted in the Eastern than in the Western Church, and which dates from well before the birth of Islam. The present author cannot claim to make any value judgements, still less to prophesy. His familiarity with original sources throughout a life of study has convinced him that Christian and Jewish documents could in their turn provide a very substantial contribution to a disheartening anthology of incomprehension and rancor. If there does in fact exist a path towards a harmonious symbiosis between men of divergent convictions, only those who are able to break with their past will be able to set out on it.[21]

DOCUMENTS: JEWS IN NORTH AFRICA AND EGYPT IN THE
NINETEENTH CENTURY

Morocco

General Domingo Badia y Leblich was a Spaniard and a scientist, sufficiently acquainted with the language and the customs of the Moors to deceive
even Sultan Sulayman himself. Passing as a Muslim (Ali Bey), he carried out
numerous "political" errands during his travels in the first years of the nineteenth century. The reliable and prolific writer on Morocco Budgett Meakin,
in a review of all works on Morocco he published in 1899, considered Bey's
Travels of Ali Bey in Morocco "a standard work" and stated that "his observations may be accepted with faith." The general description of the Jews of
Morocco that follows is confirmed by earlier and later travelers.

> The Jews in Morocco are in the most abject state of slavery; but at Tangier
> it is remarkable that they live intermingled with the Moors, without having
> any separate quarter, which is the case in all the other places where the
> Mahometan religion prevails. . . .
>   The Jews are obliged, by order of the Government, to wear a particular
> dress, composed of large drawers, of a tunic, which descends to their knees,
> of a kind of *burnous* or cloak thrown on one side, slippers, and a very small
> cap; every part of their dress is black except the shirt, of which the sleeves
> are extremely wide, open, and hanging down very low.
>   When a Jew passes before a mosque, he is obliged to take off his slip-
> pers, or sandals; he must do the same when he passes before the house of
> the Kaïd, the Kadi, or of any Mussulman of distinction. At Fez and in some
> other towns they are obliged to walk barefoot. . . .
>   On my arrival, I had two Jews amongst my servants: when I saw that
> they were so ill-treated and vexed in different ways, I asked them why they
> did not go to another country; they answered me that they could not do so
> because they were slaves of the sultan.[22]

Arthur Leared, an English doctor, had no knowledge of Arabic but,
according to Budgett Meakin (1899), his "observations" were accurate. His
book first appeared in London in 1876. His description of the Jewish condition at that time in Marrakesh is confirmed by orientalists Heinrich von
Maltzen and Joseph Halévy, who visited the southern Moroccan capital in
1859 and 1876, respectively. Dr. Leared's comments on the Jews of Marrakesh are noteworthy.

The disqualifications and indignities to which the Jews are subjected in the city of Marocco [Marrakesh], so far as they came under my own observation, were as follows:

1) They were never allowed to wear the turban.
2) In the presence of a governor, and when passing a mosque, they are obliged to remove the blue handkerchief which the head is at other times bound.
3) They must wear black instead of yellow shoes always worn by the Moors.
4) When they go from their own quarter into the Moorish town, both men and women are compelled to take off their shoes and walk barefooted; and this degradation appeared especially painful when one had occasion to walk with a Jewish friend through the filthy streets of the Moorish quarters.
5) A Jew, meeting a Moor, must always pass to the left.
6) Jews are not allowed to ride through the city.
7) They are not permitted to carry arms.
8) The use of the Moorish bath is forbidden to the Jews.
9) In the exercise of their religion they are restricted to private houses; hence there are no public buildings used as synagogues. This restriction applies equally to other parts of the empire, except Tangier.

No doubt there are other more or less annoying interferences with personal liberty which do not meet the eye. But the list given is enough to show that the grievances of the Jewish community are far from being merely sentimental. They live under the yoke of an iron despotism, and, as might be expected, betray this in their manner and appearance. The men are in general of medium height, but slender, long-visaged, and sallow. It is sad to see them walk with bowed heads and slow steps through the streets of their mother city. . . .

In the southern province of Sus the Jew is regarded as so indispensable to the prosperity of the country that he is not allowed to leave it. If he gets permission to go to Mogador to trade, it is only on condition that he leaves his wife and family, or some relation to whom he is known to be attached, as surety for his return. . . .

. . . According to Mohammedan law, neither Christian non Jew has, in legal matters, any *locus standi*. In taking evidence their oath is not received, and the presumption is always in favor of the true believer [i.e. the Muslim].[23]

Algeria

William Shaler was the United States consul in Algiers from 1816 to 1828. His *Sketches* were published four years before the French military occupation of the town in 1830. The Jews of Algiers—about ten thousand—formed roughly a quarter of its population. They became the first in any Muslim land to be granted equal rights with Muslims. Dubois-Thainville, the French consul at about the same period, and others, confirm Shaler's description.

> Independent of the legal disabilities of the Jews, they are in Algiers a most oppressed people; they are not permitted to resist any personal violence of whatever nature, from a Mussulman; they are compelled to wear clothing of a black or dark colour; they cannot ride on horseback, or wear arms of any sort, not even a cane; they are permitted only on Saturdays and Wednesdays to pass out of the gates of the city without permission; and on any unexpected call for hard labour, the Jews are turned out to execute it. . . .
>
> On several occasions of sedition amongst the Janissaries, the Jews have been indiscriminately plundered, and they live in the perpetual fear of a renewal of such scenes; they are pelted in the streets even by children, and in short, the whole course of their existence here, is a state of the most abject oppression and contumely. The children of Jacob bear these indignities with wonderful patience; they learn submission from infancy, and practise it throughout their lives, without ever daring to murmur at their hard lot. . . . It appears to me that the Jews at this day in Algiers constitute one of the least fortunate remnants of Israel existing.[24]

In 1870 the vast majority of the Jews of Algeria were granted French citizenship by the Crémieux decree.

Tunisia

The situation of the Jews of Tunisia had begun to improve in the middle of the nineteenth century. The public hanging of an innocent Jew of Tunis in 1856 on the traditional accusation of blaspheming Islam became a cause célèbre and demonstrated the precariousness of their condition. A new constitution (the Fundamental Pact) giving Christians and Jews full equality with Muslims was promulgated under French pressure by the Bey of Tunis in 1857. In the revolt of 1864, the Jews of Tunis, Nabeul, and Djerba were attacked, and the new constitution was swept away.

The description of the Jews of Tunis by the Chevalier de Hesse-Wartegg relates to conditions around 1870, prior to the French protectorate (1881). The Jews of Tunisia were nonetheless better off than their brethren in Morocco at the same period.

> The oppressions to which those latter are exposed, even to this day, are almost incredible. In Algiers the French Government emancipated them some forty years ago, but in Tunis, Morocco, and Tripolis they only got certain liberties during the last few years. Till then they had to live in a certain quarter, and were not allowed to appear in the streets after sunset. If they were compelled to go out at night they had to provide themselves with a sort of cat-o'-nine tails at the next guardhouse of the "Zaptieh," which served as a kind of passport to the patrols going round at night. If it was a dark night, they were not allowed to carry a lantern like the Moors and Turks, but a candle, which the wind extinguished every minute. They were neither allowed to ride on horseback nor on a mule, and even to ride on a donkey was forbidden them except outside the town; they had then to dismount at the gates, and walk in the middle of the streets, so as not to be in the way of Arabs. If they had to pass the "Kasba," they had first to fall on their knees as a sign of submission, and then to walk on with lowered head; before coming to a mosque they were obliged to take the slippers off their feet, and had to pass the holy edifice without looking at it. As Tunis possesses no less than five hundred mosques, it will be seen that Jews did not wear out many shoes at that time. It was worse even in their intercourse with Musulmans; if one of these fancied himself insulted by a Jew, he stabbed him at once, and had only to pay a fine to the State, by way of punishment. As late as 1868 seventeen Jews were murdered in Tunis without the offenders having been punished for it: often a Minister or General was in the plot, to enrich himself with the money of the murdered ones. Nor was that all. The Jews— probably to show their gratefulness for being allowed to live in the town, or to live at all—had to pay 50,000 piastres monthly to the State as a tax![25]

Tripolitania (Libya)

Paolo della Cella's narrative describes the condition of the Jews of Benghazi before the Ottomans reasserted their more lenient rule in Tripolitania (1835). An English naval commander confirmed the similar abject status of the Tripoli Jews at about the same time. Cella, an Italian, was physician to the ruler of Tripoli.

> The Jews form the labouring portion of the population of Bengasi, the remainder [Muslims] living in idleness at the expense of those unbelievers; in return for which, there is no species of vexation and extortion to which ·

the Israelites are not exposed. They are not permitted to have a dwelling to themselves, but are forced to pay largely for being tolerated in the house of a Mahometan, who thinks he has a right to practise every kind of knavery upon his inmate. The clothes which a poor Jew had pulled off on going to bed, I saw exposed to sale in the market next morning by the master of the house.[26]

Egypt

"The most perfect picture of a people's life that has ever been written." Edward Lane's *Modern Egyptians* describes the Egypt he knew so well from 1825 to 1835; it has retained its reputation as a classic to this day. Lane spoke fluent Arabic, bore a resemblance to a pure Arab from Mecca and, in Egypt, dressed as an Egyptian. The passage that follows is extracted from the few pages of his book in which he portrayed the Jews of Egypt. This is thirty-five years before the opening of the Suez Canal and fifty years before the British occupation of the country, when Jews and Christians finally obtained de jure legal rights with Muslims.

> The Jews have eight synagogues in their quarter in Cairo; and not only enjoy religious toleration but are under a less oppressive government in Egypt than in any other country of the Turkish empire. . . . Like the Copts, and for a like reason, the Jews pay tribute, and are exempted from military service. They are held in the utmost contempt and abhorrence by the Muslims in general . . . far more than are the Christians. Not long ago, they used often to be jostled in the streets of Cairo, and sometimes beaten for merely passing on the right hand of a Muslim. At present, they are less oppressed; but still they scarcely ever dare to utter a word of abuse when reviled or beaten unjustly by the meanest Arab or Turk; for many a Jew has been put to death upon false and malicious accusation of uttering disrespectful words against the Kuran or the Prophet. It is common to hear an Arab abuse his jaded ass, and, after applying to him various opprobrious epithets, end by calling the beast a Jew.[27]

Egypt and Libya, November 1945

The beginning of the month of November 1945 was marked in Cairo and Alexandria [and also at Mansura, Tanta, and Port Said] by very grave anti-Jewish tumults [10 Jews were killed and 350 wounded]. Student youths and mobs carried out attacks against the Jewish population, both their persons and their property. The pretext for the attacks was the anniversary of the

Balfour Declaration [November 2]. But, as the London *Jewish Chronicle* explained, in commenting on the events, all the testimonies received till now on the subject of the turmoil that occurred in Cairo concur in excluding a spontaneous outburst and show, on the contrary, that they were carefully organised. But whatever the origin, which seems difficult to detect, the real nature of the events to be understood—as with those that happened in Tripoli [Zanzur, Zawiyah, Qasabat, and Zlitan in Libya at the same period, taking the lives of 130 Jews, and wounding 450]—is the precariousness of the Jewish population in certain Arab countries, where the smallest pretext can trigger aggressions against Jews which, without being desired or approved by the majority of the Arab population, nonetheless constitute a grave danger.[28]

NOTES

The complete English version of "Protected Peoples under Islam" was published in Geneva on October 30, 1976, by the Centre d'Information et de Documentation sur le Moyen-Orient (CID). A French version followed on February 18, 1977. The last document included in the article, "Egypt and Libya, November 1945," only appeared in the French edition and has now been translated into English for this book. Shorter versions of this text by David G. Littman had already appeared in French in *L'Arche* (Paris), December 26, 1973–January 25, 1974, and then revised and enlarged for the *European Newsletter* of the World Union of Jewish Students, November 1975. All the quoted texts from French publications were translated into English in 1976 by David G. Littman.

　　1. *Dhimma* is an Arabic word describing the relationship or covenant between the dominant Muslim power and the subjected populations belonging to the revealed religions; *dhimmi* refers to "the People of the Book" (*ahl al-kitab*), that is, the Jews, the Christians, and equally the Zoroastrians and Sabeans. Others were usually given the choice between conversion to Islam or death.

　　2. Attributed, traditionally, to Umar I (634–44 CE) but, by most European orientalists, to Umar II (717–40 CE).

　　3. Y. Masriya [Bat Ye'or], "A Christian Minority: The Copts in Egypt," in *Case Studies on Human Rights and Fundamental Freedoms*, ed. Willem A. Veenhoven and Winifred Crum Ewing, vol. 4 (The Hague: Martinus Nijhoff, 1976), pp. 77–93; Bat Ye'or, *Réflexions sur la condition de l'opprimé: Le Dhimmi* (to be published). [This reference to Bat Ye'or's first book on the dhimmis has been left as printed in 1976. Nearly four years later—during which period the manuscript circulated—it found a publisher in Paris, with a modified title: *Le Dhimmi: Profil de l'opprimé en Orient et en Afrique du Nord depuis la conquête arabe* (Paris: Editions Anthropos, 1980); *The Dhimmi: Jews and Christians under Islam*, preface by Jacques Ellul (Cranbury, NJ: Fairleigh Dickinson University Press, 1985).

4. D. F. Green, ed., *Arab Theologians on Jews and Israel*, extracts from the proceedings of the Fourth Conference of the Academy of Islamic Research, 1968, 3rd ed. (Geneva: Editions de l'Avenir, 1976), p. 61. [D. F. Green was the pseudonym, for this book only, of David G. Littman ("D.") and Yehoshafat ("F.") Harkabi.]

5. Ibid, p. 91.

6. Bernard Lewis, "An Anti-Jewish Ode: The Qasida of Abu Ishaq against Ibn Nagrella," in *Salo Wittmayer Baron Jubilee Volume on the Occasion of His Eightieth Birthday*, ed. Saul Lieberman and Arthur Hyman (Jerusalem: American Academy for Jewish Research 1975), pp. 660–63.

7. Antoine Fattal, *Le Statut Légal des Non-Musulmans en Pays d'Islam* (Beirut: Imprimerie Catholique, 1958), pp. 369–72, quoted in Y. Masriya, *Les Juifs en Egypte* (Geneva: Editions de l'Avenir, 1971), p. 63.

8. See David G. Littman, "Quelques aspects de la condition du dhimmi: Juifs d'Afrique du Nord avant la colonization," *Yod, Revue des Etudes Hébraiques et juives modernes et contemporaines* (Paris) 2, no. 1 (1976): 45 (letter of 1894).

9. Louis Gardet, *La cité musulmane: Vie sociale et politique,* Etudes musulmanes, (Paris, 1954), p. 348. [Reprint Paris:Vrin, 1995.]

10. Robert Brunschwig, "Les non-Musulmans, I. Les Juifs," in *La Berberie orientale sous les Hafsides Des Origins à la fin du XX Siècle*, vol. 1 (Paris: l'Institut d'Etudes Orientales d'Alger, 1940), p. 404.

11. Gustave von Grunebaum, "Eastern Jewry under Islam: Reflections on Medieval Anti-Judaism," *Viator* (University of California) 2 (1971): 369.

12. Bernard Lewis, "The Pro-Islamic Jews," *Judaism* (New York) 17, no. 4 (1968): 401.

13. Léon Godard, *Le Maroc: Notes d'un voyageur, 1858–59* (Algiers, 1860), p. 32, quoted in Joseph Goulven, *Les Mellahs de Rabat-Salé* (Paris: Paul Geuthner, 1927), p. 123.

14. Israel Benjamin (II), *Cinq années de voyage en Orient (1846–1851)* (Algiers, 1855), p. xxviii. [English translation puplished as *Eight Years in Asia and Africa, from 1846 to 1855*, with a preface by Dr. B. Seeman Hanover, 1959.] The writer's pen name was chosen, so he recounts in a note, in memory of twelfth-century Jewish traveler Benjamin de Tulède.

15. Jacob Saphir, *Eben Sappir* (Jerusalem, 1866), p. 52, quoted in Joshua Feldmann, *The Jews of the Yemen* (London: Speaight & Sons, 1913), pp. 15–16.

16. Yomtob Sémach, *Une mission de l'Alliance au Yémen* (Paris: Alliance Israélite Universe, 1910); see also *Bulletin de l'Alliance Israélite Universelle*, 1910, pp. 48–167.

17. David G. Littman, "Jews under Muslim Rule in the Late 19th Century," *Wiener Library Bulletin* (London) 28, n.s. 35–36 (1975): 65–76; "Jews under Muslim Rule II: Morocco 1903–1912," *Wiener Library Bulletin* 29, n.s. 37–38 (1976); Littman, "Quelques aspects de la condition du dhimmi: Juifs d'Afrique du Nord avant la colonization."

18. Saïd Ghallab, "Les Juifs sont en enfer," *Les Temps Modernes,* no. 277 (June

1965): 2247, 2249, 2251. See Sadat's "Letter to Hitler" (1953) in Green, *Arab Theologians on Jews and Israel*, p. 87.

19. Green, *Arab Theologians on Jews and Israel*, for many examples.

20. Through natural increase, their number has now gone from 1.75 to 2 million souls. [In 2004, roughly half of Israel's Jewish population of 5,200,000.]

21. Georges Vajda, "L'image du Juif dans la tradition islamique," *Les Nouveaux Cahiers* (Paris), nos. 13–14 (1968): 7.

22. Ali Bey [Domingo Badia y Leblich], *Travels of Ali Bey in Morocco, Tripoli, Cyprus, Egypt, Arabia, Syria and Turkey, between the Years 1803 and 1807*, vol. 1 (London: Longman, Hurst, Reese, Orne, and Brown, 1816), pp. 33–34.

23. Arthur Leared, *Marocco and the Moors*, 2nd ed., rev. and ed. Richard Burton (London: Sampson Low, Marston, Searle & Rivington and New York: Scribner & Welford, 1891), pp. 175–76, 217, 254.

24. William Shaler, *Sketches of Algiers* (Boston: Cummings, Hilliard, 1826), pp. 66–67.

25. Chevalier de Hesse-Wartegg, *Tunis, the Land and the People*, new ed. (London: Chatto & Windus, 1882), pp. 118–19.

26. Paolo della Cella, *Narrative of an Expedition from Tripoli in Barbary to the Western Frontier of Egypt, in 1817, by the Bey of Tripoli in Letters to Dr. Viviani of Genoa . . .* , translated from the Italian by Anthony Aufrère (London: John and Arthur Arch, 1822), p. 197.

27. Edward Lane, *The Manners and Customs of the Modern Egyptian*, 2 vols. (London, 1836); reprint, 1 vol. (London: Everyman Library, 1963), pp. 559–60.

28. *Bulletin Intérieur de l'Alliance Universelle* (Paris) 1, no. 2 (November 1945): 9.

HISTORICAL AMNESIA:

5. Naming Jihad and Dhimmitude

Bat Ye'or

In Genesis 2:18–21, God has all the animals pass in front of Adam to be named. Naming is to define an object for it to be recognized by its characteristics when it next appears. A thing without a name escapes the understanding, which does not register it and consequently cannot recognize it. This can be verified also in the realm of abstract knowledge. It applies as well to the concepts of jihad and dhimmitude, yet they represent a political system that has functioned without interruption and virtually without change on three continents for fourteen centuries. Although today it is reappearing with renewed vigor, this system—because it has not been given a name—is not recognized. It is even totally ignored, even denied, whereas the proofs of its past and present existence are obvious and manifold.

Although they are intrinsically linked, jihad and dhimmitude form two separate domains. The first represents a collection of principles, strategies, and tactics of wars and conquests, based on Muslim religious ideas relating to infidels. The second represents the body of laws that the Islamic state imposes on all non-Muslim populations (dhimmis) on lands conquered and Islamized by jihad. Dhimmitude encompasses the way of life mandated by the commands of the Sharia for these subjugated indigenous peoples.

A considerable number of chronicles written by Muslims and non-Muslims exist containing information on the methods and development of jihad over the centuries. These texts make it possible to establish the synchronicity between these Islamic military practices and the prescriptions of jihad, formulated by the founders of the four schools of Islamic jurisprudence as early as the eighth century. These rules of jihad are still taught in Islamic schools

This text was prepared in August 2002. It is published here for the first time.

and institutes in Muslim countries, Europe, and the Americas. The wars currently waged by Muslim states or groups in Israel, the Sudan, Nigeria, Kashmir, the Philippines, Indonesia, Chechnya, and the United States reproduce the classic strategy of jihad.

With the technology of the twenty-first century this modern jihad reproduces the ideological principles of the jihad against infidels drawn up in the eighth century. It reveals the easily identifiable features of a worldwide jihad integrated into the process of globalization. It is easy to show the way in which current practices of war conform to the rules of jihad according to the Sharia. For example, the military conscription of pubescent and prepubescent children was used in the Iraq-Iran war, in the jihad against Israel (the *intifada*), and by Islamist militias in the Sudan. The same is true of the refusal to return enemy corpses (Lebanese Hizbollah); the taking and ransoming of hostages (Lebanon, Chechnya, the Philippines); the raids on villages and the abduction and enslavement of women and children (Sudan, Indonesia); and the terrorist campaigns against civilians regarded as enemies of Islam (infidels and apostates) and consequently deprived of all rights (terrorism in Israel, India, the United States, and Algeria).

Other manifestations of jihad include the jihad of the pen (propaganda) and jihad by way of buying hearts and minds (corrupting politicians, academics, and intellectuals). Jihad can also consist of dividing the enemy camp. For example, anti-Zionism and anti-Americanism in Europe is largely the result of political pressures exerted by the Arab-Islamic world on European political parties captivated by the oil mantra. Anti-Americanism divides two allied continents and weakens still further a Europe eroded by massive immigration, terrorism, and its economic dependence on oil. The wave of Judeophobia currently raging in Europe aims at isolating and terrorizing the Jewish communities to make them abandon their solidarity with Israel and to manipulate them against it. This policy, conceived in the Arab world, is implemented in Europe by the criminal acts of Muslim immigrants perpetrated against Jews. It is not combated by governments that are impotent in the face of Muslim criminality and prefer to deny it; at the same time they encourage it through a biased anti-Israel policy. Lastly, the Judeo-Christian rapprochement, so essential to the two Peoples of the Bible, is torpedoed by the Islamic exploitation of the traditional antisemitism/anti-Zionism of the Euro-Arab pro-Palestinian lobbies.

Thus those pulling the strings of the jihad against the infidels hide behind a screen of anti-American and anti-Zionist Westerners. An Egyptian lawyer, Fouad Abdel-Moneim Riad, who was referred to in a recent interview as a former judge of an unspecified court on war crimes, talks of creating an international moral opinion. He calls for universal mobilization of the non-governmental organizations (NGOs) and of the civil society of the Arab and international world in order to set up a "moral tribunal" that would condemn Israel for war crimes. "Such a tribunal," says magistrate Riad, "would be most effective if it were formed of great thinkers from outside of the Arab world."[1] Riad makes it clear that the condemnation for war crimes must not be limited to a few culpable politicians, as happened with Hitler, but must embrace all the people of Israel. This is an example of the essentialist and collective category of the demonization of the infidel which is a fundamental notion of jihad. Riad's idea soon found support from Archbishop Desmond Tutu in an article titled "Build Moral Pressure to End the Occupation."[2] Consciously or not, the archbishop became the Christian spokesman for Riad by describing the stages of this orchestration of hatred against Israel, comparing apartheid with Israel's self-defense against terrorism, under the accusation of "occupation."

As for dhimmitude, it dissolves in the limbo of the unknowable, having never been analyzed or given a name until recently. It is replaced by the terms "golden age" and "exemplary tolerance," propagated by pro-Muslim European lobbies. Yet dhimmitude can be observed today in most Muslim countries. A recently published book by Canon Patrick Sookhdeo throws light on some aspects of the existence of non-Muslims in Pakistan, a country governed by the Sharia.[3] This description reveals a pattern of suffering that the historical chronicles only suggest, since most often the victims disappeared without a trace. And yet, however painful it may be, this condition is not an exact replica of the past, because no Muslim country, not even Saudi Arabia and the ex-Taliban regime, imposes the requirements of the Sharia in full, as was the case in the past when it constituted the sole jurisdiction in the Muslim empires. Thus the condition known as "bonded labor" is of particular interest to the historian of dhimmitude, because it was the condition of the Jewish and Christian peasantries, so often described in their chronicles from the eighth to the nineteenth centuries. Today, in Pakistan, this subservience is still maintained by fiscal exploitation and arbitrary indebtedness that lead to expropriation and the slavery system. Likewise, Sookhdeo demonstrates how the inferior status of the non-Muslim can validate an abuse, in theory forbidden by law, and make it irreversible, as with the abduction of Christian women. This crime, also practiced in Egypt today, is a permanent component of dhimmitude.

The institution of jihad-dhimmitude constitutes a homogeneous modern pattern rooted in fourteen centuries of existence. As far as I know it has never been subject to the smallest criticism by Muslim theologians. The ideology of the jihad against the infidels and its stipulations, so often described in detail by Muslim and Christian chroniclers—namely massacres, deportations, slavery, and territorial dispossession—has never given rise to any examination. On the contrary, far from being condemned, jihad is fervently glorified and piously emulated. Judeo-Christian societies, trained to constant and rigorous self-criticism, find this total absence of relativism and historical objectivity bewildering. There are multiple reasons for it, but the principal cause lies in the fact that the eighth-century Muslim theologians rooted the institution of jihad-dhimmitude in the Qur'an and the Sunna of the Prophet, that is to say his life, his words, and his actions. These two sources are the foundation of the Islamic religion, jurisdiction, and civilization. Muslim doctrine postulates as an absolute axiom the total conformity of the divine will with the revelation (Qur'an) made to the Prophet, and with his words and his actions (Sunna).

A small booklet titled *Islam: The Essentials,* published in 1992 by the Islamic Foundation, England, lists the essential points of the faith. Among them, point 6 declares that Muhammad is "the Perfect Ideal for Mankind, the perfect servant of Allah and hence the complete and the ideally balanced manifestation of the attributes of Allah." Point 8 specifies that the believer must worship Allah according to the revelations made in the Qur'an, by the method prescribed by Muhammad, "and hence in accordance with his sayings and practice, known as Hadith or Sunnah." It is this doctrinal position that prevents any criticism or change.

Jihad and dhimmitude are compulsorily commanded by the Sharia, the sacred Islamic law, formulated by the jurists after the conquest of territories stretching from Portugal to the Indus. Their institutions are at the heart of the dynamic of Islamization specific to Muslim history and civilization that developed among the conquered infidel majorities. To criticize these institutions would throw doubt on the moral legitimacy of the Islamization of the infidels' countries that was achieved. Further, this Islamization is commanded by the dogma that proclaims the mission incumbent on the Islamic community. This mission consists of imposing the law of Allah on all mankind. To challenge the legitimacy of jihad rehabilitates infidelity, unbelief (*kufr*), the incarnation of Evil opposed to the Good (i.e., Islam), and discredits the image of the Muslim jihadist fighter. Restoring the balance in this way is inconsistent with verse 4:140, "Allah will not grant the unbelievers any way over the believers." Moreover, it is this absolute demonization of the world of infidelity that in the past had determined—and still determines today—the dogmatic rejection of its culture and influence or their adoption in an Islamized form. Thus, the Organization of the Islamic Conference has promulgated the Cairo Declaration of Human Rights in Islam (1990), which, being in accordance with the Sharia, supersedes the Universal Declaration of Human Rights (1948). This same cultural anti-Western trend led to the creation in 1981 of an International Institute of Islamic Thought (IIIT), an organization aimed at the Islamization of Western knowledge by relating it to the Sharia.[4]

If one understands, from the Muslim point of view, the theological arguments behind this lack of criticism, how can this historical negationism in the Western democracies be explained? The taboo that masks this subject leads to the claim that jihad has not made victims. Censorship presents dhimmitude in Andalusia and elsewhere under the aegis of a caliph applying the Sharia—complete with harems, eunuchs, and slaves, the majority of whom were Christians—as a perfect model of multicultural societies for the West to be emulated in the twenty-first century. This general misinformation enjoys wide outside financial support, and at the political level it justifies the European Union's laxity on the immigration question. Widely spread and taught, this myth is in keeping with Europe's security concerns and its policies of appeasement and conciliation toward Muslim countries. Servile flattery is the ransom for economic and terrorist reprisals. Quite recently Turkey applied pressure on the United States, Switzerland, France and Israel to prevent recognition of the Armenian genocide (1915–17). Thus the West has barricaded itself into a historical negationism that is the cornerstone of its economic, strategic, and security relationships with Muslim countries.

In the context of jihad-dhimmitude it should also be noted that Islamic law imposes the same status on Jews and Christians. The difference in the ways in which these two communities have evolved is linked to external demographic and political factors. At the beginning of the conquests, the Christians constituted immense majorities equipped with powerful religious and juridical institutions, capable of constituting a threat to the immigrant Muslim minority. Despite their divisions, the Muslims always suspected them of allegiance to hostile Christendoms (*dar al-Harb*, "region of war"). Depending on circumstances, these two factors specific to the Christian dhimmis played an ambivalent role in the course of history, causing sometimes bloody reprisals that spared the Jews and sometimes preferential treatment obtained by pressure or money from the Western powers. By contrast, the vulnerability of the Jews, lacking outside protection, led to the disintegration of Palestinian Jewry by Arab colonization and to the decline and even in some cases the disappearance of the numerous Jewish diasporas of Arabia, Yemen, Egypt, Syria, Iraq, Persia, and Andalusia in the twelfth century.

In the nineteenth century, the destinies of the two communities totally diverged in the Middle East. Some Lebanese and Syrian Christian movements militated on behalf of Arab nationalism. This policy, conceived by France and the papacy, aimed at unifying Christians and Muslims in one ethnic and cultural identity in order to eliminate the religious context of dhimmitude. Arabism, propagated among the Christian dhimmis by missionaries, strengthened the influence in the Holy Land of the Holy See and France, sole protector of the Holy Places of Christendom. From its beginnings, the Holy See and France utilized this movement to cement an Islamo-Christian alliance and destroy Zionism, which was supported by Protestant England. Thus the religious and political rivalries of Europe were played out by the interdhimmi conflicts. During World War II, Christian and Muslim Arab nationalists—notably from Palestine—supported the fascist and Nazi regimes.

A number of Eastern Christians were opposed to Arab nationalism, which denied their ethnic identity, their culture, their history, and their rights in their country, since Christianity had grown up in the ancient civilizations of the Orient well before Arab Islam was imported with the invaders. These Christians also rejected the extreme Judeophobia that this movement spread. In addition, they denounced the revival of dhimmitude in Arab nationalism and campaigned for autonomous Christian territories in Lebanon and Iraq. The failure of these movements, mercilessly combated by the European colonial powers and broken by bloody Muslim reprisals, fed a large flow of Christian emigration from Lebanon, Syria, Iraq, and Egypt throughout the nineteenth and twentieth centuries.

The Jews rejected Arab nationalism—a racist, Judeophobic, anti-Christian, and negationist ideology—that concealed the history, the civilizations, and the rights of the non-Arab peoples of the Middle East. Faced with Arab pogroms and fearing the fate of the Armenians, the Jews of Arab countries after World War II emigrated en masse in tragic conditions, abandoning all their possessions in these lands of dhimmitude, where for centuries they had been exploited, persecuted, and degraded.

Today, Arab-Muslim behavior toward non-Muslims has scarcely evolved since the seventh century. Israel, which symbolizes the liberation from dhimmitude of the Jewish people in their homeland, is attacked by jihad, while the remaining Christian communities live in Muslim countries under a system of dhimmitude in a precarious present and an uncertain future. The tragic consequences of Arab nationalism were revealed after the decolonization of the Muslim countries and in the process of their re-Islamization, which is bringing back the Sharia and consequently a modern dhimmitude for the Christians, and the jihad threat against the West. Thus the jihad-dhimmitude institution remains stronger than ever.

This situation is the result of the negationist culture imposed by Arab nationalism, which, in its war against Zionism, replaced the history of jihad-dhimmitude with the myth of perfect Islamo-Christian coexistence. Christian Arab nationalists destroyed their memory and their dhimmi identity, replacing them with an imaginary Arab origin. They fought—as had the janissaries in the past—against the liberation movements of their Christian brothers in order to keep them in the dhimmitude of Arabism. Ardent defenders of Islamic interests in the West, they made every effort to graft onto this amnesia a catalogue of Christian guilt toward Muslims and the latter's victimization in order to create an artificial symmetry between Islamo-Christian relations and Judeo-Christian relations.

Since Arab nationalism had been conceived and imposed by Europe, this misinformation prospered there, aggravated by circumstances connected with the expansion of the oil industries and international terrorism. In this way Europe has evolved into Eurabia, a new land of dhimmitude following the traditional pattern. The European ministers of Eurabia, like the Christian dhimmi notables, obey the commands of internal and external Islamist terrorism. While the dangers of an international nuclear jihad grew stronger, Eurabia, to assert its existence, fulminated against Israel, accusing it of threatening world peace by its refusal to surrender to Palestinian terror. The media's onslaught against Israel was encouraged by political circles. The general insecurity that is destroying democratic civil institutions, and the anti-Jewish criminal attacks, testify to the incompetence of the minister-notables of Eurabia. Like the dhimmis, whose exemplary condition they had vaunted, they are forced to deny the antisemitic rampages since they are powerless to stop clandestine immigration or Muslim criminals without incurring economic and terrorist reprisals. Thus historical amnesia has led to political impotence and the servitude of dhimmitude, which is constantly gaining ground.

NOTES

1. Fouad Abdel-Moneim Riad, "The Battle for a Moral World," *Al-Ahram* (Cairo), May 16–22, 2002, p. 8.

2. Desmond Tutu, "Build Moral Pressure to End the Occupation," *International Herald Tribune*, June 14, 2002.

3. Patrick Sookhdeo, *A People Betrayed: The Impact of Islamization on the Christian Community in Pakistan* (Pewsey, Wiltshire, UK: Isaac Publishing, 2002).

4. Amber Haque, ed., *Muslims and Islamization in North America: Problems and Prospects* (Beltsville, MD: Amana; Kuala Lumpur: A. S. Noordeen, 1999).

DHIMMI PEOPLES

6. Oppressed Nations

Bat Ye'or

Loose the bands of wickedness,
Undo the heavy burdens,
Let the oppressed go free,
And that ye break every yoke.
—Isaiah 58:6

INTRODUCTION

There are peoples roaming the earth who no longer have a soul. Flight and exile have enfeebled their memories, dimmed their sight, and stifled their speech. In glancing through history textbooks, they smile in melancholy: today their nations no longer exist. Vanquished peoples, they have been rejected by history and have joined the anonymous mass of exploited peoples, whose blood, tears, and sweat have helped to build the civilization of their oppressors. Thus they wander through the world, with neither roots nor memories, strangers, forgotten by time, atomized—bearing their nostalgia like a shackle.

When historians, peering into history through the conqueror's eyeglass, meet them at the turn of every century, eloquent in their gloomy silence, they deem "tolerant" the genocide that decimated these peoples, forgetting that the silence of nations is the same as that of the gulag. Some have survived, emaciated: these are the Samaritans. Others resist, and when their struggle explodes into violence, the world remembers the meaning of bravery: these are the Maronites. Others fight alone in the name of independence: these are

---

First published in English in 1978 by Editions de l'Avenir, Geneva, Switzerland.

the Kurds. Others despair in exile: these are the Armenians and the Assyrian Christians. Some are resigned to their fate: these are the Copts. And others dig up, from their liberated land, the ruins of their ancient culture destroyed by the occupant: these are the Israelis. So numerous and diverse, all these nations have shared a common destiny for thirteen centuries: they have resisted to the limits of human endurance in order to survive.

In this year, dedicated to the fight against racism, oppression, imperialism, and colonialism, we wish to remember them. And bearing in mind the appeal of the Native Americans at the United Nations,[1] we wondered whether martyrdom endured for thirteen centuries does not justify *at last* the recognition of the national rights and the human rights of dhimmi peoples, heirs to the national and cultural values of the most ancient civilizations.

THE DHIMMIS

> *The fundamental evil in alienation is forgetfulness.*
> —Robert Misrahi

In this article, it is impossible to go far beyond general propositions. These will be best appreciated, however, after the reader has been provided with the basic historical framework. This is why it has seemed useful to specify briefly the socioeconomic background in which the dhimmi nations evolved, while abstaining, for reasons of clarity and space, from analyzing the historical context in any depth.

After the Arab conquest, the expression *dhimmi* designated the indigenous non-Arab and non-Muslim peoples—Jews, Christians, Zoroastrians (Persians)—whose territories came under Arab-Muslim domination. It signifies "protected" because these populations—in theory, if not always in practice—were protected from pillage, slavery, exile, and massacre by the specific conditions of an agreed covenant between the victors and the vanquished. In return for such protection, the dhimmis were obliged to submit to a code or covenant (commonly referred to as the Covenant of Umar), a summary of which is given below. The need to control these foreign peoples naturally obliged the conquering Arab minority to adopt an oppressive political attitude, which became more and more severe over the years. In order to justify their oppression, the rulers based their policies on certain religious values to the exclusion of other Quranic verses recommending charity and fraternity. Thus a common geopolitical event—the conquest of foreign lands and the subjection of conquered peoples—was linked to a religious concept, the jihad, or holy war, which has as its inevitable consequence the oppression of the infidel. So, although the condition of the dhimmis is typical of religious intolerance—hardly exceptional in human history—only its political aspect, the spoliation and subjection of native inhabitants, will be examined here.

A dhimmi civilization is characterized by a language, a history, and a culture as well as specific political and juridical institutions developed in the national homeland before its annexation by the Arab conquerors. The expression *dhimmi civilization*, or *dhimmi people*, refers to a nation the ethnic origin of which is associated with a particular geographical area, regardless of that nation's present dispersion. People who belong to a dhimmi civilization are individuals who have continued to transmit to their progeny their specific heritage, despite their wanderings and their present domiciles, which have resulted from loss of their national independence through occupation, oppression, and exile. Thus, whether Westerners or Orientals, Jews are part of a dhimmi civilization if they willingly perpetuate and accept the national and cultural values of Israel. It is the same thing with the Armenians, the Assyrians, and the Maronites as well as other peoples who, after the conquest of their homeland, were subjected to a legislation that either decimated them or forced them to live in exile.

Economic Exploitation

A tax (the *kharaj*) was levied on the lands left to the indigenous dhimmis. This tax symbolized the Arabization of the land of the dhimmis, that is, its addition to the patrimony of the Arab-Islamic community. In the early period of colonization, lands given in fief were exonerated from the *kharaj*.

Each male dhimmi, with the theoretical exceptions of the aged, invalids, and slaves, had to pay a poll tax (the *jizya*), which symbolized the subjection and humiliation of the vanquished.

The dhimmis also paid double the taxes of the Muslims. In addition, ransoms (*avanias*) were frequently extorted from the local Jewish and Christian communities under threat of collective sanctions, including torture and death.

Politico-economic Discrimination

It was forbidden for dhimmis on pain of death

- to carry or possess weapons;

- to raise a hand against a Muslim, even against an aggressor unjustly determined to kill them;
- to ally themselves with the enemies of the Arabs;
- to criticize Islam, the Prophet, or the angels;
- to convert to any religion other than Islam, and having converted to Islam to revert to their original religion;
- to be linked by marriage or concubinage to a Muslim woman;
- to hold a position giving them authority over a Muslim.

The dhimmis were obliged:

- to live separated from Muslims, in special quarters of a town, the gates of which were closed every evening, or, as in Yemen, outside the limits of towns inhabited by Muslims;
- to have shorter houses than those of Muslims;
- to practice their religion secretly and in silence;
- to bury their dead hastily;
- to refrain from showing in public religious objects, such as crosses, banners, or sacred texts;
- to distinguish themselves from Muslims by their exterior aspect;
- to wear clothes distinguished not only by shape (length, style of sleeves, etc.) but also by specific colors assigned to each group of dhimmis, i.e., for Jews, Christians, and Samaritans;
- to have different types of tombs from those of Muslims.

It was forbidden for the dhimmis:

- to go near mosques or to enter certain venerated towns, which would thereby be polluted;
- to have headdresses, belts, shoes, ornate saddles, or saddles similar to those of Muslims.

Furthermore, all elements of their exterior appearance were intended to emphasize their humble and abject status. They were forbidden to ride horses or camels, since these animals were considered too noble for them. Donkeys were permitted, but they could only ride them outside towns, and they had to dismount on sight of a Muslim. In certain periods they were forced to wear distinctive badges in the public baths, and in certain regions they were even forbidden to enter them at all.

The dhimmis were obliged:

- to make haste in the streets, always passing to the left (impure) side of a Muslim, who was advised to push them to the wall;
- to walk humbly with lowered eyes;
- to accept insults without replying;
- to remain standing in a humble and respectful attitude in the presence of a Muslim;
- to leave Muslims the best places;
- never to speak to Muslims except to reply.

Any litigation between a dhimmi and a Muslim was brought before an Islamic tribunal, where the dhimmi's testimony was unacceptable.

In North Africa and Yemen, the most repugnant duties, such as executioner, gravedigger, cleaner of the public latrines, and so on were forced on Jews—even on Saturdays and holy days. Contempt for the dhimmi's life was expressed through inequality of punishments for the same offences. The penalty for murder was much lighter if the victim was a dhimmi. The murderer of a dhimmi was rarely punished, as he could justify his act by accusing his victim of blasphemy against Islam or of having assaulted a Muslim.

Muslims were strongly advised against social intercourse with dhimmis, but if contact with them could not be avoided it was recommended that they limit relations to the strictest necessities, always showing contempt.

This brief summary provides only an outline of the rules that governed a whole system of oppression, which increased or decreased according to the specific circumstances of each region. In exchange for these obligations inflicted upon the dhimmis, their existence was tolerated on their land, which was now Arabized. This tolerance was not final. It could be abrogated in two ways: the unilateral decision of the ruler to exile the dhimmis or infraction by the dhimmis of the regulations. The latter case permitted individual or collective reprisals against the dhimmi communities, ending in pillage or massacre. The enforcement or alleviation of the rules depended on the political circumstances and the goodwill of the rulers. Some orientalists have considered them "tolerant," and this was evidently the opinion of those who benefited from them. But it is obviously not the point of view of the victims. For how can oppression be justified or esteemed "tolerant" other than by denying the humanity of those subjugated by it? Every colonizing power maintains that men are not equal and considers that its yoke is benevolent and tolerant. Nor did the Arabs invent this legislation. The Byzantine clergy first elaborated it—thereby giving an ideological arm to the imperial power—in order to destroy Israel in its homeland and in the diaspora. The Arabian conquerors Islamized it, developing and using it to annihilate in their turn both oriental and North African Judaism and Christianity in the political, economic, religious, and cultural spheres.

The situation of the Christian dhimmis was alleviated following Western European pressure to protect oriental Christians, pilgrimages to the Holy Land, and commerce with the Orient. In the second half of the nineteenth century, European Jewish organizations, aided by European consuls, were able to improve the condition of the Jewish dhimmis. It was only with European colonization, which proclaimed de facto equality between Muslim, Christian, and Jew, that the dhimmis, now liberated from discrimination, could feel free and even achieve some economic progress.

After European decolonization, Arab governments adopted a policy of intensive Arabization. Wiping out the consequences of European colonization meant, amongst other things, as far as the indigenous national minorities were concerned, the reestablishment of political, economic, social, and cultural discrimination, with the aim of limiting those liberties that had been enjoyed during the colonial period. This discrimination was adjusted to new ideological formulae and was manifested with strong emphasis on the Arab-Muslim element to the detriment of the pre-Islamic ethnic cultures and nationalisms. The latter were either attacked, as in the case of the national movements of the Assyrians, Kurds, Zionists, and Maronites, or paralyzed, like the Copts of Egypt. Thus was reestablished the superiority and domination of the Arab-Muslim community over the ethnic oriental nationalisms, while pan-Arabism reaffirmed its imperialist principle of universal domination, which had been at the root of Arab colonization of the Near East, North Africa, Spain, Portugal, Sicily, and part or Italy.

Documents

Dhimmi Edict for the Jews of Yemen, 1905

The imam Said Yahya Ibn Muhammad, religious and political leader of the Yemen, wrote with his own hand the edict that follows. In 1905 the imam gave it to the Jews and promised to protect them "if they remained in their former status." In 1921 the ancient law requiring the forced conversion of Jewish orphans was renewed and rendered more severe in 1925. It remained in force until the departure of the Jews for Israel in 1948–50.

Edict promulgated in the Yemen by Imam Yahya:

In the name of Allah, the all merciful and clement

This is the regulation which I ordain for all the Jews who must remain subjected to my laws and pay the [poll] tax without any change.

I recall to mind the ancient words and their meaning; I recall to mind the obligations which the Turks have forgotten and which were observed in the time of the pious imams, before the triumph of people ignorant of the law.

The Jews can remain untroubled and be assured of their existence if they pay regularly the *gizya*.

Every male having reached the age of thirteen years is subject to this tax . . . and by this their life will be preserved under our domination.

No one can avoid paying this tax before the end of the year . . . as it is written in the Qur'an, the book received from Allah. . . .

The Jews must not:

1) Raise their voices in front of Muslims,
2) Build houses higher than the houses of Muslims,
3) Brush against Muslims whilst passing them in the street,
4) Carry on the same trade as the Arabs,
5) Say that Muslim law can have a defect,
6) Insult the prophets,
7) Discuss religion with Muslims,
8) Ride animals astraddle,
9) Screw up their eyes in perceiving the nudity of Muslims,
10) Carry on their religious devotions outside their places of worship,
11) Raise their voices during prayers,
12) Sound the shofar with much noise,
13) Lend money at interest, which can bring about the destruction of the world,
14) They must always rise in front of Muslims and honour them in all circumstances.[2]

Clothing for Dhimmi Jews (Debdou, Morocco)

They [the Jews] first obtained the usage of this scarf in Morocco [Marrakesh] and Mequinez, as a means of covering their ears. They really wanted to elude the customary insult of Moorish children, who delighted in knocking off their bonnets which were a sign of servitude. They are not allowed to fasten the scarf with a double knot below the chin. This knot must be a simple one and the scarf removed in the presence of Muslim dignitaries. . . . They are obliged always to wear the black or dark blue cloak (*yalak*); it is only by toleration that they wear the white *slam*, a small coat, useful against the hot sun. The coat's hood, made of blue cloth, must not fold over the head, lest the Jew be mistaken from afar for a Moor; for the Moor sometimes wears a hood of the same colour, except with a different rim.

Moreover the black bonnet must always be visible. Furthermore, the coat must have a little opening on the right, and the hood must fall over the left shoulder in order to trouble the movement of the arm as another sign of servitude.[3]

1851: No Justice for the Dhimmi

It is my duty to report to Your Excellency that the Jews in Hebron have been greatly alarmed by threats of the Moslems there at the commencement of Ramadan. . . .

The Jews having complained that a freed slave named Saad Allah was more obnoxious to them than any other person in Hebron and that Abderrahhman had released him almost immediately after sentencing him to imprisonment, I applied to the Pasha to have Saad Allah brought to Jerusalem.

His Excellency gave an order that the offender should be examined by the Council in Hebron, and if convicted, be forwarded to Jerusalem for punishment.

Accordingly a Council was held there during five hours, and the result was that a report (Mazbata) was drawn up and signed by the Mufti and Kadi, declaring that none but Jewish witnesses had appeared, "and we do not receive the testimony of Jews." Saad Allah was therefore dismissed.[4]

FROM DHIMMIS TO A DHIMMI STATE

> *Those who cannot remember the past are condemned to repeat it.*
> — George Santayana
> (inscription on the gate of Dachau Concentration Camp Site Museum)

Among the motivations that contributed to the elaboration of the dhimmi status, the victor-vanquished relationship in its political aspect appears as the predominant element. A distinction must be made, however, between the treatment meted out by the Arab-Muslim conquerors to non-Arab lands on the one hand and to their inhabitants on the other. The conquered lands were permanently annexed by the Arab-Muslim collectivity, that is, they were Arabized. The fate of their inhabitants depended on whether they had surren-dered as a result of defeat in battle or according to treaty, but in either case indigenous inhabitants who refused conversion to Islam were tolerated only if they accepted the dhimmi status. Arabization of the conquered lands was marked by the *kharaj* tax, which was levied only on dhimmi-owned land. The tax was paid to the Islamic collectivity, since both the dhimmis and the produce of their work were considered as belonging to the conquering com-munity of believers.

Arabization was in fact synonymous with expropriation, for it implied the dissolution of the bond between the land and its former owner. Hence-forth the dhimmis were to be "tolerated" on their own land by a foreigner who had obtained possession legally—for appropriation by force was con-sidered legal.

Exploitation of the Dhimmis

Having legitimately dispossessed the conquered populations according to the law of warfare, the conquerors tried to strengthen their hold by weakening the indigenous population through economic exploitation and inequitable laws. The decisive reason for the conqueror's tolerance of the dhimmis' exis-tence was economic. They were sedentary peoples whose daily work both on the land and in the towns was productive and necessary. The empire expanded with the aid of a Bedouin army that benefited from the spoils of war; its maintenance was guaranteed by the exploitation of the dhimmis throughout the conquered territories. Henceforth the dhimmis became merely an exploitable human mass from which corvée was obtainable at will. At some periods they were tolerated with condescension and at others with ani-mosity, according to the empire's economic and strategic needs at the time.

Submission of the Dhimmis

The victor-vanquished relationship, being one of force, compelled the master to maintain the dhimmi in a permanent state of weakness, subordi-nation, and inferiority. The dhimmi was forbidden to carry arms or keep them at home. He could be condemned to death for raising his hand against a member of the conquering religion, even in defense when criminally assaulted or attacked by a child. In certain circumstances, however, the enrollment of dhimmi mercenaries was permitted; on such occasions the latter enjoyed the same rights as Muslims.

The expropriation and economic exploitation of the dhimmi peoples required a moral justification. In order to legitimize the conquerors' right over the person and property of the vanquished, the ruling power glorified the superiority of the chosen conquering faith as well as the spiritual values it upheld, contrasting them with the perversity of the vanquished dhimmis.

It was necessary for the dominating group to illustrate by its dignity, authority, and wealth the divine grace that rewarded the just cause of the conquerors in contrast to the humility, isolation, and degradation of the vanquished. The conquerors endeavored to debase the very soul of the dhimmis by imposing on them the outward signs of moral degradation. When the politico-military danger of a massive revolt on the part of the dhimmis had passed, it was this moral and social degradation of human beings, justified by the superiority of the true believers, that characterized the dhimmi condition. But even then the political implications of the victor-vanquished relationship would survive side by side with that of the dominator-dominated, oppressor-oppressed relationship.

The dominant power felt obliged to expose publicly the imputed depravity of the dhimmis, especially as their culture—as heirs to the ancient civilizations of the Orient—was incomparably more developed than that of the conquerors. According to the renowned sheikh Damanhuri (Egypt, eighteenth century), the dhimmis "must not imitate the garb of the men of learning and honor, or wear luxurious garb, silk, or, say, fine cloth. They must be distinguished from ourselves in attire, as the local custom of each area may have it, but without adornment, so that it indicates their humiliation, submission, and abasement. Their shoelaces must not be like ours. Where closed shoes are worn, not laced footwear, their shoes should be coarse, of unpleasant color. The Companions [of the Prophet] agreed upon these points in order to demonstrate the abasement of the infidel and to protect the weak believer's faith."[5]

Debasement of the Dhimmis

A code of rules (the Covenant of Umar) based on religious and legal texts, enforced upon the already despoiled and subjugated dhimmis a moral debasement that reduced them to the outward appearance of complete contemptibility. They were deprived of all means of defense, either physical or legal, thus rendering them cowardly in comparison with the courage of their superiors; they were obliged to grovel in a servile manner such that the victor would appear more generous; they were forced to live in fear of the next day so that each day they were delivered from death would fill them with gratitude, stifling their will to revolt against their oppressors, who only spared them because of their productiveness. According to theologian Sayh Muhammad al-Magili (Maghreb, fifteenth century), on the day set aside for collecting the *jizya*, the Jews were to be assembled in a public place, such as the bazaar, at the lowest and most debasing place.

The tax collectors were to stand above the Jews in a threatening position so that it should appear to everyone that the latter were to be humiliated and despoiled of their belongings. "They will then realize what favor we bestow upon them in accepting the jizya and letting them off so easily. Then they should be dragged away, one by one. . . . While paying, the dhimmi should be slapped in the face and pushed away so that he will consider that through this form of ransom he has escaped the sword."[6]

Through isolation, infamy, vulnerability, and poverty, the dhimmis became social pariahs. The game had been won, and from then on the plundering of these subhuman beings, both their person and their possessions, was interpreted as a sign of the Divine Will rewarding the just cause of the victor. To claim that the goods and honors that certain dhimmis enjoyed were illegal and sinful was an easy next step, taken by famous jurist Ibn Taymiyya (Egypt, fourteenth century), who asserted that it was incumbent on rulers "to humiliate and oppress them [the dhimmis] by compelling them to observe the commandments of Umar; they have the duty to withdraw them from the important posts they occupy and generally to prohibit them from access to Muslim affairs."[7]

Toleration of such a despicable creature was indeed a token of the victor's generosity, but it was not to go unpaid for. Thus, according to the same jurist, the dominant community should tighten the yoke on its "protégés" so that they may realize that to flee from this condition of infamy would be punished by reprisals: at every moment they were threatened with death or exile. They were to live in an atmosphere of permanent menace. The toleration that spared their lives was not to be taken for granted—it was to be bought with gold and servility, and it could be unilaterally abolished, since the punishment of the infidel was only temporarily held at bay. This reprieve, in order to be extended, demanded more gold and more humiliation, more work, and more corruption.

Since the loyalty of the dhimmis to their religion was the cornerstone of their passive resistance to the conqueror, it was therefore necessary to debase it. The building of new religious edifices was prohibited, whereas those dating from the pre-Islamic period could be restored only under certain conditions, providing that no enlargement or embellishment should improve the original structure. In other words, any restoration merely maintained them in a constant state of disrepair. Religious objects were looked upon with scorn as symbols of contemptible practices and were frequently pillaged, burned, or profaned. Their debasement added to the degradation of the few dhimmi places of worship that had escaped destruction and confiscation.

These, then, were the political, economic, and moral motivations that produced both the dhimmi status and the whole system of myths that justify the infernal cycle of debasement of man by man. Indeed, the dhimmi condition was by no means a historical exception. A number of discriminatory practices already existed in Eastern Christendom, and these were transmitted by Arabized converts and assimilated into the historical, political, and religious values of the Arab conquerors.

History Forgotten

Nowadays, when trying to dig up the past of the dhimmi communities, historians are overwhelmed by the silences of history that cover the deaths of nations. Standing out from the ashes of abandoned places, only ruined synagogues, churches, and profaned cemeteries are to be found. Even the humiliation of the past, which symbolized the dhimmis' resistance against oppression, is forgotten, or rather denied, by their descendants—for they have been freed by the West and are eager to forget their ancestral humiliation—and by those who have deliberately falsified or concealed historical truth.

The silence that smothers the cries of past oppression and humiliation is symbolic of the dhimmi destiny. People without a past, they are also a people without rights; and in our time, when petty nationalisms spring up artificially within a decade, acquiring their national slogans at will, the rights of the dhimmis to national autonomy in their liberated homeland or equal rights with their oppressors are never mentioned. Remnants of nations—dead yet living peoples—preserved in spite of a thousand years of silence, based on the principle that all criticism of the oppressor is blasphemy, they are the embodiment of silent suffering. In the victor-vanquished relationship, they are still today victims of a totalist policy: absolutely everything for the victor, absolutely nothing for the vanquished. The conqueror may glory in a triumphantly successful imperialism, in the luster of pillaged civilizations, in the world's respect for strength and power. The vanquished must eke out a subordinate existence, affirming the grandeur of the masters and the contempt that history reserves for the weak, for the losers.

Israel: Dhimmi State

Is it necessary, it may be asked, to convey a message that no longer resounds in the hearts of a posterity that denies its past? For one who, herself a dhimmi, has in her quest for identity explored the abyss of oppression, the world today is full of dhimmis: for the system which produces them, not having been uncovered in our time, is still at work. The truth is that the dhimmi condition has reached the free world from the Orient, in the sense that the victims of the Arab economic boycott and of PLO-inspired international terrorism—banishing by death whosoever blasphemes against Arabism—are also dhimmis. Worse, there is even a dhimmi state, Israel, existing yet denied. The system of values that produced the dhimmis today decrees that to harass, assassinate, or mutilate the Israeli population and its sympathizers guilty of rebellion (Zionism) is legal and commendable. The same penalties were used to chastise the rebellious dhimmis, whose revolt was considered blasphemy—contesting as it did the dogma of the victor's superiority and the inferiority of the vanquished. Racism, imperialism, and colonialism form the hateful cloth of contempt and derision thrown on the State of Israel in order to disarm and ostracize a country, whose population, largely composed of dhimmi refugees from Arab lands liberated by Zionism, struggles for survival.

But are not references to the past detrimental to any prospects of peace in the Middle East, and should not such indictments be pushed into the background? These two points are important. The first implies that the teaching of history must submit to the political expediencies of the present, a policy that would result not only in historical falsification but also in the denial of history. If this is so, world peace will demand the destruction of all the history books of humanity, which henceforth, deprived of its memory, experience, culture, and intelligence, will revert to barbarism. Once the utility of human history has been admitted, to deny this principle to the dhimmi nations exclusively, on the pretext that their past is merely a denunciation of oppression, would raise a moral problem for history itself. Are persecuted and humiliated peoples to be rejected on the grounds that history is destined to become the narcissistic reflection of supermen and victors who boast unremorsefully of their glory, who are steeped in the blood and misery of the vanquished?

It is my belief that an objective knowledge of the past, though not itself the fundamental condition in bringing about brotherly understanding among mankind, is nevertheless a necessary stepping stone. To deny the objective data of history reflects the same mentality that once taught, in defiance of all evidence, that the sun orbits the earth.

And then, there is peace . . . and peace.

There is the *pax arabica* imposed by Khaled of Arabia in order to halt Communist progress in the Orient and to create the requisite conditions for the destruction of Israel: to isolate the Jewish State, while arming its neighbors to the teeth during a "cold war" aimed at weakening it by the return to its territory of Palestinized Arabs. That kind of peace is no more than a tactical peace in a strategy of war.

There could be another kind of peace, however, the only real peace that makes sense in the geopolitical history of the Orient. And this peace can only come about after a revolutionary recasting of the values of Arabism, which will, for the first time, bring about a renunciation of totalist concepts and the acceptance of equal rights and national autonomy for dhimmi nations. But, one might object, is Israel—a part of whose population is of European extraction—really a dhimmi nation? If the Hebrew people can resurrect on their ancestral soil the language, the institutions, the historical geography, the culture, and the pre-Islamic national traditions characteristic of this land, then Israel is truly a dhimmi nation that has achieved its decolonization. The dispersion of the Hebrew nation following an imperialist annexation of territory cannot be advanced as a justification for this annexation. In other words, the defects the victim develops as a result of oppression cannot be used by the oppressor as a pretext for his oppression (dominator-dhimmi relationship). But it is in fact this dispersion, resulting from the expropriation of the land of the Jewish dhimmis, that is invoked in order to legitimize the Arabization of the conquered territory.

Article 20 of the PLO's National Covenant claims that Jews do not form a real people and are no more than citizens of the states to which they belong. Article 1 explains the reasoning behind this attitude: "Palestine is the homeland of the Arab Palestinian people; it is an indivisible part of the Arab homeland, and the Palestinian people are an integral part of the Arab nation"[8]—which in modern terminology is the Arab empire.

The rebirth of a pre-Islamic Hebrew language and culture, in a land conquered and Arabized by force, constitutes a revolutionary defiance of the totalist mentality that has for so long conditioned the dominator-dhimmi relationship. In Israel, the Hebrew language—the pre-Arabic national vernacular—enjoys equality with Arabic and is not considered an inferior or nonexistent language, as is Kurdish, which is today struggling to survive, or Syriac, which has long since disappeared in Iraq and Syria. And Judaization or re-

Hebraization of Arabized lands reinstates a dhimmi culture—exterminated in some parts, held in contempt in others, particularly in the Land of Israel in order to affirm and maintain its Arabization—on an equal footing with the conqueror's culture. Thus it can be seen that the recognition of Israel must be not merely a tactical toleration for a limited period. A true recognition would demand from Arabism—as a necessary prerequisite for peaceful coexistence between Arabs and dhimmi nations, including respect for each other's rights—a total revision of the values that assured its expansion and domination. Such a critical revision of pan-Arabism as an ideological movement would bring to an end the historical perspective in which the dhimmi nations have been dehumanized for so long and would open the first breach in the totalist mentality.

Against the background of these historical and political motive forces, the territorial aspect of the Israeli-Arab conflict seems of secondary importance and will finally depend on the evolution of the mental attitudes elaborated in the Orient during centuries of Arabization. In order that a process toward peace may last and bear fruit between Arabs and liberated dhimmi nations, it must take into account the sociological and cultural human substratum fashioned by history. To succeed in making peace—to work for a peace that is not a temporary expedient—one must know the dhimmis history.

THE LIBERATION OF THE DHIMMIS

> *The day on which crime adorns itself with the effects of innocence, by a strange reversal, innocence is summoned to provide its own justification.*
>
> —Albert Camus

During the sessions of the colloquium on Zionism, which took place at the Collège de France (Paris, October 1976), the ideological attitudes of European Zionism were discussed by noted specialists. With the exception of Mrs. Doris Bensimon-Donath, no one appeared to remark the absence of that forgotten representative, Oriental Jewry, still waiting for the doors of history to open. It is important, not perhaps numerically (it forms only a small part of the Jewish people) but by virtue of the lessons to be learned from its history. Leaving aside the political context and the misrepresentation of Zionism as Western imperialism, it serves the interests of scientific research as well as of the Jewish people to discover this other Zionism—the Zionism of fervor, backbone Zionism, which motivated the transplantation to Israel of entire Oriental communities. It is a Zionism of the humble that was never spoken about because it was as natural and as necessary to the Oriental masses as the air they breathed. And if Oriental Jews produced neither great theoretical debates nor organizational structures, the reason is, judging by their massive Return to Israel, that Zionist teaching would have been superfluous—and also because, in Arab lands, Zionism was often forced to operate clandestinely. Moreover, if the emigration of Oriental Jewry were not set in motion until 1948, it was because its leaders understood that the saving of European Jewry was a vital priority. Besides, Arab pressure reduced the possibilities of emigration.

Certainly, it would be as well for European Jewish intellectuals—particularly for the new generation overflowing with political generosity—to turn toward this venerable ancestor of Western Jewry in order to discover the greatness and nobility of its destiny. For Western Jewry, even though it represents the majority, it does not constitute the totality of the Jewish people, and its history, although interesting, does not cover that of all the people of Israel. Oriental Jewry, whose past is torn down and used unscrupulously by political opportunists, can and must make an indispensable moral and historical contribution to the history of Israel.

The history of Oriental Jewry is interesting from many points of view. First, it gives us an insight into the significance and specific evolution of Arab-Jewish relations. Second, it explains the later development of the dhimmi nations, since the fate of the Jews of Arabia foreshadowed the fate of the dhimmis and was accepted as standard procedure throughout the period of Arab conquest. The Jewish condition in traditional Islam—similar to that of the Christian—was determined by the manner in which the Arabs in their expansion refused to recognize the national autonomy of the pre-Islamic cultures and civilizations whose lands they had usurped. But like all national histories, that of the dhimmis is not confined to a framework of cause and effect, that is, a chain of facts and political and economical phases. It spills over into a specific spiritual universe, the moral dimensions of which, forged in the course of thirteen centuries, are still noticeable in the reaction of peoples when confronted with history. And the cardinal historical event that changed Jewish life in the Orient was the massive Return to Israel in a period of less than two decades. So the traditional attitudes of the Jewish dhimmis show themselves in their return to Zion.

In the first place, this "Gathering in of the Exiles to Israel" is in keeping with the messianic current that traversed and invigorated the history of dhimmi Jewry—and only this current can explain the collective determination to remain Jewish in the face of the persecution stemming from this determination. This hope of Return is expressed in a dual attitude, apparently contradictory: a collective faithfulness to a national past, paradoxically related to a futurist vision of a better society, for every messianic expectation necessarily implies faith in the future. The massive transfer of Oriental Jews to Israel is in accordance with historic continuity; it is the fulfillment of their messianic-national aspirations, cherished throughout their exile.

In respect of their relations with the Arab world, Oriental Jews also perpetuate the traditional attitudes of the dhimmis toward the Muslim. Indeed in Islam the dhimmis have a very precise economic function, which the builders of the Muslim empire conferred upon them and which was subsequently confirmed in all the legislative texts that governed their status. Caliph Umar, who is considered the founder of the Muslim empire, had already commanded, during the conquest of Syria, that the indigenous peoples should not be shared out among the Arabs but should be subjected to taxation so that the following generations of Muslims might benefit from their labor: "Our children will live off them indefinitely for as long as they survive and these people will remain slaves to the adherents of Islam for as long as the latter endure. Therefore, strike them with the poll tax."[9] The taxes imposed on dhimmis, writes the famous jurist al-Mawardi (d. 1058), "are two burdens imposed on the polytheists by Allah for the benefit of the Faithful." The dhimmis were thus a human mass that was to be tolerated as long as it could be exploited.

When the interests of Islam required it, the community of the Faithful was duty-bound to execute dhimmi males and reduce their women and children to slavery while taking possession of their belongings; or, as an alternative, they could be expelled, and their property confiscated. Both measures were legal, and they were left to the whim of the ruler holding the religious and political authority. In modern times the second alternative was applied to Jews in many Arab countries.

It is true that Oriental Jews had *chosen* to return to Israel, but nonetheless they did not *depart* from Arab countries; in most cases they were *expelled* under the most painful circumstances, forced to leave behind them all their belongings while suffering brutality and humiliation—for, it should be added, the humiliation and degradation of the dhimmis is also the legal prerogative of the community of the Faithful. Hence, in the twentieth century, Jews were treated as dhimmis—in conformity with tradition—by the same Arab states that had just obtained their independence. And, curiously enough, the Jews reacted in exactly the traditional manner of dhimmis. As in the past, they resigned themselves to suffer massacre, rape, and pillage, being disarmed in the face of violence and the law by the prohibition to carry arms and the lack of the right of appeal to the courts. Thus in modern times they silently accepted confiscation of the fruit of generations of dhimmi labor. For thirteen centuries, men's justice had relegated them to a condition that was in reality permanent injustice. Could justice imply for them anything else but nothingness or derision? Such ideas as vindicating their rights or even imagining that they had any rights were so revolutionary that they were inconceivable to the dhimmi mentality. Thus the dhimmis never even dreamed of complaining to international organizations. Neither did they organize themselves into terrorist gangs to kill innocent Arab civilians in order to take revenge on the governments that had exploited and robbed them. They never required the international community to provide for their needs. They never exploited the compassion of public opinion for destructive political aims. Conditioned to submissiveness, to humility, and to silence by the moral aftereffects of a prolonged condition of fear, injustice, and oppression heroically endured during thirteen centuries, Jewish refugees from Arab countries were able to find within themselves the moral force necessary to overcome these ordeals. Because of this, the psychological and physical problems of social and economic integration affecting about two million Oriental Jews, including children, are today practically unknown to the world at large or even to Western Jewry.

How, then, did the modern dhimmis manage? Exactly as their forefathers when driven out, exiled, and pillaged; they had to face adversity with nothing but their own resources. They returned to their economic function as dhimmis: that of tireless creative workers. But there was one difference: they had now broken the pact of servitude and were henceforth masters of their own destiny.

The Oriental Jews returned to Israel, cultivated the desert, built up border towns, elaborated the country's industrial infrastructure, and participated in the war of national defense. And when the Arab nations, who had exploited, oppressed, and robbed them, hired terrorists to kill their children and dynamite their new homes, they replied yet again as would dhimmis, with a peace offer—in other words, with a messianic vision of the redemption of peoples, a messianism that, as has been seen, was engendered by the determination to remain dhimmis in the hope that one day their servitude would came to an end.

The Oriental Jewish refugees who emigrated to Europe and America had to confront difficulties that were in no way less arduous. Without any help whatsoever they had to integrate themselves into a highly technical society and provide for their families and the education of their children. Today, when the Arab economic boycott again threatens the efforts of these refugees, the Jews of the Orient respond once more with a call for peace.

The study of the dhimmi condition is a rich source of instruction. It invites us to ponder the destiny of exploited and oppressed human beings, not because of any fatality of theirs (race, color, social clan) but as a result of *their* deliberate choice, renewed throughout the ages, to remain on a spiritual plane higher than that of their oppressors whatever the brand of infamy imposed upon them. In the oppressor-oppressed dialectic that ensued, one can see the typical profile of the dhimmis: a courage manifesting itself in silence rather than in words, a tragedy forever overcome because chosen, the humble nobility of daily heroism reenacted time and again.

This is also the meaning of the extraordinary lesson in bravery given to the world by a handful of people ready to die, misunderstood, despised, and forsaken: the Maronites of Lebanon.

Document

Jewish Dhimmis of Jerusalem, 1839

From a report dated May 23, 1839, by W. T. Young, British Vice-Consul, Jerusalem to Viscount Palmerston, Foreign Minister, London (P.O. 78/368 no. 13):

> Agreeably to Your Lordship's commands, I have the honour to report on the state of the Jews in Palestine, so far as I am able in the present state of the country, when owing to the Quarantines, our means of communication are very limited. . . .
>
> The spirit of toleration towards the Jew, is not yet known here to the same extent it is in Europe—though their being permitted to live in the Musulman Quarter, is some evidence that the fierce spirit of oppression is somewhat abated. It should however be named that they pay more than others do for the rent of their Houses, thus they may be considered in some measure to purchase toleration.
>
> The Pacha[10] has shewn much more consideration for the Jews than His people have. I have heard several acknowledge that they enjoy more peace and tranquillity under his Government, than ever they have enjoyed here before. Still, the Jew in Jerusalem is not estimated in value much above a dog—and scarcely a day passes that I do not hear of some act of Tyranny and oppression against a Jew—chiefly by the soldiers, who enter their

Houses and borrow whatever they require without asking any permission—sometimes they return the article, but more frequently not. In two instances, I have succeeded in obtaining justice for Jews against Turks. But it is quite a new thing in the eyes of these people to claim justice for a Jew—and I have good reason to think that my endeavours to protect the Jews, have been—and may be for some little time to come, detrimental to my influence with other classes—Christians as well as Turks [i.e., Muslims].

. . . another Despatch to Her Majesty's Agent, on the subject of a new Proclamation which has been issued here, forbidding the Jews from praying in their own Houses—and reporting a most barbarous punishment of a Jew and Jewess that took place in Jerusalem this week. . . .

What the Jew has to endure, at all hands, is not to be told.

Like the miserable dog without an owner he is kicked by one because he crosses his path, and cuffed by another because he cries out—to seek redress he is afraid, lest he bring worse upon him; he thinks it better to endure than to live in the expectation of his complaint being revenged upon him. Brought up from infancy to look upon his civil disabilities everywhere as a mark of degradation, his heart becomes the cradle of fear and suspicion—he finds he is trusted by none—and therefore he lives himself without confidence in any.[11]

RETROSPECTIVE ON DHIMMI LAND

Judea and Samaria

July. The light blazes in the silence. On every side Judea. There's a hillock . . . hardly a hill, a teardrop on the Judean land. It is Bethar, where once stood the fortress of the courageous Bar Kochba, the last stronghold of ancient Hebrew resistance. The stones testify in silence, for the earth cannot lie. It confides its message to whoever listens, without even the need to turn over the soil with a trowel. All is there, laid bare as in an open book, despite the ravages of conquerors. A square tower and a wall joining two bastions bear witness to the beauty and solidity of the typical Hebrew architecture of the First Temple period. Over there, a wall and tower built by Herod more than half a millennium later. And crowning it all, Bar Kochba's fortification: a square tower faced with stones, semicircular watchtowers, and gates. Farther away the traces of the Roman encampment can still be seen. Here, on the ninth day of Ab in the year 135, the Jewish resistance was annihilated by the Roman army.

Silence. We have taken cover in the shade of an olive tree. Instantly the children have nestled in the branches, listening solemnly to our guide. Somewhere a fig tree perfumes the air . . . or is it merely the breeze of the Judean hills? Circular gesture by Yaacov Meshorer, chief curator of archaeology at the Israel Museum, renowned numismatist and former supervisor of excavations in Judea-Samaria, as he explains,

> Excavations in Judea have brought to light flourishing towns possessing numerous synagogues. The architecture as well as the ornamental patterns are typical of the attractive pre-Islamic Israelite civilization, represented in Galilee by the synagogues of Capernaum, Beth Shearim, Chorazim, Kefar Baram, Meran and other places. Between the years 70 AD and the Arab invasion and occupation in 640, these hills were dotted with Hebrew towns and villages where an intense national, religious and cultural life prospered. Deprived of its independence, the nation concentrated its genius by reflecting upon the richness of its national past. This is the period in which the Mishnah was elaborated and completed in the second century, shortly to be followed by the Talmud—monumental religious, legal and social compendia. Completed in about 400, this work was continued for another two centuries, keeping alive an intense Messianic fervor whose force was to be felt as far as Arabia.
>
> The Arab occupation scarcely modified the Hebrew place-names, and the Jewish inhabitants, now considered as dhimmis, remained on their land. It was only later that the relentless mechanism typical of every colonization gradually wiped out the indigenous population, thereby encouraging a progressive Arabization of the land.

In the former Jewish town of Bethar, there are now fifteen hundred Arabs. They call the place where the Jewish vestiges stand *khirbet al-Yahud*, the ruins of the Jews. Nevertheless, were the Israelis to return, the Arabs would not hesitate to chase them away with indignation, referring to them as foreign intruders. Mystery of the Oriental mind or logic of the occupant? These Arabs, hardly interested in a past that is not theirs, ignore totally the history of the places where they live. Of course they know that the spot was inhabited formerly by Jews, as the name indicates, but these ruins, relating to a people dispossessed and driven out, are only of interest as a quarry conveniently providing stones that others have hewn. But the excited comments from the olive tree taught me that any Jewish child knows more about the history of this place than its Arab inhabitants.

In Eshtemoa, a biblical name Arabized by the occupants into Es-Samoa, the Arab inhabitants still live in houses built almost fifteen centuries earlier. The architectural elements and decorative designs, including the menorah, are all typical of pre-Islamic Jewish art. It is common to find Arab villagers cooking on ancient mosaic floors. In the center of the village was once a three-storied synagogue, of which only two ruined floors remain. The size of the synagogue suggests that there flourished here an important community. Like many other indigenous monuments, the synagogue was destroyed at the beginning of the Arab occupation. Its stones, particularly those decorated with bas-reliefs, were used by the Arabs and today adorn their doorposts.

At Yata, the biblical name of an Israelite village, beautifully decorated Jewish ossuaries typical of the first and second centuries CE are scattered around Arab houses and used as drinking troughs for their cattle. Many troves of coins dating from the second Temple and Hasmonean periods have been found in this area.

The discrepancy between history and population in Judea and Samaria troubles the traveler constantly. It is true that the Hebrew place-names have been Arabized, that Jewish religious shrines have been Islamized—as in Hebron and elsewhere—and that Arabization has succeeded in effacing all traces of Jewish nationalism. It is also true that from afar the Arab villages seem picturesque. This is only a superficial impression, however, for if the traveler, endeavoring to account for his troubled spirit, were to look more closely he would often discover a mere heap of ruins. The neglect of the surrounding vegetation is so general that one is reminded not of a biblical landscape of wooded hillsides but of the sandy wastes of Arabia. One is struck with pity, for people do not generally live in ruins, however poor they are. Ruins are seen everywhere, so much so that they are no longer noticed.

In 1864 Arthur Penrhyn Stanley, the dean of Westminster, remarked that Palestine, more than any other country, was a land of ruins: "In Judea it is hardly an exaggeration to say that whilst for miles and miles there is no appearance of present life or habitation, except the occasional goat-herd on the hillside, or gathering of women at the wells, there is yet hardly a hill-top of the many within sight that is not covered by the vestiges of some fortress or city of former ages. Sometimes they are fragments of ancient walls, sometimes mere foundations and piles of stone, but always enough to indicate signs of human habitation and civilisation."[12]

The hillside terraces that in ancient times were planted with vineyards and olive trees are not the only aspect of destruction. What could be more distressing than these poor settlements without streets, houses—or rather, dilapidated cubes—devoid of architecture, haphazardly propped up with sculptured blocks, broken columns, and capitals ransacked from the monuments of previous civilizations. Banished or massacred, the indigenous dhimmis have completely disappeared. The nomads became sedentary; the colonists came. They camped in the houses of others, patching them up when necessary by destroying monuments they had not built. Its past hardly interested them, strangers in this land taken from others: it was not theirs. And when the relentless torment of the Exile brought the indigenous inhabitants back to their land, the fear of this continual return and the prospect of having to share the land with the despoiled victims resulted in animosity and bloodshed. Historical evidence is not wanting, but it will suffice to quote one or two testimonies from the last century. In a report to Palmerston in 1836, Colonel Campbell, the British consul-general in Egypt, describes how "their Mahomedan fellow-countrymen of Saffet took advantage of the disorderly state of the country, and fell, on the 16th June, on the innocent Jews of that town, robbed their property, violated their women, assassinated those who attempted resistance, and continued their lawless proceedings for thirty-three days."[13] At about the same time, in 1834, American traveler John Lloyd Stephens describes similar scenes perpetrated against the Jews of Hebron, who witnessed with their own eyes the rape of their wives and daughters.[14]

In 1872 English traveler Thomas Jenner was deeply moved during a visit to Nablus by the distress of two Jews, "the government having chased them from their homes and thrown them into the street with their belongings because they had need of their abode in order to quarter soldiers."[15] Nothing exceptional about such a measure, for the lodging and maintenance of Muslim troops was often an obligation imposed by the conqueror on the native dhimmis. At times of rampant anarchy the invaders were encouraged by such a law to dispossess their predecessors "legally"—especially if it is remembered that the latter were completely unarmed and their sworn testimony refused. This is only an insignificant element alongside so many others in the long chain of events that transformed the dhimmi peoples from majorities to "tolerated" minorities in their own land.

But nowhere else is the tragedy of history so poignant as in Shomron-Sebastia in Samaria. Nowhere else is the devastation so sinister as in the ruins of this ancient capital of the northern kingdom of Israel, founded about 880 BCE. Here, more than anywhere else perhaps, the contrast is striking between the present desolation and the magnificent vestiges of a flourishing and active population. There are the fortifications and palaces of Omri, Ahab, and Jezebel, the granaries of Jeroboam II (787–49). Herod built here an avenue bordered with columns. A theater, a stadium, and a city wall with gates and towers testify to the solid, elegant Israelite architecture of this period.

Today, Shomron-Sebastia is nothing more than a miserable village where thirteen hundred Arabs camp among the ruins. The church built by the Crusaders, in which lie ancient tombs attributed to Hebrew prophets Elisha and Obadiah, has become their mosque. Despite the rubble on the floor—due to an accumulation of centuries of neglect—the building remains impressive. Foreigners to this past, the present inhabitants ignore it and cover their misery in the ruins. These columns, these sculptured stones are merely used as material for repairing their poor hovels. Human distress and the cataclysms of history are brought together here to make of Shomron-Sebastia the symbol of the greatness and extermination of a people.

This people, victim of the world's longest-lasting genocide, is represented today by a remnant. Two hundred fifty Samaritans, no more, "tolerated" by forty-four thousand Arabs in their former capital of Shechem-Neapolis, Arabized to Nablus. This is not the place to describe the massacres, confiscations, and persecutions of all kinds that reduced this numerous population of farmers and skilled artisans to the size of a pathetic remnant. The interested reader can consult the article "Samaritan" in the *Encyclopaedia Judaica* (1971), where mention is made of the threat of total extermination which, in 1842, would certainly have overcome this inoffensive and dying community of 142 souls, had not another dhimmi community—the Jews of Jerusalem—come to their rescue at the last moment. Benyamin Tsedaka, a 125th-generation descendant of Manasseh (son of the patriarch Joseph), explains that the reason for the numerical difference today between Jews and Samaritans is that his people refused to go into exile: "Our principle was not to leave [the Land of] Israel."[16] This is the simple explanation of the historical anomaly of a Samaria without Samaritans and a Judea without Jews. Today the magnificent ruins of Shomron-Sebastia are among the most moving monuments in Israel. Because they were a Jewish sect attached to the soil, the Samaritans suffered their "final solution" in the obscure and humble silence in which history has buried the dhimmis.

Today the dhimmis' specter, shrouded in hatred, despoiled and despairing of all human justice, since they have been rejected by it—so often described for those who know where to look—haunts the deserted hills of Judea and Samaria, where the dhimmis' destiny was embodied.

Today the populations of these regions are Muslims, with the exception of a few pockets of Arabized Christians, remnants of the Byzantine occupation or of Crusader times, who have survived thanks to the protection of European Christendom. The Samaritans have been reduced in their homeland to 470 survivors, of whom 250 still live in Nablus. Until 1948, Jewish inhabitants of the region were massacred or expelled, and the right to reside was prohibited to them until 1967. The Arabization of the region resulted in a *judenrein* Arab province, that is, "cleaned" of all trace of its pre-Arab culture.

The indigenous peoples were replaced by Greeks, Arab-Bedouins, Persians, Druzes, Circassians, Turks, and Slavs, who were thus able to benefit from the Arabized land of the dhimmis. Yet since 1967 these peaceful villagers, with unperturbed consciences, who justified their Arab rights established by the martyrdom of the banished or annihilated native peoples, have been experiencing a nightmare. The Jews, exiled in the wake of successive waves of occupation and its sequelae, or tolerated in his own homeland but in a state of subjection—these Jews now return. And they come back no longer as dhimmis—the sole status acceptable for a native—but as citizens enjoying all the rights of free people. It is true that however scandalous it may seem, such an occurrence is not unique. Several dhimmi peoples have recovered their independence: Sicilians, Spaniards, Greeks, and Maronites, but not without leaving open wounds in the pan-Arabic consciousness. "We intend to fight in order that our Palestinian homeland will not become a new Andalusia," declared Abu Iyad, one of the principal leaders of the PLO.[17] Should one be surprised that certain Arab circles deplore the Hispanization of Spain, the Lebanization of Lebanon, and the Judaization of Israel?

Thus the Jews return. With care they search among the ruins and bring to light thousand-year-old documents bearing Hebrew inscriptions, meaningless to the villagers. The monuments and coins they discover confirm their history. The Jews, treated as foreigners, reach out to the soil that yields up its history. A perfectly harmonious dialogue in time and space is established between them.

The nightmare postponed for all these centuries by inhuman laws suddenly becomes a reality. There is no doubt about it, the natives have returned. And what if they were to take back their land, restore the destroyed hill terraces, rebuild their innumerable ruined synagogues? What if it were possible to evaluate the suffering of thirteen centuries of forced exile? If there was exile, then there must have been occupation—the two concepts are inseparable—and each knows his respective history. So a resistance is prepared against the gathering in of the exiles in an Arabized land.

But Israelis are not interested in quibbling over the past; all they want is to build a new future. Without chasing anyone away, all they want is to return home. The Arabs born and bred on this soil are in no way responsible for a thousand-year-old imperialism, even if they are its heirs and benefactors. No one is to be a foreigner; thus Israelis propose a peaceful coexistence in the land of their history, in the towns and villages that bear Hebrew names. They are ready to share with their Arab cousins, whose language is so similar to their own. It is all very simple: a discriminatory legislation, like that to which the dhimmis were submitted, does not exist in either the history or jurisdiction of Israel. Thus, from the Israeli point of view, there is nothing to impede a normal relationship of equality being established between the two parties.

The present Arab populations are faced with a choice: acceptance of peaceful coexistence and a relationship of equality between Arabs and Israelis instead of the traditional dominator-dhimmi relationship, or a continuance of the traditional jihad in massacring, exiling, or dominating the legitimate heirs in a renewed effort of total Arabization. "The civil war in Lebanon is not over and blood will continue to flow! Our war in Lebanon will save the Arabization of the Lebanon. I declare in the name of the Palestinian movement, and for the national leftwing Lebanese forces, that Lebanon will remain Arab," Yasir Arafat declared on November 30, 1975, in Damascus. This choice also concerns Oriental peoples other than Israel. It apposes a tradition of Arab domination to a revolutionary liberation movement striving for the rights of *other non-Arab Oriental peoples.*

With these thoughts in my mind, I strolled through an Arab quarter on the outskirts of Jerusalem, hardly a hundred yards from Mount Zion. Suddenly a hail of stones welcomed me. A group of Arab adolescents shielding themselves behind oil drums was hurling projectiles and curses at me while they screamed their loyalty to the PLO. The movement I made in order to protect myself took me back twenty years to the Jewish cemetery in Cairo, where I had accompanied some elderly relatives, widows who were taking leave of their departed, for, as Jewesses, they were effectively being banished from Egypt. They were startled by a hail of stones thrown by a group of Arabs. Chased off by jeers, they fled as fast as they could, as vulnerable in their old age as the mortal remains they were abandoning to probable depredations. And the gesture we then made, they to protect themselves and I to shield them, was the same as I was now making under Arab projectiles in Jerusalem, city of David, king of Israel. A gesture repeated for a thousand years by the dhimmis burying their dead in secret and in haste, or attacked and humiliated in the streets—the traditional gesture of the Arab, passed on from father to son with the same contemptuous hatred of the oppressors toward their victims.

In that same month of July 1977, the waves of bomb attacks in Israel and the attempts to wipe out the Maronites in southern Lebanon reminded me that the spilling of dhimmi blood was still lawful . . .

Documents

1884 Origin of the Palestinian Arab Population—the Example of the Plain of Sharon

It is a singular fact that the strip of coast from Haifa to Caesarea seems to have become a centre of influx of colonists and strangers of the most diverse races. The new immigrants to Caesarea are Slavs. Some of them speak a little Turkish. Arabic is an unknown tongue to them, which they are learning. Their own language is a Slav dialect. When the troubles in the provinces of Bosnia and Herzegovina first broke out [1875], which led to the Russo-Turkish war, a howl of indignation went up from the philanthropists. . . . When it [the agrarian question] was settled by handing over the provinces to Austria, the Slav-Moslem aristocracy, finding themselves in their turn persecuted by their former [Christian] peasants and the Christian power which protected them, migrated to the more congenial rule of the sultan. So the curious spectacle is presented of a Slav population migrating from Austrian rule to Asia, in order to be under a Moslem government.

Close beside the new Bosnian colony there are planted in the plain of Sharon two or three colonies of [Muslim] Circassians. These are the people who committed the Bulgarian atrocities. The irony of fate has now placed them within three or four miles of colonists belonging to the very race they massacred. They, too, fleeing from government by Christians, have sought refuge under the sheltering wing of the sultan, where, I regret to say, as I described in a former letter, they still indulge in their predatory propensities. In immediate proximity to them are the black tents of a tribe of Turcomans. They belong to the old Seljuk stock, and the cradle of their tribe gave birth to the present rulers of the Turkish Empire. They have been there for about three hundred years, and have forgotten the Turkish language, but a few months ago a new migration arrived from the mountains of Mesopotamia. These nomads spoke nothing but Turkish, and hoped to find a warm welcome from their old tribesmen on the plain of Sharon. In this they were disappointed, and they have now, to my disgust, pitched their tents on some of the spurs of Carmel, where their great hairy camels and their own baggy breeches contrast curiously with the camels and costumes of the Bedouins with whom we are familiar. . . .

The Slav colonists, whose immigration I described in my last letter, are laying out broad streets right across the most interesting ruins, using the old foundations, appropriating the beautiful masonry, the white stones which formed the temple built by Herod, and the brown limestone blocks of the cathedral of the crusaders, quarrying into ancient buildings beneath the surface of the ground, levelling down the ruins at one place, levelling them up in another, and so utterly transforming the whole picturesque area that it will soon be no longer recognizable. . . .

They were the landed aristocracy of their own country, and have, therefore, brought a considerable amount of wealth with them. A large tract of the most fertile land of the plain of Sharon has been donated to them by the Turkish government. . . .

The lower or peasant class of Bosnia and Herzegovina were not obliged, when the country was conquered by the Moslems, to change their religion, and they have continued Christians; while the descendants of their masters, who remained the proprietors of the soil, became bigoted Mussulmans. The consequence has been that now that the country has been handed over to the Austrians, the Christian peasantry have naturally found protection from the authorities against the oppression of their former masters, who, unable to endure the humiliations of seeing the tables turned, and their old servants enabled to defy them with impunity, have sold all their possessions and migrated to the dominions of the sultan, rather than endure the indignities to which they declare they were exposed from their new Christian rulers and their old Christian serfs. . . . Whether they will agree with their Circassian neighbours remains yet to be seen. They form the avant-garde of a much larger migration which is to follow as soon as arrangements can be made to receive them.[18]

The Return of the Dhimmis, about 1949

In 1881 the Jewish dhimmis of Yemen decided on a collective return to the Holy Land. Here are accounts of these immigrants:

And they celebrated the festival [Succoth] with great rejoicing. And throughout the whole festival, day and night, men and women spoke only of the subject of Eretz Israel. And all the Jews who were in Sana'a and all the Jews of Yemen agreed together to sell all their houses and all their goods in order to use the money to journey to their country. And almost all of them neither slumbered nor slept at night, out of their longing and desire and the burning enthusiasm of their love for Eretz Israel. And so strongly did this love break out in their heart, that they cast away all their money, selling all their houses and possessions at an eighth of the value, in order to find money for the expenses of the journey by land and by sea.[19]

A first caravan [of Yemenites] was fortunate enough to arrive [at Jerusalem]. . . . This second caravan, and a third one recently arrived from Sanaa and its surrounding mountains, is blocked at Hodeida. The Turkish authorities have forbidden their departure for Jerusalem. This order is most iniquitous, for it was only after these poor people had sold to the Muslims the little which they possessed that the Governor General of Yemen decided to stop their departure.[20]

The Yemenite Jews headed westwards and reached the Red Sea. They traveled on sambouks to Jedda, Hadeida and Aden and from there aboard steamships to Egypt, Palestine and European Turkey. The last caravan which left Haidan [!], one day's journey from Sa'dah, took three years to reach Jaffa. These wretched people reached the sea, and finding themselves without any means, struck out northwards on foot, crossing the land of Assyr. They rendered small services to the Arabs—the women doing needlework, the men making pieces of jewelry—and when they arrived at Jedda, they had accumulated enough money to pay their passage to Jaffa.[21]

O Lord, save thy people, the remnant of Israel.
Behold, I will bring them from the north country,
And gather them from the coasts of the earth,
And with them the blind and the lame,
The woman with child
And her that travaileth with child together:
A great company shall return thither.
They shall come with weeping,
And with supplications will I lead them:
I will cause them to walk by the rivers of waters
In a straight way, wherein they shall not stumble.

—Jeremiah 31:7–10

POSTSCRIPT

President Sadat's Visit to Jerusalem (November 1977)

To know is to understand: those who know well the obsession of the dhimmi Jew stereotype in the consciousness of the contemporary Arab—particularly of the Palestinian Arab—and its central polarizing role in the Arab-Israel conflict can understand the courage of President Sadat and the symbolic grandeur of his act. The historic meeting of Sadat and Menachem Begin and the warmth of their greetings expressed Sadat's will to refuse for the future the demonology of the dhimmi Jews—transposed into that of the Zionists— in order to discover the human face of Israel. Those 70 percent of psychological elements in the conflict, to which Sadat referred, are founded on the impurity and untouchability of the supposed dhimmi-Zionists with whom the Arabs have until now avoided all contact. Isolated in the heart of the Arab world, the Zionists became a symbol of derision, hate, and aversion. But to talk to an Israeli, to shake his hand, to accept his presence, to communicate with him by language and reason—all eminently human privileges—is to see him as an equal.

Only a knowledge of history can help one understand that this gesture breaks with traditional attitudes of the past thirteen centuries. Of course, this does not mean that the Jews should feel a frenzied gratitude because they have been promoted from subhumanity to humanity: they could as well deplore the thirteen centuries during which their humanity has been denied. What one should admire in President Sadat is the act of a man who has attempted to surmount the prejudices of the past, with all the heartbreak and all the doubts which that implies. He was a man who, first among all his own people, had set foot on a new road. It is therefore in the particular context of Arabism that Sadat acquired the stature of a man of exceptional courage and intelligence.

What Israel awaited from President Sadat, from the Egyptian people, and from the Arab peoples, was recognition of the link, depicted in history and the Qur'an, between the Jewish people and the Land of Israel—as well as the right to national sovereignty of the Jewish state in its own land. The courageous initiative of President Sadat must be warmly supported. It opened the way to the establishment of a just peace that respects the national rights of both Jews and Arabs.

NOTES

This chapter is made up of four parts first published separately in *Rond-Point* (Brussels—January, May, and October 1977) and *Centrale* (Brussels—June 1977). All the texts, revised and with documents and illustrations, were published by Editions de l'Avenir (Geneva) in a twenty-four-page booklet: *Peuples Dhimmis: Nations Mortes-Vivantes* (October 23, 1977). A postscript page was written in December 1977—after the historic visit of President Anwar el-Sadat to Jerusalem on November 17, 1977—for insertion in the first printing. It was included as part of the second printing (May 30, 1978). An English edition (*Dhimmi Peoples: Oppressed Nations*, translated by David G. Littman) was published on February 28, 1978, with the postscript. A German edition (*Dhimmi Völker: Unterdrückte Nationen*, translated by Tania Leshinsky) was published on January 15, 1980.

1. The appeal mentioned took place at the International NGO Conference on discrimination against indigenous populations in the Americas, held at the United Nations in Geneva, September 21–23, 1977.

2. Said Yahya Ibn Muhammad, quoted in Yomtob Sémach, *Une mission de l'Alliance au Yémen* (Paris: Alliance Israélite Universelle, 1910), pp. 38–40.

3. Léon Godard, *Le Maroc: Notes d'un voyageur, 1858–59* (Algiers, 1860), p. 35, quoted in Joseph Goulven, *Les Mellahs de Rabat-Salé* (Paris: Paul Geuthner, 1927), pp. 27–28.

4. Quoted in Albert M. Hyamson, ed. with an introduction and notes, *The British Consulate in Jerusalem in Relation to the Jews of Palestine, 1838–1914* (London: Edward Goldston, for the Jewish Historical Society of England, 1939), part 1 (1838–1861), p. 171.

5. Moshe Perlmann, ed. and trans., *Shaykh Damanhuri on the Churches of Cairo (1739)* (Berkeley and Los Angeles: University of California Press, 1975), p. 56.

6. Quoted in Georges Vajda, "Un traité Maghrébin: 'Adversus Judaeos' Akham Ahl al-Dimma, du Sayh Muhammad b. 'Abd al-Karim al-Magili," in *Etudes d'orientalisme dédiées à la mémoire de Lévy-Provençal*, vol. 2 (Paris: G.-P. Maisonneuve et Larose, 1962), p. 811.

7. Quoted in Martin Schreiner, "Contributions à l'Histoire des Juifs en Egypte," *Revue des Etudes Juives* (Paris) 31 (1895): 11.

8. "Palestine National Covenant of the PLO," quoted in Yehoshafat Harkabi, *Palestinians and Israel* (Jerusalem: Keter, 1974), pp. 51–69.

9. Quoted in Abou Yousof Ya'koub, *Le Livre de l'Impôt Foncier (Kitab el-Kharadj)*, trans. E. Fagnan (Paris: Paul Geuthner, 1921), pp. 217–18.

10. Here is meant Ibrahim Pacha, son of Muhammad Ali, ruler of Egypt. He conquered and controlled Syria and Palestine from 1832 to 1840.

11. Quoted in Hyamson, *British Consulate in Jerusalem*, pp. 4–7.

12. Arthur Penrhyn Stanley, *Sinai and Palestine* (London: John Murray, 1866), p. 117.

13. Quoted in John Bowring, *Report on the Commercial Statistics of Syria (Addressed to Lord Palmerston and Presented to Both Houses of Parliament)* (London, 1840; reprint, New York: Arno Press, 1973), p. 129.

14. John Lloyd Stephens, *Incidents of Travel in Egypt, Arabia Petraea, and the Holy Land* (1837; reprint, Norman: University of Oklahoma Press, 1970), p. 32.

15. Thomas Jenner, *Palestine et Liban* (Paris: Grassart and Neuchâtel: Delachaux Niestlé, 1883), p. 142.

16. Quoted in *International Herald Tribune*, March 8, 1977.

17. Quoted in *Le Monde*, January 20–21, 1974.

18. Laurence Oliphant, *Haifa: or, Life in Modern Palestine* (1887; Jerusalem: Canaan Publishing House, 1976), pp. 238–39, 241–42.

19. *The Exodus from Yemen* (Jerusalem: Keren Hayesod, n.d.).

20. Alexandre Lucciana, French vice-consul in Hodeida, Yemen, letter to the president of the Alliance Israélite Universelle, Paris, November 29, 1881; available at the AIU Archives, France VIII D 49.

21. Sémach, *Une mission de l'Alliance*, p. 109.

DHIMMITUDE

7. Jews and Christians under Islam

Bat Ye'or

Except for Asia, all the countries that were conquered by jihad (Muslim holy war) in the course of history—from Arabia to Spain and the Balkans, including Hungary and Poland—were peopled by innumerable Christians and by Jewish communities. This geographical context is therefore the true terrain of interaction between the three religions. Actually, it was in Islamic lands that they opposed, or collaborated with, one another for up to thirteen centuries. I have called this vast political, religious, and cultural span the realm of *dhimmitude*, from *dhimma*, a treaty of submission for each people conquered by jihad.

The historical field is generally studied in the context of "Islamic tolerance," but *tolerance*—or *toleration*—is an ambiguous word, since it implies a moral and subjective connotation. Moreover, the word *toleration* cannot encompass the historical density and the complexities of the numerous peoples vanquished by Islam over the centuries, as it is a vague and general notion used irrespective of space and time.

Instead of *toleration*, I have proposed the concept of *dhimmitude*, derived from the word *dhimma*. The vanquished, subject to Islamic law, become a dhimmi people, protected by the dhimma pact from destruction. Islamic legislation governing dhimmi peoples was the same for Jews and Christians, although the latter suffered more from it—declining from majorities, at the dawn of the Islamic conquest, to tiny minorities in their own countries. The domain of dhimmitude comprises all aspects of the condition of the dhimmis: that is, the Jews and Christians tolerated under Islamic law. Dhim-

Reprinted, with thanks, from *Midstream* (New York) 43, no. 2 (February–March 1997): 9–12. Written by Bat Ye'or in French, this text was translated into English by David G. Littman, with the author.

mitude as an historical category is common to, but not identical for, Jews and Christians under Islam.

Islamic law governing Christian dhimmis developed from Byzantine Christian legislation enacted from the fourth to the sixth century. It aimed at imposing legal inferiority on native Jews of Christianized countries—lands that were subsequently Islamized. These early Christian influences on Islamic law are not limited to the juridical domain but also appear at the theological level.

The study of the Jewish dhimmi condition necessarily encompasses the theological and political interaction among the three religions. During the Second Vatican Council (1962–1965), for instance, the Arab churches—yielding to pressure from their governments—strongly objected to the proposed suppression of the "deicide" accusation against the Jews. Yet the crucifixion of Jesus is not recognized in the Qur'an; therefore the accusation of deicide is meaningless for Islam. Such interferences by Arab governments in a strictly Judeo-Christian theological matter were intended to maintain the delegitimization of the state of Israel in a Christian context. Indeed, it was the deicide accusation that had structured Byzantine policy of Jerusalem's de-Judaization and the promulgation of a specific, degrading Jewish status. It was that same status that Muslim jurisconsults adapted to the jihad context with harsher modifications, imposing it equally on Jews and Christians. Clearly, Jewish-Muslim relations also comprise those Jewish-Christian relations that were transposed within an Islamic context—particularly the Jewish status in Christian legislation. Similarly, the Muslim-Christian relationship cannot obscure its Jewish dimension, because Islam associates Christians and Jews in the same dhimmi category—a specific category that was first enacted by Christians for Jews in a quite different theological context.

The study of dhimmitude comprises these multifarious aspects and requires an approach devoid of apriorisms. One can try to define the ideology that imposes dhimmitude on non-Muslim peoples: their obligatory submission by war or surrender to Islamic domination. One could examine its origin, the legal and political means used to dominate other peoples, the causes of its expansion or of its regression. Actually, it is a study of the ideology of jihad, whose jurisdiction—based on the modalities of battles and conquest—must be imposed on the vanquished peoples. How this or that land or city was conquered will determine for all time the laws to be applied there. Centuries after the Islamic conquest, Muslim jurists still consulted ancient chroniclers to determine whether churches and synagogues were legal or forbidden in towns or regions that had formerly been conquered, whether by surrender or by battles and treaties. Such regulations concerning religious buildings are still enforced in many Muslim countries today. So one discovers, throughout the ebb and flow of history, that dhimmitude is composed of a fixed ideological and legal structure. It constitutes an ideological, sociological, and political reality, since it is integrated into every aspect of the human societies it characterizes. This is proved by its geographical development, its historical perennialism, and its present resurgence.

The body of law prescribing dhimmitude originated from a single source: Islamic power. Apart from a few minor differences regarding the Sharia's (Islamic law's) interpretation, the dhimmi status constituted a homogeneous unit applied in the *dar al-Islam*. But the peoples of dhimmitude comprised all the ethnic, religious, and cultural variations of the Islamized regions of Africa, Asia, and Europe—thereby implying regional differences. One must therefore study the local history of each dhimmi group in order to detect if the causes of differentiation were of a geographical or a demographical nature, or the result of pre-Islamic local factors. Thus dhimmitude should encompass the comparative study of all dhimmi groups, for territories were not just conquered; their Islamization could take three or even four centuries, while some regions had already been Islamized by migrations prior to their military and political conquest. The study of dhimmitude, then, is the study of the progressive Islamization of Christian civilizations. In this evolution, one detects permanent structures but also different local factors that facilitated or temporarily checked this process.

The confusion of the political and economic domain is an important element in the development of the mechanism of dhimmitude. In exchange for economic advantages, non-Muslim rulers conceded to the Islamic power an essential political asset: territory. This policy appears at the start of the Muslim-Christian encounter. In modern times, the financial interests of Lebanese Christian politicians with the Muslim world were decisive in the intercommunal struggle that led to the final destruction of Lebanese Christianity. In this context of political concessions in exchange for financial gains, one should emphasize that the economic domain belongs always to the short term and the conjunctural, whereas the political sphere is long-term and implies power, notably military power. Hence, this feature of corruption—paramount in the whole system of dhimmitude—which is, in fact, the surrender of political power (territorial independence) for the economic control by the dhimmi church leaders over their communities.

It is evident that the civilizations of dhimmitude are extremely complex. The process of Islamization of such societies rested on several factors, the most important being the demographical one that transformed Christian majorities into minorities. This result was achieved through several means that combined legal disabilities and economic oppression in times of peace with destruction, deportation, and slavery in wartime and during riots or recurrent political instability. Such a transformation of civilization and of peoples also implied an extensive mechanism of osmosis, including collaboration and collusion by the elites of Christian nations that were engaged in the painful process of their self-destruction. Without this perennial collusion, the Islamic state could never have survived. Christians had collaborated in its development on all social levels and in every field, either by free choice or otherwise.

It was through Christian patriarchs and Jewish community leaders that the Islamic government imposed its authority, making of them its instruments in the control and oppression of their respective populations. Thus entire dhimmi groups collaborated in the growth of the Islamic civilization. One could also investigate the way in which different Christian and Jewish groups reacted to dhimmitude. We know that there was a strong alliance between Arab-Muslim invading troops and the local Arab-Christian tribes, as well as with the Oriental Churches. Some members of the Christian clergy not only welcomed the Muslim armies but also surrendered their cities.

The Eastern Churches were always associated with Islamic rule and benefited from it, becoming thereby the sole administrators of millions of Christians. One can examine the role of the clergy, the military class, the politicians, and the intellectuals in assisting the Islamic advance that placed their own peoples under the yoke of dhimmitude. Documents of this kind abound concerning the later Ottoman conquest of the Balkans.

The conflict of interests within the dhimmi populations indicates that different forces were at work in each community forces of collaboration and forces of resistance. Thus dhimmitude encompasses various types of relationships at all levels between the Muslim community and the dominated, tolerated, dhimmis—relationships that were regulated by laws ensuring Islamic protection and that embrace politics, history, and conjunctural situations. Modern studies on the Turkish advance in the Balkan peninsula have mentioned the mental climate that prepared a society for its surrender. One finds an evolution at all social levels, combining compromise, collusion, and the corruption that facilitated the final submission.

A similar process could have been detected in the modern history of Lebanon from the beginning of the twentieth century to the recent disintegration of Christian resistance. Here the internecine conflict between the forces of collusion and resistance brought about the collapse of the targeted

Christian groups. The situation in southern Sudan and in the Philippines provides contemporary examples of such internecine conflicts that could lead to similar situations.

Dhimmitude also encompasses the relationship between each dhimmi group, the religious rivalry among churches seeking to use the Muslim power in order to diminish or destroy rivals. This domain also overlaps with the dynastic, political, and national conflicts among Christian rulers who obtained power through Islamic help. Since the status of dhimmitude lasted from three to thirteen centuries, depending upon regions, it allows one to study numerous cases of different peoples—all theoretically subject to the same Islamic jurisdiction, with differences here and there.

What were the results of Muslim interference on the intercommunity relationships between the dhimmi peoples themselves? Did it keep their conflicts alive? How did the Muslim power manifest its protection? (The dhimmis were, of course, protected by Islamic law.) There is also the conflict between jurists, inclined toward a more severe interpretation of the law, and the caliphs or rulers, whose policies were sometimes more lenient—a problem still topical today. Therefore the domain of dhimmitude consists of the interaction of the dhimmi peoples among themselves, with the Muslim power, and with the outside world. What were the consequences of the protection afforded to each dhimmi group by the European Christian countries? How did their political and commercial rivalries affect the interrelationship of the dhimmi peoples and their situation within their Muslim environment? And to this should be added the consequences of proselytism among the various contending churches.

One might think that the history of dhimmitude had long since disappeared into a forgotten past, but this is not so. Specialists have called political Islamic radicalism a "return," thus implying the existence in the past of a political ideology that had disappeared and is now resurfacing. Optimistic analysts focus only on the economic and political factors that have contributed to the emergence of Islamic radicalism, although its ideologico-religious causes and traditional roots are so obvious that they alone would justify the use of the term *return*.

Jihad militancy and the reintroduction of some of the Sharia's provisions in countries where they had been abolished are now threatening indigenous Christians and other non-Muslim populations. The most tragic cases are found in Iran, Pakistan, Sudan, and Upper Egypt (by Islamists). Aspects of the dhimmi condition—abolished under European pressure from the mid-nineteenth century on—is returning in these countries and elsewhere.

Even antisemitic statements made by Abbé Pierre in April 1996, firmly condemned by the French episcopate and public opinion, are a reminder of a pervasive Christian dhimmitude. Abbé Pierre—one of France's most popular public figures—reiterated that, because of their iniquities since the time of Joshua, the Jews had forfeited God's promise. Apart from being a classic example of the Church's judeophobia, such a declaration was clearly aimed at pleasing the Muslims. Since the Judeo-Christian reconciliation initiated by the Second Vatican Council, the Arab Churches requested from the Vatican a strictly symmetrical attitude toward Jews and Muslims. This requirement establishes, in fact, a false symmetry between totally different theological, historical, and political contexts: the Judeo-Christian relationship and the Muslim-Christian relationship. The Jews were oppressed in Christian lands but never had any ambition to conquer them and impose their own laws there, whereas Islamic armies seized innumerable Christian lands, in which only small, vulnerable, and scattered Christian communities survive today.

Abbé Pierre's earlier meditations at Yad Vashem in Jerusalem were thus symmetrically balanced by a visit to Yasir Arafat in Gaza, where he begged forgiveness for the West's creation of the State of Israel. But the good Abbé could have spared himself such scruples, for Israel's rebirth occurred despite the genocide of European Jewry, and from the start the Vatican only supported the Palestinian cause. But a "Palestinian genocide" has become a symbolic necessity to balance the genocide of the Jews. Overlooking a span of more than three millennia, Abbé Pierre chose to link—anachronistically and in a delirious amalgamation—today's Arab Palestinians with biblical Philistines and Amalekites in the time of Joshua.

It is this desire for a specious symmetry that reduced to oblivion the tragic and painful domain of Christian dhimmitude, which could not be paralleled with a similar Jewish domination over Christian populations. Indeed, much effort has been deployed in Europe to establish similarities between Palestinians in Israel and dhimmis, especially by blaming Israeli security measures to counter Palestinian terrorism, which was conveniently glossed over as "freedom fighting." This attitude not only expresses a traditional Christian Judeophobia—now totally rejected by the Vatican and other churches—but also the complexity of Europe's relations with Israel and with Arab countries, where Christian rights are challenged by Islamists. As Europe's policy is determined mainly by its own strategic and economic interests, it shows no more sympathy to Eastern Christians than it does to Israelis. Islamic radicalism is feared, as it could provoke in Europe anti-Muslim reactions leading to economic retaliation and terrorism from Muslim states.

Since the beginning of the twentieth century, starting with the Armenian genocide (1896–1917), then the massacres of Christians in Iraq (1933) and Syria (1937), the condition of the Eastern Christians (in spite of their involvement in Arab politics) has constantly deteriorated. Thus one can see how dhimmitude still influences the interaction of different religious groups. To be sure, many scholars have studied their histories separately, but the concept of dhimmitude provides a wider and unified framework for all those varied communities that have undergone the same experience throughout history.

It is interesting to examine the different paths that each dhimmi group felt compelled to adopt, either by historical circumstances or geography, to regain its liberty and dignity. The national liberation of dhimmi peoples meant that the jurisdiction of dhimmitude, imposed by jihad, was abolished; they could then recover their proscribed language, their history, and their culture. The Christian peoples of the Balkans fought for their national sovereignty, as did the Armenians later, and the Jews in their own homeland; but Christians of the Middle East chose assimilation in a secularized Islamic society and became Arabized.

As a result of European colonialism in Arab lands, as well as the rebellions and struggle for the national liberation of Christian peoples in the Ottoman Empire, hundreds of thousands of Christians were killed during the nineteenth and early twentieth centuries in Muslim-dominated regions. Christians lived in constant fear of further atrocities. The Greeks were saved from a genocide in the early nineteenth century by the intervention of the Anglo-French and Russian armies. Their uprisings throughout that century were punished by massacres and the slavery and conversion of women and children. Similar reprisals struck both Serbs and Bulgarians in their own lands.

The genocide of the Armenians and atrocities in Iraq and Syria compelled the Lebanese Christians to create a refuge country for their persecuted brethren from neighboring lands. Some Lebanese were favorable to the restoration of a Jewish state in its historical homeland and were sympathetic to the Zionist cause, for they knew that the position of Jews and Christians under Islam was similar. But this current, led by the Maronite patriarch Antun Arida and archbishop of Beirut Ignace Mubarak, represented a small minority among the Eastern Christians, who remained, like the Vatican, adamantly hostile to a Jewish state in Palestine and especially to any Jewish sovereignty in Jerusalem. Within the context of the Jewish national liberation movement, one should remember that Muslims and the Oriental Churches were hostile to a massive return of Jews to their homeland. Jews had been condemned to suffering and exile by both Christianity and Islam, and therefore Jewish sovereignty in Palestine-Israel was totally unacceptable. How much European opposition to a Jewish state had helped the execution of the Final Solution is a question that concerns historians of the Holocaust. Clearly, antisemitism is intrinsically linked to the concept of Jewish evilness, which justifies a *judenrein* Palestine, especially Jerusalem.

Thus, one finds, in both the political and religious spheres, a hostile Muslim-Christian front against Zionism and later against the State of Israel. Many of these Oriental Christian leaders thought that this Muslim-Christian front against Zionism would help secure their position in the Arab world, first under the banner of pan-Arabism and then under the slogan "the just Palestinian cause." Palestinian anti-Zionist Christians, especially their clergy, were in the vanguard of the battle for the destruction of Israel. Some proudly participated in the worst acts of terrorism. Much of the anti-Israeli propaganda was formulated by Christian Palestinians in order to exacerbate traditional judeophobia in the West. Among them were clergymen from the Levant, such as Roman Catholic archbishop Hilarion Capucci. In fact, many in the West justified the jihad aims and tactics against Israel—and even against Jews everywhere.

The responsiveness of post-Holocaust Europe to anti-Zionism has many geostrategic and economic reasons, but it also derives from the easy channeling of traditional Judeophobia into anti-Zionism. Thus it is not surprising that the PLO's official Christian representatives were much appreciated by politicians, intellectuals, and the European media. In antisemitic circles, they were endowed with a holy mission, embodied in the historic role of the Palestinian clergy. In Byzantine Palestine, the clergy had forbidden Jews to reside and pray in Jerusalem. One of the worst massacres of Jews occurred at the instigation of the Jerusalem patriarch Sophronius, who suggested it in 628 to the emperor Heraclius (610–41). Some years later, when the Arabs conquered Jerusalem from the Greeks, Sophronius tried to persuade Caliph Umar Ibn al-Khattab to forbid any Jewish presence in Jerusalem. So we see that even at this moment of the terrible defeat, slaughter, and anguish for Christians, the Palestinian patriarch was obsessed by Judeophobia. Sophronius, later canonized, died a few years after surrendering Jerusalem to the Muslim conquerors. When welcoming Yasir Arafat in 1995 to the Church of the Nativity in Bethlehem for the traditional Christmas mass, Latin patriarch Michel Sabbah was happy to recall how Sophronius had delivered Jerusalem to Umar in 636; sixty years later—and until the 1860s—no cross could adorn a church in Jerusalem.

Throughout the centuries, Christian Judeophobia in Jerusalem and Palestine was virulent. In my books, I have reproduced nineteenth-century reports from French and British consuls who were shocked by this hatred, which led to criminal acts. In the twentieth century, anti-Zionism cemented the Palestinian Muslim-Christian alliance with Hitler's ideology; this collaboration with Nazi Germany is well known.

Whereas the Holocaust developed in a European context, anti-Zionism belongs to the domain of dhimmitude. Here the powerless Palestinian Christians—like Sophronius—had to rely on the Arab-Muslim force to prevent the restoration of a Jewish state. Among the multitude of events from the twentieth century, historians in the next millennium may well be intrigued by two particularities: the first concerns the relentlessness shown by many European politicians in exterminating and pillaging European Jewry; the second concerns post-Holocaust Europe, which is linked to the first by a similar desire of many to demonize Israel. Yet the twentieth century witnessed important Western strategic defeats in the Middle East. Armenian independence, promised at the end of World War I (in the Treaty of Sèvres) was never implemented; the same applies to the Kurds. Lebanon, considered a paragon of the realization of a Muslim-Christian symbiosis, finally collapsed in a bloody tragedy. Massacres and slavery continue to ravage the Christian and animist populations of southern Sudan; the war in the Philippines fueled by a secessionist Muslim minority group claimed 120,000 lives over the past twenty years. Genocidal massacres have been perpetrated in numerous countries, but for thirty years the main target—constantly highlighted in the media—remained Israel. This extraordinary blindness was in part caused by the Palestinian clergy, which, with its numerous religious and secular channels in Europe and elsewhere, helped to uphold the Palestinian issue as the world's first priority.

However, the militancy against Israel of the Muslim-Christian front paradoxically led to increased instability and anguish for Arab-Christians. The reasons are not difficult to find. In order to maintain this anti-Zionist front, Oriental Christians were obliged to make continual compromises. They were afraid to mention their own history of suffering and dhimmitude under Islam for fear of irritating the Muslim world; it became a taboo subject even in Europe. Eastern Christians, especially the Palestinians, thought that their support for the anti-Israeli jihad would secure their safety in a hostile environment. But this policy brought negative results: (1) The encouragement of an anti-Israeli jihad has fueled and developed a rhetoric of war hatred against Christians, because the dogma of jihad associates them with Jews. The more the Christians fought to delegitimize Israel, the more they weakened their own rights. (2) This factor had dramatic consequences for the Lebanese Christians. Like the Jews, their war for freedom in their own country was a struggle to impose on the Islamic world the respect for their rights to dignity—not to be considered as an inferior group, ready for a modernized dhimmitude. And as a result of their common destiny with Jews in Islamic dogma, the jihad aggressiveness rebounded against the Lebanese Christians inadequately prepared for such a confrontation. And since the history of dhimmitude and jihad was obfuscated in Europe—thanks to the Christian, pro-Islamic, anti-Zionist lobby—and as the Palestinian cause became *the* sacred cause of the international community, when the PLO fought the Christians in Lebanon, the latter were soon abandoned.

Hence, the concealment of dhimmi history, and of the ideology of jihad— a deliberate policy maintained for decades in the West—has facilitated a return of the past, as the same political system is now inscribed in the program of today's Islamists.

There is another, no less important, aspect of dhimmitude: the psychological and spiritual one. The dhimmi mentality appears with no great differences in its Christian or Jewish version. One could examine it either in relation to the concept of rights or to that of toleration. One should bear in mind that the study of dhimmitude necessitates an examination of the common condition of both Jews and Christians, who form one entity the "People of the Book." They are thus complementary, and the rules applied to one group likewise concern the other. Another aspect of this complex historical domain relates to their mutual relationship in the world of dhimmitude and to the manner in which each group viewed the other. Solidarity and mutual aid in time of persecutions existed, as did denunciation and revenge motivated by fear and greed. But, in general, a similar condition contributed to creating mutual bonds of understanding.

Thus, one realizes that the concept of dhimmitude—rather than the term *tolerated minorities*—covers a wide domain of research. One can study its dynamic, its evolution, its modalities, and the interactions of diverse elements within this context that shed light on the areas of fusion, interdependence, and confrontation between Islam, Christianity, and Judaism. Dhimmitude is a neutral concept and therefore a tool for historical investigation.

For me, as a Jew, this insight into Christian dhimmitude represented an intellectual experience that was not easy to undertake. This was not the domineering face of European Christendom, persecuting and triumphant, but the discovery of its persecuted, humiliated, and suffering *other* side. In short,

Eastern Christianity's history of dhimmitude under Islam is a sort of "Jewish experience"—endured this time by Christians. This is why this history was so resolutely and intensely denied by most Eastern Christians, especially Palestinians. For a Jew, this quest constitutes a moral ascesis, because it is no easy task to find expressions of the same suffering in one's persecutor. But this companionship gives a new approach to human trials and opens common perspectives of reconciliation with Muslims. It makes it easier for Jews and Christians to strive with liberal Muslims, thus freeing them from prejudices of the past and from the concepts of jihad and "tolerance," replacing them with new bonds of friendship and esteem between equals.

For the Jewish people—liberated from Christian antisemitism in its own homeland, as well as from dhimmitude imposed on them by Islam—this long task of reconciliation with Christianity and Islam could strengthen respect between the three religions and their respective peoples.

PART 4.
THE MYTH AND CONTEMPORARY GEOPOLITICS

Introduction

Robert Spencer

In the modern age we have seen not reform of the dhimmi system of intolerance, but retrenchment. Never repudiated in theory, the legal superstructure of dhimmitude was slowly set aside in part in the Islamic world during the decline and ultimate collapse of the Ottoman Empire and during the height of Western colonialism in the Middle East and other Islamic areas. Today it has been revived by radical Muslims, as part of their overall deeply traditionalist reemphasis upon the literal content of the Islamic sources. This part examines various aspects of the survival of dhimmi attitudes as a cultural hangover in Muslim countries and the revival of dhimmitude as a system as part of the program of radical Muslims worldwide.

One chilling example of this revivalism comes from Bat Ye'or's "Past Is Prologue: The Challenge of Islamism Today." She notes that "in April 1992, for instance, religious leaders in Sudan's Southern Kordofan region—who were 'publicly supported at the highest government level'—issued a *fatwa*, which stated: 'An insurgent who was previously a Muslim is now an apostate; and a non-Muslim is a non-believer standing as a bulwark against the spread of Islam, and Islam has granted the freedom of killing both of them.'" This recalled the entire ancient doctrinal system of jihad, which mandated in accord with sura 9:29 that Muslims must fight against non-Muslims until they convert to Islam or submit as inferiors under Islamic rule; as Bat Ye'or puts it, "Non-Muslims are protected only if they submit to Islamic domination by a 'Pact'—or *dhimma*—that imposes degrading and discriminatory regulations." This imperative underlies (as the documents by Walid Phares, Mark Durie, and others detail) not only the Arab-Israeli conflict but also the mistreatment of Christians by Muslims in the Middle East and Indonesia.

The same dynamic is now also changing the cultural and political landscape of Europe, as Bat Ye'or explains in her two "Eurabia" pieces included here. The pieces by Srdja Trifkovic, Daniel Pipes, and Lars Hedegaard detail just how deeply Europe is being transformed, with hardly any notice from the world community—although, as my brief piece on the Vatican's evolving position toward Islam suggests, that may be changing.

PAST IS PROLOGUE

8. The Challenge of Islamism Today

Bat Ye'or

Past Is Prologue. These words are engraved on the pediment of the National Archives building in Washington, DC. The English source is probably William Shakespeare's *Tempest*, and the original perhaps Ecclesiastes (1:9). I have chosen this motto for my statement today and shall first give a historical overview of the persecution of Christians under Islam.

To fully understand the present tragic situation of Christians in Muslim lands, one must comprehend the ideological and historical pattern that is conducive to violations of human rights, even though this pattern does not seem to be a deliberate, monolithic, anti-Christian policy. However, as this structure is integrated into the corpus of Islamic law (the Sharia), it functions in those countries that either apply the Sharia in full or whose laws are inspired by it.

The historical pattern of Muslim-Christian encounters developed soon after the prophet Muhammad's death in 632. Muslim-Christian relations were then regulated by two legal-theological systems: one based on jihad, the other on the Sharia. A jihad should not be compared to a Crusade—or to any other war. The strategy and tactics of jihad are minutely fixed by theological rules, which the caliph or ruler, wielding both spiritual and political power, must obey. The jihad practiced now in Sudan is conducted according to its traditional rules. One could affirm that all "jihad" groups today conform to these decrees.

It is a historical fact that all the Muslims countries around the southern and eastern Mediterranean were Christian lands before being conquered, during a millenium of jihad under the banner of Islam. Those vanquished populations—here I am referring only to Christians and Jews—were then

Basic text used by Bat Ye'or for US Congressional Briefing, Human Rights Caucus on the Persecution of Christians Worldwide, April 29, 1997.

"protected," providing they submitted to the Muslim ruler's conditions. Therefore "protection" in the context of a conquest is the consequence of a war, and this is a very important notion.

In April 1992, for instance, religious leaders in Sudan's Southern Kord-ofan region—who were "publicly supported at the highest government level"—issued a *fatwa* that stated, "An insurgent who was previously a Muslim is now an apostate; and a non-Muslim is a non-believer standing as a bulwark against the spread of Islam, and Islam has granted the freedom of killing both of them." This *fatwa* appears in a 1995 Report to the United Nations Commission on Human Rights by the UN Special Rapporteur on Sudan, Dr. Gaspar Biro.[1] This religious text gives the traditional definition of a harbi (someone living in the *dar al-Harb*, the "Region of War"), an infidel who has not been subjected by jihad, and therefore whose life and property— according to classical texts of Islamic jurists—is thus forfeited to any Muslim. It also gives a definition of an apostate who can be killed—the cases of Salman Rushdie in 1989, Farag Foda in 1992, and Taslima Nasreen in 1994 are other examples where the death sentence was decreed.

Non-Muslims are protected only if they submit to Islamic domination by a "pact"—or *dhimma*—that imposes degrading and discriminatory regulations. In my books, I have provided documents from Islamic sources and from the vanquished peoples, establishing a sort of classification so that the origins, development, and aims of these regulations can be recognized when they are revived nowadays. I am referring only to Christians and Jews, because they share the same Islamic theological and legal category, referred to in the Qur'an as "People of the Book"—the word *people* is in the singular. If they accept to submit to a Muslim ruler, they then become "protected dhimmi peoples"—tributaries, since their protection is linked to an obligatory payment of a Quranic poll tax (the *jizya*) to the Islamic community (the *umma*).

This protection is abolished if the dhimmis should rebel against Islamic law; give allegiance to non-Muslim power; refuse to pay the Quranic *jizya*; entice a Muslim from his faith; harm a Muslim or his property; or commit blasphemy. Blasphemy includes denigration of the prophet Muhammad, the Qur'an, the Muslim faith, the Sharia by suggesting that it has a defect, and refusing the decision of the *ijma*—which is the consensus of the Islamic community, or *umma* (sura 3:106). The moment the "pact of protection" is abolished, the jihad resumes, which means that the lives of the dhimmis and their property are forfeited. Those Islamists in Egypt who kill and pillage Copts consider that these Christians—or dhimmis—have forfeited their "protection" because they do not pay the *jizya*.

In other words, this "protector-protected" relationship is typical of a war treaty between the conqueror and the vanquished, and this situation remains valid for Islamists because it is fixed in theological texts. But it should be emphasized that other texts in the Qur'an stress religious tolerance and peaceful relations, which frequently existed. Nonetheless, early jurists and theologians—invoking the Quranic principle of the "abrogation" of an earlier text by a later one—have established an extremist doctrine of jihad, which is a collective duty.

The protection system presents both positive and negative aspects: it provides security and a measure of religious autonomy. On the other hand, dhimmis suffered many legal disabilities intended to reduce them to a condition of humiliation and segregation. These rules were established as early as the eighth and ninth centuries by the founders of the four schools of Islamic law: Hanafi, Malaki, Shafi'i, and Hanbali.

The Sharia is a complete compendium of laws based on theological sources, principally the Qur'an and Hadith—that is, the sayings and acts of the Prophet. The Sharia comprises the legal status of the dhimmis: what is permitted and what is forbidden to them. It sets the pattern of Muslims' social and political behavior toward dhimmis and explains its theological, legal, and political motivations.

It is this comprehensive system, which lasted for up to thirteen centuries, that I have analyzed in my last book, *The Decline of Eastern Christianity under Islam*, as the "civilization of dhimmitude." Its archetype—the dehumanized dhimmi—has permeated Islamic civilization, culture, and thought and is being revived through the Islamist resurgence and the return of the Sharia.

The main principles of "dhimmitude" are as follows: (1) the inequality of rights in all domains between Muslims and dhimmis; (2) the social and economic discrimination of the dhimmis; (3) the humiliation and vulnerability of the dhimmis.

Numerous laws were enacted over the centuries in order to implement these principles, which remained in practice throughout the nineteenth century and in some regions into the twentieth century.

Arab-Islamic civilization developed in conquered Christian lands, among Christian majorities that were eventually reduced to minorities. The process of the Islamization of Christian societies appears at all levels. It is part and parcel of the Christian suffering embodied in laws, customs, behavior patterns, and prejudices that were perpetuated during many centuries. Christianity could survive in some countries like Egypt and the Balkans where their situation was tolerable, but in other places they were wiped out physically, expelled, or forced to emigrate.

During the whole of the nineteenth century, European governments tried to convince Muslim rulers—from Constantinople to North Africa—to abolish the discriminations against dhimmis. This policy led to reforms in the Ottoman Empire from 1839 known as the Tanzimat—but it was only in Egypt, under the strong rule of Muhammad Ali, that real progress was made. Improvements in the Ottoman Empire and Persia, imposed by Europe, were bitterly resented by the populace and religious leaders.

European laws were introduced in the process of Turkish modernization and in some Arab countries, but it was only under colonial rule that Christian and Jewish minorities were truly liberated from centuries of opprobrium. Traditionalists, however, resented the Westernization of their countries, the emancipation of the dhimmis, and the laws imported from infidel lands. The fight for decolonization was also a struggle by the Islamists to reestablish strict Islamic law.

Why is this persecution ignored by the churches, governments, and media?

The nineteenth century—and even after World War I—was a traumatizing period of genocidal slaughter of Christians, spreading from the Balkans (Greece, Serbia, Bulgaria) to Armenia and to the Middle East. In this context of death, the doctrine of an Muslim-Christian symbiosis was conceived toward the end of the nineteenth century by Eastern Christians as a desperate shield against terror and slavery. This doctrine—which also inluded anti-Zionism—had many facets, both political and religious. In the long term, its results were mostly negative.

It is this doctrine, still professed today, that is responsible for the general silence about the ongoing tragedy of Eastern Christians. Any mention of jihad and of the persecutions of Christians by Muslims was a taboo subject, because one could not denounce persecution and simultaneously proclaim that a Muslim-Christian symbiosis has always existed in the past and the present. It is in this cocoon of lies and of a deliberately imposed silence, solidly supported by the churches, governments, and the media—each for its own reasons—that persecution of Christians could develop freely, during this century, even until now, with little hindrance. Moreover, this doctrine also blocked the memory of dhimmitude, leaving a vacuum of thirteen centuries whose emptiness was filled with a myth that was useless as a means to prevent the return of old prejudices and persecutions.

For this reason, dhimmitude—which covers several centuries of Christian and Jewish history and which is a comprehensive civilization encompassing legislation, customs, social behavior, and prejudices—has never been analyzed nor publicly discussed. It is this silence—for which academia in Europe and America bears much responsibility—that allows the perpetuation of religious discrimination and persecution today. There are many factors that explain the silence of governments, churches, academia, and the media on such a tragic issue concerning persecuted Christians in the Muslim world; they are interrelated and, although their motivations are different, they have solidly cemented a wall of silence that has buried the historical reality.

PROPOSALS FOR REDRESSING THESE VIOLATIONS OF FUNDAMENTAL HUMAN RIGHTS:

1. To define the ways and means to end this tragedy:

  (i) Not to foster an anti-Islamic current, which would be wrong, as the vast majority of Muslims are themselves victims of Islamists in Iran, Pakistan, Afghanistan, Sudan, Egypt, Turkey, Algeria, etc.

  (ii) Christians must continue to live in their historical lands because it is their right, and only they can transform traditional Muslim mentalities. These dwindling communities should be encouraged to stay, as their presence will signify that Muslims have accepted that Jews and Christians also possess the right to life and dignity in their ancient homelands—and not under a dhimmi protection, but with human rights equal to those of Muslims. If they fail, it will be our loss in the West, too. Islamic countries that once had a Judeo-Christian culture should not become monolithically Islamic—that is, Christenrein, as they have become virtually *judenrein*—through a policy of ethnic cleansing that followed a long historical period of discrimination.

  (iii) If the human rights—and the minority rights—of Christians are not respected in countries that formerly had Christian majorities, then the rights of all non-Muslims will be challenged by the Islamists' resurgence. It is for Christians worldwide—particularly in America and Europe, and for the international community also—to assure that the human rights for all religious minorities are respected worldwide.

2. We should realize that those populations are in grave danger and that even Muslim governments cannot protect them from mob violence—sometimes they pretend to be unable to do so, in order to stop foreign pressure or public campaigns. We should also remember that, from the late 1940s, the Jewish communities in the Arab-Muslim world—then more than a million, now less than 1 percent of that number, under ten thousand and fast dwindling—were the victims of persecution, terrorism, pillage, and religious hatred that forced them to flee or emigrate. Christians were left as the only non-Muslims on whom religious fanaticism and hatred could be focused. Each Christian community tried to resist the return of the old order, following the path of secularism or communism.

The Islamists reproach Christians in their countries for:

   (i) being against the implementation of the Sharia;
  (ii) demanding equal rights, basing themselves on international covenants;
 (iii) and seeking foreign help to achieve equality with fellow Muslim citizens.

For the Islamists, these three accusations alone are tantamount to rebellion. It was these same motives that justified the first great massacres of the Armenians a century ago, in 1894–1896, punished for having rebelled and for claiming the reforms that were promised.

This is why dhimmi communities were always careful to proclaim their enmity to Europe. An outward oppositon to Christian countries being their life-saving shield against threats from their environment, they have interiorized this animosity to the point that they often strive for the triumph of Islam, some of them even becoming the best and most perfect tools of Islamic propaganda and interests in Europe and America. (The late Father Yoakim Moubarac and Georges Corm in France and Edward Said in America are but three examples of many.)

3. In order to avoid mistakes and be more effective, one has to realize the difference of contexts between the campaign for Soviet Jewry in the 1970s and 1980s and the promotion of human rights for Christians in Islamic lands today. The main difficulty arises because the discrimination or persecution in some countries cannot be ascribed to a deliberate government policy. It is rather a fact of civilization: the traditional contempt

for dhimmis—not so different from that of African Americans in the past—and irritation because they are outstepping their rights and must be obliged to return to their former status.

Sometimes, however, it is imposed by the Islamists, and a weak government doesn't dare to protect the Christians, fearing to become even more unpopular, because anti-Western and anti-Christian prejudices have imbued Muslim culture and society for centuries.

There are many ways to persecute Christians; some are by legal means, like the laws concerning the building or the repair of churches; others, by terror. A Christian can be killed not because he committed a crime but simply because he belongs to a group of infidels, who, allegedly, are in rebellion—or for reasons of "spectacle terrorism" which can serve as a deterrent policy to fulfill terrorists' aims.

Another point concerns the use of a *fatwa*. If a *fatwa* is decreed against an individual, any Muslim is authorized to kill him, and by so doing he is the executor of what is considered the sentence of Allah.

4. The problem is multifarious; it is not only religious but also cultural. This aspect is more acute with Christian than with Jewish communities, because Muslims conquered Christian lands and civilization that were then subjected to a deliberate policy of Arabization and Islamization. Take, as an example, Christian pre-Islamic Coptic history: language and culture are a neglected, if not a forbidden, domain because it would imply that Muslim history had been imperialistic. But culture and history are important elements of a group's identity, and there are many Muslims intellectuals who are proud of Egypt's Pharaonic and Coptic past. It is the Islamists who reject this past as an infidel culture—a part of the *jahaliyah*, what existed before Islam, considered taboo.

Therefore, I would also suggest further goals, such as:

(i) recovering "memory," the long history of the dhimmi peoples, of dhimmitude—the collective cultural patrimony of Jews and Christians—for without their memory, and their history, peoples fade away and die; and

(ii) preventing the destruction of Christian historical monuments, either by local governments or by UNESCO, as was done with Abu Simbel and other sites that now belong to the world's cultural legacy.

5. Discussing "dhimmitude" in academia and elsewhere. This is a Judeo-Christian historical patrimony, and those whose heritage it is are entitled to know about it. The discussion of dhimmitude with Muslims, however, is fraught with difficulties. In the eyes of Islamists, any criticism of Islamic law and history is assimilated to blasphemy. For a dhimmi, it is forbidden to imply that Islamic law has a default or to contradict the *ijma*, the consensus. Moreover, the court testimony of a dhimmi against a Muslim is not accepted. Therefore, as dhimmitude is the testimony of dhimmi history—of Christians and Jews—under Islamic oppression, it would not be considered valid in traditionalist circles. Besides, the unification of religious and political power transfers the political domain into the religious one, and therefore any criticism of Islamic civilization may become, for Islamists and others, blasphemy.

   The case of Farag Foda, an Egyptian Muslim intellectual who defended the Copts and strongly criticized some Muslim religious authorities was exemplary: he was assassinated in June 1992 after a *fatwa*. In giving his testimony in an Egyptian court of law, the late Sheikh Muhammad el-Ghazali implicitly justified his assassination on the grounds of apostasy; he stated that anyone opposing the Sharia was an apostate and thus deserved death.

6. Encourage Muslim intellectuals to strive in their own countries, and in the West, for the defense of equal human rights for Christians and others. The 1981 UNESCO Declaration on Islamic Human Rights and that of Cairo in 1990, both conditional on the Sharia, are insufficient.

7. Creation of a team of experts and lawyers—and not apologists—in order to discuss the problem, always stressing that the aim is not to foster anti-Muslim or anti-Islamic feelings but to create peace and reconciliation between religions and peoples, without which the next century will become a bloodbath and a clash of civilizations.

NOTE

1. ECOSOC, E/CN. 4/1996/62, para. 97a.

ORIENTAL JEWRY AND THE DHIMMI IMAGE IN CONTEMPORARY ARAB NATIONALISM

9.

Bat Ye'or

I t is not without emotion that I, a Jewess from an Arab land, address you this evening in the country of Palmerston, Finn, Oliphant, Balfour, Churchill, and Wingate,[1] to name but six of the numerous British Zionists of the Christian faith (not forgetting Sir Harold Wilson, tonight's chairman) who have, each in his own way, from the early nineteenth century onward, demanded the recognition of the human and historical rights of an oppressed, dispossessed, and exiled people to its ancient homeland. Neither do I forget the struggle maintained by representatives of British Jewry, beginning with Sir Moses Montefiore, to restore human dignity to their persecuted brethren in the Orient and North Africa.

Twenty-one years ago, when my parents and I found refuge in Britain, I was unaware of these historical antecedents and knew little about the history of Oriental Jewry. Due to religious discrimination, I was deprived of my Egyptian citizenship and driven from my country of birth by the fanaticism of a totalitarian regime. I arrived in London a refugee, stateless and penniless. It was in England that I discovered the meaning of freedom in contrast to the constant fear for one's life experienced in Egypt. It was in London that the Jewish Refugee Committee provided me with a grant, which enabled me to study at the Institute of Archaeology. I owe a deep debt of gratitude to the British authorities and all those who received us with hospitality on these shores in 1957. I extend my special thanks to the Jews in the Arab Lands

Editions de l'Avenir, Geneva, for WOJAC (World Organization of Jews from Arab Countries), April 5, 1979. English translation from Bat Ye'or's text by David G. Littman, with the author.

Committee, which has invited me to address you this evening on the subject of Oriental Jewry.

In the thirty minutes at my disposal, I will speak of the dhimmi condition and the use of the dhimmi stereotype in modern Arab nationalism. I will not advance opinions on current political events but will suggest in my analysis how Arab leaders may be encouraged to acknowledge Jewish sovereignty in the Land of Israel.

In the middle of the nineteenth century, Oriental Jewry was in a critical situation.[2] When it came into contact with European Jewry, it was as if the gates of hope had opened. The Jews of Arab lands still lived in inhuman conditions, having miraculously survived centuries of oppression. They were dhimmis. The term *dhimmi* was applied by the Arab-Muslim invaders to Jews, Christians, and Zoroastrians after the Arabization and Islamization of their lands from the seventh century onward. Besides its religious connotations, this Arabic word has also a political meaning. It refers to those nations that were dispossessed of all their rights by conquest—including, theoretically, the right to life itself. However, a concession was granted by the victors: dhimmi peoples could buy back their rights to life and property—except land—on condition that each male adult paid a special poll tax (the *jizya*) and that the collectivity agreed to submit to humiliating regulations. Any breach of these rules, as did happen under benevolent rulers, automatically restored to the Muslim community (*umma*) its initial rights over the lives and property of the dhimmis, guilty of desiring equality with true believers.

In the case of the Jews, once their ancestral homeland had come under Islamic jurisdiction, a political dimension was added to their previous religious dhimmi status in Arabia. This political aspect of the dhimmi condition was at the root of the numerous bloody conflicts since the early nineteenth century, whenever a dhimmi people fought to regain control of its national territory from Islamic domination, whether Ottoman or Arab, that is, the Greeks, the Serbs, the Romanians, the Bulgarians, the Maronites, the Armenians, and more recently the Jews.

I would define a "dhimmi civilization" as being characterized by a language, a history, and a culture, as well as specific political and juridical institutions developed in the national homeland before its annexation by Arab-Muslim conquerors. The expression *dhimmi civilization* or *dhimmi people* refers to a nation, the ethnic origin of which is associated with a particular country Islamized by jihad (holy war), regardless of that nation's present dispersion. People who belong to a dhimmi civilization are individuals who have continued to transmit a specific heritage to their progeny, in spite of wanderings resulting from conquest and oppression. Thus, from an Islamic viewpoint, whether he is a Westerner or an Oriental, a Jew is a part of a dhimmi civilization if he willingly perpetuates and accepts the national and cultural values of Israel. This principle applies also to the Armenian and the Maronite Christians, as well as to other peoples who, after the Arab-Muslim conquest of their homelands, were subjected to a legislation that either decimated them or forced them to live in exile.

Islamic tradition maintained that from the time of Umar, the second caliph (634–644), dhimmi peoples could reside in Islamized lands only if their work was beneficial to the maintenance and expansion of Arab-Islamic rule. Later, this theory was developed into a system of legalized economic exploitation and oppression based allegedly on divine will. This is not the place for me to describe fully the dhimmi condition. It is enough to say that the indigenous peoples of the Middle East and North Africa were gradually reduced—through pillage, ransom, exploitation, oppression, dispossession, forced conversion, famine, and physical elimination—from majorities to helpless minorities. Their everyday life was governed by countless oppressive rules, and it became a religious obligation to humiliate and to revile them. In an age of violence, the law forbade them to carry arms. Lifting a hand against a Muslim, even in a case of legitimate defense, was a capital offense. In an age of injustice, their sworn testimony was refused by Muslim courts. Thus, if the aggressor was a Muslim, the judge would not accept the plea of a dhimmi. They were more defenseless than the humblest animal, protected by nature with a self-defense mechanism. Deprived even of this natural right under a system that promulgated inequality in human society and in human relations, many became servile and corrupt, the better to preserve their existence. They endeavored wherever possible to amass money secretly, because in times of great oppression they might thereby purchase their survival. Their blood was considered of an inferior quality to that of Muslims and could be shed lightly. Dhimmis rarely appealed for justice prior to the nineteenth century. To complain of pillage, murder, or massacre frequently provoked collective reprisals, thereby reminding the dhimmis of their proper place.

Dhimmis were often considered impure and had to be segregated from the Muslim community. Entry into holy Muslim towns, mosques, and public baths, as well as certain streets was forbidden them. Their turbans—when they were permitted to wear them—their costumes, belts, shoes, and the appearance of their wives and their servants had to be different from those of Muslims in order to distinguish and humiliate them; for the dhimmis should never be allowed to forget that they were inferior beings. The humble donkey was generally the sole beast of burden permitted them, and then only outside the town and on condition that they would, as a sign of respect, dismount on sight of any Muslim and mount again only after their superior was out of sight. Even their saddles had to be ugly and uncomfortable, and often they were forced to mount sidesaddle. In the street, dhimmis were obliged to walk on the left, or impure, side of a Muslim. Their gait had to be rapid, and their eyes lowered. Their graves had to be level with the ground so that anyone could walk on them, and in desert lands it was assumed that the elements would quickly obliterate their remains. These were the more common rules, which in some regions prevailed into the twentieth century; but there were other, no less vexing obligations applicable to the dhimmis and to them alone.

Our ancestors plodded on for twelve centuries in this vale of sorrow. Their world was one of distress and despair, in which they were allowed no dignity and were crushed by humiliation and misery, by oppression and a perpetual fear of death. Not all were able to resist such pressures, and many were converted. Those whose souls were not destroyed through such abasement remained faithful to an ideal of spiritual freedom. They refused to join the ranks of the oppressors, although by a simple declaration they could have ended their sufferings. They knew that they were the heirs of a great spiritual heritage, and in order to preserve it for their posterity they preferred to remain in servitude. They believed that the oppressed would be redeemed, that the slave and the captive would be freed from tyranny, that the Jews would one day return to Zion and liberate the Land of Israel. They consoled themselves in their deep distress by escaping to a world of study and mysticism. They believed that their sufferings were of a providential nature meant to strengthen their faith and their hope in a future society based on justice for all.

A letter written from Egypt by philosopher (and physician to Saladin's vizier) Moses Maimonides to the Jews in Yemen, faced with imminent forced conversion in the late twelfth century, is worth recalling. Here is an extract:

> Remember, my co-religionists, that on account of the vast number of our sins, God has hurled us in the midst of this people, the Arabs, who have persecuted us severely, and passed baneful and discriminatory legislation against us. . . . Never did a nation molest, degrade, debase and hate us as much as they. . . . Although we were dishonored by them beyond human endurance, and had to put [up] with their fabrications, yet we behave like him who is depicted by the inspired writer, "But I am as a deaf man, I hear

not, and I am as a dumb man that openeth not his mouth" (Psalm 38:14). Similarly our sages instructed us to bear the prevarications and preposterousness of Ishmael in silence. . . . We have acquiesced, both old and young, to inure ourselves to humiliation, as Isaiah instructed us, "I gave my back to the smiters, and my cheeks to them that plucked off the hair" (50:6). All this notwithstanding, we do not escape this continued maltreatment which well nigh crushes us. No matter how much we suffer and elect to remain at peace with them, they stir up strife and sedition, as David predicted, "I am all peace, but when I speak, they are for war" (Psalm 120:7). . . . May God, who created the world with the attributes of mercy, grant us the privilege to behold the return of the exiles, to the portion of His inheritance, to contemplate the graciousness of the Lord and to visit early in His Temple. May He take us out from the Valley of the Shadow of Death wherein He put us. May He remove darkness from our eyes, and gloom from our hearts. May He fulfill in our days as well as yours the prophecy contained in the verse, "The people that walked in darkness have seen a great light" (Isaiah 9:1). . . . Peace, peace, as the light that shines and much peace until the moon be no more. Amen.[3]

Those who welcomed Sir Moses Montefiore in the middle of the nineteenth century, in Cairo, in Damascus, in Jerusalem, in Marrakesh, were the descendants of the "deaf and the dumb"—the meek in spirit. But thereafter things changed.

I will not here go into historical details but only stress that thanks to the efforts of Jews and Christians in Western Europe the condition of the Jewish and Christian dhimmis greatly improved. However, the more the dhimmi peoples were emancipated from discriminatory legislation thanks to European influence and later as a result of colonial rule, the more they were hated and threatened in their Muslim environment, permeated as it was by pan-Islamic ideology and traditions. It is simple to understand why: the emancipation of the dhimmis was imposed by European powers in the name of the equality of each individual before the law. This concept was in total contrast to the values of traditional Muslim societies. Muslim religious leaders saw the social promotion of the dhimmis as a sacrilege, as an intolerable intrusion of the West, aimed at weakening Islam and humiliating it.

But there is also another, more complex and human reason: twelve centuries of oppression and humiliation have created a dhimmi stereotype—the stereotype of the Jew and the Christian in Arab-Muslim lands, or to be more precise in Arabized "dhimmi lands." This stereotype permeated history, laws, traditions, behavior, literature, and modern political ideologies. The diabolical attributes of the dhimmi stereotype were carried along in the current of

Arab-Muslim historiography and are still considered valid. And if I have spoken of the past, it is because the present is conditioned by the past. To a person familiar with dhimmi history, there can be no doubt that the dhimmi stereotype is at the very root of Arab and Muslim anti-Zionism and the present Middle East conflicts.

Modern Arab nationalism is the spiritual heir of the early-caliphate Arab empire: an empire that expanded through the Arabization of dhimmi land and by the progressive development of an antidhimmi jurisdiction. Today the goal of Arab nationalism is total Arabization, an endless struggle against all non-Arab national—even cultural—revivals of the nations that have survived one of the longest and most oppressive imperialisms of history.

And *Arabization* means a return to the dhimmi condition, a condition of alienation, of subjugation or of exile—not for Israel alone but also for the Maronite Christians and for any other movement of national independence within *dar al-Islam.*[4]

Today, Arabism and Islam are virtually synonymous for Arab nationalists. According to a Muslim religious tradition, all infidels had to be expelled from Arabia so that Arabs could only be Muslims. Arab domination is in fact Muslim domination, and this is why the traditional dhimmi stereotype—absorbed into the legal and religious structures of Arabized societies—has been reformulated by contemporary Arab nationalists.

The core of the Arab refusal and of the Charter of the Palestine Liberation Organization (PLO) is based on the very principle of the dhimmi condition: the refusal of Jewish sovereignty on its once-Arabized land. One cannot emphasize enough that in calling itself the vanguard of Arab nationalism the PLO has become an instrument to fight and suppress every non-Arab nationalism. One has seen it already in Lebanon. It is the PLO even more than Syria, which, in the name of Arab nationalism, destroyed Lebanon, the only "Arab" country where indigenous Christian remnants still enjoyed political expression. One has merely to recall the declaration of Yasir Arafat on November 30, 1975: "The civil war in Lebanon is not over and bloodshed will continue. The battle we are fighting in Lebanon is for the preservation of the country's Arab character. I declare in the name of the Palestinian revolution and the Lebanese nationalist and progressive movement that every inch of Arab land will remain Arab and Lebanon will remain Arab."[5]

It is in the name of Muslim solidarity that the PLO has raised the banner of jihad against Israel, the purpose of which has always been to reduce independent non-Muslim peoples to that of dependent dhimmis.[6]

I do not doubt the sincere desire for peace of the Egyptian people and of

President Sadat, nor the liberal views of some of Egypt's intellectuals, but one should not forget Egypt's dependence on the Arab world, particularly on the theocratic, feudal regime of Saudi Arabia. The influence of the theologians of Cairo's renowned Al-Azhar University and the Muslim Brotherhood are also not negligible factors.[7]

Before concluding, a few words on the psychological aspect of the Arab-Israel conflict are appropriate. The changeover from dhimmi to Israeli (the Jew liberating his land from Arab domination) has traumatized the Arab political consciousness. Why? Because Arab-Muslim domination and the resultant feelings of superiority were confirmed by the abasement of the dhimmi. If, however, the dhimmi can obtain equal rights, the superior feels himself doubly inferior and is thereby *humiliated*. The psychological trauma was particularly vivid for the Arabs in Palestine, where the treatment of the Jewish remnant was often more severe than anywhere else, as the conquerors' aim was to impose *their own* sovereignty. The less the Israeli image of the Jew fits into the dhimmi stereotype—a servile, cowardly, debased being—the more violent and bloodthirsty will become the efforts of the ancient oppressors to force the victims to fit into a preconceived, discriminatory mold.

Since Israel's independence, the dhimmi stereotype has been transferred to Israel and Zionism, thereby justifying the country's constant vilification in international forums. Israel is the scapegoat, responsible for every evil which afflicts the Arab world—as well as other regions. Israel is mocked and defamed, just as the dhimmis were forced to wear despicable clothes. In fact, Israel symbolizes today the isolation, the hatred, the contempt that formerly crushed the dhimmi communities. And just as death punished the rebellious dhimmis in the past when they rejected the rules that degraded them, so the dhimmi state, in rebellion against Arab domination, is today condemned to be destroyed by pan-Arab nationalism. Its existence must be illegal, for only Arab domination in such a context is considered legal. And, therefore, killing Israelis is a just cause—in the same manner as the dhimmis and their wives and children were killed in the past—not so long ago, either, as the Jewish survivors of the many massacres in Arab countries during the last generation can testify. Racism, imperialism, and colonialism are the hateful cloth of contempt and derision thrown on the State of Israel in order to disarm and ostracize a country, half of whose population is composed of descendants of dhimmis.

In our time, the weaknesses of Oriental Jewry are simply the prolongation of the helplessness engendered by the dhimmi condition. If the majority of Oriental Jewry is, politically speaking, inarticulate today, it is because its communities were reduced to a state of *nonexistence* during the past millennium.

They were destroyed to the very core by segregation and a public stigma of inferiority. They were destroyed again by their emancipation at the hands of the colonial powers, which by granting them human dignity and equal rights with Muslims broke the chains of their moral and physical prison yet alienated them culturally.

If Oriental Jewry is emerging from subjugation in our generation, it is because it has been rescued from Arab servitude and can measure itself alongside free peoples. But with this awareness goes a sense of responsibility. Perhaps we Jews of Arab lands can still change the course of history by building—with all the peoples of the Orient—a future of peace and brotherhood, rather than a future of hatred and war. With such a past, hatred is futile and debasing—and fatal to humanity.

The struggle for peace will unite us with a past, the greatness of which we have forgotten: a past characterized by the heroism of spiritual courage and nonviolence in face of violence. It is this past—not the ephemeral period of the emancipation of the dhimmis imposed upon the Arabs by Europe—that justifies the peace vocation of Oriental Jews and Christians, a duty that no one can assume in their place.

This duty consists in provoking a fundamental renovation of Arab political thought: by liberating it of its traditions of racial and imperialist intolerance and by encouraging acceptance—in terms of equality—of the *other,* the different, the non-Arab, the non-Muslim, through a reevaluation of Arab-Muslim imperial glories as seen and felt by its victims.

It is the role of Oriental Jewry to unmask in Arab anti-Zionism that "infectious current," that "plague"—surviving from the depths of the dark ages—that condemned the synagogue and the church in the Orient to debasement and to segregation—for the East also has its own "enseignement du mépris" (teaching of contempt), to use the words of historian Jules Isaac. This action should be used not to accuse but to liberate; not to hate but to seek agreement. It is a difficult path, sown with mines, but the only possible path for laying the foundations of peace between free peoples.

Courageous men and women have over the years led the struggle against every form of racism. Equality, liberty, and the respect for the rights of men and women of all creeds and colors have been the rewards for their efforts. For one cannot eradicate the concentration camps, the gulags, or, for that matter, apartheid by pretending to ignore them. Similarly, one cannot eliminate Arab anti-Zionism, the modern expression of age-old antidhimmi prejudices, by denying these prejudices. Soothing words, the temporary display of fine feelings, are incapable of modifying attitudes that have been conditioned by unchallenged stereotypes.

My conclusion is optimistic. At such a crucial epoch for the Jewish people, for Israel, and for the peace of the world, the voice that yet might restrain the Arab peoples, the voice from the past that can speak to their collective conscience by portraying the tragic history of the dhimmis—the voice of justice—has begun to speak out and to be heard.

In 1975 WOJAC (the World Organization of Jews from Arab Countries) was founded. Speaking for nearly two million Jews from Arab lands who live in Israel and in the Diaspora, WOJAC aims at contributing to the building of a bridge of friendship between Israel and the Arab countries and all the peoples of the Middle East. It also aims at achieving the realization of the rights of displaced Jews from Arab countries and a just settlement of their individual and collective claims, which, based on UN Security Council Resolution 242, is a major and essential condition for peace in the Middle East.

For centuries, we kept silent when our human dignity and rights were flouted. During the long night of exile, we held our peace rather than respond to our oppressors. During these dark centuries, we lived as if we were blind so as not to see our disgrace, as if we were deaf so as not to hear endless insults—so that we no longer knew how to see, how to hear, how to speak. We kept silent even when twenty Arab countries, covering 10 percent of the world's surface—countries that have stamped into their past and present history the degradation of the dhimmis—condemned Zionism as racism, condemned Israel of racism, that small homeland of hope and redemption to which two-thirds of the descendants of the Jewish dhimmis have returned.

We remained silent, for we reacted like a captive people, and captive peoples tend to lose their identity, their history, and the control of their destiny, remaining unaware of their rights. The recovery of our historical identity and our moral dignity will enable us to start a dialogue with the Arab peoples—as free people and not as servile dhimmis—a dialogue that may transform them and renew them spiritually. This dialogue, although inspired by the lesson of the past, nonetheless points to the future: a future of friendship and not of contempt, a future of peace and not of war, a future of mutual esteem and recognition, of understanding and of reconciliation.[8]

POSTSCRIPT 2004

After the above lecture was delivered on September 5, 1978, a question was put to Bat Ye'or regarding what might happen if the Ayatollah Khomeini were to take power in Iran. She predicted what actually happened, and her words were endorsed by Sir Harold Wilson as chairman, who stated that he had seen the shah in Iran in the spring, who told him that if ever Khomeini took power in Iran, then the West would understand the meaning of Islamic extremism and how it would affect the Middle East.

NOTES

This lecture was given at Jews College, London, on September 5, 1978, at a seminar organized by the Jews in Arab Lands Committee (Zionist Federation of Great Britain and Ireland): guest chairman Sir Harold Wilson, former prime minister; Dr. Solomon Gaon, chief rabbi, Spanish and Portuguese Jews of Great Britain; Eric Moonman, MP, chairman, Zionist Federation of Great Britain and Ireland; Percy Gourgey, chairman, Jews in Arab Lands Committee; Bat Ye'or, representative in Switzerland of the World Organization of Jews from Arab Countries (WOJAC).

1. Lord Palmerston, foreign secretary (1830–34, 1846–51), prime minister (1855–58, 1859–65); James Finn, consul, Jerusalem (1845–62); Laurence Oliphant (1829–88); Arthur James Balfour, prime minister (1902–1905), foreign secretary (1916–19); Winston Churchill (1874–1965); Orde Wingate (1903–44).

2. For simplification, all the Jews of the Middle East and North Africa are included in the expression *Oriental Jewry.*

3. Moses Maimonides, *Epistle to Yemen* (New York: Halkin Edition, 1952), pp. xviii, xx.

4. *Dar al-Islam,* House of Islam, in contrast to the rest of the world, denoted *dar al-Harb,* the House of War. Muslim jurisprudence posits a perpetual state of war between the two until Islamic rule prevails throughout the world.

5. *Voice of Falastin* (Lebanon), December 1, 1975. Broadcast of Yasir Arafat's speech of November 30, 1975, in Damascus to the administrative council of the Palestine Student Association. See also *Jerusalem Post,* December 3, 1975.

6. For a recent example, see Yasir Arafat's message of February 11, 1979, to the Ayatollah Khomeini: "I pray Allah to guide your steps on the road of faith and *jihad* in Iran, which will continue the struggle until we reach the walls of Jerusalem, where we will raise the flags of our two revolutions" (*Le Figaro* [Beirut], February 13, 1979).

7. See D. F. Green, ed., *Arab Theologians on Jews and Israel,* extracts from the proceedings of the Fourth Conference of the Academy of Islamic Research, 1968, 3rd ed. (Geneva: Editions de l'Avenir, 1976).

8. In concluding a peace treaty with Israel on March 26, 1979, Egypt courageously chose a revolutionary path, in contrast to the reactionary, PLO-led Arab Rejection Front.

ASPECTS OF THE
10. ARAB-ISRAELI
CONFLICT

Bat Ye'or

Wars, as historians of conflicts know, far from being spontaneous phenomena, are rather the climactic phases of violence resulting from conflict situations. These chronic—albeit dormant—conflicts, although they undoubtedly stem from economic and political tensions, are often affected on a psychological level by collective stereotyped images rooted in the traditions, culture, and history of peoples. This is why modern historians, notwithstanding the economic and political factors in Nazi Germany, have also included among the causes for the genocide of the Jews during World War II the influence of a Jewish stereotype in the collective German subconscious.

The relevance of such an analysis is not confined to the societies of Europe. However varied the ethnic or cultural differences that geographical diversity has produced, human behavior is determined everywhere by the same constants. My reason for citing a familiar instance from recent European history is to illustrate the importance of these pulsations resulting from the collective stereotypes that reside within each and every society, and not only in democracies where freedom of expression allows negative aspects of the collective psyche to come to light. To denounce exclusively the collective psychoses of a single particular milieu—in this case Europe—means not only to limit oneself to a partial interpretation of what is a general phenomenon, but also to patronize one oppressed group at the expense of all other victims of similar social behavior throughout the world. The only real difference is that in one case such social evils are opposed and condemned, whereas in the other they are permitted to thrive on connivance or silence.

This article was originally published in the *Wiener Library Bulletin* (Institute of Contemporary History, London) n.s., 32, nos. 49–50 (1979): 67–74. It was translated from the French by David G. Littman, with the author's collaboration.

It is with the intention of extending the application of certain theories beyond the limited European context that some of the antiracist arguments of European writers are here examined. The present article thus makes no claim to originality except insofar as it tries to utilize what has already been said or written elsewhere, in order to pinpoint the psychological element in the Arab-Israeli conflict. It will touch upon certain general aspects in the range of the emotional, historical, cultural, and traditional resonances within the Arab psyche.

Firstly, one could ask whether a Jewish archetype similar to that encountered in other societies exists in the Arab-Islamic consciousness. It can be established, without going into the causes that motivate ethnic or religious archetypes, that in the traditional Arab-Islamic *civitas*, a special legal status separated the infidels from the community of believers. The principle of cultural and religious differentiation should not be condemned outright, since it allows freedom of expression in a plural society. It becomes a manifestation of intolerance only when it is motivated by a desire to diminish politically, economically, socially, and spiritually one group in favor of another. Discrimination exists then as *intention* in the mind of the legislator, prior to its implementation through the regulations that will govern the social status of the designated group. It is clearly this discriminatory process that has progressively degraded the dhimmi,[1] whose caricature has thereby been indelibly etched into the history and customs of the Arab-Islamic peoples. This dehumanization reveals and motivates the dhimmi archetype, an archetype that in the collective mind is itself no more than the reflection of the dhimmi condition.

If the archetype of the Jewish dhimmi is in fact the principal psychological element in the Arab-Israeli conflict, and in particular in the consciousness of the Palestinian Arab, it is essential to define the specific characteristics of the dhimmi when they first become discernible under the second caliph, Umar (634–644), and especially after the period of the great Arab conquests. What is the strategy reducing an entire nation to a dhimmi people? It is the jihad, an expansionist holy war aiming at the Islamization of non-Muslim territories, that transforms a conquered people into a dhimmi people; while Islam, the force behind jihad, spreads Arab values. This is why Islam and pan-Arabism are still today inseparably linked in Arab political thinking, whereas in non-Arab Muslim countries, the acceptance of jihad will depend on the extent of the Islamization of the state institutions. The example of Iran is noteworthy. While the secular regime of the Shah accepted significant, albeit unofficial, relations with Israel, the religious leadership of the newly proclaimed Islamic Republic has joined those Arab leaders who have declared a jihad against Israel. It is of interest in this context to note Yasir Arafat's message of February 11, 1979, to the Ayatollah Ruhollah Khomeini, for whom Israel is an offense against Islam: "I pray Allah to guide your steps on the read of faith and *jihad* in Iran, which will continue the struggle until we reach the walls of Jerusalem, where we will raise the flags of our two revolutions."[2]

Bearing in mind that the concept of jihad was established in the seventh century and that it aims at the triumph of Islam, the extermination or conversion of pagans, and the conversion or humiliation of Jews and Christians, one may question the real meaning of the "secular and democratic state" slogan proclaimed by the Palestine Liberation Organization's PLO.

As jihad, according to the sacred texts, implements the divine will on earth, it starts an irreversible process of Arabization or Islamization. Consequently, any reversibility of jihad—for instance, the recuperation of national territory by a subject people—amounts to a "sacrilege." Allah's will, expressed in divine law ordaining the supremacy of the Arab-Muslim peoples and the humiliation of the dhimmis, is thereby flouted. The occupation of their homeland through jihad condemns the conquered to live forever as a landless nation. The choice is either to remain in their homeland on sufferance at the mercy of the conqueror or, threatened by extermination, to flee into exile. The subjected nation, stripped of its political rights and forbidden to carry arms, thus becomes powerless; its language, culture and values are replaced by those of the Arab metropolis, thereby modifying both populations and towns. Its national identity is completely extinguished. It is reduced from a nation to the level of a tolerated religion, by which process confessionalism was developed.

So the dhimmi condition may be considered a collective and hereditary one. It characterizes the conquered group as morally inferior, thus reducing it to permanent incapacity. The right to live is granted in exchange for the benefits accruing to the conqueror. This asymmetrical relationship between conqueror and conquered forms the basis of the covenant of tolerance. This paternalism lasts as long as the exploitation of the dhimmi is profitable, an aim that requires the dhimmi group to remain inferior and unequal. Tolerance is withdrawn if the dhimmis rebel or try to recover their homeland and their independence—or if, rejecting the imposed degrading servitude, they acquire rights and privileges reserved exclusively for the ruling class. Such "insolence"—to use the word generally applied to such abuses—substitutes an equal relationship for the asymmetrical one that guaranteed the dhimmis' existence. From then on their life and property are no longer protected, and they can legally be put to death. The covenant can also be broken if the ruler decides unilaterally to withdraw his "protection." In either case, the sentence hanging eternally over the subjected dhimmis, temporarily suspended by the grant of "protection," now becomes applicable. They can be dispossessed, massacred, or exiled, according to the method chosen by the conqueror.

The dhimmi communities are not only marginalized by their inferior status; they also serve as scapegoats. Excluded from a society that only tolerated them the better to exploit and degrade them, they are the victims of every conflict. In times of instability, brute instincts are unleashed, leading to the pillage and the massacre that periodically decimated these defenseless people, whose survival depended on a special conception of goodwill inextricably bound up with self-interest. Moreover, uncleanness and impurity is attached to the dhimmi condition. This physical repugnance leads to the death penalty for sexual relations between dhimmis and Muslim women. This desire to restrict social contact with a group considered theologically unclean motivates the numerous meticulous laws governing the clothes, segregation, and travel of dhimmis, as well as the vexing and humiliating prescriptions restricting their religious and social activities. The broad outlines of the dhimmi archetype are now clear. At the political and collective level, it represents a nation whose land has been Islamized by jihad, a process that, theologically, implies the purification of that land from sin. At the metaphysical level, the dhimmis represent evil, the perversity of the infidels who, refusing the superiority of the conquerors' beliefs, prefer their inferior faith. They suffer for their stubbornness by exile, or, if they choose to remain they purchase back their existence with an imposed condition of humiliation, destitution, and servility.

Can it be affirmed today that the dhimmi condition remains, from an Islamic viewpoint, applicable to Jews and Christians in *dar al-Islam*?[3] This question necessitates a distinction between the archetype and the actual juridical status of the dhimmis. Although the legal status is based on a complex of laws and customs, the archetype seems at first to be an abstract and fluid purpose. The archetype determines the status, which is merely its implementation in reality. Enriched by popular imagery, nourished on the degradation of the discriminated group, the archetype is petrified over the centuries into a phantasm that justifies and consecrates the condition of the dhimmis. Archetype and condition are dialectically linked, the one reinforcing the other. Contingent political circumstances may abolish the dhimmi condition by ending the asymmetric relationship, but the archetype will not necessarily be destroyed, since it exists within the collective psyche, independent of written laws, from whence it inspires the ideology. Deriving from history its obsessive force, it selects from the political currents of the present those elements favoring its realization at a more propitious time. Thus the archetype conserves and projects the condition into the future, even if it is temporarily suspended or abolished by historical contingencies such as the successful revolt of a dhimmi people or its expulsion from *dar al-Islam.* Thus the archetype, even emptied of its substance, survives in its own ideological structure, whose function is to elaborate and select the factors that will implement it.

To know to what extent the dhimmi condition still keeps its validity, one would have to examine how its ideological structure is formulated in present-day Muslim societies. In this article, only the more obvious manifestations will be mentioned. The jihad, for example—which may be considered as the basis of the dhimmi condition—has often been proclaimed against the state of Israel. Its strategy as well as its tactics are applied by the PLO and the Arab Rejection Front. The dhimmi condition which results automatically from jihad (i.e., the Islamization of a land) is implicitly confirmed for the Jews of Israel. Even on the philological level, the claim that the land of Israel is Arab implies that the Israelis are a landless people condemned to accept Arab suzerainty over its homeland. In the logic of Arab history, "Arab Palestine" and Jewish dhimmi status are synonymous. They are two aspects of the same reality—the conqueror's usurpation and domination, and the exploitation and subjection of the conquered. One can therefore maintain that the whole political and ideological context of the slogan "Arab Palestine" is influenced by the Jewish archetype—a dispossessed people whose land has been definitively Islamized. The terms "Arab Palestine" and even "Palestine"—the latter inherited from Roman imperialism—foreshadow the implementation of the dhimmi condition for the Jews, when the propitious hour will come.

Should this condition once again bring about a national dissolution for the Jews in their homeland, they would find themselves obliged, as before in their history, to seek refuge among other nations in order to survive. Thus the factors conducive to exile, persecution, and degradation would be reunited according to the dhimmi archetype, which, from an abstract project—albeit permeating the present ideology—would be fulfilled in reality. One could therefore answer the question raised above by unmasking the dhimmi archetype behind the frequent calls to jihad, in the affirmation that the land of Israel is Arab, and, more directly and concretely, in the numerous declarations by Muslim political or religious leaders which explicitly or implicitly confirm that the dhimmi condition is an obligatory status for Jews within *dar al-Islam.*

As far as the realization today of the archetype is concerned, or the extent to which Jews have actually been obliged to live as dhimmis, collective measures taken by Arab leaders against Jews in Arab countries and the specific attitudes of their peoples show that even until recently Jews were considered as dhimmis. Once the process of decolonization was over, the unofficial policy of Arab leaders (with the exception of King Hassan of Morocco and President Bourguiba of Tunisia) was either to expel Jews or hold them as hostages. Other measures included arbitrary confiscation of property; political, economic, and social discrimination, including deliberate humiliation; physical maltreatment and imprisonment; and summary executions and expulsions. As a justification for such measures, the political and theological authorities referred to the traditional status of the dhimmi. Today—with the exception of Morocco, Tunisia, and, more recently, Egypt—the situation of the Jews remaining in Arab countries perpetuates all the essential characteristics of the dhimmi condition: insecurity, marginalization, discrimination, and humiliation.[4] The fact that the victims—some young people, but the majority old men and women—are unable to escape to freedom, nor even to imagine its existence, and bow to their fate, does not alter their objective situation. The submission of serfs does not mean that their state of serfdom has ended.

At the collective level, the bloody pogroms suffered by Oriental Jewry illustrate the extent to which it was used as a scapegoat in an Arab world traumatized by colonization and Western penetration. In his study of the Libyan pogroms of 1945, Harvey E. Goldberg examines the symbolic meaning behind the social pattern of these bloody scapegoat rituals.[5] These outbursts were not confined to Libya but were repeated throughout the Arab world. Moreover, the virulent Judeophobia found in Arab countries is rooted in the traditional demonizing of the dhimmis, even if some observers, unaware of the various aspects of the dhimmi condition, maintain that it stems from Western ideology. Thus not only pronouncements by political and religious leaders but also modern literature and the collective behavior of the masses all point to the survival of the dhimmi archetype. It took on concrete shape against Israel, its avatar, or against the still-existing Jewish communities within the Oriental Diaspora.

Obviously neither the average Muslim nor the popular consciousness understand the archetype and the dhimmi condition as clear concepts. Carried in the ebb and flow of history from the collective unconscious to a political formulation, they appear at many levels—in proverbs and popular speech, in literature and jurisprudence, in customs, tradition, collective psychosis, and political ideology. A critical reflection on the national rights of dhimmi peoples would consequently imply not only a complete reversal of contemporary Arab values but also a reinterpretation of Arab imperialism along universalist values and not, as heretofore, in terms of an Arab epic. Sociocultural conditioning and the lack of freedom of speech are only two of the many reasons why such a reevaluation—which would amount to nothing more than an acknowledgment of the human and political rights of the *other*—has never been undertaken by the Arab intelligentsia. Instead, the latter attempts to update traditional modes of thinking so as to adapt them to changing historical circumstances. With regard to the submissive and sometimes servile behavior of dhimmi communities—resulting from unconcealed threats, discrimination and insecurity—it stems from their dual role as scapegoats and hostages. To this should be added the almost total destruction of their national identity. Today, as in the past, "tolerance" is granted to victims only if they accept their inferior status. Complications arise should they reject this role, refuse to play the game, and, breaking the chains of moral alienation, claim emancipation and liberty. In the case of the Jews, the psychosis at the core of the Arab-Israeli conflict is precisely the traumatism caused by the desynchronization between the millenary archetype of the Jew and the claims of the Israeli liberating his homeland from Arab-Muslim domination.

Numerous books on the racial persecution of Jews, blacks, and Arabs within Western societies reveal the harmful effects of caricatural archetypes on the collective consciousness. It has been shown that a modification of the relations between oppressors and oppressed—whether through emancipation, assimilation, or, as in the case of the colonized Arabs, national liberation—does not necessarily dispel the demonological archetypes attached to the discriminated groups. On the contrary, the emancipation of dehumanized collectivities gives rise to new forms of morbid, collective psychoses. In fact, the more the reality is different from the traditional image, the more emphasis will be laid on the stereotype in order to bridge the traumatizing gap between phantasm and reality. Hence, the more the Israelis differs from the archetype of the dhimmi Jews, the more hideous becomes their caricature and the more violent and bloody are the oppressors' attempts to adjust reality to the phantasm. Arab societies being no different in this respect to European, Arab attitudes towards their colonized peoples (the dhimmis) are hardly different from those of other colonizing powers in analogous situations. The only really different element is that of time. The longer and more reassuring the implantation, the fiercer becomes the hatred against the rebellious victim, and conversely the louder are the victim's cries for justice and right.

These general principles appear at two levels in the Arab-Israeli conflict. First, they influence collectively Arab attitudes toward Zionism and toward the remaining Jewish communities in the Arab world. Second, and on a far more traumatic level, they explain the relationship of the Palestinian Arabs to Zionism. Whereas in the Diaspora the relationship of the Jews to their environment is that of a religious minority, in the land of Israel it is determined by four thousand years of history and is, and always will be, that of a people despoiled of its national territory. And this is true whatever the demographic asymmetry resulting from oppression. The discrimination against Jews was greater in Palestine than anywhere else because of a political dimension— territorial usurpation. The special relationship between Palestine and the Jewish people motivated a persecution that was crueler there than elsewhere. Never was a nation so systematically humiliated and destroyed in its national expression (demography, history, language, and culture) than was the Jewish remnant in its own homeland. The conquerors' goal being to impose *their* sovereignty and values eternally over the country, the land of Israel was thus rendered *judenrein* (the use of this anachronism is justified, as the policy preceded the invention of the word).

The reason for such a policy is that the Arabs had no doubts about their imperialist mission, in which they gloried. The Qur'an, as they are well aware, makes frequent mention of both the land of Israel and its people, and Muslim chronicles and other sources have made the Arabs familiar with the history and progress of the conquest. They also know that the only town they founded during thirteen centuries in Palestine was Ramla and that the towns, land, and cultivated areas that they appropriated belonged to others. They are also aware—from the Qur'an Arab legends, and the *hadith* (opinions attributed to the Prophet)—that the Jews would one day return to their ancestral homeland. The persecution of the Jews of Palestine helped consolidate Arab foreign penetration, forcing Israel to wander in exile for thirteen centuries. In modern times, however, an ever-changing situation worked against the occupant under whose rule the country had become a desert, supporting only 10 percent of its former population. The weakness of the Turkish government allowed European countries to protect the non-Muslims of the Ottoman empire from the persecutions and massacres that had been their lot as dhimmis.

Development of the press as well as modern means of communication and transportation enabled Zionism to emerge into a coherent, worldwide movement of national liberation. Modern technology compensated for numerical inferiority. The times had changed: the small regional waves of returning Jews—previously neutralized by the persecution, expulsion and massacre that awaited survivors reaching Palestine—grew into a movement of mass emigration that was to result finally in the establishment of an independent Jewish state.

This historic context explains the traumatic effect that the progress of Zionism had on the Arab consciousness. On the level of the collective image, the behavior of European Jews was at variance with the classic archetype of the dhimmis (the Oriental Jews or Christians), whose dehumanization confirmed and justified feeling of superiority and domination of the Muslim community (*umma*). The rise of the dhimmi to equality with their oppressors was considered by the latter as a degrading humiliation, reducing them to the level of their former victims whom they had regarded as a social outcast for twelve centuries, to be tolerated only as long as they were useful. Politically, the rebellion of the dhimmis came as a tremendous shock to the Arab political consciousness, throwing into question the legitimacy of Arab sovereignty over territories conquered by jihad and threatening to undermine the foundations of Arab nationalism's ideology. For this ideology—in which "nationalism" has a meaning so ambiguous as to be almost contrary to the European sense of the term—is to create an Arab empire on the model of the Arab-Islamic empire, an empire that was only able to expand by jihad, by territorial usurpation outside Arabia and by the political and spiritual oppression of indigenous populations, reduced to the dhimmi status.

Consequently, contemporary Arab nationalism as the heir to territorial spoils of jihad and the guardian of its values has recast the dhimmi archetype in modern form. It has answered any expression of non-Arab nationalism by eliminating the few pockets of resistance that for thirteen centuries have withstood one of the longest and most alienating oppressions in history. Oriental Christendom, more directly threatened by the dhimmi archetype than Israel, has recently discovered what a Herculean task it is to secularize Arab nationalism. This much is evident from the conflict in Lebanon. There it was the PLO that, as the spearhead of Arab nationalism, massacred the Maronites in the name of Arabism. As the PLO considers itself the vanguard of Arabism, it conceives its mission as a struggle against all non-Arab and non-Muslim liberation movements in the Middle East. Christians of Lebanon (ancient Phoenicia) and Jews of Israel, who for centuries had shared the common bond of dhimmi existence, thus came to renew their historic ties.

The religious implications of an ideology that retrieves the values of the past are evident: the revolt of the dhimmis contests the divine will expressed in jihad-inspired conquests. The result entails metaphysical chaos and the rule of Satan. Israel is an "inexpiable sin" by its very existence, an apocalyptic sacrilege. The demographic concentration of dhimmis accentuates their demonological characteristics. These project on the dhimmi state, as on a "gigantic mirror," the horrific features of the dhimmi archetype. Israel, the symbol of the dhimmi state—half of whose population is composed of descendants of dhimmis—is the reflection of the dhimmi status. Israel is made the scapegoat responsible for every evil that afflicts the Arab world—as well as other regions—and is defamed in international forums. In fact, Israel symbolizes the isolation, the hatred, and the contempt that formerly crushed the dhimmi communities. Arab ideas about the dhimmis and their destiny are found underlying Arab (particularly Palestinian Arab) writing on Israel, even the most sophisticated.[6]

It is scarcely surprising, therefore, that all these various elements are heightened in the consciousness of the Palestinian Arabs, who are directly concerned by the territorial aspect of the conflict. That a land Arabized by jihad should have been lost to a dhimmi people by the beneficiaries of the dhimmi condition during thirteen centuries is considered a catastrophe of cosmic dimensions. For the Arabs to have to live now under the law of Israel when for thirteen centuries the opposite had been the case can only be a sin against Allah. The Palestinian Charter shows a total commitment to the ideology and the conquests of jihad: "Palestine is the homeland of the Arab Palestinian people; it is an indivisible part of the Arab homeland, and the Palestinian people is an integral part of the Arab nation" (art. 1). Such a claim necessarily denies the national sovereignty of the Jewish people. Thus "claims of historical and religious ties of Jews with Palestine are incompatible with the facts of history and the true conception of what constitutes statehood" (art. 20).[7]

The ideas of uncleanness and impurity associated with the dhimmis are transposed to the Israelis. The Israeli presence on the esplanade of Solomon's Temple in Jerusalem or at the tombs of the Hebrew patriarchs in Hebron offends the Islamic mind; for the Jewish dhimmi religion is encroaching on the privileges of the "superior" Muslim religion. In a UNESCO declaration, PLO representative Ibrahim Souss [who later became Arafat's brother-in-law] stated that the Israelis were desecrating the sanctity of the mosques in those places.[8] Nostalgia for former times, when death punished dhimmi entering the precincts of sacred Muslim shrines? The PLO spokesman did not limit himself to this religious observation but declared that the Israeli (hence Jewish) presence was defiling the whole of Palestine. The link with tradition and with the archetype is unmistakable: it was this religious idea of impurity that prompted the expulsion of the Jewish and Christian Arab tribes in the seventh century from the pure soil of Arabia. To this day, no church or synagogue is permitted to "defile" it.

The *Jerusalem Post* carried a report that a group of Arab villagers in Israel, rejoicing at a wedding celebration, had been heard chanting, "The Arabs will soon be cutting the throats of the Jews." The words "Arabs" and "Jews"—these simple villagers were ignorant of the niceties of propaganda—express that visceral connection with times past, when the law was Arab and the dhimmis were animals to be stripped and slaughtered. Every available weapon, from burning trees and fields[9] to expulsion and massacre, from terrorism to corruption at the United Nations in order to obtain votes, all these tactics of jihad have been and are still used to further its strategy against the rebellious dhimmis.

Researchers have demonstrated how the successful liberation of a colonized people may traumatize their colonizers. The impotent rage of the oppressors at the victims' revolt is expressed through hatred, revenge, and a desire to exterminate—that is, commit politicide, in the case of a state. The attainment of equal rights by a dehumanized group *humiliates* the dominant group, which, deprived of its superiority, seeks compensation through bloody phantasms. The mechanism has been closely analyzed in the literature dealing with racist phenomena.

Arab leaders officially distinguish between Judaism—the tolerated religion of a dhimmi people—and Zionism, the national liberation movement of the same people in rebellion against Arab-Islamic domination on its land. Whereas Jews are tolerated if they submit to the system, Zionists deserve death. This theological and political conception justifies PLO-inspired terrorism: Israelis and Zionists are fought by jihad in accordance with its sanctions against the enemies of Islam or any subject people in rebellion. This policy is not new; it was applicable whenever possible.

For example, during the nineteenth and twentieth centuries the Ottoman government strove to crush the national revivals of its subject peoples by carrying out wholesale massacres of Christian Greeks, Serbs, Romanians, Bulgarians, Maronites, and Armenians; on the other hand, it took measures—often inadequate—to protect these same peoples, scattered throughout the empire, where they were resigned to their traditional status.

This demonstrates that anti-Zionism in the Arab-Islamic geopolitical context is, in many respects, different from European antisemitism. It also explains the motivation behind the various campaigns launched by some Arab leaders, especially the PLO—and by the Ayatollah Khomeini—to win over Jews. Such attitudes, deliberately aimed at isolating and weakening the State of Israel, are nothing but political tactics that the laws of jihad allow. Thus Jews are to be used in fighting against their own national interest. History provides many examples of alienated members of a religious or national group being manipulated by the dominant power. Christian Arab nationalists are themselves a vivid illustration of this phenomenon. If it is true that the destruction of racist myths is a necessary precondition for establishing a better world, by the same token it must follow that the elimination of the dhimmi archetype is a precondition for true peace in the Middle East. Such a precondition would imply a recognition of the link, depicted in history and the Qur'an, between the Hebrew people and the land of Israel—as well as the right to national sovereignty of the Jewish people in its own land. For the Arabs it would imply an acceptance that the gains of jihad are reversible, that the holy war is not a divinely infallible decree but has a terrestrial dimension common to all imperialistic exploits and that decolonization is a universal process applicable to Arabs also. Pernicious myths that are not denounced will continue to determine the collective behavior of peoples and consequently the fate of the world, in spite of the seductive ideological dress in which they may masquerade.

Seen in the perspective of history, the destiny of the Jews as dhimmis has specific meaning as a special testimony, since Israel's struggle is none other than a fight to destroy a dhimmi archetype that has bewitched the Arab consciousness with a destructive and nostalgic dream of hegemony, irreconcilable with principles of decolonization or with the rights and liberties of peoples. This context gives the peace initiative of President Sadat, supported by the Egyptian people, a revolutionary significance, in contrast to the reactionary position of the PLO-led Arab Rejection Front. Not only has it thrown off the weight of the past, but it has also created new realities, new trends of thought. It has abolished the asymmetric relationship between a dominant Arab-Muslim people and the Jews, thereby opening the road to a future of peace and mutual esteem among all the peoples of the Middle East. One can only hope that, in spite of considerable obstacles, this courageous policy will triumph over that of the reactionary opposition.

NOTES

1. The term *dhimmi* designates the "People of the Book" (*ahl al-kitab*): Jews, Christians, and Zoroastrians, whose lands were Islamized by the conquering Arabs. They were obliged to pay to the Islamic community (*umma*) an annual poll tax (*jizya*) symbolizing the repurchase of their lives. The word *dhimma* applied to the relationship or covenant between the dominant Muslim power and the subject peoples.

2. Quoted in *France Soir*, February 13, 1979.

3. *Dar al-Islam* means "House of Islam"—the regions under Muslim rule.

4. Out of nearly one million Jews who lived in Arab countries in 1948, just over thirty thousand remained in 1978: twenty thousand in Morocco; five thousand in Tunisia; and forty-five hundred in Syria. Two-thirds of these Jewish refugees represent today, with their children, 41 percent of Israel's Jewish population (about 1.3 million).

5. Harvey E. Goldberg, "Rites and Riots. The Tripolitanian Pogrom of 1945," *Plural Societies* (The Hague) 8, no. 1 (Spring 1977): 35–56.

6. See Yehoshafat Harkabi, *Arab Attitudes to Israel* (Jerusalem: Keter/Israel Universities Press, 1971); D. F. Green, ed., *Arab Theologians on Jews and Israel*, extracts from the proceedings of the Fourth Conference of the Academy of Islamic Research, 1968, 3rd ed. (Geneva: Editions de l'Avenir, 1976); S. Abraham [Shmuel Moreh], "The Jew and the Israeli in Modern Arabic Literature," *Jerusalem Quarterly*, no. 2 (Winter 1977): 119–36.

7. Quoted in Yehoshafat Harkabi, *Palestinians and Israel* (Jerusalem: Keter, 1974), pp. 51, 63.

8. *Le Monde*, April 2, 1976.

9. Martin Gilbert, *The Arab-Israeli Conflict: Its History in Maps* (London: Weidenfeld and Nicolson, 1974), pp. 20–22. In the year 1936 alone, tens of thousands of trees belonging to Jews were destroyed by Arabs under order from the mufti of Jerusalem, Hajj Amin al-Husseini, who collaborated with Hitler during World War II.

11. EURO-ARAB ANTI-ZIONISM

Bat Ye'or

Peace in the Middle East implies the peace of religions. We will try to clarify here the pathways from Judeophobia to anti-Zionism in Christianity and Islam, respectively, and their convergence and fusion on the theological and political levels. This analysis will require a study of past and current zones of confrontation, including brief retrospective surveys of theological and historical developments.

It must be emphasized that the anti-Zionist policies analyzed here do not represent the full range of European and Eastern Christian opinion. Anti-Zionist attitudes are contested and in some quarters strongly opposed. Nevertheless they still shape the anti-Israel policy that has prevailed in postwar Europe. The obsessive pathological denigration of the Jewish state, officially or secretly encouraged by governments and religious institutions, has conditioned reticent public opinion. Like the antisemitism of past centuries, anti-Zionism is now integrated into the European mindset and fulfills an essential function in Europe's international politics. Modifications in Judaism and the emergence of a sovereign Jewish state have led to the transfer of theological Judeophobia to the political sphere of state anti-Zionism.

Text written in 1998, two years before the courageous pilgrimage of Pope John Paul II in Israel. His moving presence at Yad Vashem and the Temple Wall is a symbol of friendship, reconciliation, and peace between the two religions. This analysis was originally published as "L'Antisionisme Euro-Arabe," chap. 1 in *[Nouveaux] visages de l'antisémitisme: Haine-passion ou haine historique?* (Paris: NM7 éditions, 2001), pp. 23–70. This version, adapted by the author, was translated by Nidra Poller.

THE HISTORICAL CONTEXT

The name *Palestine* does not belong exclusively to Arab Muslim-Christianity. The Roman conquerors of Judea (*Judaea Capta*, in 70 CE) coined the name in 135 to designate the Jewish province of their empire. In Byzantine Palestine, torn by intra-Christian conflicts, Jewish demography remained important, especially in Galilee, despite persecution by monks starting in the fourth century. A juridical corpus, the *Jerusalem Talmud,* was composed during this period. Hadrian's edict (135) prohibiting Jewish presence in Jerusalem did not apply to the rest of Palestine, and, in fact, the prohibition had gradually lost its force until it was recuperated and applied with great severity in fourth-century Christianized Palestine. Christian persecution of Palestinian Jews was stimulated in the fifth and sixth century by the anti-Jewish laws of emperors Theodosius II and Justinian, inspired by the Church Fathers. In the seventh century, Jewish depopulation was aggravated by the insecurity and expropriation resulting from Arab clans emigrating from Arabia and settling in the countries conquered by jihad. The devastation of the Arab conquests, attested by Christian and Muslim chroniclers, was not restricted to the Jews; Christians and other non-Muslim indigenous peoples were also victims in all the lands Islamized by jihad. Muslim chroniclers recorded the Arab tribal settlements in the colonized territories, including Palestine.[1] These irrefutable historical documents show that the Arab-Muslim Palestinians are definitely not the descendants of the Canaanites, Jebuzites, or Philistines. The Islamization of Palestine was achieved by land expropriation of native populations as prescribed by the injunctions of jihad and according to the regime of dhimmitude imposed in the Arab colonization of the Middle East and elsewhere.

THEOLOGICAL ASPECTS OF ANTI-ZIONISM

Christianity

Judea became the site of the most intense conflict between the burgeoning Church and Palestinian Judaism integrated into its ancestral homeland for more than a millennium. The alliance between the reigning political authority and the Church hardened the anti-Judaism of the Church Fathers, namely those from the Orient, into theory and jurisdiction. Saint Augustine (354–430), bishop of Hippo (Bona), stated the classic view of the Jewish people: a fallen deicidal people cursed by God, who rescinded the promise and condemned them to exile, wandering, and abjection. Because of its geographical localization, the Palestinian Church stood thereafter as the intransigent guardian and support of this condemnation, proclaiming itself the *Verus Israel* and rightful heir of the Jewish heritage. The replacement theology justified the exclusion of Jews from Jerusalem and their oppression in their own country. The suffering and destitution of the Jews *testified* to the election of the Church, the *true* Israel. The Palestinian Church, guardian of this belief, persecuted and humiliated the Jews in their homeland, while other dioceses implemented the same policy in the Diaspora.

The first massacre of the Jews (ca. 628) in the Byzantine Empire was decreed after the Persian wars by the emperor Heraclius, at the instigation of Sophronius, Patriarch of Jerusalem. Some years later, according to Christian sources, Sophronius entreated the Muslim conquerors to maintain the total exclusion of Jews from Jerusalem, based on the Christian theological principle of rejection.[2] Thus Christian Judeophobic policy was passed to Islam.

After the Arab conquest of Palestine (634–640) the Christians lost their privileged and dominant position. Palestinian Jews and Christians, expropriated by the jihad laws that applied throughout the *dar al-Islam,* endured the scourges of conquest and colonization by Bedouin tribes emigrating massively from Arabia to inhabit the Byzantine territories. Palestine was divided into provinces attached to different Syrian administrative towns, as it had been in the Byzantine period, losing its geographically circumscribed national unity, while Jerusalem lost the centrality it had in the Jewish kingdom. Insecurity prevailed in a country devastated by Bedouin migrations following the transhumance of their herds. In the course of time the dhimmis were reduced to a few agglomerations with prestigious biblical names, where they paid dearly for a precarious security.

Over the centuries, conscious of their role as guardians of the infamous Jewish status, Orthodox Christian and Roman Catholic clergy inflicted endless humiliations on Palestinian Jews, especially in Jerusalem. Invoking an imaginary *firman*, they legalized the murder of Jews who dared to pass in front of the Church of the Holy Sepulchre, a punishment maintained until the turn of the twentieth century. Various religious orders and the masses of Christian pilgrims, notably at Easter, exacerbated the latent popular fanaticism. Their hostile acts, aimed at persecuting the Jews in their own country, illustrated the election of the New Alliance and the abrogation of the Old, making the persecution of Israel in its homeland an act of piety. It is precisely this religious theory that explains the extreme Judeophobia characteristic of

Palestinian Christianity throughout history, which scandalized many Western Christians.

Islam

Quranic replacement dogma is formulated in approximately the same terms as Christianity's assertion to be the accomplishment of Judaism. Islam claims to precede the two biblical religions that it completes and corrects (sura 5:52). Islam, religion of God (sura 3:17), existed at the origin of Creation and the biblical characters, including Jesus, were Muslim prophets, preaching Islam. However, the Quranic and biblical notions of prophecy, revelation, election, and exegesis differ. The influence of the Church Fathers appears in the Quranic anti-Jewish polemic, which echoes the Judeophobic imprecations of John Chrysostomus and Saint Augustine's image of the Jewish peddler (sura 62:5).

These Islamic borrowings of Christian anti-Judaism and replacement theology mark important zones of convergence and fusion of Muslim-Christian anti-Zionism and Judeophobia. Christian condemnation of the Jews to exile and degradation is recuperated by the Islamic doctrine but incorporated into a different theological construction that associates Christians and Jews and includes all infidels in one and the same infamy.

JURISDICTION

Christianity: Jewish Statute

Discriminatory dispositions against the Jews, often couched in insulting terms, were introduced into civil law codes and juridical collections on the basis of council decisions and pressure exerted by bishops on the Byzantine emperors and subsequently on the royal authority. This is the origin of the Jewish statute applied with variations throughout Christendom, in the West as in the East, where it originated. Abolished in some European countries in the eighteenth and nineteenth centuries by secularization and modernization movements, the statute was reinstated by the Nazis (1933), the Italian fascists (1938), and the collaborationist Vichy government of France (1940).

Islam: Statute of Jews and Christians (Dhimmitude)

The ideology of jihad demands the implementation of Sharia (Islamic jurisdiction) in all lands taken from the infidels. Under Islamic law the Jews, who
were a minority within the conquered populations, had the same statute as the
Christians, whereas Zoroastrians and other pagan peoples were relegated to
inferior categories and more severely oppressed.

Reciprocal borrowings between Islam and Christianity were not limited
to the theological sphere. Caliphs and sultans governed multitudes of subject
peoples under a jurisdiction that, though based on interpretations of the
Qur'an and the Hadith,[3] had integrated pre-Islamic laws and customs of the
conquered countries into an Islamic structure. This system of governing vanquished peoples (dhimmis), which I call "dhimmitude," has determined the
demographic, religious, and ethnic modifications of lands occupied by jihad.
The term *dhimmitude* encompasses all aspects and complexities of this political system, which shaped Jewish and Christian civilizations of dhimmitude
over the centuries.

Some of the humiliating discriminatory dispositions imposed on Jewish
and Christian dhimmis are the same as those imposed on Jews in Christendom: obligatory segregation; exclusion from all honorific and public positions giving authority over a Muslim; and prohibition against owning land,
acting as a witness, and building places of worship, to name a few examples.
The reciprocity of borrowings is obvious: distinctive signs, hats, and badges
imposed on the Jews by the Fourth Latran Council in 1215 were directly
inspired by Islamic codes going back to the eighth century, which obliged
Jewish and Christian dhimmis to wear distinctive discriminatory clothing
and colors. European Jews in the late Middle Ages had to wear ostensible
signs reminiscent of discrimination much more perverse and severe that was
imposed on non-Muslims throughout the Muslim empire from the eighth
century on.

The dhimmi status in Islam was shared by Jews and Christians, but the
latter perceived this equal treatment as a deliberate, supplementary humiliation imposed by Islam. That attitude contributed to the willful obfuscation of
the history of dhimmitude, that is, the same juridical and theological rules for
both Jews and Christians.

Dhimmitude does not only apply to relations between Islam and the
People of the Book (Jews and Christians); it also concerns relations between
Christians and Jews. Christian anti-Jewish doctrine and legislation are inte-
grated into dhimmitude. Thus the Arab-Israeli conflict is an exemplary case

of dhimmitude because it encompasses—albeit with dissimulation—a Judeo-Christian conflict. Interactions among these three monotheistic religions throughout the twentieth century and up to the present have remained within these traditional historical patterns, which constantly reproduce the same conflictive relations. It is important, therefore, to recognize the structures and mechanisms of these interactions if we are to master their noxiousness in the twenty-first century.

The Arab-Israeli conflict is but a small recent element in the vast geographic confrontation provoked and sustained for centuries by jihad ideology. Islam considers its relations with Jews and Christians from a theological and a political viewpoint. Theologically, they are assigned a legal status as tolerated but inferior tributary infidels (dhimmis or rayas) in their own country Islamized by jihad. The political aspect—linked to Zionism in the Jewish case—falls into the problematic of a dhimmi people that has liberated its country from the dhimmitude imposed by the laws of jihad. The political disposition in the case of rejection of dhimmitude, meaning refusal of the legal framework imposed on submissive infidels, remains the same for Jews and Christians.

Muslim countries are torn today by numerous conflicts involving different aspects of Islamist combat. Jihad strategies of territorial reconquest operate in Kashmir, the Philippines, Indonesia; in Sudan and elsewhere in Africa; on several fronts in Europe; and in Israel and Lebanon. Other Muslim countries, for example, Algeria, are ravaged by bloody politico-religious intra-Muslim wars. The Islamist concept of jihad against the infidels has filtered through to the general public in recent years. From Sudan to Afghanistan, from Gaza to Madrid and New York, from Egypt to Algeria, calls for jihad repeat the same themes inscribed in the same ideological structure. Such homogeneity cannot be improvised and cannot result from external circumstantial conditions. On the contrary, it is inherent to a historical constant based on juridical, ideological, and cultural foundations.

ANTI-ZIONISM

Anti-Zionism refers to the strategy aimed at the elimination of the State of Israel. This strategy uses various techniques: military warfare, local and international terrorism, delegitimization through a defamatory campaign with strong media support, and usurpation of Israel's history.

Though anti-Zionism is composed of two currents, Muslim and Christian, the latter is not easily identifiable because it hides behind the Islamic movement that it guides and enriches with traditional Christian anti-Judaism.

The Islamic Current

Islamic anti-Zionism is rooted in the politico-religious concept of jihad, which proscribes all non-Islamic political authority. It grants in theory peace and security to the People of the Book (Jews and Christians) in exchange for their territory and solely on condition of their submission to dhimmitude. This is the base of the Muslim peace with non-Muslims. The war against Israel is a war against dhimmis who rebelled, a war to restore the supremacy of Islamic law. Muslim countries that repudiated these outdated concepts and made a commitment to modernity, such as Turkey or the shah's Iran, have had good relations with Israel. In the nineteenth century, Ottoman Turkey was forced by the European powers to recognize the autonomy and independence of its former Euro-Christian provinces. It integrated into its empire, notably in Armenia, Palestine, and Syria, millions of Muslim refugees chased out of the new central European Christian states, liberated from centuries of dhimmitude after bloody wars.

Muslim anti-Zionism denies all national features of the Israeli people—language, history, civilization—recognizing only the religious rights of dhimmis, as it does with other Christian ethnic groups. This ambiguity between war and tolerance has misled many analysts who are unaware of the jihad and dhimmitude context.

The Muslim-Christian Current

Islamized Christianity, a historical current that has been active since the origins of Islam, was a fundamental force throughout the history of Islamic conquests and their hold over subjected Christian peoples. This current, which encompasses intra-Christian rivalries and conflicts, led to the political and military collusion and collaboration of some Christian religious hierarchies. It appeared in a syncretic religious form when countless Eastern Christian and European monks were Islamized in the course of invasions and wars. We will examine it here only in its modern anti-Zionist expression, forged in the Holy Land by religious missions polarized by the theological and political rivalries of European powers. However, it is also a potent anti-Christian and pro-Islamic movement instrumentalized by jihadist policies.

The Palestinian Context

European policies toward Palestine that were forged in the nineteenth century held the Jewish people both hostage and victim to a genocidal war in the twentieth century. These policies were articulated around the geostrategic and economic rivalries of European powers with the Ottoman Empire, and they were envenomed by divergent theological and eschatological Christian visions of the Holy Land and the Jewish people.

Since Napoleon Bonaparte's Egyptian expedition, France had dreamed of lording over a great Arab empire in the Levant. To this end France tried to reinforce the power of Muhammad Ali, Egyptian pasha and vassal of the Turks. In 1829, planning to unite the three regencies of Tripoli, Tunis, and Algiers with Egypt, France encouraged its protégé Muhammad Ali to conquer Syria, Palestine, and Mesopotamia. In 1832, Ibrahim Pasha was able to undermine the power of the local chiefs and place Syria, Lebanon, and Palestine under the government of the Egyptian pasha. As protector of Vatican religious interests, France was authorized to develop a network of Catholic institutions there. This was the beginning of a grand Franco-Egyptian strategy to ensure French and Catholic predominance in the Mediterranean. Publications praised the splendid virtues of the Arabs and the incalculable benefits expected from close collaboration with them.[4] But the fiscal exactions and cruelty of Ibrahim Pasha in Syria provoked Druze and Maronite rebellions. The British government rushed to help the insurgents with English advisers, money, and arms, determined to counter the expansion of French ambitions in the Arab Ottoman provinces, which, combined with the increasing influence of the Holy See, endangered strategic British interests.

Theological Conflicts

The breakup of the Ottoman Empire opened Palestine to political and religious competition among the three dominant Christian currents: Catholic, Protestant, and Orthodox. All three developed missionary activity directed at Jewish and Christian rayas (dhimmis) and obtained political and financial support from governments to intensify programs of pilgrimage, construction and restoration of churches and monasteries, and, from 1836 on, to foster the Christian population of Jerusalem and the Holy Land by land acquisition. Under French diplomatic protection the Holy See broadened its implantation in the Orient by way of Uniatism, profiting from substantial subsidies for the Uniate raya churches. This attachment of the raya churches to Rome incited the sultan to issue a *firman* in 1834 prohibiting passage from one Christian communion to another. Contributions for the holy sites flowed into Palestine from Catholics everywhere while Russia, concerned by the Uniate movement that transferred Orthodox rayas from Russian tutelage to that of France and the Holy See, reinforced its religious and political implantation.

This policy of re-Christianization of the Holy Land by two rival Christian currents conflicted with certain Protestant notions favoring the restoration of Israel in its heritage as a prelude to its millenarian conversion. Thus, three opposing projects divided Christianity: the Russian Orthodox worked through the Orthodox rayas; the Roman Catholics, hiding behind Arabism, used the Catholic rayas to infiltrate and extend the influence of France and the Holy See; and the millenarian Protestant movement envisaged the return of the Jews to their homeland and pursued its own penetration in the Holy Land. A fundamental debate in Christian teaching about the Jewish people—deicide or chosen people—was being played out in the Palestinian context of dhimmitude.

In the 1830s, under the impetus of Lord Shaftesbury, the Protestant current strove to grant British consular protection to Palestinian Jews, thereby providing them security from Muslim and Christian fanaticism. This protection widened the British zone of influence and introduced a Protestant presence in the Holy Land, where a French religious protectorate had dominated since 1535. In 1838 the British obtained authorization from the Ottoman sultan to open the first vice consulate in Jerusalem, with responsibilities extended throughout Palestine. The British authority used biblical history as a basis for mapping the limits of the Palestinian territory at a time when it didn't exist on maps and when its districts were administratively attached to separate provincial capitals. As the only country with a consulate in Jerusalem at that time, Great Britain also obtained authorization from the sultan to build a large Protestant church, Christ Church, near the Citadel and the Armenian Quarter.

This encroachment of Anglo-Saxon and Prussian Protestantism troubled the French, who had exercised an exclusive protectorate of the Christian sanctuaries since the seventeenth century (through the *firman* of 1620, confirmed in 1740). French influence in the Ottoman Empire was further reinforced by support for the papal politics of Uniatism that assembled raya churches under the wing of the Holy See. Paris and ultramontane circles opposed British penetration in the Holy Land, which competed with France's closely connected religious and economic interests and its ambitions for political expansion. The ultramontanes detected a double danger looming behind the Protestant advance, because the British did not hide their intentions to protect the Jews and favor their restoration. This Jewish return to the homeland contradicted the doctrine of the fallen deicide people condemned to expiate the crucifixion by wandering and exile. On the political level, the emergence of a Jewish state threatened French prestige and expansionism in the Holy Land.

The French supported the claims to Syria and Palestine of their ally Muhammad Ali, using him to instrument their Arab policy and oppose the proto-Zionist British Protestant penetration. The implantation of numerous Roman Catholic missionary institutions under French protection in the Levant united native Catholic and Uniate Christians under French patronage, favoring France's political and religious influence in the region. A tug-of-war between London and Paris for the control of Syria and the holy sites ensued. Beyond the French-English strategic and economic rivalries, two fundamentally opposed theological conceptions collided: the French-Catholic notion of the Jewish deicidal people and the Protestant restorationist view. Meanwhile, populations revolted against the excesses of Egyptian oppression. In Crete the Egyptian governors, backed by French officers, terrorized Christians and Turks, threatening them with a general massacre.[5] In Syria the whole Lebanese mountainous region rose up against Ibrahim; the Maronites, who had been allies of France for centuries, rallied to the British, who promised the restoration of Israel in the Holy Land and a Christian state in Lebanon— both opposed by Paris. France's position was seriously compromised.

Political Conflicts

It was in this context, where the political and religious interests of the great powers tangled and conflicted in the Levantine region and especially in Palestine, that the alleged assassination of Father Thomas, a Capuchin monk under French protection, and his servant Ibrahim Amara provoked a grave crisis. In February 1840 the French consul in Damascus, Count Benoît Ulysse-Laurent-François Ratti-Menton, and the Egyptian governor, Sherif Pasha, accused the Jewish community of Damascus of blood libel. Crowds of Christians and Muslims, stirred up by ecclesiastics from the highest hierarchical level of all the communities, called for the massacre of the Jews and the plunder of their belongings.[6] The Father Thomas blood libel broke out at a time when hard bargaining divided the Quadruple Alliance (Great Britain, Prussia, Russia, and Austria), led by the British, who were determined to expel Muhammad Ali from Syria and Palestine. France, excluded from the alliance, would be isolated and cornered if it persisted in backing the pasha and would have to fight alone against the European powers. French prestige was tarnished. Great Britain had shattered the dream of a French Arab empire extending from Algeria to Alexandretta (Turkey). The Egyptian pasha was ordered to restitute to the sultan Crete and the Syrian provinces, where even the Maronites had abandoned France. Moreover, Austria and the Protestant countries condemned the barbaric behavior of the French consul in Damascus. In Europe, Catholic and especially Protestant theologians revolted against the accusations of blood libel and the torture inflicted on the Jewish martyrs of Damascus.

In France, the Thiers government gave full support to its consul, while ultramontane and government newspapers exploited the affair with a continuous campaign demonizing Judaism. Throughout Europe books, commentaries, and articles related with sadistic details the alleged ritual crimes of Christian victims attributed to the Jews. Ratti-Menton became a national hero invested with the sacred mission of revealing to Christians and Muslims, united in their horror of Judaism, the satanic actions of the Jews and their hatred of Christians. Alone in the face of the occult corrupting forces of "international Jewry" he defended the prestige and glory of France and Catholicism.

This demonization of the Jews by the French government spread in a European political context that strongly opposed Jewish emancipation, while serving the precise objectives of France's Arab policy. The struggle against Great Britain led to a close association of French ambitions with those of Muhammad Ali. The French consul—supported by the Egyptian governor of Syria, who was Muhammad Ali's son-in-law—proclaimed France's right to protect all the Catholics of the Ottoman Empire against the alleged crimes of Israel. This maneuver restored a tarnished French influence in the Orient and on the international scene. In Europe, the criminalization of the Jews strengthened all the currents hostile to their emancipation.

In the Orient, the French tactic of defaming Israel discredited the British vision of Jewish restoration in a Palestine that was escaping French control. Furthermore, it aimed at excluding the Jews from the edict of Gulkhane, promising the abolition of the dhimmi status, promulgated two months previously on November 2, 1839. Oriental patriarchs felted that emancipation should be granted only to the Christian rayas in the Ottoman Empire but not to the Jews. Both Orthodox and Catholic communities in the Holy Land protested against the abolition of the legal degradation of the Jews; invoking the accusation of deicide, they insisted that they alone were worthy of equality with the Muslims.

The accusations of murder in Damascus could not be substantiated, and the corpses of the alleged victims were never found, but France refused to reopen the trial as requested by Jewish delegates from France and Great Britain: Adolphe Crémieux, Sir Moses Montefiore, and Solomon Munk. The delegates cast doubt on the alleged assassinations and confessions extorted under torture and pressure, including the arrest of children, taken from their parents and jailed in a house. Those confessions of fabricated Jewish crimes were useful for the constitution of a political case against Jewish emancipation in Europe and as a means of countering the Protestant proto-Zionist movement in a context of French-British and Catholic-Protestant rivalries. These rivalries were pursued during the nineteenth and twentieth centuries throughout the Orient and especially in Palestine. When, by the subterfuge of foreign protections, Ottoman Christians were able to own land, they rejected the extension of these rights to the Jews who, as dhimmis, should not have the right to own land in Muslim countries. Humiliated by an emancipation granted also to the Jews, Levantine Christians exacerbated a Judeophobic climate by a defamatory press and frequent accusations of blood libel. The Zionist movement and the Balfour Declaration (1917) backed by Protestant Great Britain aggravated this trend.

France's hopes for a great Arab uprising against the Ottoman sultan failed in 1839 for lack of a unifying concept among ethnically diverse and mutually hostile populations. Missionaries rushed to the Levant to make up for this lack. From the 1840s, they undertook to teach and modernize the Arab language, which would be the centralizing pole of a future Arab nation that would separate the Arabophone provinces from Turkey. Thus the concept of the Arab nation was born in the French Catholic missions.

The "Damascus Affair" marked the beginning of French anti-Zionist strategy. It combined the political and economic interests of French imperialism in the Arab world with the exploitation of anti-Judaism. This policy promoted the Arabization of Eastern Christians in a perspective of Muslim-Christian rapprochement and political patronage. The Damascus Affair initiated a defamatory anti-Jewish tactic that was renewed by frequent accusations of blood libel, pursued in the Ottoman Empire as in Eastern Europe and Russia up to the period of World War I (Beilis affair, 1911–13). France, asserting its right of patronage of Catholicism in the Turkish Empire, united all the Levantine Catholics in its Arab anti-Zionist policy. This was the beginning of the polarization of Eastern Christianity, Arabized by the Catholic missions and enlisted in the combat against the Jews.

In the second half of the nineteenth century, migratory flows toward

Palestine included European colonists, Jews, Christians escaping from Muslim massacres in the Levant (1840–60), and Muslim emigrants from Egypt, Russian Crimea, the Christian Balkans, and French Algeria. European powers started acquiring large estates and fostered the Christianization of the Holy Land, where Christian demography had dropped to a minimum after a millennium of dhimmitude. The Holy See was able to reestablish the Latin Patriarchate in 1847 and strengthen its implantation in the Holy Land by purchasing land and creating a network of religious and educational foundations, encroaching by Uniatism on rival Orthodox ambitions.

Waves of Syro-Lebanese Christian immigrants in Palestine were followed, after World War I, by Armenian, Syriac, and Nestorian Christian refugees fleeing from Muslim massacres in Anatolia, Iraq, and Syria. Christianity in the Holy Land was, consequently, distinguished by its heterogeneity, unlike the other ethno-religious dhimmi groups rooted in their ancestral homeland: Assyrians, Copts, Armenians, Maronites, Greeks, Serbs, Bulgarians. This historical context explains the specific characteristics of Christians in Palestine.

FROM ANTI-JUDAISM TO ANTI-ZIONISM

Antisemitic passions were unleashed in Europe by the return of the Jews to their homeland, concomitant with the immigration of Levantine Christian refugees in Palestine. The essential themes that would determine the extermination of European Jews a century later were already manifest in the 1840s: the Jewish-Freemason conspiracy, allied with Anglo-Saxon Protestantism to reestablish the kingdom of Israel; the satanic essence of this kingdom; its war to destroy Christianity and the Church. These themes that present the Jews and Zionism as irreducible enemies of the Christians polarized the strategy of war waged on them by antisemitic parties in the nineteenth and twentieth centuries.

The progress of Zionism in Ottoman Palestine in the 1880s provoked hysterical propaganda and warnings of an imminent "Jewish peril" that threatened to engulf all of Christendom in unspeakable suffering and humiliation. At the turn of the century, religious and extreme right parties in France demanded the abolition of Republican laws, the confinement of Jews in ghettos, reestablishment of their traditional discriminatory statute, and the abolition of their civil and political rights. The Eastern Churches—especially in Palestine—associated closely with European antisemitic movements and integrated the mechanism of hatred that would lead to the Holocaust, serving as transmission and connections in the Euro-Arab war against the Jews.

In Europe, the anti-Zionist reaction developed in both theological and political strategy involving European interests in Muslim countries. France intended to keep the privileged position it had maintained for centuries as protector of the Christian holy sites in the Holy Land. After the first Zionist Congress in Basel in 1897, *The Protocols of the Elders of Zion* were fabricated and used in the joint Muslim-Christian anti-Zionist war. We will limit our study to the latter aspect here.

After the Balfour Declaration (1917) and especially after the recognition by the League of Nations of a Jewish national homeland in Palestine (1922), *The Protocols* became a success, particularly among Levantine Christians and Europeans. The themes of *The Protocols* were used in a racist perspective in Hitler's *Mein Kampf* and spread all over Europe, making the project of spoliation and extermination of the Jews an acceptable banality. Many studies have been devoted to political anti-Zionism in Europe in its numerous aspects. In the period of European colonization of the Middle East, anti-Zionism was a primordial factor in the Christian rapprochement with Islam by focusing Muslim hostility on Israel.

Christian immigration, apace with Jewish immigration in the Holy Land in the nineteenth century, furthered a policy of re-Christianization in a situation of European religious rivalries and Muslim persecution of Christians. The Christian immigration was sustained by political and financial means far beyond what the Jews could muster, drawn from competing European powers: France, the Holy See, the Austro-Hungarian Empire, and later Germany for the Protestants, and Russia and Greece for the Orthodox. In this context of Christian political and religious imperialism, Zionism was perceived as a danger that could not be fought by military means because the Jews were a civilian population dispersed in many different countries and protected by their respective governments. Consequently, the war against the Jews used different strategies, such as defamation, incitement to hatred, and calls for extermination that intensified as Zionism progressed in Palestine.

The anti-Jewish strategy spread over Europe and the Ottoman Empire, especially through religious channels, playing on political, racist, and religious registers. In Palestine itself, primary focus of Christian interest, European anti-Zionist propaganda could intervene only through local Christians. But the Christians were politically powerless, scattered, divided minorities detested by the Islamic environment. The only way European antisemites could defeat Zionism was by making alliances with the Muslims; Islam would thus become the savior of Catholicism and Orthodoxy, endangered by the return of the Jews to their homeland. It must be stressed that this policy was specific to Euro-Arab antisemitic movements; it was not shared by all European or Eastern Christians.

The religious heterogeneity of Christians in the Holy Land and the fragility of traumatized Christian refugees made them a privileged medium for intrigues and manipulation by foreign imperialists. By uniting Christians and Muslims in the war against the Jews, Arab nationalism compensated for fragmentation and centrifugal shifts in the churches. However, this policy was not unanimously accepted by Eastern Christians. Many opposed both antisemitism and national self-denial in the form of Arabization, imposed by the clergy and Western imperialists protecting their own religious and political interests. In the Holy Land, Christian advocates of Arabism found recruits among sympathizers in religious hierarchies, the civil service, Western Arabists, and intellectuals with strong ties to the Vatican and France.

Meanwhile, irrepressible Jewish immigration undermined the *judenrein* policy for the Holy Land that had been maintained by Christian and Muslim replacement theology for over a millennium. The Syro-Palestinian Christians, charged with the sacred historical mission of fighting the Jews, denounced Jewish immigrants and acquisition of land to the Turkish authorities, and they maintained a virulent Judephobic press campaign aimed at Muslims. Nevertheless, anti-Jewish discrimination in Palestine was subverted by European emancipation, Zionist funds, and Christian support. We can follow the exacerbation of antisemitism in the French press at the turn of the century in step with the growing assertion of Zionism. Though national factors such as the Dreyfus Affair also came into play, demands by antisemites before World War II for application of the Jewish statute and confiscation of Jewish property were intended also to neutralize Zionism.

Palestinian Christians, especially the clergy, poisoned the Muslim world with European antisemitism transmitted through their networks to all corners of the Levant. The Arab-fascist and Nazi movements that collaborated with the Axis forces developed within the Palestinian Christian communities; the extermination of European Jewry was the final solution for Zionism.

Christian attitudes in Palestine can be divided into an Arab phase, from 1922 to 1967, followed by a Palestinian phase, from 1967 to date. In the first phase, Christians were exclusively committed to Arabism, refusing all regional nationalisms, including Palestinian, which was claimed only by the Jews under the Mandate. The Palestinian phase initiated a search for identity built in opposition to Israel but modeled on Jewish identity and, consequently, drawing on Christian sources because Christianity, unlike Islam, adopted the Bible. By Christian mediation the Bible was confiscated from the Israelis and transferred to the Palestinians. Differences between these two phases are superficial; in both phases Arab Palestinians acknowledge that they belong to the Arab nation and claim legitimacy from historical precedence over Israel. We can thus distinguish three different but convergent currents in anti-Zionism:

- The *Arab-Islamic current* articulated within jihad ideology places Israelis with the countries of miscreants destined to disappear. This current is as much anti-Christian as anti-Jewish.
- The *Arab-Christian theological current* dissimulates traditional Oriental and European Judeophobia behind the Arab cause. The Christian contribution is revealed in political discourse structured to seduce Western opinion with various registers of Christian antisemitism screened by ideological disguises. More sophisticated Christological themes and the replacement theology that transfers Israel's historical heritage to the Arabs are easily identifiable. We have seen that the concept of an Arab nation was a French fabrication, reworked by religious establishments in the Levant. The Vatican's engagement in the Palestinian cause and its ties with the PLO are common knowledge.[7] The combat for Arab Palestine is simply the Christian mask of the war against Israel; the aims are the same, only the rhetoric is different.
- The *European political current* sustains, guides, and supports the Arab-Christian theological current both financially and politically. The serious doubts on Israel's legitimacy expressed by Charles de Gaulle at his November 27, 1967, press conference opened the way to French ideological and political support for the elimination of the Jewish state.[8]

RELIGIOUS ANTI-ZIONISM

The Christian concept of the Jews as a fallen deicidal people fuses theological anti-Judaism and political delegitimization of the State of Israel. Writing from Jerusalem in a letter dated January 25, 1919, and forwarded to British prime minister Lloyd George, Cardinal Bourne declared that Zionism "appears to be quite contrary to Christian sentiment . . . but that they [the Jews] should ever again dominate and rule the country would be an outrage against Christianity and its Divine Founder."[9] In the course of debate at the League of Nations on the modalities of the British Mandate for Palestine, Lord Balfour complained that "the extent of the campaign undertaken can scarcely have been realised in London." Lord Balfour added that one could, without exaggeration, attribute the hostility of countries like France, Poland, Spain, Italy, and Brazil to objections communicated to their governments by papal delegates.[10] In 1922 Gen. Ronald Storrs, military governor of Jerusalem, made a voyage to Rome at his own expense to reassure Pope Pius XI, who "had evidently been receiving alarmists reports as to the 'preponderating influence of Jews.'"[11]

In his analysis of *The Protocols*, Pierre-André Taguieff points out its clerical origins and anti-Zionist motivation.[12] The revised 1905 version of *The Protocols* claims to reproduce the "minutes" of the First Zionist Congress in 1897. The manuscript was written in French in Paris.

POLITICAL ANTI-ZIONISM

The symbiosis between Arab nationalism and *The Protocols* is revealed in *Le Réveil de la Nation Arabe* (The awakening of the Arab nation) by Syrian Negib Azoury, published in Paris in January 1905.[13] Azoury, a Catholic close to the Jesuits and former deputy of the Turkish governor of Jerusalem, lived in Paris at the turn of the century.

In his book, Azoury entreats the whole Christian and Muslim world to unite under the banner of France and the joint moral authorities of an Arab caliph and the Vatican to crush evil, meaning the future Jewish state. This imminent cosmic danger calls for an immediate alliance of Islam and Christianity, which can only operate through the mediation of Arabism. Since all the Churches of Christendom are dispersed throughout the Arab territories and, whatever their doctrinal differences, they are all represented within the Arab nation, it follows that Palestine contains this Christian totality in miniature. Consequently, Arabism is the link that assembles and unites the various branches of Christianity. Moreover, Arabism welds the alliance of Christendom with Islam within the Arab nation. This Arab nation, which represents the alliance of Islam and the whole of Christianity, is endowed with the sacred mission of protecting humanity from the "universal Jewish peril." What is this Jewish peril that threatens the world? It is Zionism, the return of the Jews to restore their independence in their homeland, including Jerusalem, thus annulling Jewish expiation for the crucifixion. Zionism is sacrilege and, as proclaimed in a widespread slogan of the period, it is the enemy of Christianity: "The Jews, that's the enemy!" was the slogan launched by Abbé Chabauty in 1882, taken up by Abbé Martinez in 1890, and by Abbé Hippolyte Gayraud in 1896, who declared, "I consider it axiomatic, theologically, historically, and canonically, that the Jew is the enemy."[14]

In his preface, Azoury points out that the Arab movement "comes to destroy Israel's project of universal domination just when it is so close to success." And he announces the publication of his second book, *Le Péril Juif Universel: Révélations et Études politiques* (The universal Jewish peril: Revelations and political studies), which completes the first. "With the aim of facilitating intelligence of the Jewish peril," he explains, "I will limit my study to the detailed geography of Palestine, which is an accomplished miniature of the future Arab empire." Azoury claims that *Le Réveil de la Nation Arabe* and *Le Péril Juif Universel* "will allow the reader to grasp the unique idea that we envisage in these two works." This idea is to prove the reality of a universal Jewish peril that endangers humanity and to propose the sole solution—an Arab movement uniting the joint combat of Christians and Muslims to destroy Israel.

In the foreword, Azoury claims to expose the universal nature of the Jewish peril from an entirely original new viewpoint. He says that he resigned from his post "to undertake a sacrosanct work of patriotism, justice, and humanity," and spent six years in Palestine studying this question. During the period of gestation of *Le Réveil de la Nation Arabe* and *Le Péril Juif Universel*, the author, living in Paris and Cairo, remained "intimately linked with our compatriots and in constant contact with the Jews," watching their "silent and pernicious efforts." In his calls for Muslim-Christian unity— under the joint spiritual authority of the pope and the caliph in an Arab nation under a French protectorate—Azoury proclaims himself the author of *Le Péril Juif Universel* and develops the themes of an anonymous pamphlet that would appear later that same year: *The Protocols of the Elders of Zion*.

The Christian tradition condemning the Jews to wandering, exile, and debasement, which remained unchanged until the Second Vatican Council (1962–1965), together with the Islamic doctrine of Jewish dhimmitude, sealed the Muslim-Christian anti-Zionist alliance.

It is important to study the anti-Jewish arguments that united Christians and Muslims because they determine political developments from the early twentieth century to the present day. In a letter addressed to General Storrs, military governor of Jerusalem, on March 23, 1919, the Palestinian Muslim-

Christian Association (MCA), Jerusalem Section, wrote, "One of the most important rules of the country is preventing the Jews from permanently settling in Palestine, but they are allowed to stay for a short period after which they are required to return from whence they came."[17]

This is the foundation of the religious policy of exclusion of Jews from Palestine that resulted in their expropriation and the sufferings of imposed exile. The MCA stated the following principles:

- The exile and dispersion of the Jewish people is required and must be maintained.
- Palestine belongs exclusively to Christians and Muslims who should inhabit and control it—the Jews don't belong there.
- The Jews have no religious relics or any other connection with Palestine and, consequently, no historical rights there.
- The Arabs lived in Palestine before the Jews.
- Arabic is the only recognized language—the use of Hebrew as official language is rejected, as is the use of biblical names of cities and provinces.
- The peril of a State of Israel is demonstrated by the numerous diabolical characteristics of the Jews, borrowed from European antisemitic press and literature.
- The Arabs are the creators of the sciences and civilization, and the Jews are the agents of evil and destruction.[18]

The Interwar Period

The MCA themes, constantly hammered in by the Euro-Arab current, combine the Christian views of replacement and deicide with the Muslim theological principles of jihad. The MCA statutes were drawn up on May 20, 1920, under British aegis, represented by Chief of Staff Col. B. H. Waters Taylor. In 1922 Storrs observed that Arabism was practically nonexistent "even when reinforced by the Vatican and by the relics of pan-Islam."[19] The British military and civil Administration reinforced the Arab Muslim-Christian camp: "Zionism had at least united (for the first time in history) the Arab Muslims and Christians, who now oppose a single front to the Mandatory."[20]

From the start, the association received financial and moral support from the British administration,[21] which was so violently antisemitic that Colonel Wedgwood, testifying in 1937 before the Peel Commission, described it as "an Administration of 'crypto-fascist bureaucrats,' whose objections to Parliament had taken the place of objections to the Jews."[22]

On the occasion of his visit to the seven basilicas of Rome on April 17, 1937, Msgr. Eugenio Pacelli, the future Pope Pius XII, declared, "Bow your head, my Christian brethren, before these sacred altars and remember that a crucified God intended to make us the Chosen People, and that He, destroying the only Temple which the ancient deicide people had been granted, revealed the infinity of his compassion by taking delight in being with us and among us."[23]

Even after World War II, *L'Osservatore Romano* could declare, concerning the foundation of the State of Israel, "Modern Zionism is not the true heir of biblical Israel, it is a secular state and for this reason the Holy Land and its sacred places belong to Christendom, the true Israel" (Vatican City, May 14, 1948).[24] An article published in *La Documentation Catholique* in Paris on July 17, 1949, stated that "[we] have now, after careful investigation, arrived at least at part of the truth, and we can only agree with a statement frequently heard that Zionism is Nazism in a new guise."[25]

EURO-ARAB ANTI-ZIONISM: THE PALESTINIAN CAUSE

Shortly after World War I, the mechanism of anti-Zionism in Muslim-Christian and Euro-Arab relations was set in motion with (1) Muslim-Christian rapprochement; (2) the alliance and cooperation of Euro-Arab antisemitic Nazi movements, notably in the extermination of the Jews during World War II; and (3) the deflection onto Israel of the hostility of Muslims colonized and humiliated by European powers.

A variety of factors are involved in the political operation of European anti-Zionism. Government anti-Zionist policies were tailored to the nation's economic and geostrategic interests in their Muslim colonies; these policies hardly differed from the nineteenth-century "Eastern Question," concerning Christian peoples of the Ottoman Empire. However, public opinion tried to temper government cynicism when it affected Christians and their churches but, with some exceptions, accepted Judeophobia with general consensus. Guilt feelings were aroused by the Armenian genocide (1915–17) that Europe could prevented and by the sacrifice of Armenia on the altar of Euro-Muslim entente. The situation evoked this bitter commentary from Ronald Storrs: "The supposed indignation of 'His Majesty's sixty million loyal Indian subjects,' who appeared alternatively under the journalese disguise of

'Moslem Susceptibilities,' delayed many reforms in the Near and Middle East, kept several million Orthodox Christians as '*Rayahs*' under Ottoman domination; and helped to paralyse intervention in the torture and massacre of countless innocent Armenians."[26]

In the first years of World War I, a Christian people was massacred by Muslims in the Turkish provinces of Anatolia, Iraq, Syria, and later in the Caucasus. They were not rescued by the countries of the Entente. Guilt toward the Armenians, particularly from Germans and Austrians, who were allies of the Turks, was poured on the Jews, who were instrumental in the United States in joining the war to defeat Germany. At the end of the war, a policy of appeasement of Muslims and Arabs blocked the emergence of a Christian Assyria and lent a deaf ear to Armenian voices. However, the League of Nations recognized the "Jewish national homeland," despite an unprecedented campaign of defamation and French efforts to have Palestine attached to Syria in their zone of attribution.

Historians have shed light on the sources and mechanisms of Judeo-phobia in the interwar period, a genocidal structure that led to the Holocaust. Irreducible opposition to the restoration of a Jewish state had filled the Judeophobic press and literature since the 1840s. The propagation of hatred conditioned public opinion for determined political purposes. Religious channels spread this hatred on an international level. Repeated calls for war on the Jews and their total extermination led inexorably to the Holocaust. Palestine was active in this war: Hajj Amin al-Husseini, president of the MCA and mufti of Jerusalem, encouraged the *farhud* (massacre) of the Jews of Baghdad (June 1–2, 1941), precipitated by allegations made by his Greek Orthodox Lebanese friend Georges Antonius, an advocate of Arabism. Al-Husseini fled Baghdad at the end of May and reached Berlin on November 6, 1941, where he and a number of his Palestinian Christian colleagues took refuge with the Nazis. In 1941 an Arab-Nazi military unit (*Deutsch-Ara-bische Lehrabteilung*), wearing Nazi uniforms, started operating in Greece, reinforced by Bosnian and Albanian Muslim volunteers recruited by al-Husseini. Muslims from the Caucasus were integrated into SS units and sent to Poland. At the end of 1944 the mufti assembled Palestinian Arabs for military training by the Nazis in Holland.[27] Hunted by the Allies in 1945 as a war criminal, al-Husseini took refuge in France under the protection of de Gaulle's government; the mufti claimed that de Gaulle intervened personally in his favor and encouraged his political activities.[28]

THE MODERN PERIOD

Even after the Holocaust and the restoration of the State of Israel, the anti-Zionist war was pursued in Europe in the 1960s by defamation, incitement to hatred, delegitimization, negationism, and, above all, by moral support for Palestinian terrorism. Although many Arab clergymen collaborated with this terrorism, other Christian intellectuals and theologians debated, denounced, and fought against these abuses.

The Second Vatican Council, or the Tactics of Ambiguity

The rapprochement with Judaism initiated by the Second Vatican Council provoked virulent opposition from Eastern Churches and Arab states. The latter went so far as to threaten the existence of local Christian communities, taking the Vatican and the process of Judeo-Christian reconciliation hostage and, further, interfering in theology and biblical exegesis to impose Islamic demands on Catholics. The *Nostra Aetate* (In Our Era) declaration provoked violent Arab demonstrations against Christians. However, Arab concerns proved to be unfounded because the Vatican compensated for this rapprochement with the Jews by faithfully supporting the PLO and intensifying the Catholic campaign against Israel. In this way the principle of the condemnation to wandering prevailed, and reconciliation with Judaism could accommodate the eventual disappearance of Israel. Moreover, the condemnation of antisemitism did not include complete rehabilitation of the Jews. This ambiguity facilitated the association of visceral hatred of Israel with compassion for the Jews, whose suffering testified to divine wrath as established in the conception of the "witness."

In the same way that the Jews were accused by antisemites of being the source of all evil, Israel was blamed for all Euro-Arab problems. The transition was abetted by the tireless activism of Palestinian and Arab Churches allied with the PLO and Western sister Churches in one and the same circuit of political indoctrination. The liberation of Jerusalem in 1967 exacerbated this trend. Over a period of three decades Western media, in different degrees, shaped anti-Israeli public opinion that reproduced, on the political level, the theological teachings of contempt. This constant attack was aggravated by the passage of United Nations Resolution 3379, assimilating Zionism with racism, by UNESCO in 1974 and in November 1975 by the General Assembly. It should be mentioned, however, that other, more positive positions were expressed in national episcopate declarations in France and other countries in 1974 and thereafter, while there was also significant progress on the level of liturgy, theology, and teaching.

We will outline here the most common Judeophobic anti-Zionist themes.

Political Themes

Europe as Protector of Palestine and the Muslims from Israel

Europe's attitude as the protector of Muslims against the rapacious Jews appeared simultaneously in French Algeria and Palestine toward the end of the nineteenth century. French colonists in Algeria, claiming that "Arabs [were] exploited, expropriated, impoverished" by the Jews, demanded the abolition of the Crémieux decree (1870) and the restoration of the Jewish statute, which is the Christian version of dhimmitude. "The antisemite presented himself as the Muslim's friend and teacher, his natural protector against the rapacious Israelite."[29] Geneviève Dermenjian notes: "The stamp of the anti-Jewish league showed a colonist and an Arab stepping on a Jew lying on the ground. It should be noted that the antisemites who made it their duty to protect 'Arabs against the Jews' and who had long reckoned on Arab antisemitism, wanted to associate Arabs with the Europeans in anti-Jewish engravings."[30]

The same structure was transferred to Palestine, where Arab Christians, the Vatican, and European antisemitic parties acted as self-proclaimed protectors of the Arabs against the Jews. After the Holocaust and decolonization, former Vichy collaborators and bureaucrats, ministers, and intellectuals stationed in Algeria slipped into the ministries under presidents de Gaulle, Giscard d'Estaing, and Mitterrand. The ideological Judeophobic arsenal was later recycled in the "Palestinian cause." Interlocking economic and strategic interests had nourished the Euro-Palestinian war to delegitimize Israel pursued over the past thirty years, with its postcolonial transfer of guilt feelings. The globalization of the Palestinian cause, conceived and developed in post-Holocaust Europe, followed the same religious, intellectual, political, and media channels as the internationalization of antisemitism in the interwar period. It shifted onto Israelis the hatred of Muslims colonized by Western European powers and the Soviet Union. Palestine was an opportunity for an absolving transfer, combined with neocolonialist economic development in Muslim countries. The Arab-Israeli conflict was maintained through political support for Palestinian radicalism, reinforcing European collaboration with the Arabs against the common enemy and procuring profitable military contracts. Some European anti-Zionist currents, disappointed by Israeli-Palestinian peace agreements, abandoned Arafat, considered too conciliatory, and turned their support to Hamas.

Inversion

We will cite just two out of the multiple inversion attitudes: (1) The exoneration of the persecutor by transfer of the crime to the victim; Nazism is projected onto Israel. The diabolization of Israel counterbalances revelations by historians of collusion among the Nazis, Arab nationalists, and the ecclesiastic networks that helped Nazis escape, notably to Arab countries. (2) The inversion of ignominious Palestinian dhimmitude into fair and just government; Israel is held guilty of liberating itself from this condition. In other words, Israel's dhimmitude in Palestine ratifies the criteria of justice.

Isolationist Strategy

Euro-Arab anti-Zionism isolated Israel and confined it in a political ghetto. Islamic theology actually associates Jews and Christians in numerous Quranic verses, hadiths, and legal dispositions of theologian-jurists; Christians, particularly Syrians, humiliated by being placed on the same level as Jews, rejected this common condition. Modern analysts claim that Quranic verses that mention Jews and Christians together refer to a Christian sect that disappeared back in the eighth century. But this argument is belied by a millennium of jihad against Christian countries, pursued long after the disappearance of this sect, and it is contradicted by the prevalence of Christian dhimmitude in some Muslim countries today.

Verses that mention friendship between Jews and Christians are also attributed to that extinct sect and interpreted as a reference to friendship of Christians with Christians and Jews with Jews, given that Jews and Christians cannot be friends with each other. The most virulent critics of my research on dhimmitude take me to task for studying Christian dhimmitude "in tandem" with Jewish dhimmitude—as if dhimmitude could be something other than a common, complementary condition of Jews and Christians. I am criticized for adulterating the images of churches in my book by placing them close to illustrations of synagogues. Thus principles of separation of Jews and Christians maintain division and hostility among the People of the Book, in accord with Islamic desiderata.

Christological Themes

Replacement

The theme of replacement, which has been strongly opposed by both secular Christians and theologians, was transferred to Palestinian Arabs, making them the heirs to biblical Israel. The State of Israel is stripped of its history and identity and treated as an impostor that has usurped a name and a land to which it has no rights: Zionism in Zion is labeled imperialism, and the Jews in Judea are called colonists.

In the same way that the Nazis Aryanized Jewish property, Israel's heritage is Palestinized. It should not be forgotten that up to the period of the Mandate, individual ownership of real estate in Palestine was prohibited under the rules of Islamic conquest, which designates land confiscated from conquered non-Muslim indigenous peoples as war booty (*fay*) that belongs to the caliph. Except for a few properties conceded by the sultan to European states in the nineteenth century or purchased under a regime of Capitulations, all the land in Palestine belonged to the Ottoman authority. With rare exceptions, neither the Arabs nor the non-Muslims in Palestine owned their land. Calling Israelis living in Judea "colonists," when the Arabs had extended their dominion to Africa, Asia, and Europe and the French had colonized the entire Maghreb, Syria, and Lebanon, not to mention lands in Africa, Asia, and the Americas, is cynical to an extreme.

The theme of delegitimization fits into the precedent: the transfer of Israel's historical heritage to the Palestinians, who replace the Jews, leads automatically to the delegitimization of the state of Israel. This replacement policy is the work of Christians, as illustrated by Palestinian recuperation of David's slingshot, the favorite replacement image of Western media, which does not figure in the Qur'an.

Demonization

The theme of demonization is expressed in various registers. Nonreligious Christians like Jacques Berque or Georges Corm project onto Israel the image of a deicide people of diabolic essence: Israel, being evil, is mentioned only in a negative way. The religious and political spheres are fused, and Israel is held responsible for discrimination against Christians in Muslim states and the latter's animosity against the West. In fact, this discrimination is inherent in the laws of jihad and Sharia, drafted starting in the eighth century, and Muslim hatred is a reaction to European colonization. The Arab-Israeli conflict is used to disguise a whole range of factors that explain Muslim-Christian contention, and Israel is held responsible for Islamic Christophobia. This strategy of incriminating the Jews for Muslim persecution of Christians and Christian persecution of Muslims, as occurred during the war in Lebanon, has been employed regularly throughout a millennium of dhimmitude. In our day it serves to spare European political interests that are tributary to Muslim-Christian anti-Zionism. The vital node of this Euro-Arab alliance is the myth of fraternal Muslim-Christian empathy that was destroyed by the State of Israel—a pious lie exposed by the widespread, albeit obscured, return of dhimmitude.

The Crucifixion

The thematic of a Muslim-Christian Palestine crucified by the deicidal Israelis was used as a means of pressure on the Second Vatican Council. The theme has been widely exploited for the past thirty years by Muslims and Christians, often conjointly even if the Christian hand is dissimulated under a Muslim signature. The Islamophile scholar Norman Daniel wrote that if there is any hope of a future for Islamo-Christian ecumenism, this is the direction it must take[31]—meaning that the Judeophobe concept of a deicide people is the sole grounds for Muslim-Christian rapprochement.

Perverse Symmetry

On the theological level, the principle of perverse symmetry is illustrated by the use of anti-Zionism, which contributes to Arab policies, as a counterforce to the Vatican's rapprochement with the Jews. This strategy presumes symmetry between Israelis and Palestinian Arabs with respect to Europe and Christianity. But no such symmetry exists. The theological reconciliation of the Church with Judaism emerged out of the context of the Holocaust and the theology of replacement and deicide; this unique situation, specific to Judeo-Christian relations, is effaced by the imposture of false symmetries. The Church proclaimed itself the new Israel, never the new Islam. The Holocaust was the response of European antisemitism to Zionism, which had been fiercely opposed by the Vatican and many Reform churches fervently militating for a Muslim-Christian Palestine. Worldwide propaganda for the Palestinian cause, which contrasts sharply with the consensus of silence that reigned during the Holocaust, illustrates the principle of replacement and consequent delegitimization of the State of Israel. The façade has been redecorated, but the dogmatic positions stood unchanged. The rehabilitation of Judaism served as a screen to hide the demonization of Israel. Christian love and compassion was poured on the fallen people, while Jewish national sovereignty was unstintingly opposed. Judeo-Christian rapprochement was being poisoned by the perverse principle of false symmetry between Israel and Palestine.

On the historical level, perverse symmetry wipes out thirteen centuries of Jewish dhimmitude in Palestine, placing Jewish victims and Arab oppressors on grounds of equality. Arab Palestinians, who claim membership in the Arab nation, call for the destruction of the State of Israel on its national territory, whereas the Israelis do not contest Arab independence in its historical homeland, Arabia, or in any of the vast countries Arabized by jihad. The perverse symmetry that equates totally opposite policies obscures Israel's specificity and subtly reinstates the concept of replacement.

The Palestinian Dodge

This strategy was articulated by the Lebanese Abbé Youakim Moubarac who declared, immediately following the Second Vatican Council, that the Christian conscience must "know that [henceforth] the Judeo-Christian dialogue, whatever the occasion, will always and essentially include a third party, the Muslim world."[32] This assigns Islam the role of referee in Judeo-Christian relations, as if the Vatican had to examine two thousand years of Christian Judeophobia through the Muslim-Palestinian prism. And the Palestinian cause, used by Christians to dodge a doctrinal reform of their relations with Jews, is enhanced with immense symbolic value. This Palestine-idolatry, vulgarized since the mid-1960s, rehabilitates anti-Judaism and hinders Judeo-Christian reconciliation. There is no equivalence between the Christian persecution of the Jews and the Palestinian cause other than the falsified equivalence used to justify keeping the Jews in dhimmitude by the negation of Jewish rights in their own country.

Arab Christians and European Guilt

Europe's guilt toward Arab Christians is freely expressed in anti-Zionist circles. Kenneth Cragg, a former Anglican deputy bishop of Jerusalem, imputed Muslim reprisals against Eastern Christians to European resistance against the jihad armies.[33] According to his reasoning Europe bears a heavy historical and moral responsibility for fighting against the invaders and conse-quently inviting the destruction of Eastern Christianity by Muslim powers.

Cragg deplores the lack of European guilt feelings; in fact this guilt is inferred from Christian reflection on anti-Judaism and the Holocaust. Cragg seems unaware that the Christians he abusively calls Arabs (Copts, Greeks, Armenians, Syriacs) were not always scattered powerless minorities; they were national majorities, they had armies. Their tragic fate, for which they are partially responsible, was a result of intra-Christian conflict and corrupt religious and political elites. There is no symmetry between these situations, however tragic they may be, and the belief of deicide with the ensuing legal and political consequences for Jewish minorities in the Christian Orient and Occident. Christian reflection on relations with Israel is situated on an alto-gether different theological and political plane from these false symmetries. Cragg blithely concocts a parallel between the history of jihad on three con-tinents, the history of Europe along the same paths, and the history of a recent Jewish settlement in Gush Emunim—or orthodox religious Jews in Judea! Apparently unafraid of appearing ridiculous, he gives equal weight to a mil-lennium of worldwide Islamic and Christian imperialism and a tiny political group in Israel.

In the same vein, the Latin patriarch of Jerusalem, Michel Sabbah, sug-gested that "just as Western Christians had had to repent for the treatment of Jews, so Jews would have to repent for their treatment of Palestinians."[34] In other words, the Jews should apologize for breaking the chains of dhimmi-tude imposed on them in their own land by Christians and Muslims.

DEMONIZATION OF ISRAEL AND TRANSFIGURATION OF PALESTINE

The above-mentioned mechanisms, and many other similar means developed by European and Arab Christian theologians, operate within a fixed theolog-ical system in which the Jews and Israel symbolize the essence and the empire of evil, an eternal evil enemy of the good and of justice, equated with Palestine. The Palestinians, incarnation of Jesus, crucified on the Cross, wearing the crown of thorns, stand in the face of this demonic principle embodied by the Zionist state or Zionism. This is why, insists Cragg, Pales-tinity bears an indissoluble essentiality—as evil is essential to Israel—that does not exist in any other nationalism in the world. This Palestinian essen-tiality lies in its eternal mission to denounce by its suffering the nature of evil, which is Israel. This denunciation should be tireless and endless so that evil will never be forgotten or ignored but always proclaimed, pilloried, unmasked in its true nature. Thus penetrating the heart it is integrated into the person who perceives it instinctively in its essentiality. "Evil," says the author, "that one can compare to Judas Iscariot and to the crown of thorns." "It is not," he continues, "a political solution, draws no maps on territories, negotiates no treaties. But it liberates from the evil imprisoning the future and releases hope from the bondage of the past."[35] In other words, the constant demonization of Israel will produce the fruits of this hatred in the future—a second Holocaust. When Cragg explains why the Palestinians are a martyred people, as were the Poles and the Armenians, we must assume that he is unaware that the latter were also victims of Syrian Arabs. And he insists that an eventual peace settlement will change nothing, because the evil and injustice (Israel's restoration) will remain. So the war must continue by other means, in the form of theological hatred, to restore the former state of justice, which is the nonexistence of Israel.

If the mission of Palestinian Arabs is to suffer in order to denounce evil, we can understand why the Arab Churches and their Western relays are pathologically obsessed with proclaiming the demonic essence of Israel and exposing it to shame. Publications on the genocide of the Jews provoke a reactive transfer of this Jewish martyrology to the Palestinians. The more horrible the Holocaust, the more guilty the victim of bearing witness, the more indispensable to the persecutors the Palestinian mediation in the symbolism of the transfer. This Palestine crucified by the State of Israel is a morbid, essential necessity uniting the passions of all the neo-Nazi and Judeophobic currents of Europe. As figurehead of the conquest of the Orient and idol made in Europe, this crucified Palestine propels an insidious war against Israel. What does it matter if the Palestinian Christians were never more than a barely tolerated dhimmi minority who used their Judeophobia to facilitate integration? What does it matter if the Palestinian Muslims have at their disposal at least twenty countries where dhimmitude made millions of victims, where Jews were plundered and massacred and forced to flee, leaving all their property behind? What does it matter if Christian wars of liberation from dhimmitude in the Balkans provoked large-scale exodus and massacres of Muslims and, incidentally, reprisals against the Jews, prologue to their extermination in Central Europe during World War II? And what does it matter if behind this Palestine of justice, an image created and imposed by Europe, flows the blood of Christian Lebanon, the stifled cries of the Copts, the mutilated victims of Saddam Hussein, the victims of genocide in southern Sudan—while Europe and its Churches stand by in silence?

Is Palestinian Christianity innocent of the role it is made to assume in this Euro-Arab policy against Israel? Yes and no. Here, as elsewhere, attitudes toward Israel are not uniform. Forced to wear a costume tailored by two thousand years of Christian Judeophobia and hide from view the real criminals, Palestinian Christianity is torn and divided precisely in this confrontation with Israel.

CONCLUSION

As mentioned in the introduction, this incomplete survey of the thematic of Judeophobic anti-Zionism does not represent the full range of opinions about Israel. This cannot be emphasized enough, in tribute to those who fought against that policy at the cost of immense sacrifices. The spectacular progress of Judeo-Christian reconciliation results from the constant efforts of secular Christians and theologians, famous and anonymous, an immense transnational population, partner in history and in solidarity with the spiritual adventure of Israel. Despite the importance of these fertile reunions, they can only be mentioned in passing here.

And we will not be able to examine here the situation of the silenced Eastern Christians subject to dhimmitude, hostage to Europe's determination to protect its interests, its Western religious institutions, and their dhimmi relays. This has aroused strong tension in communities in Lebanon, Sudan, and Pakistan, for example, as well as in the Coptic Diaspora. And the determinant factor in this somber tableau can be mentioned only in passing: the colossal political and economic pressure exerted on the West by Islamic anti-Zionism, with its international terrorist potential and threats of reprisal against Arab Christians. In addition, it is difficult to determine whether the anti-Zionism of Europe's media and culture is motivated by traditional Judeophobia, hunger for profits, or surrender to threats of massacre of vulnerable Christian communities in Arab countries. Perhaps all three at the same time. The fact remains that two Muslim countries, Turkey and the shah's Iran, were able to have friendly relations with Israel while protecting their own non-Muslim communities. Thus it seems that from the beginning anti-Zionism resulted from the fusion of European and Arab Judeophobia.

This clarification results from our analysis of zones of convergence and fusion in European and Arab currents of political and theological anti-Zionism. The analysis of relations among the three religions, which of course pertains to the field of dhimmitude, is transposed to the political sphere with the emergence of the State of Israel.

The consequences of a century of hostility against Israel are dramatic. Europe lost its soul in the Holocaust. The ensuing political anti-Zionism shaped Euro-Arabian policy and collusion with international Palestinian terrorism. The teachings of theological contempt were replaced by forty years of constant anti-Israeli indoctrination. The survival of Eastern Christianity was sacrificed to the Palestinian cause, keystone of an illusory, self-defeating Euro-Arab policy. In 1982 Lebanon's president-elect Bashir Gemayel attributed to Europe's traditional Judeophobia the abandonment of Lebanese Christianity, sacrificed on the altar of the demonization of Israel.

The strategy of isolating Israel economically, politically, and diplomatically operated notably by pressure from France and the Vatican on third-party countries. Support for a Muslim-Christian Palestine to oppose Israel was a deathly cause for Europe. It gave momentum to the process of extermination of the Jewish people during World War II, with the deliberate consensual silence of governments and religious hierarchies. In the postwar period its ideologists and agents, camouflaged by various political labels, recycled the war against Israel into "the Palestinian cause," integrating the Christian concept of deicide and the Muslim doctrine of dhimmitude, even though the latter applies to Christians as well as Jews. The varied anti-Zionist strategies that reject the fraternity of Jews and Christians led Euro-Arabism and Muslim-Christian relations into political and ideological traps.

Support for the Palestinian cause, conceived as an arm for the destruction of Israel, had consequences on both a political and a theological level.

Political Level

1. Support for jihad against Israel justified the same jihad policies against Christians in Arab countries, condemning them to silence under the yoke of dhimmitude. Negation of the rights of one of the Peoples of the Book developed the same process of necrosis against its twin, regardless of Christians' belief in their own superiority.

2. Thirteen centuries of Jewish and Christian history in Islamicized countries were obscured for the following reasons: (i) the Muslim-Christian union against the Jews was weakened by acknowledging persecutions endured by the dhimmis; (ii) these facts of history rehabilitate Zionism; (iii) dhimmitude places Jews and Christians in the same condition with regard to Islam. This leaves the crucifixion, in that it rejects Israel, as the only theme that upholds Muslim-Christian ecumenism.

Theological Level

Historical amnesia blocks efforts for critical Islamic exegesis, notably concerning relations with the People of the Book and other infidels; this exegesis is all the more urgent now that millions of Muslims have emigrated to Europe.

Christian anti-Zionism could not possibly strengthen Christianity because it is based on theological prejudice that is rejected and opposed by the majority of Christians today. Maintaining these prejudices encourages the excesses of pagano-Christianity and the Islamization of Christian theology. The latter current, reworked by Louis Massignon, is the source of Palestinian liberation theology—meaning, of course, liberation from Judaism. The Islamization of Christian theology by rejecting its Jewish roots unwittingly sustains the same Quranic replacement principle that denounces Christianity as a falsification of its original prior form, which is Islam.

Perverse symmetries gave Christianity guilt feelings toward Islam modeled on its relations with Judaism, but these situations have nothing in common.

This guilt is based on the fabrication of artificial symmetry between five million Israeli Jews living in their tiny country and a billion Muslims, of whom several hundred million live in countries that used to be Christian. These false symmetries are political traps today.

This triangular context reveals the signification of Israel. By liberating itself from the bonds of a definition imposed by Christianity, Israel also liberated Christianity from a source of self-destruction and barbarian excesses and allowed it to achieve its true mission in human history.

By the abolition of dhimmitude, Israel obliges Islam to redefine its relations with the People of the Book, and with all peoples, in a perspective of equality and reconciliation. This liberates Muslims from the baneful concepts of jihad and dhimmitude and encourages deepening of the Quranic spiritual message. The Return of the Exiles after so many deserts crossed brings Israel out of the swamps of history. Universal reconciliation can flourish in the multiple faces of human diversity united by mutual respect of other religions.

NOTES

1. Moshe Gil, *A History of Palestine, 634–1099*, ed. and trans. from Hebrew by Ethel Broido (Cambridge and New York: Cambridge University Press, 1992).

2. Ibid., p. 71; for the buildup of the Haram al-Sharif mosque, see the article by Heribert Busse, "The Temple of Jerusalem and Its Restitution by 'Abd al-Malik b.

Marwan," in Bianca Kühnel, ed., *The Real and Ideal Jerusalem in Jewish, Christian and Islamic Art* (Jerusalem: Journal of the Center for Jewish Art, Hebrew University, 1998), pp. 23–33.

3. The Hadith comprises words and deeds attributed by tradition to Muhammad and collected in a corpus. The Hadith and the Qur'an form the major bases of the Sharia.

4. Edouard Driault, *Histoire diplomatique de la Grèce de 1821 à nos jours*, vol. 1, *L'insurrection et l'indépendance (1821–1830)* (Paris: PUF, 1925), p. 456.

5. Edouard Driault and Michel Lhéritier, *Histoire Diplomatique de la Grèce de 1821 à nos jours*, vol. 2, *Le règne d'Othon—La grande idée (1830–1862)* (Paris: Presses Universitaires de France, 1925), p. 190.

6. Jonathan Frankel, *The Damascus Affair: "Ritual Murder," Politics, and the Jews in 1840* (Cambridge: Cambridge University Press, 1997).

7. On this subject see George Emile Irani, *Le Saint-Siège et le conflit du Proche Orient*, trans. Dominique Eddé (Paris: Desclée de Brouwer, 1991).

8. Jacques Frémeaux, *Le monde arabe et la sécurité de la France depuis 1958* (Paris: PUF, 1995), p. 52, mentions the connivance of French politics with PLO terrorists.

9. Doreen Ingrams, comp. and annotator, *Palestine Papers 1917–1922: Seeds of Conflict* (London: John Murray, 1972), p. 60.

10. Ibid., p. 168.

11. Ronald Storrs, *Orientations* (London: Nicholson & Watson, 1943), p. 432.

12. Pierre-André Taguieff, *Les protocoles des sages de Sion : Faux et usages d'un faux*, 2 vols. (Paris: Berg International, 1992). See the thorough, profound study of antisemitism, from the origins of Christianity to the present day, by Religious Studies emeritus professor William Nicholls: *Christian Antisemitism: A History of Hate* (Northvale, NJ, and London: Jason Aronson, 1995); and Pierre Pierrard, *Juifs et Catholiques français: D'Edouard Drumont à Jacob Kaplan (1886–1994)* (Paris: Éditions du Cerf, 1997).

13. Negib Azoury, *Le Réveil de la Nation Arabe dans l'Asie turque . . .* (Paris: Plon, 1905).

14. Quoted in Pierrard, *Juifs et Catholiques français*, pp. 28, 124.

15. Azoury, *Le réveil de la nation arabe*, pp. iii, iv.

16. Ibid., pp. vi, viii.

17. Israel State Archives (ISA), Stet GR 2, 5/155.

18. Ibid. Memorandum of the MCA addressed to the Conférence de la Paix in Paris, February 3, 1919, following a General Assembly of the MCA in Jerusalem, January 27, 1919.

19. Storrs, *Orientations*, p. 358.

20. Ibid., p. 371; parentheses in the original.

21. Yehoshua Porath, *The Emergence of the Palestinian Arab National Movement, 1918–1929* (London: Cass, 1974), p. 32.

22. Quoted in Storrs, *Orientations*, p. 378.

23. Quoted in Friedrich Heer, "The Catholic Church and the Jews Today," *Midstream* (New York), May 1971, pp. 20–31.

24. Quoted in ibid., p. 22. For connections and collaboration of Catholic prelates with the Nazis, see Annie Lacroix-Riz, *Le Vatican, l'Europe et le Reich de la Première Guerre mondiale à la guerre froide* (Paris: Armand Colin, 1996).

25. Quoted in Heer, "The Catholic Church and the Jews Today," p. 23.

26. Storrs, *Orientations*, p. 358.

27. Zvi Elpeleg, *The Grand Mufti* (London: Cass, 1993), pp. 69–73; for the allegations of Antonius, see ibid., pp. 61–62.

28. Ibid., p. 75.

29. Geneviève Dermenjian, *La crise anti-juive oranaise, 1895–1905: L'antisémitisme dans l'Algérie coloniale* (Paris: L'Harmattan, 1986), p. 206.

30. Ibid., p. 135.

31. Norman Daniel, *L'Islam et l'Occident* (Paris: Éditions du Cerf, 1993), p. 390.

32. Youakim Moubarac, *L'Islam et le dialogue islamo-chrétien*, 5 vols. (Beirut: Éditions du Cénacle Libanais, 1972–73), 3:172.

33. Kenneth Cragg, *The Arab Christian: A History in the Middle East* (London: Mowbray, 1992), p. 68.

34. Quoted in Haïm Shapiro, "Jewish-Christian Dialogue: Root and Branch," *Jerusalem Post*, February 23, 1997.

35. Cragg, *The Arab Christian*, p. 275. Cragg dedicates the book to the son of a Syrian Presbyterian pastor, Fayez A. Sayegh, close collaborator of the PLO and initiator of the 1975 resolution assimilating Zionism and racism, in Taguieff, *Protocoles*, 1:326, n. 17.

THE OPPRESSION OF MIDDLE EAST CHRISTIANS

12. A Forgotten Tragedy

Walid Phares

Extraordinary diplomatic efforts in recent years have been undertaken to resolve some of the world's most complex, divisive conflicts—in Ireland, Bosnia, and the Middle East. However, the latter is no closer to resolution. For in the troubled Middle East, Islamic fundamentalism, which is seeking to reignite the Arab-Israeli conflict, is targeting Christians, Jews, and other non-Muslims throughout the Islamic world.

MIDEAST CHRISTIANS: LOCATION AND NUMBERS

Egypt. The Copts of Egypt—Orthodox, Catholics, and Protestants—are estimated to be between 10 to 12 million, dispersed across the country. They are the descendants of the ancient Egyptian people living under the pharaohs. Their number shrunk after the Arab-Muslim invasion in 740 CE and flourished under the British in the nineteenth century. One million Copts live in the diaspora, particularly in the United States and Canada.

Iran: Five hundred thousand Persian, Armenian, and Assyrian Christians of all denominations live in constant fear under the Islamic Republic of Iran. Christian spiritual leaders are executed by the government.

Iraq. About one million Christian Assyrians, Nestorians (Orthodox), Chaldeans (Catholics), and others (evangelicals, Jacobites) live in Iraq. Most of the Christians are concentrated in the north. The Assyrians are submitted

Reprinted with permission from *Chaldeans On Line*.

to cultural and political repression. Around one million Christian Mesopotamians live in North America, Europe, and Australia.

Lebanon. The Christians—Maronites, Orthodox, Melkites, and other communities, including Protestants—number about 1.5 million. Since 1975, hundred of thousands were massacred, displaced, or exiled. After 1990, the Christian areas of Lebanon are under Syrian occupation. There are more than 7 million Lebanese Christians in the diaspora. More than 1.5 million Americans are of Lebanese descent.

Sudan. Seven million black Africans live in the south. Most of these tribes are Christians—Anglicans, other Protestants, and Catholics. Since the Islamic conquest, the Africans of Nubia were displaced to the south. As a result of an Islamist takeover in the north in 1989, they are submitted to ethnic cleansing and forced to abandon their faith. One million south Sudanese are exiled.

Syria. One million Christians are Syrian citizens. Deprived of their cultural and educational rights, Syria's Aramaeans, Armenians, Orthodox, and Melkites are present in the northeast and the major cities.

MIDEAST CHRISTIANS UNDER ATTACK

In Lebanon, where Christians enjoyed constitutionally guaranteed equality until a few years ago, hundreds of Christians are arrested, tortured, and jailed by pro-Syrian forces. In the south of Lebanon, thousands of Christians are bombarded constantly by Hizbollah. In the event of an Israeli withdrawal, the Christian community would be threatened by Islamist militias. Similarly, dozens of Christian villages in Egypt are routinely attacked by the Islamists. As an example, the village of Manshiet Nassr in Upper Egypt has been attacked by Islamic fundamentalists repetitively. Dozens have been killed or injured. Today, south Sudanese Christians are being killed by the Islamist forces of Khartoum. Entire villages are being destroyed by the Arab government of the north. Yet these tragedies, like others in the Muslim world, go unreported by the Western media and unchallenged by Western leaders.

These examples are not isolated events. Nor is the neglect they receive from the press and world governments. Thus the public in the United States is largely unaware of the "Middle East" that non-Muslims of the region know all too well. Non-Muslims are targeted by Islamic fundamentalists, who are tacitly encouraged by governments of the region, who, at best, do nothing to stop them and, at worst, are actively leading the pogroms.

THE COLLECTIVE SUFFERING

Middle East Christians suffer collectively. Yet few people in the West are aware of the size of the Christian communities in the Middle East. The common image of Middle Eastern Christianity is that it is limited to a few groups or individuals among the Palestinian population. In reality the Palestinian Christians are only a fragment of the millions of Christians from Sudan to Armenia: more than 10 million Copts live in Egypt, 7 million Christians and animists in south Sudan, 1.5 million Christians in Lebanon, about one million Assyro-Chaldeans in Iraq, 1 million Christians in Syria, and five hundred thousand in Iran, among others. The fact is that the Middle East is neither entirely Arab nor entirely Muslim. The Arab-Israeli confrontation is not the only conflict in the Middle East. Centuries earlier, a major invasion occurred from Arabia, ushering in domination by Arabs and Muslims in Syria, Mesopotamia, Palestine, and Egypt. Gradually the new conquerors attempted to assimilate millions of Christians, transforming the conquered nations into "Arabized" and "Islamized" populations. Those who were not assimilated by the Arabs became second-class citizens called dhimmis, deprived of their basic political, social, and economic rights.

SURVIVAL AND RIGHTS

Despite the continuous oppression of these Middle Eastern communities for thirteen centuries, many national groups survived and struggled to restore their freedom. At the beginning of the twentieth century the Copts of Egypt, the Assyro-Chaldeans of Iraq, the south Sudanese, and the Lebanese Christians tried to obtain independence. But the Arab powers in the region denied these Christians their natural right to self-determination. At the expense of the Middle East Christians, Arab identity and Islamic domination were established in the region.

THE IMPACT OF ISRAEL

The creation of the state of Israel was perceived as a major positive development in the eyes of other non-Arabs. Indeed, Middle East Christians considered the rebirth of Israel and the ingathering of the Jewish people on its historical land as a promise of their own future liberation. The Jewish success demonstrated that Christians can achieve similar goals. For decades, secretly or openly, Christians from countries including Lebanon, Iraq, and Sudan have praised the Israeli model and attempted to imitate it. This attraction between Israel and Middle East Christians challenged the Arab-Islamic order in the region.

THE ARABIST STRATEGY

In reaction to the Jewish state, the Arabist strategy since the forties has been the following:

- To claim that the Middle East is an Arab and Muslim region; this claim is directed not only at Israel, but all non-Arab, non-Muslim populations in the region;
- To isolate non-Arab, non-Muslim groups from one another;
- To eliminate minorities within their borders, by one means or another.

These strategies have been in effect in the Middle East for decades. The Assyrians were massacred in Iraq, then the south Sudanese, followed by the Christians of Lebanon and the Copts in Egypt. For example, in 1982, the Arabs applied overwhelming pressure to the United States and other Western governments, using all their influence to abort any agreement between Lebanon and Israel. This episode was followed by the massacre of thousands of Lebanese Christians throughout the eighties and the invasion of their free enclave in 1990.

To continue with the example of Lebanon because it is instructive and consistent with patterns throughout the area, one should also note how the Arabist strategy has carefully included a disinformation campaign in the United States. Throughout the war, which dragged on for about fifteen years, the "Arabs" were wrongly referred to by the press as a collective group and were routinely portrayed as the victims. Israel was the "aggressor," whereas the Syrians were carelessly called "peacekeepers" by all too many. What is worst, the public has been all too often misled by Middle Eastern Christians, often of Lebanese descent, who have historically been the leaders of the Arab lobbies in this country. These individuals, who do not represent the causes of their motherland, perpetuated the interpretation (and sometimes even advocated the demands) of the Arabists, both in the region and in the United States.

Another trend was to block favorable US policies toward the Christians of the Middle East and toward Israel, within the administration and throughout the various bodies of government. More particularly, efforts were aimed at destroying any attempt to build bridges between the Middle Eastern (specifically Lebanese) Christians and the Jewish community. The Arab lobby waged several campaigns to discredit the Middle East Christians.

THE MIDDLE EAST CHRISTIAN STRATEGY

Since its inception, the Middle East Christian Committee (MECHRIC) has advanced the following strategy as a way to rebuild the legitimacy of the Christian cause in the Middle East:

- To confront the Islamist strategy through alliance. This effort is currently aimed at building a coalition of Copts, Lebanese Christians, Assyrians, and south Sudanese in order to represent these forgotten Christian nations. As of 1992, MECHRIC is speaking on behalf of these resistance movements in the diaspora;
- To reach the American, European, and worldwide Christian public and involve them in supporting the struggle of Middle Eastern Christians;
- To build an open and historical alliance between American and Middle East Christians on the one hand and American Jews and Israelis on the other. This union could offer testimony that could expose the Islamist falsifications and lay the grounds for the emergence of a free and democratic Middle East, which includes and protects all its nations, and in which the Christian peoples of the Middle East, the Jews of Israel, and the Arab Muslims can live in harmony.

A CHRISTIAN MINORITY

13. The Copts in Egypt

Bat Ye'or

The clashes that began in 1971 but broke out in 1972 between Christian Copts and Muslims in Egypt prompted the Egyptian government to set up a parliamentary commission of inquiry to investigate the causes of these disturbances. According to the official report, they "were the result of tensions aroused by a strong religious undercurrent, tinged by fanaticism."[1] According to the same report, one of the causes of unrest was a law, passed in 1934, that permitted churches to be built only if ten conditions were fulfilled, one of which was the absence of any mosque in the vicinity. In practice, however, no sooner was any plot of land set aside for the building of a church than a mosque was immediately erected nearby, thereby dashing the hopes of the Christian community.

The Coptic population numbers about six million today out of a total Egyptian population of approximately forty million.

THE PAST

The Copts descend from the early Egyptian Christians. Before the Arab invasion, Egypt was a province of the Byzantine Empire. Egypt's inhabitants

This article in French under the pen name Y. Masriya was published by the Geneva Centre d'Information et de Documentation sur le Moyen-Orient on January 19, 1973. It was enlarged, revised, and corrected by the author and translated into English by David G. Littman for *Case Studies on Human Rights and Fundamental Freedoms: A World Survey*, ed. Willem A. Veenhoven and Winfred Crum Ewing, published for the Foundation for the Study of Plural Societies, vol. 4 (The Hague: Martinus Nijhoff, 1976), pp. 79–93.

were primarily Christians, and the land was covered with numerous churches and monasteries.

At the end of the second century, the famous Catechetical School of theology and exegesis of early Christianity was founded in Alexandria, then the centre of Hellenistic culture. It was renowned due to the writings and teachings of Pantaenus, Clement of Alexandria, and Origen, who opposed Hellenistic paganism. After Alexandria became the spiritual capital of Christianity, cenobitic life extended into the desert along the valley of the Nile and deep into the oases. Communities of anchorites and monks were founded under the leadership of Paul, Anthony, and Pachomius (292–346), who established the monastic rules and vows that were to serve as a model for the religious orders of Europe in the Middle Ages. In 323 Constantine the Great declared Christianity the state religion of the Roman Empire. Religious strife broke out throughout the Empire among pagans, Christians, and heretics. The national struggle of Egypt against the Byzantine yoke took a religious form. The Church of Alexandria, orthodox at first, later adopted the monophysite creed (one nature of Christ) and fought against the Byzantine Orthodox Church. At the time of the Arab conquest, Egypt was the scene of bloody religious battles between the Melkites, followers of Byzantium, and the more numerous Jacobites, adherents of the monophysite doctrine.

In 640 some Egyptians welcomed the Arab conquerors, but most opposed them. The Arab army of occupation made no changes in the administration of the conquered territories, and the Copts retained their posts. But this tolerance was due to the particular circumstances of the conquest—the necessity for the Arab army to control a large Christian population—and was short-lived. In fact, the relations between the Arab army and the subjected indigenous population changed as the Arab domination grew firmer and became an irreversible phenomenon of history as a result of the elaboration of a system of colonization: the *dhimma*.

Originally, the *dhimma* was the treaty concluded between Muhammad and those he subdued. The tolerant character of these pacts, defining the obligations and duties that bound the indigenous populations to the conquering Arab Muslims, determined the sedentary populations of the towns and villages to capitulate before the advancing Bedouin armies. In theory, life and property—as well as religious liberty—were guaranteed to those who accepted this pact, on the condition that they did not transgress any of its stipulations; but very soon the interpretation and the application of its conditions transformed the *dhimma* into a codified system of legal tyranny that was spiritual in theory but in practice often led to genocide and was at the base of the

Arabization and Islamization of the Christian Orient. Its evolution, in the course of centuries, was governed throughout by the irrefutable belief in the superiority of Islam and in its universal supremacy. The following words are attributed to the caliph Mu'awia: "I found that the people of Egypt were of three sorts, one-third men, one-third like men, and one-third not men, i.e. Arabs, converted foreigners, and those who pretend to be Muslims, the Copts."[2]

THE PACT OF UMAR

The Pact of Umar, generally attributed to Umar II (717–740), regulated the discriminatory status imposed upon the dhimmis, the non-Muslim native population living under the domination of Islam. They had to pay the *jizya*, a poll tax symbolizing their subjection to Islam, and also higher commercial taxes than were paid by the Muslims. The ownership of their land passed to the Muslim community, and in order to have the right to cultivate it they had to pay a special land tax, the *kharaj*. Very often, whole communities were burdened with arbitrary impositions. At the beginning of the conquest, the Muslim occupants paid no taxes, and therefore the Arab state and army were subsidized by the non-Muslim peasants and town dwellers.

The construction of new churches or the restoration of old ones, as well as the use of bells, banners, sacred books, crosses on churches or borne in procession, and any other non-Muslim cult object were prohibited. So as not to disturb Muslims, the dhimmis had to hold their services in silence and abstain from lamentation at funerals. The social discrimination of the dhimmis and their exigency for security compelled them to live in separate areas. Their inferior and humble dwellings and tombs had to differ from those of the Muslims in size and decay. Marriage, sexual intercourse with a Muslim woman, and blasphemy against Islam were all punishable by death. Relations between dhimmis and Muslims were forbidden, but as this proved impracticable, relations were strongly discouraged. The dhimmis were not allowed to exercise any authority over Muslims and could not testify in a legal tribunal against them. Their movements were restricted, and they had to go unarmed.

As the dhimmis were considered inferior to Muslims, they had to differ in their outward appearance—for instance, in early Islam Christians had to shave their brows. They were denied the use of certain colors—such as green, which was the color of the Prophet—and were forbidden to wear the clothes, belts, shoes, and turbans worn by Muslims. Numerous decrees regulated in detail the colors and shape of clothes, ill-fitting and ridiculous headgear, belts and shoes that the dhimmis and their slaves were obliged to wear so as to be easily recognized and humiliated in the streets. A little bell around the neck, or a similar distinctive sign, made them recognizable at the public baths. Noble mounts such as horses and camels were reserved for Muslims; the dhimmis were only allowed to ride donkeys and use pack saddles. In some periods they were forbidden to ride their donkeys within the towns; in other periods the Christians were humiliated by being forced to ride their donkeys facing the tail.

Other vexing measures also governed their everyday life, such as the obligation to stand up and remain standing in the presence of Muslims, to address them in low and humble tones, and to give them right of way on the sidewalk by walking along the narrowest section of the street, on their left side—the impure side, for a Muslim. Dhimmis could not assemble in groups to converse. For a more detailed study of the life of dhimmis (Jews and Christians in Muslim lands), the reader should consult the authoritative monographs on this subject.[3]

The *jizya* was paid in the course of a ceremony during which dhimmis were publicly humiliated by receiving a slap in the face or a blow on the back of the neck. The dhimmis were then issued with a receipt that allowed them to travel; however, should they lose it, they could be put to death. When a census was taken of monks in Egypt (715–717) they were obliged to wear a metal bracelet bearing their name and the date and name of their monastery. Any monk found without his bracelet was liable to have his hand cut off or be executed.

The *kharaj*, the tax on non-Muslim land, reduced the Copts to destitution: they abandoned their fields and mass conversions occurred, but they were forcibly brought back by the army and obliged to pay the taxes (694–714). To prevent the Copts from abandoning their villages, the Arab army conducted a census and branded them on the hand and brow (705–717). No Christian could travel without a passport. Boats on the Nile that carried Christians without passports were set on fire. In 724, twenty-four thousand Copts converted to Islam to escape ruinous taxes. The conversions impoverished the state; to discourage them, the *jizya* was also imposed on new converts. Furthermore, they were forbidden to sell their lands to Muslims, as these lands would then have been exempt from the *kharaj*; later a fixed sum was levied on the Coptic community, which covered any lost revenues from new converts. At the beginning of the eighth century, Usame ben Zaid, governor of Egypt, wrote to Caliph Abdel Malik (715–717), "I draw milk; if it stops, I draw blood; if it clots, I press the skin." The same caliph used to say, "Draw milk until it ceases to flow, draw blood until it is exhausted."

In Tinnis, in the eastern Delta, taxes reduced the Copts to such destitution that they abandoned their children in slavery to the Arabs.[4] Those who did not pay were thrown into jail or tortured. Under the Abbasids, dhimmis who could not pay their taxes were put into cages with wild animals. Church leaders were often held responsible for the sums levied on the community. If unable to pay, they were thrown into jail and tortured. Around 718, Abdel Malik ben Rifaa, governor of Egypt, had Patriarch Michael thrown into a windowless cell dug into the rock, had a block of wood attached to his feet, and had a heavy collar put around his neck. He remained in this cell for thirty-one days until the required sum was paid. The exorbitant taxes and the tortures used to extort them provoked numerous revolts, which were brutally crushed. Thousands of Copts were killed, women and children enslaved, their property confiscated by the Arabs, who thus became more numerous in towns and villages.[5]

As the Pact of Umar forbade dhimmis to exert any authority over a Muslim, they could neither become civil servants nor join the army. In every period, numerous decrees resulted in the dismissal of Christians from the posts they held unless they converted to Islam. However, the Copts were indispensable, as all the Egyptian bureaucracy was in their hands. The Muslims accused them of purposely trying to complicate the administration in order to retain their posts. These deviations from the *dhimma* provoked riots: the mob would then plunder the Christian quarter, massacre the Copts, and destroy their churches.

In every period, monasteries and churches were despoiled, burned, and destroyed. Caliph al-Hakim (996–1020) renewed the clauses of the Pact of Umar. All the churches and synagogues in his empire (Egypt, Syria, and Palestine) were then looted and demolished or converted into mosques. The mob pillaged the Christian and Jewish quarters, and the caliph forced the dhimmis to convert or leave his dominions. At the end of his reign, he allowed them to return to their religion and to rebuild their places of worship. In 1058 all churches were closed, the patriarch and the bishops thrown into jail, and the Copts ransomed for seventy thousand dirhams. The slightest incident could provoke a massacre. In 1377 the mob was incensed at the sight of a Christian maltreating a Muslim and immediately clamored for the dismissal of Christian and Jewish public servants in the service of the emirs and then for their conversion or death. The Christians went into hiding, but the mob ransacked their quarter, massacred them, and forced the women into slavery. Some Christians were grouped in a horse market; a pit was dug into which they were to be thrown and set alight—all converted to Islam.[6] A Christian was riding by the Al-Azhar mosque; his spurs and handsome saddle angered the Muslims, who pursued him with the intention of killing him. Riots broke out, forcing the sultan to summon the leaders of the Jewish and Christian communities and remind them that they were subject to the shame and humiliation of the *dhimma*. When they left the sultan, they were attacked by the mob, which tore their clothes and beat them until they agreed to apostasize. Stakes were set alight for the Jews and the Christians. The churches and houses of dhimmis that rose higher than those of the Muslims were destroyed. The dhimmis even feared to go out into the streets. In 1343, Christians were accused of starting fires in Cairo; in spite of the sultan's efforts to protect them, they were seized in the street, burned, or slaughtered by the mob as it left the mosques. Anti-Christian violence raged in the main towns. To enable Christians to go out into the streets, Jews would sometimes lend them their distinctive yellow turbans.

The history of the Copts is a lengthy tale of persecution, massacre, forced conversion, and devastated and burned churches. Thousands of Copts fled to Abyssinia, but the greater part found refuge by accepting Islam.

THE PRESENT

The founder of modern Egypt, Muhammad Ali (1801–1846), undertook the cultural and industrial revolution of his country with the help of a team of French scientists. Tolerant and politically minded, he tried to mitigate religious discrimination in the face of the opposition of a traditionalist population. The Copts made use of this period to build schools and acquire modern skills; when the British occupied the country (1882) the Christians were prepared to act as civil servants in a modern administration. The British occupation brought stability and economic development to Egypt. Schools were founded, and new opportunities were created in the developing commerce, industry, and agriculture. The Copts perfected their skills and distinguished themselves in the liberal professions and in government service.

In spite of the liberal, albeit limited, trend that favored the secularization of the state and the equality of its citizens, the rise of the erstwhile dhimmis did not occur without shocking, even traumatizing, Muslim susceptibilities— as their former abject status had been the basis of the superiority and domination of Islam. To make matters worse, the abolition of the discriminatory laws against non-Muslims in 1856 did not stem from an evolution sui generis in the Arab mentality but was imposed by the West.[7] In retaliation, thousands of Christians were slaughtered in the Syrian provinces in 1860. This massacre prompted France's brief intervention—in agreement with the other European powers—and the establishment of an autonomous Christian region in Lebanon, which remained nonetheless under Ottoman suzerainty.

Having thus been emancipated by Europe, the Christians—remnants of pre-Islamic cultures—in a cynical paradox of history, were automatically associated with imperialism. Their hard-won equality was considered by the Arabs as an additional humiliation imposed on them by the Western powers. This is the reason that the struggle for national independence, with its rejection of the West and its return to Islam, has also manifested itself in the persecution of minorities. In fact, justified as it may have been, the anticolonial struggle was never conceived of as a national war in the European sense. It was a jihad—a holy war of Islam against Christianity. Inevitably then, religious fanaticism linked Eastern Christians to the West, which had not only liberated them, but, furthermore, by protecting them, had delivered them from a traditional humiliation, thus violating the tenets of Islam established in the eighth century.

Worse, the situation of the minorities became more complicated by the fact that in any litigation between Muslims and non-Muslims, Islamic law was applicable, and then, as neither the testimony nor the oath of a non-Muslim was admissible due to the infidel's congenital depravity, the Muslim was automatically acquitted. In order to protect their lives and property, the minorities tried to obtain consular protection or a foreign citizenship, thus benefiting from the system of Capitulations. By this device, they could escape from the discriminatory Islamic courts; on the other hand, this link with the West compromised them even more. Thus, in the short or long run, no matter what they did, the political situation of the religious minorities was foredoomed.

Under the British protectorate, the fact that a few Copts and Jews became high government officials created the illusion of liberalization, despite a violently xenophobic pan-Islamic current that was the manifestation of the revolt of Islam against the political and cultural supremacy of the West. Professor W. C. Smith has written, "Most Westerners have simply no inkling of how deep and fierce is the hate, especially of the West, that has gripped the modernizing Arab."[8] This same hatred has accused the minorities of collusion with Western imperialism.

Charles Issawi attributes these anti-Coptic feelings in part to the high intellectual level of the Copts, but primarily to Islamizing tendencies, which resulted in economic discrimination against the Christians in the early thirties.[9] During this period the Egyptian monarchy led an active pan-Islamic campaign in the Arab countries. The progressive Islamization of national life inspired the rector of Al-Azhar, the renowned Islamic University of Cairo, to declare in 1928 that nationality is religion.[10]

Already in 1927, Muslim political and religious associations proliferated, such as the Society of Young Muslims, the Society for the Benevolence of Islamic Morals, the Good Islamic Way, the Society for the Preaching of Islamic Virtues, the Society for the Revival of Religious Law, the Salafiya Society, the Muslim Brotherhood, and Young Egypt. Cairo became the center of a religious nationalism from which missionaries went forth to the Sudan, Japan, and India.[11] This proselytism carried with it a current of xenophobia, which manifested itself also against European orientalists, accused of undermining the faith of Islam. In March and April 1928 the activities of Christian missionaries were violently criticized. They were accused of utilizing dangerous drugs and hypnosis to gain new converts.[12] In 1933, in Kafr el Zayat, the Franciscan Sisters of Mercy were forced by a menacing crowd to release the pupils in their care.[13] The nationalist element in this religious current is best illustrated by the words of Christian author Salama Moussa, who stated in 1930, "Islam is the religion of my country, my duty is to defend it."[14]

In 1936 Makram Ebeid, the Coptic finance minister, declared, "I am a Christian, it is true, by religion, but through my country I am a Muslim."[15] From which it follows that to be an Egyptian it was necessary to act as a Muslim.

In 1937 King Farouk, with the help of his former tutor, Mustapha el-Maraghi, rector of Al-Azhar, attempted to abolish the constitutional government and transform Egypt into a theocratic state. The Wafd, the nationalist party, which was very popular, became the main obstacle to royal ambition. In order to discredit the Wafd, Maraghi resorted to religious xenophobia, accusing the Wafd of being controlled by the Copts, whom he described as "foxes" in a radio broadcast in February 1938. Friendship between Copts and Muslims is contrary to divine law, he declared.[16] In pursuit of his anti-Copt campaign, the rector of Al-Azhar stated that Egyptian policy must draw its inspiration only from Islamic principles, which, as far as the relations with Christians were concerned, meant the reintroduction of the *dhimma*. Anti-Coptic and antimissionary feelings were aroused, and the reputation of the Wafd was ruined.

At the same time, the Muslim Brotherhood considerably increased the number of its members as well as its hold on the economic and political sectors of the country. The Brotherhood attempted to turn Egypt into an essentially religious state, governed according to the strictest interpretations of Islamic law. It condemned democratic parliamentarianism, which, in its eyes, was a corrupt institution imported from the West. Divided into cells, the Brotherhood owned printing presses, clinics, schools, bookshops, and recreation centers, and it possessed its own secret terrorist organization and paramilitary "army."

The part played by the Brotherhood is still a determining factor in Egypt. Remarkably well organized, it became the most powerful party in the country. Thanks to the support of the king and the army, it had ramifications throughout the country—as well as in the Sudan, in Yemen, and particularly in Palestine, where from 1948 to 1956 it provided the fedayeen with arms and money. After World War II, the Brotherhood became the most powerful party in Egypt and was at the zenith of its glory. Its fanaticism, the wave of murders and bloody riots instigated by its terrorist organizations, maintained xenophobia at a fever pitch and created an atmosphere of terror and discrimination against non-Muslims. Possessing arms and training grounds, it set up military organizations and units of shock troops, which applied unbearable pressure on the Egyptian government and plunged the country, with the king's consent, into the 1948 war against Israel. After the defeat of the Arab forces, it started a regime of terror in Egyptian cities. The government, not having the means to control them, could only reestablish comparative stability by imposing martial law.

Gamal Abdel Nasser needed the help of the Brotherhood to seize power, and Anwar el-Sadat collaborated with Hassan el-Banna, the Brotherhood's Supreme Guide.[17] Yasir Arafat, born in Cairo in 1929, learned from members of the Brotherhood how to make bombs and other explosives.[18] When the party was outlawed by Nasser, thousands of its members were imprisoned; others found refuge in Syria and especially in Jordan, where they joined the ranks of the Palestinian fedayeen organizations.

Though it never had a definite program for social reform, the activity of the Muslim Brotherhood was varied and affected every sphere of life, whether social, economic, political, educational, or cultural. In its pursuit to create an essentially Muslim society governed by the most rigorous precepts of Quranic law, it established, within the framework of the state, its own banks, industries, schools, and army. If it can be said that the Muslim Brotherhood introduced reforms for the protection of wage earners, it is no less true to say that, by religious intransigence, it contributed to the spread of a destructive hatred of the West, the foreigner, and the nonbeliever, using for this end numerous publications and inflammatory sermons pronounced from mosques.

To understand Islamic pan-Arabism, which in Western disguise ("secular and democratic Palestine," "progressive Muslim Lebanon") stirs the Arab world today, it is necessary to trace the steps of its evolution.

After the 1860 Syrian massacres, the Christians tried to promote an Arab nationalism based on cultural identity. But this Arab nationalism, inspired by European conceptions, irritated the Muslims, who looked upon it as an attempt by the West to divide and weaken them. The majority therefore rallied to the pan-Islamic movement, which advocated a return to traditional Islam. Thanks to the theologians of Al-Azhar, the two movements, antagonistic at first, fused into Islamic pan-Arabism. Today it is clear that Islam and Arabism are inseparable terms and that, in fact, pan-Arabism is synonymous with the cultural, social, and political rebirth of Islam. To be more precise, it is possible to be a Muslim and not an Arab, but the reverse is impossible: a true Arab must be a Muslim. As long as modern Egypt proclaims itself to be "essentially an Arab and Muslim land," uncertainty will continue to weigh on the Copts, the only remaining native religious minority after the forced departure of eighty thousand Jews.

When Nasser came to power, Egypt resolutely turned its face toward Arabism and became its staunchest champion. Cairo proclaimed Islamic unity and pursued an active policy of pan-Arabism, which identified Islam with Arabism.

The precarious situation of the minorities became even more acute. Was it possible to be a Christian and an Arab? The problem was obsessively debated in literature and in the press, and the solution was invariable: since Muhammad was an Arab and the sacred Qur'an was revealed in Arabic, only a Muslim could identify fully with Arabism.

In addition, Islam gave the Arab civilization strength and grandeur. These beliefs were formulated by the Christian founder of the Baath Party, Michel Aflak, who urged his coreligionists to convert, for, as he maintained, "Islam is Arab nationalism."[19]

It was quite clear that in the context of this essentially religious nationalism, no religious minority could ever participate in the political life of the country. The Islamization of the country led inevitably to discrimination against the Copts at all levels. Edward Wakin's book on this subject is particularly enlightening.[20] An article published by the late Georges Henein, a

Coptic writer, gave valuable information on the economic discrimination imposed on the Copts during Nasser's rule.[21]

In August 1957 the Copts protested against persecutions that revived, in modern Egypt, a familiar, thirteen-century-old tradition: restrictions in building churches; new laws affecting the personal status of Christians; discrimination against Christians in public office, in the distribution of land, in housing, and for posts in the mass media.[22] These events must be examined in the context of the *dhimma*—churches destroyed by villagers, houses and shops burned down, bishops and Coptic congregants stoned.[23] The campaign of intimidation, inspired by *The Protocols of the Elders of Zion* as described by Henein in the above-mentioned article, is not unlike that instigated against the Jews in the fifties, which resulted in their total expulsion. Was the rebirth of religious fervor in Egypt a consequence of the Islamization of governmental institutions, with President Sadat's tacit approval, or was it the work of the resurgent Muslim Brotherhood, organized into semiclandestine cells?

The remarks made [in 1957] by orientalist W. C. Smith on the Muslim Brotherhood of the fifties could well apply to certain trends prevalent later on in the Arab world:

> The reaffirmation of Islam endeavors to counter the failure of modern life but may not succeed in transcending it. Unfortunately, for some of the members of the Ikhwan (Muslim Brotherhood) and even more for many of their sympathizers and fellow-travellers the reaffirmation is not a constructive program based on cogent plans and known objectives, or even felt ideas; but is rather an outlet for emotion. It is the expression of the hatred, frustration, vanity, and destructive frenzy of a people who for long have been the prey of poverty, impotence, and fear. All the discontent of men who find the modern world too much for them can in movements such as the Ikhwan find action and satisfaction. It is the Muslim Arab's aggressive reaction to the attack on his world which we have already found to be almost overwhelming—the reaction of those who, tired of being overwhelmed, have leapt with frantic sadistic joy to burn and kill. The burning of Cairo (26th January 1952), the assassination of Prime Ministers, the intimidating of Christians, the vehemence and hatred in their literature—all this is to be understood in terms of a people who have lost their way, whose heritage has proven unequal to modernity, whose leaders have been dishonest, whose ideals have failed. In this aspect, the new Islamic upsurge is a force not to solve problems but to intoxicate those who cannot longer abide the failure to solve them.[24]

The lessons of the past and the present [1973] isolation of the Copts does not augur well for the future. When Nasser seized power and forbade all political parties, no one dared question or criticize the dictatorial government of the military oligarchy. This was particularly distressing in view of the fact that, at the beginning of the century, Egyptian intellectuals were the first from the Arab world to focus on the problems created by the clash with the modern Western world.

Although the more liberal regime of President Sadat loosened the totalitarian control in the political and intellectual spheres of the state's institutions, it hardly diminished anti-Christian discrimination in the political, economic, and educational fields.[25] The actual resurgence of Islam,[26] the massacre and flight of Lebanese Christians as a result of the union of Islamo-Palestinian forces, Syrian president Hafez al-Assad's military intervention in Lebanon, allegedly to protect Christians, can only favor a general traditional policy of Arab-Islamic domination.

As a confirmation of this tendency, at a manifestation of the Muslim Brotherhood in Cairo, some Egyptian members of parliament demanded that Quranic law should henceforth be the only source of the country's legislation.[27]

The moment has come for Arab Muslim intellectuals to recognize, courageously, that if the Arabs can condemn Western imperialism, so have the Eastern Christian communities the right to demand equality of rights in the lands successfully colonized by Arab imperialism.

DOCUMENT

Telegram Addressed to President Anwar el-Sadat, Summer 1972, by the Assembly of Christian Churches in Egypt

The National Assembly of the heads of the Copt-Orthodox, Copt-Catholic, and Copt-Evangelical churches met at the Orthodox-Coptic Patriarchate in Alexandria. The delegates were shocked by recent provocations and the planned persecutions publicly announced by the Ministry of WAKFS (Muslim Ministry of Religion) and its various sections. These projects are intended to inflame the populace to hatred and to discrimination, which can only lead to our annihilation. In spite of all this, no responsible department of the administration has done anything to stop these perfidious intrigues against national unity. Those intriguing knew very well that their action would lead to clashes between the two groups of the nation—the Muslims and the Copts— and this at a time when there is a great need to preserve our unity in order to create a united front against the enemy. All this has happened, even though on several occasions we have complained to those in authority.

We, members of this Assembly, subjected to considerable pressure engendered by all these injustices, which are occurring throughout the country, conscious also that the Constitution guarantees liberty to all citizens, we request, Sir, that

1. Sectarian and mischievous projects of the Ministry of WAKFS and other departments of this Ministry cease.
2. Restrictions imposed by the officials of the Administration concerning the construction of new churches be abolished. The argument used, according to which this prohibition is based on an old Ottoman decree, is invalid as this law was abrogated by the new constitution.
3. Entrance to the universities must be based solely on the final examination results at secondary school and not on a private interview. Furthermore, it should be forbidden for University courses to be held in mosques and Islamic institutions.
4. Studies of our religion from a negative viewpoint, such as "Israel and Universal Zionism" and "Conference on Christianity," should not be published.
5. All discrimination regarding employment in certain departments of the universities and the Institutes of Advanced Studies should be abolished, as well as the QUOTA system applicable to Christian students in specialized schools and similar institutions.
6. It should be forbidden to publish books or articles attacking our faith and our Holy Scriptures, in particular the Old Testament.
7. It is essential to apply the CHARTER and protect the Christian family against the dangers that menace it through the pretext of granting legal protection. Divorce must be made more difficult in that part of the law relating to the personal status of non-Muslims.
8. The projects that are aimed at preventing Christians from acceding to high [government] posts should be abolished.

Sir, we await your reply, as soon as possible, to our just requests. We do not accept being humiliated in this country that is ours. The delegates have called a further assembly in Cairo for Tuesday, 29 August 1972. There is thus sufficient time for our just requests to be accepted. If this will not be the case, martyrdom is preferable to a life of servitude.

We are sure of your wisdom, as we are sure that you will overcome this dangerous situation. May God protect you and through your efforts grant victory to our nation.

[signed]

For the Copt-Orthodox Patriarchate: The Reverend MENA, Patriarchal Vicar

For the Copt-Catholic Church:

The Reverend GIBRAEL GHATTAAS, Patriarchal Vicar

For the Copt-Evangelical Church: Pastor Labib QALDAS

NOTES

1. *Le Monde*, December 2, 1972; see the document.

2. Arthur Stanley Tritton, *The Caliphs and Their Non-Muslim Subjects* (London: F. Cass, 1970), p. 1.

3. Ibid.; Antoine Fattal, *Le Statut Légal des Non-Musulmans en Pays d'Islam* (Beirut: Imprimérie Catholique, 1958); Eliahu Strauss (Ashtor), "The Social Isolation of Ahl-Adh Dhimma," in *Etudes orientales à la mémoire de Paul Hirschler*, ed. O. Komlos (Budapest, 1949), pp. 73–94.

4. Tritton, *The Caliphs*, p. 145.

5. Ibid., p. 144.

6. Ibid., p. 33.

7. Moshe Ma'oz, *Ottoman Reform in Syria and Palestine, 1840–61* (Oxford and London: Clarendon Press, 1968), p. 27. By the Hatt-i Hümayun edict of 1858, European powers forced the Ottoman sultan, who was still the nominal suzerain of Egypt, to proclaim equality among Muslims, Christians, and other minorities throughout his empire.

8. Wilfred Cantwell Smith, *Islam in Modern History* (Princeton, NJ: Princeton University Press, 1957), p. 164.

9. Charles Issawi, *Egypt: An Economic and Social Analysis* (Oxford: Oxford University Press, 1947), pp. 161–62.

10. Marcel Colombe, *L'évolution de l'Egypte, 1924–1950* (Paris: G. P. Maisonneuve, 1951), p. 171.

11. Ibid., p. 144.

12. Ibid., p. 143.

13. Ibid.

14. Ibid., p. 146.

15. Ibid.

16. Elie Kadourie, *The Chatham House Version* (London: Weidenfield & Nicolson, 1970), pp. 199–200. Maraghi no doubt alludes to the verses in the Qur'an (sura 5:51) and to the Hadith (acts and words attributed to Muhammad) that forbid or strongly discourage relations between Christians and Muslims. The segregation of the dhimmis was at the root of their social and political ostracism by the Islamic community (*umma*).

17. Anwar Sadat, *Revolt on the Nile* (London: A. Wingate, 1957), p. 30.

18. Thomas Kiernan, *Yasir Arafat* (London: Abacus, 1976).

19. Quoted in Silvia Haim, *Arab Nationalism* (Berkeley: University of California Press, 1962), p. 64.

20. Edward Wakin, *A Lonely Minority: The Modern History of Egypt's Copts* (New York: Morrow, 1963).

21. Georges Henein, *L'Express*, November 20–26, 1972.

22. See Wakin, *A Lonely Minority*, pp. 53, 88.

23. *Le Monde*, November 16, 1972.

24. Smith, *Islam in Modern History*, pp. 163–64.

25. Josette Alia, "Les Chrétiens d'Orient," *Le Nouvel Observateur*, no. 581, December 29, 1975–January 4, 1976.

26. Bernard Lewis, "The Return of Islam," *Commentary* 61, no. 1 (January 1976): 39–49.

27. *Le Monde*, March 26, 1976.

14. EASTERN CHRISTIANS TORN ASUNDER

Challenges—New and Old

Bat Ye'or

The dhimmi mentality cannot be easily defined and described. An endless variety of reactions has been provoked by the evolving historical situations in the civilization of dhimmitude, which spans three continents and close to fourteen centuries. Generally speaking, dhimmi populations can be described as oscillating between alienation and submission and, at the other extreme, a self-perception of spiritual freedom.

The basic aspects of the dhimmi mentality are related to characteristics of its status and environment, because dhimmitude operates exclusively within the sphere of jihad. Contrary to common belief, jihad is not limited to holy war conducted militarily; it encompasses all strategies, including peaceful means, aimed at the unification of all religions within Islamic dogma. Furthermore, as a juridical-theological construction, jihad determines all aspects of relations between the *umma*—the Islamic community—and non-Muslims. According to the classical interpretation, these are classified in one of three categories: enemies, temporarily reconciled, or subjected. Because neither jihad nor dhimmitude has been critically analyzed, we can say today that the Islamist mentality—currently predominant in many Muslim countries—establishes relations with non-Muslims in the traditional jihad categories of war, truce, and submission/dhimmitude.

In our times dhimmis are found among the residues of indigenous populations of countries that were Islamized during a millenium of Muslim conquests: Christians, Hindus, and a scattering of Jews and Zoroastrians. Chris-

First published in French under the title "Les déchirures des chrétiens d'Orient," in *L'Observatoire du Monde Juif* 6/7 (June 2003): 24–26. It was translated in a modified version by Nidra Poller in collaboration with the author and published by *National Review Online*, September 18, 2003. Distributed by United Feature Syndicate Incorporated.

tians would seem to be the most familiar group, closer to Westerners by proximity, culture, and religion, and subject to the same status under Islam as the Jews, the other *ahl al-kitab*, "People of the Book"—the Bible. But this impression is often deceiving, since the reassuring appearance of similarity is misleading.

The behavior of Christian dhimmis varies according to the country, the social category, and their association with the ruling classes as, for example, their participation in the Iraqi or Syrian Baath parties or the PLO, a militarist organization engaged in the Arab jihad against Israel. Christian dhimmis appointed to important positions by Muslim rulers have often served as agents between the Arab world and strategic centers in the West: churches, governments, industries, universities, media, and so on.

Because Christian dhimmi populations are on the whole highly skilled and better educated than the surrounding population, they often suffer from malicious jealousy coupled with the traditional anti-Christian prejudices of the *umma*. The persistence of Christianity in Muslim environments testifies to qualities of endurance and adaptability. Yet survival in dhimmitude had its price: the dhimmi pathology.

Briefly summarized, Christian attitudes can be classified in three categories: active resistance, passive resistance, and collaboration. These three attitudes are manifest within one and the same population, but certain geographical or historical situations favor one or another.

ACTIVE RESISTANCE

Recent examples of active resistance are noteworthy. The repression of the Christian rebellion against the establishment of Sharia in the Sudan in 1983 caused more than two million dead and over four million displaced. Lebanese Christians fought against the Islamization of their country during the civil war that began in 1975. At the dawn of the twentieth century, Armenian and Assyrian Christians were punished by genocide for their attempts at independence. In the present day, active Christian resistance against Islamization in Indonesia, Nigeria, and other African countries is manifest in the massacre of Christian civilians, the burning of villages, and the flight of populations. Westerners, and especially Europeans, turn a deaf ear to the sufferings of Christians who actively resist Islamization, frequently blaming them for their own misfortunes.

PASSIVE RESISTANCE

Examples of passive resistance can be found in Egypt, Pakistan, and Iran. Egyptian Christians denounce the violence of which they are victims and strive to protect their dignity, reduce legal and professional discrimination, and secure basic rights such as permission to build or renovate churches. Here again, the West prefers to ignore their dire situation or underplay it with episodic attention. Christians engaged in active or passive resistance exhaust their meager resources in vain efforts to alert their fellow Christians and enlist their help.

COLLABORATIONIST CHRISTIANS

Collaborators are recruited among Christians who identify themselves as Arabs. This type of collaboration, which has caused endless fratricidal battles over the centuries, has been denounced by dhimmis struggling for centuries against an Islamic domination that progressed with the help of Christians.

Christian collaborationism has taken different forms in the course of history, according to circumstances and political opportunity. It is expressed today in a two-pronged political and theological project. The political project is implemented in a trans-Mediterranean fusion, with the construction of an economic, cultural, political, and geographical entity composed of the European Union and Arab and African countries. This policy of association and integration, active in all international forums, works to counterbalance American policy, under cover of a notion of "international legitimacy," albeit a legitimacy of sanguinary totalitarian Arab dictators.

Collaborationist Christian dhimmis function as the intellectual and economic mechanism of this project because they belong to both worlds. Their role is to invent the idyllic Muslim-Christian past that upholds the political construction of a future Eurabia and to dissimulate the anti-Christian foundations of Islamic doctrine and history.

Dhimmi collaboration on the theological level is oriented in two directions: toward Christianity and toward Islam. It finds its most radical expression in "Palestinian Liberation Theology," meaning nothing less than the liberation of Christianity from its Jewish matrix. The spiritual center of this theology is the al-Liqa Institute in Jerusalem, created in 1983 for the study of the Muslim and Christian heritage in the Holy Land. This strongly politicized institute, sponsored by international Christian organizations, specializes in disseminating anti-Israeli propaganda through its international religious and media channels.

Uniting Marcionist and Gnostic theological currents, this Palestinian theology strips away Jesus' Jewishness and turns him into a sui generis Arab-Palestinian Jesus, a twin of the Muslim Jesus (Isa). Christianity, thus liberated from its Jewish roots, can be transplanted in Arab-Islamism. This would place Palestine, and not Israel, at the origin of Christianity, making Israelis usurpers of the Muslim-Christian Palestinian homeland. This theory denies the historical continuity between modern Israel and its biblical ancestor, the locus of nascent Christianity.

The theology of Palestinianism, integrating all the anti-Jewish themes of replacement theology, is reworked to fit the new Palestinian fashion and is addressed to Christians all over the world, inviting them to gather together around an Arab-Palestinian Jesus, symbol of a Palestine crucified by Israel. The theme goes back to the nineteenth century. However, in those days when the idea of an Arab-Palestinian entity differentiated from the Arab world did not even exist, the unifying role of Palestine was assigned to Arab nationalism.

Palestinist theology shores up the Euro-Arab policy of Christian-Muslim and European-Arab fusion: the modern state of Israel—considered a temporary accident of history—is bypassed, and Europe's Christian origins are anchored in an Muslim-Christian Palestine. Having fulfilled its historical role of uniting the two enemies—Christianity and Islam—opposed to its very existence, Israel can now disappear, sealing the fusion between Europe and the Arabs. The unifying role devolves on Muslim-Christian Palestine; the reconciliation of Islam and Christianity can finally be consummated on the ashes of Israel and its negation. This is why the European Union—and especially France—designates Israeli "injustice" and "occupation" as the unique sources of conflict between Europe and the Arab/Muslim world, as well as the cause of international, anti-Western Islamist terrorism.

The contribution of dhimmi Christian collaborationism to Islam is even more important. It satisfies three objectives: (1) its propaganda shores up the mythology of past and present peaceful Muslim-Christian coexistence and confirms the perfection of Islam, jihad, and Sharia; (2) it promotes the demographic expansion and proselytism of Islamic propaganda in the West; (3) in the theological sphere it eliminates the Jewish Jesus and implants Christianity in the Muslim Jesus; in other words, it facilitates the theological Islamization of all of Christendom.

According to Islamic dogma, Islam encompasses Judaism and Christianity, both of which are falsified posterior expressions of the first and fundamental religion, which is Islam. All the characters of the Bible, from Adam to Abraham, Moses to David, the Hebrew prophets, Mary, Jesus, and the apostles, were Muslim prophets who preached Islam, and it is only in their quality as Muslims that they are recognized and respected. They belong to the Qur'an, not to the Bible. From this viewpoint the bond between Judaism and Christianity is a falsification, because the filiation of Christianity is Islamic, not Judaic. Christianity descends from Islam, the first religion of all humanity (*din al-fitra*). Christianity is a falsified expression of Islam, and belongs to Islam. According to a hadith, when Isa, the Muslim Jesus, returns, he will break the cross, kill the pig, abolish the *jizya* (poll tax for infidels), and money will flow like water. Exegetes interpret the destruction of symbols attached to Christianity—the cross and the pig—as the extinction of that religion; the suppression of the *jizya* means that Islam has become the only religion; and the abundance of wealth refers to the booty taken from infidels. In other words the return of the Muslim Jesus could lead to the destruction of Christianity.

The global jihad has made the problems of dhimmitude a worldwide reality. Europe's creeping dhimmitude, expressed in a refusal even to mention in its proposed constitution the "Judeo-Christian" values of its civilization, is one of the major elements of the current European-American divide.

CHRISTIANS IN THE
15. MUSLIM WORLD

Patrick Sookhdeo

We in the Western nations are free to follow our religious beliefs as we wish, and as Christians it is all too easy to forget the suffering and fear that so many of our fellow believers are living with in many Islamic countries today. They increasingly find themselves an embattled minority with dwindling rights who are trapped in poverty and uncertainty.

There are around 40 million Christians living as minorities in Muslim-majority countries in the world today. In some parts of the world these Christian minorities are of substantial size—at least 15 million in Indonesia, about 9 million in Egypt, and 3 million in Pakistan. In other places, there may be no more than a few dozen national Christians in the whole country, for example, the Maldives. In countries such as Saudi Arabia national Christian believers must keep their faith secret, or they would be executed. It is impossible to know exactly how many Christian believers there are in these countries.

Christians living in Muslim countries are generally treated as second-class citizens. They meet frequent discrimination in education, employment, and even from the police and judiciary. They are despised and distrusted, often suspected of giving their primary loyalty to the "Christian" West rather than to their homeland. The basis of this lies in the traditional Islamic teaching that Christians and Jews—the "People of the Book"—should be subjugated by force and made to pay a special tax called *jizya*. sura 9, verse 29 of the Qur'an instructs Muslims as follows:

Reprinted with permission from http://www.c4israel.org/articles/english/e-I-02-2-sook-christiansinm .htm.

Fight those who believe not
In God nor the Last Day,
Nor hold that forbidden
Which hath been forbidden
By God and His Apostle,
Nor acknowledge the Religion
Of Truth, (even if they are)
Of the People of the Book,
Until they pay the Jizya
With willing submission,
And feel themselves subdued.

These subjugated peoples were designated dhimmis. As well as the *jizya*, there were many other conditions imposed on dhimmis, most of which were designed to underline their inferior status. Though these rules are not followed strictly nowadays, the general attitude still prevails across the Muslim world. Christians are very often discriminated against in employment, education, and other social contexts, as well as by the police and the judiciary.

In some countries there is legalized discrimination against Christians. In other cases, it is community and society that treat them unfairly, despite fair laws and constitutional rights. Often it is a mixture of the two, as in Egypt, for example. One of the greatest difficulties facing Egyptian Christians concerns church buildings. They have to get permission from the president himself to build a new one, a process that can take many years and has no guarantee of success. Even permission to repair existing church buildings is hard to obtain, and on top of this they often find their buildings attacked. In lawless areas of rural upper Egypt they face much violence to themselves, their homes, and their fields from Islamic extremists, some of whom demand payment of *jizya*. The government seems unable to protect rural Christians from these militants.

Pakistan's Christians have two particular handicaps. First, they are very vulnerable to false accusation under the so-called blasphemy law, which lays down a death sentence for the crime of "defiling" the name of the prophet Muhammad. Although none have yet been executed, several Christians accused in malice under this law have been murdered by zealous Muslim individuals who believe this is pleasing to God. Second, in the Islamic court system, the witness of Christians does not carry as much weight as the witness of Muslims, putting the former at a severe disadvantage.

In Nigeria Christians slightly outnumber Muslims but are concentrated in the south of the country, with Muslims forming a majority in the north.

In the "middle belt," Christians and Muslims are roughly equal in number. Since 2000 twelve northern and middle-belt states have introduced full Islamic law (Sharia). Despite promises that Christians in these states would not be affected, they face a variety of restrictions and difficulties with such matters as church buildings, Christian schools, women's dress, and public transportation. Furthermore, there have been many incidents of violent rioting, in which thousands of Christians have been killed and thousands more made homeless. Many churches have been destroyed.

Anti-Christian violence on an even greater scale has been occurring in parts of Indonesia, the world's most populous Muslim nation. Until a few years ago, this country was an example of harmonious Christian-Muslim relations and real equality between the two communities. Now, however, Christians in are being targeted by Islamic militants in a systematic genocidal campaign to eliminate them. Initially the attacks were predominantly in the Malukus; then the main area of violence moved to Sulawesi and are now spreading to West Papua. Many thousands of Christians have been killed, as village after village has been burned to the ground, and almost half a million have been made refugees. In addition, at least seven thousand Christians have been forcibly converted to Islam. Many of these were forcibly circumcised as a sign of their new Islamic faith. This includes men and women, young and old, and the circumcisions were usually performed without antiseptic or anesthetic.

The Sudanese government has been ruthless in attacking African Christians and animists in southern Sudan, who refuse to accept its policies of Islamization and Arabization—hence the brutal civil war, which began in 1983 and resulted in the destruction of the entire infrastructure of the south. Several peace agreements have been signed, but real peace has not yet come. Millions of southerners have fled, either to the north or to neighboring countries. In the north they find themselves discriminated against in many ways. The shantytowns where they live are often bulldozed, and truckloads of Christians have been forcibly dumped in the desert with no food, water, or shelter. Many Christians are also enslaved by Arab Muslims.

WORSE THAN EVER

Following the September 11, 2001, attacks on the World Trade Center and the Pentagon, and the subsequent US-led "war on terror" with attacks on Afghanistan and Iraq, the situation for Christians in the Muslim world has become even more tense and dangerous. They are an easy local target on which Muslims can vent the anger they feel against the United States.

In the weeks following September 11, 2001, numerous attacks on Christians occurred around the world. For example, on September 20, a thirteen-year-old Christian stallholder in Pakistan was beaten to death by a gang of Muslims who refused to pay for the food they had bought from him. They told him to "take your payment from America." Two churches in Isiolo, Kenya, were burnt down on September 26, and the words "God is great" and "We condemn America" carved into the charred remains. In Israel on October 8, a Christian convert from Islam was stabbed to death by a supporter of Osama bin Laden, who shouted, "You are an apostate!" In Malaysia eight Christian workers at the headquarters of the National Evangelical Christian Fellowship were hospitalized on October 23 after coming into contact with an envelope containing white powder. The powder was sent with an offensive letter, claiming the powder was anthrax and promising the death of the staff, the destruction of their office, and a curse on Christians in general. In Iraq it is reported that some Christians are now being left out of the distribution of government food rations and are being mockingly told to ask America for their food instead. They have become too frightened to wear a cross in public any more. On October 28, fifteen Christians at Sunday worship were shot dead by Islamist gunmen who burst into their church in Bahawalpur. The gunmen shouted, "Pakistan and Afghanistan, graveyard of Christians," "God is great," and "This is just the start." The massacre occurred several weeks after some Islamic religious leaders in Pakistan had announced a *fatwa* that two Pakistani Christians would be killed for every Muslim who died in airstrikes on Afghanistan.

These attacks that took place in the immediate aftermath of September 11 have now increased in intensity, and many Westerners and missionaries are being targeted as well as national Christians.

Hope for the Future?

What does the future hold for Christian minorities in Islamic contexts? The trend in the last two decades has been consistently toward the erosion of their rights and status, the increase of pressure, discrimination, and violence. These developments have gone largely unremarked by the world in general, including the Western Churches. Christians in Muslim countries feel themselves forgotten by their Christian brothers and sisters elsewhere who are blessed with greater freedoms, and this only adds to their pain and hopelessness.

But perhaps the new interest in Islam that has resulted from the events of

September 11 could result also in greater publicity for the plight of the suffering Church under Islam, which has continued for fourteen centuries. Perhaps, too, it could result in a debate leading to a reformation of Islam, to move it on from its present laws and values, which have remained unchanged since the Middle Ages, toward modern standards of human rights and religious liberty.

16. PERSECUTION OF JEWS AND CHRISTIANS

Testimony versus Silence

Bat Ye'or

I have no pleasure in the death of the wicked;
but that the wicked turn from his way and live.

—Ezekiel 33:11

Ladies and Gentlemen,

I wish to thank Elliott Abrams for giving me the privilege of sharing with you some reflections on the meaning of "testimony versus silence." But we must first ask ourselves—testimony about what? And also, testifying for which purpose?

To answer the first question, we can say that the Bible—to mention but this aspect—testifies to a suprahuman and an immanent order of values or, more simply, to a divine presence within the universe and humanity. The divine spirit abolished chaos, fixed the limits in human behavior of what is allowed and what cannot be transgressed on the basis of the universal sanctity of the human being, as announced in Genesis 1:27: "in the image of God created he him; male and female created he them." The immanence of the divine in man creates an alliance, a partnership between God and man, a dual responsibility freely accepted by man, for keeping or testifying to these supreme ethical norms based on the sanctity of all humans, which cannot be transgressed. The Bible illustrates the constant struggle between the testifier and the destroyer of life, or the hater of man.

Bat Ye'or originally delivered this address at the Ethics and Public Policy Center, Washington, DC, on April 2, 1998. The EPPC's president, Elliott Abrams, chaired the session and the respondents on the podium were George Weigel and Paul Marshall. This text was translated into English by David G. Littman, with the author.

In the context of my remarks today, the meaning of *testimony* is to stand up against a tyrant, to denounce injustice, and to proclaim the dignity of all humanity. Although the testifier gives testimony because he has to do so and cannot escape from this duty, his act implies an inherently optimistic hope and faith in man—the hope that the heart of the tyrant will change. With the words in the Psalm, "I will speak of thy testimonies also before kings, and will not be ashamed" (119:46).

In the long, sad, and painful history of the Judeo-Christian relationship, the people of Israel have always assumed the role of the witness or testifier, not because it is any better than others but because history made them victims of dehumanizing laws. This is the well-known status of Jewry in Europe, which was abolished in the French Revolution of 1789, and later, in the nineteenth century, throughout Western Europe. Because of the Jewish roots of Christianity, this tradition of dialogue and of the contestation of power was integrated into the dynamic of history. The emancipation of European Jewry was a Christian political decision, made on humanitarian principles—the Jews later joining in the fight for the equality of civil rights. Because Jews and Christians claim the same ethical values of the Bible, Christians raised their voices against the deliberate dehumanizing policy of the people who had first proclaimed their knowledge of God. Jewish testimony was joined, promoted, and sustained by a Christian engagement. Before, during, and after the Holocaust, this partnership held firm despite overwhelming hatred and cruelty. Since then, Christian engagement in a redemptive work within the Church has become more forceful.

But testifying is no easy task, as it also brings persecution, loneliness, and despair. Challenging "evil," unveiling it from behind its ubiquitous masks, is dangerous, an unending life struggle. For the lonely surviving remnant of Israel, constantly bearing testimony to the Holocaust in an indifferent world was an agonizing process. In a world of ashes, Jews unceasingly proclaimed the dignity and sanctity of man. And they were not alone in testifying. Many Christians joined them: writers, theologians, and anonymous voices, too. Jews and Christians testified together. The result of this common action, what I consider a common prayer—by acts and deeds—led to the revolutionary theological transformation of Church dogma concerning the Jews. By testifying together, Jews and Christians initiated profound spiritual changes. One might even say that through the very act of the rehumanization of the Jewish victim, the Church rehumanized itself in an internal process of humility, thereby deepening its own theological reflection.

Now, if we turn to the Islamic lands, we find a very different situation, where Jews and Christians often declare their "gratitude" to the Islamic society, and yet few Jews exist today in Arab-Muslim lands, and the Christians are on the same road of exile. By the early nineteenth century, Judaism was nearly extinguished in Palestine, the very cradle of Jewish history and civilization. A similar historic process was at work for Eastern Christianity, whose roots are in the Middle East, nowadays usually referred to as Arab-Muslim lands. Except for the Copts of Egypt, who still form a sizable minority, Christianity would hardly have survived in its Oriental homeland—especially in Palestine—without the permanent support and protection of Europe.

Islamic law, the Sharia, provides "protection" and security for the People of the Book—the Bible; it is, indeed, a basic theological principle. However, Muslim theologians and jurists attached so many conditions and humiliations to this real protection that the status of the protected Jews and Christians—the dhimmis—soon became a status of oppression, deprivation, and insecurity.

This status was regulated by several laws that bound them within a social pattern of discriminations and insecurity. Instead of "Islamic tolerance," or "toleration," I have called this vast political, religious, and cultural world— from Arabia to Spain and the Balkans, including, for some time, part of Hungary and Poland—the realm of "dhimmitude," from the Arabic word *dhimma*: a treaty of submission for those peoples conquered by jihad. The laws that were applied to the dhimmis I have called the laws of dhimmitude, and the special type of civilization that dhimmis developed I have called the civilization of dhimmitude.

The civilization of dhimmitude is based on two main elements: jihad— that is, a compulsory religious war of conquest that brings non-Muslim lands into the realm of Islam; and the subjugation of its native populations. In other words, the choice is between perpetual war or submission. The civilization of dhimmitude developed in the context of subjugation and insecurity. Its main features were the payment of the *jizya*, a Quranic tribute that became a poll tax. For early Muslim jurists, the *jizya* had two purposes: to enrich the *umma*, the Islamic community, and—a symbolic meaning—it suspended the jihad threat, which was death, slavery, or the expulsion of non-Muslims. The payment of the *jizya* procured for the dhimmis the security for their lives, their families, and their personal possessions. One important aspect of dhimmitude is the principle of the dhimmis' inferiority to Muslims in every walk of life. This civilization of dhimmitude expanded on three continents, representing millions of people. Over the centuries, populations and entire civilizations disappeared, or barely survived. The civilization of dhimmitude is composed of numerous ethnic groups, mainly Christian, and rival Eastern Churches. Documentation abounds, and a few sources may be found in my books.

The civilization of dhimmitude is based on the principle of "protection," which is the security for life and property pledged by a Muslim ruler to non-Muslims, who are subjected to certain conditions—tribute money, or as a temporary protection (*aman*). This concept implies that the right to security of life and property are denied to non-Muslims and are only granted by the Muslim community according to its own conditions. In other words, the principle of natural rights for all human beings is denied. The civilization of dhimmitude is engendered by war and conquest.

Today, Eastern Christianity looks as if it will disappear from the very cradle of its birthplace, the Middle East, and one may well ask, Is there an adequate Christian "testimony" of this drama? Let us see how the various peoples of dhimmitude conceive their own history. The Greeks recounted their trials under the Turkish yoke; Serbs did the same in the pre-Communist era, as well as Hungarians, Bulgarians, and other Balkan peoples. The Armenians have written abundantly on the Armenian genocide. Yet the Chaldean Assyrians of Iraq have hardly protested against their tribulations. Although the Copts testified from the beginning of the century, few in the West paid much attention to their grievances. Recently, Coptic associations in America and Canada have succeeded in having their courageous protests published in the national press about the sufferings of their people and the abuses of their fundamental human rights. Lebanese Christianity fought, suffered, and succumbed with little protest coming from Europe or America. The Sudanese Christians still suffer from an Islamic regime: jihad and slavery, abduction, forced conversions, and destruction have been their lot for decades, and only recently have their cries been heard. Last year, a Christian Coalition for the defense of oppressed Eastern Churches began a human rights campaign here in Washington. Only last week, Paul Marshall, my husband, and I were in Columbia, South Carolina, participating with others at the First National Conference on the Persecuted Church, titled "Shattering the Silence." So we see that there are peoples who are still subjected nowadays to dhimmitude. A whole Judeo-Christian, Aramaic civilization from pre-Islamic times is slowly agonizing, while a profound silence prevails. Recently, a handful of books have been written on the subject in French, but generally there is an unwritten consensus to praise the historico-religious record of "Islamic tolerance" toward non-Muslims. Let me enumerate some of the reasons that have led to this.

CAUSES RELATED TO THE MUSLIM SOCIETY

The idea that Jews and Christians have suffered under Islamic law is totally rejected by the dominant group—the Muslims—and this for several reasons, based on theological grounds: (1) Islamic law cannot be defective since it must be perfect, being considered a divine law. Therefore it cannot be unjust, and the suffering of infidels under that rule is deserved since it represents the justice of Allah. (2) The Sharia should not be criticized, and Christians and Jews cannot say it has any defect whatsoever. (3) Whereas in the Bible the religious function is separated from the political one, in Islam political and religious power must be united. The nonseparation of politics and religion confer a fixed religious and sacred character to politics. (4) An absence of Muslim support on behalf of dhimmis since the conception of their relations with non-Muslims is determined by the principles of jihad and protection, which granted to the Muslims the feeling of being generous. Without this "passport" of protection (*aman*), no *harbi*—the name for all non-Muslims from the *dar al-Harb*, the region of war—could enter the *dar al-Islam*, the region of Islam, unless he agreed to become a dhimmi.

CAUSES RELATED TO THE DHIMMIS

The cause most closely related to the dhimmis is the divisions and conflicts between the diverse dhimmi Churches. Any protests against the oppression of the laws implies a minimum of consensus between Armenians, Maronites, Assyrians, Copts, Melchites, Greeks, and the Slavonic Churches. Since the laws of dhimmitude apply equally to Jews and Christians, this also requires a consensus with the Jews, and this has been impossible for the Eastern Churches.

There are other reasons to explain this political impotence: the vulnerability of small, insecure Christian communities; the religious leadership's subservience to the Muslim power; their economic interests; and the total and deliberate obfuscation of their dhimmi past.

CAUSES RELATED TO THE WESTERN POWERS

Here we can mention the pro-Islamic policy of the Western powers, their economic interests in the Muslim world, the all too frequent concealment of the truth by the media and Western governments, and their deliberate refusal to transmit this local reality to the public, for fear of (1) Muslim terrorism (2) anti-Islamic reactions in the West, and (3) economical and political retaliations from Muslim countries.

Denouncing the injustice of dhimmitude means a feeling of solidarity with all its victims—Christians of all denominations, as well as Jews. It means having the profound conviction that all humans are equal and that no one should be demonized. Laws that are unjust for Christians cannot be considered just for Jews—unless Jews are first demonized. Testifying to the great tragedy of dhimmitude implies a sense of togetherness that has never existed.

I am convinced that Christian involvement in the Arab-Islamic jihad, first against Zionism in the late nineteenth century and then against Israel throughout the twentieth century, was the main cause for the obfuscation of dhimmi history and the lack of testimony about the sufferings of Christian dhimmis. The source of all evil had to be projected onto Zionism and Israel, whereas it is a historical fact that the causes for Christian oppression in the East are rooted in the doctrine of jihad and in the laws and civilization of dhimmitude. Because the trials and tribulations of Christians in Islamic countries and their causes—the rules of dhimmitude—had to be hidden, dhimmi Christian history became a well-guarded secret, a secret that had to be concealed and never revealed. The Muslim-Christian alliance in an anti-Zionist crusade led the Christians to testify against Israel. And because the significance of the restoration of Israel in this region of the world symbolizes the abolition of jihad and of the laws of dhimmitude, the engagement of Christians in the anti-Israel jihad has contributed to the decline of Christianity itself.

Let me conclude these brief remarks on a complicated subject. It is this lack of testimony that has brought back the evils and the prejudices of the past—the jihad mentality and the laws of dhimmitude that were only abolished by the colonial European powers. And now, more and more, because of this lack of testimony, we see moderate Muslims themselves being persecuted. Because they were indifferent to the humiliation of Jews and Christians, because they remained silent and aloof, they now find themselves—in Algeria, Egypt, and elsewhere—suffering from cruel injustices and barbarism. Testifying together, giving testimony against dhimmitude, would have allowed Muslim intellectuals to rethink their whole relationship with the People of the Bible—and with all non-Muslims, and this without renouncing their faith. Such an attitude would have brought all of us together in the fight against tyrannical oppression, against the process of dehumanization. This is what could have been done but what was not done.

17. WHAT IS HAPPENING IN INDONESIA?

Mark Durie

In all the discussion of the Bali tragedy, many Australians have searched for a reason for so many innocent people to have been killed. Surely such hatred must have some explanation. Could it be something we have done? Was it East Timor? The "war on Iraq"? Our lifestyle? Our indifference to world poverty?

This bomb attack, and others like it, must be understood in terms of the strategic goals and worldview of the Islamic terrorist organizations that carry them out. All these groups aim to establish the Islamic Sharia, or "Islamic way," as the law of the land. They oppose existing regimes in Muslim countries that are rejected as un-Islamic. A second belief they share is that jihad is the best method for bringing this objective about.

Countless books, tracts, and training schools emphasize these two principles. At the time of independence from the Dutch in 1945, calls for Indonesia to become an Islamic state were successfully resisted. The authors of Indonesia's constitution opted instead for pluralism, affirming a diversity of religions, including Islam, Christianity, Hinduism, and Bhuddism. The national motto is "Unity in Diversity."

However, during the 1980s President Suharto, to prop up his ailing presidency, began to court Islamic radicals, who grew rapidly in influence. One of the effects of this political shift has been an escalation of attacks on Christian communities in Indonesia. The Barnabas Fund (UK) reported at the end of 2000 that half a million Christians have become internally displaced, more than five thousand people have been killed, and as many as seven thousand

---

This piece was written for use at a memorial service at St. Hilary's, Kew, after the Bali terrorist attacks in 2002.

have been forcibly converted to Islam. Local Muslim communities have also experienced great suffering in the violent confrontations.

There are renewed calls today for Indonesia to become a Sharia state. However, an obstacle to imposition of the Sharia, apart from the many moderate Muslims, is the handful of provinces with significant Christian populations, or, in the case of Bali, a majority Hindu population.

In November 2000 the Laskar Jihad militia announced, "We intend during this Ramadan to . . . carry out various activities paving the way for full Sharia at least in places that have now become exclusively Islam, such as the islands of Ternate, Tidore and Bacan." This is a kind of code for religious cleansing of Christians from those regions. The town of Poso in Central Sulawesi used to have a population of forty thousand, mostly Christian. By the end of 2002 it had been reduced to an exclusively Muslim population of five thousand, with all of its churches destroyed. Reports of the Laskar Jihad's operations in Ambon and Sulawesi describe a systematic progression through villages and towns, sometimes using equipment such as bulldozers, petrol tankers, rocket launchers, and other military hardware. Villages are looted, burned out, and razed to the ground.

The Laskar Jihad is known to include fighters from Afghanistan, Pakistan, Saudi Arabia, and the Philippines. Susilo Bambang Yudhoyono, Indonesia's top political and security minister, has said of them, "They also play a role in defending truth and justice that is expected by Muslims in Indonesia. For me, as far as what they are doing is legal and not violating the law, then this is OK."

The Laskar Jihad has proven links to al Qaeda, which by its title is officially dedicated to worldwide jihad against "Jews and Crusaders" (*Crusaders* means Christians in terrorist-speak). An al Qaeda training center near Poso was used by the Laskar Jihad as a staging base for many attacks against local Christians, constantly frustrating local attempts at reconciliation between Muslims and Christians during 2001. More recently the Laskar Jihad has proclaimed West Papua as its next theater of operations.

Thousands of militants have been gathering there to prepare the way for the next jihad campaign. Although the Laskar Jihad claims to have disbanded just hours before the Bali atrocity, its troops remain in Papua.

The label "sectarian violence," used so irresponsibly by the media for all this terror, has served to conceal and minimize the overall impact of the radical jihad groups' activities within Indonesia. The world has allowed destabilization, terror, and displacement to advance a very great way already.

The shift from jihad against Indonesian citizens to attacks on foreigners heralds a new phase in the struggle. Yet the goal of this operation must still be measured in terms of the way it could forward the pro-Sharia cause. It has certainly greatly weakened Hindu Bali, and, by dealing the tourist trade a deadly blow, it will serve to isolate Indonesia from Western scrutiny and influence. Forcing Indonesian president Megawati Sukamoputri to take action against militants could hasten her political demise and leave the way open for a more acceptable replacement. It also helps the Sharia cause that the operation was conducted in Bali, where Muslims would be much less likely to have been hit as collateral damage.

As we mourn the lost and express sympathy and sorrow for the suffering of survivors from the Bali attack, let us work and seek for peace in Indonesia, a return to religious harmony, and a stable future for this great nation.

DOCUMENTATION OF OPPRESSION OF
18. RELIGIOUS FREEDOM IN ACEH, INDONESIA

Mark Durie

The following document was imposed on the Christian community in the District of Aceh Singkil, in the Province of Aceh, Indonesia, on October 11, 2001. This "mutual agreement" was imposed in order to ward off the threat of destruction of all church buildings and a real threat against the lives of Christians in the area: this is what the document refers to as "unwanted consequences." This oppression of religious freedom was triggered by one church expanding the size of its building. It was claimed by the Muslim leadership that this violated previous "agreements" in 1979 not to build any more churches.

This "agreement" would appear to be in the spirit of the Quranic framework given for struggle against the People of the Book. A doctrinally acceptable outcome of this struggle is submission of the Christian community to Islam through means of a pact or treaty. Classically this would have involved payment of a head tax to the Muslim community, as well as restrictions on places of worship. The "agreement" below focuses on places of worship and also prohibits Christian religious meetings from being held in private homes. It is a characteristic of Muslim perspectives on such pacts is that they show "Islamic tolerance" (cf. 3b, below). The guarantee of peace implicit in point III.1 is also typical of Islamic understandings of such covenants: the Christians will not experience struggle (jihad) if they adhere to the pact. Characteristic also is that the Christians are seen to be the cause of potential conflict (I). No parallel constraints or appropriation are placed upon the Islamic community.

AGREEMENT BETWEEN THE ISLAMIC AND CHRISTIAN COMMUNITIES IN THE COUNTIES OF SIMPAN KANAN, GUNUNG MERIAH, AND DANAU PARIS IN THE DISTRICT OF ACEH SINGKIL

I. In recent times the Islamic Communities in the Counties of Simpang Kanan, Gunung Meriah and Danau Paris have been disturbed by the activities of the Christian Community in building and renovating a Church in contravention to a Statement between the Islamic Community and the Christian Community in the County of Simpang Kanan dated July 11, 1979, and an Agreement to live in harmony together dated October 13, 1979.

II. To avoid the possibility of unwanted consequences which could instigate the destruction of unity and oneness between the religious Communities (Islam and Christian) Tuesday, October 9, in the Board room at the office of the District Mayor of Aceh Singkil, we the Leaders of the Islamic religion and the Christians of the Counties of Simpang Kanan, Gunung Meriah and Danau Paris, conducted a Consultative meeting in a family atmosphere, good ethics and the meeting was continued on Thursday, October 11, 2001.

III. The Consultation was undertaken and witnessed to by the County Council of Government Leaders [Mayor, Speaker of Parliament, Military, Police, Courts] of Simpang Kanan and the District Council of Government Leaders of Aceh Singkil which resulted in the following agreement:

1. We the Islamic Community wish to live peacefully alongside and to mutually assist in the completeness and unity as a clear implementation/form of compact unity between the Islamic Community and the Christians which has been long developed.
2. We the Islamic Community and the Christian Community continue to respect and obey the points of a combined statement between the Islamic Community and the Christians in the County of Simpang Kanan dated July 11, 1979, and the Agreement of unity together dated October 13, 1979.
3. We the Islamic Community and the Christian Community have agreed upon the number of Churches and small Houses of Worship [small church building or hut used for worship] in the Counties of Simpang Kanan, Gunung Meriah and Danau Paris, that is 1 (one) Church building and 4 (four) small Houses of Worship, each consisting of:

a. 1 (one) Church building in the Village of Kuta Kerangan which has a Government permit measuring 12 × 24 meters and not multi-level.

b. 4 (four) small Houses of Worship as a sign of Islamic tolerance, each consisting of:

—1 (one) small House of Worship in the Village of Keras;

—1 (one) small House of Worship in the Village of Napugaluh;

—1 (one) small House of Worship in the Village of Suka Makmur;

—1 (one) small House of Worship in the Village of Lae Gecih.

4. Other than the Church building and small Houses of Worship mentioned in point 2 above there are still other Church buildings in other places in the Counties of Simpang Kanan, Gunung Meriah and Danau Paris which must be eliminated/destroyed by the Christian Community themselves.

5. We the Christian Community will not engage in religious activities in the homes of residents, nor conduct any missionary activity.

IV. This is the result of the consultation between the Islamic Community and the Christian Community with all sincerity and a sense of brotherhood to create an atmosphere of living in harmony between the religious communities in the Counties of Simpang Kanan, Gunung Meriah and Danau Paris specifically and in the District of Aceh Singkil generally.

Singkil, October 11, 2001
We who conducted the Consultation
a. Islamic Community b. Christian Community
[List of 42 names] [List of 32 names]
[Signed by 23] [Signed by 20]

Witnessed by Members of the District Council of Government Leaders of the District of Aceh Singil and County Councils of Govt Leaders of Simpang Kanan, Gunung Meriah and Danau Paris.

1. Mayor of Aceh Singkil
2. Speaker of District Parliament of Aceh Singkil
3. Assistant Mayor of Aceh Singkil
4. Chief Prosecutor of the District of Aceh Singkil

5. Chief Judge of the District Court of Aceh Singkil
6. District Secretary of Aceh Singkil
7. Head of Military for South Aceh in Singkil
8. Chairman of MPU District of Aceh Singkil
9. Member of Provincial Parliament of Aceh
10. Head of the Department of Religion of Aceh Singkil
11. Head of the Office of Social Politics
12. County Mayor of Simpang Kanan
13. County Mayor of Gunung Meriah
14. County Mayor of Simpang Kanan
15. Police Chief of Simpang Kanan
16. Police Chief of Singkil
17. Military Commander of Simpang Kanan
18. Military Commander of Singkil
19. Naval Commander of Singkil
20. Captain Zainul

JIHAD AND HUMAN RIGHTS TODAY

19. An Active Ideology Incompatible with Universal Standards of Freedom and Equality

Bat Ye'or

Human rights and the concept of jihad are two incompatible ideas. In Judeo-Christian societies, the concept of human rights is based on the biblical interdiction against killing and the equality of all human beings. Though it has religious roots, this notion of human rights evolved mainly from the nineteenth century in a secular European and American framework. It then acquired a universal character, proclaiming the equality of all human beings and the inviolability of their natural human rights. But it was only after World War II that this concept became the core of an international legal system, as a tool to prevent political abuses and to protect civil populations from genocidal policies.

Other major civilizations—including the Chinese, Hindu, and Islamic—have also conceived legal systems that protect the rights of their citizens. However, in the Islamic case, specifically, the fifty-four Muslim countries of the Organization of the Islamic Conference have conceived their own human rights charter, contained in the 1990 Cairo Declaration on Human Rights in Islam.

This document states in its preamble and in articles 24 and 25 that all its provisions are in conformity with the Sharia, the religious Islamic law, which has primacy. Moreover, it proclaims that God has made the Islamic community (*umma*) the best nation—and, hence, its role is to guide humanity. We can see here the differences between the Cairo Declaration and the Universal Declaration of Human Rights, which does not refer to any religion or to the

This text ("Human Rights and the Concept of Jihad") was first used by Bat Ye'or at a US Congressional Human Rights Caucus Briefing (with Habib Malik and David G. Littman) on February 8, 2002. It was reedited, with the assistance of Dr. Andrew G. Bostom, and published by the *National Review Online* on July 1, 2002. Distributed by United Feature Syndicate Incorporated.

superiority of any group over another but stresses the absolute equality of all human beings.

The institution of jihad belongs to a religious, Islamic domain, outside the realm of Western universalism and secularism. These two domains do not meet. Secular laws can be changed, abrogated, or ameliorated, but jihad regulations are believed to express divine commands. By definition, human beings can neither discuss nor scrutinize the divine will, and so those jihad obligations—attributed by the theologians to Allah—place jihad in the domain of faith. I would like to emphasize strongly that jihad is a special domain of Islamic law. Not all Muslims know it, and many reject its ideology. It would be a great mistake to believe that each and every Muslim identifies with the jihad war ideology.

The ideology of jihad was formulated by leading Muslim theologians and scholars from the eighth century onward. Their voluminous writings make clear the notion of jihad as a holy war of conquest. Ibn Abi Zayd al-Qayrawani (d. 966), for example, stated, "Jihad is a precept of Divine institution. . . . We Malikis [adherents of one of four schools of Muslim jurisprudence] maintain it is preferable not to begin hostilities with the enemy before having invited the latter to embrace the religion of Allah, except where the enemy attacks first. They have the alternative of either converting to Islam or paying the poll tax [*jizya*], short of which war will be declared against them."[1]

Jihad ideology separates humanity into two hostile blocs: the community of Muslims (*dar al-Islam*), and the infidel non-Muslims (*dar al-Harb*). Allah commands the Muslims to conquer the entire world in order to rule it according to Quranic law. Hence Muslims must wage a perpetual war against those infidels who refuse to submit. This is the motivation for jihad. It is based on the inequality between the community of Allah and the infidels, as was reemphasized in the Cairo Declaration. The first is a superior group that must rule the world; the second must submit. The current relevance of this ideology is apparent, and disturbing.

For example, *Al-Muhajiroun, the Voice, the Eyes, the Ears of the Muslims*, an Islamist newspaper in London, published an article on January 27, 2001, which declared, "Upon the establishment of the Islamic State, the whole world will potentially be *Dar ul Harb* since the foreign policy of the Islamic state is aimed at conquering the world. . . . Once the Islamic State is established anyone in *Dar ul Harb* will have no sanctity for his life or wealth; hence, a Muslim in such circumstances can then go into Dar ul Harb and take the wealth from the people unless there is a treaty with that state. If there is no treaty, individual Muslims can even go to Dar ul Harb and take women to keep as slaves."[2] Such an attitude assumes that the infidels have no rights and are totally dehumanized. It breeds hatred and contempt and has led to historical negationism and the destruction of non-Muslim cultures. Moreover, such views are not confined to the most radical Islamists. They were confirmed in the Proceedings of the Fourth Conference of the Academy of Islamic Research, held in 1968 (Cairo: General Organization for Government Printing Offices, 1968), and regularly since then by eminent Islamic scholars. These authoritative pronouncements have recapitulated the theory of jihad in a manner completely consistent with the *Al-Muhajiroun* statements.

The theory of jihad against the infidels is composed of two parts: the ideology and the military institutions aimed at implementing this ideology. According to these rules the infidels without a treaty have no rights at all: they can be deported, reduced to slavery, abducted for ransom, or killed. Women and children can be taken into slavery. Infidels can be spared by a temporary treaty, which should not go beyond ten years. The treaty must conform to Islamic rule and serve Islamic interests; hence a ransom should be paid. Infidels who submit to Islamic rulers are given a pledge of security against the rules of jihad, as long as they accept a condition of humiliation and of total inferiority to Muslims.

Jihad is therefore a genocidal war, according to the modern definition of genocide. It encourages terrorism against civilians and does not differentiate between innocent civilians and soldiers. All infidels without a treaty of protection can be killed. Jihad does not recognize universal human rights, for there is no equality between Muslims and infidels and no reciprocity between Muslims and infidels in legal matters. Jihad warriors do not accept that either the Geneva Conventions or the conventional rules of war have any validity for them.

Jihadists have associated the notion of a reward in paradise with the practice of killing infidels. Killing at war was, and still is, practiced by all societies. In the Judeo-Christian tradition, wars, because they imply the acts of killing, are hateful, and peace is praised. In the jihadist ideology, it is war that is praised, along with the killing of the infidels. Tragically, jihad ideology will not disappear soon. It is shaping the minds of a generation of young Muslims in many countries. Jihad ideology is a well-constructed system, created after the death of the prophet Muhammad. It has remained alive and well since then—except under secularized Muslim governments like that of Turkey, after the Kemalist revolution. It is delusional and dangerous to maintain that this ideology is rooted in social deprivation, backwardness, injustice, or despair. Moreover, paying subsidies to suspend global jihad terrorism is tantamount to paying a tribute to terrorist states, and buying one's own peace and security as temporarily ransomed privileges—instead of living by the principles of universal human rights, which proclaim the inviolability of every human being. Societies that pay a tribute to survive are destined to disappear.

NOTES

1. *La Risala* (*Epître sur les éléments du dogme et de la loi de l'Islam selon le rite mâlikite*), 5th ed., trans. from Arabic by Léon Bercher (Algiers, 1960), p. 163.

2. See www.onlyam.com/islamics/newtopics/foreign_policy/land_policy/land _classification.html.

CULTURE OF HATE

20. A Racism That Denies the History and Sufferings of Its Victims

Bat Ye'or

At the dawn of the new millennium, the world is being confronted with an absolute culture of hate, characterized by paroxysms of international terrorism against civilians and religious intolerance. This culture of hate has multiple heads, from Algeria to Afghanistan to Indonesia, via Gaza and the West Bank, Damascus, Cairo, Khartoum, Teheran, and Karachi. It scatters the seeds of terrorism from one end of the earth to the other.

This hate, which suppresses freedom of thought and condemns difference, calls itself Islamic jihad. It draws on religious texts whose interpretation other Muslims dispute. Moreover, because these moderate Muslims challenge this interpretation of jihad, wishing to live in peace with the non-Muslim peoples and nations of the world, their lives are threatened. There is constant bloodshed in Algeria. Jihad is disseminating death and terror in Israel. In southern Sudan, jihad has caused the death of some two million people, generated an even larger number of refugees, led to the enslavement of tens of thousands, and produced deadly famines.

In Indonesia, some two hundred thousand deaths resulted from jihad violence in East Timor. Christians have been pursued and massacred, and their churches burned down by jihadists, in the Moluccas and other Indonesian islands. The death toll in these violent attacks is over ten thousand, whereas an additional eight thousand Christians have been forcibly converted to Islam,

This text originated as a brief address on July 31, 2001, in French ("La Culture de la Haine") at an NGO symposium organized at the United Nations (Geneva) by the Association for World Education during the fifty-third session of the UN Subcommission on Human Rights. Translated by David G. Littman, with the author, an enlarged English version (with editing help from Dr. Andrew G. Bostom) was published by the *National Review Online*, on August 2, 2002. Distributed by United Feature Syndicate Incorporated.

including many who were subsequently circumcised. Atrocities are also being committed by jihadists in both the Philippines and some northern Nigerian states. Hundreds of innocent people died when jihad struck at the Jewish Community Center of Buenos Aires in Argentina and the US embassies in Kenya and Tanzania. In Egypt jihadists have massacred Copts in their churches and villages and murdered European tourists. Christians in Pakistan and in Iran live in terror of accusations of blasphemy, which, if "proven," can yield a death sentence. And a cataclysmic act of jihad terror resulted in the slaughter of nearly three thousand innocent civilians of multiple faiths and nationalities in New York on September 11, 2001. None of these victims were guilty of any crime. They were murdered and mutilated out of hate.

It is this hate that Israel is fighting. The Durban World Conference against Racism—where the culture of hate was rehabilitated, not condemned—ended only three days before the jihad terror attacks on the World Trade Center and the Pentagon. When proposals were made condemning Zionism, this conference was encouraging jihad, the culture of the war against infidels, while ignoring the principles of freedom and human rights. This was negationist racism. The word *Zion*, which designates the land of Israel and its capital Jerusalem, exists in texts dating back almost three millennia. It was the Emperor Hadrian who first called the country Palestine in 135 CE. In this Palestine, Arabic was not the common language, the Bible and not the Qur'an was taught, and the population was mainly Jewish. Palestine was colonized five centuries later by the Arab armies of the Islamic jihad. Many Jews were massacred at that time, others deported to Arabia as slaves, the whole population expropriated and reduced to the condition of dhimmis, as were all indigenous Jews and Christians in the southern Mediterranean countries conquered by jihad, and later those in many European countries as well.

Should these countries conquered by Islam—Portugal, Spain, Sardinia, Sicily, Crete, and the southern regions of France and Italy, for example—still be considered Arab Muslim lands? Turkish jihad conquests imposed the Sharia as far north as Hungary and southern Poland, as well as of central Europe within the Ottoman Empire, including regions of Greece, the former Yugoslavia, Romania, and Bulgaria until the end of the nineteenth century. Are these countries also to be identified as Muslim lands, in which non-Muslim inhabitants must return to the condition of dhimmis, whose testimony concerning Muslims is rejected by Islamic courts? Will they again be required to don discriminatory garments, such as the Taliban demanded of the Hindus, or be subject to the continuing prohibition on building and renovating their churches, like the Copts in Egypt?

If the liberation movement of the Jews in their ancestral homeland is interpreted as racism, then all the movements of liberation from expropriation and servitude imposed by jihad are racist. Such a stance reinstates the imperialism of the Islamic jihad, which has claimed millions of victims over three continents during more than a millennium, deported an incalculable number of slaves, and annihilated entire peoples, destroying their history, their monuments, and their culture. Have the Copts of Egypt a right to their history and their language? Do the Kabili of North Africa have a right to theirs? We must acknowledge all the victims of the racism that jihad creates, a racism that denies the history, sufferings, and memories of those conquered.

Arab racism consists of calling the Land of Israel Arab land, whereas no Palestinian province, village, or town, including Jerusalem, is mentioned either in the Qur'an or in any Arabic text before the end of the ninth century. On the contrary, these locations are mentioned in the Hebrew Bible, which represents the religious and historical heritage of the Jewish people. The Bible, which tells the history of this country, tells it in Hebrew, the language of the country, and not in Arabic. Palestinian racism consists of asserting that the whole history of Israel, biblical history, is Arab, Islamic, and Palestinian history. The kings and prophets of Israel were Arab, Palestinian, and Muslim kings and prophets, as were Jesus, his family, and the apostles. This Arabization and Islamization of the Bible thus robs not only the Jews but also the whole of Christianity of their history. New theologies of substitution are developed, transferring Israel's heritage to Arab and Muslim Palestine.

The imperialism of jihad consists of appropriating the whole history and identity of the peoples who were conquered and thrown into the nonexistence of dhimmitude. This is a total negation of the other, a refusal to acknowledge it as equal. Israel's battle is not a battle of colonists, as some European political circles like to claim, because Europe itself had a colonial history on all continents, which it projects onto Israel. Similarly, Europe projects its own history of Nazism on to the Israelis, thereby revenging itself on the revelations of historians. Israel's battle is not a battle against the Muslim world; it is a battle against the unbridled hate of jihad. Israelis are struggling to maintain their liberation from the yoke of dhimmitude, which was imposed in order to eradicate the Jews in their indigenous homeland. That is why Christians who reject the new theologies of substitution are joining Israel in its fight, as are Muslims who refuse to allow the values of Islam to be perverted by the ideology of jihad. It is through this common effort that reconciliation between peoples can be achieved, replacing the culture of hate with a culture of friendship.

21. THE DHIMMITUDE OF THE WEST

Mark Durie

Dhimmitude is an Islamic phenomenon. It defines the condition of submissive surrender to Islamic rule without conversion to the Islamic faith. Under classical theological formulations developed in the first centuries of Islam, the region where Islam rules is known as *dar al-Islam*. the "House of Islam."

From the very beginning the *dar al-Islam* included many non-Muslims; indeed, they were normally in the majority after initial conquest. Based on the example of Muhammad's dealings with the conquered Jewish farmers of Khaybar, Fadak, Tayma, and Wadi-l Qura, the institution of the *dhimma*, or "pact of protection," was developed to provide for those who refused to convert to Islam. The *dhimma* was granted by the conquerors as one possible outcome of military jihad. It assured the vanquished an institutional legal framework that guaranteed their religious freedom, and determined their social and economic place in the Islamic state. In return the people of the pact, or dhimmis, were required to pay tribute in perpetuity to the Muslim community (*umma*), and to adopt a position of humble servitude to the *umma*.

The Quranic verse that dictates this fundamental character for dhimmitude is sura 9:29: "Fight against those who do not believe in Allah nor in the Last Day, and do not make forbidden what Allah and His Messenger have made forbidden, and do not practice the religion of truth, of those who have been given the Book [i.e., Jews and Christians], until they pay the *jizya* [head tax] readily and are humbled."

Reprinted with permission from the *Newsletter for the Centre for Islamic Studies*, London Bible College.

Within the Islamic state, all non-Muslims who are not objects of war are considered to be dhimmis—communities who are allowed to exist within the *dar al-Islam* by virtue of surrender under the conditions of a dhimmi pact. These are the permanently conquered peoples of Islam.

Historian Bat Ye'or has documented the social, political, economic, and religious conditions of dhimmi communities—Jews and Christians—in the Middle East. It is a sad history of dispossession and decline. Legal provisions applying to dhimmis ensured their humiliation and inferiority, and to this was added the often crippling taxes that were allocated to support the Muslim community. Under conditions of dhimmitude there was also a constant risk of jihad conditions being reinvoked—of massacre and dispossession—if the dhimmi community was considered to have failed to live up to the conditions of their pact. History records many examples where dhimmis were attacked by their fellow Muslim citizens on such grounds—for example, the massacres of the Jews of Granada in 1066 and of the Christians of Damascus in 1860.

Like sexism and racism, dhimmitude is manifested not only in legal and social structures but also in a psychology of inferiority, a will to serve, which the dominated community adopts in self-preservation.

> The law required from dhimmis a humble demeanor, eyes lowered, a hurried pace. They had to give way to Muslims in the street, remain standing in their presence and keep silent, only speaking to them when given permission. They were forbidden to defend themselves if attacked, or to raise a hand against a Muslim on pain of having it amputated. Any criticism of the Koran or Islamic law annuled the protection pact. In addition the dhimmi was duty-bound to be grateful, since it was Islamic law that spared his life.
>
> The whole corpus of these practices . . . formed an unchanging behavior pattern which was perpetuated from generation to generation for centuries. It was so deeply internalized that it escaped critical evaluation and invaded the realm of self-image, which was henceforth dominated by a conditioning in self-devaluation. . . . This situation, determined by a corpus of precise legislation and social behaviour patterns based on prejudice and religious traditions, induced the same type of mentality in all dhimmi groups. It has four major characteristics: vulnerability, humiliation, gratitude and alienation.[1]

As one Iranian convert to Christianity put it, "Christianity is still viewed as the religion of an inferior class of people. Islam is the religion of masters and rulers, Christianity is the religion of slaves." Often dhimmi Christians can be seen to collude to conceal their own condition, finding themselves psychologically unable to critique or oppose it.

Although many of the laws of dhimmitude were dismantled during European colonization, today they are making a comeback. Islam is exerting an increasingly important influence in the destiny of Western cultures. Through immigration, oil economics, cultural exchange, and even terrorism, the remnants of what was once Christendom now find themselves having to attend to Islam and its distinctive "take" on the world. We increasingly hear that we have an "Abrahamic" civilization—an Islamic perspective, not a Judeo-Christian one.

Within the Islamic self-consciousness, there are limited options for the roles that non-Muslim communities can play. The only real alternative to "enemies of Allah" for such communities is dhimmitude.

The requirement that dhimmis affirm and serve Islam greatly limits the repertoire of responses that dhimmified Christians can have toward it. Where there are grounds for confrontation, the only way of struggling permitted to the dhimmi is by saying soft things. Such political correctness is itself an injustice that needs to be exposed and challenged. This dynamic, when combined with the meanings of "struggle" (jihad) that Islam claims as its divine right without apology of any kind, can intimidate and debilitate Christians who are free and do not live under Islam. The cumulative effect can be that the gross injustices come to seem as somehow excusable or unexceptional. An infamous example is the weak international response today to the persecution of non-Muslims (not just Christians) under Islam. This is epitomized in the slavish attitude adopted by Mary Robinson, UN High Commissioner for Human Rights, in a statement she read to an Organization of the Islamic Conference Symposium on Human Rights in Islam, held at the Palais des Nations in Geneva in 2002. After offering praise Robinson adopts the strategy of affirming the inherent righteousness of Islam:

> It is important to recognize the greatness of Islam, its civilizations and its immense contribution to the richness of the human experience, not only through profound belief and theology but also through the sciences, literature and art.
>
> No one can deny that at its core Islam is entirely consonant with the principle of fundamental human rights, including human dignity, tolerance, solidarity and equality. Numerous passages from the Qur'an and sayings of the Prophet Muhammad will testify to this. No one can deny, from a historical perspective, the revolutionary force that is Islam, which bestowed rights upon women and children long before similar recognition was afforded in other civilizations. . . . And no one can deny the acceptance of the universality of human rights by Islamic States.[2]

Observe here the dhimmi themes of gratitude, affirmation of moral superiority of Islam (with the implication of inferiority of the infidel), and the denial of any possible voice of protest against human rights abuses in Islamic states. It is a classical dhimmi strategy to avoid confrontation by affirming what is best in Islam. Change for the better is only allowed to arise from values that Muslims can see as springing from their faith itself. This strategy conceals and disempowers the moral worth of non-Muslim value systems. It is the strategy of those whose existence is marginal and threatened.

For those living in liberal democracies, this is not in the end a healthy way to engage with the "other" that is Islam. It establishes a framework in which Islam takes on the role of a dominator that expects to be praised, admired, and stroked. The reaction to deserved criticism, when it manages to find a voice, can be shock, denial, and outrage.

For Christians there is a special challenge here. In adapting to this requirement of grateful service, Christians can interpret their own submissiveness in gospel categories of forgiveness and service. But from the Islamic side this just looks like "submission"; that is, the program of Islam itself is working. Islam interprets such submissiveness as its rightful due, not an expression of grace, and affords itself the privilege of feeling generous. Likewise, international aid is interpreted as tribute, a rightful due. This perception is reinforced when the most peaceful Islamic nations receive the least aid.

Another cost of this dynamic is a widespread Islamic pattern of claiming the role of victim while inculpating others for problems not of their making. Since Islam is not confronted about its own difficulties, while having its virtues affirmed, Muslim communities have permission to feel themselves aggrieved. This is enormously costly for the ongoing social and economic development of Islamic nations, and it is costly for Western societies.

In Victoria, Australia, our Equal Opportunity Commission has a "Stand Up to Racism" campaign, which announces to the community that Islam is a religion to be admired—this is called "dispelling myths." Yet the majority of attacks on Australian religious buildings since September 11 have been against churches and synagogues. Our EOC's tactic distorts the whole meaning of "tolerance" and undermines social harmony. This issue is especially urgent now that significant numbers of Westerners are embracing Islam.

Appeasement and the "softly, softly" approach only buys time. Sooner or later the will to dominance inherent in the jihad stream of the Qur'an and Sunna will rear its head when a faithful believer reads the Qur'an and finds that it says to struggle against unbelievers and subjugate them. Frank exposure and critique offers the best way to contain this outcome.

NOTES

1. Bat Ye'or, *Islam and Dhimmitude: Where Civilizations Collide* (Cranbury, NJ: Fairleigh Dickinson University Press, 2002), pp. 103–104.

2. Mary Robinson, speech delivered at the Organization of the Islamic Conference Symposium on Human Rights in Islam, Geneva, March 15, 2002.

22. BEYOND MUNICH

The Spirit of Eurabia

Bat Ye'or

Allow me first to make a preliminary observation about the title of this session: the "return of the spirit of Munich"—a title that I find some-what optimistic.[1] At Munich in 1938, France and England, exhausted by the death toll of the Great War, abandoned Czechoslovakia to the Nazi beast in the hope that by doing so they would avoid another conflict. The "spirit of Munich" thus refers to a policy of states and of peoples who refuse to confront a threat and attempt to obtain peace and security through conciliation and appeasement, or even, for some, an active collaboration with the criminals. For my own part, I would say that we have gone beyond the spirit of Munich, and the present situation should be seen not in the context of the World War II but in the present jihadist context.

In fact, for the past thirty years France and the rest of Europe have been living in a situation of passive self-defense against terrorism. This began with Palestinian terrorism and then became Islamic terrorism, not to speak of the local European terrorism, including the IRA in Great Britain, ETA in Spain, the Baader-Meinhof group in Germany, and the Red Brigades in Italy.

One need only look at our cities, airports, and streets, at the schools with their security guards, even the systems of public transportation, not to mention the embassies and the synagogues, to see the whole astonishing array of police and security services. The fact that authorities everywhere refuse to name the evil does not negate that evil. Yet we know perfectly well that we have been under threat for a long time; one has only to open one's eyes, and our authorities know it better than any of us, because it is they who have ordered these very security measures.

This text, a lecture delivered on June 6, 2004, in Paris, was translated from French by Hugh Fitzgerald with assistance from David G. Littman.

In his book *La vie quotidienne dans l'Europe médiévale sous domination arabe* (Daily life in medieval Europe under the Arab domination), published in 1978, Charles-Emmanuel Dufourcq, a French specialist on Andalusia (Islamic Spain) and the Maghreb, described under the subheading "Une grande peur" (A great fear) the conditions of life for the indigenous non-Muslim peoples in the Andalusian countryside.[2] Today, Europe itself is living with this great fear.

At Munich, war had not yet been declared. Today the war is everywhere. And yet the European Union and the states that it comprises have denied that war's reality, right up to the terrorist attack in Madrid of March 11, 2004. If there is a danger as Europe proclaims *urbi et orbi* ("from the city to the world"), that danger can only come from America and Israel. What should one understand? For can anyone seriously maintain that it is the American and Israeli forces that threaten us in Europe? No, what must be understood is that American and Israeli policies of resistance to jihadist terror provoke reprisals against a Europe that long ago ceased to defend itself. So that peace can prevail throughout the world, those two countries, America and Israel, need only adopt the European strategy of constant surrender, based on the denial of aggression. How simple it all is . . .

This strategy is less worthy than even Munich's connivance and cowardice. At Munich there was some sort of future contemplated, even if war, or peace, were to determine the future. There was a choice. In the present situation there is no choice, for we deny the reality of the jihad danger. The only danger comes, allegedly, from the United States and Israel. We conduct a propaganda campaign in the media against these two countries before entering into a yet more aggressive phase; it's so much easier, so much less dangerous . . . and we conduct this campaign with the weapons of cowardice: defamation, misinformation, the corruption of venal politicians.

In the time of Munich, one could envisage that there would be battles that might be won. There was at least the Maginot Line for defense. In Europe today, dominated by the spirit of dhimmitude—the condition of submission of Jews and Christians under Muslim domination—there is no conceivable battle. Submission, without a fight, has already taken place. A machinery that has made Europe the new continent of dhimmitude was put into motion more than thirty years ago at the instigation of France.

A wide-ranging policy was then first sketched out, a symbiosis of Europe with the Muslim Arab countries that would endow Europe—and especially France, the project's prime mover—with a weight and a prestige to rival that of the United States.[3] This policy was undertaken quite discreetly, outside of official treaties, under the innocent-sounding name of the Euro-Arab Dialogue. An association of European parliamentarians from the European Economic Community (EEC) was created in 1974 in Paris: the Parliamentary Association for Euro-Arab Cooperation. It was entrusted with managing all of the aspects of Euro-Arab relations—financial, political, economic, cultural, and those pertaining to immigration. This organization functioned under the auspices of the European heads of government and their foreign ministers, working in close association with their Arab counterparts and with the representatives of the European Commission and the Arab League.

This strategy, the goal of which was the creation of a pan-Mediterranean Euro-Arab entity, permitting the free circulation both of men and of goods, also determined the immigration policy with regard to Arabs in the European Community (EC). And, for the past thirty years, it also established the relevant cultural policies in the schools and universities of the EC. Since the first Cairo meeting of the Euro-Arab Dialogue in 1975, attended by the ministers and heads of state from both European and Arab countries and by representatives of the EC and the Arab League, agreements have been concluded concerning the diffusion and the promotion in Europe of Islam, of the Arabic language and culture, through the creation of Arab cultural centers in European cities. Other accords soon followed, all intended to ensure a cultural, economic, political Euro-Arab symbiosis. These far-ranging efforts involved the universities and the media (both written and audiovisual) and even included the transfer of technologies, including nuclear technology. Finally, a Euro-Arab associative diplomacy was promoted in international forums, especially at the United Nations.

The Arabs set the conditions for this association: (1) a European policy that would be independent from, and opposed to, that of the United States; (2) the recognition by Europe of a "Palestinian people" and the creation of a "Palestinian" state; (3) European support for the PLO; (4) the designation of Arafat as the sole and exclusive representative of that "Palestinian people"; (5) the delegitimizing of the State of Israel, both historically and politically, its shrinking into nonviable borders, and the Arabization of Jerusalem. From this sprang the hidden European war against Israel, through economic boycotts and in some cases academic boycotts as well, through deliberate vilification, and through the spreading of both anti-Zionism and antisemitism.

During the past three decades a considerable number of nonofficial agreements between the countries of the EC (subsequently the EU) on the one hand, and the countries of the Arab League on the other, determined the evolution of Europe in its current political and cultural aspects. I will cite here only four of them: (1) it was understood that Europeans who would be dealing with Arab immigrants would undergo special sensitivity training, in order to better appreciate their customs, their *moeurs*; (2) Arab immigrants would remain under the control and the laws of their countries of origin; (3) history textbooks in Europe would be rewritten by joint teams of European and Arab historians—naturally the battles of Poitiers and Lepanto, or the Spanish *reconquista*, did not possess the same significance on both Mediterranean littorals; (4) the teaching of the Arabic language and of Arab and Islamic culture were to be taught, in the schools and universities of Europe, by Arab teachers experienced in teaching Europeans.

THE SITUATION TODAY

On the political front, Europe has tied its destiny to the Arab countries and thus become involved in the logic of jihad against Israel and the United States. How could Europe denounce the culture of jihadic venom that exudes from its allies, while for so many years it did everything to activate the jihad by hiding and justifying it by claiming that the real danger comes not from jihadists themselves but from those who resist the Arab jihadists, the very allies that Europe serves at every international gathering and in the European media.

On the cultural front, there has been a complete rewriting of history, which was first undertaken during the 1970s in European universities. This process was ratified by the parliamentary assembly of the Council of Europe in September 1991, at its meeting devoted to "The Contribution of the Islamic Civilization to European Culture." It was reaffirmed by President Jacques Chirac in his address of April 8, 1996, in Cairo, and reinforced by Romano Prodi, president of the European Commission, through the recent creation of a "Foundation on the Dialogue of Cultures and Civilizations" (May 2004) that was to control everything that was said, written, and taught on the new continent of Eurabia, which encompasses Europe and the Arab countries.

The dhimmitude of Europe began with the subversion of its culture and its values, with the destruction of its history, and its replacement by an Islamic vision of that history, supported by the romantic myth of Andalusia. Eurabia adopted the Islamic conception of history, in which Islam is defined as a liberating force, a force for peace, and the jihad is regarded a "just war." Those who resist the jihad, like the Israelis and the Americans, are the guilty ones, rather than those who wage it. It is this policy that has inculcated in us, the Europeans, the spirit of dhimmitude that blinds us, that instills in us a hatred for our own values and the wish to destroy our own origins and our own history. "The greatest intellectual swindle would be to allow Europe to continue to believe that it derives from a Judeo-Christian tradition. That is a complete lie," Tariq Ramadan has stated.[4] And thus we despise George W. Bush because he still believes in that tradition. What simpletons, those Americans . . .

The spirit of dhimmitude is not merely that of submission without fighting, not even a surrender. It is also the denial of one's own humiliation through this process of integrating values that lead to our own destruction; it is the ideological mercenaries offering themselves up for service in the jihad; it is the traditional tribute paid by their own hand, and with humiliation, by the European dhimmis, in order to obtain a false security; it is the betrayal of one's own people. The non-Muslim protected dhimmi under Islamic rule could obtain an ephemeral and delusive security through services rendered to the Muslim oppressor and through servility and flattery. And that is precisely the situation in Europe today.

Dhimmitude is not only a set of abstract laws inscribed in the Sharia; it is also a complex set of behaviors developed over time by the dhimmis themselves, as a way both to adapt to and to survive oppression, humiliation, and insecurity. This has produced a particular mentality as well as social and political behaviors essential to the survival of peoples who, in a certain sense, would always remain hostages to the Islamic system.

Dhimmis are inferior beings who endure humiliation and aggression in silence. Their aggressors, meanwhile, enjoy an impunity that only increases their hatred and their feeling of superiority, guaranteed by the protection of the law. The culture of dhimmitude expanding throughout Europe is that of hate, of crimes against non-Muslims that go unpunished, a culture that is imported from the Arab countries along with "Palestinianism," the new European subculture that has been raised to the level of a European Union cult, and its exalted war banner against Israel.

At Munich in 1938, France had not renounced its own culture or its own history, thereby becoming German; it did not proclaim that the source of its own culture was the German civilization. The spirit of dhimmitude that today blinds Europe springs not from a situation imposed from without but from a choice made freely and systematically carried out, in its political dimensions, over the course of the last thirty years.

Well-known scholar of Islam William Montgomery Watt, himself an

Islamophile, described the disappearance of the Christian world from the countries that had been Islamized, and often Arabized as well, in his book *The Majesty That Was Islam* (1974): "There was nothing dramatic about what happened; it was a gentle death, a phasing out."[5] But Watt was wrong; in fact, the long death throes of Christianity under Islam were extremely painful and tragic, as can be seen even in the twentieth century, with the genocide of the Armenians, the Lebanese Christians' resistance in the 1970s and 1980s, for the last decades the genocide in the Sudan, and finally the relentless Arab jihad against Israel, which is only one of the examples of the age-old struggle by people devoted to fighting for freedom against dhimmitude, for the dignity of man against the slavery of oppression and hate. But the observation by Watt—about the "gentle death, the phasing out"—applies perfectly to Europe today.

NOTES

1. This lecture ("Vers un retour à l'esprit de Munich") was originally delivered at a seminar ("La Démocratie à l'épreuve de la menace islamiste") in the French Senate on June 6, 2004, organized by the B'nai B'rith (France).

2. Charles-Emanuel Dufourcq, *La vie quotidienne dans l'Europe médiévale sous domination arabe* (Paris: Hachette, 1978). This book examines the Arab conquest and colonization of Andalusia; see esp. chap. 1, "Les jours de razzia et d'invasion." I am grateful to Dr. Andrew Bostom for having brought Dufourcq's works to my attention.

3. Pierre Lyautey (the nephew of Maréchal Lyautey, French governor of Morocco), "Le nouveau rôle de la France en Orient" (The new role of France in the Middle East), *Comptes rendus-des séances de l'Académie des Sciences d'Outre-mer* May 4, 1962 (Paris), p. 176. See also Jacques Frémaux, *Le Monde Arabe et la Securité de la France depuis 1958* (Paris: PUF, 1995).

4. Tariq Ramadan, "Critique des (nouveaux) intellectuels communautaires," Oumma.com, October 3, 2003.

5. William Montgomery Watt, *The Majesty That Was Islam: The Islamic World, 661–1100* (London: Sidgwick & Jackson, 1974), p. 257.

EURABIA

23. The Road to Munich

Bat Ye'or

September 11, 2001, was for millions worldwide a day of sorrow, pain, and profound sadness; a day of solemn solidarity, self-sacrifice, and prayer. For others it was a day of rejoicing, a revengeful exultation, a long-awaited triumphalism born from the death and suffering of thousands of innocent victims. They were saying: That'll teach them! America deserves it and must repent! And many were asking maliciously: Don't you have remorse for your wrongs? Why don't you ask yourself why you are hated? If we hate you, it can only be your own fault. Emerging from the ruin and distress that they had endured, Americans asked themselves: What have we done? We have been vilely attacked, yet we are accused. Why do they hate us?

And that's the snare. For iniquity engulfs those who hate, who kill—and not the hated victim. It is those who hate who are sick: sick from envy; sick from the frustration of having failed to achieve an absolute, pathological domination; sick from a schizophrenic lust for power. To heal these societies one must first diagnose the evil and not mask it under the excuse of "poverty" and "underdevelopment." Terrorism is not a consequence of poverty. Many societies are poor, yet they do not produce an organized criminality of terror. To subsidize societies that nourish ideologies of hate will not suppress terrorism; rather, such pusillanimity will reinforce it.

America should not choose European ways: the road back to Munich (see chap. 22 for explanation) via appeasement, collaboration, and dhimmitude. For decades, at the instigation of France, Europe backed Arafat—the godfather of modern terrorism—as the champion of liberty, and their hero.

This essay was translated from French by David G. Littman, with the author, and was first published in the *National Review Online*, October 9, 2002. Distributed by United Feature Syndicate Incorporated.

After the Yom Kippur War and the Arab oil blackmail in 1973, the European Community (EC) created a structure of cooperation and dialogue with the Arab League. The Euro-Arab Dialogue (EAD) began as a French initiative composed of representatives from the EC and Arab League countries. From the outset the EAD was considered a vast transaction: The EC agreed to support the Arab anti-Israeli policy in exchange for wide commercial agreements. The EAD had a supplementary function: the shifting of Europe into the Arab-Islamic sphere of influence, thus breaking the traditional trans-Atlantic solidarity. The EAD operated at the highest political level, with foreign ministers on both sides, and the presidents of the EC—later the European Union (EU)—with the secretary general of the Arab League. The central body of the Dialogue, the General Commission, was responsible for planning its objectives in the political, cultural, social, economic, and technological domains; it met in private, without summary records, a common practice for European meetings.

Over the years, Euro-Arab collaboration developed at all levels: political, economic, religious, and in the transfer of technologies, education, universities, radio, television, press, publishers, and writers' unions. This structure became the channel for Arab immigration into Europe, of anti-Americanism, and of Judeophobia, which—linked with a general hatred of the West and its denigration—constituted a pseudoculture imported from Arab countries. The interpenetration of European and Arab policies determined Europe's relentless anti-Israel policy and its anti-Americanism. This politico-economic edifice, with minute details, is rooted in a multiform European symbiosis with the Arab world.

West German foreign minister Hans-Dietrich Genscher expressed the aims clearly in his opening speech to the Hamburg Symposium's Euro-Arab Dialogue of April 11–13, 1983 (at a time when West Germany held the presidency of the European Community):

> The Euro-Arab Dialogue would indeed remain incomplete if the political side were to be ignored or not taken seriously. Both parties to the Dialogue, both partners, should always remind themselves of the joint Memorandum issued in Cairo in 1975, the Charter of the Dialogue. The Memorandum contains the following quote: "The Euro-Arab Dialogue is the outcome of the common political will which strives for the creation of a special relationship between the two groups." We Europeans spoke out in a clear and convinced manner for a revival of the Euro-Arab Dialogue in the Vienna Declaration of June 13, 1980. Since then, the various working groups within the Dialogue have become more active and the prospects for the future are more promising.

Our Arab partners in the Dialogue have also indicated that they are in favour of continuing and intensifying this Dialogue. Both in the course of this joint venture, our Symposium, and through its outcome, it will become clear that we are determined to give the Euro-Arab Dialogue a new and long lease of life.

Europe's economic greed was instrumentalized by Arab League policy in a long-term political strategy targeting Israel, Europe, and America. Arab economic ascendancy over the EC influenced the latter's policy toward Israel. The EAD was the vehicle for legitimizing the propaganda of the PLO, procuring it international diplomatic recognition and conferring on Arafat's terrorist movement honor and international stature by supporting Arafat's address to the General Assembly of the United Nations on November 13, 1974. Through the labyrinth of the EAD system, a policy of Israel's delegitimization was planned at both the EC's national and international levels. Approved instructions from the highest political, religious, and academic authorities functioned within the EAD's multiple commissions, implicating the media, universities, and diverse cultural activities. The EAD was the mouthpiece that diffused and popularized throughout Europe the defamation of Israel. France, Belgium, and Luxembourg were then the most active agents of the EAD.

Strategically, the Euro-Arab cooperation was a political instrument for anti-Americanism in Europe, whose aim was to separate and weaken the two continents by an incitement to hostility and the permanent denigration of American policy in the Middle East. The cultural infrastructure of the EAD allowed the traditional cultural baggage of Arab societies, with its anti-Christian and anti-Jewish prejudices and its hostility against Israel and the West, to be imported into Europe. The discredit heaped on the infidel Judeo-Christian culture was expressed by the claim of the superiority of the Islamic civilization, at which source European scholars, over the centuries—it was said—had humbly slaked their thirst for knowledge. Drowned in this wave of Arab cultural and religious expansionism that was integrated into the cultural activities of the EAD, Europeans adopted the Arab-Islamic conception of history. The obsequiousness of certain academics, subjected to a political power dominated by economic materialism, is reminiscent of the worst periods of the decline of civilizations. The suppression of intellectual freedom imported from undemocratic Muslim countries, attached to a culture of hate against Israel, has recently led to the exclusion and boycott of Israeli academics by some of their European colleagues.

The cogs created by the EAD led the EC to tolerate Palestinian terrorism

on its own territory, to justify it, and finally to finance Palestinian infrastructure—later to become the Palestinian Authority—and hate-mongering educational system. The ministers and intellectuals who have created Eurabia
deny the current wave of criminal attacks against European Jews, which they,
themselves, have inspired. They deny the antisemitism, as they have
neglected the attacks against the fundamental rights of their own citizens by
delinquency and the terrorist threats, which they have allowed to develop
with impunity in their countries, in exchange for financial profits. The silence
and the negligence of the public authorities faced with this wave of antisemitic aggression is but the tip of the iceberg of a global policy. The EAD,
which had tied Arab strategic policies for the destruction of Israel to the
European economy, was the Trojan horse for Europe's inclusion in the orbit
of Arab-Muslim influence.

With the support of parliaments and ministries, the EAD concealed
behind the Arab-Israel conflict the global jihad being perpetrated on all continents. Europe's subservience to Arab policy led the EU to give an artificial
and absolute priority to the Arab-Israel conflict in international affairs. It
could have been solved from the start by the integration of about five hundred thousand Arab-Palestinian refugees into the Arab League countries,
foremost into the Emirate of Transjordan—created by Great Britain in 1922
from 78 percent of the total League of Nation–mandated area of Palestine,
the historical Holy Land on both sides of the Jordan river. After the 1947–49
Arab League war against Israel, this territory was increased to 83 percent of
Palestine, with the occupation of what became the "West Bank" of the
Hashemite Kingdom of Jordan.

Europe's pathological obsession with the Arab-Palestinian conflict has
obscured the criminal ongoing persecution of Christians and other minorities
in Muslim lands worldwide, as well as the sufferings and slavery of millions
from jihad wars in Africa and Asia.

The sudden collapse of the World Trade Center's twin towers, the recent
threat of an American boycott of what was perceived as an antisemitic
Europe, President Bush's ironic criticism of Europe's moral haughtiness, and
especially the rise of extreme-right parties brought responsible politicians to
their senses. They had been blinded by a Palestinian fantasy ("Jenin-grad");
racist, genocidal accusations; and massive media disinformation arousing
hatred on their radios and televisions against small, vulnerable Jewish communities, tracked, aggressed, criminalized, and terrorized—while the leaders
of their countries looked the other way and pretended that Israel was responsible for the violent aggressions against Jews in Europe by Arab-Muslim

immigrants. Then they saw criminal bands terrorizing their city suburbs, as well as the terrorist networks and rampant fanaticism, that they had over-looked for decades. Today the likely war against Iraq has caused shivers throughout Europe, which is trembling at the possible collapse of its Arab alliances, built on foundations that implied a rupture with America and the demise of Israel. Europe had tied its Arab-Muslim friendly alliances and prosperity to a cooperation with Middle East tyrants, and by supporting Yasir Arafat's criminal policies.

Hence the desperate move to save Arafat recently, backed by a wide-spread and slanderous antisemitic media campaign, together with criminal acts in Europe against Jews that were neither checked nor condemned. Over fifty years ago the Holocaust was the response to Zionism. Today, diaspora Jews and Israel would do well to foresee a possible vengeful reckoning after Saddam Hussein falls and Arafat is marginalized—an Arafat who was courted by the EU, which greatly increased its funding to the Palestinian Authority after the Oslo Accords of 1993, without adequate controls. The recent anti-Jewish hysteria in Europe was an advertisement to neutralize diaspora Jews and the Israeli self-defense mechanism against Palestinian terror, which is why it was so superbly overlooked by the highest authorities. This complacent attitude has scandalized many European friends of Israel, who are much more numerous than the EAD censorship organs and the Euro-Arab terrorist networks would have us believe. Yet the majority of Euro-peans, who are not antisemitic, are totally unaware of most of the EAD's policy, since its key deliberations are unrecorded. More research and publi-cations are needed in this field.

The cracks between Europe and America reveal the divergences between the choice of liberty and the road back to Munich on which the European Union continues to caper to new Arab-Islamic tunes, now called "occupa-tion," "peace and justice," and "immigrants' rights"—themes that were com-posed for Israel's burial—and for Europe's demise.

THE ISLAMIC CONQUEST
24. OF BRITAIN

Srdja Trifkovic

The latest disclosures (December 19) that trained al Qaeda terrorists are present in the United Kingdom and operate in classic small-cell structures came only a day after the arrest of seven suspected Muslim terrorists in London and Edinburgh.[1] According to British government sources, the most likely threat from such groups may take the form of a "truckful of explosives left in a public place" and attacks on "transport, particularly using aviation . . . clearly a favourite technique." A Whitehall official acknowledged on December 18 that even if counterterrorist operations succeeded in disrupting al Qaeda, its ideology would live on in others: "My prediction is that we are in for the long haul."

The official did not say, but we know, that the "long haul" is open-ended. It is certain to go on for as long as Great Britain continues to have one of the largest Muslim diasporas anywhere outside the Islamic world. This "long haul" may well end up in Britain becoming an Islamic country by the end of this century, with Sharia law replacing common law and the Qur'an replacing the magnificent edifice of its unwritten constitution. If current demographic trends continue—with native Britons aborting and birth-controlling themselves to death, with Muslims already settled in Britain having third world birth rates, and with rampant immigration continuing unabated—the writing is clearly on the wall. London and a host of industrial cities in the Midlands already have a nonnative majority.

An early sign of what was about to hit England came exactly twenty years ago in a declaration issued by the Islamic Foundation in the industrial city of Leicester, one hundred miles north of London. It stated that the

Reprinted with permission from *Chronicles*, http://www.ChroniclesMagazine.org.

Islamic movement is "an organized struggle to change the existing society into an Islamic society based on the Qur'an and the Sunna and make Islam, which is a code for entire life, supreme and dominant, especially in the socio-political spheres." This demands clear acceptance "that the ultimate objective of the Islamic movement shall not be realized unless the struggle is made by locals. For it is only they who have the power to change the society into an Islamic society."

A generation later mosques have multiplied all over Britain and provided the backbone to terrorist support networks. This was partly due to the British Home Office routinely approving priority entry into the country to Muslim clerics from countries such as Pakistan, who speak no English and do not want to control extremists who control the mosques.[2] On the first anniversary of the September 11 attacks, to take but one notable example, Muslim leaders gathered at the Finsbury Park mosque in north London "to hail Osama bin Laden as a hero and to evoke the 'positive outcomes' of the attacks in New York and Washington."[3] This mosque has long been known as a recruiting ground for radical Muslims, and it has been visited by Zacarias Moussaoui and Richard C. Reid. Abu Hamza al-Masri, the Egyptian-born imam of the Finsbury Park mosque, is wanted in Yemen on terrorism charges.

Nevertheless, the conference organized at the Finsbury Park mosque under the title "September 11: A Towering Day in History" and advertised by posters depicting hijacked planes smashing into the World Trade Center, was an act of supreme contempt for the host society that also indicated an impressive level of self-confidence. No outsiders were allowed to attend, but the spirit of the proceedings could be gleaned when one of the 150 participants, Muhammad al-Massari from Saudi Arabia, said at a news conference that the September 11 onslaught "wasn't the wisest thing, but legitimate, yes. An eye for an eye as an old book says. But it was only one eye for 100 eyes. There is still much more to do." Bin Laden, he said, was "fighting according to his beliefs. Anyone who fights according to his beliefs is a hero." The convention was organized by a group called al-Muhajiroun, led by Syrian-born Omar Bakri Mohamed. Before the meeting, the al-Muhajiroun Web site said the "positive outcomes" of September 11 included "the clear crystallization of the two camps of Islam and Kufr (non-Islam), of believers and hypocrites."

Such remarks, and the fact that the conference went ahead at all, indicate the extent to which the British authorities are reluctant to move against radical Muslim elements, which have been routinely linked to the recruitment of young British Muslims to fight in conflicts abroad. The British security services, like the government, have long been in a state of denial regarding the Islamist threat. Time and again the British courts have interpreted criminal, asylum, and terrorism laws in a manner damaging to the security of the realm and favorable to the Islamic underground. British police have repeatedly ignored warnings that the recruiting agents for extremist groups prey on mosques, universities, and community centers. There are now over three hundred after-hours schools run by militant groups all over Britain, in which the children are indoctrinated, Taliban-style. Maintaining the loyalty of the Muslim diaspora in Britain has been the mullahs' top priority, and Islamic religious instruction has been carried out by immigrant imams, who have a clear agenda aimed at inculcating their British-born wards with disdain and even hatred for their surroundings.

"We will remodel this country in an Islamic image," Sheikh Omar bin Bakri, the organizer of September 11 conference, declared three years ago. He still belongs to the International Islamic Front for Jihad against Jews and Crusaders, founded by bin Laden, and boasts, "We collect funds to be able to carry on the struggle; we recruit militiamen; and sometimes we take care of these groups' propaganda requirements in Europe."[4] Bakri also heads the London branch of Hizb ut-Tahrir (Arabic for "Islamic Revolutionary Party"), which has some fifty branches all over Western Europe. When the Afghan war started in October 2001, Bakri declared, "We will replace the Bible with the Kuran. . . . Christians have to learn that they cannot do this to Islam. We will not allow our brothers to be colonialised. If they try it, Britain will turn into Bosnia."[5]

Remarkably, this same Mr. Bakri (who does not seem to realize that the Bible has long been replaced in Great Britain by Mr. Blair's therapeutic state) was expelled from Saudi Arabia in 1985 as a dangerous agitator for creating al-Muhajiroun, a branch of the Islamic Revolutionary Party. He has lived in London since 1986, drawing five hundred dollars a week a week in welfare and calling on young Muslims to take up arms against the "opponents of Islam"—ultimately meaning everyone who is not Muslim or who does not subscribe to his vision of Islam. While living in Britain at its taxpayers' expense he denounces the host country as "the spearhead of blasphemy that seeks to overthrow Muslims and the Islamic caliphate." As early as 1991, during the Gulf War, Bakri said that then prime minister John Major "is a legitimate target. If anyone gets the opportunity to assassinate him, they should take it. It is our Islamic duty and we will celebrate his death."

We can only guess how many thousands of Bakris operate freely in Boston, Michigan, New Jersey, or, for that matter, in Paris, Berlin, Toronto,

Amsterdam, or Milan. They take full advantage of the host countries' laws and often operate under the guise of charities. A notable example was the International Development Foundation (IDF), with offices in London's Curzon Street, which was named in a French parliamentary report in 2001 as a financial front for al Qaeda. Its trustees were four brothers belonging to the wealthy bin Mahfouz family, one of Saudi Arabia's most powerful, with a fortune estimated at over four billion dollars. The British Charity Commission says that the IDF was connected to Khalid bin Mahfouz, a Saudi businessman and Irish citizen who had hosted bin Laden at his mansion in Buckinghamshire and who is under investigation for his links to al Qaeda. The Mahfouz brothers and IDF trustees denied any knowledge of Khalid when first approached by British investigators, but it was then discovered that he is also their brother![6] In addition Khalid had had connections to BCCI with the former Soviet Union.

"Our own legal framework stops us from dealing with extremist religion," concludes a Pakistani-born British Anglican who grew up as a Muslim. Historically, Islam has never learned to live as a minority and cannot reconstruct itself in Western societies: "My own feeling is that what will happen in the British society—I am waiting to see whether it will happen in the US—is Muslim societies will emerge within Western countries where they will develop their own patterns of social sharia [Islamic law]. In Britain today, where Islam controls the inner cities, we have major social exclusion and the development of sharia. We have had churches burned, Christians attacked and a mission center destroyed. The media has deliberately kept everything off the air."[7]

Indeed, jihad has never had it so good as over the past two decades. The Muslim population of the world has been exploding, not only in Asia and Africa but also in Europe and the United States. Most Muslim countries regard demography as a political weapon. They gladly export their surplus population to Europe and America, aware that the bigger the diaspora, the greater the political influence it will exert, and the more concessions the Islamic world will be able to extort from the West. Open-ended population explosion in every predominantly Muslim country in the world is the underlying reality behind immigration trends, fortifying the impression that tomorrow belongs to Islam. A Muslim woman has between five and six children on average, compared to fewer than two children for women in the developed world. Even when they move to Britain, Muslims from the Subcontinent procreate at three times the host country average. As we enter the century that will see fresh confrontation between Islam and the rest, the outcome is sadly preordained if poet T. S. Eliot is to be proven right in his warning that the West would end "not with a bang but a whimper."

The example of Britain indicates what happens when a vast and so far utterly unsupervised subculture of intrinsically hostile non-Western immigrants is allowed to emerge within a Western society. British politicians have permitted the emergence of an alternative social and political structure in their midst in which terrorists can operate. Seeking to appease that structure by granting it special privileges will only prompt demands for more. There is no sign that any mainstream Muslim group in Great Britain today understands that some soul-searching and critical examination of their faith's assumptions, however tentative—as opposed to mere lip service to "peace and tolerance"—may be a necessary prerequisite for the community's claim to the permanent enjoyment of the rights and privileges enjoyed by other citizens of the country to which they freely chose to migrate.

It is wrong to conclude that Muslims have simply "replaced" communists as the main threat to the West; they are but two faces of the same menace of the closed society and the closed mind, and they have been the one *real threat* all along. Ideological divisions have not given way to communitarian ones. The totalitarian nature of Islam, akin to communism and Nazism in aspects, makes the threat different in degree to that faced during the cold war, but not in kind. It demands a similar response. Like communism, Islam relies on a domestic fifth column—the Allah-worshiping Rosenbergs, Philbys, Blunts, and Hisses—to subvert the civilized world.

Islam also relies on an army of fellow travelers, the Qur'an-reading Blairs in the world of politics and on "Islamic studies specialists" in the ivory towers, on "liberal academics and opinion-makers [who] sympathize with Islam partly because it is a leading historical rival of the Western civilization they hate" and partly because they long for a romanticized and sanitized Muslim past that substitutes for the authentic Western and Christian roots they have rejected.[8]

Those roots must be defended, in the full knowledge that "those who subscribe to Islam and its civilization are aliens, regardless of their clothes, their professions or their places of residence."[9] They sense Western weakness and expect that if Islam supplies the only old religious tradition left standing fifty years hence, it may attract mass conversion. That would indeed be the end of the West, its final surrender to the spirit masterfully depicted by Jean Raspail in the preface to the 1985 French edition of his *Camp of Saints*: "[T]he West is empty, even if it has not yet become really aware of it. An extraordinarily inventive civilization, surely the only one capable of meeting the challenges of the third millennium, the West has no soul left. At every level—nations, race, cultures as well as individuals—it is always the soul that wins the decisive battles."

The story that Raspail tells is rooted in a "monstrous cancer implanted in the Western conscience." Its roots are in the loss of faith and in the arrogant doctrine—rampant in "the West" for three centuries now—that man can solve the dilemma of his existence by his unaided intellect alone. If that loss is not reversed the game is over anyway, proving yet again that where God retreats, Allah advances.

NOTES

1. *Times* (London), December 19.

2. *Times* (London), December 27, 2001.

3. *New York Times*, September 13, 2002.

4. *Il Giornale* (Milan), October 14, 2000.

5. *Observer* (London), October 27, 2001.

6. James Doran, "UK Assets of Islamic Charity Are Frozen," *Times* (London), January 16, 2002.

7. Quoted in *Washington Times*, January 16, 2002.

8. Philip Jenkins, *Chronicles*, September 2001.

9. Sam Francis, "Mass Immigration Let Terrorists Operate," VDARE.com, http://www.vdare.com/francis/specter.htm (accessed September 20, 2004).

SOMETHING ROTTEN
25. IN DENMARK?

Daniel Pipes and Lars Hedegaard

A Muslim group in Denmark announced a few days ago that a thirty-thou-sand-dollar bounty would be paid for the murder of several prominent Danish Jews, a threat that garnered wide international notice. Less well known is that this is just one problem associated with Denmark's approximately two hundred thousand Muslim immigrants. The key issue is that many of them show little desire to fit into their adopted country.

For years, Danes lauded multiculturalism and insisted they had no problem with the Muslim customs—until one day they found that they did. Some major issues:

- *Living on the dole.* Third world immigrants—most of them Muslims from such countries as Turkey, Somalia, Pakistan, Lebanon, and Iraq—constitute 5 percent of the population but consume upwards of 40 percent of the welfare spending.
- *Engaging in crime.* Muslims are only 4 percent of Denmark's 5.4 million people but make up a majority of the country's convicted rapists, an especially combustible issue given that practically all the female victims are non-Muslim. Similar, if lesser, disproportions are found in other crimes.
- *Self-imposed isolation.* Over time, as Muslim immigrants increase in numbers, they wish less to mix with the indigenous population. A recent survey finds that only 5 percent of young Muslim immigrants would readily marry a Dane.
- *Importing unacceptable customs.* Forced marriage—promising a new-born daughter in Denmark to a male cousin in the home country, then

Reprinted with permission from the *New York Post*, August 27, 2002.

compelling her to marry him, sometimes on pain of death—is one problem. Another is threats to kill Muslims who convert out of Islam. One Kurdish convert to Christianity, who went public to explain why she had changed religion, felt the need to hide her face and conceal her identity, fearing for her life.

- *Fomenting antisemitism.* Muslim violence threatens Denmark's approximately six thousand Jews, who increasingly depend on police protection. Jewish parents were told by one school principal that she could not guarantee their children's safety and were advised to attend another institution. Anti-Israel marches have turned into anti-Jewish riots. One organization, Hizb ut-Tahrir, openly calls on Muslims to "kill all Jews . . . wherever you find them."
- *Seeking Islamic law.* Muslim leaders openly declare their goal of introducing Islamic law once Denmark's Muslim population grows large enough—a not-that-remote prospect. If present trends persist, one sociologist estimates, every third inhabitant of Denmark in forty years will be Muslim.

Other Europeans (such as the late Pim Fortuyn in Holland) have also grown alarmed about these issues, but Danes were the first to make them the basis for a change in government. In a momentous election last November, a center-right coalition came to power that—for the first time since 1929— excluded the socialists. The right broke its seventy-two-year losing streak and won a solid parliamentary majority by promising to handle immigration issues, the electorate's first concern, differently from the socialists.

The next nine months did witness some fine-tuning of procedures: Immigrants now must live seven years in Denmark (rather than three) to become permanent residents. Most nonrefugees no longer can collect welfare checks immediately on entering the country. No one can bring into the country an intended spouse under the age of twenty-four. And the state prosecutor is considering a ban on Hizb ut-Tahrir for its death threats against Jews.

These minor adjustments prompted howls internationally—with European and UN reports condemning Denmark for racism and "Islamophobia," the *Washington Post* reporting that Muslim immigrants "face habitual discrimination," and a London *Guardian* headline announcing that "Copenhagen Flirts with Fascism."

In reality, however, the new government barely addressed the existing problems. Nor did it prevent new ones, such as the death threats against Jews or a recent Islamic edict calling on Muslims to drive Danes out of the Norrebro quarter of Copenhagen.

The authorities remain indulgent. The military mulls permitting Muslim soldiers in Denmark's volunteer International Brigade to opt out of actions they don't agree with—a privilege granted to members of no other faith. Sheikh Omar Bakri, the London-based self-proclaimed "eyes, ears and mouth" of Osama bin Laden, won permission to set up a branch of his organization, al-Muhajiroun.

Contrary to media reports, the real news from Denmark is not flirting with fascism but getting mired in inertia. A government elected specifically to deal with a set of problems has made minimal headway. Its reluctance has potentially profound implications for the West as a whole.

FOLLOW-UP LETTERS

Multiculturalism and Denmark

National Post
September 6, 2002
Letters
From: Elisabeth Arnold and Elsebeth Gerner Nielsen, Members of the Danish Parliament

As Danish politicians, we are offended by the way integration problems in Denmark were portrayed by Daniel Pipes and Lars Hedegaard and we wish to set the record straight ("Muslim Extremism: Denmark's Had Enough," Daniel Pipes and Lars Hedegaard, Aug. 27).

The authors claim that 40 percent of Danish welfare expenses are consumed by Muslim immigrants. Denmark has a much broader spectrum of welfare costs than countries in North America. We include not only unemployment benefits and social security but also substantial allocations to housing, transport, homecare, early retirement, protected workplaces, daycare and other smaller schemes. Muslim immigrants do not receive 40 percent of those allocations even though they represent a substantial part of the clients. The main reason being: It is hard to compete on a job market not interested in employing immigrants.

The further assumption that more than half of all rapists in Denmark are Muslims is without any basis in fact, as criminal registers do not record religion.

Mr. Pipes and Mr. Hedegaard mention that only 5 percent of young Muslims in Denmark wish to marry a Dane. A sign of self-inflicted isolation, indeed. We welcome the brave 5 percent who accept intermarriage—they are true pioneers for peaceful coexistence and human contact across cultures. However, the new Danish government has made it extremely difficult for Danish citizens to bring a foreign spouse to Denmark. The ruling opinion obviously is that intermarriage should be avoided.

Mr. Pipes and Mr. Hedegaard also claim that Muslim violence threatens the six thousand Jewish citizens in Denmark. Rumours—also hitting the front pages of major newspapers—tell that identified Jewish Danes figure on a death list. Danish authorities consider death threats very serious, but police investigators have so far found no evidence of real threats.

During the coming decade, Denmark will need one hundred thousand new pairs of hands in the workforce. The Danes produce fewer children and live longer. Integration must work better and immigrants admitted to Denmark should be welcomed. On this point, we take inspiration from Canadian society, which is open to other cultures and religions.

Re: Multiculturalism and Denmark

National Post
September 10, 2002
Letters
From: Daniel Pipes and Lars Hedegaard, Philadelphia, PA

Elisabeth Arnold and Elsebeth Gerner Nielsen, two members of the Danish parliament, are "offended" by our article "Muslim Extremism: Denmark's Had Enough" (Aug. 27).

Most Canadian readers may not realize that both writers are politicians belonging to the Socialist-Radical Liberal government that was defeated last November—indeed, Ms. Nielsen was its minister of culture. They have an axe to grind.

Both protest our conclusion that Muslims "make up a majority of the country's convicted rapists," saying that because Danish statistics do not correlate religion with crime, this assertion "is without any basis in fact." Statistics Denmark does, however, produce numbers on immigrants from third world countries and their descendants, which it reports makes up 5 percent of the population; and it is known that Muslims make up four-fifths of this element. The latest police figures show that 76.5 percent of convicted rapists in Copenhagen belong to that 5 percent of the population, and from that we drew our understated conclusion.

Our critics then sow confusion about the word *welfare*. We wrote in English for an English-speaking readership, and used *welfare* in the conventional English sense of meaning public assistance in the form of cash or food stamps—not in the Danish sense of including "housing, transport, homecare, early retirement, protected workplaces, daycare and other smaller schemes" as mentioned by the two politicians.

As for the numbers involved, former Socialist spokeswoman for immigration and integration Ritt Bjerregaard has leaked figures from an unpublished study showing that in 1999, the 5 percent of the Danish population made up of third world immigrants received 35 percent of all welfare payments (Danish: *kontanthjaelp*). This percentage is higher today and therefore we wrote that that 5 percent consumes "upwards of 40 percent of the welfare spending."

Both MPs may not believe Danish Jews are threatened but the Jewish population itself believes it is under siege. This obliviousness of Ms. Arnold and Ms. Nielsen is part of a larger problem, whereby they have long been among the most vocal cheerleaders of massive immigration and completely blind to the problems this creates. Unfortunately for them, Danish voters do see the problems and threw their coalition out of office last November.

Finally, we are at a loss to explain the notion our critics forward that the current government believes "intermarriage should be avoided" between Danes and foreigners, an outrageous accusation which no one of any political stature has advocated. To the contrary, the policy of the government is integration, not segregation.

PART 5.

HUMAN RIGHTS AND HUMAN WRONGS AT THE UNITED NATIONS

Introduction

David G. Littman and Robert Spencer

The material in this section—comprising thirty-four articles, papers, appeals, and numerous oral and written statements, all directly related to the UN Commission on Human Rights (UNCHR)—has been selected by Robert Spencer with my collaboration. Since 1986, I have been accredited to the UNCHR in Geneva by several nongovernmental organizations (NGOs) at different periods and am currently a representative of the Association for World Education (AWE) and of the World Union for Progressive Judaism (WUPJ).[1]

This part begins with two descriptive articles, followed by a full analysis (chapter 29) of the 1997 UN "Blasphemy Affair," written in collaboration with my colleague René Wadlow, the main representative of the AWE. These studies provide a detailed overview of the blatant contradictions between the International Bill of Human Rights (and the other ratified international covenants), which should be binding, and the Cairo Declaration of Human Rights in Islam, which has primacy for many of the Muslim countries. Some aspects of cultural relativism described here illustrate a growing "soft-power" Islamism, initiated first by Iran over twenty years ago and diligently pursued at the UNCHR and other UN bodies by the fifty-six-member-state Organization of the Islamic Conference (OIC). Here, and in some of the other texts, overlapping could not be avoided without making major cuts. The editor decided to retain most of this material for the sake of coherence and clarity.

The oral statements that follow (beginning with chapter 27) are repro-duced as pronounced and made available at the UNCHR and the UN Sub-Commission on Human Rights. Passages not spoken due to time constraints remain in their original square brackets. Where there is duplication in an oral and a related written statement, some passages have been omitted. The expressions "Mr. Chairman," "Sir," "Madam," and "Thank you" were deleted. Written statements submitted by NGOs are reprinted with paragraph numbering—without the cover page—as posted on the official UN Office of the High Commissioner for Human Rights section of the UN Web site.

The four papers (chapters 44–47) of the seminar on "Apostasy, Human Rights, Religion, and Belief"—sponsored on April 7, 2004, by the Associa-tion for World Education, the Association of World Citizens, and the Inter-national Humanist and Ethical Union, in the context of the sixtieth session of the UNCHR—are reproduced as used and circulated.

My lecture delivered in November 1994 at the University of Lund regarding an imagined future Middle East Confederation is the final docu-ment (chapter 48). Inspired by Churchill's historic address at the Univer-sity of Zurich (September 19, 1946) on a future "United States of Europe," I had proposed a "United States of Abraham" in my March 6, 1990, state-ment to the UNCHR. Using Churchill's formulae—and backed by my col-league, historian Martin Gilbert, Churchill's official biographer—I spoke in my then capacity as WUPJ's main representative. The major obstacles that continue to wreck the peace and mar the prospects of all such utopian ideas for the Middle East region—including the failed Oslo Agreement of 1993 and the unworkable "Road Map"—were referred to in 1990, and later too. (AWE's written statement E/CN.4/2004/NGO/7, available on the UN Web site, is mentioned in a note but has not been reproduced to avoid duplication.)

NOTE

1. "Human Rights and Human Wrongs" (available at the US Library of Con-gress, the New York Public Library, and many other libraries) was the title used for eleven publications (nos. 1–11) published by the WUPJ in Geneva. They contain all the verbatim oral—and written—statements made by its representatives in Geneva to the UNCHR and the UN Sub-Commission on Human Rights from 1986 to 1991.

Postscript by Robert Spencer

This section of documents related to the UN Commission on Human Rights illustrates just how far modern Islamic states are from embodying the mythical Islamic tolerance. After an initial concern with antisemitism and Judeophobia, the focus broadens to show that the concerted attacks on Israel by Islamic states are not singular but are part of an overall pattern of behavior that is guided by principles of Islamic theology and law that are anything but tolerant.

Of particular interest is the attempt to make "blasphemy" in an Islamic context forbidden at the United Nations, which would effectively silence all critics—including an apostate such as Ibn Warraq, who speaks so eloquently here about the freedom of conscience—and make any reform impossible.

ISLAMISM GROWS STRONGER AT THE UNITED NATIONS

26.

David G. Littman

I n recent years, representatives of some Muslim states have demanded, and often received, special treatment at the United Nations, mostly via the Commission on Human Rights (UNCHR). As a result, nondiplomatic terms such as "blasphemy" and "defamation of Islam" have seeped into the United Nations system, leading to a situation in which non-Muslim governments accept certain rules of conduct in conformity with Islamic law (the Sharia) and acquiesce to a self-imposed silence regarding topics touching on Islam. This pattern of behavior has emerged with regard to a host of issues—Salman Rushdie, Muslim antisemitism, Islamic alternatives to the Universal Declaration of Human Rights (UDHR), a "defamation of Islam" resolution, and the actions of the Sudanese government.

SALMAN RUSHDIE

The United Nations took little interest when Ayatollah Khomeini issued an edict in February 1989 that condemned British writer Salman Rushdie to death for his novel *The Satanic Verses*, which is "in opposition to Islam, the Prophet, and the Qur'an," as the edict affirms; if anything, most member states tried to ignore the whole episode. It took four full years before the greatest freedom-of-expression case of our time found an even implicit mention in a UNCHR resolution (the one that annually criticizes Iran for human rights violations): "[The UNCHR] also expresses its grave concern that there

Reprinted from the *Middle East Quarterly* 6, no. 3 (September 1999): 59–64. This article is also available on the Middle East Forum Web site at http://www.meforum.org/article/477/.

are continuing threats to the life of a citizen of another State which appears to have the support of the Government of the Islamic Republic of Iran and whose case is mentioned in the report of the Special Representative."[1]

By 1999, the UNCHR chose to accept at face value "the assurances given by the Government of Iran in New York in September 1998,"[2] when foreign minister Kamal Kharazi said his government would no longer seek to end Rushdie's life. In the process, the commission preferred to ignore Kharazi's acknowledgment that he was saying nothing new ("We did not adopt a new position with regard to the apostate Salman Rushdie, and our position remains the same");[3] it also disregarded statements by leading regime officials threatening Rushdie's life. For example, it made no difference that Ayatollah Hasan Sanai, head of a leading foundation, stated on February 14, 1999, that "Iran is serious and determined in the execution of God's order. The idea of Rushdie's annihilation is a living idea looking for an appropriate opportunity."[4]

This attitude of indifference emboldened member states of the Organization of the Islamic Conference (OIC) sympathetic to the enhancement of the Sharia, and they proceeded to try to introduce Khomeini-style restrictions on freedom of speech about certain political aspects of Islam to the United Nations itself. Thus did the "Rushdie rules" begin affecting UN bodies, and especially the Commission on Human Rights, eating away at international norms.

"HUMAN RIGHTS IN ISLAM"

The Cairo Declaration

On August 5, 1990, the nineteen Islamic Conference of Foreign Ministers adopted the Cairo Declaration on Human Rights in Islam (CDHRI). The CDHRI is very precise: according to the official English version, "All the rights and freedoms stipulated in this Declaration are subject to the Islamic *Shari'a*" (article 24), and "The Islamic *Shari'a* is the only source of reference for the explanation or clarification of any of the articles of this Declaration" (article 25). In other words, by establishing Sharia law as "the only source of reference" for the protection of human rights in Islamic countries, the Cairo Declaration gives it supremacy over the Universal Declaration of Human Rights.

In spite of this self-evident contradiction between the CDHRI and the UDHR, the Office of the High Commissioner for Human Rights published the former document in December 1997,[5] thereby seeming to give it a certain authority within the United Nations. And, sure enough, the CDHRI then became a quotable source at the United Nations. For example, the twenty-six members of the Sub-Commission on Human Rights referred to it in the preamble to a resolution adopted on August 21, 1998, on the situation of women in Afghanistan: "*Deeply concerned* at the situation of the female population of Kabul and other parts of Afghanistan controlled by the Taliban; *dismayed* by the Taliban's claim that Islam supports their policies concerning women; *fully aware* that the Cairo Declaration on Human Rights in Islam, adopted by the Organization of the Islamic Conference in 1990, guarantees the rights of women in all fields."[6]

An "Islamic Perspectives" Seminar

On the initiative of Iran's foreign minister Kamal Kharazi, who called for a "revision of the Declaration [UDHR]" in his address to the UNCHR on March 17, 1998, the Office of the High Commissioner for Human Rights hosted a seminar in Geneva entitled "Enriching the Universality of Human Rights: Islamic Perspectives on the Universal Declaration of Human Rights," on November 9–10, 1998. At the event, which was financed by the OIC countries at a cost of nearly five hundred thousand dollars, twenty Muslim experts on Islam presented papers with the aim of "expounding the Islamic perspectives as to human rights and recall the contribution of Islam to the laying of the foundations of these rights through which Islam aimed at leading people out of the obscurities and into enlightenment, at ensuring dignity in their life and non-submission to anyone but God, and at asserting their freedom and their right to justice and equality on the basis of the two sources of Islamic Shari'a: Qur'an and Sunna and on Fiqh jurisprudence."[7]

Although the seminar's stated purpose was "to promote understanding and respect among peoples," the audience of over 250 representatives from more than eighty states, intergovernmental and UN bodies, and forty-one nongovernmental organizations (NGOs) had no chance to speak, for the discussion was restricted to participants. The invitation noted that to promote "understanding and respect among peoples, we have designed the seminar to have a scholarly focus and to be a venue for exchanges of scholarship, views, and opinions. It will not be called upon to reach conclusions, adopt positions, or review country practices."[8] Understanding and respect may have been the stated goal, but in fact the seminar rendered impossible the open discussion of issues. Observers agreed that this format was unprecedented within the

United Nations system; certainly, it was much deplored, even by some diplo-mats from OIC member states.

No Muslim Antisemitism

The governments of the Organization of the Islamic Conference reached a decision in 1996 at their summit held in Tehran that Ambassador Munir Akram of Pakistan would later explain to the Commission on Human Rights as calling for "pragmatic and constructive steps to counter the negative pro-paganda against Islam; to remove and rectify misunderstandings; and to pre-sent the true image of Islam: the religion of peace and tolerance."[9]

Four months later, the OIC began to apply this decision at the United Nations. On the very last day of the UNCHR's 1997 session, the representa-tive of Indonesia, Agus Tarmidzi, speaking on behalf of the OIC countries, took the floor to protest a passage in a report by Benin's Maurice Glélé-Ahanhanzo, the UN special rapporteur on racism. Focusing on information under the subheading "Islamist and Arab Anti-Semitism," the Indonesian ambassador referred to a quotation from a book on antisemitism that reads, "The use of Christian and secular European antisemitic motifs in Muslim publications is on the rise, yet at the same time, Muslim extremists are turning increasingly to their own religious sources, first and foremost the Qur'an, as a primary anti-Jewish source."[10]

Tarmidzi called this a "defamation of our religion Islam and blasphemy against its Holy Book Qur'an." That same evening, the UNCHR's fifty-three member states—including the United States and several Western countries—adopted a decision by consensus that "[e]xpress[ed] its indignation and protest at the content of such an offensive reference to Islam and the Holy Qur'an; affirmed that this offensive reference should have been excluded from the report; requested the chairman to ask the special rapporteur to take corrective action in response to the present decision."[11]

That request was promptly carried out, and the "offensive reference" was duly excised.[12] But this was not enough. On July 22, 1997, at the Geneva ses-sion of the UN Economic and Social Council (ECOSOC), Indonesia, speaking for the OIC, again referred to the "outrageous reference to Islam and to the Qur'an" contained in the report on racism, which had been excised in a corrigendum two weeks earlier. Some of the OIC speakers even demanded that the very subheading, "Islamist and Arab Anti-Semitism," be excised—a demand subsequently reiterated by Iran and Sudan.[13]

Interestingly, not one of these representatives attempted to refute the "outrageous reference"; instead, heaping scorn on it and making sure it was not repeated sufficed for them. Perhaps their reluctance to deal with the facts of the matter has to do with the irrefutable evidence that Islamists constantly use religious sources for what is spoken and written critically on the subject of Jews in Arabic and Persian. Thus the accusation of "blasphemy" amounts to an attempt to make special rapporteurs exercise self-censorship.

And, indeed, such self-censorship has occurred, as can be seen in the 1999 report of the special rapporteur on racism, where the subheading that caused the furor in 1997, "Islamist and Arab Anti-Semitism," is now conspicuously absent.[14] Although Glélé-Ahanhanzo again refers to the same Israeli publication as he did in 1997, he omits any reference to its twenty-five pages on antisemitism in Arab countries and Iran.[15] In fact, he does not even mention any evidence of antisemitism in the Muslim world. [This remained the same throughout his mandate until 2002.]

"DEFAMATION OF ISLAM"

In contrast to the last-minute efforts in 1997, the OIC countries began their efforts to pass a resolution (under the agenda item "racism") condemning what they called the "defamation of Islam" right at the start of the UNCHR's 1999 session. They claimed—in negotiations with the European Union (EU), the United States, and other delegations—that "Islam, one of the principal religions of the world, is being slandered in different quarters, including in human rights fora."[16] On behalf of the OIC countries, Pakistani ambassador Akram introduced draft resolution L.40, titled "Defamation of Islam," on April 29, 1999. To justify this text, he compared "the emergence of a new manifestation of intolerance and misunderstanding and misconception of Islam and Muslim peoples in various parts of the world" to "antisemitism in the years of the past."

Akram built his argument in part on the 1997 "blasphemy" decision: "It has already been claimed that Islamic scriptures incite Muslims to violence. This assertion was even included in a human rights report and excised only after the commission acted on this blasphemy."[17] More assertively, Akram made large claims for his religion: "It was Islam which gave the world the first Charter of Human Rights in the Holy Qur'an; the Declaration of Human Rights in prophet Muhammad's last address; and the first Refugee Convention in the *mithâq-i-Medina* [Constitution of Medina]."[18]

The Western countries refused, however, to accept a resolution that had the provocative title of "Defamation of Islam." As German ambassador Wilhelm Höynck put it, on behalf of the European Union, the OIC's draft resolution was selective in nature, focusing "exclusively on what its authors perceive as a negative stereotyping of Islam." Attempts to find a compromise between the two sides were getting nowhere, leading to a threat from Pakistan's ubiquitous ambassador that if the EU and others maintained their position "this will have a lasting impact in the Muslim world."[19] Both sides preferred to avoid a vote—with its unpredictable repercussions—so Höynck, noting that "the European Union is attached to freedom of thought, conscience, and religion, as well as to tolerance for all religions," proposed as a title, "Stereotyping of Religions." This the OIC refused.

Finally, the two sides reached a compromise: the title of what became Commission Resolution 1999/82 would be "Defamation of Religions," and the text would not refer exclusively to Islam.[20] Despite this apparent compromise, no one will be misled as to the intent of this resolution. Islam is the only religion mentioned in the text (a preambular paragraph refers to the seminar on "Islamic Perspectives on the Universal Declaration of Human Rights" in November 1998), and the operative paragraph also expresses "deep concern that Islam is frequently and wrongly associated with human rights violations and with terrorism." Thus a Reuters dispatch dated April 30, 1999, reported that "the U.N. Speaks against Anti-Islam in the Media," and went on to explain that the UNCHR "expressed concern . . . that Islam was often wrongly blamed for being behind crimes and terrorist acts." The Reuters news item also (correctly) noted that this "was the first time that the panel had adopted a text on defamation of religion."

SUDAN

The case of Sudan's behavior illustrates how concepts such as the "defamation of Islam" have progressed at the UNCHR and affected decision making there. Back in 1994, the Sudanese ambassador circulated a letter to all representatives at the UNCHR, accusing the UN special rapporteur on Sudan, Gaspar Biro, of making a "vicious attack on the religion of Islam," because portions of his first report indicated inconsistencies between the international human-rights conventions (to which Sudan has been a signatory party since 1986) and some provisions of Sudan's Criminal Act of 1991 that follow the Sharia.[21] However, with no backing from the OIC, the Sudanese government got precisely nowhere; the commission called on it "to comply with applicable international human rights instruments."[22]

Five years later, the situation had changed completely. Appearing at the UNCHR on March 23, 1999, John Garang, chairman of the Sudan Peoples' Liberation Movement (SPLM) and head of the Sudan Peoples' Liberation Army (SPLA), the southern, mostly Christian rebel force fighting the government of Sudan and its Sharia law since 1983, was prevented from speaking by the Sudanese representatives. Although Garang had been properly accredited by a nongovernmental organization, Christian Solidarity International (CSI), before he could reach the second sentence of his speech, on "the genocidal character of the war waged by the present regime in Khartoum," the Sudanese representative stopped him on a "point of order." The chair ruled Garang in order. Then Sudan requested a vote and, after a few exchanges and a recess, the chair gave Garang the floor, only to rule him out of order on a point of procedure (namely, that "the statement being made by the representative of CSI was not germane to the agenda item").

Technically speaking, the Sudanese government had a point: CSI had made two minor errors (Garang's statement was not as integrated into the agenda item as the rules of procedure required, and his statement was distributed on SPLM letterhead, not CSI's). With this, the most important leader of the southern Sudanese people was silenced, unable to ask the UNCHR plenum what just one day earlier he had asked an audience of representatives from governments and nongovernmental organizations and at a press conference: "In 1992 the regime in Khartoum declared jihad against the people of southern Sudan and the Nuba Mountains. Since then jihad has been declared again and again. I ask this very important question: is the jihad a religious right of those who declare and wage it, or is it a violation of the human rights of the people against whom it is declared and waged?"[23]

Nor was this all. The government of Sudan, angered by CSI's constant denunciation of its many human rights violations, particularly slavery, seized on this technical pretext to oust CSI from all UN bodies. On June 17 in New York, twelve of the nineteen members of the UN Committee on NGOs (Sudan, Pakistan, Algeria, Tunisia, Lebanon, Senegal, Ethiopia, Turkey, India, China, Russia, and Cuba) voted to recommend that the Economic and Social Council (ECOSOC) withdraw CSI's accreditation; four abstained, and the United States cast the only no vote. Seth Winnick, the US representative, later commented, "The committee acted grossly in violation of the norms of due process. This committee is not competent to act."[24] Then, at a final ECOSOC meeting of July 30, 1999, a decision by consensus sent the flawed recommendation back to the Committee on NGOs, allowing CSI until August 31 to submit a report and a response. [CSI's accreditation was then withdrawn.] The ECOSOC verdict on CSI is potentially a precedent of considerable importance, for it is often by votes on relatively minor issues such as this that one sees which way the wind is blowing at the United Nations.

CONCLUSION

The new rules of conduct being imposed by the OIC and acceded to by other states, give those who claim to represent Islam an exceptional status at the United Nations that has no legal basis and no precedent; it therefore gives ample reason for apprehension. Will a prohibition of discussion about certain political aspects of Islam become generally accepted at the United Nations and beyond, contradicting "the right to freedom of opinion and expression" promised by article 19 of the Universal Declaration of Human Rights? Unless farsighted states, both Muslim and non-Muslim, make it their business to assert and reassert the need for freedom of speech, this precious liberty is at risk of being eroded throughout the system of international organizations.

NOTES

1. UNCHR resolution 1993/62, para. 5.

2. UNCHR resolution 1999/13, 1(f). However, the same resolution, under 3(e), "expresses its concern . . . [a]t continuing threats by the Fifteen Khordad Foundation to the life of Mr. Salman Rushdie including the increase in the bounty announced by the foundation."

3. *Voice of the Islamic Republic of Iran*, October 3, 1998.

4. Quoted in an article on the UNCHR, Reuters, February 14, 1999.

5. *Human Rights: A Compilation of International Instruments*, vol. 2, *Regional Instruments* (New York and Geneva: United Nations, 1997), pp. 474–84.

6. The reference is to CDHRI article 6(a): "Woman is equal to man in human dignity, and has rights to enjoy as well as duties to perform."

7. From the introductory address by Dr. Azeddine Laraki, secretary-general of the OIC, provisional publication of the UN Office of High Commissioner for Human Rights: HR/IP/SEM/1999/1, part 1, March 15, 1999, p. 6 (GE.99-40940).

8. Reply from the Office of the High Commissioner for Human Rights, October 16, 1998, to the letter from René Wadlow and David Littman, representatives of the

Association for World Education to the United Nations, Geneva, to Mary Robinson, September 24, 1998.

9. UN recording, April 29, 1999, at the sixty-first meeting. (The *Summary Record*, E/CN.4/1999/SR.61 omits this introductory passage.)

10. Dina Porat et al., eds., *Anti-Semitism Worldwide, 1995–96* (Tel Aviv: Anti-Defamation League and World Jewish Congress, 1996), p. 4; see also UNCHR: E/CN/1997/71, E-3, chap. 2, para. 27.

11. UNCHR 1997/125, in E/CN.4/1997/SR.70.

12. UNCHR report on racism, E/CN.4/1997/71; corrigendum, E/CN.4/1997/71/Corr. 1 of July 8, 1997.

13. At the August 1997 Sub-Commission on Human Rights and at the 1998 UNCHR. See E/CN.4/1998/SR.11, para. 50, and E/CN.4/1998/SR.12. para. 10.

14. UNCHR report on racism, E/CN.4/1999/15, para. 78 and 79 (D. Anti-Semitism).

15. Dina Porat et al., eds., *Anti-Semitism Worldwide, 1997–98* (Tel Aviv: Anti-Defamation League and World Jewish Congress, 1998), pp. 181–205.

16. This quotation, later dropped, is from the original draft resolution, "Defamation of Islam."

17. UN recording, April 29, 1999, and partially in E/CN.4/1999/SR.61, paras. 1–2.

18. Other speakers, such as Sheikh Jasim bin Nasir ath-Thani, the head of Qatar's delegation, concurred with this argument: "There is no doubt that Islam, which preceded the Universal Declaration on Human Rights by fourteen centuries, was first in declaring equality among humans in all rights and responsibilities, and in defining rights and freedoms both for individuals and groups." Quoted from the delegation's text, delivered on April 1, 1999 (also E/CN.4/1999/SR.13, para. 95). [For a scholarly analysis of the historical document mentioned by Ambassador Akhram, see Moshe Gil, "The Constitution of Medina: A Reconsideration," *Israel Oriental Studies* (Jerusalem) 4 (1974): 44–65.]

19. UN recording, April 29, 1999, and partially in E/CN.4/1999/SR.61, paras. 1–2.

20. UN recording, April 29–30, 1999; E/CN.4/1999/SR.61–62.

21. Letter dated February 18, 1994 (E/CN.4/1994/122); report on Sudan by Dr. Gaspar Biro (E/CN.4/1994/48).

22. UNCHR resolution 1994/79 (5), and subsequently 1995/77 (9), 1996/73 (8), 1997/59 (9), 1998/67 (8), and 1999/15 (4).

23. From the undelivered statement of John Garang, point 2, and from the circulated SPLM press statement, point 8, March 22, 1999.

24. Quoted in article on ECOSOC meeting, Associated Press, New York, June 18, 1999; Reuters, June 18, 1999.

27. UNIVERSAL HUMAN RIGHTS AND "HUMAN RIGHTS IN ISLAM"

David G. Littman

ISLAMIC PERSPECTIVES ON THE 1948 UNIVERSAL DECLARATION OF HUMAN RIGHTS

For years now, a systematic effort has been made at the United Nations by certain member states to replace some of the dominant paradigms of international relations. For example, representatives of the Islamic Republic of Iran continue—in all fora—to press their objections to the universal character and indivisibility of human rights, as interpreted in the Universal Declaration of Human Rights (UDHR), which according to them is a Western secular concept of Judeo-Christian origin, incompatible with the sacred Islamic Sharia.

We shall examine here a few major developments of concern that have occurred in the past decade at some of the top UN watchdog bodies on human rights: the Geneva-based Commission on Human Rights, its Sub-Commission on Prevention of Discrimination and Protection of Minorities, the Office of the High Commissioner on Human Rights, and the Human Rights Committee, a major treaty body.

In November 1998 a seminar was held at the United Nations in Geneva under the auspices of the Office of the High Commissioner but was totally financed by the Organization of the Islamic Conference (OIC) at a cost of almost half a million dollars. That event—called "Enriching the Universality of Human Rights: Islamic Perspectives on the Universal Declaration of Human Rights"—could not, and did not, break the deadlock created by regular calls for "revision" of the 1948 UDHR. But one could ask—what led to the decision to organize it, and how was it justified?

Reprinted from *Midstream* 45, no. 2 (February/March 1999): 2–7.

On March 17, 1998, the first speaker at the Jubilee Commemoration of the UDHR—at the Commission on Human Rights in Geneva, after the ceremonial speeches by secretary-general Kofi Annan, Vaclav Havel, and Elie Wiesel—was Iranian foreign minister Dr. Kamal Kharazi (Iran then held the presidency of the OIC). His statement contained an appeal for a "revision of the Declaration," followed by a request that "the High Commissioner invite commentaries on the UDHR as a prelude to dialogue and encourage all states and organizations to join the exercise."[1]

As a result of Kharazi's appeal—coming soon after Mary Robinson's visit to Tehran in February, when the matter was first raised—the Office of the High Commissioner began preparations, jointly with the OIC, for a two-day seminar; it finally took place on November 9–10. 1998. For this unique UN event, twenty Islamic experts from the fifty-six OIC countries—one each from Iran, Saudi Arabia, and Sudan—presented their papers on "Islamic Perspectives on the UDHR." Discussions were restricted to the experts, while the more than 250 participating representatives from more than eighty states, intergovernmental and UN bodies, as well as forty-one nongovernmental organizations (NGOs), listened without any opportunity to ask questions.

The aims of the seminar were clarified in Robinson's October 29, 1998, letter of invitation to all members of UN treaty bodies, working groups of the subcommission and special rapporteurs: "The seminar is being organized during this 50th Anniversary year of the UDHR as part of the process of providing Islamic perspectives on the UDHR. I accept responsibility for the process in response to the invitation made by the Minister of Foreign Affairs of the Islamic Republic of Iran, during his address to the 54th session of the Commission on Human Rights (1998). I believe this process will help promote understanding and respect among peoples."

UNITED NATIONS SEMINAR WHERE "ISLAM IS UNDERSTOOD IN TERMS OF 'SHARI'A' (QUR'AN AND HADITH)"

An earlier explanation from Mary Robinson's office (October 16) stated, "In order to achieve this objective ['to promote understanding and respect among peoples'], we have designed the seminar to have a scholarly focus and to be the venue for exchanges of scholarship, views and opinions. It will not be called upon to reach conclusions, adopt positions or review country practices. Further, we have agreed that for the purpose of this seminar, Islam is understood in terms of 'Shari'a' (Qur'an and Hadith) and not in terms of traditions or practices that may vary and mix with historical heritages. This will allow the seminar to focus on the Islamic perspective with a minimum of potential controversy which could overshadow the central purpose."[2]

Two weeks after the event, a Muslim researcher from the European Institute at the University of Geneva, Hasni Abidi, wrote an article in the *Tribune de Genève*, "Human Rights à la carte," asking: "Are we going toward a new Universal Declaration of Human Rights? . . . to accept this type of manifestation risks opening a breach in the universality of human rights. Worse, this seminar could constitute support for political attitudes totally in contradiction with the fundamental principles of human rights."[3]

Aside from two revealing papers,[4] the fact that this seminar led nowhere is not surprising, as UN-sponsored seminars and costly megaconferences usually end with no effect on the real world. The problem is that these efforts to undercut international paradigms, which have been at the core of the world order since 1945, are henceforth guaranteed an institutionalized forum and legitimacy within the UN system.

The relationship between the sacred, as announced in the Qur'an, and the political is one of the ongoing, controversial debates within Islamic countries. There is today a wide range of views as to what is covered by the Sharia, the nature of the state's legal system, the nature of the authority for its legal codes, the nature of these codes themselves, and the modalities for modifying them. In the light of the more and more frequent appeals to the authority of the Sharia by Islamist groups— in order to sanctify violence or highly restrictive social measures imposed by them upon defenseless people under their ideological and totalitarian control—more and more voices are being raised for the separation of the political from the traditional legal and religious doctrine in Islam.

One such voice is that of imam Soheib Bencheikh, the mufti of Marseilles. Speaking at the Commission on Human Rights on March 23, 1998— under the auspices of the Association for World Education—in relation to the savagery being perpetrated in Algeria, he called on Muslim theologians and thinkers to strive for a "desacralization of Islamic law" and a reform of Islamic theology. By repeating that call at the UN seminar on November 10, 1998, he again contributed a clear message.[5]

THE INTERNATIONAL BILL OF HUMAN RIGHTS AND THE 1993 VIENNA DECLARATION AND PROGRAM OF ACTION

Among the efforts to codify universal human values in the last half century, the UDHR is among the best known and most widely cited, both by governments and civil society. In today's planetary society, where people from so many different nations and cultures intermingle with increasing frequency, there should be common standards and a general acceptance of the International Bill of Human Rights—that is, the UDHR (1948)—as well as the International Covenant on Economic, Social, and Cultural Rights and the International Covenant on Civil and Political Rights (ICCPR), both adopted in 1966.

These three basic texts have been developed in a subsequent series of international human rights instruments, which were published by the United Nations in *A Compilation of International Instruments.*[6] Thus an allegation that certain states were absent from the drafting process of the UDHR prior to its adoption on December 10, 1948, is specious, as third world countries and other states have had ample opportunities since then to contribute—as was done!—to the later elaboration and codification of the principles and rights contained in the UDHR. Therefore, no calls for a "revision of the Declaration"—along the lines requested by Khazari on March 17, 1998—are justified.

In this context, one should not forget the clear provisions contained in article 29 of the UDHR:

1. Everyone has duties to the community in which alone the free and full development of his personality is possible.
2. In the exercise of his rights and freedoms, everyone shall be subject only to such limitations as are determined by law solely for the purpose of securing due recognition and respect for the rights and freedoms of others and of meeting the just requirements of morality, public order and the general welfare in a democratic society.
3. These rights and freedoms may in no case be exercised contrary to the purposes and principles of the United Nations.

The corpus of international instruments on human rights adopted after 1948 constitutes a sufficiently flexible framework for their full implementation in all regions and countries in the world, provided the political will exists. The preamble of the UDHR begins with the words, "Whereas recognition of the inherent dignity and of the equal and inalienable rights of all members of the human family is the foundation of freedom, justice and peace in the world." This idea is reiterated in article 1: "All human beings are born free and equal in dignity and rights."

In June 1993, in order to reaffirm the UDHR and the other international human rights instruments, the United Nations organized in Vienna a World Conference on Human Rights. The 171 participating states adopted the Vienna Declaration and Program of Action, thereby reasserting the universality of all human rights as the birthright of all human beings and recognizing that their protection and promotion were the prime concerns of governments that guaranteed to uphold them.

The preamble affirms "that all human rights derive from the dignity and worth inherent in the human person." The UN General Assembly endorsed, by consensus, the Vienna Program of Action and thereby the crucial importance of the recognition of the principle of human dignity inherent in the UDHR. The 1993 Vienna Declaration reaffirmed that "the universal nature of these rights and freedoms is beyond question."

TWO CRITICISMS OF THE 1948 UNIVERSAL DECLARATION OF HUMAN RIGHTS

The year 1998 marked the five-year review of the implementation of the Vienna Declaration and Program of Action. In the past, the universality and indivisibility of the rights set out in the UDHR came under criticism from two sources. The first was a Western, largely American-led criticism on economic, social, and cultural rights. This was a reflection in the 1980s of an extreme neoliberalism, which maintained that the state should play a minimal role in the economic and social sphere.

But as a whole the international community did not yield to these pressures. Today, there is a realization of a need for a strong civil society and a widespread consensus in Western countries, demanding governmental leadership in fields of health, education, employment, housing, and social security—all areas considered as "rights" in the UDHR. As a result, the earlier Western criticisms were much toned down, and vigorous poverty reduction programs are now functioning within the UN system.

The second source of attacks came from third world countries that have earlier, ancient legal systems and are constantly calling for human rights to be viewed in the historical and cultural context of each country or civilization. China, India, and several countries of the Islamic world—notably Iran, Sudan, Pakistan, Afghanistan, and Saudi Arabia—have been stressing this position off and on. Although many third world countries are reluctant to follow this reasoning, few oppose it openly.

Already in September 1992, six months before the Vienna Conference, the Final Declaration of the Conference of the 108 Non-Aligned Countries, held in Jakarta, Indonesia, stressed "differences in cultures" and implied that differences in the interpretation of human rights should be recognized. Since then, the new Indonesian government, led by B. J. Habibie, appears to be less vocal on the issue of "Asian values."   Clearly all religions and traditional societies deserve respect, without however losing sight of the goals laid down in the International Bill of Human Rights. But any reinterpretation of human rights beyond the existing framework of international norms—that is, the various forms of "cultural relativism"—quickly leads to grave human rights abuses by some rulers whose states are signatories to the International Bill of Rights and to the other international human rights instruments.

Thus any future "compromises" on the UDHR—based upon the proclaimed differences in culture, traditions, religion, or socioeconomic customs—rather than leading to peaceful reconciliation could, however worthy the intentions, insert uneven cobblestones, thus paving new paths of uncertainty in the coming century for the international community and all peoples of the world.

IRAN'S STEADFAST UN POSITION ON THE UDHR SINCE 1981

In 1981—two years after the Iranian revolution—the new government's position was clearly stated at the thirty-sixth UN General Assembly session, when its representative affirmed that the UDHR represented a secular interpretation of the Judeo-Christian tradition, which could not be implemented by Muslims; if a choice had to be made between its stipulations and "the divine law of the country," Iran would always choose Islamic law.[7] This was the same year, 1981, in which the Universal Islamic Declaration of Human Rights (UIDHR) was presented with much fanfare to the United Nations Educational, Scientific, and Cultural Organization (UNESCO) in Paris, attended by Ahmad ben Bella of Algeria, Mukhtar Ould Daddah of Mauretania, Saudi Arabia's Prince Muhammad al-Faisal, and Pakistani president Zia al-Haq's advisor. It was prepared under the auspices of the Islamic Council, a London-based organization affiliated with the Muslim World

League, an international nongovernmental organization (NGO). As Prof. Ann Elizabeth Mayer explains in her meticulously documented study *Islam and Human Rights*, "In a casual reading, the English version of the UIDHR seems to be closely modeled after the UDHR, but upon closer examination many of the similarities turn out to be misleading. In addition, the English version diverges from the Arabic version at many points."[8]

In his December 7, 1984, statement to the UN General Assembly's Third Committee, the Iranian representative, Rajaie-Khorassani, again put on record his country's position on the UDHR:

> In his delegation's view, the concept of human rights was not limited to the Universal Declaration of Human Rights. Man was of divine origin and human dignity could not be reduced to a series of secular norms. . . . Certain concepts contained in the Universal Declaration of Human Rights needed to be revised. [Iran] recognized no authority or power but that of Almighty God and no legal tradition apart from Islamic law. As his delegation had already stated at the thirty-sixth session of the General Assembly, conventions, declarations and resolutions or decisions of international organizations, which were contrary to Islam had no validity in the Islamic Republic of Iran. . . . The Universal Declaration of Human Rights, which represented a secular understanding of the Judeo-Christian tradition, could not be implemented by Muslims and did not accord with the system of values recognized by the Islamic Republic of Iran; his country would therefore not hesitate to violate its provisions, since it had to choose between violating the divine law of the country and violating secular conventions.[9]

Since then, this basic Iranian position has been reiterated. It was clearly expressed on October 30, 1992, in a reply by Ambassador Sirous Nasseri to the Human Rights Committee (the UN treaty body that supervises the 1966 ICCPR), regarding comments and questions by the Committee's independent members to Iran's second periodic report:

> It could, of course, be argued that each State party to the Covenant should simply apply its provisions to the letter. Yet many peoples were not satisfied with the rigid application of human rights instruments and wanted account taken of their traditions, culture and religious context in order to evaluate the human rights situation in a country.
>
> A revival of Islam, which some call fanaticism or extremism and others renaissance, was obviously taking place. . . . It should be borne in mind that certain Islamic countries—and by no means the least important—had not subscribed to the Universal Declaration of Human Rights. An even larger

number had not yet acceded to the Covenant. There were reasons for that. It was easy to reject the argument that the representatives of Islamic countries had participated in the discussions that had led to the elaboration of the Universal Declaration of Human Rights and the Covenant, for it was clear that at that time the Islamic countries had not carried the political weight they deserved—which was still true at the present time. The Islamic countries had therefore elaborated an Islamic Declaration of Human Rights [CDHRI]. Members of the Committee had asked whether the Islamic Republic of Iran had specific reservations to make concerning the Universal Declaration of Human Rights and the Covenant; an examination of the Islamic Declaration of Human Rights revealed what, in the view of the Islamic countries, was lacking in those two instruments.

[Iran] had reached the conclusion that those two instruments were compatible with Islamic law. . . . Discrepancies . . . between domestic legislation and the Covenant should not be exaggerated. . . . Those differences could be overcome and a better understanding of Islam, of Islamic law and of international law achieved only by means of dialogue approached with an open mind.[10]

THE 1990 "CAIRO DECLARATION OF HUMAN RIGHTS IN ISLAM" AND THE 1981 UNIVERSAL ISLAMIC DECLARATION

The controversial Cairo Declaration on Human Rights in Islam (CDHRI) was adopted in Cairo on August 5, 1990, by the Nineteenth Islamic Conference of Foreign Ministers (session of "Peace, Interdependence, and Development") of the forty-five member states of the Organization of the Islamic Conference (OIC), subsequent to the Report of the Meeting of the Committee of Legal Experts held in Tehran, December 26–28, 1989. The CDHRI establishes the Sharia law as "the only source of reference" for the protection of human rights in Islamic countries, thus giving it supremacy over the UDHR. The CDHRI was presented for approval at the OIC Summit Meeting of Heads of State and Government, held in Dakar, Senegal, on December 9, 1991. This was averted following a press release from the Geneva-based International Commission of Jurists (ICJ). The dangers of the CDHRI were enumerated in the press release and again spelled out in a joint statement to the UN Commission on Human Rights by Adama Dieng, its Muslim secretary general and a prominent Senegalese jurist, who alerted the international community to the grave negative implications that would result. Speaking for the ICJ and the Paris-based International Federation of Human Rights at the

Commission on Human Rights in February 1992,[11] he declared, among other things, that

1. It gravely threatens the intercultural consensus on which the international human rights instruments are based;
2. It introduces, in the name of the defense of human rights, an intolerable discrimination against both non-Muslims and women;
3. It reveals a deliberately restrictive character in regard to certain fundamental rights and freedoms, to the point that certain essential provisions are below the legal standards in effect in a number of Muslim countries;
4. It confirms, under cover of the Islamic Sharia, the legitimacy of practices, such as corporal punishment, which attack the integrity and dignity of the human being.

The ICJ's fears—and those of the NGO community—concerned the intercultural consensus that forms the heart of the UDHR and the international covenants ratified by most states, thus making them binding under international law.

Although traditions, cultures, and religious background may be different, human nature is universally the same. The aim of those who drafted and approved the UDHR was precisely to affirm this universal human identity, separating it from particular and religious contexts, which introduce and sanctify differences and discriminations. Any attempt to bring in cultural and religious particularisms would simply remove the specifically universal character of the UDHR.

Neither the UIDHR nor the CDHRI is universal, because both are conditional on Islamic law, which non-Muslims do not accept. The UDHR places social and political norms in a secular framework, separating the political from the religious.

In contrast, both the UIDHR and the CDHRI introduce into the political sphere an Islamic religious criterion, which imposes an absolute decisive and divine primacy over the political and legal spheres. Therefore the latter texts cannot be considered universal, since they endorse all the differentiations between individuals as spelled out in the Islamic Sharia law.

APPLICATION OF THE SHARIA LAW IN PAKISTAN AND OTHER MUSLIM COUNTRIES

The case of Pakistan is exemplary because in August 1998 the government of Prime Minister Nawaz Sharif introduced a controversial constitutional amendment to scrap any remaining British laws in Pakistan and replace them with laws based on the Qur'an, giving the government sweeping powers to "prescribe what is right and forbid what is wrong." The National Assembly passed the amendment in September, but it still awaits a vote in the Senate where the prime minister's Pakistan Muslim League does not have an absolute majority. This notwithstanding, on January 16, 1999, an ordinance signed by the governor of the Northwest Frontier, representing the federal government, imposed Islamic Sharia in tribal areas of the northwest part of the country, between the provincial capital, Peshawar, and the border with Afghanistan, where similar punishments were imposed by the Taliban religious army. These include public flogging, amputations of hands and feet, stoning for adultery, and executions. All civil and criminal cases will now be decided according to the Qur'an, in courts headed by Muslim clerics. "Opposition parties, human rights groups and non-Muslim minorities bitterly oppose the prime minister's efforts to introduce Islamic laws saying they violate the Constitution."[12]

The 1985 constitution distinguishes between human rights that can be derogated and those that cannot—freedom of religion being in the first category. During the presidency of Gen. Zia al-Haq (1977–1988), the Federal Shariat (legal) Court (FSC) was instituted, with full "jurisdiction over convictions or acquittals from district courts in cases involving . . . Islamic criminal laws; exclusive jurisdiction to hear [petitions] . . . challenging 'any law or provision of law' as repugnant to the Holy Qur'an; exclusive jurisdiction to examine 'any law or provision of law' for repugnancy to the Holy Qur'an."[13]

Although non-Muslims may not appear before the FSC to give testimony, they are subject to its rulings. Ordinance 20 (1984), which was incorporated into the 1985 constitution, established the Islamic Hudood (punishment) to "define crimes against Islam" and "enforce punishment for those who commit such crimes." In such cases, testimony from a non-Muslim male is considered to be worth half that of a Muslim male. In 1986, section 295-C was inserted into Pakistan's penal code, making the death penalty mandatory for anyone convicted of blaspheming the prophet Muhammad. From 1986 to 1993, over two hundred Ahmadi Muslims were charged with "blasphemy," but none were convicted. More than a dozen Christians were charged, four of whom were reportedly killed in detention, but none executed. On May 6, 1998, John Joseph, bishop of Faisalabad, chairman of the Human Rights Commission established by the Catholics Bishops' Conference of Pakistan, killed himself in protest against these blasphemy laws.[14]

In the Sharia legal system—practiced in Saudi Arabia, Pakistan, Afghanistan, Iran, Sudan, and in other Muslim countries—the testimony of a Muslim man is equal to the testimony of two Muslim women. Other examples from the Sharia, strictly applied or in abeyance, abound. The demands of Islamist groups in Algeria, Egypt, and elsewhere usually relate to traditional extremist interpretations of the Sharia.

ENGLISH AND ARABIC VERSIONS MAY DIFFER, BUT THE SHARIA LAW PREVAILS

As with the 1981 UIDHR, there exists both an English version for general purposes as well as an Arabic version of the 1990 CDHRI, each conveying a somewhat different message. Nonetheless, articles 24 and 25 in the English version of the CDHRI are very precise and leave no doubt as to the overall meaning:

> All the rights and freedoms stipulated in this Declaration are subject to the Islamic Shari'a. (article 24)

> The Islamic Shari'a is the only source of reference for the explanation or clarification of any of the articles of this Declaration. (article 25)

In spite of the self-evident contradiction with the UDHR, the CDHRI was published in December 1997 by the Office of the High Commissioner for Human Rights in volume 2 of *International Instruments*, which would seem to give it a certain authority, even if the volume title refers to *Regional Instruments*, whereas the title of volume 1 (in two parts) is *Universal Instruments*.

It is difficult to understand why the CDHRI is the concluding document in volume 2, under the section "E. Organization of the Islamic Conference"—as the OIC is not a specific regional body, nor is the CDHRI a "regional instrument."[15]

"Cairo Declaration on Human Rights in Islam" at the UN

The CDHRI was supposed to "serve as a general guidance for Member States in the field of human rights," and its preamble states,

> The Member States of the Organization of the Islamic Conference, *Reaffirming* the civilizing and historic role of the Islamic Ummah which God made the best nation that has given mankind a universal and well-balanced civilization in which harmony is established between this life and the hereafter and knowledge is combined with faith; [and] . . . believing that fundamental rights and universal freedoms in Islam are an integral part of the Islamic religion . . . as they are binding divine commandments, which are contained in the Revealed Books of God and were sent through the last of His Prophets to complete the preceding divine messages thereby making their observance an act of worship and their neglect or violation an abominable sin, and accordingly every person is individually responsible—and the Ummah collectively responsible—for their safeguard.

The CDHRI thus claims supremacy over the UDHR, based on divine revelation.

Volume 2 was circulated to all eighteen "independent experts" of the subcommission, who referred to the CDHRI in the preamble to a resolution adopted on August 21, 1998. It reads, among other things,

> 1998/17: *Situation of Women in Afghanistan*:
>
> *Deeply concerned* at the situation of the female population of Kabul and other parts of Afghanistan controlled by the Taliban,
>
> *Dismayed* by the Taliban's claim that Islam supports their policies concerning women,
>
> *Fully aware* that the Cairo Declaration on Human Rights in Islam, adopted by the Organization of the Islamic Conference in 1990, guarantees the rights of women in all fields.

The reference is to article 6(a) of the CDHRI, which states, "Woman is equal to man in human dignity, and has rights to enjoy as well as duties to perform." These "rights to enjoy" are "subject to the Islamic Shari'a" (article 24), and the "duties" are also prescribed by the Islamic Sharia.

Two Previous UN Examples Related to "Blasphemy"

In a letter dated February 18, 1994, addressed to all delegates at the Commission on Human Rights,[16] the Sudanese ambassador requested an immediate withdrawal of any reference—from the report of the UN special rapporteur on Sudan—in which certain inconsistences were indicated between the international human rights conventions and the provisions of Sudan's Criminal Act of 1991. The ambassador alleged that the report "contained abusive, inconsiderate, blasphemous and offensive remarks about the Islamic faith." A further Sudanese circular titled *Attack on Islam* claimed that portions of the report "represent a vicious attack on the religion of Islam and contain a call for the abolition of its Islamic Penal Legislation."

In reply, the commission adopted resolution 1994/79, calling on the government of Sudan "to comply with applicable international human rights instruments and to bring its national legislation into accordance with the instruments to which Sudan was a party." In spite of death threats published in the government's newspaper, *Horizon*,[17] Dr. Gaspar Biro continued investigations into the many human rights violations in Sudan, fully described in his later reports submitted to the General Assembly and to the Human Rights Commission.[18] He was supported by resolutions condemning the government of Sudan.

On April 18, 1997, another "blasphemy" charge was leveled.[19] This time the alleged offending words were from a quoted passage contained in the report of the special rapporteur on racism, Mr. Maurice Glélé-Ahanhanzo from Benin (under "Islamist and Arab Anti-Semitism").[20] This new "blasphemy" charge succeeded after the representative of Indonesia intervened on the last day of the ccommission—in the name of the OIC's fifty-six Islamic states, on the initiative of Iran—claiming that Islam had been defamed and "blasphemy" committed against the Holy Qur'an. This led to the fifty-three-member-state commission's consensus decision 1997/125, obliging the special rapporteur to take a "corrective action."[21]

Hence a very dangerous precedent: the censorship of a UN special rapporteur, *in his capacity as an independent expert*, and of his report, on grounds of "blasphemy"—*although the facts he quoted are exact*—provides a concrete example of how the consequences of a cultural-relativist approach were imposed, by consensus, on the UN Commission on Human Rights, thereby avoiding a "religious-cultural" conflict. As a result, the only choice for the special rapporteur became censorship or resignation.[22]

A year later, on March 23, 1998, the representatives of Iran and Sudan were still calling for the Commission on Human Rights to act even more harshly in regard to its "blasphemy" censorship decision 1997/125.[23] One should not be surprised if such pressures persist in this case and others, as a result of the seminar jointly organized by the Office of the High Commissioner and the OIC—to quote Robinson's letter of "invitation"—as part of the process of providing Islamic perspectives on the UDHR.

Regarding Islamic perspectives on human rights, in general, Ann Elizabeth Mayer made a pertinent point in her authoritative study: "Since most current theorists of Islamic human rights persist in talking exclusively in terms of an idealized vision of Islamic social harmony, even though the historical record and the acts of current governments have manifestly demonstrated the inadequacy of the very scheme that they propose, one may doubt that their Islamic human rights schemes were actually devised to deal with contemporary political problems or to improve protections for human rights in contemporary Middle Eastern societies."[24]

THE UNIVERSAL CHARACTER OF HUMAN RIGHTS IS OF STRATEGIC IMPORTANCE

Debates on the nature of the Sharia in Islamic countries and elsewhere can be of intellectual interest, but they are not relevant to the UDHC, nor to the intergovernmental decisions based on it. The principal aim of the UDHR was to create a framework for a world society that needs some universal codes based on mutual consent in order to function. It is the universal character of the UDHR that makes it a common base for relations between peoples across national and cultural frontiers.

Today, people understand the importance of the respect for the dignity and uniqueness of every human being. At the same time, there is a common awareness of dignity disregarded. There are many reasons, however, to consider the issue of human rights as of strategic importance, beyond any past experience in the cold war. The human dignity of every single human being can be properly affirmed and given effective protection only within the framework of an interrelated system of norms, principles, and institutions. Human rights issues in international relations are frequently interpreted as belonging to the moral sphere, despite existing legally binding international instruments that developed the principles of the UDHR. One of the lessons of the cold war in this regard is that only a firm and noncompromising stand regarding the most fundamental questions can lead to the effective implementation of the ideals and objectives of the International Bill of Human Rights and other relevant instruments.[25]

NOTES

1. From official text; see also UN summary record E/CN.4/1998/SR.2, para. 9.

2. See also the seminar's descriptive circular.

3. Hasni Abdi, "Droits de l'homme à la carte," *Tribune de Genève*, November 25, 1998. Translated from the French text.

4. Soheib Bencheikh, "L'Islam et la liberté religieuse," HR/IP/SEM/1998/WP.11; Ridwan el Sayyed (Lebanon), "Human Rights in Contemporary Muslim Thought," HR/IP/SEM/1998/WP.13.

5. "It was necessary that Muslim theologians and thinkers should break their shameful silence and appeal for a reform of their theology and a rereading of the Koran," (E/CN.4/1998/SR.21, para. 66, March 23, 1998); see also "Le problème des musulmans est d'avoir sacralisé l'Islam," *Le Courrier* (Geneva), November 14–15, 1998.

6. *A Compilation of International Instruments*, vol. 1, *Universal Instruments*, 2 parts, 5th rev. (St/HR/I/Rev.5) (New York and Geneva: UN Centre for Human Rights, 1993–94), pp. 418, 950.

7. The new Iranian Constitution (December 1979) referred to human rights in article 20, without endorsing the UDHR. See A/C.3/37/SR.56, paras. 53–55, for a 1982 demand to transform the UDHR "through sincere dialogue and honest scholarly endeavour."

8. Ann Elizabeth Mayer, *Islam and Human Rights: Tradition and Politics* (Boulder, CO: Westview Press; London: Pinter, 1991), p. 27.

9. A/C.3/39/SR.65, paras. 91–95.

10. *Official Records of the Human Rights Committee, 1992–93, CCPR/12 (International Covenant on Civil and Political Rights)*, vol. 1, 46th session, 1196th meeting (New York and Geneva: UN (ICCPR), 1996), paras. 55–59.

11. E.CN.4/1992/SR.20, paras. 17–20. See also International Commission of Jurists press release, Geneva, December 5, 1991.

12. "Pakistan Imposes Strict Islamic Law," Associated Press, January 17, 1999. [For a detailed description of this and what followed, see Patrick Sookhdeo, *A People Betrayed: The Impact of Islamization on the Christian Community in Pakistan* (Pewsey, Wilt. UK: Isaac Publishing, 2002), pp. 151–58.]

13. Pakistani constitution of 1985, article 203-D [1], quoted in C. H. Kennedy, "Repugnance to Islam—Who Decides? Islam and Legal Reform in Pakistan," *International and Comparative Law* 41, part 4 (October 1992): 772.

14. Association for World Education, "Blasphemy Legislation in Pakistan's Penal Code," NGO Written Statement, E/CN.4/Sub.2/1998/NGO/3.

15. *A Compilation of International Instruments*, vol. 2, *Regional Instruments* (New York and Geneva: UN Office of the High Commissioner for Human Rights, 1997), pp. 478–84.

16. See E/CN.4/1994/122.

17. *Agence France Press*, February 14, 1994.

18. See General Assembly interim reports A/48/601, A/49/539, A/50/569, A/51/490, and A/51/510, as well as CHR reports E/CN.4/1994/48, E/CN.4/1995/58, E/CN.4/1996/62, E/CN.4/1997/58, and E/CN.4/1998/66. Extracts from Biro's 1993–95 reports, detailing slavery and forced conversions to Islam, were summarized in a documentary article with an introduction by David G. Littman, "The U.N. Finds Slavery in the Sudan," *Middle East Quarterly* 3, no. 3 (September 1996): 90–94.

19. See René Wadlow and David G. Littman, "Dangerous Censorship of a UN Special Rapporteur," *Justice* no. 14 (September 1997): 10–17 (reprinted in this book as chapter 29); "Blasphemy at the United Nations?" *Middle East Quarterly* 4, no. 4 (December 1997): 85–86; "UN Special Rapporteur Censured on 'Islamist and Arab Antisemitism,'" *Midstream* 44, no. 2 (February–March 1998): 8–13.

20. E/CN.4/1997/71, subheading E.3, chap. 2.

21. E/CN.4/1997/SR.70, paras. 22–23.

22. See E/CN.4/1998/71, corr. 1.

23. E/CN.4/1998/SR.11, para. 50, and SR.12, para. 10. For another "blasphemy" case in relation to the 1948 Genocide Convention, see the 1997 written statement by the Association for World Education, E/CN.4/Sub.2/1997/NGO/15.

24. Mayer, *Islam and Human Rights*, p. 67. In chapter 5, "Discrimination against Women and Non-Muslims," she concludes, "In these circumstances, reference to Islamic criteria on rights is not likely to result in respect for the principles of equality and equal protection of the law as mandated in international human rights law; instead, such references tend to undermine the rights involved and to afford legal rationales for discrimination" (p. 108). A recent attempt at an analysis of this problem led another author to conclude, "Although doctrinal Islam does not stand in dire need of reinterpreting its juridical tenets, it surely needs reformulation of its human rights doctrine specifically in reference to gender, non-revealed religions, and equality between and among Muslims and non-Muslims." Mahmood Monshipouri, "The Muslim World Half a Century after the Universal Declaration of Human Rights: Progress and Obstacles," *Netherlands Quarterly of Human Rights* 16, no. 3 (September 1998): 287–314.

25. On this idea, see Gaspar Biro, "The Universal Declaration of Human Rights and the Cold War," statement to an international colloquium titled "La Déclaration universelle des droits de l'homme, 1948–1998: Avenir d'un idéal," at the Sorbonne, Paris, September 14–16, 1998 (See their Web site: www.cncdh@cncdh.org.

"BLASPHEMY" AT THE UNITED NATIONS AND JUDEOPHOBIA IN THE ARAB-MUSLIM WORLD

28.

David G. Littman

We are again reminding the Commission on Human Rights of a regrettable landmark event that took place seven years ago, well-known as the "Blasphemy Affair," which resulted in a the censorship cecision 1997/125 of April 18, 1997. Our subcommission written statement in 1997 gave details,[1] and three academic articles followed to sound the warning bells of what might follow if Judeophobia in the Arab/Muslim world is not properly analyzed and condemned as a violation of basic human rights norms.[2]

[As a result of self-censorship, the then special rapporteur on racism, Maurice Glélé-Ahanhanzo (of Benin), avoided any reference to Judeophobic antisemitism in the Arab-Muslim world in all his subsequent reports (1998–2002). Last year, the new special rapporteur, Mr. Doudou Diène (of Senegal), devoted nine lines on this subject in his forty-three-page report, where he referred to "allegations of large-scale distribution in the Middle East and in Europe of *The Protocols of the Elders of Zion.*"[3]]

[Judeophobia—under the guise of "anti-Zionism"—is now generally recognized as endemic in the Arab/Muslim world, being nourished by a general "culture of hate" that is creeping into Europe and beyond. The annual adoption since 1999 of a commission resolution—sponsored by the OIC's fifty-six Muslim states, with the Palestinian Authority—against any "defamation of religions" has had no effect whatsoever on these dangerous attitudes. Resolution 2003/4, *Combating Defamation of Religions*, under its

---

NGO oral statement prepared and delivered by David G. Littman—a representative of the Association for World Education (AWE)—on March 23, 2004, at the sixtieth session of the UNCHR, Geneva. The passages in square brackets were not spoken within the three-minute time limit, but the entire text was circulated with AWE written statement E/CN.4/2004/NGO/5, as reproduced in chapter 30 of this volume.

paragraph 6, "[e]xpresses deep concern at programmes and agendas pursued by extremist organisations and groups aimed at the defamation of religions, in particular when supported by Governments."]

A meaningful analysis of Judeophobia in the Arab/Muslim world requires a close look at the recent past. Therefore, our written statement titled *Judeophobia Today=Anti-Judaism/Anti-Zionism/Antisemitism: A Growing "Culture of Hate"*[4] includes a 1971/1976 preface by D. F. Green to a compilation, *Arab Theologians on Jews and Israel*, in which he warned of the genocidal dangers of such racist manifestations of hate as were expressed at the 1968 Fourth Conference of the Academy of Islamic Research, Al-Azhar University, published by the Egyptian government press in 1970.

[Green also reproduced in that publication some comments on Jews by the renowned Egyptian writer Anis Mansour, who has written prolifically for over thirty years in newspapers on cultural, historical, and religious subjects—and who represented Egypt in November 1975 at the Fortieth International Pen. One startling opinion from Mansour was reported in *Le Monde* on August 21, 1973: "The world is now aware of the fact that Hitler was right and that the cremation ovens were the appropriate means of punishing such contempt of human values, principles, religions and law."]

[At this same period, an "official" Saudi text of Sayyid Qutb's essay from the early 1950s, "Our Struggle with the Jews" (*Ma'rakatuna Ma'a al-Yahud*), was reprinted with similar articles in 1970 and widely distributed by the Saudi government—at the same time as the *Proceedings of the Fourth Conference of the Academy of Islamic Research* was published by the Egyptian government.][5]

However, three decades later we are faced with the gravest dangers. As eminent French sociologist Pierre-André Taguieff recently wrote in his book, *La nouvelle judéophobia* (The new Judeophobia), in the chapter titled "Silences Regarding the New Judeophobia: Blindness, Indulgence, or Connivance?"[6]: "The culture of hate and death has imperceptibly become, at the start of the third millennium, a social, transnational movement armed with an unscrupulous jihadist vanguard."[7] [This excellent analysis by a leading expert on racism, the director of research at the Centre Nationale de la Recherche Scientifique (CNRS) in Paris, is now translated into English under the title *Rising from the Muck: The New Anti-Semitism in Europe.*[8]]

His new study on this burning issue says it all in the title: *Prêcheurs de haine: Traversée de la judéophobie planetaire* (Preachers of hate: Crossing into global Judeophobia).[9] [A quotation from his conclusion is reproduced here, with the author's permission: "The vast revolutionary program for the destruction of the 'old world' in order to rebuild it 'on new foundations' is giving way to an exterminatory dream of the arsonist and vandal: eliminate the Jewish state and transform America into a field of ruins. However that may be, the ideological corruption of great causes has never been more radical nor more glaring. Nor more repugnant. It is in this last aspect of the great confusion of the epoch that one can find reasons to hope: if the ideological confusion and the corruption of ideas are from now on more and more visible and audible, to the point of being blinding and deafening, it becomes less and less possible to refuse to open one's eyes and to decide at last to hear."[10]]

We solemnly appeal to the commission, to the various UN special rapporteurs concerned, and all the competent UN bodies to speak out *now* and condemn this specific "culture of hate and violence"—so reminiscent of the 1930s, when the Palais des Nations was in construction—and also to act urgently in promoting education for interfaith understanding and reconciliation.

NOTES

1. E/CN.4/Sub.2/1997/NGO/3.

2. See René Wadlow and David G. Littman, "Dangerous Censorship of a UN Special Rapporteur," *Justice* (Tel Aviv), no. 14 (September 1997): 10–17 (reprinted in this book as chapter 29).

3. E.CN.4/2004/24, p. 15.

4. E/CN.4/2004/NGO/5.

5. See Ronald L. Nettler, *Past Trials and Present Tribulations: A Muslim Fundamentalist's View of the Jews* (London: Pergamon, 1987), pp. 71–87; see also Yigal Carmon, "Contemporary Islamist Ideology Permitting Genocidal Murder," paper presented at the Stockholm International Forum on Preventing Genocide, January 25, 2004, Middle East Media Research Institute (MEMRI) special report no. 25.

6. Original title: "Silences sur la nouvelle judéophobie: aveuglement, complaisance ou connivances?"

7. The original French is as follows: "La culture de la haine et de la mort est imperceptiblement devenue, en ce début du troisième millénaire, un mouvement sociale transnational doté d'une avant-garde djihadist sans scrupules." David G. Littman read the French version when he gave his oral statement at the UNCHR on March 23, 2004.

8. Pierre-André Taguieff, *Rising from the Muck: The New Anti-Semitism in Europe* (Chicago: Ivan R. Dee, 2004).

9. Pierre-André Taguieff, *Prêcheurs de haine: Traversée de la judéophobie planetaire* (Paris: Ed. Fayard/Mille et une nuits, 2004).

10. "Le vaste programme révolutionnaire de la destruction du 'vieux monde' en vue de le reconstruire 'sur de nouvelles bases' tend à faire place à un rêve exterminateur d'incendiaire et de vandale: éliminer l'État juif et transformer l'Amérique en champ de ruines. Quoi qu'il en soit, la corruption idéologique des grandes causes n'a jamais été plus radicale ni plus éclatante. Ni plus répugnante. C'est dans ce dernier caractère de la grande confusion de l'époque qu'on peut trouver des raisons d'espérer: si la confusion idéologique et la corruption des idées sont désormais de plus en plus visibles et audibles, au point d'être aveuglantes et assourdissantes, il devient de moins en moins possible de refuser d'ouvrir les yeux et de se décider enfin à entendre.

DANGEROUS
CENSORSHIP OF A UN
29. SPECIAL RAPPORTEUR

René Wadlow and David G. Littman

Two incidents, that seriously limited rational discussion and debate marred the fifty-third session of the United Nations Commission on Human Rights, held in Geneva, March 10–April 18, 1997.

AIDS LIBEL ACCUSATION AGAINST ISRAEL BY PALESTINIAN REPRESENTATIVE

We shall not discuss in detail here the first incident, a statement made on March 11 by the observer of the Palestine Authority in which he alleged that "the Israeli authorities have infected by injection 300 Palestinian children with the HIV virus during the years of the *Intifadah*." As the representatives of a nongovernmental organization (NGO), the Association for World Education, we reacted immediately in correspondence and direct discussions with the chairman. This calumny became known to the public following two articles in the *Jerusalem Post* and an Anti-Defamation League advertisement in the *New York Times* and the *International Herald Tribune*.[1] It was again raised on July 22, by Israeli ambassador Yosef Lamdan and US deputy permanent representative Seth Winnick, at a meeting of the Economic and Social Council (ECOSOC),[2] and in his previous letter of July 18 (including two annexes) to the president of the council.[3]

There, Winnick strongly expressed his "abhorrence at, and rejection of, the malicious, patently false and uncorrected statement by the observer from

Reprinted from *Justice* (Journal of the International Association of Jewish Lawyers and Jurists, Tel Aviv) 14 (September 1997): 10–17. It is reproduced here with permission.

the Palestinian Liberation Organization," yet Ambassador Nabil Ramlawi refused either to apologize or to correct his AIDS libel. As of September [1997], this malicious calumny still remains in the record of the Commission on Human Rights.[4]

"BLASPHEMY" CHARGE AT THE UNITED NATIONS COMMISSION ON HUMAN RIGHTS

The second incident, the main subject of our article, was a last-minute accusation on the grounds of "blasphemy"—leveled against the special rapporteur on racism, Maurice Glélé-Ahanhanzo—and a demand for censorship. It concerned the section of his report subheaded, "Islamist and Arab Anti-Semitism." This dangerous precedent can be used in future sessions if it is allowed to pass unchallenged. The censuring of reports of UN special rapporteurs, after they have been printed and discussed, weakens an essential structure of the protection and promotion of human rights. Thus this report merits our attention. The possibility of the wider use of the accusation of "blasphemy" to limit analysis at any UN debate was raised on August 27 at the forty-ninth session of the Sub-Commission on Prevention of Discrimination and Protection of Minorities, when the Indonesian representative, speaking for the Organization of the Islamic Conference (OIC), expressed satisfaction at "the excision of a blasphemous reference to the Holy Qur'an in the report of the Special Rapporteur on Contemporary Forms of Racism, Racial Discrimination, Xenophobia and Related Intolerance. We are glad that this offensive reference was excised by the Special Rapporteur *in consultation with the parties concerned*."[5]

AN ABORTED 1994 "BLASPHEMY" CHARGE BY THE GOVERNMENT OF SUDAN

Already at the 1994 commission meeting, the Sudanese ambassador, in a letter of February 18, addressed to all representatives and observers,[6] requested "an immediate withdrawal of those references" from the report of the special rapporteur on the situation of human rights in the Sudan,[7] in which certain inconsistencies were indicated between the international human rights conventions to which the Sudan is a signatory party since 1986 and some provisions of its Criminal Act of 1991.

This letter stated that the paragraphs underlining these inconsistencies "contained abusive, inconsiderate, blasphemous and offensive remarks about the Islamic faith." In resolution 1994/79 of March 9, however, the Commission on Human Rights accepted the analysis and the recommendations made by Dr. Gaspar Biro, the special rapporteur, on this subject and, inter alia, called upon the government of Sudan "to comply with applicable international human rights instruments and to bring its national legislation into accordance with the instruments to which the Sudan was a party." This call upon the government of Sudan was reiterated in all subsequent resolutions by the Commission, including its latest resolution, 1997/59, on the situation of human rights in the Sudan. In his 1994 introductory statement, the special rapporteur had an opportunity to develop his arguments, as he was supported by the majority of the fifty-three member states. The Sudanese request to introduce modifications that included deletions of paragraphs in the report was unanimously rejected, both procedurally and in substance.

The Importance of Precedent at UN Human Rights Bodies

The Commission on Human Rights, as well as the Sub-Commission on Prevention of Discrimination and Protection of Minorities, have rules of procedure, but in practice much of the work is done on precedent; once something has been accepted, it serves as an example. One can be fairly sure that this example will be cited again when a similar situation turns up; hence the importance of an analysis of precedents in the Commission on Human Rights and in the subcommission, which is one of the important strengths of Bertrand G. Ramcharan's book *The Concept and Present Status of the International Protection of Human Rights.*[8]

Strong remedial measures should be initiated to facilitate the constructive work of the UN human rights bodies, especially as the Commission on Human Rights is presently preparing a new World Conference on Racism and Discrimination, in whose preparation both the commission and its subcommission are to play major roles.

The Facts about the 1997 "Blasphemy" Charge at the United Nations

Let us now examine how the second accusation of "blasphemy" at the United Nations succeeded, thereby becoming a dangerous precedent.

By its resolution 1993/20, the Commission on Human Rights nominated Maurice Glélé-Ahanhanzo as special rapporteur, later mandating him "to examine incidents of contemporary forms of racism, racial discrimination, any form of discrimination, *inter alia*, against Blacks, Arabs and Muslims, xenophobia, negrophobia, anti-Semitism and related intolerance, as well as governmental measures to overcome them, and to report on these matters on a yearly basis to the Commission." His latest report was submitted to the commission's fifty-third session.[9] In this report, there is a section on antisemitism that contains a subheading titled "Islamist and Arab Anti-Semitism,"[10] which concludes with a quotation taken from an annual survey, *Anti-Semitism Worldwide*,[11] and forwarded to the special rapporteur on racism by Israel's ambassador and permanent representative in Geneva:

> The use of Christian and secular European anti-Semitism motifs in Muslim publications is on the rise, yet at the same time Muslim extremists are turning increasingly to their own religious sources, first and foremost the Qur'an, as a primary anti-Jewish source.

The original Arabic sources to which the quoted extracts refer are not included in the UN report. No question was raised on this wording when the special rapporteur introduced his report at the start of the ccommission. But on the last morning of the session—in the absence of Glélé-Ahanhanzo, who had returned home—and at the time of the explanation of votes on the resolution accepting his report and supporting his mandate, the Indonesian representative, speaking on behalf of the OIC, referred to this passage and stated, "This amounts to the defamation of our religion, Islam, and blasphemy against its Holy book, Qur'an. We are infuriated that such a statement has been included in the report of the Special Rapporteur. The Commission on Human Rights cannot become a silent spectator to this defamation against one of the great religions of the world. We, therefore, call on the Commission to express censure for this defamatory statement against Islam and the Holy Qur'an and ask you, Mr. Chairman, to express this censure on behalf of the Commission."[12]

Prior to this, the Turkish representative (whose government was then led by an Islamist prime minister), a cosponsor of the Draft Resolution on Racism, also objected to the alleged "blasphemy," as did the representatives of Egypt, Pakistan, Algeria, and Bangladesh. Soon afterward, negotiations began in private, over lunch and in hallways where NGOs could have no input. At a late, final evening meeting, the chairman read out an agreed draft decision, adopted by consensus, that became decision 1997/125.[13] In it, the commission

1. Decided, without a vote, to express its indignation and protest at the content of such an offensive reference to Islam and the Holy Qur'an;
2. Affirmed that this offensive reference should have been excluded from the report;
3. Requested the Chairman to ask the Special Rapporteur to take corrective action in response to the present decision.

For an initial account of this event and the dangers of such a precedent, see René Wadlow, "Shooting the Messenger," in *Human Rights Tribune*.[14]

FREEDOM OF EXPRESSION IN UN REPORTS: AN EMPIRICAL APPROACH

The reports of all UN human rights special rapporteurs must be open to questioning, comment, and debate. It is in this spirit of dialogue that the special rapporteurs have an essential role to play in the defense of human rights. To force modification of a report is to denature their role and to weaken possibilities for effective action. Moreover, to consider the analysis by the special rapporteur on racism of discriminatory attitudes contained in current religious preaching and literature as "blasphemy" is to mask from examination a large segment of public discourse. Religious teachings constitute an important avenue for the transmission of ideas and attitudes. As with all bodies of ideas, religious doctrines should be examined carefully in their historical context.

Such analysis of religious attitudes in UN documents is rare, for religion deals with highly sensitive issues and deeply set emotional attitudes. However, as the quotation under question deals in large part with religious teachings, we believe that the offensive reference merits close attention as well as some bibliographical indications, so that further research can be carried out in this field. We believe that statements in thematic reports require some bibliographical references in order to meet high standards of evidence, so that the exactitude of the facts put forward by the special rapporteur may be examined. The inclusion of such references to support a sound analysis will ensure a constructive discussion aimed at remedial action. In the spirit of this empirical approach, it is necessary to provide examples of the accuracy of the above-mentioned controversial quotation that was used as an excuse to justify the introduction of a "blasphemy" accusation and a peremptory request to censure a report at the Commission on Human Rights. The crux of the matter concerns the validity or not of the sentence that provoked the "blasphemy" charge. Thus on July 15 we submitted a written statement to the subcommission, in which we indicated some of the factual background needed to analyze the above-mentioned three currents of antisemitism.[15]

While such information is no doubt familiar to readers of *Justice*, we shall here highlight a few passages, as the analysis of religious and ideological currents is rare at UN meetings, and this fifteen-hundred-word written statement by the Association for World Education may serve as a "positive precedent."

CHRISTIAN, SECULAR EUROPEAN, AND ISLAMIST AND ARAB ANTISEMITISM

We shall now briefly examine the three trends of antisemitism that appear in the controversial phrase on Christian, secular European, and Islamist and Arab antisemitism.

Christian Antisemitism

On the origins of Christian antisemitism, we have chosen a quotation from emeritus professor William Nichols's major work, *Christian Antisemitism: A History of Hate*: "[B]ecause the Jews rejected and killed Christ, they in turn have been rejected as God's chosen people. The Jews have broken their ancient covenant with God, and he has made a new covenant, sealed in the blood of Christ, gathering to himself a new people, drawn from the Gentiles. This new people has now superseded the old Israel. . . . The Jews have lost their status as the covenant people, and the new Israel is now the true Israel. As a punishment for their cosmic crime, the Jews have lost their Temple and been exiled from their land. Until the return of Christ, they will remain homeless wanderers upon the earth. What theologians are beginning to call the theology of supersession joins hands with the myth of the deicide, Christ-killing people to make the Jews a permanent target for Christian hostility and contempt."[16]

Since the early twentieth century, there has been a strong and active school of Christian scholarship whose aim has been to analyze the historical, social, and political context in which Christianity developed. There have been patient efforts to understand all the positions in these first-century debates, where theology, politics, sociology, and the quest for identity are all mixed together. Such scholarship is essential for the study of all religious traditions, so that religious texts, attitudes, laws, and institutions are seen against their historical background. In the last two decades, this scholarship has become irrefutable, but "it will take time to be more widely absorbed."[17] In this context, one should recall the 1965 historic *Nostra aetate* declaration of the Second Vatican Council.

There are two major themes in Christian anti-Jewish thought that are used in Islamist publications. The first theme is the current irrelevance of the Jews in God's plan of salvation for humanity—the early alliance of God with the Jews has been superseded. The second theme is of a collective Last Judgment—on a whole people, as well as upon each individual. These themes were reiterated in a subsequent article by an Islamist Egyptian writer, Dr. Mustafa Mahmoud, who uses both of these Christian themes as well as a dozen quotations from the Qur'an as a *primary anti-Jewish source*, predicting the millennial destruction of Israel in his conclusion: "Israel is continuing in the haughtiness that the Qur'an talks about. The small haughtiness is leading to the great haughtiness."[18]

Blood-Libel Accusation and World Conspiracy Theories

There are many secular European strands of anti-Jewish thought being widely spread in Arab and Islamist publications; more and more, the denial of the Holocaust, but especially "conspiracy theories" of history and the 1840 "Damascus Affair" blood-libel, which surfaced during the Gulf War at the United Nations Commission on Human Rights. On February 8, 1991, the representative of Syria, holding aloft a copy of *The Matzah of Zion*, declared, "We should like to launch an appeal to all members of this Commission to read this very important work that demonstrates unequivocally the historical reality of Zionist racism." In its preface by Syrian minister of defense Maj. Gen. Mustafa Tlass, one reads, "The Jew can . . . kill you and take your blood in order to make his Zionist bread. . . . I hope that I have done my duty in presenting the practices of the enemy of our historic nation. Allah aid this project."[19]

This dangerous "conspiracy theory" myth consists in the belief that a Jewish-led conspiracy seeks to control the world, a plot seen at work in every revolution, in every war since time immemorial, and in all international organizations, including the United Nations. The most widespread of these conspiracy theories of history is contained in a forged document called *The Protocols of the Elders of Zion*. This forgery was fabricated in Paris at the turn of this century for the use of the Russian czar's secret police, the Okhrana. It inspired Hitler's genocidal antisemitism. The long history of *The Protocols* has been documented in full by French sociologist Pierre-André Taguieff in his work, *Les Protocoles des Sages de Sion (Faux et Usages d'un faux).*[20]

The Protocols are still widely disseminated, having been reprinted in the last decades in at least ten European countries. However, it is in the Arab/Islamic world that it remains a best-seller of hate and can be found in the main centers of the Middle East and the Maghreb. An Arabic edition of *The Protocols*, available in the West, includes a preface with a rare example of religious and racial hatred against the Jews that concludes with the prophesy of Israel's destruction: "This destruction is what we believe and teach to our children, striving toward its realization and asking for success from Allah, the Exalted One."[21] (On "conspiracy theories," see our written statement of March 25, 1997, submitted to the Commission on Human Rights, titled *Constitution of the Islamic Resistance Movement Hamas: 18 August 1988*.)[22]

Islamist and Arab Antisemitism as a Growing World Phenomenon

On the question of whether Islamists regularly use "religious sources, first and foremost the Qur'an, as a primary anti-Jewish source?" a full documentation on such recurring themes may be found in *The Fourth Conference of the Academy of Islamic Research* (September 1968).[23] This book contains research papers given by twenty-two theologians and scholars. Extracts were reproduced in *Arab Theologians on Jews and Israel*, edited by D. F. Green [the joint pseudonym of coeditors David G. Littman and Yehoshafat Harkabi]. Green writes in the introduction, "The ideas expounded in this volume could lead to the urge to liquidate Israel (politicide) and the Jews (genocide)."[24] The 1988 charter of Hamas—a blueprint for genocide—is full of idiosyncratic interpretations of the Qur'an that we shall not quote here. But a controversial Hadith, or saying attributed to the Prophet—now a commonplace with Islamists worldwide—concludes its article 7: "the Hamas aspires to implement Allah's promise, whatever time that may take. The Prophet, Allah bless him and grant him salvation, has said: 'The Day of Judgement will not come about until Muslims will fight the Jews (and kill them), until the Jews hide behind rocks and trees, which will cry: O Muslim! there is a Jew hiding behind me, come on and kill him.'" This article precedes the Hamas slogan contained in article 8: "Allah is its goal, the Prophet its model, the Qur'an its Constitution, *Jihad* its path and death for Allah's cause its most sublime belief."

Numerous examples of this trend have been documented in various publications over the last thirty years, beginning with Yehoshafat Harkabi's *Arab Attitudes to Israel*.[25] Here are the words used by Moshe Ma'oz then: "Arab Judeophobia draws essentially upon Islamic religious literature and religious teaching, because of the centrality of Islam in modern Arab ideologies and cultural tradition."[26]

These facts cannot be denied or dismissed as "blasphemous" when Islamists are quoted in such works, as well as those reproduced on cassettes and on the Internet.[27]

ANTISEMITISM WITHIN THE PARAMETERS OF A FORTHCOMING CONFERENCE ON RACISM

Even after the publication of Glélé-Ahanhanzo's "corrective action" that removed the "offensive reference,"[28] the campaign continued at the substantive session of ECOSOC, when, on July 22, the representative of Indonesia—on behalf of the OIC—referred to the "outrageous reference to Islam and to the Qur'an" and requested that his statement—which also cited the Hebron case of "blasphemy"—be distributed as an official UN document at the Security Council and at the forthcoming session of the General Assembly. The representatives of Egypt, Syria, Lebanon, Saudia Arabia, Sudan, Iraq, Jordan, and Iran intervened on this issue to support Indonesia's request and to make further negative comments about the "offensive reference to Islam and the Holy Qur'an"—some of them demanding that the subheading "Islamist Arab Anti-Semitism" also be removed from that report.[29]

We maintain—having demonstrated this in our detailed written text[30]—that the so-called "offensive reference" is accurate. If anything, it is a euphemism in regard to what is *actually* being said publicly on this subject and published regularly in Arabic and otherwise. Remedial action on all forms of racial discrimination—including antisemitism and anti-Christian attitudes—should not be blocked by invoking respect for religious belief and practice. We must examine closely and without fear the ways in which discriminatory attitudes are formed and transmitted. In this way, the preparation for a new World Conference to Combat Racism will not be a bureaucratic exercise but part of an important process to modify in a positive direction many negative attitudes and practices. The conclusion of our written statement to the subcommission was borrowed from the conclusion of Prof. Inge Lenning's report on a notorious Swedish case of antisemitism—"Radio Islam" or the "Rami-Bergman Affair." A former rector of the University of Oslo, he sent us an abridged English version for use at the United Nations and to be forwarded to the then assistant secretary general for human rights, Ibrahim Fall, for transmission to the special rapporteur on racism: "The general lesson to be learnt from the 'Rami-Bergman Affair' should be that the challenge of manifest antisemitism should be faced by all citizens, but first and foremost by those in charge of central institutions in society, like church and universities. Representatives of the academic and the religious community should, in their double capacity of citizens and professionals, have a special awareness and a special obligation to meet the challenge in an adequate manner."

Our above-mentioned written statement to the subcommission (E/CN.4/Sub.2/1997/NGO/3) was circulated to all eighteen independent members of the Human Rights Committee (HRC) and the Committee for the Elimination of Racial Discrimination at their respective sessions held in Geneva in late July and early August. Christine Chanet, the HRC's chairperson, raised this grave matter on September 16 at a meeting of persons chairing the human rights bodies. She was followed the next day by Paulo Pinheiro, chairperson of the special rapporteurs, representatives, experts, and chairpersons of working groups of the Commission on Human Rights and the Advisory Services Programme, which on May 23 resolved unanimously "that the Special Rapporteurs should not be requested to amend their Reports merely because certain passages are deemed to be offensive by a particular Member State or group of Member States."

On September 18, at the new high commissioner's first meeting with NGOs, we asked Mary Robinson if she would add her "voice of support for the total independence of all the Special Rapporteurs." This she agreed to do in her meeting with the chairpersons of the human rights bodies the following day. It is of crucial importance that all strongly defend the independence of the special rapporteurs before this dangerous precedent of "censorship" becomes a UN norm.

THE AMBIGUOUS QUIBBLE OVER THE TERM
ANTI-SEMITISM/ANTISEMITISM

As the word *antisemitism* is frequently misused at UN sessions—most recently in the statements mentioned above, made at the meeting of

ECOSOC on July 22—it is necessary to clarify a certain ambiguity about the term itself, which was first coined in 1879 by Wilhelm Marr, a German journalist. To quote Emeritus Professor Nicholls: "Antisemites were and are not opposed to all so-called Semites but only to Jews, and not always to all of them as individuals but primarily to Jews as a group in society."[31] As proposed in James Parkes's classic work *The Conflict of the Church and the Synagogue: A Study in the Origins of Antisemitism*,[32] the term *antisemitism* should be spelled as one word, without a hyphen—as in French and German—and not as two words, with a capital *S* (*anti-Semitism*), as is customary in America and at the United Nations. This way of spelling leads to a semantic legerdemain, a curious quibble that is often heard: "How can Arabs be antisemites? They are Semites themselves." If Arabs truly felt that the term "antisemite" also encompassed them as "Semites," they would not have insisted on adding the words "Arabs" and "Muslims" to the list of those specifically concerned by "any form of discrimination" in the 1993 resolution on racism. Perhaps a better word would have been *anti-Jewish*." Indeed, it would be interesting to know why "Christians" were not mentioned in this resolution, in the same way as "Muslims," especially as in the last decades Christians are increasingly suffering from all forms of discrimination and persecution worldwide, both ethnic and religious.

THE DANGERS OF CENSORSHIP AND SELF-CENSORSHIP AT THE UNITED NATIONS

We have described this censorship in some detail, for there is a danger that unless there is a strong defense of the independence of the special rapporteurs from within the UN system and from NGOs, such censorship will become an irreversible trend. We see three aspects to this very real danger:

1. After the recent censorship—"in consultation with the parties concerned"—there is a real danger of self-censorship by the special rapporteurs or by the editors of the report in the Centre for Human Rights, such that "Islamist and Arab anti-Semitism" would in the future be largely passed over, with little or no analysis of what is being preached in mosques, by radio, video, and television, or on tapes and on the Internet. Only the persistence of traditional antisemitism in the West and "Christian and secular European anti-Semitism motifs in Muslim publications" would be mentioned for fear of the "blasphemy" charge.

2. Were such self-censorship to occur in the yearly reports of the special rapporteur, it is likely that antisemitism—especially in the Muslim world—would be downplayed or only condemned ritually in the preparations for the forthcoming World Conference on Racism. The intellectual and policy preparations for this conference are likely to be difficult, and consensus is reached by neglecting awkward questions.

3. The third danger, which merits serious attention, is the use of the theological accusation of "blasphemy"—Molière had the same problem three hundred years ago with Catholic clerics when *Tartuffe* was first performed—an ill-defined term, which can be expanded to mean anything an accuser dislikes. There is a proper sensitivity to the belief systems of government representatives that is part of diplomatic culture, but sensitivity should not induce blindness. Some accusations of "blasphemy" can be ill-disguised death threats, which should have no place in civilized relations between governments. It is more dangerous when they are used against representatives NGOs or special rapporteurs—the threat to Dr. Gaspar Biro was explicit—who do not have the backing of a government.

CONCLUSION

The last years of this second millennium of the common era is not a time to allow this form of "cultural relativism" to restrict freedom of opinion and expression at the United Nations—in Geneva, not far from the homes of both Voltaire and Jean-Jacques Rousseau. It is a dangerous precedent for charges of "blasphemy" to be given credence and even consecration at the UN Commission on Human Rights and other UN bodies. Rather, it is a real analysis that is needed if we are to come to grips with all forms of racism and discriminatory attitudes, including those that are transmitted by religious thought and teaching—from whatever the source. The struggle to combat racism in all its forms—including antisemitism—through serious scholarship and freedom of thought, opinion, and expression should not be curtailed at the United Nations by self-censorship, as a result of doctrinal accusations of "blasphemy," whose demands are legion.

NOTES

For two recent special issues related to this topic, see "Anti-Semitism: Then and Now," *Justice* (Tel Aviv), no. 34 (Winter 2002); and also *Antisemitism International* (Journal of the Vidal Sassoon International Center for the Study of Antisemitism, Hebrew University of Jerusalem) (2003).

1. See *Jerusalem Post*, March 26 and April 11, 1997; *New York Times*, April 21, 1997.

2. See E/1997/SR.37.

3. See E/1997/105.

4. The US ECOSOC document E/1997/105 was introduced to the fifty-fourth session of the Commission on Human Rights, March–April 1998. [Ramlawi was obliged to retract the accusation before the session could begin.]

5. Our italics, from his verbatim statement, para. 6; and E/CN.4/Sub.2/1997/SR35.

6. E/CN.4/1994/122, March 1, 1994.

7. E/CN.4/1994/48.

8. Bertrand G. Ramcharan, *The Concept and Present Status of the International Protection of Human Rights* (Dordrecht: Martin Nijhoff, 1989).

9. E/CN.4/1997/71.

10. E.3, chap. 2.

11. Dina Porat et al., eds., *Anti-Semitism Worldwide* (Tel Aviv: Tel Aviv University, 1996).

12. Verbatim text; see also the summary record, E/CN.4/1997/SR.68.

13. E/CN.4/1997/SR.70.

14. René Wadlow, "Shooting the Messenger," *Human Rights Tribune* (Ottawa) 4, nos. 2–3 (June 1997): 10–11.

15. E/CN.4/Sub.2/1997/NGO/3.

16. William Nicholls, introduction to *Christian Antisemitism: A History of Hate* (Northvale, NJ, and London: Jason Aronson, 1993), p. XIX.

17. Ibid. p. 437.

18. Mustafa Mahmoud, "The Israeli Haughtiness, and How It Will End" [in Arabic], *Al-Ahram International* (Cairo), May 17, 1997.

19. See preface, by Mustafa Tlass, to *The Matzah of Zion* [in Arabic] (Damascus: Tlass edition, 1983/1985). For full UN documentation of the Syrian representative's declaration, see *Human Rights and Human Wrongs*, nos. 10 and 11 (Geneva: Editions de l'Avenir and World Union for Progressive Judaism, 1991).

20. Pierre Taguieff, *Les protocols des sages de Sion (Faux et usages d'un faux)*, 2 vols. (Paris: Berg International, 1992).

21. *The Protocols of the Elders of Zion* [in Arabic], 2nd ed. (Beirut: Dar an-Nafais, 1990).

22. René Wadlow and David G. Littman, *Constitution of the Islamic Resistance Movement Hamas: 18 August 1988*, E/CN.4/1997/NGO/85.

23. *The Fourth Conference of the Academy of Islamic Research* (Cairo: Government Printing Offices, 1970); Arabic edition in 2 vols., 1968.

24. D. F. Green, ed., *Arab Theologians on Jews and Israel* (Geneva: Editions de l'Avenir, 1971; see 3rd ed., 1976), p. 9.

25. Yehoshafat Harkabi, *Arab Attitudes to Israel* (Jerusalem: Israel Universities Press, 1971); Hebrew ed., 1968.

26. Moshe Ma'oz, *The Image of the Jew in Official Arab Literature and Communications Media*, at a July 1975 "Continuing Presidential Seminar on World Jewry and the State of Israel" (Jerusalem: Shazar Library and Hebrew University of Jerusalem, 1976), p. 7. See also Olivier Carré, "Juifs et Chretiens dans la Societé islamique ideale d'après Sayyid Qutb," *Revue des Sciences Philosophiques et Théologiques* (Paris) 68 (1984): 50–72; Olivier Carré, *Mystique et Politique: Lecture revolutionnaire du Coran par Sayyid Qutb, Frère Musulman Radical* (Paris: Editions du Cerf, 1984); Olivier Carré, *L'Utopie islamique dans l'Orient arabe* (Paris: Presses de la Fondation Nationale des Sciences Politiques, 1991); Gilles Kepel, *The Prophet and Pharaoh: Muslim Extremism in Contemporary Egypt*, preface by Bernard Lewis (London: Al Saqui, 1985; American ed., Berkeley and Los Angeles: University of California Press, 1986; original French ed., Paris: La Découverte, 1984); Johannes J. G. Jansen, *The Neglected Duty: The Creed of Sadat's Assassins andIslamic Resurgence in the Middle East* (New York and London: Macmillan, 1986); Rivka Yadlin, *An Arrogant Oppressive Spirit: Anti-Zionism as Anti-Judaism in Egypt* (Oxford and Elmsford, NY: Pergamon Press, 1989); Raphael Israeli, *Muslim Fundamentalism in Israel* (London and McLean, VA: Brassey's, 1993); Bat Ye'or, *Juifs et Chretiens sous l'Islam: Les dhimmis face au defí intégriste* (Paris: Berg International, 1994); Daniel Pipes, *The Hidden Hand: Middle East Fears of Conspiracy* (New York: St. Martin's Press, 1996); Martin Kramer, *Arab Awakening and Islamic Revival: The Politics of Ideas in the Middle East* (New Brunswick, NJ, and London: Transaction, 1996); and the annual reports on antisemitism worldwide of the American Jewish Committee, the Anti-Defamation League, and the World Jewish Congress.

27. See Emmanuel Sivan, "Eavesdropping on Radical Islam," *Middle East Quarterly* (Philadelphia) 2, no. 1 (March 1995): 13–25; David Sitman, "Propagating Anti-Semitism on the Internet," *Justice* (Tel Aviv), no. 12 (March 1997): 7; and Jeff Stein, "Look at What Hate Groups Say," *Baltimore Sun*, April 5, 1997, reprinted in the *International Herald Tribune*, April 6, 1997.

28. E/CN.4/1997/71/Corr. 1.

29. E/1997/SR.37.

30. E/CN.4/Sub.s/1997/NGO/3.

31. Nicholls, *Christian Antisemitism*, p. 325.

32. James Parkes, *The Conflict of the Church and the Synagogue: A Study in the Origins of Antisemitism* (London: Soncino Press, 1934).

JUDEOPHOBIA TODAY = ANTI-JUDAISM / ANTI-ZIONISM / ANTISEMITISM

30.

A Growing "Culture of Hate"

1. Judeophobia—under the guise of "anti-Zionism"—is now generally recognized as endemic in the Arab/Muslim world, being nourished by a general "culture of hate" that is creeping into Europe, and beyond. The annual adoption since 1999 of a commission resolution—sponsored by the OIC's fifty-six Muslim States—against any "defamation of religions" has had no effect whatsoever on these dangerous attitudes. Resolution 2003/4, "Combatting Defamation of Religions," states under its paragraph 6: "Expresses deep concern at programmes and agendas pursued by extremist organisations and groups aimed at the defamation of religions, in particular when supported by Governments."[1]

2. Yet the farewell address—with its controversial Judeophobic diatribe by [Malaysian president Muhammad bin Mahathir], president of the tenth Summit of the Organisation of the Islamic Conference on October 16, 2003—received a standing ovation. Although Malaysia is one of fifty-three Member States of the Commission on Human Rights, there was no official reaction from any UN personality.

3. In a written statement last year,[2] we pointed out that antisemitism in the Arab and Muslim world has been totally ignored in all reports of the special rapporteur on racism since 1998, after the "blasphemy affair" that occurred on the last day of the fifty-third session. Following a very brief mention in the special rapporteur's 2003 report, we are promised a fuller analysis for 2004.

NGO written statement E/CN.4/2004/NGO/5—submitted by the AWE to the sixtieth session of the UNCHC, and posted on the UN Web site—was prepared by David G. Littman, with advice from René Wadlow.

4. In that statement,[3] we reproduced the "Urgent Appeal" of December 10, 2002, which we sent to the High Commissioner for Human Rights, the late Sergio Vieira de Mello. This was directly related to the event that occurred in Egypt during the Muslim holy month of Ramadan (October–November 2002), when the Egyptian Dream Satellite TV channel serialized—with government authorization—forty-one episodes of *Knight without a Horse,* a melodrama based on the one-hundred-year-old-forgery, *The Protocols of the Elders of Zion.*

5. Below is our "Urgent Appeal" of December 10, 2003, to Dr. Bertrand Ramcharan, the Acting High Commissioner for Human Rights, regarding the reuse in Egypt during the recent Ramadan (2003) of *The Protocols*; and of the "blood-libel" on Arab TV—again with a Syrian contribution:

6. URGENT APPEAL FOR HUMAN RIGHTS DAY (DECEMBER 10, 2003) TO ACTING HIGH COMMISSIONER FOR HUMAN RIGHTS DR. BERTRAND RAMCHARAN

A Growing Phenomenon of a Revived Culture of Hate:
The Continuing Use of The Protocols of the Elders of Zion
and the Medieval "Blood-Libel"

On the fifty-fifth anniversary of the General Assembly's adoption of the Universal Declaration of Human Rights, we wish to express to you and all your colleagues in UN bodies our deep dismay and grave concern over the continuous use of a genocidal century-old forgery, *The Protocol of the Elders of Zion*, as well as the medieval "blood-libel" accusing Jews of killing Christian children each year to mix their blood in the Passover *Matzah.* Two very recent examples highlight this revived culture of hate, which is regularly propagated in Arab/Muslim lands—and not condemned.

The new Alexandria Library was recently renovated with the help of the governments of Egypt and Italy and the collaboration of UNESCO—and in memory of the great Hellenistic Library of antiquity that had been a unique foundation of world knowledge and understanding. Thus, it was with consternation and sadness that we learned of the first exhibition in its manuscript museum that purported to display the sacred texts of the three monotheistic religions, while including an Arabic translation of *The Protocol of the Elders of Zion,* exhibited alongside the Hebrew Bible or Torah [*sic*] in the display case concerning Judaism. As director Dr.

Yusef Ziedan has explained: "[I]t is only natural to place the book [*The Protocols*] in the framework of an exhibit of Torah [scrolls]," as "it has become one of the sacred [tenets] of the Jews, next to their first constitution."[4]

This Arabic translation by Muhammad Khalifa al-Tunsi of the English version of *The Protocols* was first published in 1951 in Egypt, and often reprinted.[5]

In Syria and elsewhere, there has been a continued rehash of the 1840 Damascus "Blood-Libel" accusation, particularly by Defense Minister Mustafa Tlass in his *The Matzah of Zion* (1983), constantly reprinted since as a Tlass-editions best-seller in several languages, and confirmed by him again in 2003. This, even after the sinister scandal at the 1991 Commission on Human Rights, when Syria's delegate brandished an illustrated and gory Arabic edition of *The Matzah of Zion*—to prove "the historical reality of Zionist racism." General Tlass actually wrote in the preface: "The Jew can kill you and take your blood in order to make his Zionist bread."[6]

During last month's [November 2003] Ramadan, Hizbollah's satellite TV channel Al-Manar—viewed worldwide—broadcast *Al-Shatat* ("Diaspora"), a thirty-part Judeophobic / antisemitic "Syrian TV series recording the criminal history of Zionism."[7] Episode 20 depicts a rabbi teaching Jews of the perennial, spiritual need to cut a Christian child's throat and mix in his blood and then, ritually, "taste the holy Passover matzo."

Fortunately, a protest from UNESCO's director-general Koichiro Matsuura early last week led to the withdrawal on December 6 of *The Protocols* from the Alexandria Library,[8] a welcome example of the power of enlightened protest. We await a protest against this latest Syrian-inspired "blood-libel."

On June 17, 2003, at a symposium in Vienna on "antisemitism,"[9] you stated: "Denial is not an option. Many people of course would like to deny the reality of anti-Semitism." Your message then was clear: "So when you reflect on anti-Semitism as a continuing concern, I would invite you to consider programmes of educational activities that can help deal with this phenomenon." In your posted "Human Rights Day Message,"[10] you "plead for stronger messages of protection, nationally, regionally, and internationally," asking: "what more can be done to strengthen human rights protection. . . . Today I plead for stronger human rights protection."

Therefore, we solemnly call upon you as Acting High Commissioner for human rights—and to the whole human rights community—to speak out and redouble UN efforts for the elimination of all hate-generating, especially genocidal, forgeries on Web sites and in the media, and to engage in wide educational programs which will develop understanding and mutual respect among peoples and between religious communities.

René Wadlow   David G. Littman
    (Representatives, Association for World Education to the UN Office, Geneva)

7. The genocidal dangers of such racist manifestations of hate were expressed by historian D. F. Green over thirty years ago in an introduction to *Arab Theologians on Jews and Israel*,[11] being extracts from the proceedings of the 1968 Fourth Conference of the Academy of Islamic Research, linked to Cairo's Al-Azhar University.

8. This introduction—three-quarters of which is reproduced with the author's permission—is as relevant today as when it was first published over thirty years ago. It may help the commission to combat an ongoing politicidal and genocidal phenomenon.

From D. F. Green's Introduction to Arab Theologians on Jews and Israel[12]

9. On June 23, 1961, the Academy of Islamic Research was founded and linked to Cairo's prestigious Al-Azhar University by a resolution passed by the National Assembly of the United Arab Republic. At the same time, the faculties and administration of Al-Azhar were reorganized and the university itself was attached to the office of the president of the Republic, through the appointment of a special ministry. This resolution of the National Assembly specified that the academy should comprise fifty Egyptian members and up to twenty foreigners, all appointed by the president of the Republic. Its first three conferences took place in March 1964, May–June 1965, and October 1966.

10. The Fourth Conference of the Academy of Islamic Research was convened in Cairo during September 1968 to discuss the fundamentals of the Middle East conflict, particularly its spiritual-theological significance, and its historical antecedents. Mr. Hussain al-Shafe'i

(vice president of the United Arab Republic under presidents Nasser and Sadat) greeted the participants, seventy-seven Muslim ulema and invited guests, on behalf of President Nasser.

11. Some of the proceedings were reproduced immediately after the conference in *Majallat Al-Azhar*, the university's monthly. The complete transactions were published in 1970 in Arabic (3 vols.) and in English (1 vol., 935 pp.). In the latter, it is stated on the title page that the book was printed in Cairo by the General Organisation for Government Printing Offices, which signifies governmental support. The efforts involved to have these transactions translated into English indicate that the authorities did not hesitate to publicize the proceedings, thereby propagating to the world the views contained in this volume.

12. The Arab-Israeli conflict is often considered as of a political nature stemming from a territorial litigation. Such conflicts however tend to spill over into other domains. The need to substantiate one's position can lead to an attempt to buttress it by giving it the form of an ideology, or even—as in the present case—the conflict may be theologized as an extreme measure to justify one's position and condemn that of the adversary.

13. It is disheartening to witness some of the principal leaders of the Arab-Muslim world convening for the sake of vilifying another religion and people, shunning neither expressions of abuse, nor the worst invectives. [E.g., vice-principal of Tanta Institute, Egyptian Sheikh Kamal Ahmad Own, "The Jews Are the Enemies of Human Life as Is Evident from Their Holy Book."]

14. Islam, from its origins, includes extreme anti-Jewish and anti-Christian components. These traditional attitudes relating to Jews are now being invested with new life and vigor by the spiritual leaders who took part in this Fourth Conference, in the subsequent Fifth Conference, and in similar learned gatherings held from time to time in other Arab centers.

Recurring Themes in the Proceedings:
Fourth Conference of the Academy of Islamic Research

15. The superiority of Islam over all other religions is brandished as a guarantee that the Arabs will ultimately triumph. The grandeur of Islam must be reflected in future secular successes. Arab defeats and

reverses are explained away as having been ordained by a providential design, in order to teach the Arabs a lesson because of their spiritual negligence—and as a purgatorial ordeal.

16. Jews are frequently denoted as the "enemies of Allah" or the "enemies of humanity." This latter expression is even to be found in the opening speech of Vice President al-Shafe'i. The expression "dogs of humanity" is used by Mr. Hassan Khaled, the mufti of the Lebanon.

17. The State of Israel is the culmination of the historical and cultural depravity of the Jews. It has to be destroyed, having been established through aggression, which is its congenital and immutable nature. This task should be achieved by a *jihad,* a Holy War.

18. Many participants reiterate that it is outrageous for the Jews—traditionally kept by Arab-Islam in a humiliated, inferior status, and characterized as cowardly—to defeat the Arabs, have their own state, and cause the contraction of the "abode of Islam" (*dar al-Islam*). All these events contradict the march of history and Allah's design.[13]

19. Furthermore, if the picture of the Jews and Judaism as portrayed by the venerable participants of this conference is, in fact, as they contend the traditional image of the Jews in the eyes of Islam, it is inconceivable that it would not have affected the feelings and behavior of Arabs toward Jews over the centuries. For it to have been otherwise would have amounted to a schizophrenia which is very implausible.

20. The ideas expounded in this volume could lead to the urge to liquidate the State of Israel (politicide) and the Jews (genocide). If the evil of the Jews is immutable and permanent, transcending time and circumstances, and impervious to all hopes of reform, there is only one way to cleanse the world of them—by their complete annihilation. Did the participants of this conference intend this, and were they conscious of the dangers concealed in such reasoning? Yet its inner logic could easily lead to such a conclusion.

21. The fact that these sages have witnessed the moral havoc that similar ideas of hatred had wrought in Nazi Germany and were not inhibited from resorting to them only testifies to the vehemence of their attitudes. [In his *Mein Kampf,* and elsewhere, Hitler cited *The Protocols of the Elders of Zion*—using this crude forgery, proven since 1921—to justify his "Final Solution."]

22. The seriousness of this compilation is increased because it is a post-

Nazi opus. These learned religions dignitaries and academics knew exactly what they were saying, and meant it. The view sometimes aired that the Arabs are unfortunate victims of their language is merely a slander. Language is an instrument. Choosing abusive terms does not stem from exuberance but is a deliberate choice. Furthermore, the lectures reprinted in this book were made in the serenity of an academic environment and were not frenzied harangues to a euphoric public.

23. Arab spokesmen contend that they differentiate meticulously between Zionism and Judaism and that they are against Zionism and not against Judaism. There cannot be a more trenchant disproof of this explanation than the arguments used at the Fourth Conference of the Academy of Islamic Research, at least as regards its participants. The odium of Zionism is described as emanating from the perversity of Judaism. Zionists and Jews are treated synonymously.

24. One may query the direct influence of the Arabic and English editions of these volumes, as their distribution can hardly have been very large. Their importance, however, lies in their being a symptom. It is known that such attitudes are frequently repeated by preachers during the Friday religious services and are mentioned by Arab political leaders.

25. The position of a state and its policies should not be assessed merely through the narrow vista of its concrete behavior or the official pronouncements of its leaders. A political analysis which is based only upon such external realities will be inadequate. Ideologies, beliefs, aspirations, and emotions are part of the inner realities on which policies evolve, and they should also be taken into consideration. Deliberations such as those that took place at the Fourth Conference may shed some light on the substratum of Arab attitudes toward Jews and Israel. Herein lies their political significance.

26. The absolutist self-righteous tenor which pervades all the deliberations of the Fourth Conference is most repelling. It stands in blatant contradiction to what I consider a moral imperative in molding positions in international conflicts: relativism, that is, the understanding that one's adversary also has rights and virtues. In these deliberations, and the attitudes underlying them, there is not a modicum of such relativism, only a pretentiousness that all justice and all rights belong to the Arabs and the Muslims, who represent everything that is good. The Jews and Israel are denigrated as utterly wrong, without any rights, and their cause is considered as devoid of any merit.

27. The aim here is not to pour fuel on the flames of this conflict: its blaze has already caused enough suffering, and its calamities have perverted the souls of many. It is to be hoped that this appeal may serve as a general exhortation against the dangers lurking in the ideologization (or worse, in the theologization) of a political conflict.
28. When such books, published under government auspices, cease to appear a step toward reconciliation will have been made.

——D. F. Green, London, August 1976[14]

29. The Association for World Education again appeals to the Acting High Commissioner for Human Rights; the Commission and the Sub-Commission on Human Rights; the UN Special Rapporteurs; and all other UN bodies and representatives to act urgently, and publicly, on this grave matter—and to promote actively education for interfaith understanding and mutual respect.

NOTES

1. On April 4, 2002, the Grand Sheik of Al-Azhar, Muhammad Sayyid Tantawi, the highest ranking cleric in the Sunni Muslim world (his nomination needs approval by Egypt's president), referred to the Jews as "the enemies of Allah, descendants of apes and pigs." This is a commonplace statement made today by numerous Arab theologians (www.palestine-inf/arabic/palestoday/readers/mashoor/120401/htm). For a detailed study on this racist phenomenon, see Aluma Solnick, "Based on Koranic Verses, Interpretations, and Traditions, Muslim Clerics State: The Jews Are the Descendants of Apes, Pigs, and Other Animals" and English trans. in *MEMRI*, Special Report no. 11, November 1, 2002, http://memri.org/bin/opener.cgi?Page=archives&ID=SR01102. See Also Ahmad Abd al-M'uti Higazi, "An Egyptian Intellectual Campaigns to Change the Religious Discourse Led by Al-Azhar," *Al-Sharq Al-Awsat* (London), September 16, 2002 ("Those who quote [religious scriptures] and impose the word [namely, the chief clerics] are the ones responsible for producing fundamentalist terror."), see English trans., http://memri.org/bin/opener.cgi?Page=archives&ID=SP43602, in *MEMRI*, Special Dispatch no. 436, November 3, 2003. Al-M'uti Higazi sharply criticized Al-Azhar University and Sheikh Muhammad Sayyid Tantawi and Egyptian mufti, Dr. Ahmad al-Tayyeb. See also Yigal Carmon, president of MEMRI, "Harbingers of Change in the Antisemitic Discourse in the Arab World," http://memri.org/bin/opener.cgi?Page=archives&ID=IA13503, English trans. in *Inquiry and Analysis Series,* no. 135, April 23, 2003. A New Recommendation by Al-Azhar: Stop Calling Jews "Apes and Pigs" (March

2003). This decision followed a decisive request to the Islamic Research Institute from the Egyptian Foreign Ministry to examine the matter, after receiving strong complaints from the Egyptian Embassy in Washington, DC.

2. E/CN.4/2003/NGO/4.

3. Ibid.

4. *Al-Usbu* (Egypt), November 17, 2003.

5. The first Arabic edition was translated from the French and appeared in 1925 and 1927.

6. David G. Littman, "Syria's Blood Libel Revival at the UN: 1991–2000," *Midstream* (New York) 46, no. 2 (February/March 2000): 2–8.

7. As described in the *Syria Times* (Damascus), November 11, 2003.

8. *International Herald Tribune*, December 8, 2003.

9. At the Organization for Security and Cooperation in Europe (OSCE), held in the Vienna Hofburg.

10. "Human Rights Day Message," dated December 5, 2003.

11. D. F. Green, *Arab Theologians on Jews and Israel* (Geneva: Editions de l'Avenir, 1971; 3rd ed., 1976).

12. Ibid., 3rd ed., pp. 7–10.

13. See the lecture by Lebanese Sheikh Nadim al-Jisr: "Good Tidings about the Decisive Battle between Muslims and Israel, in the Light of the Holy Qur'an, the Prophetic Traditions, and the Fundamental Laws of Nature and History."

14. From the 3rd edition of *Arab Theologians on Jews and Israel*. D. F. Green was the joint pseudonym of David G. Littman [D.] and Yehoshafat (Fati) Harkabi [F.], used once for this publication, in English (three editions), French (two editions), and German (one edition) from 1971 to 1976. Yehoshafat Harkabi (d. 1994) participated in the Israeli-Arab armistice negotiations held in Rhodes in 1949. From 1955–1959 he served as chief of Army Intelligence of the Israel Defense Forces and was in charge of Strategic Research in the Israel Ministry of Defense. He received academic degrees from the Hebrew University of Jerusalem and Harvard, becoming a full professor at the Hebrew University. His first major study, *Arab Attitudes to Israel* (Hebrew, 1967) was published in English (1971); *Palestinians and Israel* in 1974 (French ed. *Palestine et Israël* [Geneva: Editions de l'Avenir, 1972]). Several books and articles followed.

THE IDEOLOGY OF JIHAD

31. Antisemitism/Genocide/ Slavery in the Sudan

Robert S. Wistrich

I t is fitting for this commission to address the alarming wave of anti-semitism that today characterizes not only Europe but a growing part of the Arab/Muslim world. To continue to turn a blind eye is to ignore a major motivating force behind the ideology of jihad responsible for the shocking acts of Islamist terror that have left a bloody trail in Manhattan, Washington, Bali, Istanbul, Riyadh, Djerba, Casablanca, Jerusalem, Ashdod, and the recent atrocity in Madrid [March 11, 2004]—a clear warning to Europe of what lies ahead.

[The deadly cocktail of terrorism—jihad and antisemitism embodied in Islamist organisations from al Qaeda to the Palestinian Hamas movement—represents a potent totalitarian threat to the open society and the cause of human rights and civilization. These totalitarian Islamists have hijacked and blackened the name of Islam and are as much a threat to Muslims as they are to Christians, Jews, and millions of other peaceful citizens going about their daily business.]

Europe's reaction to this scourge has thus far been disappointing. It con-tinues to permit Islamists to preach openly their antidemocratic values and poisonous Judeophobia in the heart of Europe—a continent on which only sixty years ago the Jewish people suffered the greatest mass slaughter in its history. In the last three years there has been an unprecedented wave of

This oral statement prepared by Prof. Robert S. Wistrich—a guest representative of the WUPJ to the sixtieth session of the UNCHR—with aid from David G. Littman should have been delivered by Pro-fessor Wistrich on March 26, 2004. In the end, it was delivered by David G. Littman on March 29, with a concluding paragraph by him, when a reliable source provided information on another poten-tial "slavery" tragedy in Sudan. This text was circulated at the UNCHR with WUPJ's written state-ment, E/CN.4/2004/NGO/15, reproduced as chapter 32 in this volume.

attacks on Jewish institutions, synagogues, and individual Jews throughout the European Union.

[Not only that, but the constant double standards applied to Israel, its denigration, defamation, and delegitimization are a chilling reminder of Nazi propaganda in the 1930s. Everyone understands that no state is immune to criticism. Israelis themselves are Olympic gold medalists when it comes to criticizing their own government. That is not the same as seeking the demise and disappearance of a member state of the United Nations. Such discourse is now heard even in mainstream circles in Europe, as has long been the case in the Middle East. It feeds antisemitism and it must be stopped.]

[I should like to remind this commission that just as Palestinians have human rights that deserve to be respected, so, too, do all the victims of totalitarian Islamism. Israelis also have human rights—the right to walk down a street, to go to a shopping mall, to take a bus, to sit in a bar, a cafeteria, a pizzeria, to go to the cinema, the theater, a disco, or any other public place, to pray in the House of God, or to study on a university campus, without being blown to pieces by a jihadist bomber. At my own University in Jerusalem, on July 31, 2002, I witnessed such an atrocity, carried out by the Hamas organisation.]

[Like other Islamists, Hamas uses antisemitic/Judeophobic language, full of hatred toward Jews, ever since its foundation in 1987. In its Sacred Covenant (August 18, 1988), there are frequent references to *The Protocols of the Elders of Zion*, which would have gladdened the hearts of Hitler and Goebbels. It is difficult to see what any of this has to do with spirituality, works of charity, dialogue, or the search for peace.]

At the beginning of the twenty-first century, jihadist terrorism, antisemitism, and racism have become globalized. The struggle against these evils is an indivisible part of the worldwide campaign for human rights. One blatant, recurring "crime against humanity" was highlighted ten days ago by the UN resident coordinator in Sudan, Mukesh Kapila, who referred to "ethnic cleansing" in Darfur in a BBC interview. Last Thursday's major article in the *New York Times*, "Don't Let Sudan's Ethnic Cleansing Go On," deplored "a campaign of murder, rape and pillage by Sudan's Arab rulers that has forced 700,000 black African Sudanese to flee for their lives."[1] Already in his 1995 report on Sudan, the first UN special rapporteur, Gaspar Biro, wrote, "The racial aspect of the violations cannot be disregarded."[2]

[Nicholas Kristof added in his above-mentioned article, "If we turn away simply because the victims are African tribespeople who have no phones and live in one of the most remote parts of the globe, then shame on us." Mukesh

Kapila, the UN resident coordinator to Sudan, speaking to the BBC on March 19, said that more than one million people were being affected by ethnic cleansing: "It is more than just a conflict. It is an organised attempt to do away with a group of people. . . . This is ethnic cleansing, this is the world's greatest humanitarian crisis, and I don't know why the world isn't doing more about it." This crime against humanity is being carried out by Arab militias, fully backed by the Sudanese government, who have driven hundreds of thousands from their homes. A month ago, said Kapila, seventy-five people were killed in the village of Tawila: "over 100 women were raped, six in front of their fathers who were later killed," he said. All these people are black African Muslims. This matter and that of the thousands of enslaved Sudanese Christians, animists, and Muslim black Africans should again be addressed urgently by this commission, and by Western and African countries too.]

Thirty-two hundred years ago, the children of Israel fled from the Egyptian house of bondage. In three days, Jews begin the celebration of the festival of Passover, which has inspired many peoples and many faiths ever since—especially Christianity and Islam. It is a celebration that should remind all of us that we were once "slaves." Indeed, the Exodus from Egypt was a foundation stone for universal human rights: [a commandment to Jews—and, indeed, all mankind—to show solidarity with the poor, the needy, and the oppressed, without distinction of race or creed]. The biblical call to Pharoah, "Let my people go!" is as relevant today as ever before!

We here include a "special sitting appeal" to the chairman and the commission—to act urgently on this massive humanitarian tragedy—and also on the latest news to reach us from Sudan. An exodus of slaves was underway as this commission convened. Five hundred three non-Muslim Africans—mainly women and children—are currently held in a government CEAWC [Committee for the Eradication of the Abduction of Women and Children] compound in Mieram [near the border between northern and southern Sudan—cf. Radio Omdurman and other government sources]. But last week the government-backed PDF [Popular Defense Forces] militias halted this official exodus, threatening that the slaves would never reach their southern homes alive. They are now in imminent danger of becoming enslaved again or perishing in the wilderness. This commission should take urgent action for their immediate liberation, so that before both Passover and Easter begin, these five hundred three slaves too will rejoice in that universal dream, reaffirmed by Martin Luther King Jr. forty years ago: *"Free at last! Free at last! Thank God almighty, we are free at last!"*[3]

Notes

1. Nicholas D. Kristof, "Don't Let Sudan's Ethnic Cleansing Go On," *New York Times*; reprinted in the *International Herald Tribune*, March 25, 2004.

2. E/CN.4/1996/62, para. 52.

3. Conclusion to his speech at the march on Washington, DC, August 28, 1963.

THE ALARMING GROWTH OF JUDEOPHOBIA/ANTISEMITISM SINCE THE VIENNA WORLD CONFERENCE ON HUMAN RIGHTS (1993) AND THE UN DECADE FOR HUMAN RIGHTS EDUCATION: 1995–2004

32.

1. The World Union for Progressive Judaism wishes to stress the appeal
   made last year by High Commissioner Sergio Vieira de Mello—tragically assassinated six months later by terrorists in Baghdad—in his
   first report to the Commission (Human Rights and Follow-up to the
   World Conference on Human Rights): "I call the Commission and,
   through it, the international community at large to conscience . . ."/
   "Actions, not words, is what matters. Protection, not rhetoric is
   needed. We cannot shield gross violations of human rights—wherever they occur—behind the veneer of sovereignty or the chicanery
   of diplomatic procedures."[1]

2. In his report on "Information and Education: Study on the Follow-up
   to the UN Decade for Human Rights Education (1995–2004)," the
   high commissioner suggested: "A second decade would need to be
   properly structured, also through the organization of regular periodical events to create momentum and continuity."[2]

3. A preamble to last year's Commission Resolution 2003/30, under
   agenda item 4 reads: "*Reaffirming* the views of the World Conference

---

This NGO written statement E/CN.4/2004/NGO/15—submitted by the WUPJ to the sixtieth session
of the UNCHR, and posted on UN Web site—was prepared by David G. Littman, with Professor
Wistrich's June 19, 2003, Vienna address, and his approval.

on Human Rights held in Vienna in 1993, on the urgency of eliminating denials and violations of human rights."

4. In an address to a symposium on antisemitism held in Vienna (June 17, 2003) by the Organization for Security and Cooperation in Europe (OSCE), the acting high commissioner, Dr. Bertrand Ramcharan, reiterated that "denial is not an option. Many people of course would like to deny the reality of anti-Semitism." He then went on to recommend "programs of educational activities that can help deal with this phenomenon."

5. Two days later, a renowned historian and world expert on antisemitism Prof. Robert Wistrich delivered his address, as an independent expert, on "Antisemitism in Europe Today" to the same symposium, hosted by the OSCE.

6. Twenty years ago (October 1984), in the preface to his *Hitler's Apocalypse. Jews and the Nazi Legacy*, Wistrich predicted that "the evidence I have been able to marshal concerning the continuity of a radical and murderous antisemitism into the post-war era convinced me that we are dealing with a highly dangerous and fateful phenomenon which may possibly determine the future of our planet."[3] Today this is a certainty.

7. Again, concluding his global remarks at the opening meeting of the sixtieth session of the commission on January 19, 2004, Acting High Commissioner Bertrand Ramcharan stressed that "the duty of conscience and the duty of protection go hand in hand." He reiterated—and may well have had it in mind—the late high commissioner's call to the commission, and the international community, to "conscience"—quoted above under our paragraph 1.

8. At the close of the United Nations Decade for Human Rights Education (1995–2004), the World Union for Progressive Judaism is reprinting in full, with his permission, Prof. Robert Wistrich's important text delivered at a very special event which should create momentum.[4]

9. "Antisemitism in Europe Today," address by Prof. Robert S. Wistrich at a symposium in Vienna on June 19, 2003, to the Organization for Security and Cooperation in Europe.

Speaking to you this afternoon from the majestic setting of the Hofburg in Vienna, I am very mindful of certain historic events that can never be erased. Sixty-five years ago, in the Heldenplatz, only a few hundred meters from this building, hundreds of thousands of cheering Austrians greeted Adolf Hitler with a truly hysterical enthusiasm. In the next three years following the 1938 Anschluss, the Jews of Austria were subjected to indescribable humiliations and cruelties. Over one-third of Austria's Jews (over sixty thousand) were sent to the death camps in Poland—a highly symbolic microcosm of the six million Jewish men, women, and children across Europe who would suffer a similarly horrible fate. Today, shocking to relate, the specter of antisemitism has once more returned to haunt Europe, although it is assuming some radically new forms that require a different approach if we are to deal effectively with the challenge. This session is devoted to education, a subject of great importance. But let us not delude ourselves that education or enlightenment in themselves offer any quick fix or magic wand which will dissipate the dark clouds that are gathering around us. What goes on in the school classrooms, in colleges, in the universities, or in adult education is not divorced from standards of behavior in the broader culture, from family and socialization patterns, from the media and politics. Let us remember, before we assume that knowledge alone is the answer, that the "educators" themselves must be educated (or reeducated!) to quote that highly unfashionable nineteenth-century thinker Karl Marx!

Let us also recall that although this conference is devoted to Europe, thus far no speaker has seriously addressed the burning issue of contemporary Muslim antisemitism, something highly relevant to our topic. Today, we are witnessing a dangerous, toxic, and potentially genocidal form of antisemitism in the Arab-speaking Middle East. The scale and extremism of this literature and commentary—in newspapers, journals, magazines, caricatures, on Arab and Islamic Web sites, on the radio and TV news, in documentaries, films, and soap-operas like the Egyptian-produced version of *The Protocols of the Elders of Zion—Rider without a Horse*—is comparable only to Nazi Germany at its worst. The educational materials of the Arab world are soaked in this poison, made even more inflammatory by what is regularly preached in the mosques. The motifs and symbols of this genocidal antisemitism combine the worst slanders of European anti-Jewish bigotry (including the Christian blood-libel) with Nazi-style caricatures, the myth of the world Jewish conspiracy, and the tendentious use of Islamic sources, including the holy Qur'an. The Islamists (but not only them) have hijacked Islam and are producing a new and more deadly anti-Jewish cocktail, one which is now being reexported back to Europe. It has already infected part of the Muslim youth in France, Holland, Belgium, Great Britain, Germany, Sweden, and other European countries. This rebound effect has brought

Middle Eastern fanaticism and a violent new antisemitism right back into the heart of Europe. No educational strategy that turns a blind eye to the acuity of this problem can possibly succeed.

Educational methods also need to be revised in the light of the highly mediatized global village in which we now all live. This has made the transmission and amplification of antisemitic images and ideas so much more mobile, transnational, and globalized. Today's educators have to confront libels that whiz through cyberspace at the speed of light—malicious disinformation of the kind that accuses not only the Israeli army but "the Jews" per se of infanticide (cold-bloodedly murdering Palestinian children), libels which blame dark "Jewish cabals" for pushing the United States into the Iraq war; or accuse "neo-cons" (a codeword for East Coast Jewish intellectuals) of seeking a "war of civilization" with Islam. Then, there are the grotesque fantasies claiming that the Mossad or the Jews orchestrated the September 11 attack on America. Millions of credulous people out there believe these lies!

Contemporary antisemitic conspiracy theories often hide under the mask of anti-Zionism, anti-Israel prejudice, and/or anti-Americanism. Their purveyors are far more likely to be Islamists that Christians. They often come from the Left more than they do from the Right; they are not outwardly racist and frequently adopt an "antiracist" disguise. They almost never call themselves "antisemitic," unlike their predecessors of sixty or one hundred years ago. Indeed, the "new Judeophobes" invariably wax indignant at the very suggestion that they are against the Jews. Their main focus is on demonizing Israel, on dissolving the so-called Zionist entity and making the world Judenstaatrein—cleansed of the world's only Jewish state.

We cannot deal educationally with this "new look" antisemitism unless we tackle its changing dynamics head-on and expose the pretensions of its new intellectual garb. This is not the ethnic, nationalist, racist, or Nazi antisemitism of six decades ago, which had its roots in late nineteenth-century Europe. All the delegates we have heard from today appear united in their opposition to that type of brutal racist antisemitism, in their rejection of Neo-Nazism, right-wing populism, and xenophobia. That is, of course, gratifying and I welcome it. But we will accomplish little if we think that this is the real problem confronting us in 2003.

Let me, then, share with you some heretical thoughts. Antisemitism at the dawn of the twenty-first century comes nicely wrapped in the radiant and beatific glow of human rights. It is an "antisemitism without antisemites," an antisemitism with a good conscience! Not only that, but some of its most prominent spokesmen think of themselves as being in the forefront of the struggle against racism, fascism, and other related evils. In its "anti-Zionist" masquerade, this style of antisemitism is part of the new religion of Humanity—adapted to a postnational utopia without frontiers—which Israel's existence is allegedly and bizarrely obstructing. Already, at the UN Conference against Racism in Durban[5] we witnessed the shameful spectacle of how such a worthy cause as "antiracism" can be hijacked and turned into an ugly hatefest against Israel and the Jewish people.

We must also contend with the twisted use of the Holocaust as a propaganda weapon against the Jewish state and the Jewish people. I am not just talking about Holocaust denial. What does an educator do when he or she is confronted with the numerous examples of European intellectuals, artists, clerics, journalists, and caricaturists who today twin the Nazi swastika with the Star of David? Here are just a few random examples from an ever-expanding dossier: The Greek caricature in *Ethnos*[6] showing two Israeli soldiers somewhere in the disputed territories. One says to the other: "Don't feel guilty, my brother! We were not in Auschwitz and Dachau to suffer but to learn!" Or the Nobel prize winner for literature from Portugal, José Saramago, who last year compared what was happening in Ramallah to Auschwitz; or the well-known British poet Tom Paulin, who periodically offloads his venom against the so-called Zionist SS; or Abbé Pierre, one of France's most revered Catholic priests, who informs us: "The Jews, once victims, have become executioners."[7]

This is the surreal climate of "democratic," "humanistic," *bienpensant* stereotyping of Jews as Nazis and the libeling of the Jewish state as an apartheid, racist monster engaged in the "ethnic cleansing" of Palestinians. Worse still, it is the intellectual and political elites of Europe who seem to encourage, repeat, aid, and abet such falsehoods under the impeccably respectable but deeply misleading label of "criticizing" Israel. There is a world of difference between criticism and defamation. The disproportionate and relentless singling out of Israel alone for human rights violations is a sure sign of discriminatory practice.

In the media, churches, universities, and in the mainstream politics of the European Union there is an elusive but unmistakable whiff of antisemitism, which we ignore at our peril. What kind of "Enlightenment" is it, for example, when the more "progressive" European media use archaic Christian motifs, to suggest that Ariel Sharon is a deicidal Jew and Yasir Arafat is Jesus Christ? At the end of December 2001, the

French left-wing daily *Libération* ran a cartoon about the fact that Arafat, a Muslim, was not allowed by the Israeli government to go to Bethlehem to celebrate Christmas. Sharon was shown preparing a cross for the Palestinian leader, with hammer and nails at the ready (an Israeli tank in the background) and a caption underneath stated that Arafat would be welcome for Easter—that is, for the Crucifixion!

Then there is *La Stampa*[8]—a liberal Italian paper which is certainly not antisemitic—but which could nevertheless run a caricature showing the baby Jesus, asking when "they" (i.e., the Israelis/Jews) are going "to annihilate me once more." Britain's liberal newspaper, the *Independent*, depicts Ariel Sharon crunching a Palestinian baby in a clear echo of the medieval blood-libel. The Press Complaints Commission in the UK did not censure the paper, claiming that nobody in Britain today knows what the ritual murder accusation means! So while we talk about education against antisemitism, it transpires that highly educated journalists in the UK are so ignorant of the history of antisemitism, they do not even know what the blood-libel is or why it matters! Who needs to be educated?

The problem, ladies and gentlemen, is not to engage in well-meaning, ritualized indictments of racism and antisemitism. We have to address the fact that even some highly educated people do not recognize Jew-hatred except when it is dressed up for them in a Nazi uniform. The problem is that a Heil Hitler salute is no longer the main criteria for measuring antisemitism.

Of course, echoes of the Nazi past are still with us in Europe, America, the Middle East, and beyond. Indeed they must not be ignored. Jewish cabals and conspiracies are once again the flavor of the month, as they were back in 1938. We hear a great deal about warmongering Jews, about Sharon, Israel, and the "Jewish lobby" who allegedly control America and would like to control the whole world. Even the much-respected BBC encourages documentaries about these "dangerous liaisons" in tones uncomfortably reminiscent of darker times.

Great Britain, it should be said, has not been a major bastion of anti-semitism in modern times. Yet, the much revered Labor MP Tam Dalyell recently alleged that British Foreign Secretary Jack Straw—who apparently has a Jewish grandfather—was also a member of the "Jewish cabal" behind the Anglo-American assault on Saddam Hussein. According to such a reckoning, this would make Mr. Straw a Mischling Zweiten Grades—a second-degree Mischling (mixed race) as defined by the Nazi racial laws of 1935. Tam Dalyell is a pacifist, a strong critic of Mr. Blair, a pro-Palestinian advocate, and a passionate opponent of the Iraq war. There are many like him who have begun to move from pro-Palestinian advocacy down the slippery slope of intemperate Israel-bashing to outright anti-Jewish mythologizing. This greatly complicates our task.

It is made even more difficult where there is obstinate denial that the phenomenon even exists, as happened in France, until about one year ago. I still remember the incredible spectacle of the president of the French Republic, declaring that there was "no antisemitism in France" and Mr. Shimon Peres, then foreign minister of Israel, nodding in agreement. That was before the last French presidential elections, at a time when synagogues and community centers were going up in flames, schools and Jewish students were attacked, and individual Jews harassed on a scale unknown since 1945.

There are ten times as many Muslims as there are Jews in France today. But since September 2000 there have been three to four times as many racist acts against Jews as compared to Muslims on French soil. That is an alarming statistic. I am the first to deplore and denounce Islamophobia, but the truth must be told. The majority of antisemitic attacks in France in the past three years have been carried out by North African Arab Muslims. There have been no comparable attacks by Jews on French Muslims!

In the "milieu scolaire" since 2000, things are especially serious, though the French government has at least begun to deal with the problem. Let me recommend that you read *Les Territoires Perdus de la République*,[9] which gives outsiders a flavor of what Jewish pupils and teachers have been experiencing, primarily at the hands of North African Arab students in French schools. Any teacher trying to communicate materials on the Holocaust in French lycées in the banlieux or the so-called *quartiers difficiles* is liable, especially since September 2000, to be subject to frightening abuse.

This last example brings me squarely back to the educational sphere and contemporary antisemitism, which a decade ago in my book on the subject I described as the "Longest Hatred."[10] But it is not only its longevity and persistence that make it so difficult to eradicate. Antisemitism is endlessly protean, adapting itself to the Zeitgeist—like an extraordinarily cunning virus which flares up with renewed force just when it is pronounced extinct.

The old slogans and tactics employed against Nazism, racism, and xenophobia—some of which have been repeated here—are not enough. Indeed, they may even be feeding the very evil—antisemitism—which they are supposed to defang. To "Nazify" Israel and the Jewish people is, for example, a contemporary form of Holocaust inversion that palpably incites antisemitic feelings. The kind of mindless "antiracism" that pillories Israel as an apartheid state produces exactly the same effect. Moreover, the constant effort to subsume antisemitism under the general category of racism is not only untenable historically—it denies the specificity of anti-Jewish bigotry just as it diminishes the distinctive features of other forms of prejudice. The hostility to Jews predated the emergence of racism and racial ideology by many centuries.

To successfully combat antisemitism today—educationally, morally, legally, or politically—we must be alive to its changing contours. We must go beyond conventional pieties about tolerance, pluralism, and multiculturalism—important though it is to uphold these values in practice. We must put an end to the disgraceful international campaign to delegitimize, defame, demonize, dismantle, or destroy the Jewish state. We must also condemn classic antisemitic tools employed in the political war against Israel, such as economic, academic, scientific, or cultural boycotts. For such boycotts are not only intrinsically discriminatory but contradict the principles of free scholarly exchange and of an open democratic society. In the matter of antisemitism, as with terrorism and human rights, this impressive international gathering must call things by their proper name. The very act of holding this meeting here in Vienna is an important statement—that the time of denial is over.

NOTES

1. Under item 4: E/CN.4/2003/14, para.1, 4.
2. Under item 17: E/CN.4/2003/101, para. II. A (a) 10.
3. Robert Wistrich, *Hitler's Apocalypse: Jews and the Nazi Legacy* (London: Weidenfeld & Nicolson, 1985).
4. "Zionism: One of the Earliest Examples of a National Liberation Movement," written statement E/CN.4/2004/NGO/89.
5. The UN Conference against Racism was help in Durban in August 2001.
6. *Ethnos*, April 7, 2002.
7. In French: "Les Juifs, de victimes sont devenus bourreaux."
8. *La Stampa*, April 3, 2002.
9. *Les Territoires Perdus de la République: Antisémitisme, racisme et sexisme en milieu scolaire* (Paris: Mille et une nuits, 2002).
10. *Antisemitism: The Longest Hatred* (London: Thames Methuen, 1991).

"FREE AT LAST"

33. Slaves in Sudan/ Disappearing Jews of Iran: Their History

David G. Littman

In our statement on Monday [March 29, 2004] we called for "urgent action" after learning the tragic news from Sudan that 503 African slaves—mainly women and children—due to be liberated by the official CEAWC Committee had become hostages in a compound in Mieram, near the southern Sudan border, by PDF [Popular Defense Forces] militia forces. We appealed to the commission to do something for their immediate liberation. This plea was heard! It may well be that it was the acting high commissioner's prompt action that convinced the government of Sudan to intervene. We are overjoyed to announce here that yesterday—three days after our appeal—374 slaves reached the town of Warawar in SPLA-controlled southern Sudan, led by James Aguer and others. They were met by Christian Solidarity International representatives with humanitarian aid, who were greatly moved to tears in seeing with their eyes the fulfillment of that dream immortalized by Martin Luther King Jr.: "Free at last! Free at last! Thank God almighty, we are free at last!" To the high commissioner we wish to express our deepest thanks, adding that biblical passage concerning the prophet Elijah: that "the Lord" was not in the wind, nor the earthquake, nor the fire, but "in a still small voice" (1 Kings 19:12). May that "still small voice"—from wherever it may come—continue to be used, rather than fire and brimstone, to liberate soon the tens of thousands of slaves in northern Sudan. [. . .]

In 2003 the International Committee of the Red Cross held several conferences on "The Missing: End the Silence," the last with the Red Crescent in early December. On December 11, in a written text submitted as an offi-

---

NGO oral statement, prepared and delivered by David G. Littman for the WUPJ on April 2, 2004 (item 11), to the sixtieth session of the UNCHR. Thirteen lines were deleted. The entire text was circulated at the UNCHR with WUPJ written statement E/CN.4/2004/NGO/87, as reproduced in chapter 34.

cial question to Iranian president Khatami, when he spoke at the World Council of Churches, we called on the Iranian government to end the long "silence" regarding twelve missing Jews, secretly incarcerated for more than a decade, simply because they tried to leave Iran. The freeing of these missing prisoners, still held "incommunicado" without trial, would be a welcome sign now. All the facts and details, including names, are in our written statement that incorporates the text submitted to President Khatami for the Iranian government. It also provides a brief historic overview of the ancient Jewish community of Persia, from the time of Cyrus the Great, as well as the Shiraz "show trial" of 2000.[1]

NOTE

1. "The Ancient Jewish Community of Iran: End Silence on Disappearances, Discrimination, 'Dhimmitude,'" E/CN.4/2004/NGO/87. This report has been included in the present book as chapter 34.

34. THE ANCIENT JEWISH COMMUNITY OF IRAN

End Silence, Disappearances, Discrimination, "Dhimmitude"

I. PROLONGED "DISAPPEARANCES"/"THE MISSING: END THE SILENCE"

1. An international ICRC conference of governmental and nongovernmental experts was held February 19–23, 2003 in Geneva on the theme "The Missing: End the Silence." "Uncertainty about the fate of their relatives is a harsh reality for countless families in armed conflict and internal violence." The purpose in launching this process was to "respond to the need of families that have lost contact with their loved ones; raise this concern higher on the agendas of governments, the United Nations and NGOs." This theme was stressed at the Twenty-eighth International Conference of the Red Cross and Red Crescent in Geneva (December 2–6).

2. On December 2, 2003, the executive vice chairman of the Conference of Presidents of Major Jewish Organizations, Malcolm Hoenlein, and the secretary general of the Iranian American Jewish Federation, Sam Kermanian, wrote to UN secretary general Kofi Annan on the subject of twelve missing Iranian Jewish males and requested his intervention: "We believe that this is a priority humanitarian issue given the length of their detention, separation from families and denial of even the most fundamental rights." They recalled that three years earlier relatives had written a letter to President

This written statement, E/CN.4/2004/NGO/87—submitted by the World Union for Progressive Judaism (WUPJ) to the sixtieth session of the UNCHR and posted on the UN Web site in March 2004—was prepared by David G. Littman.

Mohammad Khatami on this matter (with a copy sent also to the UN secretary-general).

3. *Text submitted to President Mohammad Khatami at WCC meeting:*[1]

Your Excellency, Member States which have ratified UN Human Rights Conventions remain bound, under all circumstances, by the provisions of those Universal Instruments—and also by the obligations under customary international law.[2] The Working Group on Arbitrary Detention (WGAD) has referred to many aspects[3] of the Institutional and Legal Framework for Detention in its report to the 2004 Commission on Human Rights.[4]

Last February the International Committee of the Red Cross convened in Geneva in its first ever International Conference of Government and Non-Governmental Experts, to discuss the issue of missing persons. At the Conference it was unanimously agreed that families had the right to know the whereabouts of their loved ones.

Question: Your Excellency, nearly ten years ago, twelve young Iranian Jews disappeared on their way to the border with Pakistan, with the aim of immigrating to the West. A few months ago a member of the Majles (Parliament) disclosed to Iranian reporters that he knew of ten people from a non-Muslim minority who were detained in Iranian prisons for long periods. Nobody knows where they are. Secrecy surrounds their imprisonment. The list of these persons is provided below, aged from fifteen to forty-five, some from the same family. I appeal to you to give this forum, comprised of religious leaders of different denominations, your assurance regarding an investigation into the whereabouts of the twelve missing Jews. This is a humanitarian appeal, unconnected with politics. On these grounds alone, I make this plea in the form of a "question."

1. Babak TEHRANI was fifteen when he "disappeared" in a city near the border with Pakistan.
2. Shahin Nik-Khou ZAHEDAN, a young person, "disappeared" along with TEHRANI.
3. Behzad SALARI was arrested in 1994, when he was twenty years old.
4. Farhad EZZATI "disappeared" along with Behzad SALARI.

5. Homayoun BALA-ZADEH "disappeared" when he was in his thirties—is now about forty-five.
6. Omid SOLOUKI, born in 1972, "disappeared" at the same time.
7. Reuben BEN-MATZLIAH, who also "disappeared" then, was born in Shiraz.
8. Abraham BEN-MATZLIAH "disappeared" with his brother, and Omid SOLOUKI.
9. Cyrus GHAHREMANI, who also "disappeared" then, was born in Kermanshah.
10. Abraham GAHREMANI, probably the brother of Cyrus, "disappeared" at the same time.
11. Nourollah RABII'-ZADEH
12. Yitzhak Hassis KHORAM-ABAD was arrested near Hamadan and then "disappeared."

4. The WGAD's report on its visit to Iran states: "*2. Second cause: abuse of 'solitary confinement'* (para.54–55) Solitary confinement covers the generalized use of 'incommunicado' imprisonment. . . . The Working Group considers that owing to the absence of guarantees such 'imprisonment within imprisonment' is arbitrary in nature and must be ended. . . . Furthermore, such absolute solitary confinement, when it is of long duration, can be likened to inhuman treatment within the meaning of the Convention against Torture."

5. Last year's ICRC conferences and that of the Red Cross and Red Crescent unanimously established a fundamental human right that families had the right to know about the whereabouts of their loved ones.

II. ANCIENT JEWISH COMMUNITY OF IRAN: BRIEF HISTORICAL OVERVIEW FROM ANTIQUITY TILL NOW

6. An important Jewish community existed in Mesopotamia (later Iraq) and Persia from biblical times. Tens of thousands of Jews were successively deported to Assyria from the northern kingdom of Israel (after 732 BCE) and to Babylonia from the southern kingdom of Judea (597–581 BCE), particularly after the fall of Jerusalem and the destruction of the First Temple, built by King Solomon in the tenth century BCE, nearly three thousand years ago. After conquering Babylon in 538 BCE, the new Persian ruler, Cyrus, autho-

rized the Jews to return to their homeland. About fifty thousand did, while thousands remained in exile "by the rivers of Babylon." The remembrance of his magnanimity is mentioned in several books of the Bible, and Cyrus the Great is extolled—almost in messianic terms—in the late Isaiah: "That saith of Cyrus, He is my shepherd . . . even saying to Jerusalem, Thou shalt be built; and to the temple, Thy foundations shall be laid. Thus saith the Lord to his anointed, to Cyrus." (44:28–45:1). Jewish community life then flourished during two hundred years of Persian rule in Judea (local coins bear the name *Yehud*) and in Persia-Mesopotamia for a millennium.[5]

7. All the regions invaded by the conquering Arab armies from the seventh century CE were henceforth governed by Islamic legislation. The native majority inhabitants either converted to Islam or became dhimmis, that is: non-Muslim peoples "protected" by the dhimma—a pact granted to them by a treaty of submission that ended the jihad onslaught. The application of this inferior status ("dhimmitude") for the indigenous populations—Christians, Jews, Samaritans, Sabeans, Zoroastrians, and others—varied in different regions and periods, but in Iran, Yemen, and North Africa it survived in its harshest form into the twentieth century. This traditional climate of tolerated contempt is revealed in thousands of Islamic juridical and other texts, as well as in historical dhimmi sources. The legal inequality of dhimmis with Muslims is exemplified by the invalidity of their testimony in an Islamic court, which was based on a strict interpretation of the traditional Sharia law.

8. Over the centuries, the Jews of Shiraz—like their coreligionists in other places of Iran—were the target of constant discrimination and persecution from the clergy, who considered them impure. One example from the early twentieth century is relevant: in 1910 their entire quarter was destroyed by a fanatical mob, following a false "blood libel" accusation; twelve Jews were killed, fifty wounded, and six thousand left homeless and in tatters.[6]

III. Jews of Shiraz: "Show Trial" of 2000—A Landmark Case of Religious Discrimination

9. In the 1990s the pious Jews of Shiraz were considered by the authorities to be an "assertive community," mainly because they refused to

close their shops on Friday and open them on the Sabbath—one of the more plausible reasons for the arrest of thirteen Jews on Passover eve in 1999, among whom were a rabbi, three teachers of Hebrew, and a kosher butcher. This, in spite of the fact that articles 12 and 13 of Iran's Islamic Constitution purports to accord "full respect to their religion."

10. The Jewish community of Iran, which numbered approximately 120,000 in 1948, had declined to 70,000 in 1978, many of them leaving for Israel and the West. Their number is now under 20,000, and this remnant is again—as so often in the past—in danger of customary scapegoat discrimination and of disappearance as a religious minority. One obvious aim of the Shiraz "show trial" was to create a situation of insecurity, so that most Iranian Jews would follow those who had previously abandoned their homes, before and after the 1979 Islamic revolution. Since the first Shiraz arrests and the television "show trial"—all the accusations of espionage stemmed from contacts with their relatives in Israel—the departures have continued, achieving this objective.

11. Before the trial began, President Mohammad Khatami guaranteed that, under Islamic law, the "protected minorities"—this includes Christians and Jews and Zoroastrians but not the persecuted Bahais—had civil rights and freedom from persecution. But in its resolution 1999/13, *Situation of Human Rights in the Islamic Republic of Iran*, the Commission on Human Rights, in its operative paragraph 3(c), expresses its concern "at the continuing discrimination against religious minorities"; this was reiterated in resolution 2000/28.

12. In his wide-ranging report on Iran to the fifty-sixth session, in 2000, special rapporteur Maurice Danby Copithorne devotes a section to the status of minorities.[7] In his conclusion, he declares that "one of the backwaters of the human rights situation in Iran is the status of minorities, ethnic and religious." In annex 2, he referred, to the case of the thirteen arrested Jews. He also mentioned that Iran's thirteenth, fourteenth and fifteenth periodic reports on the *Elimination of All Forms of Racial Discrimination* were closely considered at the August 1999 session of the CERD.[8] On August 4, 1999, the plight of Iran's Jewish community was raised by a member, Regis de Gouttes of France; Iran's promised "written response" on the question of Iranian Jews—and on other Iranian minorities—was never received.

13. The show trial of the thirteen Jews was "balanced" for the media with eight Muslims, but no outside observers or lawyers were accepted. The court-appointed defense lawyers were quoted in the Iranian press as saying that their clients were guilty. The head of the local judiciary stated that four of the defendants had confessed and had asked for mercy. This was denied by defense attorney Esmail Naseri. Just before the trial began (May 1, 2000), the executive director of the Middle East and North African division of Human Rights Watch, Hanny Megally, was quoted as saying, "The defence lawyers have not had access to all the files in the case, even for the minimum five-day period required by Iranian law." In September 2000, the appeals court reduced slightly the harsh sentences handed down against ten of the thirteen Iranian Jews, three of them being acquitted.

14. In two urgent appeals addressed to the high commissioner for human rights (July 3, and September 21, 2000, copies of which were sent to the special rapporteur on Iran and to the special rapporteur on the independence of judges and lawyers, Param Cumaraswamy), the Association for World Education (AWE) raised a key point in this trial. It related to the fact that while thirteen of the accused were Jews and eight Muslims, yet all the trial proceedings—held in an Islamic court, behind closed doors "for security reasons"—appear to have been separate for each religious group. No details of the trial of the eight Muslims were ever provided, other than that they were acquitted, or received light sentences. None of them went to prison. Experts on Islamic law explain this anomaly by the fact that, under the traditional interpretation of the Islamic Sharia law—whether Sunni or Shi'ite—any testimony by a non-Muslim in regard to a Muslim never had validity in an Islamic court and consequently could not have any validity today in the Islamic Republic of Iran.[9]

15. On the initiative of Iran's President Mohammad Khatami—soon after he took office in 1997—the year 2001 was officially designated by the United Nations General Assembly as the "United Nations Year of Dialogue among Civilizations." On May 3–5, 1999—acting on behalf of the Organization of the Islamic Conference—Teheran hosted a widely publicized "Islamic Symposium on Dialogue among Civilizations." In an official paper, under "General principles, A.9," the Islamic Republic of Iran set out its official position: "Compliance with principles of justice, equity, peace and solidarity, as well

as the fundamental principles of international law and the United Nations Charter."[10]

16. The high commissioner was encouraged by the AWE to initiate a special procedures mechanism, via Param Cumaraswamy, "to enquire whether it is true that, in the Shiraz trial, any testimony from a Jew with regard to a Muslim was considered invalid by the court, because of the traditional and imperative obligations of the sacred Islamic sharia law which forbids it. If this is still the actual situation in the Islamic Republic of Iran, then 'justice' would have been basically flawed, and the appropriate UN body should intervene immediately to insist that all international human rights norms (ratified by Iran) be upheld for all in this case—and from now on." In February 2001 [during her visit to Tehran], she did not receive "a satisfactory answer" on this point.

17. A decade earlier, the special rapporteur on Iran, Galindo Pohl, had suggested in his final report that there was a need for "an academic study on the compatibility of Islamic and international law."[12]

18. As indicated by special rapporteur Maurice Danby Copithorne, no trial of the eight accused Muslims ever took place. Fortunately, the remaining Shiraz Jews, unjustly incarcerated, were finally released from prison by 2003 after much media attention, external pressure, and constant reminders at UN bodies by the Association for World Education.

19. Despite this welcome decision by the Iranian judiciary, the World Union for Progressive Judaism calls upon this commission to examine diligently this landmark case, particularly in regard to the "universality of justice." We also call upon special rapporteur Leila Zerrougi to examine all the ramifications in her coming report on discrimination in the criminal justice system, as requested at the sub-commission on August 6, 2003, by an NGO.[12]

20. The WUPJ calls on the government of the Islamic Republic of Iran to end the long "silence" regarding the twelve "missing" Jews, secretly incarcerated for more than a decade. The freeing of these missing prisoners, held "incommunicado" without trial, would be a welcome sign. Such a gesture would be a clear response to the recent report of the WGAD after its February 2003 visit to Iran, and also to the humanitarian conferences held in 2003 by the ICRC, as well as the Twenty-eighth International Conference of the Red Cross and Red Crescent.

21. The international human rights norms set out in the international covenants—all are binding on Iran—should be firmly upheld on all occasions by the commission, UN bodies, and by all UN member states. An effective implementation of these international instruments should be mandatory for all national institutions.

NOTES

1. Comments and questions on December 11, 2003, from David G. Littman, representative at the United Nations Office in Geneva of the World Union for Progressive Judaism (delegated by Rabbi François Garaï to participate for him): floor open for written questions and comments to Mohammad Khatami, president of the Islamic Republic of Iran, after his lecture "Inter-religious Dialogue and International Relations at the Commission of the Churches on International Affairs" (World Council of Churches, Geneva). The original text was handed in as a "question" to be selected, or not, by the WCC officer on the podium. In the end, President Khatami replied at great length to the first "set of questions," and then time ran out. He asked for all the written questions to be given to him so that he could reply in writing. No direct answer was received to this appeal.

2. Cf. letter from the OHCHR of September 14, 2000, chapter 42, p. 425.

3. See E/CN.4/2004/3/Add.2, paras. 12–15..

4. Visit to Islamic Republic of Iran, February 15–27, 2003: E/CN.4/2004/3/Add.2, June 27, 2003.

5. For a historical overview and nineteenth-century documents from the archives of the Alliance Israélite Universelle (Paris), see David G. Littman, "Jews under Muslim Rule: The Case of Persia," *Wiener Library Bulletin* (London) 32, n.s. 49–50 (June 1979): 2–15.

6. Ibid., pp. 12–14. The vivid description in the original French was published in David G. Littman, "Les Juifs en Perse avant les Pahlevi," *Les Temps Modernes* 395 (June 1979): 1910–35 (reprint, Geneva: Editions de l'Avenir, 1979). An English version was republished by Bat Ye'or as "Destruction of the Jewish Quarter, Shiraz (Iran)," appendix 2 in *Islam and Dhimmitude: Where Civilizations Collide* (Madison, NJ: Fairleigh Dickinson University Press, 2002), pp. 403–405.

7. E/CN.4/2000/35.

8. See the fifteenth periodic report of states' parties. Add. Islamic Republic of Iran: CERD/C/338/Add. 8 of October 28, 1998. In regard to Christians, Bahais, and Jews, see also in Bat Ye'or, "Countries Applying the *Shari'a*: Iran," in *Islam and Dhimmitude*, pp. 225–28.

9. E/CN.4/2000/35, para. 7.

10. Ibid., para. 9.

11. This matter was raised in some detail then—with reference to the special rap-

porteur's report on Iran—by the representative of the WUPJ, a year after the "Rushdie Affair" (February 14, 1989). See the oral statement by David G. Littman on February 20, 1990 (E/CN.4/1990/SR.31), verbatim in *Human Rights and Human Wrongs*, no. 8, pp. 25–28 (statement of the observer from Iran on February 28, 1990, in E/CN.4/1990/SR. 43).

12. See also E/CN.4/2003/19/Add.1, "Report of the Joint OHCHR/UNESCO Workshop," under H. Topic 8, which refers to Leila Zerrougui's background paper: HR/PARIS/SEM.3/2003/BP.8.

THE REMNANT DHIMMI POPULATIONS OF THE MIDDLE EAST AND NORTH AFRICA

35.

Forgotten Jewish Refugees and Persecuted Indigenous Christian Communities

David G. Littman

We are once again reminding this commission of a neglected issue—here and elsewhere: the modern exodus of Jews from Middle East and North African countries since the 1940s—that "forgotten million," who suffered the habitual religious cleansing—whether by violent means or otherwise—from Arab countries, now virtually *judenrein*, with barely a remnant one-half of 1 percent—under five thousand. They and their progeny now number over 3 million, of whom 2.5 million make up more than 50 percent of Israel's 5.2 million Jews.[1]

It is a historical fact that the tragedy of the Arab refugees of mandated Palestine occurred because of the refusal of the Arab League and the Palestinian leadership to accept "international legality" in 1947, and their unashamed aim of eliminating the nascent State of Israel, a policy maintained for forty years, which has been reactivated by some states—and by those Islamist groups like Hamas. On the other hand, the Jewish refugees from Arab countries—far from the war zones—were victimized simply because of their religion.

. . . Worse, everything is simply denied—even the documented condition of "dhimmitude" for thirteen centuries alongside their fellow dhimmi Christians.[2] . . .

[We wish also to mention that only twelve days ago, US Senate Resolu-

---

NGO oral statement, prepared and delivered by David G. Littman for the WUPJ on April 13, 2004 (item 14), to the sixtieth session of the UNCHR. Several lines indicated in square brackets have been omitted. The entire text was circulated at the UNCHR with WUPJ written statement E/CN.4/Sub.2/2003/NGO/35 (July 2003) from the fifty-fifth session of the UN Sub-Commission on Human Rights, as reproduced in chapter 36 of this volume.

tion 325 was submitted and referred to the Committee on Foreign Relations on "The Creation of the Refugee Populations in the Middle East, North Africa and the Persian Gulf area as a result of Human Rights violations." We have this text.]

There is a commonplace saying in the Middle East: "After Saturday comes Sunday!" The World Union of Progressive Judaism wishes to recall the petition two years ago that was deposited with the high commissioner [on April 11, 2002] by the Christian Barnabas Fund (UK). Signed then by over 123,000 persons from seventy countries—and many more since—it requested indigenous "Christian minorities in Muslim-majority countries to be given the same rights and freedoms as those enjoyed by Muslim minorities in Western countries." A UN truism, indeed!

Gravely concerned at this shameful collective "blindness" by the international community, we are once again calling on the acting high commissioner, the commission, and appropriate UN bodies—and to all Church leaders (Catholic, Protestant, and others), and particularly Muslim spiritual and lay leaders, to hear the lamentations of the remnant Christian dhimmi communities, who often must endure persecutions and discrimination as an inferior, religious minority, while being falsely accused by their oppressors.

Albert Camus defined this situation well: "The day on which crime adorns itself with the effects of innocence, by a strange reversal . . . innocence is summoned to provide its own justifications."[3]

NOTES

1. See "Historical Facts and Figures: The Forgotten Jewish Refugees from Arab Countries" (E/CN.4/2003/Sub.2/NGO/35), reprinted as chapter 34 in this book. See also the one-page article from the *New York Times* of May 16, 1948—the day after five Arab armies invaded Israel—with the title: "Jews in Grave Danger in All Muslim Lands."

2. Cf. Bat Ye'or, *The Dhimmi: Jews and Christians under Islam* (Rutherford, NJ: Fairleigh Dickinson University Press, 1985); *The Decline of Eastern Christianity under Islam* (Madison, NJ: Fairleigh Dickinson University Press, 1996); and *Islam and Dhimmitude: Where Civilizations Collide* (Madison, NJ: Fairleigh Dickinson University Press, 2002).

3. English translation. It was spoken in the original French: "Le jour où le crime se pare des depouilles de l'innocence, par un curieux renversement . . . c'est l'innocence qui est sommée de fournir ses justifications."

HISTORICAL FACTS
36. AND FIGURES

The Forgotten Jewish Refugees from Arab Countries

INTRODUCTION

1. On November 29, 1947, the UN General Assembly adopted its resolution 181. Called the "Partition Plan," it delineated the land west of the Jordan river into two parts: an Arab state and a Jewish state, with an international *corpus separatum* for Jerusalem. It comprised about 22 percent of the roughly 120,000 square kilometers of the original 1922 League of Nations area of Palestine. All the land east of the Jordan river—78 percent, about 94,000 square kilometers of the entire mandatory area—had been transferred to Emir Abdullah of Arabia by Britain, thus creating the de facto Emirate of Trans-Jordan, later to be renamed in 1949 the Hashemite Kingdom of Jordan.

2. This 1947 Partition Plan was categorically refused by all the Arab League States and also by the Arab-Palestinian leadership, still nominally headed by the mufti of Jerusalem, Hajj Amin al-Husseini, who found refuge in Egypt in 1946 (he moved to Beirut in 1962). Recently praised by Yasir Arafat in an interview, Husseini was declared a war criminal in 1945 after his sojourn in Germany during the Second World War, where he participated in the creation of a

The original form of this article was NGO written statement E/CN.4/Sub.2/2003/NGO/35—submitted by the WUPJ to the fifty-fifth session of the Sub-Commission on Human Rights in Summer 2003 and posted on the UN Web site and prepared by David G. Littman. With the author's permission, this written statement—with several modifications by him—is based on his "The Forgotten Refugees: An Exchange of Populations," *National Review Online*, December 3, 2002, www.nationalreview.com/script/asp?ref=/comment/comment-littman120302.asp.

Bosnian and an Arab brigade to fight alongside Nazi SS units. He
was received officially by Hitler on November 28, 1941, "to discuss
the Arab-Nazi alliance and the methods to exterminate the Jews."[1]
Known for his "ominous role in the extermination of European
Jewry,"[2] he broadcast genocidal appeals to the Arab world on Radio
Berlin, even three months before D-Day: "Kill the Jews wherever
you find them. This pleases Allah, history, and religion. This saves
your honour. Allah is with you."[3]

3. On November 24, 1947, when addressing the Political Committee of
the UN General Assembly, Egyptian delegate Heykal Pasha warned
about the Partition Plan for Palestine: "The United Nations . . .
should not lose sight of the fact that the proposed solution might
endanger a million Jews living in the Muslim countries. . . . If the
United Nations decides to partition Palestine, it might be responsible
for very grave disorders and for the massacre of a large number of
Jews . . . if a Jewish state were established, nobody could prevent
disorders. Riots would spread through all the Arab states and might
lead to a war between the two races."[4]

4. Seven weeks later, the president of the World Jewish Congress, Dr.
Stephen S. Wise, appealed to US secretary of state George Marshall
to intervene, and his political director, Dr. Robert S. Marcus,
referred to al-Husseini's involvement in the June 1941 Baghdad
pogrom (*farhud*), warning about the menacing situation for Jews in
Arab countries: "This conspiracy is inspired by the Mufti, notorious
war criminal, who participated in the Nazi plans to exterminate the
Jews of Europe. . . . Acts of violence already perpetrated, together
with those contemplated, being clearly aimed at the total destruction
of the Jews, constitute genocide which under the resolutions of the
General Assembly is a crime against humanity."[5]

5. The title of a detailed article in the *New York Times* of May 16,
1948—a day after Israel declared its independence—echoed this dire
official warning: "Jews in Grave Danger in all Moslem Lands: Nine
Hundred Thousand in Africa and Asia Face Wrath of Their Foes."

THE INDIGENOUS JEWS FROM ARAB COUNTRIES BEFORE 1948 AND WHY THEY FLED OR CHOSE EXILE

6. During the first half of the twentieth century thousands of Jewish
men, women, and children, the young and the old, were brutally

massacred in Arab countries in North Africa, Iraq, Syria, Egypt, Libya, and Aden—even under French and British colonial rule—and also in Palestine by lawless gangs soon after the British conquest in 1918 and throughout the Mandate period.

7. Already in Iraq (1936, and especially the Baghdad *farhud* of 1941), Syria (1944, 1945), Egypt and Libya (1945), and Aden (1947), murderous attacks had killed and wounded thousands. All these events occurred before Israel's independence. Here is a description from the official firsthand report in 1945 by Tripoli's Jewish community president Zachino Habib on what happened to Libyan Jews in Tripoli, Zanzur, Zawiya, Casabat, and Zitlin on November 4–5, 1945: "The Arabs attacked Jews in obedience to mysterious orders. Their outburst of bestial violence had no plausible motive. For fifty hours they hunted men down, attacked houses and shops, killed men, women, old and young, horribly tortured and dismembered Jews isolated in the interior. . . . In order to carry out the slaughter, the attackers used various weapons: knives, daggers, sticks, clubs, iron bars, revolvers, and even hand grenades."[6]

8. A recent example of such terrorist acts was perpetrated on April 11, 2002, when the jihadist bombing of the ancient al-Ghariba synagogue of Djerba in Tunisia killed seventeen and badly wounded many others, most of them elderly German tourists. A spokesman for al Qaeda claimed responsibility for the bombing. Tunisia's remaining Jewish community of about one thousand—a remnant of an indigenous community with roots in the country's Phoenician past—will probably soon seek security in Israel and elsewhere, as have 99 percent of their coreligionists since the late 1940s.

9. In 1945 about 140,000 Jews lived in Iraq; 60,000 in Yemen and Aden; 35,000 in Syria; 5,000 in Lebanon; 90,000 in Egypt; 40,000 in Libya; 150,000 in Algeria; 120,000 in Tunisia; 300,000 in Morocco, including Tangiers—a total of roughly 940,000 (and approximately 200,000 more in Iran and Turkey). Of these indigenous communities, less than 50,000 Jews remain today—and in the Arab world their number is barely 5,000, one-half of 1 percent of the overall total at the end of the World War II.

10. Pogroms and persecutions—and grave fears for their future—regularly preceded the mass expulsions and exoduses of these indigenous Jews, whose ancestors had inhabited these regions from time immemorial, over a millennium before the successive jihad waves of

Arab invaders from the seventh century. Beginning in 1948–49, more than 650,000 of these Oriental Jewish refugees, stripped of everything, were integrated into Israel's sparse area of 20,000 square kilometers—even as the new state was being threatened with extinction by neighbouring Arab states. A further 300,000 or so Jewish refugees found asylum elsewhere, in Europe and the Americas.

11. About half of Israel's 5.2 million Jews—from a population of about 6.5 million, of whom roughly 20 percent are Arab, Druze, and Bedouin Israelis—is composed of these forgotten refugees and their descendants, who received no humanitarian aid from the United Nations and did not ask for it. It was Israel alone, with the help of Jewish communities just emerging from the Holocaust, which achieved their humanitarian survival and integration into a nascent society.

12. No parallel political commitment was made for the integration of the less numerous Arab refugees from Palestine (numbering about 550,000 in 1949, although an inexact figure of 750,000 and above is often claimed—rising to 4 or even 6 million today in the world's media). The Arab League countries cover 15 million square kilometer—about 10 percent of the world's land surface—and many states possess immense oil and gas reserves, yet little was done to alleviate the plight of their Arab brethren. But the full moral responsibility lies exclusively with the Arab League and the Arab Palestinian leadership, which defied international legality, beginning in 1947—a "refusal" clearly echoed by Farouq al-Qaddoumi, head of the PLO political bureau and the secretary-general of Fatah's Central Committee, when he stated in 2003: "The [Palestinian] problem was created by the United Nations when it decided on a partition resolution."[7]

13. George Orwell's saying about everyone being equal, but some being more equal than others, could also be applied to refugees in general since the 1940s. Some refugees *are*, indeed, considered more equal than others. The forgotten million Jewish refugees from Arab lands were not helped by the United Nations, nor were they kept—as were the Palestinian Arabs—for over half a century in "refugee camps," breeding hopelessness, frustration, and also a religious-inspired culture of hate and death in which jihadist bombers are thriving.

14. The transfer of populations on a large scale, a consequence of war or for political reasons, has been a characteristic of human history, particularly in the Islamic Orient. Deportations, expropriations, and

expulsions of the dhimmis—Jews, Christians, and other indigenous peoples—were recurrent throughout the long history of dhimmitude, after Arab jihad wars of conquest, expropriation, and occupation, including Palestine.[8] One should question the real motivation of a selective, historically flawed memory that systematically spotlights Arab refugees from a part of Palestine during an Arab League war to destroy Israel.

15. UN Security Council Resolution 242, of November 22, 1967, was also rejected by the Khartoum Arab League Summit Conference, with the unchanging line, *"No peace with Israel, no recognition of Israel, no negotiation with Israel, no concessions on the questions of Palestinian national rights."* Yet resolution 242 also referred to *"a just solution to the refugee problem"*—a term that included the Jewish refugees from Arab countries (dixit President Carter in 1978).

16. The dire hardships endured by the great majority of these indigenous Jewish refugees from Arab countries have never been examined—certainly not at the United Nations—nor has the loss of their inestimable collective heritage dating back from two to three millennia and their vast personal property rights. This great injustice should be addressed at the United Nations, within the context of an equitable global solution to the ongoing Middle East tragedy and as a just contribution to the current "Road Map" to peace and mutual recognition.

17. The question of these forgotten Jewish refugees from Arab countries—now over three million—has often been raised by the WUPJ at the Commission on Human Rights and its subcommission. At the fifty-eighth session of the commission (April 24, 2002), speaking in "reply," a representative of Iraq, Saad Hussain—after the usual ad hominem attack against the speaker—declared, "The Arab history, the Arab and Islamic history for fourteen centuries, has not witnessed any harm to the Jews—quite the contrary. The Jews have lived, and continue to live in peace, and their sacred places and their property have been protected until today. . . . They live in Arab countries today in perfect safety, despite the events—the horrible events in Palestine."[9]

18. Such gross official denials contrast with the irrefutable historical facts that Jews have been forbidden to reside in Arabia since the advent of Islam (except for Yemen and a part of the Gulf region)—and in Jordan since 1922. Today, there are no Jews in Libya, less

than 100 in Egypt and Syria, and scarcely 5,000 in the Arab world. Before the Arab conquest, Iraq was populated only by Christians and Jews, with smaller communities of Zoroastrians. When Iraq's representative addressed the commission, only 33 elderly Jews remained in Iraq from a 1948 population of over 140,000. All their ancient Scrolls of the Law (*Sifrei Torah*) had been confiscated in the 1960s and stacked one against another in a locked room at the Medressa al-Moustansariyya, a market near the Souk al-Haraj in Baghdad.[10] The survival of these ancient sacred scrolls and other libraries is still uncertain.

19. The major stumbling block to peace in the Middle East remains the necessary establishment of democratic institutions and, above all, the acceptance by all Arab states, including the Palestinian Authority and Hamas, of the inalienable and legitimate de jure rights and existence of the State of Israel within a part of its historic homeland.

20. There is also the divisive question of a return of, or compensation for, Arab refugees as a result of two Arab wars to destroy Israel. The refusal in 1947—and for forty years and more, by Arab Palestinian leaders and the Arab League—of Israel's existence in any part of the biblical "Land of Israel" is the fundamental reason for a double refugee tragedy. But the deliberately targeted victims—far from any war zone—were, indisputably, the totally innocent and indigenous Jewish communities from ten Arab countries, which have now become virtually *judenrein* ("cleansed" of all Jews). These facts can no longer be denied.

21. The World Union for Progressive Judaism solemnly calls on the High Commissioner for Human Rights, the High Commissioner for Refugees, all competent UN bodies, and particularly the Commission on Human Rights and its subcommission—as well as the Arab League—to recognize formally the fundamental and equal human rights of these Jewish minorities, those forgotten millions—indigenous Jewish refugees from their former countries.[11] This key recognition of a great historic injustice could usefully be addressed in the future work of the Working Group on Minorities, and especially "on peaceful and constructive approaches to situations involving minorities," as well as the subcommission's work on "The return of refugees' or displaced persons' property" under item 4.[12]

NOTES

1. Bat Ye'or, *Islam and Dhimmitude: Where Civilizations Collide* (Cranbury, NJ: Fairleigh Dickinson University Press, 2002/2003), p. 172.

2. Lucasz Hirszowicz, *The Third Reich and the Arab East* (London: Routledge and Kegan Paul, 1966), p. 26, quoted in Bat Ye'or, *Islam and Dhimmitude*, p. 300.

3. Broadcast March 1, 1944; quoted in Maurice Perlman, *Mufti of Jerusalem: The Story of Haj Amin el Husseini* (London: Gollancz, 1947), p. 51; and quoted in Bat Ye'or, *Islam and Dhimmitude*, p. 283.

4. UN Official Records of the Second Session of the General Assembly, Ad Hoc Committee on the Palestinian Question, SR., September 25–November 25, 1947, p. 185.

5. Full details can be found in a full-page article by Richard A. Yaffe, "Arab Pogroms Endanger 800,000 outside Palestine: Jews Slain, Homes and Synagogues Burned Down," *PM* (World Jewish Congress), January 18, 1948.

6. Renzo di Felici, *Jews in an Arab Land: Libya, 1835–1970*, trans. Judith Roumani (Austin: University of Texas Press, 1985), pp. 193–94, 365, n. 19. See the recent testimony by Giulia Boukhobza (born in Libya in 1951), "Justice for Jews from Arab Nations," *International Herald Tribune*, July 1, 2003, p. 9.

7. Interview with Qaddoumi, in *Kul al-Arab* (Israeli Arab newspaper), January 3, 2003.

8. For documentation, see Bat Ye'or, *The Dhimmi: Jews and Christians under Islam* (Cranbury, NJ: Fairleigh Dickinson University Press, 1985/2003); Bat Ye'or, *The Decline of Eastern Christianity under Islam: From Jihad to Dhimmitude: 7th to 20th Century* (Cranbury, NJ: Fairleigh Dickinson University Press, 1996/2003); and Bat Ye'or, *Islam and Dhimmitude*.

9. UN English interpretation as recorded verbatim from statement delivered in Arabic (E/CN.4/2002/SR.54).

10. Photograph by Yossef Yinnon (1972) on the back cover of an eight-page publication by Bat Ye'or, *Oriental Jewry and the Dhimmi Image in Contemporary Arab Nationalism*, lecture for Jews in Arab Lands Committee, World Organisation of Jews from Arab Countries (WOJAC), Jews College, London, September 5, 1978 (Geneva: Editions de l'Avenir, 1979). This text appears as chapter 9 in this book.

11. Malka Hillel Shulewitz, ed., *The Forgotten Millions: The Modern Jewish Exodus from Arab Lands* (London and New York: Cassell, 1999; New York: Continuum, 2000); Shmuel Trigano, ed., *L'exclusion des Juifs des pays arabes: Aux sources du conflit israélo-arabe* (Clamecy, France: In Press Editions, 2003).

12. Cf. Working Group on Minorities, ninth session, May 12–16, 2003, under item 4, the update reports by Asbjorne Eide, and under item 4 of the Sub-Commission on Human Rights, the reports undertaken by Paulo Sérgio Pinheiro.

DISCRIMINATION IN THE EGYPTIAN CRIMINAL

37. JUSTICE SYSTEM

The Exemplary Case of Dr. Neseem Abdel Malek— Grave Attacks and Discrimination against Copts

1. The commission and the subcommission have long been greatly concerned with the protection of human rights in "state of emergency" conditions worldwide, especially that of minorities. Egypt is an example of the constant misuse of military tribunals and of a "state of emergency" system that was reintroduced and reinforced in 1981 after the assassination of President Anwar el-Sadat. Although Egypt is not officially at war, this "emergency system" was again extended for a further three years in February 2003; it automatically refers any civilian to a military court by a presidential decision if the case falls under the general category "act of terrorism."[1]

2. Since 1998, the case of Dr. Neseem Abdel Malek has been highlighted by the Association of World Education at several UN bodies as an exemplary case. It illustrates very clearly how Egypt's iniquitous criminal justice system functions, via a "military tribunal," to provide discriminatory ad hoc condemnations without appeal on what is often blatantly false or totally inadequate evidence.

3. This discrimination in the criminal justice system affects all citizens,

---

This text—with the exception of paragraphs 9, 10, and 11—comprises all of the AWE's written statement E/CN.4/2004/NGO/90 (titled "Discrimination in the Egyptian Criminal Justice System: 'State Security'/ 'States of Emergency'/ 'Military Tribunals' / An Exemplary Case: Dr. Neseem Abdel Malek/ Discrimination against Copts"). It was submitted to the sixtieth session of the UNCHR and posted on the UN Web site in March 2004. It was prepared for publication by David G. Littman, with advice from René Wadlow.

as illustrated by the case of Prof. Saad Eddin Ibrahim—director of the Cairo-based Ibn Khaldun Center for Development Studies, a staunch human rights defender, advocate of democracy and women's rights, and of the Christian Coptic minority—recently released from prison after an international outcry. But millions of members of the indigenous Christian Coptic minority are even more vulnerable to such arbitrary decisions due to their perceived inferiority—resulting from their traditional dhimmi status under the Islamic "protection pact" (*dhimma*) granted to non-Muslims by the Sharia law. An Islamist trend has led to the return of a "jihad ideology," conducive to a form of "dhimmitude" status today.[2]

4. Thus, Dr. Abdel Malek, a Christian, was considered responsible for the crime committed by a Muslim, Saber Farahat Abu Ulla, who—aided by his brother—killed nine German tourists and their Egyptian driver on September 17, 1997. Although Saber had been confined to a mental asylum after killing four foreign tourists outside the Cairo Semiramis hotel in 1993, his testimony was accepted as valid. He first alleged that he had obtained a special weekend furlough by bribing Dr. Sayed el-Qut, then deputy health minister and the former head of another mental institute, although el-Qut had signed a certificate of insanity four years earlier, thus saving Saber from the gallows. However, Saber later retracted this "testimony" and then accused Dr. Abdel Malek, the Christian Copt, director of the El-Khanka mental hospital since mid-1992, of having accepted his bribes.

5. "Thus, the doctor who had signed the certificate [of insanity in 1993] was duly acquitted and Dr. Abdel Malek found guilty in his place."[3] In this way, a Copt was accused of corruption by a certified madman, even though he was absent from the El-Khanka clinic on that fatal September 1997 weekend. By a "religiously correct" sleight of hand, the false testimony of a condemned killer—duly certified insane and incompetent—was accepted,[4] even though this allegation was contradicted in court by Saber's own mother. No other plausible evidence or "proof" was provided to justify a verdict against the Christian doctor. The original bribe allegations against a high-ranking Muslim doctor were dropped.

6. During an interview on Egyptian television—widely reported just before both brothers were executed in May 1998—Saber proudly stated that his murderous actions were a part of his "jihad for Allah." He had only one sincere regret: that he had not killed more "infidels."

7. Opinion 10/1999 (Egypt) of the Working Group on Arbitrary Detention detailed all these facts and asked the Egyptian government to
review the case of Dr. Abdel Malek, unjustly condemned to twenty-
five years' imprisonment with hard labor by a military court. The
AWE's 2001 written statement contains this opinion, the brief
"Reply of the Government of Egypt," and some of our comments.[5]

8. The conclusion of opinion 10/1999 states, "The deprivation of liberty of Dr. Neseem Abdel Malek is arbitrary, as being in contravention of articles 9 and 10 of the Universal Declaration of Human
Rights and articles 9 and 14 of the International Covenant on Civil
and Political Rights and falls within category III of the applicable
categories to the consideration of the cases submitted to the Working
Group" (para. 19). "Consequent upon the opinion rendered, the
Working Group requests the Government: to take the necessary
steps to remedy the situation, and bring it in conformity with the
standards and principles set forth in the Universal Declaration of
Human Rights" (para. 20). . . .

12. Five years after submission, the recommendations of the WGAD in
its opinion 10/1999 have been ignored by the government of Egypt.
However, the arbitrary sentence by a military tribunal under the
"state of emergency" regulations was reduced from twenty-five to
ten years in January 2000, two-thirds of which have been served by
Abdel Malek.

13. In a statement to the commission last year (April 9, 2003), the
AWE's representative explained that this matter had been referred to
Param Cumaraswamy, the then special rapporteur on the indepen-
dence of judges and lawyers, asking him to pursue it under his man-
date with respect to resolution 2002/43 and especially 2002/37,
Integrity of the Judicial System. He sent a communication to the
Egyptian government before the fifty-ninth session of the commis-
sion, which has remained unanswered until this date.

14. The AWE again calls on the WGAD—in the light of the continued
arbitrary detention of Dr. Abdel Malek—to reconsider his case,
taking into account the findings made in opinion 10/1999, and the
more recent action taken by former special rapporteur Param
Cumaraswamy last year.

15. In a statement to the Sub-Commission on Human Rights (August 6,
2003), we also appealed to the new special rrapporteur on discrimination in the criminal justice system, Ms. Leïla Zerrougi, to examine

this clear case of discrimination in her forthcoming "detailed study of discrimination in the criminal justice system with a view to determining the most effective means of ensuring equal treatment . . . for all persons without discrimination, particularly vulnerable persons."

16. Anyone reading opinion 10/1999 will wonder why a former director of the Cairo El-Khanka Hospital for Mental and Neurological Health—a distinguished Copt—should remain incarcerated while thousands of Islamists, condemned for violent crimes, regularly receive presidential pardons on Muslim holidays. If such an obvious "discrimination in the criminal justice system" of Egypt cannot be corrected five years after a WGAD opinion, what does it say about this UN mechanism?

17. As Egypt's "'state of emergency'" system allows no appeal from a military tribunal ruling, the Association for World Education is once again reiterating its appeal to President Hosni Mubarak—based solely on WGAD opinion 10/1999—to free Dr. Abdel Malek on compassionate grounds by a presidential pardon before the Coptic Easter of 2004, so as to reverse this grave miscarriage of justice with a humanitarian gesture that would be warmly welcomed even now.

IMPUNITY: THE MASSACRE OF TWENTY-ONE COPTS AT AL-KHOSHEH (JANUARY 2000) AND THE BRUTAL ATTACK AT AL-GIRZA (NOVEMBER 14, 2003)

18. The case of Dr. Abdel Malek is but one of many examples of religious discrimination in the Egyptian criminal justice system. There are many others in which members of the Coptic minority are victims. We have constantly referred to this grave situation, highlighting the ghastly al-Khosheh village massacre—the fortieth collective attack on Copts since 1972—when twenty-one Copts were massacred and their property destroyed by Muslim mobs over the weekend of December 31, 1999–January 2, 2000. Already in August–September 1998, over one thousand innocent Copts from the same village—including women and children—were brutally tortured by the local police, as reported by Hafez Abu Saada, the then secretary general of the Egyptian Organization for Human Rights; this resulted in his being gravely intimidated by the government and even officially accused of disseminating false accusations.

19. On February 27, 2003 an Upper Egyptian criminal court freed all the criminals involved in the massacre of the Copts at Al-Khosheh, leaving the bereaved Coptic families of victims in total shock. Youssef Sidhom, a member of the Coptic Community Council and editor of *Watani Weekly*, lamented, "The case of El-Khosheh with its painful weight of victims and losses cannot be forgotten."[6]

20. As recently as November 2003 a mass attack took place against the Coptic village of Al-Girza by Muslim mobs, when all their property, crops, and chattel were either looted or destroyed—with no protection from security forces.[7] In this case—as with that of Al-Khosheh, and the scores of other attacks that have been the bitter lot of the indigenous Egyptian Christian Coptic minority for over thirty years—the Egyptian criminal justice system has been shown to be gravely flawed.

21. Many Egyptian Muslims have opposed this iniquitous discrimination, like Farag Foda, defender of secularism and of the Copts (assassinated on June 8, 1992), the above-mentioned Hafez Abu Saada and Saad Eddin Ibrahim, and the well-known writer Hassanein Heikal in his book *Al-Koutoub: Weghat Nazzar* (Books: Viewpoints) (March 2000), when he appealed to President Hosni Mubarak to act now on this matter. Indeed, it is a truism that "Egyptian laws are autocratic by nature." This was the verdict of Neged Borai in July 2002—a leading lawyer and political reform advocate—who courageously contradicted the oft-repeated general affirmations in Egypt's last report to the CERD that portrayed Egypt as a land of democracy and justice in the Middle East where universal human rights norms were taught in all elementary schools—and implemented nationally.[8]

22. The Al-Khosheh massacre of 2000, the subsequent acquittals and release of the murderers, and the recent attacks on Al-Girza provide an urgent reminder to the commission, to special rapporteur (on "discrimination in the criminal justice system") Leïla Zerrougi, and to human rights defenders in general. It is time to monitor this grave situation of a martyred dhimmi people—the Christian Copts of Egypt, the direct heirs to one of humanity's oldest civilizations—painfully forced to choose between the creeping renewal of a modern form of "dhimmitude" in Egypt or freedom in Western democracies.

23. The Association for World Education is appealing to this Human

Rights Commission—called by the UN secretary-general "the conscience of humanity"—to find the proper means and to take the effective measures to stop the recurrence of these massacres and mass sectarian attacks, as well as the injustice and discrimination systematically committed against the defenseless and besieged Coptic community. To this end, the AWE appeals also to all UN competent bodies and special rapporteurs. Now is the time to call on the government of Egypt to ensure that inquiries and trials be conducted openly, with the active participation of prominent human rights defenders and international observers.

NOTES

1. Art. 6, act 52, 1966.

2. Bat Ye'or, *Islam and Dhimmitude: Where Civilizations Collide* (Madison, NJ: Associated University Presses, 2002), pp. 180–82, 231–34, and in the index under "Egypt." For earlier details, see Y. Masriya [Bat Ye'or], "A Christian Minority: The Copts in Egypt," Case Studies on Human Rights and Fundamental Freedoms: A World Survey. (The Hague: Martinus Nijhoff, 1976), 4:79–93 (reprinted in this book as chapter 13).

3. WGAD opinion 10/1999, para. 6.

4. Military felony case 66/97.

5. AWE statement: E/CN.4/2001/NGO/49; opinion: E/CN.4/2000/4/Add. 1, pp. 52–55; "Reply," E/CN.4/2000/4, paras. 27–28.

6. Youssef Sidhom, Arabic article in *Watani Weekly* (Cairo), November 30, 2003, p. 1.

7. Youssef Sidhom, Arabic article in *Watani Weekly*, March 16, 2003, p. 1.

8. Quoted by Nadia Abou el-Magd in an Associated Press article, July 29, 2002, from Cairo (Neged Borai was reacting to the latest court decision at that time on Prof. Saad Eddin Ibrahim).

"RUSHDIE AFFAIR"

38. Syndrome and Historical Overview—the Right to Life and Human Rights Mechanisms

1. On February 14, 2004, the 15 Khordad Foundation declared in a press release that the *fatwa/hukm* death sentence on Salman Rushdie remained valid. On February 15, 2004, the Teheran daily, *Jomhouri Islami*, announced that "the committee for the glorification of the martyrs of the Muslim world" had offered a $100,000 bounty to anyone who killed Rushdie.[1]

2. Last year, on February 14, 2003, Iran's Revolutionary Guards renewed the death sentence on Salman Rushdie with a clarification: "The historical decree on Salman Rushdie is irrevocable and nothing can change it."[2]

3. On the fifteenth anniversary of Ayatollah Ruhollah Khomeini's *fatwa* against the British writer, the Association for World Education is submitting a substantive documentation on the "Rushdie Affair"—the greatest freedom-of-opinion-and-expression issue of our time—and also on the silence and, alternatively, the efforts of United Nations human rights bodies to address that issue.

4. Although the Association for World Education sent an "Urgent Appeal on the Rushdie Affair Syndrome" on February 17, 2004, to Iranian president Mohammad Khatami, we maintain that a clear condemnation of the fatwa by the Organization of the Islamic Conference (OIC) and by its member states, at the sixtieth session of the Commission on Human Rights, would be a real contribution to the protection of article 19 of the Universal Declaration of Human

---

This NGO written statement, E/CN.4/2004/NGO/252, was submitted by the AWE to the sixtieth session of the UNCHR and posted on the UN Web site in April 2004—enlarged by David G. Littman from an earlier text submitted to the UNCHR.

Rights—and for the struggle against terrorism and any arbitrary execution of dissident writers. The OIC is the appropriate body to make this condemnation, as representatives of the government of the Islamic Republic of Iran constantly stress that the *fatwa* is binding on all Muslims, not just on Iranians.

5. The Iranian government has repeatedly cited the declaration adopted at the eighteenth meeting of foreign ministers of the OIC, held in Riyadh (Saudi Arabia) on March 13–16, 1989, which "had proclaimed, in unambiguous terms, the apostasy of Salman Rushdie." Indeed, the forty-four foreign ministers present at that meeting did promulgate a ban on *The Satanic Verses*, but they did not comment on the *fatwa* that sentenced its author and publishers to death. However, they did pronounce Salman Rushdie to be an apostate. As the traditional interpretation of Sharia law requires that the punishment (*hadd*) for an apostate (*ridda*) should be death—one of the three cases where a Muslim's blood may be legally shed—we maintain that it is the OIC that should declare the *fatwa* contrary to all the human rights norms that UN member states have ratified.

6. The *fatwa* has remained for fifteen years a constant threat against the life of Salman Rushdie and of others—and is an impediment to the normal functioning of the Islamic Republic of Iran within the world community and an example and encouragement to others, and to states.

7. Meeting with British foreign secretary Robin Cook on September 24, 1998—ten years after the publication of *The Satanic Verses*—the foreign minister of the Islamic Republic of Iran, Dr. Kamal Kharazi, declared that the Iranian government "has no intention, nor is it going to take any action whatsoever to threaten the life of the author of *The Satanic Verses* or anybody associated with his work, nor will it encourage or assist anybody to do so. Accordingly, the government dissociates itself from any reward that has been offered in this regard and does not support it."

8. Although this statement allowed the British government to resume full diplomatic relations with Tehran, broken off in 1989, it soon became evident that these assurances were similar to those expressed by Iranian diplomats in June 1989, soon after the death of Ayatollah Khomeini, and since then. Foreign Minister Kharazi readily acknowledged that he was saying nothing new: "We did not adopt a new position with regard to the apostate Salman Rushdie,

and our position remains the same as that which has been repeatedly stated by the Islamic Republic of Iran's officials." Since Iran considers that Islam does not allow a division between religion and government, the separation of this *fatwa* from government policy would violate that principle.

9. It is important to distinguish between two types of religious rulings in Iran: a *fatwa* and a *hukm.* The former remains valid only during the lifetime of the religious authority who issues it; the latter continues in effect beyond his death. Despite the Western habit of referring to the edict against Rushdie as a *fatwa,* Iranian spokesmen have universally regarded it as a *hukm.*[3]

10. Ayatollah Khomeini's *fatwa/hukm* of February 14, 1989, states, in the English translation, "I inform all zealous Muslims of the world that the author of the book entitled *The Satanic Verses*—which has been compiled, printed, and published in opposition to Islam, the Prophet, and the Qur'an—and all those involved in its publication, who were aware of its content, are sentenced to death. I call on all zealous Muslims to execute them quickly, wherever they may be found, so that no one else will dare to insult the Muslim sanctities. . . . Whoever is killed on this path is a martyr."

11. On February 17, 1989, President Seyyed Ali Hoseyni Khamanei declared that if Rushdie were to repent, "it is possible that the people may pardon him." But two days later, following Rushdie's inadequate apology, Ayatollah Khomeini confirmed his "execution order": "Even if Salman Rushdie repents and becomes the most pious man of [our] time, it is incumbent on every Muslim to employ everything he has, his life and his wealth, to send him to hell. If a non-Muslim becomes aware of his whereabouts and has the ability to execute him quicker than Muslims, it is incumbent on Muslims to pay a reward or a fee in return for this action."[4]

12. On March 1, 1989, the UN special rapporteur on summary or arbitrary executions, Amos Wako, referred to this unusual call for an arbitrary execution when introducing his annual report to the commission: "The Human Rights Committee has observed that arbitrary killings are forbidden and the law must strictly control and limit the circumstances in which a person may be deprived of his life. . . . The right to life is a right from which all other rights flow."

13. In a subsequent reply to the special rapporteur's March 3, 1989, cable from the Centre for Human Rights, the Iranian government

made its position clear: "The Special Rapporteur's intervention in the case of Salman Rushdie's criminal offence against Islam and the world Muslim community was outside his mandate and thus unwarranted."[5]

14. In an interview four years later, Iranian president Ali Akbar Hashemi Rafsanjani referred to the *fatwa/hukm* against Salman Rushdie: "This is prescribed by an Islamic law that has been in existence for a thousand years. Even if the Imam [Ayatollah Khomeini] had not pronounced a *fatwa*, it could have been traced in the books of great Islamic scholars. It is written that anyone cursing the Prophet is condemned to death."[6]

15. Soon after the *fatwa*'s proclamation, the Iranian ambassador to the Holy See even declared that he would kill Salman Rushdie with his own hands, and Iranian interior minister Ali Akbar Mohtashemi called on Hizbollah agents worldwide to execute him. Also, on February 15, 1989, Ayatollah Hassan Sanai, head of the 15 Khordad Relief Agency Foundation—created on June 15, 1979, by the Iranian government—appeared on Iranian television and offered $3 million [on the inflated official rate of 200 million rials], to any Iranian, and $1 million to a foreigner, who killed Rushdie. This was raised to $2 million in March 1991—and then "with additional expenses" on June 17, 1992.[7] On November 2, 1992, he called on "all Muslims of the world to unite and make an effort to end the life of the apostate Rushdie." Three days after Ayatollah Sanai announced that the 15 Khordad Foundation would "send volunteers abroad to execute the death sentence," Iranian supreme guide Ali Khamanei reappointed him—and nine others—as a member of the official Council on Expediency and Discernment.[8] Yet in December 1997, when Ayatollah Sanai once more raised the bounty for a non-Muslim assassin to $2.5 million, President Rafsanjani casually announced that "this foundation is a non-governmental foundation and its decisions are not related to government policies."

16. On July 3, 1991, Ettore Caprioli, the Italian translator of *The Satanic Verses*, was grievously injured, and on July 12 Hitoshi Igarishi—professor of literature and an admirer of Islamic civilization, who had translated the book into Japanese—was assassinated in Tokyo. William Nygaard, the Norwegian translator, was later knifed.

17. On June 30, 1992, 147 out of 270 deputies of the newly elected Majles (Iranian National Assembly) signed a letter condemning the

British Parliament for receiving Salman Rushdie. It stated, "We deputies of the Majles, in obedience to the decisive views of the eminent leader, His Eminence Ayatollah Ali Khamanei, declare that the Imam's historic *fatwa* on the apostasy of Salman Rushdie remains in force as before and that all Muslims and all the world's hezbollah forces are duty-bound to carry it out."

18. In November 1992 Iran's chief justice, Ayatollah Morteza Moqtadi, also confirmed that Ayatollah Khomeini's *fatwa/hukm* was irrevocable.

19. On February 14, 1993, Ayatollah Ali Khamanei, who had succeded the Ayatollah Khomeini in June 1989 as Iran's supreme guide, confirmed that the death sentence must be carried out whatever the circumstances: "Imam Khomeini has shot an arrow at this impudent apostate. The arrow is moving to its target and will sooner or later hit it. The verdict must undoubtedly be carried out and will be carried out. . . . Solving the Rushdie issue is possible only with the handing of this apostate and infidel person to Muslims."

REACTIONS BY UN BODIES TO THE AYATOLLAH KHOMEINI'S DEATH EDICT AGAINST RUSHDIE

20. The Committee on Economic, Social, and Cultural Rights dealt explicitly with the "Rushdie Affair" in its concluding observations on Iran's initial report.[9]

21. On October 30, 1992, during the examination of Iran's second periodic report at its forty-sixth session, three experts of the Human Rights Committee[10] raised the case of Salman Rushdie, concerning the incompatibility between the International Covenant on Civil and Political Rights and the Ayatollah Khomeini's 1989 *fatwa*.[11]

22. On April 7, 1993, at the forty-seventh session, the representative of Iran's Judicature, Hussain Mehrpour, replied, "Several members had referred to the death sentence passed on the writer Salman Rushdie and had requested an explanation of its relationship to the Covenant. The Western world must understand that Mr. Rushdie's book was a severe insult not to Iran but to Islam and to the Prophet, a person considered by all the Islamic world as the messenger of God's Word. That insult had caused a reaction in many countries besides Iran. . . . Moreover, it was important to point out that the Iranian Parliament

had not passed any law calling for Mr. Rushdie's execution, nor had any court condemned him. Any action taken in response to that decree would be based on an individual's religious belief, not on a formal judicial decision."[12]

23. It is most regrettable that for four years, until 1993, neither the commission nor the subcommission passed a resolution, nor did anything to condemn the *fatwa* or the subsequent public incitements to murder Rushdie. Finally, in its resolution 1993/62, *Situation of Human Rights in the Islamic Republic of Iran*, the commission made a brief reference to it: "*Also expresses its grave concern* that there are continuing threats to the life of a citizen of another State which appears to have the support of the Government of the Islamic Republic of Iran and whose case is mentioned in the report of the Special Rapporteur" (para. 5).

24. A year later, resolution 1994/73 added "to the life of Mr. Salman Rushdie, as well as to individuals associated with his work" (para. 5). This wording remained in resolutions 1995/68 and 1996/84; in 1997/54, after lobbying, two additions were added: "and deeply regrets the increase announced in the bounty offered for the assassination of Mr. Rushdie by the 15 Khordad Foundation" (para. 2(d)); and "*Calls upon* the Government of the Islamic Republic of Iran . . . to provide satisfactory written assurance that it does not support or incite threats to the life of Mr. Rushdie" (para. 3(f)). Resolution 1998/80 went further, stating, "and deeply regrets the failure of the Government to condemn the bounty for the assassination of Mr. Rushdie by the 15 Khordad Foundation" (para. 3(e)); and, "*Calls upon* to provide satisfactory written assurances . . ."(para. 4(i)).

25. Resolution 1999/13 echoed the words of foreign minister Kharazi on September 24, 1998 (para. 7 above): "*Welcomes*: The Assurances given by the Government of the Islamic Republic of Iran that it had no intention of taking any action whatsoever to threaten the life of Mr. Salman Rushdie and those associated with his work or of encouraging or assisting anyone to do so, and that it dissociates itself from any reward offered in this regard and does not support it" (para 1(f)). No reference was made to this matter in the resolutions for 2000 and 2001 concerning Iran—and nothing since, even though on February 14 of each year the death threat is restated, as in 2004.

26. Today, there is near unanimous agreement in Iran, and elsewhere, that the religious edict against Rushdie is a permanent decree, one

which both constitutes government policy and at the same time is beyond the competence of the government to change. Therefore, neither the Iranian president nor the foreign minister can speak for the government of Iran on this subject. Theoretically, only the Ayatollah Khamanei, successor to the Ayatollah Khomeini, could act, and he has steadfastly supported the death edict.

27. The "Rushdie Affair" began as a somewhat exotic matter that many—especially in the United Nations—tried to ignore. But the infection festered, eating away at international norms, attacking the very heart of the International Bill of Human Rights, particularly the right to freedom of opinion and expression. Waves of Islamist-inspired assassinations have struck several Muslim countries, killing and maiming writers—beginning with Egyptian Nobel laureate for literature Naguib Mahfouz—journalists, artists, intellectuals, and anyone considered by religious extremists as a "heretic" or an "apostate," and therefore a legitimate target for arbitrary execution.

28. Regarding "insults against Islam," there has been an escalation of death edicts emanating from Iran and elsewhere, against individuals and entire groups—even incitements to genocide by Ayatollah Muhammad Yazdi, the head of the Iranian judiciary, in a sermon on July 4, 1997, broadcast by Tehran's Voice of the Islamic Republic of Iran.[13] Since 1989, a new form of religious-inspired terrorism has developed, leading to the September 11, 2001, climacteric, all of which has been characterized by some as a "clash of civilizations" and differently by others.[14]

29. The Association for World Education maintains that an authoritative revocation of the Ayatollah Khomeini's *fatwa/hukm* of February 14, 1989, which arbitrarily sentenced Rushdie to death—to be executed by any Muslim or non-Muslim assassin—can no longer be postponed at UN bodies. We therefore call upon the Organization of the Islamic Conference (OIC) to make a clear and firm declaration indicating that the fifteen-year-old *fatwa/hukm* is not compatible with international human rights norms that are binding.

30. The Association for World Education also calls upon the Commission on Human Rights at its sixtieth session to condemn the February 14, 2004, reconfirmation of the arbitrary death edict of the Ayatollah Khomeini by the 15 Khordad Foundation, which annually declares it to be valid, as well as the announcement by a new "committee for the glorification of the martyrs of the Muslim world,"

which has offered a further bounty of $100,000 to any assassin of Salman Rushdie.

31. An appropriate declaration by the ambassador of the Islamic Republic of Iran—on behalf of Iran's president or spiritual leader—would give hope to many millions worldwide, who will never accept that any authority, whether religious or secular, can arbitrarily condemn a person from any country to death by decree—for either heresy or apostasy, for an opinion or a book.

32. We wish to conclude by endorsing the words of Libyan ambassador Najat Al-Hajjaji, the chairperson of the fifty-ninth session of the Commission on Human Rights, pronounced at last year's tenth meeting of special rapporteurs and representatives, independent experts, and chairpersons of Working Groups of the Special Procedures of the Commission on Human Rights and of the Advisory Services Programme (June 23–27, 2003). This opinion is particularly applicable to the "Rushdie Affair," especially with regard to human rights mechanisms and the special procedures: "I would like to exhort all of you to continue your work. Speak freely as you have done in the past. Continue to do so in the interests of truth, of justice, irrespective of the pressure that is brought to bear upon you by Governments. Even if what you say is contrary to the interests of the Government, there are thousands, millions, of victims who look upon the Commission, the special procedures, as the conscience of humanity, of mankind. So I would just like to exhort you once again, urge you, to continue. . . . Stand firm, let nothing stand in the way of truth."[15]

NOTES

1. *AFP*, February 15, 2004.

2. Official IRNA news agency, as reported by Reuters on February 14, 2003.

3. Ayatollah Javardi-Amoli is quoted as saying in February 1997, "This is not a *fatwa* which died with the death of the religious leader who issued it. . . . It is a *hukm* which is permanent and it will stay in place until it is carried out."

4. Daniel Pipes, *The Rushdie Affair: The Novel, the Ayatollah, and the West* (New York: Birch Lane Press, 1990), pp. 27, 30.

5. E/CN.4/1990/22, para. 254.

6. *Time International*, May 24, 1993.

7. *Iran Times*, June 26, 1992.

8. *Iran Times*, November 13 and 20, 1992.

9. E/1994/23-E/C.12/1993/19, para. 128.

10. Rhein A. Myullerson, Christine Chanet, and Rosalyn Higgins.

11. 1196th meeting, paras. 23–32; CCPR/12, vol. 1, pp. 104–105.

12. 1230th meeting, para. 9; CCPR/12, Vol. 1, p. 246.

13. BBC World Service report; see written statement E/CN.4/Sub.2/1997/NGO/15.

14. German foreign minister Joschka Fischer prefers the "definition of the world's central problem . . . as 'the new totalitarianism' of 'destructive jihadist terrorism.'" See the recent article by John Vinocur, "Europe's Old Axis Has Lost Its Luster," *International Herald Tribune*, February 19, 2004, p. 8. See also Samuel P. Huntington, *The Clash of Civilizations and the Remaking of World Order* (New York: Simon and Schuster, 1996); and Bat Ye'or, *Islam and Dhimmitude: Where Civilizations Collide* (Cranbury, NJ: Associated University Presses, 2002).

15. E/CN.4/2004/4. Consultations with the expanded bureau of the Commission on Human Rights, para. 44, p. 14.

39.
BLASPHEMY LEGISLATION IN PAKISTAN'S PENAL CODE

1. The Association for World Education submits the present written statement in memory of a prominent human rights defender, the late John Joseph, bishop of Faisalabad, chairman of the Human Rights Commission established by the Catholic Bishops' Conference of Pakistan, who killed himself on May 6, 1998, to protest the continued application of Pakistan's blasphemy laws.

2. Bishop Joseph's suicide was related to the "blasphemy" case of Ayub Masih, who had been incarcerated in solitary confinement since October 14, 1996, and sentenced to death on April 27, 1998, by Sessions Court Judge Rana Abdul Ghaffar. Distinguished lawyer Asma Jahangir, who had secured the release of Salamat and Rehmet Masih in 1995 on a similar charge of blasphemy, is also involved in the defense of Ayub Masih. The appeal against the death sentence is still pending in the High Court.

3. A few hours before his tragic death, Bishop Joseph publicly declared that the charges were false and were merely concocted to force fifteen Christian families to drop a local land dispute with Muslim villagers. In his last circular letter, published on May 7, in the Lahore edition of the newspaper *Dawn*, he strongly urged Church leaders, parliamentarians, Muslims, Christians, Hindus, and all segments of society in Pakistan to support the campaign for the repeal of the iniquitous blasphemy laws. This legislation violates the international instruments that were signed and ratified by Pakistan.

This NGO written statement, E/CN.4/Sub.2/1998/NGO/3 (July 1998), was submitted by the AWE to the fiftieth session of the UNCHR's Sub-Commission and was posted on the UN Web site. It was prepared by David G. Littman and René Wadlow.

BACKGROUND TO THE INTRODUCTION OF THE BLASPHEMY LEGISLATION

4. During the presidency of Gen. Zia ul-Haq (1977–1988), a Federal Shariat (legal) Court (FSC), was instituted, which was granted "jurisdiction over convictions or acquittals from district courts in cases involving . . . Islamic criminal laws; exclusive jurisdiction to hear [petitions] . . . challenging 'any law or provision of law' as repugnant to the Holy Koran; exclusive jurisdiction to examine 'any law or provision of law' for repugnancy to the Holy Koran"[1] Although non-Muslims may not appear before the Shariat Court, they are subject to its rulings.

5. President Haq introduced the *hudood* (punishment) ordinances in 1984, which "define crimes against Islam" and "enforce punishment for those who commit such crimes." In *hudood* cases, the testimony of a non-Muslim is considered to be worth half that of a Muslim. Section 298-B and 298-C of the Pakistan Penal Code singles out, pejoratively, the "non-Muslim" minority group Ahamadiyya—considered by Sunni theologians to be heretics.

THE SUBCOMMISSION'S 1985 REACTION TO ORDINANCE XX (1984)

6. Ordinance XX was incorporated into the 1985 constitution. That year, the subcommission adopted resolution 1985/21, in which it

1. *Expresses its grave concern* at the promulgation by Pakistan of Ordinance XX of 28 April 1984 which, prima facie, violates the right to liberty and security of the person, the right to freedom of thought, expression, conscience and religion, the right of religious minorities to profess and practise their own religion, and the right to an effective legal remedy;

2. *Further expresses its grave concern* that persons charged with and arrested for violations of Ordinance XX have been reportedly subjected to various punishments and confiscation of personal property, and that the affected groups as a whole have been subjected to discrimination in employment and education and to the defacement of their religious property;

3. *Requests* the Commission on Human Rights to call on the Government of Pakistan to repeal Ordinance XX and to restore the human rights and fundamental freedoms of all persons in its jurisdiction.

7. In 1986 the government of Pakistan used the power granted it by Ordinance XX to insert section 295-C into the Pakistan Legal Code, making the death sentence mandatory for anyone convicted of blaspheming the prophet Muhammad. From 1986 to 1993, over two hundred Ahmadis were charged with "blasphemy," but none were convicted. Soon this law, originally directed at the Ahmadis, was being used primarily against Christians and also against Muslims, several of whom have been convicted.

8. In 1993 a further bill, generally supported by anti-Shia groups as a means of persecuting Shias, was introduced to extend the law to the defiling of the Prophet's family and companions.

9. An editorial in the Pakistani newspaper the *Frontier Post* stated,"Now, not only has theocracy been presented as a model for law and procedure, but discrimination on the basis of religion has become a part of the law."[2]

10. On February 10, 1995, the United Nations special procedures system was used to send an urgent appeal to the government of Pakistan regarding the cases of a thirteen-year-old illiterate boy, Salamat Masih—accused of having written blasphemous words on a mosque wall—and his uncle, Rehmet Masih. A reply was received within four days, and the international outcry in this case resulted in their release from prison; they fled to Europe.

11. Over a dozen Christians have been jailed under the blasphemy laws, four of whom were reported killed in detention. Ayub Masih is the fourth Christian to be condemned to death; the other three were acquitted on appeal and fled Pakistan. This is the background for Bishop Joseph's tragic "sacrificial death."

A Death Sentence for "Blasphemy" Is Illegitimate

12. The Association for World Education questions the legitimacy of Pakistan's blasphemy laws under the international instruments, the 1981 Declaration on the Elimination of All Forms of Intolerance and of Discrimination Based on Religion or Belief, and fundamental human rights standards.

13. In addition to questioning the legitimacy of such blasphemy laws, our association wishes to raise questions concerning the conditions in which trials for blasphemy are conducted: the right to a fair and

speedy trial; the independence of the judiciary; the safety of defense lawyers; and the holding of the trial in a serene atmosphere, isolated from political, social, and religious pressures. We ask the subcommission to undertake inquiries as to whether Pakistan's courts are meeting these international human rights standards in all trials related to charges of blasphemy.

14. In particular, we wish to stress five points in regard to blasphemy charges under the section 295 of Pakistan's Penal Code: (a) blasphemy, as a civil crime under section 295-B and 295-C, is tried in civil courts, where only Muslim judges may hear cases; (b) the death penalty is a punishment for blasphemy under section 295-C; (c) blasphemy accusations may be applied to non-Muslims, whose testimony is given less weight in court than Muslims; (d) blasphemy charges may be used to mask other, more material or political, motivations; and (e) blasphemy charges are being increasingly used as a way of limiting discussion and debate—what has been called since 1989 the "Rushdie syndrome."

15. In a statement on August 21, 1992, to the forty-fourth session of the subcommission, a member of the subcommission, Claire Palley, declared, "This is not a century—and certainly the twenty-first century is not one—in which the death penalty should exist for heresy. I hope the Sub-Commission will, as a body, make it clear that both *fatwa*s and the death penalty for heresy are themselves gross violations of human rights."[3]

A SUBCOMMISSION RESOLUTION ON "BLASPHEMY" CHARGES IS A NECESSITY

16. In the same spirit, the Association for World Education calls on the fiftieth session of the subcommission to adopt a resolution along the lines that "this is not a century, nor is the twenty-first century one, in which the death penalty should exist for blasphemy."[4]

17. The use of an accusation of "blasphemy"—an ill-defined term that can be expanded to mean anything that any accuser dislikes—merits serious attention. Some accusations of "blasphemy" can be ill-disguised death threats—as was the case in 1994 regarding the UN special rapporteur for Sudan, Gaspar Biro—and when they are not, they can be considered as sufficiently dangerous to lead to kowtowing, and even censorship at the United Nations.

18. The Association for World Education has provided essential facts about the "UN Blasphemy Affair" of April 18, 1997, in a subcommission written statement,[5] in several oral statements made to last year's subcommission, to the fifty-fourth session of the commission, and more fully in two out of three articles recently published.
19. Such rigid doctrinal accusations of "blasphemy"—charges that are constantly revived to the detriment of basic human rights in Pakistan and elsewhere—merit unreserved condemnation by the United Nations now.

NOTES

1. Charles H. Kennedy, "Repugnancy to Islam—Who Decides? Islam and Legal Reform in Pakistan," *International and Comparative Law* 41, part 4 (October 1992): 772. [See a recent study by Patrick Sookhdeo, *A People Betrayed: The Impact of Islamization on the Christian Community in Pakistan* (Pewsey, Wilt. UK: Isaac Publishing, 2002).]

2. Peter Jacob Dildar, "Minorities under the Law," *Frontier Post* (Islamabad, Pakistan), June 18, 1994.

3. Verbatim transcription; see also E/CN.4/Sub.2/1992/SR.27, paras. 70–71.

4. René Wadlow and David G. Littman, "Dangerous Censorship of a U.N. Special Rapporteur," *Justice*, no. 14 (September 1997): 10–17 (reprinted in this book as chapter 29); "Blasphemy at the United Nations?" *Middle East Quarterly* (December 1997): 85–86; "UN Special Rapporteur Censured on 'Islamist and Arab Antisemitism,'" *Midstream* (February–March 1998): 8–13.

5. E/CN.4/Sub.2/1997/NGO/3.

UNIVERSALITY OF
4O. INTERNATIONAL HUMAN
RIGHTS TREATIES

David G. Littman

Our written statement entitled *International Bill of Human Rights: Univer-sality/International Standards/National Practices*[1] concludes with the following passage from the new high commissioner's ground-breaking report to the commission:[2] "I. THE NEED FOR STRONGER PROTEC-TION OF HUMAN RIGHTS. In the 55 years since the Universal Declara-tion of Human Rights was adopted, the international community has devel-oped a solid body of international norms of human rights and humanitarian law aimed at the tangible protection of human rights. A global consensus has been strengthened around the universality and the irreducibility of human rights" (para. 7). "An adequate national protection system is one in which international human rights norms are reflected in the national constitution and in national legislation" (para. 11).

A key aspect of universality as a fundamental basis of world human rights law was strongly stressed in General Comment no. 18 of the thirty-seventh session (1989) of the Human Rights Committee, under *Non-discrimination*: "Non-discrimination, together with equality before the law and equal protection of law without any discrimination, constitute a basic and general principle relating to the protection of human rights. Thus article 2, paragraph 1 of the International Covenant on Civil and Political Rights obligates each State party to respect and ensure to all persons . . . the rights recognized in the Covenant without distinction of any kind, such as race, colour, sex, language, religion, political or other opinion, national or social origin, property, birth or other status."[3]

This NGO oral statement was prepared and delivered by David G. Littman for the AWE on July 30, 2003, at the fifty-fifth session of the UN Sub-Commission on Human Rights. This text was circulated with written statement E/CN.4/Sub.2/2003/NGO/15, reprinted in this book as chapter 42.

General Comment no. 22, adopted by the Human Rights Committee, 48th session (1993) declares:

> The right to freedom of thought, conscience and religion (which includes the freedom to hold beliefs) in article. 18.1 is far-reaching and profound.
> . . .
>
> Article 18 protects theistic, non-theistic and atheistic beliefs, as well as the right not to profess any religion or belief. The term "belief" and "religion" are to be broadly construed.
>
> Article 18 is not limited in its application to traditional religions or to religions and beliefs with institutional characteristics or practices analogous to those of traditional religions. The Committee therefore views with concern any tendency to discriminate against any religion or belief for any reason, including the fact that they are newly established, or represent religious minorities that may be the subject of hostility on the part of a predominant religious community.
>
> Article 18 distinguishes the freedom of thought, conscience, religion or belief from the freedom to manifest religion or belief. It does not permit any limitations whatsoever on the freedom of thought and conscience or on the freedom to have or adopt a religion or belief of one's choice. These freedoms are protected unconditionally, as is the right of everyone to hold opinions without interference in article 19.1. In accordance with articles 18.2 and 19, no one can be compelled to reveal his thoughts or adherence to a religion or belief.[4]

The aims of article 18 are further developed in the Declaration on the Elimination of All Forms of Intolerance and of Discrimination Based on Religion or Belief, proclaimed by the General Assembly in 1981, with concern for "manifestations of intolerance and by the existence of discrimination in matters of religion or belief still in evidence in some areas of the world."

Twenty years later the situation is more alarming. On this grave matter, we wish to call attention to an appeal, dated today [July 30, 2003], to be submitted tomorrow by the Barnabas Fund (UK) to the Acting High Commissioner for Human Rights, the Chairpersons of the Human Rights Committee, the CHR, the subcommission, and the special rapporteur on religious intolerance: "The Suffering of Muslims Who Adopt Another Belief." It deals with apostasy in Islam and criminal pressures against those who are accused of changing their belief. Their appeal also refers to a motion of the British Parliament,[5] which has already received the signatures of 45 MPs [the total reached 92 by November 2003]. On this religious freedom and belief issue, the motion states: "That this House supports liberal Muslims, human rights campaigners and others who are calling for an end to cruel traditional punishments for apostasy."

In a similar context, we wish to recommend a remarkable book, *Leaving Islam: Apostates Speak Out*, by Ibn Warraq, containing moving and courageous testimonies from Muslims accused of "apostasy" and then physically menaced.[6]

This commonplace situation should neither be ignored by the UN secretary general, the high commissioner for human rights, nor by the commission and the subcommission, nor by special rapporteurs and human rights treaty bodies! Our appeal will also be delivered to the chairman and all members of the Human Rights Committee currently in session, whose comments have been quoted extensively here on this crucial matter. We therefore call upon the subcommission to take action now through an appropriate resolution.

On the fundamental right of freedom of thought and speech and religious tolerance, we shall conclude with the words of Spinoza, a glowing beacon of light, from the seventeenth century:

> I have thus shown:
> —That it is impossible to deprive men of the liberty of saying what they think. . . .
> —Every man should think what he likes and say what he thinks.[7]

NOTES

1. E/CN.4/Sub. 2/2003/NGO/15.

2. E/CN.4/2003/14.

3. HRI/GEN/1/Rev.6 of 22 May 2003, p.146.

4. UN Human Rights Committee, 48th sess., General Comment no. 22, pp. 155–56.

5. Early Day Motion 1290, May 22, 2003.

6. Ibn Warraq, *Leaving Islam: Apostates Speak Out* (Amherst, NY: Prometheus Books, 2003).

7. Conclusion of *Tractus Theologico-Political Treatise of 1670*. For the English translation given, see R. H. M. Elwes, *The Works of Spinoza*, vol. 1 (New York: Dover, 1955), pp. 264–65.

41. HOMAGE TO UN HIGH COMMISSIONER SERGIO VIEIRA DE MELLO

David G. Littman

Last year, on March 21, 2003, we concluded a joint statement under item 4 by warmly welcoming the new high commissioner for human rights, Sergio Vieira de Mello: "Sir, you have a long task before you, not an easy one, but we are confident that with sustained collective efforts you will overcome, always bearing in mind Shakespeare's advice, in the words of John of Gaunt: 'Small showers last long, but sudden storms are short;/He tires betimes that spurs too fast betimes.'"[1]

Today, we wish to pay a worthy homage by quoting key passages from last year's groundbreaking report, E/CN.4/2003/14, by the high commissioner.

However utopian it may sound here, point 5 of the introduction has a very pertinent message: "Membership of the Commission on Human Rights must carry responsibilities. I therefore wonder whether the time has not come for the Commission itself to develop a code of guidelines for access to membership of the Commission and a code of conduct for members while they serve on the Commission. After all, the Commission on Human Rights has a duty to humanity and the members of the Commission must themselves set the example of adherence to the international human rights norms—in practice as well as in law."

Indeed, a courageous suggestion from a courageous man, and appreciated by many NGOs. . . .

This NGO joint oral statement was prepared and delivered by David G. Littman on April 19, 2004 (item 18), for the Association for World Education (AWE), the International Humanist and Ethical Union (IHEU), and the World Union for Progressive Judaism (WUPJ), at the sixtieth session of the UNCHR. This is an abridged version, omitting some passages. The entire text was circulated at the UNCHR with AWE's written statement E/CN.4/Sub.2/2003/NGO/15, International Bill of Human Rights: Universality/International Standards/ National Practices reprinted in this book as chapter 42.

We also endorse the conclusion in paragraph 55: "Without universal respect for human rights, the vision of the Charter of a world of peace grounded in respect for human rights and economic and social justice will remain an illusion. Let us vindicate the Charter's vision by being faithful to the universal implementation of human rights. In doing so we shall continue in the direction of history, rather than allowing ourselves to be diverted from the course we know to be just."

Our association's written statement entitled *International Bill of Human Rights: Universality/International Standards/National Practices* provides much useful data on this matter.[2]

Mr. Chairman, Acting High Commissioner for Human Rights [Dr. Bertrand Ramcharan], you will remember that in his inaugural statement on March 17 2003, Sergio referred with dismay to terrorists who would kill anyone at any time in any place—and yes! they killed him five months later! To Osama bin Laden—who in his message just last week once again threatened the United Nations, as well as the United States and others[3]—and to all the bloodthirsty jihadists, who dare to champion (and defame) Islam by killing and mutilating in Allah's name while threatening the entire world by their crimes against humanity, our answer can only be Winston Churchill's.

Speaking [to the City Carlton Club] on June 28, 1939, and referring to Hitler's "March of Folly" only two months before World War II began, which resulted in fifty million deaths, Churchill declared, "Is he going to blow up the world or not? The world is a very heavy thing to blow up! An extraordinary man at a pinnacle of power may create a great explosion, and yet the civilised world may remain unshaken. The enormous fragments and splinters of the explosion may clatter down upon his head and destroy him . . . but the world will go on."

We should all make it clear here to those "jihadist bombers"—the term *suicide bomber* is inaccurate—that the civilized world will never surrender to their vile threats. Only a total victory over such ignominious religious depravity and terror will bring salvation for the free world, for free people—and for those still to be freed! We ask the commission—in a true homage to Sergio Vieira de Mello—to make that point crystal clear. Sergio would have appreciated it—and, surely, Churchill's words too!

NOTES

1. *Richard II*, act 2, scene 1, lines 35–36.

2. E/CN.4/Sub.2/2003/NGO/15; reprinted in this book as chapter 42.

3. Al-Jazeera television (Qatar) and Al-Arabiya television (United Arab Emirates), April 15, 2004; English trans. from Arabic in "Osama Bin Laden Speech Offers Peace Treaty with Europe, Says Al-Qa'ida 'Will Persist in Fighting' the U.S.," MEMRI Special Dispatch 695, April 15, 2004, Middle East Media Research Institute Web site, http://www.memri.org/bin/articles.cgi?Page=archives&Area=sd&ID=SP69504 (accessed September 27, 2004). See also "Terrorism (Al-Irhaab): The Fashion of the 21st Century," al-Muhajiroun Web site, March 31, 2004.

INTERNATIONAL BILL OF
42. HUMAN RIGHTS

Universality/
International Standards/
National Practices

1. The secretary general's note on specific human rights issues indicates that as of June 1, 2003, 146 states had ratified, acceded to, or succeeded to the International Covenant on Economic, Social and Cultural Rights; and 149 states to the International Covenant on Civil and Political Rights.[1] Section 5 of this note relates to the "Effective Implementation of International Instruments on Human Rights, including Reporting Obligations of States Parties to the United Nations Instruments in the Field of Human Rights"; it also mentions the Meeting of Chairpersons of Human Rights Treaty Bodies of 2002 and that of June 23–27, 2003.

2. The principal aim of the 1948 Universal Declaration of Human Rights (UDHR) was to create a framework for a universal code based on mutual consent. The early years of the United Nations were overshadowed by the division between the Western and Communist conceptions of human rights, although neither side called into question the concept of universality. The debate centered on *which* rights—political, economic, and social—were to be included among the universal instruments. In the 1960s, with the arrival of a large

---

NGO written statement E/CN.4/Sub.2/2003/NGO/15—submitted by the AWE to the fifty-fifth session of the UN Sub-Commission on Human Rights (July 2003) and posted on the UN Web site—is based on an article by David G. Littman, "Human Rights and Human Wrongs: Sharia Can't Be Exception to International Human-Rights Norms," *National Review Online*, January 19, 2003, http://www.nationalreview.com/script/printpage.asp?ref=/comment/comment-littman011903.asp (accessed September 27, 2004). This text—with additions by the author—was edited with pertinent modifications by René Wadlow. It was circulated at the fifty-fifth session of the Sub-Commission on Human Rights and at the sixtieth session of the UNCHR, with the respective oral statements (July 30, 2003, and April 19, 2004).

number of third world states that had not been present in 1948, there were discussions as to whether new states were bound by covenants that had been adopted before they became independent and joined the United Nations. In general, by 1975 (the Helsinki Accords), consensus was reached on the universality of human rights.

3. A crucial part of the debate has consisted in bringing national legislation into conformity with the universal human rights standards, as defined in what is usually called the International Bill of Human Rights, comprising the UDHR; the International Covenant on Economic, Social, and Cultural Rights; and the Covenant on Civil and Political Rights. Usually, states that ratified, or acceded to, the international covenants modified their legislation if it was not in conformity.

4. Nevertheless, there are states that consider that the UDHR is not a universal standard for all legislation, and they continue a policy of selective conformity. For instance, the Web site of Saudi Arabia's embassy in London contains a new document titled, "Saudi Arabia—Questions of Human Rights." There, in a response to a question whether Saudi Arabia accepts "universally accepted human rights," it is officially stated, "No, Saudi Arabia doesn't accept that. Some human rights are controversial, and yet others are an anathema to a large portion of humanity."[2]

5. Likewise, a bill in the Iranian parliament to raise the marriage age for girls from nine to fourteen was refused three years ago by religious groups on the grounds it would be against Islamic teachings to make changes to the current law, since "Islamic scholars had put a lot of efforts into these laws" (Muhammad Ali Sheikh, quoted in parliament.) Yet, in 1994, Iran had signed and ratified the Convention on the Rights of the Child, whose article 1 specifies, "For the purposes of the present Convention, a child means every human being below the age of eighteen years unless under the law applicable to the child, majority is attained earlier."[3] After the 1979 Islamic revolution, Sharia law had effectively halved the girl child's marriage age to nine years.

6. When encouraged to bring their national legislation into agreement with the UDHR, some states have responded negatively. In his first report, dated February 1, 1994, the then special rapporteur on Sudan, Gaspar Biro, called upon "the Government of Sudan to bring its legislation into accordance with international instruments to which it is

a party. "On February 18, 1994, the Sudanese ambassador, Ali Ahmed Sahloul, sent a letter to all permanent representatives and observers at the United Nations in Geneva. This followed a similarly worded text circulated by the Sudanese delegation the previous day at the Commission on Human Rights, boldly titled "Attack on Islam." In its official "Comments on the Report," Sudan declared, "All Muslims are ordained by God to subject themselves to Sharia Laws and that matter could not be contested or challenged by a Special Rapporteur or other UN agencies or representatives."[4]

7. The continuing need to have international human rights norms reflected in national legislation has been one of the themes of the World Decade for Human Rights Education, in which the Association for World Education has been active.

8. In addition to the issue of selective conformity within national legislation, there has been a greater challenge to the universalistic framework of the UDHR with the presentation of an alternative, more narrowly based human rights system. This alternative framework was presented primarily by the Islamic Republic of Iran, shortly after the 1979 Islamic revolution.[5]

9. Already at the thirty-sixth session of the UN General Assembly, in 1981, the representative of Iran expressed the Iranian government's position, reaffirmed at the GA's thirty-ninth session, in 1984: "It recognises no legal tradition apart from Islamic law. . . . Conventions, declarations and resolutions or decisions of international organisations, which were contrary to Islam, had no validity in the Islamic Republic of Iran. . . . The Universal Declaration of Human Rights, which represented a secular understanding of the Judeo-Christian traditions, could not be implemented by Muslims and did not accord with the system of values recognised by the Islamic Republic of Iran." If a choice had to be made between its stipulations and "the divine law of the country," Iran would always choose Islamic law. Since then, Iran has led the constant effort to modify the UDHR.[6]

10. These efforts led to the Universal Islamic Declaration of Human Rights, proclaimed at UNESCO in 1981, and to the Cairo Declaration of Human Rights in Islam (CDHRI), adopted on August 5, 1990, in Cairo by the nineteenth Islamic Conference of Foreign Ministers of the 45 (now 57) Member States of the Organization of the Islamic Conference (OIC), subsequent to the Report of the

Meeting of the Committee of Legal Experts, held in Tehran from December 26–28, 1989.[7]

11. It is significant that article 24 of the English CDHRI states, "All the rights and freedoms stipulated in the Declaration are subject to the Islamic Sharia," and article 25 confirms, "The Islamic Shari'ah is the only source of reference for the explanation or clarification of any of the articles of this Declaration." Thus it is clear that the Sharia law has supremacy, and the 1990 Cairo Declaration primacy—in the view of its authors—over the International Bill of Human Rights (the UDHR included) and all other UN covenants.

12. When the CDHRI was tabled for adoption at the Summit Meeting of OIC Heads of State and Government, held in Dakar on December 9, 1991, the Geneva-based International Commission of Jurists (ICJ) warned in a press release, "The ICJ wishes, however, to call the attention of the Muslim communities and world public opinion to the negative implications which might follow the Summit's adoption of the Islamic Draft Declaration on Human Rights in Islam, as elaborated on 5 August 1990 in Cairo during the Nineteenth Islamic Conference of Foreign Ministers." In February 1992, its secretary general—Adama Dieng, a preeminent Senegalese jurist—declared in a joint statement to the Commission on Human Rights on behalf of the ICJ and the Paris-based International Federation for Human Rights, in regard to the 1990 CDHRI:

    i. It gravely threatens the intercultural consensus on which the international human rights instruments are based;

    ii. It introduces, in the name of the defense of human rights, an intolerable discrimination against both non-Muslims and women;

    iii. It reveals a deliberately restrictive character in regard to certain fundamental rights and freedoms, to the point that certain essential provisions are below the legal standard in effect in a number of Muslim countries;

    iv. It confirms under cover of the "Islamic Sharia (Law)" the legitimacy of practices, such as corporal punishment, that attack the integrity and dignity of the human being.[8]

13. Representatives of the Islamic Republic of Iran have continued to present the CDHRI as an alternative framework for human rights.

Iranian foreign minister Kamal Kharazi—the first speaker at the Jubilee Commemoration of the UDHR to address the commission on March 17, 1998—called for a "revision of the UN's Universal Declaration of Human Rights." On November 9–10, 1998, the Office of the High Commissioner for Human Rights jointly hosted a seminar with the OIC, titled, "Enriching the Universality of Human Rights: Islamic Perspectives on the Universal Declaration of Human Rights," at which twenty Muslim experts on Islam presented papers.[9]

14. In his opening address the secretary-general of the OIC, Azeddine Laraki, stated, "An elite of Muslim experts in the field of Sharia and Law are thus being offered the opportunity to present researches which expound the Islamic perspective as to human rights and recall the contribution of Islam to the laying of the foundations of these rights through which Islam aimed at leading people out of the obscurities and into enlightenment, at ensuring dignity in their life and non-submission to anyone but God, and at asserting their freedom and their right to justice and equality on the basis of the two sources of Islamic Shari'a: Qur'an and Sunna and on Fiqh jurisprudence, away from politicking, demagogy or reliance on local practices and mores which are subject to variations according to historical legacies."[10]

15. In a prior letter to all delegations, the then High Commissioner for Human Rights, Mary Robinson, explained, "We have agreed that for the purpose of this seminar, Islam is understood in terms of *'Sharia'* (*Qur'an* and *Hadith*) and not in terms of tradition or practices that may vary and mix with historical heritage."

16. A follow-up seminar, organized by the OIC alone—Symposium of Human Rights in Islam—was held March 14–15, 2002, just prior to the fifty-eighth session of the Commission on Human Rights. It covered much the same ground as the 1998 seminar. The first paper, titled "War against Terrorism: Impact on Human Rights," was delivered by Ahmad al-Mufti; after having threatened Biro in 1994 and 1995, he had been reprimanded implicitly in a UN General Assembly resolution (December 5, 1995). No longer a senior official in the Sudanese Justice Department, he had become director general of the Khartoum International Centre for Human Rights. His written paper concluded with an affirmation: "We believe that Islam adds new positive dimensions to human rights, since, unlike inter-

national instruments, it attributes them to a divine source thereby adding a new moral motivation for complying with them."[11]

17. On March 15, 2002, the high commissioner addressed the OIC Conference Symposium. In her statement she declared, under the heading "A Greater Need for an Understanding of Islam,"

> No one can deny that at its core Islam is entirely consonant with the principles of fundamental human rights, including human dignity, tolerance, solidarity and quality. Numerous passages from the Qur'an and sayings of the Prophet Muhammad will testify to this. No one can deny, from a historic perspective, the revolutionary force that is Islam, which bestowed rights upon women and children long before similar recognition was afforded in other civilisations. Custom and tradition have tended to limit these rights, but as more Islamic States ratify the Convention for the Elimination of Discrimination against Women, ways forward for women are being found and women are leading the debate. And no one can deny the acceptance of the universality of human rights by Islamic States.

18. At the back of the room where she spoke could be found various written statements by the participants, as well as copies of the 1990 Cairo Declaration of Human Rights in Islam[12]—but not the 1948 Universal Declaration of Human Rights, normally available in five official languages.

19. To date, no other religiously based human rights declarations have been put forward in discussions at the United Nations. Rather, the universality of the UDHR is increasingly stressed.

20. Moreover, on September 14, 2000—in a reply to the Association for World Education's formal request concerning the inexplicable inclusion of the CDHRI in the UN's 1997 volume 2 of *International Instruments*—the legal advisor to the then high commissioner confirmed the official UN opinion: "The Member States which have acceded to and ratified United Nations Human Rights Conventions remain bound, under all circumstances, by the provisions of those texts, as well as the *erge omnes* obligations under customary international law."

21. Today, we see a broad international consensus that the UDHR should be the common framework for all states as reflected both in their national legislation and in their dealings with citizens of other states. This consensus was clearly stressed by the new HCHR,

Sergio Vieira de Mello, in his groundbreaking report to the fifty-ninth commission:[13]

I. THE NEED FOR STRONGER PROTECTION OF HUMAN RIGHTS. "In the 55 years since the Universal Declaration of Human Rights was adopted, the international community has developed a solid body of international norms of human rights and humanitarian law aimed at the tangible protection of human rights. A global consensus has been strengthened around the universality and the irreducibility of human rights:[14] "An adequate national protection system is one in which international human rights norms are reflected in the national constitution and in national legislation."[15]

NOTES

1. E/CN.4/Sub.2/2003/25.
2. See "Saudi Arabia—Questions of Human Rights," Royal Embassy of Saudi Arabia, London, Web site, http://www.saudiembassy.org.uk/publications/questions-of-human-rights/questions-of-human-rights.htm (accessed September 27, 2004). Recent English translation in "The Website of the Saudi Embassy in London," MEMRI Special Dispatch 529, June 26, 2003, Middle East Media Research Institute Web site, http://www.memri.org/bin/articles.cgi?Page=archives&Area=sd&ID=SP52903 (accessed September 27, 2004). For an earlier explanation, see the *Memorandum on Human Rights* (Riyadh, 1972), and *Colloques de Riyad*, by the Saudi Ministry of Information (p. 57), in answer to a request from the UN Human Rights Committee. The document was subsequently removed from the Saudi Web site.
3. "Iran Bill to End Marriage at 9: Guardian Consent Still Needed," *International Herald Tribune*, August 10, 2000.
4. See the UNSR's report, E/CN.4/1994/48 (February 1, 1994), and the government of Sudan's reply, E/CN.4/1994/122 (March 1, 1994).
5. See Sami A. Aldeeb Abu-Sahlieh, "Dialogue conflictuel sur les droits de l'homme entre Occident et Islam," *Islamochristiana* (Vatican City) 17 (1991): 53–82; Gérard Conac and Abdelfattah Amor, eds., *Islam et droits de l'homme*, with a preface by Ibrahima Fall (Paris: Economica, 1994); Anne Elizabeth Mayer, *Islam and Human Rights: Tradition and Politics*, 3rd ed. (Boulder, CO: Westview Press, 1999); Mahmood Monshipouri, "The Muslim World Half a Century after the Universal Declaration of Human Rights: Progress and Obstacles," *Netherlands Quarterly of Human Rights* 16, no. 3 (September 1998): 287–314.
6. See A/C.3/37/SR.56, paras. 53–55 (1982), and A/C.3/39/SR.65, paras. 91–95 (December 7, 1984).
7. See the written statement by the Association for World Education,

E/CN.4/2000/NGO/3; see also resolution 49/19-P on the CDHRI, in *Human Rights: A Compilation of International Instruments*, vol, 2, *Regional Instruments* (New York and Geneva: Office of the High Commissioner of Human Rights, United Nations, 1997), pp. 477–84.

8. International Commission of Jurists press release, Geneva, December 5, 1991; and E/CN.4/1992/SR.20, paras. 17–20.

9. For full details on this question, see David G. Littman, "Universal Human Rights and Human Rights in Islam," *Midstream* 45, no. 2 (February–March 1999): 2–7 (reprinted as chapter 27 in this book); and David G. Littman, "Islamism Grows Stronger at the United Nations," *Middle East Quarterly* (Philadelphia) (September 1999): 59–64 (reprinted as chapter 26).

10. HR/IP/SEM/1999/1, part 1, March 15, 1999, p. 6.

11. OIC/SEM/2002/3, part 2, para. 2, p. 14.

12. Annex to resolution 49/19-P (OIC/SEM/2002/2) (LEG1-5. DISK NO.6/24-ICFM).

13. See E/CN.4/2003/14.

14. Ibid., para. 7.

15. Ibid., para. 11.

43. COMBATING DEFAMATION OF RELIGIONS

Roy Brown

In relation to the adaptation and strengthening of the UN machinery for human rights, the International Humanist and Ethical Union notes the additions made to the text of resolution 2004/L.5, "Combating Defamation of Religions," and in particular to points 3 and 4, which urge states to commit themselves, inter alia, to ensuring equal access to education for all; to refrain from measures leading to racial segregation in schooling, and to ensure access to free primary education for both girls and boys. We regret, however, that the resolution does not call upon states to refrain from measures leading to *religious* segregation in education. The IHEU has long held that unsegregated education for all children, based on our shared human values, regardless of race *or* religion, are the surest safeguard against sectarianism, hatred, and violence in the future.

We also note with some concern that the word *defamation* is undefined in the text of the resolution.[1] We urge the commission and the special rapporteur [on contemporary forms of racism, racial discrimination, xenophobia, and related intolerance] to accept the distinction between *defamation* of a religion and *valid criticism* of its practices, in particular when those practices are in contravention of the Universal Declaration of Human Rights and related instruments. In this regard we note with concern that when, under agenda item 11 [at this sixtieth session of the commission], we raised the issue of the treatment of those accused of apostasy in some Islamic countries, this was construed by one delegation [Pakistan] as an attack on Islam. We

---

This NGO oral statement was prepared and delivered by Roy Brown, the main representative and president of the International Humanist and Ethical Union (IHEU) on April 15, 2004 (item 18), to the sixtieth session of the UNCHR.

respectfully request all states to address honestly and openly [the] concerns [that may be expressed] about genuine abuses of human rights. Accusations of defamation of religion should not be allowed to stifle legitimate criticism [of the laws and practices of any country].

We would also urge the commission and the special rapporteur to be mindful of the distinction between *defamation* of a religion and the publication of academic research into its origins, history, and practices. We all deplore defamation and falsehood. But it would be a tragedy if concerns about *defamation* were allowed to stifle honest inquiry and the publication and expression of factual data. [We would also urge all states to recognize that with so many differing beliefs current in the world, genuine differences will arise. The honest belief of one man should not be treated as defamation of his religion by another.]

Finally, we would urge those states whose laws are based on their understanding of God's law not to treat calls for the change or repeal of any law as defamation of their religion, or worse, as blasphemy or as evidence of apostasy. Allow me to conclude, Mr. Chairman, by quoting Mr. Abdelfattah Amor, [special rapporteur on freedom of religion or belief], who said here [at a parallel session] on April 2, "There are two problems—when religion is the property of the state, and when the state is the property of religion."

NOTE

1. See resolution 2004/L.5.

44. APOSTASY, HUMAN RIGHTS, RELIGION, AND BELIEF— NEW THREATS TO THE FREEDOM OF OPINION AND EXPRESSION

A General Overview of Apostasy

Ibn Warraq

The very notion of apostasy has vanished from the West, where one would talk of being a lapsed Catholic or nonpracticing Christian rather than an apostate. There are certainly no penal sanctions for converting from Christianity to any other religion. In Islamic countries, on the other hand, the issue is far from dead.

The Arabic word for apostate is *murtadd,* the one who turns back from Islam, and apostasy is denoted by *irtidad* and *ridda. Ridda* seems to have been used for apostasing from Islam into unbelief (*kufr* in Arabic), and *irtidad* from Islam to some other religion.[1] A person born of Muslim parents who later rejects Islam is called a *murtadd fitri—fitri*, meaning "natural," can also mean "instinctive, native, inborn, innate." One who converts to Islam and subsequently leaves it is a *murtadd milli*, from *milla*, meaning "religious community." The *murtadd fitri* can be seen as someone unnatural, subverting the natural course of things, whose apostasy is a willful and obstinate act of treason against God and the one and only true creed, and a betrayal and

---

This paper was delivered (in part, over twenty minutes) at a panel discussion on "Apostasy, Human Rights, Religion, and Belief" at the Palais des Nations, Geneva, April 7, 2004, during the sixtieth session of the UNCHR. Sponsors included the Association for World Citizens, the Association for World Education, and the International Humanist and Ethical Union. The full text was widely circulated at the UNCHR and to the UN media. The final section is an NGO oral statement prepared by Ibn Warraq and delivered for him on April 2 (item 11) by Roy Brown at the sixtieth session of the UNCHR.

desertion of the community. The *murtadd milli* is a traitor to the Muslim community and equally disruptive.

Any verbal denial of any principle of Muslim belief is considered apostasy. If one declares, for example, that the universe has always existed from eternity or that God has a material substance, then one is an apostate. If one denies the unity of God or confesses to a belief in reincarnation, one is guilty of apostasy. Certain acts are also deemed acts of apostasy, for example, treating a copy of the Qur'an disrespectfully, by burning it or even soiling it in some way. Some doctors of Islamic law claim that a Muslim becomes an apostate if he or she enters a church, worships an idol, or learns and practices magic. A Muslim becomes an apostate if he defames the Prophet's character, morals, or virtues, or denies Muhammad's prophethood and that he was the seal of the prophets.

QUR'AN

It is clear quite clear that under Islamic law an apostate must be put to death. There is no dispute on this ruling among classical Muslim or modern scholars, and we shall return to the textual evidence for it. Some modern scholars have argued that in the Qur'an the apostate is threatened with punishment only in the next world, as for example in sura 16:106, "Whoso disbelieveth in Allah after his belief—save him who is forced thereto and whose heart is still content with the Faith but whoso findeth ease in disbelief: On them is wrath from Allah. Theirs will be an awful doom." Similarly, in sura 3:90–91, "Lo! those who disbelieve after their (profession of) belief, and afterward grow violent in disbelief, their repentance will not be accepted. And such are those who are astray. Lo! those who disbelieve, and die in disbelief, the (whole) earth full of gold would not be accepted from such an one if it were offered as a ransom (for his soul).Theirs will be a painful doom and they will have no helpers."

However, sura 2:217 is interpreted by no less an authority than al-Shafii (died 820 CE), the founder of one of the four orthodox schools of law of Sunni Islam, to mean that the death penalty should be prescribed for apostates. Sura 2:217 reads, "But whoever of you recants and dies an unbeliever, his works shall come to nothing in this world and the next, and they are the companions of the fire for ever." Al-Thalabi and al-Khazan concur. Al-Razi, in his commentary on sura 2:217, says the apostate should be killed.[2]

Similarly, sura 4:89: "They would have you disbelieve as they themselves have disbelieved, so that you may be all like alike. Do not befriend them until they have fled their homes for the cause of God. If they desert you seize them and put them to death wherever you find them. Look for neither friends nor helpers among them." Baydawi (d. c. 1315–16), in his celebrated commentary on the Qur'an, interprets this passage to mean, "Whosover turns back from his belief (*irtada*), openly or secretly, take him and kill him wheresoever ye find him, like any other infidel. Separate yourself from him altogether. Do not accept intercession in his regard."[3] Ibn Kathir, in his commentary on this passage, quoting al Suddi (d. 745), says that since the unbelievers had manifested their unbelief they should be killed.[4]

Abul Ala Maududi (1903–1979), the founder of the Jamaat-i Islami, is perhaps the most influential Muslim thinker of the twentieth century, being responsible for the Islamic resurgence in modern times. He called for a return to the Qur'an and a purified *sunna* as a way to revive and revitalize Islam. In his book on apostasy in Islam, Maududi argued that even the Qur'an prescribes the death penalty for all apostates. He points to sura 9 for evidence: "But if they repent and establish worship and pay the poor-due, then are they your brethren in religion. We detail our revelations for a people who have knowledge. And if they break their pledges after their treaty (hath been made with you) and assail your religion, then fight the heads of disbelief. Lo! they have no binding oaths in order that they may desist"(9. 11–12)[5]

HADITH

In the Hadith we find many traditions demanding the death penalty for apostasy. According to Ibn Abbas, the Prophet said, "Kill him who changes his religion," or "behead him."[6] The only argument was as to the nature of the death penalty. Bukhari recounts this gruesome tradition:

> Narrated Anas: Some people from the tribe of Ukl came to the Prophet and embraced Islam. The climate of Medina did not suit them, so the Prophet ordered them to go to the (herd of milch) camels of charity to drink their milk and urine (as a medicine). They did so, and after they had recovered from their ailment they turned renegades (reverted from Islam, *irtada*) and killed the shepherd of the camels and took the camels away. The Prophet sent (some people) in their pursuit and so they were caught and brought, and the Prophet ordered that their hands and legs should be cut off and that their eyes should be branded with heated pieces of iron, and that their cut hands and legs should not be cauterised, till they die.[7]

Abu Dawud has collected the following saying of the Prophet: "'Ikrimah said: Ali burned some people who retreated from Islam. When Ibn Abbas was informed of it he said, 'If it had been I, I would not have them burned, for the apostle of Allah said: 'Do not inflict Allah's punishment on anyone.' But I would have killed them on account of the statement of the Apostle of Allah, 'Kill those who change their religion.'"[8]

In other words, kill the apostates (with the sword) but certainly not by burning them—that is Allah's way of punishing transgressors in the next world. According to a tradition of Aisha's, apostates are to be slain, crucified, or banished.[9] Should the apostate be given a chance to repent? Traditions differ enormously. In one tradition, Muadh Jabal refused to sit down until an apostate brought before him had been killed "in accordance with the decision of God and of His Apostle."[10]

Under Muslim law, the male apostate must be put to death, as long as he is an adult and in full possession of his faculties. If a pubescent boy apostatizes, he is imprisoned until he comes of age, when if he persists in rejecting Islam he must be put to death. Drunkards and the mentally disturbed are not held responsible for their apostasy. If a person has acted under compulsion he is not considered an apostate, his wife is not divorced, and his lands are not forfeited. According to Hanafis and Shia, a woman is imprisoned until she repents and adopts Islam once more, but according to the influential Ibn Hanbal, and the Malikis and Shafiites, she is also put to death. In general, execution must be by the sword, though there are examples of apostates tortured to death, or strangled, burned, drowned, impaled, or flayed. Caliph Umar used to tie them to a post and had lances thrust into their hearts, and Sultan Baybars II (1308–1309) made torture legal.

Should attempts be made at conversion? Some jurists accept the distinction between *murtadd fitri* and *murtadd milli* and argue that the former be put to death immediately. Others, leaning on sura 4:137—"Lo! those who believe, then disbelieve and then (again) believe, then disbelieve, and then increase in disbelief, Allah will never pardon them, nor will he guide them unto a way"—insist on three attempts at conversion, or have the apostate imprisoned for three days to begin with. Others argue that one should wait for the cycle of the five times of prayer and ask the apostate to perform the prayers at each. Only if he refuses at each prayer time is the death penalty to be applied. If he repents and embraces Islam once more, he is released.[11]

The *murtadd*, of course, would be denied a Muslim burial, but he suffers other civil disabilities. His property is taken over by the believers; if he returns penitent he is given back what remains. Others argue that the apostate's rights of ownership are merely suspended; only if he dies outside the territory under Islam does he forfeit his property to the Muslim community. If either the husband or wife apostasizes, a divorce takes place ipso facto; the wife is entitled to her whole dower, but no pronouncement of divorce is necessary. According to some jurists, if husband and wife apostasize together their marriage is still valid. However, if either the wife or husband were singly to return to Islam, then their marriage would be dissolved.[12] According to Abu Hanifa, legal activities such as manumission, endowment, testament, and sale are suspended. But not all jurists agree. Some Shii jurists would ask the Islamic law toward apostates to be applied even outside the *dar al-Islam*, in non-Muslim countries.

Finally, according to the Shafiites, it is not only apostasy from Islam that is to be punished with death, but also apostasy from other religions when this is not accompanied by conversion to Islam. For example, a Jew who becomes a Christian will thus have to be put to death since the Prophet has ordered in general that everyone "who adopts any other religion" shall be put to death.[13]

Article 18 of the Universal Declaration of Human Rights [UDHR, 1948] states, "Everyone has the right to freedom of thought, conscience and religion; this right includes freedom to change his religion or belief, and freedom, either alone or in community with others and in public or private, to manifest his religion or belief in teaching, practice, worship and observance."[14]

The clause guaranteeing the freedom to change one's religion was added at the request of the delegate from Lebanon, Charles Malik, who was a Christian.[15] Lebanon had accepted many people fleeing persecution for their beliefs, in particular for having changed their religion. Lebanon especially objected to the Islamic law concerning apostasy. Many Muslim countries, however, objected strongly to the clause regarding the right to change one's religion. The delegate from Egypt, for instance, said that "very often a man changes religion or his convictions under external influences with goals which are not recommendable such as divorce." He added that he feared in proclaiming the liberty to change one's religion or convictions the UDHR would encourage without wishing it "the machinations of certain missions well-known in the East, which relentlessly pursue their efforts with a view to converting to their faith the populations of the East."[16] Significantly, Lebanon was supported by a delegate from Pakistan who belonged to the Ahmadi community, which, ironically, was to be thrown out of the Islamic community in the 1970s for being non-Muslim. In the end all Muslim countries except Saudi Arabia adhered to the UDHR.

During discussions of article 18 in 1966, Saudi Arabia and Egypt wanted to suppress the clause guaranteeing the freedom to change one's religion. Finally a compromise amendment proposed by Brazil and the Philippines was adopted to placate the Islamic countries. Thus, "the freedom to change his religion or belief" was replaced with "the freedom to have or adopt a religion or belief of his choice."[17] Similarly, in 1981, during discussions on the Declaration on the Elimination of All Forms of Intolerance and Discrimination Based on Religion or Belief, Iran, under its new Islamic regime, reminded everyone that Islam punished apostasy by death. The delegate from Iraq, backed up by Syria, speaking on behalf of the Organization of the Islamic Conference, expressed his reservations about any clauses or terms that would contradict the Islamic Sharia, while the delegate from Egypt felt that they had to guard against such a clause being exploited for political ends to interfere in the internal affairs of states.[18]

The various Islamic human rights schemes or declarations—such as the Universal Islamic Declaration of Human Rights (1981) are understandably vague or evasive on the issue of the freedom to change one's religion, since Islam itself clearly forbids apostasy and punishes it with death. As Anne Elizabeth Mayer says, "The lack of support for the principle of freedom of religion in the Islamic human rights schemes is one of the factors that most sharply distinguishes them from the International Bill of Human Rights, which treats freedom of religion as an unqualified right. The [Muslim] authors' unwillingness to repudiate the rule that a person should be executed over a question of religious belief reveals the enormous gap that exists between their mentalities and the modern philosophy of human rights."[19] Islamic human rights schemes are clearly not universal since they introduce a specifically Islamic religious criterion into the political sphere, whereas the UDHR of 1948 places human rights in an entirely secular and universalist framework. The Islamic human rights schemes severely restrict and qualify the rights of individuals, particularly women, non-Muslims, and those, such as apostates, who do not accept Islamic religious orthodoxy.

As for the constitutions of various Muslim countries, many do guarantee freedom of belief (Egypt, 1971; Syria, 1973; Jordan, 1952), some talk of freedom of conscience (Algeria, 1989), and some of freedom of thought and opinion (Mauritania, 1991). Islamic countries, with two exceptions, do not address the issue of apostasy in their penal codes: the two exceptions are Sudan and Mauritania. In the Sudanese Penal Code of 1991, article 126.2, we read, "Whoever is guilty of apostasy is invited to repent over a period to be determined by the tribunal. If he persists in his apostasy and was not recently converted to Islam, he will be put to death." The Penal Code of Mauritania of 1984, article 306 reads, "All Muslims guilty of apostasy, either spoken or by overt action will be asked to repent during a period of three days. If he does not repent during this period, he is condemned to death as an apostate, and his belongings confiscated by the State Treasury." This applies equally to women. The Moroccan Penal Code seems to only mention those guilty of trying to subvert the belief of a Muslim or those who try to convert a Muslim to another religion. The punishment varies between a fine and imprisonment for anything up to three years.[20]

The absence of any mention of apostasy in some penal codes of Islamic countries of course in no way implies that a Muslim in the country concerned is free to leave his religion. In reality, the lacunae in the penal codes are filled by Islamic law. Mahmud Muhammad Taha was hanged for apostasy in 1985, even though at the time the Sudanese Penal Code of 1983 did not mention such a crime.[21]

In some countries, the term *apostate* is applied to some who were born non-Muslim but whose ancestors had the good sense to convert from Islam. The Bahais in Iran in recent years have been persecuted for just such a reason. Similarly, in Pakistan the Ahmadi community were classed as non-Muslims and are subjected to all sorts of persecution.

There is some evidence that many Muslim women in Islamic countries would convert from Islam to escape their lowly position in Muslim societies or to avoid the application of an unfavorable law, especially Sharia law governing divorce.[22] Muslim theologians are well aware of the temptation of Muslim women to evade the Sharia laws by converting from Islam, and take appropriate measures are taken. For example, in Kuwait an explanatory memorandum to the text of a law reform says, "Complaints have shown that the Devil makes the route of apostasy attractive to the Muslim woman so that she can break a conjugal tie that does not please her. For this reason, it was decided that apostasy would not lead to the dissolution of the marriage in order to close this dangerous door."[23]

The following is just one recent example among many (others are discussed in my book, *Leaving Islam: Apostates Speak Out*:

> A Somali living in Yemen since 1994, Mohammed Omer Haji converted to Christianity two years ago and adopted the name "George." He was imprisoned in January 2000 and reportedly beaten and threatened for two months by Yemeni security police, who tried to persuade him to renounce his conversion to Christianity. After he was rearrested in May, he was formally put on trial in June for apostasy under article 259 of Yemen's criminal law.

Haji's release came seven weeks after he was given a court ultimatum to renounce Christianity and return to Islam or face execution as an apostate. Apostasy is a capital offense under the Muslim laws of "sharia" enforced in Yemen.

After news of the case broke in the international press, Yemeni authorities halted the trial proceedings against Haji. He was transferred on July 17 to Aden's Immigration Jail until resettlement could be finalized by the UNHCR, under which Haji had formal refugee status. One of the politicians who tabled a motion in July 2000 in the British House of Commons was David Atkinson: "Early Day Motion on Mohammed Omer Haji. That this House deplores the death penalty which has been issued from the Aden Tawahi Court in Yemen for the apostasy of the Somali national Mohammed Omer Haji unless he recants his Christian faith and states that he is a Muslim before the judge three times on Wednesday 12th July; deplores that Mr Haji was held in custody for the sole reason that he held to the Christian faith and was severely beaten in custody to the point of not being able to walk; considers it a disgrace that UNHCR officials in Khormaksar stated they were only able to help him if he was a Muslim; and calls on the British Government and international colleagues to make representations immediately at the highest level in Yemen to ensure Mr Haji's swift release and long-term safety and for the repeal of Yemen's barbaric apostate laws."[24]

Amnesty International adopted Haji as a prisoner of conscience in an "urgent action" release on July 11, 2000, concluding that he was "detained solely on account of his religious beliefs." The government of New Zealand accepted Haji and his family for emergency resettlement in late July after negotiations with the Geneva headquarters of the United Nations High Commissioner for Refugees (UNHCR).[25]

However, charges of apostasy, unbelief, blasphemy, and heresy, whether upheld or not, clearly go against several articles in the UDHR of 1948, and the legally binding International Covenant on Civil and Political Rights [ICCPR] of 1966, to which 147 states are signatories.

General Comment no. 22, adopted by the UN Human Rights Commission at its forty-eighth session (1993) declares: "Article 18 protects theistic, non-theistic and atheistic beliefs, as well as the right not to profess any religion or belief. The term 'belief' and 'religion' are to be broadly construed."[26]

As with my statement to the UN Human Rights Commission delivered by the president of the International Humanist and Ethical Union, we urge the UN Human Rights Commission to call on all governments to comply with applicable international human rights instruments like the ICCPR, to bring their national legislation into accordance with the instruments to which they were a party, and to forbid *fatwas* and sermons preaching violence in the name of God against those holding unorthodox opinions or those who have left a religion.

NOTES

1. See al-Raghib al-Isfahani (d. 1108 CE), *Al-mufradat fi harib al-Qur'an* (Cairo, 1890).

2. Samuel M. Zwemer, *The Law of Apostasy in Islam* (London and New York: Marshall Brothers, 1924), pp. 34–35. See also al-Razi, *al-Tafsir al-Kabir,* vol. 2 (Cairo,1890), ll. 17–20.

3. Quoted in Zwemer, *Law of Apostasy,* pp. 33–34.

4. Ibn Kathir, *L'interpretation du Coran,* trans. Fawzi Chaaban (Beirut: Dar al-Fikr, 1998), 2:128.

5. Abul Ala Maududi, *The Punishment of the Apostate According to Islamic Law,* trans. Syed Silas Husain and Ernest Hahn (Lahore, Pakistan: Islamic Publications, 1994); also available at http://www.answering-islam.org/Hahn/Maududi/ (accessed September 28, 2004).

6. Ibn Maja, *Hudud,* chap. 2; al-Nisai, *Tahrim al-Dam,* chap. 14; al-Tayalisi, no. 2689; Malik, *Aqdiya* tradition 15; al-Bukhari, *Institabat al-murtadin,* chap. 2; al-Tirmidhi, *Hudud,* chap. 25; Abu Dawud, *Hudud,* chap. 1; Ibn Hanbal i. 217, 282, 322.

7. Al-Bukhari, *Sahih,* trans. Ahmad Hasan (Delhi: Kitab Bhavan, 1987), 8:519–20.

8. Abu Dawud, "Punishment of an Apostate," hadith no. 4337, chap. 1605 in *Kitab al-Hudud,* vol. 3 of *Sunan,* trans. Ahmad Hasan (Delhi: Kitab Bhavan, 1990), p. 1212.

9. Al-Nisai, *Tahrim al-Dam,* chap. 11; Qasama, chap. 13; Abu Dawud, *Hudud,* chap. 1

10. Al-Bukhari, *Maghazi,* chap. 60; *Istitabat al-Murtaddin,* chap. 2 Ahkam, chap. 12; Muslim, *Imara,* tradition 15; Abu Dawud, *Hudud,* chap.1; Ibn Hanbal, l, v. 231.

11. Al-Shafii, *Umm, I 228*; Abu Yusuf, Kharaj, 109

12. "Apostasy from Islam," in *Dictionary of Islam,* ed. Thomas Patrick Hughes (Delhi, 1885), p. 16.

13. T. W. Juynboll, "Apostasy," in *Encyclopaedia of Ethics and Religion,* ed. James Hastings (Edinburgh: T&T Clark Publishers, 1910), p. 626.

14. "Fiftieth Anniversary of the Universal Declaration of Human Rights," United Nations Web site, http://www.un.org/rights/50/decla.htm (accessed September 28, 2004).

15. Sami A. Aldeeb Abu-Sahlieh, "Le délit d'apostasie aujourd'hui et ses conséquences en droit arabe et musulman," *Islamochristiana* (Vatican City) 20 (1994):

93–116; Ann Elizabeth Mayer, *Islam and Human Rights: Tradition and Politics* (Boulder, CO: Westview Press, 1991), p. 164.

16. Abu-Sahlieh, "Le délit d'apostasie," p. 94.

17. Ibid.

18. Ibid.

19. Mayer, *Islam and Human Rights*, p. 187.

20. Abu-Sahlieh, "Le délit d'apostasie," p. 98.

21. Sami A. Aldeeb Abu-Sahlieh, *Les Musulmans face aux droits de l'homme* (Bochum, Germany: Winkler, 2001), p. 110.

22. Mayer, *Islam and Human Rights*, p. 167.

23. Ibid., pp. 167–68.

24. Ibn Warraq, ed., *Leaving Islam: Apostates Speak Out* (Amherst, NY: Prometheus Books, 2003), p. 98.

25. *Christianity Today,*, August 28, 2000.

26. General Comment no. 22, HRI/GEN/1/Rev.6, May 22, 2003, pp. 155–56.

45. APOSTASY, HUMAN RIGHTS, RELIGION, AND BELIEF— NEW THREATS TO THE FREEDOM OF OPINION AND EXPRESSION

A Concrete Proposal

Shafique Keshavjee

I wish to thank again the organizations that invited me to participate in this roundtable. The subject is not theoretical and touches the concrete lives of millions of men and women worldwide.

For many years, I have been active as a pastor in the promotion of dialogue between the Churches and other religions.

Along with others, I direct a center dedicated to this dialogue in Lausanne, Switzerland.[1] There, Christians of all denominations—Catholics, Orthodox, and Protestants—Jews, Muslims, Buddhists, Hindus, and Bahais meet in order to build bridges of harmony, and, as our charter says, "without confusion of doctrine or proselytizing pressure." By means of the pen, I have also stimulated this dialogue in many countries all over the world through my novel dedicated to this subject, *The King, the Sage, and the Fool: The Great Tournament of Religions*, which has been translated into more than fifteen languages—from most of the European languages to Chinese and Japanese, as well as Turkish (but unfortunately not yet into English).[2]

When we think of apostasy and the dramatic misdeeds that result from it, most glances are turned toward contemporary Islam. Hardly a day passes without some terrible news reaching us, in which we learn that a Muslim who has become a Christian, Bahai, Buddhist, or atheist has been persecuted for

This paper was delivered in French (translated by Robert Spencer, with assistance from David G. Littman) at a panel discussion on "Apostasy, Human Rights, Religion, and Belief" at the Palais des Nations, Geneva, April 7, 2004, at the sixtieth session of the UNCHR.

his beliefs.[3] An important aspect of Islamophobia—a regrettable phenomenon that must be resisted—is rooted in this lack of respect for the religious convictions of others.

By way of an introduction to my brief presentation, I must recall that the pressures experienced by apostates, or what are perceived as such—pressures from strong psychological constraints to the threat of being killed—are not unique to Islam. The great monotheistic religions of the past, like new religious movements of today, have been, or can be, extremely violent.

I was involved in the funeral service of the Order of the Third Personality in the Solar Temple, which, on October 4, 1994, caused the collective suicide (voluntary or not) of forty-eight of its members. Who really chose to commit suicide, and who was forced to do so? We will never know. I have also met many people belonging to sectarian movements such as Scientology or Jehovah's Witnesses who have experienced enormous pressure once they wished to leave the movement. It is well to recall that over the centuries the Christian Churches could—despite all the love taught by Christ—hate, torture, banish, and put to death apostates and heretics. For the past two centuries, thank God—and the promotion of respect for human rights, notably in Protestant countries—these practices virtually disappeared. But it took time! It was only when the Churches gave up using—generally by constraint and sometimes by choice—their privileged position within the state to exercise power over consciences that changes took place. This dark picture could have raised hope that atheist states ought to have and could have been more tolerant. As you know, it did not happen. During the twentieth century, it was the most antireligious states that caused the death of the greatest number of people because of questions of conscience and belief.

After a short recapitulation of the etymology of the word *apostasy*, my presentation will articulate three points: (1) some religious and social bases of violence toward apostates; (2) some juridical implications; and (3) a practical proposition.

In the word *apostate* there are two Greek roots: *apo*, "far from," and *statos*, "that which is stable, that which is stationary." The root *sta*, of Indo-European origin, is found elsewhere among Latin words as *statio*, in German as *stehen*, and in English as *stand*.

An apostate is one who is separated from that which is stable and stationary. An apostate is resented as a menace to the stability of a community or a society, as a traitor to the Truth, which is regarded as *stationary* and eternal. Through a personal choice differing from the majority, the apostate seems to put in danger the stability and constancy of the community. That is true for religious communities, but not only for them. I have had contacts with senior Chinese officials responsible for religious affairs. I have particularly noticed that they also can perceive unregistered religious communities—wrongly or rightly—as menaces to the stability of the State.

SOME RELIGIOUS AND SOCIAL FOUNDATIONS OF VIOLENCE TOWARD APOSTATES

In Judaism, foundational texts justify the killing of apostates.[4] In Deuteronomy 13, one can read, "If your brother . . . or your friend who is as your own soul, entices you secretly, saying, 'Let us go and serve other gods,' . . . you shall not yield to him or listen to him . . . but you shall kill him" (6, 8–9). The apostate, in this text, is not only one who abandons the God of his father but one who invites his contemporaries to change gods. Because of centuries of domination and persecution by Christians and Muslims, it was not until recently that Jews could have reactivated such texts. But to my knowledge, no rabbi takes this text literally.

In Christianity, Jesus, who died for all and was raised up by God, has been perceived as the fulfillment of the Truth announced to the Jews. To abandon that Truth after having known it could not but be perceived as a disaster. A severe text from the Epistle to the Hebrews affirms, "For if we sin deliberately after receiving the knowledge of the truth, there no longer remains a sacrifice for sins, but a fearful prospect of judgment, and a fury of fire which will consume the adversaries" (10:26).

Because of such passages in particular, Martin Luther had doubts about the authenticity of this epistle. Over the centuries, the Church justified physical violence against apostates and heretics as aimed at saving them from a future "devouring fire" that would come from God. Fortunately, over the last two centuries, the mentality of the clergy has largely changed. What has facilitated matters is that there is no text of the Gospels that can be cited to justify physical violence toward, or the killing of, an apostate.

In Islam, the message of the Qur'an is considered to be the final revelation. To leave would be a "step backward" (*ridda*). A hadith—a saying attributed to Muhammad—affirms, "Whoever changes his religion, kill him." According to a Muslim's degree of openness, this hadith must be applied literally or set aside as being of doubtful authenticity. (It pertains to the category *ahad*; that is to say, it was reported by only one person.) In Islamic centers, the debate is extremely virulent; we may hope that the interpretation that respects the liberty of conscience will triumph.

Here is what Mohamed Charfi, emeritus professor on the faculty of juridical sciences of Tunis and president of the League of Human Rights, wrote,

> God is not a fanatic, but the ulema of yesterday, like the ulema and the fundamentalists of today, are. . . . As Sami Abu Sahlieh recalled, the classical Muslim jurists prescribed "in keeping with their contemporary Jewish and Christian colleagues, the death penalty for all people who abandoned their religion. In fact, religious freedom for the jurists is a liberty in one unique sense: the freedom to enter, but a prohibition to leave."[5]
>
> The Christians and Jews abandoned that shameful law. Islam has not abandoned it, because of the theologians and fundamentalists. It is a question of development. Underdevelopment is not solely economic or social; it is also cultural and intellectual. Fundamentalism, with us, is the most obvious expression of our underdevelopment.[6]

Also according to Charfi, the accusation of apostasy is a weapon brandished by the theologians against every intellectual who proposes a new idea; then they put pressure on the state for him to be judged. The first to suffer from this are the Muslims themselves—those choosing to revive the static interpretation of Islam or those choosing to change their religion, or even to become atheists. That is true in their own countries. But not only there. One well-known pastor in French-speaking Switzerland, a convert from Islam, escaped from an attack by a member of his own family, who felt dishonored by his choice. Fortunately, this pastor was not killed, and with the passage of years he may, while always guarding his Christian faith, be reconciled with them.

The foundations of the accusation of apostasy are religious. However, in these times of globalization and the acceleration of planetary exchanges, and of the economic, technological, and financial domination of the West, religion has become a rampart against the loss of identity and a form of resistance. Amid the fragmentation of our world, the apostate is perceived, wrongly in my opinion, as a destroyer of the social bond.

SOME LEGAL IMPLICATIONS

There is, as you know, tension between juridical and religious norms.

Article 18 of the Universal Declaration of Human Rights (1948) states, "Everyone has the right to freedom of thought, conscience and religion; this right includes freedom to change his religion or belief."

This clause on "freedom to change his religion" was added at the recommendation of the representative of Lebanon, a country where many people who were persecuted for having changed their faith were refugees. In the Canton of Vaud, where I live, I was part of the assembly that wrote a new constitution. As my contribution, I proposed that there be included an article that stipulated, "All persons have the right to join the community of their choice *or to leave it*" (article 16). And that was fully accepted.

Religious liberty, to be realistic, must be able to include not only the freedom to enter a community but especially that of being able to *leave* it.

However, for the partisans of a traditionalist reading of their religion, to leave the community is a menace to the stability of their faith. It is also a door opened to all the aggressive forms of missionary activity coming from outsiders. For the right to abandon or change one's religion to become effective, it is important to reassure those who hold to the religious tradition in three ways: first, by emphasizing that one who changes religion is not necessarily an enemy of the common good—quite to the contrary; second, by stating that the genuine freedom to leave a religious community is not a sign of weakness, but rather of strength; and third, by declaring that this liberty is not synonymous with a "religious free market," in which all forms of militant proselytism are accepted. In the same way that multinational corporations must be regulated by political laws, religious communities should be subjected to ethical principles. Any abuse of them should be denounced vehemently.

A CONCRETE PROPOSITION

The special rapporteur on contemporary forms of racism, racial discrimination, xenophobia, and associated intolerance wrote an alarming report about the situation of Muslim and Arab populations in various areas of the world.[7] It notes that Islamophobia tends to spread in the West. In his report, he suggests that the Office of the High Commissioner for Human Rights create "a center to monitor the contemporary phenomena of racism, antisemitism and Islamophobia." In our global society, the phenomenon of conversion from one faith to another will multiply. To avoid violent reactions and to end situations of increased violence, throughout the world, I suggest, if a suitable place does not yet exist, that such a center can collect throughout the year testimonies from the entire world where the act of leaving one's religion is a source of persecution. This would be a significant contribution to the reinforcement of human rights, while offering to the victims of flawed justice the certitude of being heard.

The United Nations has the goal notably to "maintain international peace and security" (Charter of the United Nations, art. 1, para. 1) and to realize international cooperation in "encouraging respect for human rights and for fundamental freedoms for all, without distinction as to race, sex, language, or religion" (art. 1, para. 3).

The fundamental freedom to change one's religion is menaced today. The credibility of the Commission of Human Rights depends on its protection.

NOTES

1. The author can be reached at Maison de l'Arzillier, av. de Rumine 62, 1005 Lausanne, Switzerland, or at skeshavjee@hispeed.ch.

2. The original French version was published by Éditions du Seuil in Paris, 1998.

3. For the often difficult situation of Christians, see, for example, Jean-Marie Gaudeul, *Appelés par le Christ, ils viennent de l'Islam* (Paris: Editions du Cerf, 1991).

4. See, for example, "Apostasie," in *Dictionaire encyclopédique du judaisme* (Paris: Editions Robert Laffont, 1996), p. 81.

5. Sami A. Aldeeb Abu-Sahlieh, "Le délit d'apostasie aujourd'hui et ses conséquences en droit arabe et musulman," *Islamochristiana* (Vatican City) 20 (1994): 95.

6. Mohamed Charfi, *Islam et liberté: Le malentendu historique* (Paris: Albin Michel, 1998), p. 79.

7. E/CN.4/2004/19.

APOSTASY, HUMAN RIGHTS, RELIGION, AND BELIEF— NEW THREATS TO THE FREEDOM OF OPINION AND EXPRESSION

46.

Pakistani Blasphemy Law

Muhammad Younus Shaikh

Muslims are the first victims of Islamism. In a novel and unethical way, Pakistani mullahs have started abusing the dreadful Islamic blasphemy laws to terrorize liberal and moderate Muslims.

I am a Pakistani doctor, a physiologist, a patriotic and law-abiding citizen, a Muslim by birth. I trained as a surgeon and worked for some years in the United Kingdom. I gave up my job there in order to return to Pakistan to serve the people of my own country. I obtained a position as a lecturer in physiology at the Capital Homeopathic Hospital, Islamabad.

One of my reasons for returning to Pakistan was to campaign for human rights and civil liberties in Pakistan: to work for the Pakistan-India peace movement; to struggle for liberalism, secularism, and humanism; and to counter the forces of religious extremism and fundamentalism.

MY TRIAL

If you are accused of blasphemy in Pakistan, you will usually be denied bail and held in custody until trial. If found guilty, you will face a mandatory

This paper was delivered (in large part over a twenty-minute span) at a panel discussion on "Apostasy, Human Rights, Religion, and Belief" at the Palais des Nations, Geneva, April 7, 2004, at the sixtieth session of the UNCHR. Sponsored by the Association of World Citizens, the Association for World Education, and the International Humanist and Ethical Union.

death sentence. My trial was held in a series of sessions throughout the summer of 2001. Although neither a body of crime was established nor did the evidence prove any occurrence of blasphemy, I was pronounced guilty on August 18, 2001, fined one hundred thousand rupees, and sentenced to death—nearly nine months after my arrest.

The specific charge on which I was found guilty was "Insulting the Prophet." To many European observers it might seem illogical that a death sentence could be pronounced without proving the incidence or establishing the body of crime; however, that is the way blasphemy cases are adjudicated upon in the very Islamic Republic of Pakistan.

For the next two years, I was held in solitary confinement in a very small death cell in the Central Jail, Rawalpindi, a dark and dirty death cell with unbearable, stinking, and distasteful food. There was no facility for walking or exercise, and I was without books, newspapers, medication, or treatment for my worsening diabetes. I remained constantly under threat of murder by Islamic fundamentalist inmates in jail for murder and gang rape, as well as by some religiously minded prison warders. I appealed. My appeal was heard over several sessions lasting fifteen long months before the two judges managed to disagree over their verdict; one Islamic-minded judge rejected the appeal without giving any legal grounds for doing so, while the other, legal-minded judge stated that the prosecution had failed to prove the case beyond reasonable doubt and that the witnesses were neither trustworthy nor reliable. The referee High Court judge took another year and sent the case for retrial.

The retrial was held in November 2003 at the Court of the Session in Islamabad. Because of threats and harassment no lawyer was ready to plead my case, and I was forced to defend myself for my survival, which I did after secretly smuggling law books into my death cell. At the retrial the courtroom was full of mullahs and the Pakistani Taliban. The two mullah advocates and the public prosecutor tried to exploit the religious feelings of the court, but I confined my defense to legal arguments. I was inspired by the defense speech of Sir Thomas More in *A Man for All Seasons*. Fortunately, the outcome in my case was different. The judge accepted my legal arguments and found the charges against me baseless. My accusers, the two mullahs and the Islamist students, had lied under oath. I was acquitted on November 21, 2003.

MY ORDEAL

I feel I have been a victim of Islamic mullah terrorism through the abuse of the state apparatus and the civil law. My first trial was a show trial, almost reminiscent of the trials and tortures of the infamous Spanish Inquisition and the trials and burning of European women as witches. After my acquittal and release, I wanted to stay in my country with my family and friends, but instead I found myself under a *fatwa* by the same mullahs that I should be killed. I had to say goodbye to my loved ones and flee to Europe for my safety.

I am very thankful to the International Humanist and Ethical Union, the various humanist organizations and individual humanists, and all of the other human rights organizations who campaigned on my behalf: Amnesty International, Physicians for Human Rights USA, the Jubilee Campaign USA, the many honorable senators and congressmen from the United States, and the UK members of Parliament. I also want to thank the Swiss and US embassies in Islamabad and the Swiss government for their ceaseless support for justice and equity in my case. I am very grateful to the Swiss government for granting me refugee status in Switzerland.

WHAT IS BLASPHEMY?

What, then, constitutes blasphemy? Unfortunately the Pakistan Penal Code provides little guidance. The law is vague and the term is undefined. In view of the mandatory death penalty for the offense, this would seem to be an important oversight. The law is a relic of 1860 British Colonial criminal law but was modified in 1926 again under the British, then in 1986 by General Zita to make it more strictly in accordance with the Sharia, and finally in 1992 when the death penalty was made mandatory—this under the democratically elected prime minister Nawaz Sharif. Whereas the original law had been even-handed and applied equally to all religions, under the revised law the death penalty applies only to blasphemy against Islam. More than a hundred victims are currently in jail awaiting trial, fifteen of whom face the death penalty under section 295-C of the Pakistan Penal Code. Mercifully, none have so far been executed.

In another famous case, a Christian, Ayub Masih, was condemned to death for blasphemy on the unsupported evidence of a neighbor, Muhammad Akram, who was involved with him in a land dispute and who was awarded property belonging to the accused after the case was decided. The verdict and the sentence were upheld by the Lahore High Court on July 25, 2001. However, after seven long years of unnecessary incarceration in a death cell, he was found innocent and acquitted by the Supreme Court.

Despite there successes in obtaining convictions, the fundamentalists have not been willing to leave judgment and execution to the courts. Several people have been murdered by Islamic zealots after having been acquitted by the courts. Others accused of blasphemy have been murdered in jail while awaiting trial, and even a High Court judge was murdered after finding one prisoner not guilty.

PAKISTAN'S SHAME

The blasphemy law has brought shame on Pakistan. The law itself is unjust and inequitable, the offense it treats is poorly defined and open to abuse, and its operation has been widely misused and abused. Since the introduction of Sharia law in Pakistan in 1986, the blasphemy law has been used on hundreds of occasions by fundamentalists to silence moderate opponents, to intimidate non-Muslims, and to settle personal scores.

While praising President Gen. Pervez Musharraf for his liberal and secular steps, and for his courageous fight against Islamic jihadi terrorism, I appeal to him to curb this menace of Islamic mullah terrorism: the abuse of Pakistani Islamic blasphemy laws. I call upon the Commission on Human Rights to press the government of Pakistan

1. To urgently review the cases of all those currently charged or convicted of blasphemy and awaiting execution, including an urgent judicial review of all cases currently subjudice;
2. To immediately review the application of the blasphemy law and to introduce safeguards against its abuse;
3. To replace the blasphemy law by laws which respect the human rights of individuals in conformity with the Universal Declaration of Human Rights, to which Pakistan is a signatory; and finally,
4. To compensate the victims of these unjust and iniquitous laws and to punish the false accusers and untruthful witnesses.

47. APOSTASY, HUMAN RIGHTS, RELIGION, AND BELIEF—NEW THREATS TO THE FREEDOM OF OPINION AND EXPRESSION

The Problem of Apostasy in an Islamic-Christian Context

Paul Cook

I am very pleased to be here as part of the panel. I would like to take this opportunity to share with you some of the work Barnabas Fund has been doing over the past fifteen months through our campaign on the issue of apostasy.

In the nine years since Barnabas Fund was established, our work has brought us into direct contact with hundreds of Muslims who have adopted another belief from many different countries. It is tragic to relate that of these hundreds, fewer than ten informed us that their families recognized and respected their decision to adopt another belief and have been supportive and understanding. The rest have faced widespread hostility and aggression from their families and communities. Some have endured imprisonment, death threats, torture, and beatings because of their decision. A few have been executed; others have died in prison or disappeared.

It is astonishing that at the beginning of the twenty-first century such abuses are still being perpetrated against human beings merely for exercising such a basic human right as freedom of belief. More astonishing still is the silence that surrounds this issue.

This paper was delivered at a panel discussion on "Apostasy, Human Rights, Religion, and Belief" at the Palais des Nations, Geneva, April 7, 2004, at the sixtieth session of the UNCHR. Sponsored by the Association of World Citizens, the Association for World Education, and the International Humanist and Ethical Union.

BARNABAS FUND'S APOSTASY CAMPAIGN

In January 2003 Barnabas Fund launched a major international campaign designed to break this silence and draw attention to the crucial issue of apostasy and the suffering of Muslims who adopt another belief. What we are calling for is no more than an affirmation of the basic human right to "change" one's religion as affirmed in article 18 of the Universal Declaration of Human Rights. We believe that a Muslim (or any other person) who chooses to change his belief (whether to Christianity, Buddhism, atheism, or any other faith or belief) should be free to do so without having to face violence, intimidation, and persecution as a result.

Prejudice and persecution is directed against "apostates" in many religious traditions. In Eritrea today many Orthodox Christians who choose to adopt certain forms of Evanglical Protestantism face persecution. In India Hindus adopting Buddhism or Christianity often similarly suffer. In Sri Lanka those who convert from Buddhism to another belief may be persecuted. However, it is Muslims choosing to adopt another belief who face the greatest suffering in the world today.

The prejudice and persecution with which apostates are viewed in most traditional Muslim societies does not occur in a vacuum. It is a direct result of traditional teachings found in Islamic law (Sharia) that adult Muslim men who choose to adopt any other belief and refuse to return to Islam should be put to death. Some schools of Sharia teach that this should be applied to women as well. Other punishments prescribed by the Sharia include the annulment of marriage, the removal of children, and the loss of all property and inheritance rights. This tradition is still upheld and taught by most Muslim religious leaders around the world today.

This is a tradition that affects not only individuals who choose to adopt another faith but also whole communities, such as the Ahmadis in Pakistan and the Bahais in Iran. The accusation of apostasy is also used by extremists to victimize many liberal and secular Muslim academics and journalists, including many prominent human rights defenders. In Sudan in January 1985 Mahmoud Muhammad Taha, a renowned Islamic scholar, liberal, and reformer, was executed for apostasy for publishing a leaflet calling for the reform of Islamic law to make it more just and humane.

As long as this tradition goes unchallenged by Muslim leaders and other religious and political figureheads, this persecution will continue. Only when more reformist and moderate interpretations that fit better with the religious freedoms enshrined in the International Bill of Rights become widely accepted as normative will this persecution cease.

To this end over seventy-six thousand people from more than thirty different countries have now signed an international petition launched by Barnabas Fund in July 2003. The petition calls upon "Muslim religious leaders and Islamic organizations to make a public call for a reform or reinterpretation of Shari'ah, so that Muslims who change their faith will not have to face intimidation, harassment, persecution or death as a result." The petition also urges the Commission on Human Rights, Western governments, and other international institutions to "raise this as a matter of urgency with Muslim leaders and organizations, and to exercise their influence by speaking out in support of this call."

This is not a matter of concern for Christians only. The petition has also been signed by peoples of other religious and nonreligious backgrounds. This includes members of the Muslim community in Britain, several of whom have signed even in the face of obvious intimidation by others in the community. Noted signatories of the petition include several bishops and a former president of Trinidad and Tobago.

The campaign has also been supported in Britain's House of Commons, where ninety-two MPs last year signed an Early Day Motion. The motion states "[t]hat this house supports liberal Muslims, human rights campaigners and others who are calling for an end to cruel traditional punishments for apostasy."

Also in conjunction with the campaign, last July Barnabas Fund made an appeal to the high commissioner for human rights, the chairman of the Human Rights Committee, and the chairpersons of the commission and the subcommission. We asked them to give the issue of apostasy within the Islamic tradition "the serious attention that it deserves under the international covenants." We urged them to "lend their support to the voice of liberal Muslims, human rights campaigners and British parliamentarians who are speaking out on behalf of Muslims who have adopted another belief."

Supporters of the campaign have been writing literally hundreds of letters to Muslim leaders, parliamentarians, heads of state, public figures, and religious leaders around the world. They have been alerting them to the suffering of Muslims who adopt another belief and urging them to make public calls for a reform of Sharia and an end to the death sentence and other cruel penalties.

Among British MPs alone, lobbying has raised the level of awareness of this issue significantly over the past year. In January 2003 many MPs were expressing astonishment and admitting that they had never heard of the persecution of apostates from Islam before. By October 2003 the British Foreign and Commonwealth Office said apostasy was one of the top seven human rights issues on which they were most lobbied.

The campaign has also received some coverage in the media, with interviews, articles, letters and debates appearing on the BBC, on the *Times* of London, and Reuters news agency stories, among others.

BREAKING THE SILENCE

Yet despite all of this activity and attention the silence of political and religious leaders remains deafening. Despite receiving hundreds of letters the Muslim Council of Britain has failed to issue any kind of reply or make any statement on this issue. The offices of British prime minister Tony Blair and Prince Charles, the heir to the throne, have both produced very noncommittal replies despite being lobbied by hundreds of people. Christian leaders have also largely failed to speak out on this issue, despite being extensively lobbied. Many privately acknowledge the terrible suffering of apostates and admit to the gravity of the situation but are unprepared to speak out publicly.

During the past fifteen months, while the campaign has been running, Muslims who have adopted another belief have continued to suffer. On February 17, 2003, Ziwar Muhammad Ismail was shot dead in Zakho, in the Kurdish-authority area of North Iraq. His killer later admitted while in police custody that he had murdered Ziwar because he had converted to Christianity.

In the same month that Ziwar was killed, an extremist group in Somalia issued a press release calling for Somali Christians to be executed as apostates in accordance with Islamic law.

In October 2003 police in Alexandria, Egypt, launched a series of raids against twenty-two converts and their supporters living in the city under false identities in order to avoid persecution. They faced interrogation, beatings, torture, and abuse during their time in police custody. They are now released on bail with charges pending.

REITERATING THE CALL

Distinguished representatives, it is good to have the opportunity this panel provides to reiterate once more at the United Nations the call for political and Muslim religious leaders to issue prominent public statements calling for a reform or reinterpretation of Sharia. We believe that at the beginning of the twenty-first century no religion (be it Islam, Christianity, or any other) can justify the intimidation, harassment, and persecution of individuals simply for exercising their freedom of belief.

It is a tragic day when no political or religious leader can be found who is prepared to simply publicly affirm the most basic of human rights enshrined in the Universal Declaration of Human Rights and International Covenant on Civil and Political Rights.

It is our hope, and I am sure the hope of the rest of the panel, that this meeting will help to draw more much-needed attention to the persecution of Muslims and other persons who adopt another belief. It is also our hope that the meeting will encourage the members of the commission and other UN representatives to respond with a public condemnation of such persecution. Finally, it is our hope that the commission will issue a similar public encouragement to Muslim religious leaders to publicly condemn the persecution of converts and to denounce it as something unworthy of the Islamic faith.

48.

UTOPIA: A "UNITED STATES OF ABRAHAM"

David G. Littman

I wish to thank Dr. Samuel Rubenson for suggesting, and Prof. Bo Holm-berg for accepting, that I address you today on the Middle East. To be more precise: on the origins and development of an "idea"—an idea that may be considered by many, not excluding myself, a "utopia"—and the relationship of that idea to the present Middle East peace process, within a context of regional reconciliation.

In this context, the words of seventeenth-century English philosopher John Locke are worth recalling: "All men are liable to error; and most men are, in many points, by passion or interest, under temptation to it."[1]

Such temptations to propose utopian ideas on the Middle East can easily turn out to be pipe dreams, yet the example of Europe comes to mind. Richard Coudenhove-Kalergi, Aristide Briand, Winston Churchill, Gustav Stresemann, Maurice Schuman, and Jean Monnet—to name but six key fig-ures—were the prophets for thirty years, while the hermits hibernated, hyp-notized by the syndrome of gloom and doom that gripped Europe in the after-math of the two world wars.

Only last month [October 1994] a centenary commemoration took place in Vienna to honor Count Coudenhove-Kalergi, who first launched the pan-European "idea" in 1922. Today, thirty years after Winston Churchill's death, I would like to preface my statement on the Middle East by quoting from his 1930 article in the *London Saturday Evening Post*, in which he wrote of that

This chapter was originally delivered by David G. Littman as an address to the Society for Semitic Studies (Semitiska Sällskapet), Department of Middle Eastern Languages, Lund University, Sweden, on November 23, 1994.

nascent pan-European "idea" with his characteristic imagery. It may serve as a fitting introduction to my address:

> Ideas are born as sparks fly upward. They die from their own weakness; they are whirled away by the wind; they are lost in the smoke; they vanish in the darkness of the night. Someone throws on another log of trouble and effort, and fresh myriads of sparks stream ineffectively into the air. Men have always tended these fires, casting into them the fruits of their toil— indeed, all they can spare after keeping body and soul together. Sometimes, at rare intervals, something exciting results from their activities. Among innumerable sparks that flash and fade away, there now and again gleams one that lights up not only the immediate scene, but the whole world. What is it that lights up not only the immediate scene but the whole world? What is it that distinguishes the fortunes of one of these potent incendiary or explosive ideas from the endless procession of its fellows? It is always something very simple and—once the surroundings are illuminated— painfully obvious. In fact we may say that the power and vitality of an idea result from a spontaneous recognition of the obvious.[2]

Sixteen years later, on September 19, 1946, no longer prime minister, Churchill made his famous appeal at the University of Zurich for a future "United States of Europe." That dream has taken nearly half a century to take form, and his vision of a united Europe has yet to come to full fruition, although more and more candidates are pressing at the gates. Sweden's recent yes vote and Finland's ratification have opened the Nordic road to Europe, with Norway's decision awaited next week [which turned out negative]. It should be remembered that, at the time when Churchill made his speech, the very idea that France and Germany should together begin the building of a new Europe seemed not only utopian but even totally unrealistic to most Europeans. Barely a year after the World War II, the very name of Germany was still anathema as a result of the Nazi plague that had dragged the world into the depths of hell, snuffing out the lives of over forty million and leaving half of Europe enslaved by an equally ruthless Communist tyranny that has only recently been relegated to the dustbin of history.

This is a subject that deserves more time than is available to me here. It raises issues about what fundamental changes in a society are needed for democracy to triumph. Notwithstanding the admirable work accomplished by the Russian organization Memorial, founded by Andrei Sakharov, too little attention has been paid to "memory" or "atonement," let alone to "redemption," for decades of countless crimes against humanity—against ecology too!—in the name of an ideological system that systematically reduced men and women to robots while callously destroying nature itself in the name of an allegedly socialist ideal. Recently, Russian historian Dmitry A. Volkogonov indicated a figure of 21.5 million victims of Stalinist purges between 1929 and 1953, and Aleksandr S. Yakovlev, the father of glasnost, referred to the 1917 Bolshevik coup d'état as the most tragic event in Russia's thousand-year-old history.

I came across Churchill's 1946 speech in autumn 1989 and, as an NGO representative to the United Nations in Geneva, was inspired to adapt it, with the essential aid of sustained metaphor, to the Israel-Jordan-Palestinian predicament. I hoped that his memorable peace framework, proposed at a tragic period of Europe's history, might yet serve not only as an inspiration, but as a model for those who have no alternative other than to find a peaceful solution to generations of conflict. By chance, over five hundred delegates—including ambassadors and heads of delegations—were present at the Palais des Nations in Geneva on March 6, 1990, awaiting the voting procedure on resolutions of the forty-sixth session of the Commission on Human Rights, when the chairman gave me the floor as the last speaker of the six-week session. That [World Union for Progressive Judaism] statement was printed verbatim soon after and published on Christmas Eve 1990 in *Al-Fajr*, the Palestinian Jerusalem English weekly, as a contribution to Middle East dialogue—and a month later, during the Gulf War, it again appeared in an abridged French version in *La Tribune de Genève*, just prior to the opening of the 1991 UN Commission on Human Rights.[3]

With Dr. Rubenson's encouragement, I have welcomed the opportunity to repeat here in Lund that Churchill-inspired Middle East "dream," following which I shall explain its antecedents and in what manner the International Fellowship of Reconciliation (IFOR) [unnumbered note, pp. 467–68] has endeavored to propagate that "idea" in UN circles and elsewhere—as well as the chances of its fulfillment, if not in the remaining five years of this century, perhaps by the beginning of the twenty-first century.

> I wish to speak today about the tragedy of the Middle East. This noble ancient region is the fountain of the three Abrahamitic faiths. It is the spiritual origin of more than half of humanity. If the Middle East were united in the sharing of its common inheritance, there would be no limit to the happiness, to the prosperity and the glory which its tens of millions of people would enjoy. Yet it is within the Middle East that have sprung frightful nationalist and religious quarrels, which have wrecked the peace and marred the prospects of that vast area of the world.

Yet all the while there is a remedy, which, if it were generally and spontaneously adopted by the great majority of people in these lands, would as if by a miracle transform the whole scene, and would in due time make all of the Middle East, or the greater part of it, as free and as happy as Switzerland is today. What is this sovereign remedy? It is to create a "Family of Abraham," or "Family of Ibrahim"—dependent on one's pronunciation of that revered personage—and to provide it with a structure under which it can dwell in peace, in safety and in freedom. We must build a kind of "United States of Abraham." The process is simple. All that is needed is the resolve of millions of men and women to do right instead of wrong and to gain as their reward blessing instead of cursing.

And why should a future United States of the Middle East not take its rightful place with other great groupings and help to shape the onward destinies of man? In order that this should be accomplished, there must be an act of faith in which millions of men and women, speaking their diverse languages, must consciously take part. With regard to the past, there must be what that great nineteenth century British statesman, William Gladstone, called "A blessed act of oblivion." All must turn their backs upon the horrors of the past. All must look to the future. One cannot afford to drag forward across the years that are to come the hatreds and revenges which have sprung from all the various injuries of the past. If the Middle East is to be saved from infinite misery, and indeed from final doom, there must be this act of faith in the concept of a "Family of Abraham"—a "Family of Ibrahim"—and this act of oblivion against all the crimes and follies of the past.

Can the peoples of the Middle East rise to the height of these resolves of the soul and of the instincts of the spirit of man? If they can, the wrongs and injuries which have been inflicted will have been washed away on all sides by the miseries which have been endured. Is there any need for further floods of agony? Is the only lesson of history to be that mankind is unteachable? Let there be justice, mercy and freedom. The peoples have only to will it, and all will achieve their hearts desire.

I am now going to say something that will astonish you. The first step in the creation of this Family of Abraham—or Ibrahim—must be a partnership between Israel, Jordan and the Palestinians within that geographical area designated as "Palestine" in the original 1922 League of Nations Mandate for Palestine. The structure of a future United States of Abraham, if well and truly built, will be such as to make the material strength of a single State less important. Small Nations will count as much as large ones and gain their honour by the contribution to the common cause. The ancient Peoples, Nations and States of the Middle East, freely joined together for mutual convenience in a Federal—or other—system, might eventually take their individual places within this unifying concept, or condominium. I shall not try to make a detailed programme for tens of millions of peoples who want to be happy and free, prosperous and safe. If this is their wish, if this is the wish of so many peoples living in so many lands—comprising the very cradle of the most ancient civilisations of the Near East—they have only to say so, and means can certainly be found, and machinery erected, to carry that wish to full fruition.

But I must give a warning: time may be short. At present there is a breathing-space. The cannons have ceased firing. There is a lull in the fighting, but the dangers have not yet stopped. If there is to be a United States of Abraham, or whatever name it may take, work on this concept must begin now.

I must now sum up. Under and within the world concept of the United Nations Organisation, one must create the Family of the Middle East in a regional structure called, it may be, the United States of Abraham, and the first practical step would be to form a Council of Abraham. If at first all the Peoples, Nations and States of the Middle East are not willing or able to join the Union, one must nevertheless proceed to assemble and combine those who will and those who can. The salvation of all the peoples in the Middle East must be established on solid foundations. In all this urgent work, Israel, Jordan and the Palestinians must take the lead together. The United Nations Organisation, the European Community, the British Commonwealth of Nations, America and Russia—for then indeed all would be well—must be the friends and sponsors of the new Community and must champion its right to live and shine. Therefore I say to you: Let Abraham, let Ibrahim arise!

Winston Churchill's vision of Europe has taken nearly half a century to become reality. May Arab and Israeli political leaders and intellectuals—and also the representatives of all the region's minorities—act with determination, so that peace and reconciliation will come at last to the Middle East, in an upsurge of enthusiasm. If this should be the people's desire, surely wise leaders would wish to achieve, within the next decade, genuine peace and reconciliation (*sulh* in Arabic/*shalom* in Hebrew). Was it not written in the prophetic biblical Book of Joel (2:28), "Your old men shall dream dreams, your young men shall see visions." May the dialogue begin now—

And, I then added, "perhaps even here at this Commission!"

Since making this proposal at the United Nations nearly five years ago, I have became more and more aware that other persons and groups have had similar "ideas" and "dreams" over the past decades, sometimes federalist, sometimes confederalist, sometimes far-flung utopias or visions. But then even Churchill himself did not believe that Great Britain would necessarily restrict its participation to Europe. He always spoke of three overlapping circles: Britain and its Commonwealth, the United States, and the future United States of Europe.

The term *United States of Abraham*, however, was new; it was again used last December for the title of a long article by British historian Martin Gilbert, Churchill's official biographer, in which he assessed the potential global benefits that could flow from a secure Middle East peace. He pointed out that Col. T. E. Lawrence ("Lawrence of Arabia") first suggested that "the Jews might act as a 'leaven' for the whole Arab world, a leaven necessary, in his view, for the Arab world to take full advantage from the emerging nationalism and economic advances of the 20th century." He pointed out that Lawrence's idea contributed to both the Feisal-Weizmann Agreement and the Feisal-Frankfurter Correspondence of January 1919. That agreement was signed at Akaba, where in June of this year, seventy-five years later, Israeli prime minister Yitzhak Rabin and King Hussein of Jordan signed their own historical breakthrough in Israel-Jordan relations.

Let me quote more fully from that article by Gilbert, published on a whole page of the weekly *London Jewish Chronicle* of December 31, 1993:

> Lawrence wanted the Arabs, whose national cause he had espoused, to be able to benefit from the European experience and Middle East aspirations of the Jews. The vision of a federal Middle East, in which a vibrant Jewish state would form an integral and constructive part, was put forward by Churchill in April 1945, when he met the Saudi Arabian ruler, Ibn Saud, at the Fayyum oasis in Egypt. It has been revived several times since, Abba Eban being one of its earliest advocates. Today, the work of Yitzhak Rabin and Shimon Peres, and their negotiations with the PLO, brings it closer to reality, despite the momentary setbacks that give such cause for concern. . . . In 1946, in Zurich, Churchill launched his United States of Europe concept. In March 1990, a year and a half before the Madrid conference, David Littman, [WUPJ] representative in Geneva, read out Churchill's speech [at the UNCHR] as a model for a "United States of Abraham," whose kernel would be a partnership to be worked out freely among Israel, Jordan and the Palestinians.[4]

A few days after that article was published, Joseph Abileah, an Austrian-born musician, died in Haifa, aged eighty. It was he who founded a movement called the Middle East Confederation in 1972, while Ibrahim Siman served as chairman; Dr. Hugh Schonfield was a cosponsor; and Sir Yehudi Menuhim a longtime supporter. At that time I had not related to such ideas, although three years earlier the *Journal de Genève* highlighted, on its international page, a long letter in which I had proposed a future Israelo-Palestinian economic union (or *Zollverein*).[5] For those interested in a comprehensive study of federalist research, I would recommend the book by Daniel J. Elazar, *Two Peoples—One Land: Federal Solutions for Israel, the Palestinians, and Jordan.* Another thought-provoking publication with original suggestions is *Palestinians between Israel and Jordan: Squaring the Triangle,* by Raphael Israeli; and from a Palestinian viewpoint, there is Emile A. Nakhleh's article, "Palestinians and Israelis: Options for Coexistence," in the *Journal of Palestinian Studies.*[6]

So many "ideas," from here and there, those logs of trouble and effort, are starting to gleam in the Middle East's fiery firmament, now that the surroundings have been sufficiently illuminated by so many dramatic events since the cataclysmic Gulf War. Yet the fundamental question remains—to borrow again that vibrant image from Churchill's 1930 article: will the power and the vitality of such ideas take root, now that there appears to be a spontaneous recognition of the obvious?

The position of IFOR on the Middle East issue was subsequently set out in numerous statements and in a joint article by IFOR's representatives to the United Nations in Geneva, René Wadlow and myself, under the title "A Time for Every Purpose under Heaven: The Peace Process and New Forms of Regional Integration." Headlined by *Al-Fajr* in Jerusalem on May 31, 1993, at a crucial period in the Middle East negotiations, it was widely distributed in June to Israeli and Palestinian leaders in Israel and to hundreds of delegates at the Vienna World Conference on Human Rights. An updated version of this article was published in the September 1993 issue of the journal of the Vienna-based International Institute for Peace. On September 13, 1993, Prime Minister Yitzhak Rabin movingly recited at length that same timeless passage from the book of Ecclesiastes in his memorable White House speech, when the river of time stood still, as he announced: "The time for peace has come!"

In the context of a future confederation, comprising Israel, Jordan, and the Palestinians, it might be useful to circulate for those interested—as was done at the United Nations in Geneva on several occasions—IFOR's press release of February 2, 1993, and the above-mentioned two articles, which contain the precise declarations made on this subject by Prime Minister Rabin, the Palestinian spokesman Faisel Husseini, and King Hassan II of Morocco, who—in an interview published in *Le Monde* on September 2, 1992—spoke of "[that idea for an Israeli-Palestinian-Jordanian Confederation and its positive aspects for peace in that region of the world, and of] that dream of a multi-religious and multi-racial peace which would be an extraordinary thing for all the sons of Abraham." To this may be added [the words of Prime Minister Yitzhak Rabin at the Knesset Foreign Affairs and Defence Commission on September 22, 1992: "I place great importance on the transitory period and on the intermediate agreements with the Palestinians. But I do not exclude the possibility of a union with them which would guarantee Israel's security and its right to develop within the framework of a confederation or a federation between us, the Palestinians and Jordan" (*Jerusalem Post*, September 23, 1992)]; foreign minister Shimon Peres's words ten weeks before the Oslo breakthrough was announced in August 1993: "I suggest the establishment of an Israelo-Palestinian-Jordanian Confederation";[7] and King Hussein of Jordan's moving declaration in his White House speech of July 25, 1994: "For many, many years and with every prayer I have asked God Almighty to help me be a part of forging peace between the children of Abraham." Three months later, on signing the Israel-Jordan peace treaty with Yitzhak Rabin, the king of Jordan was more emphatic: "This is an honorable peace, a balanced peace, a peace that will last because from the first instance it was our determination to make it so." To which Prime Minister Rabin replied, "I believe this is the most beautiful act, to end not the state of war, but to establish the structure of peace to build the relations of peace." He added his hopes that Israel's treaty with Jordan, like the September 1993 interim agreement with the Palestinians, would be a model for other Arab neighbors.

This is indeed the crux of the matter. We believe that there must be a wide range of possibilities for new forms of regional integration, which should include regional security, individual security, economic cooperation and development, and a spirit of mutual acceptance. Regional security will require conventional arms control (including, eventually, chemical and nuclear weapons), military confidence-building measures along the lines developed in the CSCE process by the Warsaw Pact and NATO, and transparency in arms production, sales, and purchases. Regional security will also require a more balanced relation between Syria and Lebanon, whose independence should be guaranteed after the withdrawal of all foreign troops from its soil, linked to a broad economic and social integration between Lebanon, Syria, Jordan, Israel, and the future Palestinian entity or state. Any Israeli withdrawal from the Golan plateau is only possible in a spirit of mutual confidence, backed by solid military guarantees that could include an American military presence, as has existed in the Sinai over the past dozen years. Syria is the key to regional peace, and that key is in the hands of President Hafez al-Assad, who assumed power over twenty years ago and has since ruled the country with an iron fist but is ailing and still undecided. This present uncertainty notwithstanding, the momentum of the peace process has attracted other Arab countries further afield; Morocco and Tunisia have already taken giant steps along the road to reconciliation, and some of the smaller Gulf states too have been encouraged to board the "Orient Express."

Economic cooperation got off to an encouraging start during the Middle East and North Africa Economic Summit held in Casablanca last month, sponsored by Morocco, the Council on Foreign Relations, and the World Economic Forum, based in Geneva. Symbolic contacts were conspicuous between Israelis and Arabs, and the most ambitious of the proposed regional agencies was a Middle East Development Bank. Many reports were submitted, the most grandiose of which was the World Bank's program to develop the Jordan Rift Valley and address some of the region's critical water issues. In addition, two regional agencies were proposed in the summit's declaration: a tourist board and a chamber of commerce and business council, intended to place the proper emphasis on promoting the region, disseminating information and transferring expertise, as pointed out by the World Economic Forum's president. Agricultural markets and industrial joint ventures were envisaged in many fields. All this, and more, is intended to cement the peace process with a model of cooperation throughout the region, where the stakes are enormous should essential economic reforms succeed alongside mutual trust. There can be future stability in these regions only if the peoples of the Middle East and North Africa see the economic dividends of peace; and there can be peace only if they earnestly wish it. Once peace is achieved, the interrelationship of the Mediterranean world and economic links with the European Union and its neighbors will follow as surely as day follows night, ushering in a new era for a new millennium.

This brings me to the most critical issues, which will determine whether a new spirit of mutual acceptance will be allowed to flourish—and which also includes an essential goal: individual security for all! Without that spirit and that guarantee, the vision of a confederation, leading to an even wider regional grouping—of the United States of Abraham utopia, for instance—would remain a barren dream, a pipe dream, no more, no less!

First, it must be stressed that such visions can only develop if democratic institutions and respect for human rights become the natural bedrock of civil society in all the countries of the Middle East. Egypt and Jordan, each in its own manner, have begun that process. The time has come for the Palestinians to prove that their fledgling efforts to build a new society will provide a beacon of democracy for other Arab neighbors. An excellent beginning may be found in the "Draft Document of Principles of Women's Rights" released on August 3 in Jerusalem by the Palestinian Women's General Union. It declares in its preamble that "human dignity will be safeguarded by means of a parliamentary democratic system of governance, itself based on freedom of expression and freedom to form parties." It calls for the constitution to be "based on the United Nations Conventions, the Universal Declaration of Human Rights, and other international documents and conventions pertaining to political, civil, economic, social and cultural rights, specifically the Conventions on the Elimination of All Forms of Discrimination Against Women."[8]

Opposed to this enlightened democratic trend in Palestinian society, there is the ugly face of fundamentalist Islam, whose ideological hatred leads its adepts to terror, murder, massacre, and genocide, whenever possible—all carried out in the name of Allah! Islamic Jihad and Hamas derive their inspiration from the Lebanese Hizbollah organization, and all of them are mainly financed by the Islamic Republic of Iran. They are part and parcel of a Fundamentalist International, which held a mass meeting in London's Wembley Stadium on August 7 this year [1994] under the banner of "The Khilafah Conference" (calling for the return of the caliphate), attended by over eight thousand supporters from Europe, Africa, the Maghreb, and the Middle East. It was organized by the Hizb ut-Tahrir, or HUT, the Islamic Liberation Party, Britain's most active fundamentalist group. Among the conference's seven-point declaration, point 4 states, "All agreements with Israel are invalid—not binding on Muslims. There can be no peace with Israel until the State of Israel is demolished." The chairman, at this particular point, added, "Tell that to Arafat and [King] Hussein!" which was greeted by a thunderous chorus of "Allahu Akbars!" Point 7 declares, "All international organisations, e.g. the United Nations . . . the World Bank, etc. are the tools of Imperialists and are rejected by Islam." The HUT is the same organization that, earlier in the year, called for the murder of Jews worldwide in order to accelerate the coming of the Last Day, and then, following outraged protests, provided an eschatalogical explanation for their genocidal appeal.

Distinguished French Arabist Olivier Carré has described and documented in a recent study the irrefutable fact that virtually all of today's militant Islamists expound a Judeophobic or antisemitic doctrine, one of whose major ideological props is *The Protocols of the Elders of Zion*, which they pretend is an authentic Jewish blueprint for world domination—just as Adolf Hitler maintained seventy years ago in *Mein Kampf*.[9]

Concocted nearly one hundred years ago by certain Jesuit circles reacting to the Dreyfus Affair in France, this apocryphal "document" was fabricated in Paris at the turn of the century for the use of the Russian czar's secret police, the Okhrana. The long history of this forgery was recently analyzed and documented by French sociologist Pierre-André Taguieff in his monumental work, *Les Protocoles des Sages de Sion: Faux et Usages d'un faux.*[10] In August 1922, over seventy years ago, the *Times* of London published three articles from its Istanbul correspondent, Philip Graves, who demonstrated, irrefutably, the apocryphal nature of *The Protocols.* The same conclusion resulted from a 1935 court case in Bern, when a Swiss judge again declared *The Protocols* to be a forgery that had caused much harm and might still cause even worse evils.

This dangerous racist myth consists in the belief that a Jewish-led conspiracy seeks to control the world, a plot that is seen at work in every revolution, in every war, in the workings of all international organizations, and in the efforts of most transnational associations—since the French Revolution and even from time immemorial! *The Protocols* have had a long life because they still help to reinforce this grotesque belief, which inspired Hitler's radical antisemitism and helped pave the way to World War II and all its horrors.

Not surprisingly, the August 18, 1988, covenant of the Palestinian Hamas movement splatters in these murky waters, declaring with regard to Zionists—and Jews as a whole, "Their plan is embodied in *The Protocols of the Elders of Zion.*"[11] Article 22 provides evidence to "prove" that the Jews have been responsible for all evils in the world for centuries—including the founding of the League of Nations and the United Nations, after World War I and II, for which they were also responsible.

It is a tragic reflection on our times—sixty years after the 1930s and their apocalyptic aftermath—that *The Protocols* are still widely disseminated, having been reprinted over the last decade in ten European countries: Great Britain, France, Italy, Spain, Yugoslavia, Greece, Poland, and Russia, and also in the United States.

But it is in the Arab/Islamic world that *The Protocols* remains a repulsive bestseller of hatred, running into the hundreds of thousands of copies. As Professor Taguieff points out, Saudi Arabia is the largest producer and exporter of this gross incitement to hatred,[12] which is to be found in the main centers of the Middle East and the Maghreb. The Islamic Republic of Iran provides the needs of the Iranian market, spilling over into European languages for Western consumption.

Here in Sweden, *The Protocols* was one of the main "sources" used by Radio Islam (the Swedish Islamic Association) to "prove," inter alia, that there was a Jewish world conspiracy and that the Holocaust was a Jewish "hoax."

Radio Islam began broadcasting its antisemitic propaganda in 1987 from the vicinity of Stockholm, which led to the longest and most extensive court trial of its kind two years later, when the attorney general successfully prosecuted Ahmad Rami, a Moroccan Muslim, for "incitement against an ethnic group." Here is one quote from Rami's words, referred to by the district attorney in the trial: "Jews will conquer the whole world and kill everyone who resists Jewish world domination and enslave all the other peoples."[13]

The evening newspaper *Expressen* published several articles about Rami in May 1992, revealing the sources of his financial support, which included Iran. Rami lost his lawsuit against *Expressen* in August 1992. The radio was closed down as a result of the October 1992 Stockholm District Court's condemnation of David Janzon, who was legally responsible for the radio station and is a member of the Nazi Swedish National League.

I have here with me this blatant bombshell of religious and racial hatred, which for a century has incited people to kill and to justify their crimes. It is a 1990 Arabic edition of *The Protocols*, published in Beirut by Dar an-Nafais, the "House of Precious Things."[14] It is being sold freely in the Muslim Bookshop, at 233 Seven Sisters Road, London, which prides itself— as indicated in its visiting card—on being "London's Window on Islam," but is in fact inciting hatred and genocide.

The cover of this second edition shows a white Star of David torn into pieces against a crimson background. Superimposed is a Jewish menorah, made of barbed wire, which is dripping blood. The sole illustration shows a spider grasping the globe of the world, with a crude human head, a typical Stürmer-like caricature of a Jew, with the revealing title *Le Péril Juif: Texte intégral des Protocols des Sages d'Israël*, which is then explained in Arabic: "This is the cover of the French edition, whose title is *The Jewish Peril*, from which the present translation was made." In fact, it is the replica of the 1938 Paris edition, sold extensively in France during the Nazi occupation.

The conclusion of the preface is revealing: "They [the Jews] believe that they are God's chosen people, returning to the Promised Land in order to act immorally and foment trouble in whatever way they can. But the inevitable course of history and the Arab and Muslim awakening, as well as the Will of Providence, will make [the destruction of] Israel a lesson for all the people of the world to see. This [destruction] is what we must believe and teach to our children, striving toward its realisation and asking for success from Allah the Exalted One."

A savage onslaught of antisemitic, racial hatred has been launched by the evil forces of extremist obscurantism in their desire to derail the Middle East peace process—and to kill any Jews indiscriminately! A series of wholesale massacres of innocent civilians, committed by religious fanatics in their ongoing war against the Jews, killed 96 persons and wounded 230 in central Buenos Aires on July 18 [1994]. Soon afterward, a Panamanian airliner was blown up, killing 21 persons, most of whose targeted passengers were also Jews. The two bombings in London on July 26–27 [1994] continued the series of hallmark missions of death and destruction, and a third international crime was committed in Tel Aviv on October 19, killing a further 23 persons.

I have gone to some length to demonstrate the real problems that must be faced if one is to overcome the fundamentalists' negation of any kind of peace or reconciliation with Jews and Israel; or, for that matter, with the non-Muslim world—for one should never forget that, in traditional Islamic doctrine, the condition and destiny of Jews and Christians is identical. Now it is the Christians and the West who are accused of fomenting a conspiracy in order to destroy Islam by secularization. Here is, indeed, the major flaw, which could wreck the peace and mar the prospects of all our dreams and visions. It must be squarely faced on all sides if the backlog of suffering and suspicion is to be overcome. This is a highly dangerous and fateful phenomenon, which—in its worldwide ramificatications—may possibly determine the future of our globe during the coming generation.

Although comparisons would be inappropriate, there is also the serious problem of Jewish religious extremism, which has led to outrageous acts of criminality against Muslims in Israel, particularly the Hebron massacre of February 25, 1994, which took the lives of twenty-nine Palestinian men at prayer in the holiest of sanctuaries. The government and people of Israel must find a legal way to marginalize these Jewish extremists and muzzle the fanatics among them—and that brings me to the question of Jewish settlements in the West Bank and Gaza.

We believe that strong ties must encompass full guarantees for the rights of minorities within the geographical area of each party's sovereignty and the autonomous area. The recent statistics indicate Israel's population at about 5,400,000 [in 2004, 6,500,000], of whom nearly 1 million, or 18 percent [in 2004, 1.3 million, or 20 percent], may be categorized as belonging to the country's non-Jewish minorities (about 120,000 Christians), whose equal rights as citizens are inscribed in the country's basic laws. The West Bank and Gaza combined have a population of just under 2 million [in 2004, over 3 million], with a dwindling Palestinian Christian minority of scarcely 35,000 (not counting about 10,000 living in East Jerusalem); and there are about 120,000 Israeli settlers in Judea, Samaria, and Gaza (aside from those living within the municipal bounderies of Greater Jerusalem). The Christian minority thus forms 2 percent [in 2004, about 1 percent] of the Palestinian population in these territories, and the Jewish settlers about 7 percent, outside of the Jerusalem area [in 2004, about 8 percent]. Surely, all the minority groups throughout these regions should share the same "rights of minorities" referred to in the above-mentioned women's draft document. Yasir Arafat is on record as having supported this point of view on several occasions, according to the well-known Palestinian journalist Hanna Siniora, with whom I discussed this matter early last August in Jerusalem.

There is no reason why Jews and Christians cannot live without fear in any Middle East country, just as Muslims and Christians live peaceably as citizens in Israel. I have no doubt that the Jordanian Citizen Law no. 6, dated February 4, 1954, will soon be revoked. It states under subsection 3, "Any man will be a Jordanian subject if he is not a Jew."[15] In the future, neither Jordan nor any other country in the Arab world should be considered *judenrein*.

One could ask, What is the minimum degree of changed attitudes necessary to provide a motivation for economic, social, and political integration? Having given the European example as a model, one should recall that the integration of Western Europe was a slow process, seen by many leaders as politically—and, to a lesser extent, economically—necessary, when popular attitudes toward Germany were still colored by the sufferings of World War II. But such examples are perhaps inappropriate, as Israel is still the only Western-type democracy in the region, and without a general process of democratization the peace process will simply run out of steam. We need to ask, To what extent can extremist forces stop the process of integration? To begin with, all institutional forms of discrimination on both sides must be eliminated, and new forms of cooperation, leading to attitudinal changes, are essential.

Paradoxically, the question of Jerusalem—the City of Peace—is probably the greatest stumbling block to all those now genuinely striving toward "a new spirit of mutual acceptance." Many proposals have been made on this subject, but I prefer to abstain, remembering Alexander Pope's well-known warning: "For fools rush in where angels fear to tread." Unfortunately, Jerusalem has been short of its full quota of angels for some time now! Nonetheless, competent historians can be trusted to put the facts before us, which is what Martin Gilbert has done, in a seminal paper titled "A Tale Of One City," published last week (November 14), in the much-read American weekly the *New Republic*. As this subject is not scheduled to come up for discussion till 1996, perhaps the "new spirit" of cooperation that is beckoning on the horizon will coincide with a memorable event—the trimillennial celebration of the anointing in Jerusalem of David as king of Israel, a great historic figure, recognized by Muslims as a prophet, whose psalms are called *zabour* in Arabic. King David is, of course, a revered person in the Christian tradition, too. There is a motto that says, The Past Is Prologue. With that thought in mind, let me conclude with an ancient "dream."

At such a grand climacteric, when a highway is seriously being planned from Egypt to the Arab Middle East via Israel, some may turn their eyes to the book of Isaiah, where it is written in chapter 19, verses 23–25, "In that day shall there be a highway out of Egypt to Assyria, and the Assyrian shall come into Egypt, and the Egyptian into Assyria, and the Egyptians shall serve with the Assyrians. In that day shall Israel be the third with Egypt and with Assyria, even a blessing in the midst of the land. Whom the Lord of hosts shall bless, saying, Blessed be Egypt my people, and Assyria the work of my hands, and Israel mine inheritance."

Notes

The "United States of Abraham" statement was first prepared by Littman and delivered at the UNCHR on March 6, 1990, when he was the main NGO representative (at the UN's Geneva headquarters) of the World Union for Progressive Judaism. He was greatly encouraged by historian Martin Gilbert, official biographer of Winston Churchill, several times a guest NGO representative for the WUPJ, speaking on Soviet Jewry at the UNCHR in the late 1980s. From 1992 till 1995, Littman was a representative of the International Fellowship of Reconciliation (IFOR), whose main representative was René Wadlow. As a team, they have represented the Association for World Education (AWE) since 1996. A written statement was submitted to the sixtieth session of the UNCHR by the AWE: *14 Years after the Proposal at the UNCHR of a Future "United States of Abraham" (1990)*, E/CN.4/2004/NGO/7, which was posted on the UN Web site in March 2004. Much of this text is to be found in the 1994 lecture; several passages that have been added above [in square brackets] have been integrated from this text. (The following paragraph is based on note 5 in the AWE written statement.)

This documentation was widely circulated in UN, Israeli, and Palestinian circles. Among the correspondence is one of several letters from Eitan Haber, then Israel advisor to Prime Minister Rabin, who wrote to Littman on November 5, 1992, "I am writing on behalf of the Prime Minister, Mr. Yitzhak Rabin, to thank you for your fax dated September 25 and your warm wishes for the New Year. As you know, peace negotiations are currently taking place, and we are hopeful that an agreement will be reached to the satisfaction of all citizens of this region, which will enable Jews and Arabs to live in peace and security. We also have for acknowledgment copy of your release dated 25 August." (The moving conclusion of Prime Minister Rabin's historic speech on the White House lawn is from the same passage in Ecclesiastes 3:1 as in the title published in the *Al-Fajr* weekly of May 31, 1993: "To every thing there is a season, and a time to every purpose under heaven.") On August 17, 1993—a month before the White House ceremony—Israeli foreign minister Shimon Peres wrote to Littman personally: "Thanks for your fax dated June 30. I have read with great interest the proposal and article which you sent me earlier. I appreciate your words of support and your offer of assistance on behalf of your organization, regarding relevant documentation. Best wishes. Sincerely, Shimon Peres."

1. John Locke, *Essay on the Human Understanding*, bk. 4, chap. 20, sec. 17.

2. Winston Churchill, *London Saturday Evening Post*, February 15, 1930.

3. See "Human Rights and Human Wrongs," World Union for Progressive Judaism statement no. 8, Geneva, April 17, 1990, pp. 36–39. It was recorded at the UNCHR; a greatly abridged summary record (E/CN.4/1990/SR.52) omitted mention of Churchill. And *Tribune de Geneve*, January 26–27, 1991.

4. Martin Gilbert, "United States of Abraham," *London Jewish Chronicle*, December 31, 1993.

5. David G. Littman, letter to the editor, *Journal de Genève*, May 9, 1969.

6. Daniel J. Elazar, *Two Peoples—One Land: Federal Solutions for Israel, the Palestinians, and Jordan* (Lanham, MD: University Press of America, 1991); Raphael Israeli, *Palestinians between Israel and Jordan: Squaring the Triangle* (London: Praeger, 1991); Emile A. Nakhleh, "Palestinians and Israelis: Options for Coexistence," *Journal of Palestinian Studies* (Berkeley, CA) 23, no. 2 (Winter 1993).

7. Quoted in *Ha-Aretz* (Tel Aviv), June 24, 1993.

8. "Draft Document of Principles of Women's Rights," *Jerusalem Times*, August 5, 1994.

9. Olivier Carré, *L'utopie islamique dans l'Orient arabe* (Paris: Presses de la Fondation nationale des sciences politiques, 1991), p. 210.

10. Pierre-André Taguieff, *Les Protocoles des Sages de Sion: Faux et Usages d'un Faux*, 2 vols. (Paris: Berg International, 1992), p. 1223.

11. Art. 32.

12. Taguieff, *Les Protocoles*, 1:380.

13. The court transcripts used are from the report on the "Bergman Affair" provided by the Swedish Committee against Antisemitism, Stockholm.

14. Translated by Ihsan Haqqi (Beirut: Dar an-Nafais; 1st ed., 1988; 2nd ed., 1990).

15. In an amendment to this law, enacted April 1, 1963, and called law no. 7 of 1963, "Law Amending the Jordanian Citizenship Law," it became subsection 2 of section 3 of the 1954 law.

YASIR'S TERRORIST
49. JESUS

David G. Littman

I n the past two thousand years there have been numerous descriptions of Jesus of Nazareth, but the image of an Arab Jesus—"the first Palestinian *fedayin* who carried his sword"—as depicted by Yasir Arafat at a sideshow of the United Nations in 1983—during a conference on Palestine—was probably the most grotesque. Present at his first press conference at the Palais des Nations in Geneva on September 2, 1983, I heard the words from the UN simultaneous English interpretation of his spoken Arabic:

> We were under Roman imperialism. We sent a Palestinian fisherman, called St. Peter, to Rome. He not only occupied Rome, but also won the hearts of the people. We know how to resist imperialism and occupation. Jesus Christ was the first Palestinian militant *fedayin* who carried his sword along the path on which the Palestinians today carry their Cross.[1]

There was a full house, but no one expressed either shock or disbelief, nor was there any later protestation from representatives of the Holy See or the World Council of Churches, even after my letter quoting his words was published in three Swiss newspapers.[2] Yet few could ignore the historic fact that it was in 135—one hundred years after the death of Jesus—that the Roman emperor Hadrian reconquered Judea, changing its official name from Judea to Palestina. ("Now when Jesus was born in Bethlehem of Judea in the days of Herod..." Matthew 2:1.)

It was neither the first nor the last time that Arafat, and others, would

---

This article was posted by *FrontPage* magazine on November 15, 2004 (frontpagemag.com), and is reproduced here with the deletion of about seven lines and an additional note.

steal the symbol of Jesus, transforming the Jews of Judea into "Arab Pales-tinians," inhabitants of ancient "Palestine." According to Greek Catholic Archbishop François Abu Mokh, when Arafat was received by Pope John Paul II two weeks later, on September 15, 1983, he told the pope that he felt at home in the Vatican, seat of the successors to St. Peter, "the first Pales-tinian exile."[3] And Arafat repeated his "Jesus" / "Super-*fedayin*" story to columnist Flora Lewis six months later in Paris.[4]

This theme of Jesus and "Palestine" became a constant in the framework of Palestinolatry. . . . In 1974—after a formal complaint—Geneva's authori-ties banned the entry and display of Arafat-Fatah posters representing Jesus nailed to a Star of David, with the caption "Palestine."

Two more recent crude examples, from dozens, illustrate this "religious" tactic. In 1997, at Har Homa, a stony hillside in the Judean desert over-looking East Jerusalem, three Arabs had themselves bound to crosses at Easter to protest the building of houses on land owned by a Jew. The only protest about this sacrilegious utilization of the Cross seems to have come from two foreign Christian residents of Jerusalem, who wrote to express their indignation:

> The continued and blasphemous abuse of the symbols of our faith by the followers of another. . . . Not only did it denigrate our Lord, it was also an unsubtle attempt to resurrect, in the minds of viewers worldwide, the libel of deicide which prompted centuries of Jewish suffering.[5]

Probably the most heinous insult /"defamation" to both Judaism and Christianity occurred on December 11, 2000, two weeks before the Christmas Jubilee, ten weeks after the second intifada began with the savage *fedayin* attacks on Israeli civilians. A new Palestinian daily, *Intifada*, dis-played on one-half of its front page a provocative caricature, showing a cru-cified young woman called "Palestine"—with blood flowing from her pierced hands and feet. A long spear transfixes her body to the cross, its pro-truding point embossed with a star of David and an American flag at the shaft end. Blood spurts from her martyred body down upon a trio of huddled, car-icatured Oriental Jews, who are looking up and grimacing at the crucified young woman, clearly meant to symbolize Jesus and "Palestine." On December 14, *Intifada* went a step further. Alongside a battered cross appeared a pious prayer to: "My Lord the Betrayed ... betrayed by the con-temptible treasonable kiss," and ending: "O Son of the Virgin, they cannot overcome you twice."[6]

There was no official Church reaction before or after Christmas to this gross defamation of Christianity—and of hate propaganda against Jews and Judaism—at the close of the Jubilee Year 2000, after the earlier memorable visit of Pope John Paul II to Jerusalem. However, in Geneva, an ecumenical letter of protest was sent on December 17, 2000, to the Association for World Education (AWE) by Abbé Alain-René Arbez and the Reverend Bernard Buunk. It asked that their "Appeal"("Abuse of a Religious Symbol: A Parody of a Prayer, and Crucifixion in Palestine") be submitted as a formal complaint to the appropriate UN bodies. This was done before Christmas by AWE, which forwarded the joint letter and the caricatures to the UN special rapporteurs on Religious Intolerance (Abdelfattah Amor) and on Racism (Maurice Glélé-Ahanhanzo), asking them to act under Commission on Human Rights Resolution "Defamation of Religions" and record and condemn this blatant travesty. Nothing came of it.[7]

In October 2002, two years after he approved the bloody second Aqsa intifada, Arafat gave an interview to a correspondent from the London Arabic-language daily *Al-Hayat*. On Jerusalem, he was explicit: "They [the Israelis] found not a single stone proving that the Temple of Solomon was there, because historically the Temple was not in Palestine."[8]

In 1983 at the UN—when he called Jesus "the first Palestinian *fedayin* who carried his sword along the path on which the Palestinians today carry their Cross"—and in 2002—when he reiterated a refusal to admit that the Temple of Solomon had ever existed in Jerusalem ("in Palestine")—Arafat demonstrated a classic example of the pillage of Jewish history in the Land of Israel, and a denigration of Christianity—both of which he strove to supplant in order to assume an Arab-Palestinian legitimacy. He would have been more convincing if, in building his "Palestine" as a part of the "Arab Nation," he had researched Arab history, rather than Arabizing and Palestinianizing the history of the Jewish people. If one is obliged to fabricate a history, and a legitimacy by endeavoring to pillage others, it demonstrates a historical dearth.

In an Islamic context, 'Isa—the Muslim name of Jesus—is considered to have preached Islam. He was the awaited Messiah, but did not die on the Cross. In two hadiths, it is alleged that he will return at the end of time, kill the Evil One (the one-eyed Dajjal), break the cross, and kill pigs (thus ending Christianity). He will abolish the *jizya* (poll tax for non-Muslims), and the booty will be abundant, for there will be no religions except Islam, which will reign supreme.[9]

Yasir Arafat would certainly have known these hadiths, including the favorite one of Hamas (his allies since 2000), which concludes article 7 of their genocidal 1988 Constitution—still not condemned at the United Nations!: "The Day of Judgement will not come until Muslims fight the Jews, killing them, when the Jew will hide behind stones and trees. The stones and trees will say, 'O Muslim, there is a Jew behind me, come and kill him.'" And as an epitaph, the slogan of Hamas (article 8)—which has become the slogan of all the Islamikazes—fits Arafat like a glove: "Allah is its target, the Prophet is its model, the Qur'an its Constitution; Jihad its path and death for the sake of Allah is the loftiest of its wishes."[10]

NOTES

1. UN press conference tape, September 2, 1983, in Bat Ye'or, *Islam and Dhimmitude: Where Civilizations Collide* (Madison, NJ: Fairleigh Dickinson University Press, 2002), pp. 319, 466, n. 42.

2. David G. Littman, "Arafat, Jésus et l'histoire," *Dimanche Tribune* (Lausanne), September 11, 1983; *Tribune de Genève*, September 14, 1983; *La Vie Protestante* (Geneva), October 7, 1983.

3. François Abu Mokh, *Les Confessions d'un Arabe Catholique. Entretiens avec Joëlle Chabert et François Mourvillier* (Paris: Centurion, 1991), p. 195; for English see Bat Ye'or, *Islam and Dhimmitude*, p. 466, n. 42.

4. Flora Lewis "The Remarkable Resiliance of Chairman Arafat," *International Herald Tribune* (Paris), March 9, 1984; letter by David G. Littman, "Arafat and Jesus," *International Herald Tribune* (Paris), April 4, 1984.

5. Patrick and Nicola Goodenough, *Jerusalem Post*, April 5, 1997, and in Bat Ye'or, *Islam and Dhimmitude*, pp. 275–76.

6. Documentation from Palestinian Media Watch (PMW), Jerusalem, in Bat Ye'or, *Islam and Dhimmitude*, p. 276.

7. Documentation from Palestinian Media Watch (PMW), and Association for World Education, in Bat Ye'or, *Islam and Dhimmitude*, p. 276.

8. Interview with Arafat, October 5, 2002. English translation in MEMRI, Special Dispatch—Palestinian Authority, no. 42, October 11, 2002, http://www.memri.org/bin/articles.cgi?Page=archives&Area=sd&ID=SP42802.

9. Mark Durie, " 'Isa, the Muslim Jesus," chapter 53 in this volume.

10. Raphael Israeli, *Islamikaze: Manifestations of Islamic Martyrology* (London: Frank Cass, 2003).

PART 6.

THE MYTH IN CONTEMPORARY ACADEMIC AND PUBLIC DISCOURSE

Introduction

Robert Spencer

Today, despite the mountain of evidence provided by the historical record, the myth of Islamic tolerance reigns supreme in the academic and public spheres. Ibn Warraq's seminal debunking of the pretensions of Edward Said is particularly important, for Said is a myth in himself. The influence of his *Orientalism* is so great today that any questioning of the myth of Islamic tolerance brings charges of racism—but as Ibn Warraq demonstrates, once again the reality is quite different.

This section also includes a number of brief pieces that attempt to cut through the fog of misinformation and disinformation that currently constitutes the public debate about Islam. The aggressive nature of this disinformation campaign and its bland acceptance by politicians and opinion makers indicate that patient and thorough spadework must be done today on a large scale in order to restore truth and sanity to the non-Muslim world's dialogue and interaction with the House of Islam. Ibn Warraq, Bat Ye'or, Daniel Pipes, and Mark Durie do some of the necessary work in the documents included here.

Only when the historical record is acknowledged, along with the current teachings of learned Islamic jurists about jihad and dhimmitude, can true Islamic reform become possible. Only then might we see the birth of a genuine form of Islamic tolerance.

EDWARD SAID AND THE
50. SAIDISTS

Or, Third World Intellectual Terrorism

Ibn Warraq

Consider the following observations on the state of affairs in the contemporary Arab world:

> The history of the modern Arab world—with all its political failures, its human rights abuses, its stunning military incompetences, its decreasing production, the fact that alone of all modern peoples, we have receded in democratic and technological and scientific development—is disfigured by a whole series of outmoded and discredited ideas, of which the notion that the Jews never suffered and that the holocaust is an obfuscatory confection created by the Elders of Zion is one that is acquiring too much—far too much—currency. . . . [T]o support Roger Garaudy, the French writer convicted earlier this year on charges of holocaust denial, in the name of "freedom of opinion" is a silly ruse that discredits us more than we already are discredited in the world's eyes for our incompetence, our failure to fight a decent battle, our radical misunderstanding of history and the world we live in. Why don't we fight harder for freedom of opinions in our own societies, a freedom, no one needs to be told, that scarcely exists?[1]

It takes considerable courage for an Arab to write self-criticism of this kind; indeed, without the personal pronoun *we* how many would have guessed that an Arab, let alone Edward Said himself, had written it? And yet, ironically, what makes self-examination for Arabs and Muslims, and particularly criticism of Islam in the West, very difficult is the totally pernicious influence of Edward Said's *Orientalism.*[2] This work taught an entire generation of Arabs the art of self-pity—"were it not for the wicked imperialists,

Reprinted with permission from www.secularislam.org/articles/debunking.htm.

racists, and Zionists, we would be great once more"—encouraged the Islamic fundamentalist generation of the 1980s, and bludgeoned into silence any criticism of Islam, even stopping dead the research of eminent Islamologists who felt their findings might offend Muslim sensibilities and who dared not risk being labeled "Orientalists." The aggressive tone of *Orientalism* is what I have called "intellectual terrorism," since it does not seek to convince by arguments or historical analysis but by spraying charges of racism, imperialism, Eurocentrism, from a moral high ground; anyone who disagrees with Said has insult heaped upon him. The moral high ground is an essential element in Said's tactics; since he believes his position is morally unimpeachable, Said obviously thinks it justifies him in using any means possible to defend it, including the distortion of the views of eminent scholars, interpreting intellectual and political history in a highly tendentious way—in short, twisting the truth. But in any case, he does not believe in the "truth."

Said attacks not only the entire discipline of Orientalism, which is devoted to the academic study of the Orient but which Said accuses of perpetuating negative racial stereotypes, anti-Arab and anti-Islamic prejudice, and the myth of an unchanging, essential "Orient"; he also accuses Orientalists as a group of complicity with imperial power and holds them responsible for creating the distinction between Western superiority and Oriental inferiority, which they achieve by suppressing the voice of the "Oriental" and by their antihuman tendency to make huge but vague generalizations about entire populations, which in reality consist of millions of individuals. In other words, much of what was written about the Orient in general, and Islam and Islamic civilization in particular, was false. The Orientalists also stand accused of creating the "Other"—the non-European, always characterized in a negative way—as for example, passive, weak, and in need of civilizing (Western strength versus Eastern weakness).

But "Orientalism" is also more generally "a style of thought based upon an ontological and epistemological distinction made between "the Orient" and (most of the time) "the Occident" (p. 2). Thus European writers of fiction, epic, travel, social description, customs, and people are all accused of "orientalism." In short, Orientalism is seen "as a Western style for dominating, restructuring, and having authority over the Orient." Said makes much of the notion of a discourse derived from Foucault, who argued that supposedly objective and natural structures in society—which, for example, privilege some and punish others for nonconformity—are in fact "discourses of power." The putative "objectivity" of a discipline covered up its real nature; disciplines such as Orientalism participated in such discourses. Said continues, "[W]ithout examining Orientalism as a discourse one cannot possibly understand the enormously systematic discipline by which European culture was able to manage—even produce—the Orient politically, sociologically, militarily, ideologically, scientifically, and imaginatively during the post-Enlightenment period" (p. 3).

From Pretentiousness to Meaninglessness

There are, as I shall show, several contradictory theses buried in Said's impenetrable prose, decked with postmodern jargon ("a universe of representative discourse," "Orientalist discourse" [p. 71]) and pretentious language that often conceals some banal observation, as when Said talks of "textual attitude " (pp. 92–93), when all he means is "bookish" or "bookishness." Tautologies abound, as in "the freedom of licentious sex" (p. 190). (And some kind editor really ought to explain to Said the meaning of *literally* [see pp. 19, 87, 93, 138, 179, 218, 307] and the difference between *scatological* and *eschatological* [see p. 68]).

Or take the comments here:

> Thus out of the Napoleonic expedition there issued a whole series of textual children, from Chateaubriand's *Itinéraire* to Lamartine's *Voyage en Orient* to Flaubert's *Salammbô*, and in the same tradition, Lane's *Manners and Customs of the Modern Egyptians* and Richard Burton's *Personal Narrative of a Pilgrimage to al-Madinah and Meccah*. What binds them together is not only their common background in Oriental legend and experience but also their learned reliance on the Orient as a kind of womb out of which they were brought forth. If paradoxically these creations turned out to be highly stylized simulacra, elaborately wrought imitations of what a live Orient might be thought to look like, that by no means detracts from their strength of their imaginative conception or from the strength of European mastery of the Orient, whose prototypes respectively were Cagliostro, the great European impersonator of the Orient, and Napoleon, its first modern conqueror. (pp. 89–88)

What does Said mean by "out of the Napoleonic expedition there issued a whole series of textual children" except that these five very varied works were written *after* 1798? The pretentious language of "textual children" issuing from the Napeolonic expedition covers up this crushingly obvious fact. Perhaps there is a profound thesis hidden in the jargon, that these works were somehow influenced by the Napoleonic expedition, inspired by it, and could not have been written without it. But no such thesis is offered. This arbitrary group consists of three Frenchmen, two Englishmen, one work of romantic historical fiction, three travel books, and one detailed study of modern Egyptians. François-René Chateaubriand's *Itinéraire* (1811) describes superbly his visit to the Near East; *Voyage en Orient* (1835) is Alphonse de Lamartine's impressions of Palestine, Syria, and Greece; *Salammbô* (1862) is Gustave Flaubert's novel of ancient Carthage; Edward William Lane's *Manners and Customs of the Modern Egyptians* (1836) is a fascinating firsthand account of life in Egypt, particularly Cairo and Luxor, written after several years of residence there (1825–1828; and 1833–1835); Richard Francis Burton's account of his audacious visit to Mecca was first published in three volumes between 1855 and 1856. Lane and Burton both had perfect command of Arabic, classical and colloquial, while the others did not, and Lane and Burton can be said to have made contributions to Islamic studies, particularly Lane, but not the three Frenchmen.

What on earth do they have in common? Said tells us that what binds them together is "their common background in Oriental legend and experience but also their learned reliance on the Orient as a kind of womb out of which they were brought forth." What is the background of Oriental legend that inspired Burton or Lane? Was Flaubert's vivid imagination stimulated by "Oriental legend," and was this the same legendary material that inspired Burton, Lane, and Lamartine? "Learned reliance on the Orient as a kind of womb" is yet another example of Said's pretentious way of saying the obvious, namely that they were writing about the Orient about which they had some experience and intellectual knowledge.

Why are all these disparate works "imitations"? Take Lane and Burton's works; they are both highly accurate accounts based on personal, firsthand experience. They are not imitations of anything. James Aldridge, in his study *Cairo* (1969), called Lane's account "the most truthful and detailed account in English of how Egyptians lived and behaved."[3] Burton's accurate observations are still quoted for their scientific value, as in F. E. Peters's *The Hajj*.[4] Said also says of Lane, "For Lane's legacy as a scholar mattered not to the Orient, of course, but to the institutions and agencies of his European society" (p. 164). There is no "of course" about it—Lane's *Arabic Lexicon* (5 vols., 1863–74) is still one of the first lexicons consulted by any Muslim scholars wishing to translate the Qur'an into English; scholars like Maulana Muhammad Ali, who began his English translation in 1909 and who constantly refers to Lane in his copious footnotes, as does A. Yusuf Ali in his

1934 translation. What is more, the only place where one can still buy a reasonably priced copy of Lane's indispensable work of reference is Beirut, where it is published by the Librairie du Liban.

What profound mysteries are unraveled by Said's final tortuous sentence in the passage above? Count Alessandro Cagliostro (1743–1795) was a Sicilian charlatan who traveled in Greece, Egypt, Arabia, Persia, Rhodes, and Malta. During his travels he is said to have acquired considerable knowledge of the esoteric sciences, alchemy in particular. On his return to Europe, Cagliostro was involved in many swindles and seems to have been responsible for many forgeries of one kind or another, but he found time to establish many masonic lodges and secret societies. He died in prison in 1795. He did not contribute anything whatsoever to the scientific study of the Near or Middle East, neither of its languages nor of its history or culture. He was not a distinguished Orientalist in the way Lane was. Indeed, apart from "Letter to the French People" (1786), I do not think Cagliostro ever wrote anything worthy to be called scientific. Cagliostro, according to Said, was the prototype of "their [the above five authors'] imaginative conception." Is he suggesting that they, too, forged or made up their entire knowledge of the Egypt, Near East, and Arabia? If that is what Said means, it is false for reasons that I have already indicated above.

For Said, Napoleon was the prototype of the "strength of European mastery of the Orient," since he was the Orient's first modern conqueror. This would be fine as a rather contrived metaphor—Lane and Burton mastered Arabic in the way Napoleon mastered Egypt—but unfortunately, in the rest of his book, Said seems to suggest something far more literal and sinister in the complicity of Orientalists with the imperial powers.

Orientalism is peppered with meaningless sentences. Take, for example, "Truth, in short, becomes a function of learned judgment, not of the material itself, which in time seems to owe its existence to the Orientalist" (p. 67). Said seems to be saying that "truth" is created by the experts or Orientalists and does not correspond to reality, to what is actually out there. So far, so good. But then "what is out there" is also said to owe its existence to the Orientalist. If that is the case, then the first part of Said's sentence makes no sense, and if the first part is true, then the second part makes no sense. Is Said relying on that weasel word *seems* to get him out of the mess? That ruse will not work either; for what would it mean to say that an external reality independent of the Orientalist's judgment also seems to be a creation of the Orientalist? That would be a simple contradiction.

Here is another example: "The Orientalist can imitate the Orient without the opposite being true" (p. 160). Throughout his book, Said is at pains to point out that there is no such thing as "the Orient," which for him is merely a meaningless abstraction concocted by Orientalists in the service of imperialists and racists. In this case, what on earth could "the Orient cannot imitate the Orientalist" possibly mean? If we replace "the Orient" by the individual countries, say between Egypt and India, do we get anything more coherent? No, obviously not: "India, Egypt, and Iran cannot imitate the Orientalists like Renan, Bernard Lewis, Burton, et al." We get nonsense whichever way we try to gloss Said's sentence.

CONTRADICTIONS

At times, Said seems to allow that the Orientalists did achieve genuine positive knowledge of the Orient, its history, culture, and languages, as when he calls Lane's work *Manners and Customs of the Modern Egyptians* "a classic of historical and anthropological observation because of its style, its enormously intelligent and brilliant details" (p. 15); or when he talks of "a growing systematic knowledge in Europe about the Orient" (p. 34), since Said does not have sarcastic quotation marks around the word "knowledge," I presume he means there was a growth in genuine knowledge. Further on, Said talks of Orientalism producing "a fair amount of exact positive knowledge about the Orient" (p. 52). Again, I take it Said is not being ironic when he talks of "philological discoveries in comparative grammar made by Jones" (p. 98). To give one final example, Said mentions Orientalism's "objective discoveries" (p. 203).

Yet these acknowledgements of the real discoveries made by Orientalists is contradicted by Said's insistence that there is no such thing as "truth " (p. 272) or when he characterizes Orientalism as "a form of paranoia, knowledge of another kind, say, from ordinary historical knowledge " (p. 73). Or again, "It is finally Western ignorance which becomes more refined and complex, not some body of positive Western knowledge which increases in size and accuracy" (p. 62). At one point Said seems to deny that the Orientalist had acquired any objective knowledge at all (p. 122), and a little later he also writes, "The advances made by a 'science' like Orientalism in its academic form are less objectively true than we often like to think" (p. 202). It is true that the last phrase does leave open the possibility that *some* of the science may be true, though less than we had hitherto thought. Said also of course wholeheartedly endorses Abdel Malek's strictures against Orientalism and its putatively false "knowledge" of the Orient (pp. 96–97).

In his 1994 afterword, Said insists that he has "no interest in, much less capacity for, showing what the true Orient and Islam really are" (p. 331). And yet he contradicts this outburst of uncharacteristic humility and modesty when he claims that "[the Orientalist's] Orient is not the Orient as it is, but the Orient as it has been Orientalized" (p. 104), for such a formulation assumes Said knows what the real Orient is. Such an assumption is also apparent in his statement that "the present crisis dramatizes the disparity between texts and reality" (p. 109). In order to be able to tell the difference between the two, Said must know what the reality is. This is equally true when Said complains, "To look into Orientalism for a lively sense of an Oriental's human or even social reality . . . is to look in vain" (p. 176).

HISTORICAL AND OTHER HOWLERS

For a work that purports to be a serious work of intellectual history, *Orientalism* is full of historical howlers.[5] According to Said, at the end of the seventeenth century, Britain and France dominated the eastern Mediterranean, when in fact the Levant was still controlled for the next hundred years by the Ottomans. British and French merchants needed the permission of the sultan to land. Egypt is repeatedly described as a British colony when, in fact, Egypt was never more than a protectorate; it was never annexed, as Said claims (p. 35). Real colonies, like Australia or Algeria, were settled by large numbers of Europeans, and this manifestly was not the case with Egypt.[6]

The most egregious error surely is where Said claims Muslim armies conquered Turkey before they overran North Africa (p. 59). In reality, of course, the Arabs invaded North Africa in the seventh century, and what is now Turkey remained part of the Eastern Roman Empire and was a Christian country until conquered by the Seljuk Turks in the late eleventh century.[7] Said also writes, "Macdonald and Massignon were widely sought after as experts on Islamic matters by colonial administrators from North Africa to Pakistan" (p. 210). But Pakistan was never a colony; it was created in 1947 when the British left India. Said also talks rather oddly about the "unchallenged Western dominance" of the Portuguese in the East Indies, China, and Japan until the nineteenth century (p. 73). But Portugal only dominated the trade, especially in the sixteenth century, and was never, as historian J. M. Roberts points out, "interested in the subjugation or settlement of large areas."[8] In China, Portugal only had the tiniest of footholds in Macao. The first decades of the seventeenth century witnessed the collapse of much of the

Portuguese empire in the East, to be replaced by the Dutch. In the early eighteenth century there was a Dutch supremacy in the Indian Ocean and Indonesia; however, the Dutch, like the Portuguese, did not subjugate "the Orient" but worked through diplomacy with native rulers and through a network of trading stations.[9]

Said thinks that Carlyle and Newman were "liberal cultural heroes"! It would be more correct to characterize Carlyle's works as the intellectual ancestry of fascism.[10] Nor was Newman a liberal, rather a High Church Anglican who converted to Catholicism. Said also seems to think that Goldziher was German (p. 18); Goldziher was, of course, Hungarian. (One hopes that it is simply a typographical error in his 1994 afterword that was responsible for the misspelling of Claude Cahen's name.)[11] Said thinks *Muslims* designates a race (p. 99).

INTELLECTUAL DISHONESTY AND TENDENTIOUS REINTERPRETATIONS

The above errors can be put down to ignorance; Said is no historian, but it does put into doubt his competence for writing such a book. On the other hand, we can only qualify as intellectual dishonesty the way he deliberately misinterprets a distinguished scholar's work and conclusions. Said quotes with approval and admiration some of the conclusions of R. W. Southern's *Western Views of Islam in the Middle Ages*:

> Most conspicuous to us is the inability of any of these systems of thought [European Christian] to provide a fully satisfying explanation of the phenomenon they had set out to explain [Islam]—still less to influence the course of practical events in a decisive way. At a practical level, events never turned out either so well or so ill as the most intelligent observers predicted; and it is perhaps worth noticing that they never turned out better than when the best judges confidently expected a happy ending. Was there any progress [in Christian knowledge of Islam]? I must express my conviction that there was. Even if the solution of the problem remained obstinately hidden from sight, the statement of the problem became more complex, more rational, and more related to experience. . . . The scholars who labored at the problem of Islam in the Middle Ages failed to find the solution they sought and desired; but they developed habits of mind and powers of comprehension which, in other men and in other fields, may yet deserve success.[12]

Now here is Said's extraordinary misinterpretation of the above quote from Southern: "The best part of Southern's analysis . . . is his demonstration that it is finally Western ignorance which becomes more refined and complex, not some body of positive Western knowledge which increases in size and accuracy" (p. 62). According to Said, Southern says that positive Western knowledge of the Orient did not increase. This is *not* what Southern is saying. Southern explicitly asks a question and replies, "Was there any progress [in Christian knowledge of Islam]? I must express my conviction that there was." Yes, I am firmly convinced that Western knowledge did progress—that is what Southern states. Then Southern goes on to say that medieval scholars' methodology became more and more sophisticated; they were more mature intellectually since they developed habits of mind and powers of comprehension that would pay dividends later. How Said can claim, with his usual pretentious vocabulary of "Western ignorance which becomes more refined," otherwise is a mystery, but all in keeping with his intellectual dishonesty and his overriding concern to paint the West in as negative a fashion as possible? Incidentally, and ironically, the very same passage from Southern contradicts one of Said's principal theses about Oriental Studies being a cause of imperialism. All this thinking about the Orient failed, Southern says, "to influence the course of practical events in a decisive way."

Said also seems to reproach Friedrich Schlegel for holding views that are in fact correct: "[Although by] 1808 Schlegel had practically renounced his Orientalism, he still held that Sanskrit and Persian on the one hand and Greek and German on the other had more affinities with each other than with Semitic, Chinese, American, or African languages" (p. 98). One can only conclude that Said does not know that what Schlegel held is indeed the case: Sanskrit, Persian, Greek, and German all belong to the same family, the Indo-European, and have more in common with each other by definition, than with any other language in any other family, like Semitic.

Said quotes Sir William Jones's famous encomium on Sanskrit and its affinities to Greek and Latin as though it were of some sinister significance, by prefacing the quote with remarks that can only be described as plain silly:

> [Jones's] most famous pronouncement indicates the extent to which modern Orientalism, even in its philosophical beginnings, was a comparative discipline having for its principal goal the grounding of the European languages in a distant, and harmless, Oriental source: "The Sanscrit language, whatever be its antiquity, is of a wonderful structure; more perfect than the Greek, more copious than the Latin, and more exquisitively refined than either, yet bearing to both of them a stronger affinity, both in the roots of

verbs and in the forms of grammar, than could possibly have been produced by accident; so strong indeed, that no philologer could examine them all three without believing them to have sprung from some common source." (pp. 78–79)[13]

What does Said mean by saying modern Orientalism had as its goal "the grounding of the European languages in a distant, and harmless, Oriental source"? It is pretentious nonsense. Jones was not the first one to see that there were remarkable similarities between Sanskrit and Greek and Latin— as early as the sixteenth century Filippo Sassetti, and in 1767 P. Coeurdoux, had noticed them—but Jones's independent reflections led him to conclude that there was a similarity, and this was a *discovery*, a very exciting scientific discovery that has since been amply confirmed. To say that Orientalists wanted to ground the European languages in Oriental sources is absurd; they *discovered* that they were related in some way—they did not concoct some theory to fit their desire to "ground European languages in Oriental sources." What on earth does a "harmless, Oriental source" mean, in any case? Greek and Latin do not have their "sources" in Sanskrit; they simply belong to the same genetic family, possibly descended from some common ancestral proto-Indo-European language.

As Prof. K. Paddaya of Pune, India, said in his appreciation of Sir William Jones, "[I]t was genuine curiosity and admiration which made some of these officers [of the East India Company like Jones] voluntarily take up the study of [India's] past conditions."[14] Jones's eulogy on Sanskrit is still quoted with pride by many Indian scholars, who honored Jones's memory by holding conferences in Calcutta and Pune in April 1994 to mark the bicentenary of his death. The bicentenary of the establishment of the Asiatic Society, which Jones founded, was celebrated in 1984 in New Delhi and Calcutta.

Said also does not come across as a careful reader of Dante and his masterpiece, *The Divine Comedy*. In his trawl through Western literature for filth to besmirch Western civilization, Said comes across Dante's description of Muhammad in hell and concludes, "Dante's verse at this point spares the reader none of the eschatological [*sic*] detail that so vivid a punishment entails: Muhammad's entrails and his excrement are described with unflinching accuracy" (p. 68). First, Said does not know the difference between scatological and eschatological, and second, we may ask how he knows that Dante's description is unflinchingly accurate. He simply means, I presume, that it was highly graphic.

Said then makes much of the fact that earlier in the *Inferno*, three Muslims turn up in the company of virtuous heathens like Plato and Aristotle.

Said continues, "[B]ut the special anachronisms and anomalies of putting pre-Christian luminaries in the same category of 'heathen' damnation with post-Christian Muslims does not trouble Dante. Even though the Qur'an specifies Jesus as a prophet, Dante chooses to consider the great Muslim philosophers [Avicenna and Averroës] and king [Saladin] as having been fundamentally ignorant of Christianity." This fatuous comment betrays Said's fundamental ignorance of Christian doctrine, even though he himself is a Christian. Although these people of much worth—*gente di molto valore*—had not sinned, according to Christian doctrine, they could not be saved outside the Church, that is, without baptism, which is the first sacrament and thus the "gateway to the faith." The three Muslims were in the outer circle of hell not because they were ignorant of Christianity but because they had died unbaptized. Since these regions of hell are timeless and its inhabitants are there forever, the question of anachronism does not arise, especially as these historical figures have an allegorical significance. Said was surely aware that Virgil, who died in 19 BCE, was Dante's guide and fulfills an allegorical function; Virgil's voice is that of reason or philosophical wisdom. Allegory is central to any understanding of the *Divine Comedy*: *literra gesta docet, quid credas, allegoria*—the literal sense teaches the facts; the allegory what you should believe.

Furthermore, these illustrious Muslims were included precisely because of Dante's profound reverence for all that was best in the non-Christian world, and their exclusion from salvation, inevitable under Christian doctrine, saddened him and put a great strain on his mind—*gran duol mi prese al cor quando lo 'ntesi*—"great grief seized me at heart when I heard this." Dante was even much influenced by the Averroistic concept of the "possible intellect." The same generous impulse that made him revere non-Christians like Avicenna and their nobleness made Dante relegate Muhammad to eternal punishment in the eighth circle of hell, namely, Dante's strong sense of the unity of humanity and of all its spiritual values—*universalis civilitas humani generis*—the universal community of the human race. He and his contemporaries in the late thirteenth and early fourteenth century had only the vaguest of ideas about the history and theology of Islam and its founder. Dante believed that Muhammad and Ali were the initiators of the great schism between Christianity and Islam. Dante, like his contemporaries, thought Muhammad was originally a Christian and a cardinal who wanted to become pope. Hence Muhammad was a *divider* of humanity, whereas Dante stood for the unity—the essential organic unity—of humankind. What Said does not see is that Dante perfectly exemplifies Western culture's strong tendency toward universalism.[15]

Self-pity, Postimperialist Victimhood, and Imperialism

In order to achieve his goal of painting the West in general, and the discipline of Orientalism in particular, in as negative a way as possible, Said has recourse to several tactics. One of his preferred moves is to depict the Orient as a perpetual victim of Western imperialism, dominance, and aggression. The Orient is never seen as an actor, an agent with free will, or designs or ideas of its own. It is to this propensity that we owe that immature and unattractive quality of much contemporary Middle Eastern culture, self-pity, and the belief that all its ills are the result of Western-Zionist conspiracies.[16] Here is an example of Said's own belief in the usual conspiracies, taken from "The Question of Palestine": It was perfectly apparent to Western supporters of Zionism like Arthur James Balfour that the colonization of Palestine was made a goal for the Western powers from the very beginning of Zionist planning: Herzl used the idea, Weizmann used it, every leading Israeli since has used it. Israel was a device for holding Islam—later the Soviet Union, or communism—at bay.[17] So Israel was created to hold Islam at bay!

As for the politics of victimhood, Said has "milked it himself to an indecent degree."[18] Said wrote, "My own experiences of these matters are in part what made me write this book. The life of Arab Palestinians in the West, particularly in America, is disheartening. There exists here an almost unanimous consensus that politically he does not exist, and when it is allowed that he does, it is either as a nuisance or as an Oriental. The web of racism, cultural stereotypes, political imperialism, dehumanizing ideology holding in the Arab or the Muslim is very strong indeed, and it is this web which every Palestinian has come to feel as his uniquely punishing destiny" (p. 27).

Such wallowing in self-pity from a tenured and much-feted professor at Columbia University, where he enjoys privileges that we lesser mortals only dream of and a decent salary, all the while spewing forth hatred of the country that took him in and heaped honors on him, is nauseating. As Ian Buruma concluded in his review of Said's memoir, *Out of Place*, "The more he dwells on his suffering and his exile status, the more his admirers admire him. On me, however, it has the opposite effect. Of all the attitudes that shape a memoir, self-pity is the least attractive."[19]

The putative conquest of Egypt by Napoleon plays an important symbolic role in Said's scheme of showing all that is evil in Orientalism. For Said, Napoleon conquered, dominated, engulfed, possessed, and oppressed Egypt (pp. 83–88). Egypt is described as the passive victim of Western rapacity. In reality, the French were defeated and had to retreat hastily after less than four years; Napoleon arrived in July 1798, and left it for good just over a year later, and the French forces stayed until September 1801. But during this brief interlude, the French fleet was destroyed at the Battle of the Nile, and the French failed to capture Murad Bey. Riots also broke out when a house act was introduced in Cairo, and the French general dupuy, lieutenant governor of Cairo, was killed. Further riots broke out among the Muslims in Cairo when the French left to confront the Turks at Mataria, but the chief victims were Christians, many of whom were slaughtered by the Muslims. Jean-Baptiste Kléber, the French general, was also assassinated. Far from seeing the Egyptians as the "Other," and far from denigrating Islam, right from 1798, the French were highly sensitive to Muslim opinion, with Napoleon showing an initimate knowledge of the Qur'an. Perhaps the ultimate irony was that after the assassination of Kléber, the command of the French army passed to Gen. J. F. Baron de Menou, who had converted to Islam and who set about enacting various measures to conciliate the Muslims.

Naguib Mahfouz, the Nobel Prize–winning Egyptian novelist, once said it is thanks to Napoleon's campaign in Egypt that his country has emerged out of centuries of obscurantism. Egypt owes all her modernity to Napoleon![20] So much for the evils of the "conquest of Egypt."

Had he bothered to pursue the subsequent history of Egypt, Said would have put all Western imperialism in perspective, since he would have come across the history of Muhammad Ali, often considered the founder of modern Egypt. It was never in the interest or even the intention of the Western powers to see the dismemberment of the Ottoman Empire, which time and time again sought and received European support for the preservation of its imperial possessions. After the humiliating retreat of the French, the Ottomans' greatest challenger was a Muslim, the able but ambitious governor of Egypt Muhammad Ali Pasha, "who aspired to nothing less than the substitution of his own empire for that of the Ottomans."[21] Inspired by Napoleon, Muhammad Ali modernized many of Egypt's archaic institutions. In his imperial dreams, Ali was thwarted by the Ottomans with the help, once again, of the great powers, Britain, Russia, Austria, and Prussia, which did not wish to use the sultan's plight to expand their imperial possessions. A little later Muhammad Ali's grandson, Ismail, also dreamed of transforming Egypt into a modern imperial power. By the mid-1870s "a vast Egyptian empire had come into being, extending from the Mediterranean in the north to Lake Victoria, and from the Indian Ocean in the east to the Libyan desert."[22]

I have dwelled on these historical details to put nineteenth-century imperialism in context and to show that Middle Eastern history was created by

Middle Eastern actors who were "not hapless victims of predatory imperial powers but active participants in the restructuring of their region."[23] But this, of course, does not serve Said's purpose at all, which is to show "the Orientals" as passive victims of Western imperialism, unable to control their own destiny. It is Said who is guilty of the very sins that he accuses the Orientalists of, namely, suppressing the voice of the people of Egypt, the true history of the Near East, which was created by indigenous trends, desires, and actions freely chosen.

In *Orientalism*, Said writes, "Both before and during World War I secret diplomacy was bent on carving up the Near Orient first into spheres of influence, then into mandated (or occupied) territories" (p. 220). This is totally false; here is how two historians see it:

> [T]he chain of events culminating in the destruction of the Ottoman Empire and the creation of the modern Middle East was set in motion *not* by secret diplomacy bent on carving up the Middle East, but rather by the decision of the Ottoman leadership to throw in its lot with Germany. This was by far the single most important decision in the history of the modern Middle East, and it was anything but inevitable. The Ottoman Empire was neither forced into the war in a last-ditch bid to ensure its survival, nor maneuvered into it by an overbearing German ally and an indifferent or even hostile British policy. Rather, the [Ottoman] empire's willful plunge into the whirlpool reflected a straightforward [Ottoman] imperialist policy of territorial aggrandizement and status acquisition.[24] (emphasis in the original)

Prime Minister Asquith noted in his diary in March 1915, "[Foreign secretary Sir Edward Grey and I] both think that in the interests of our own future the best thing would be if at the end of the War we could say that we had taken and gained nothing." Similarly, the Bunsen Committee of April–May 1915 had a clear preference for the maintenance of an independent but decentralized empire comprising of five major provinces: Anatolia, Armenia, Syria, Palestine, and Iraq-Jezirah. Nearly a year after the outbreak of World War I, Britain still did not wish to see the destruction of Turkey in Asia.[25] It was an Arab, Sharif Hussein of Mecca, who wanted to establish his own empire on the ruins of that of the Ottomans.

Similarly, when referring to T. E. Lawrence, Said writes, "The great drama of Lawrence's work is that it symbolizes the struggle, first, to stimulate the Orient (lifeless, timeless, forceless) into movement; second, to impose upon that movement an essentially Western shape" (p. 242). Again, it is *Said* who is assuming the Arabs were passive and had decisions taken for and imposed upon them, as though they were children or imbeciles incapable of having desires and acting freely. Certainly, the forceful personalities of the sharif of Mecca, Hussein Ibn Ali, and his son Faisal played the most important part during World War I and were as responsible for what emerged after it as the Western powers.

Thus Said's use of emotive language concerning Western imperialism with all its supposed evils conceals the real overall historical background of the entire region. Whereas the French presence lasted less than four years, when they were ignominiously expelled by the British and Turks, the Ottomans had been the masters of Egypt since 1517, a total of 280 years! Even if we count the later British and French protectorates, Egypt was under Western control for 67 years, Syria for 21 years, and Iraq for only 15. And, of course, Saudi Arabia was never under Western control. Contrast this with southern Spain, which was under the Muslim yoke for 781 years, Greece for 381 years, and the splendid new Christian capital that eclipsed Rome—Constantinople—is still in Muslim hands.[26] But I do not know of any Spanish or Greek politics of victimhood.

SAID'S ANTI-WESTERNISM

In the rather disingenuous 1994 afterword Said denies that he is anti-Western; he denies that the phenomenon of Orientalism is a synecdoche of the entire West and claims that he believes there is no such stable reality as "the Orient" and "the Occident," that there is no enduring Oriental reality and even less an enduring Western essence, and that he has no interest in, much less capacity for, showing what the true Orient and Islam really are (pp. 330–33).

Denials to the contrary, an actual reading of *Orientalism* is enough to show Said's anti-Westernism. While he does occasionally use inverted commas around "the Orient" and "the Occident," the entire force of Said's polemic comes from the polar opposites and contrasts of the East and the West, the Orient and Europe, Us and the Other, that he himself has rather crudely set up.

Said wrote, "I doubt that it is controversial, for example, to say that an Englishman in India or Egypt in the later nineteenth century took an interest in those countries that was never far from their status in his mind as British colonies. To say this may seem quite different from saying that all academic knowledge about India and Egypt is somehow tinged and impressed with, violated by, the gross political fact [of imperialism]—and yet *that is what I am saying* in this study of Orientalism" (p. 11; emphasis in original).

Here is Said's characterization of all Europeans: "It is therefore correct that every European, in what he could say about the Orient, was consequently a racist, an imperialist, and almost totally ethnocentric" (p. 204). In other words, not only is every European a racist, but he must *necessarily* be so. Said claims he is explicitly antiessentialist, particularly about "the West." But here is Said again: "Consider first the demarcation between Orient and West. It already seems bold by the time of the *Iliad*. Two of the most profoundly influential qualities associated with the East appear in Aeschylus's *The Persians*, the earliest Athenian play extant, and in *The Bacchae* of Euripides, the very last one extant. . . . The two aspects of the Orient that set it off from the West in this pair of plays will remain essential motifs of European imaginative geography. A line is drawn between two continents. Europe is powerful and articulate; Asia is defeated and distant" (pp. 56–57).

Keith Windschuttle comments on the above passage,

> These same motifs persist in Western culture, [Said] claims, right down to the modern period. This is a tradition that accommodates perspectives as divergent as those of Aeschylus, Dante, Victor Hugo, and Karl Marx. However, in describing "the essential motifs" of the European geographic imagination that have persisted since ancient Greece, he is ascribing to the West a coherent self-identity that has produced a specific set of value judgements—"Europe is powerful and articulate; Asia is defeated and distant"—that have remained constant for the past 2500 years. This is, of course, nothing less than the use of the very notion of "essentialism" that he elsewhere condemns so vigorously. In short, it is his own work that is essentialist and ahistorical. He himself commits the very faults he says are so objectionable in the work of Orientalists.[27]

Just in case the above were not enough to prove Said's anti-Western essentialism, here is another gem: "The Orient was Orientalized not only because it was discovered to be 'Oriental' in all those ways considered commonplace by an average nineteenth-century European, but also because it could be—that is, submitted to being—*made* Oriental" (p. 6). Here we have Said's ultimate reductionistic absurdity: the average nineteenth-century European!

A part of Said's tactics is to leave out Western writers and scholars who do not conform to Said's theoretical framework. Since, for Said, all Europeans are a priori racist, he obviously cannot allow himself to quote writers who are not. Indeed, one could write a parallel work to *Orientalism* made up of extracts from Western writers, scholars, and travelers who were attracted by various aspects of non-European cultures, which they praised and contrasted favorably with their own decadence, bigotry, intolerance, and bellicosity.

Said makes much of Aeschylus's *Persians* and its putative permanent creation of the "Other" in Western civilization. But Aeschylus can be forgiven his moment of triumphalism when he describes a battle in which he very probably took part in 480 BCE, the battle of Salamis, on which the very existence of fifth-century Athens depended. The Greeks destroyed or captured two hundred ships for the loss of forty, which for Aeschylus was symbolic of the triumph of liberty over tyranny, Athenian democracy over Persian imperialism, for it must not be forgotten that the Persians were ruthless imperialists whose rule did not endear them to several generations of Greeks.

Furthemore, had he delved a little deeper into Greek civilization and history, and bothered to look at Herodotus's great history, Said would have encountered two features that were also deep characteristics of Western civilization and that Said is at pains to conceal and refuses to allow: the seeking after knowledge for its own sake and its profound belief in the unity of mankind—in other words, its universalism. The Greek word *historia*, from which we get our *history*, means "research" or "inquiry," and Herodotus believed his work was the outcome of research: what he had seen, heard, and read but supplemented and verified by inquiry. For Herodotus, "historical facts have intrinsic value and rational meaning." He was totally devoid of racial prejudice—indeed, Plutarch later branded him a *philobarbaros*, whose nearest modern equivalent would be "nigger lover"—and his work shows considerable sympathy for Persians and Persian civilization. Herodotus represents Persians as honest—"they consider telling lies more disgraceful than anything else"—brave, dignified, and loyal to their king. As to the religions of the various peoples he studied, Herodotus showed his customary intellectual curiosity but also his reverence for all of them, because "all men know equally about divine things."[28]

Even in the Middle Ages, we find figures in the Christian Church ready to make, in the words of Maxime Rodinson, an "outstanding effort . . . to gain and to transmit an objectively based scientific knowledge of the Islamic religion." Rodinson is talking about the remarkable Peter the Venerable, Abbot of Cluny (c. 1094–1156). Rodinson is convinced that Peter the Venerable was not only motivated for polemical reasons but "was moved by a disinterested curiosity."[29]

A number of thinkers, writers, and scholars in Europe from the sixteenth century onward took up the theme of the noble savage as a means to criticize their own culture and to encourage tolerance of others outside the West. Perhaps the real founder of the sixteenth-century doctrine of the noble savage was Peter Martyr Anglerius (1459–1525). In his *De Orbo Novo* of 1516, Peter Martyr criticized the Spanish conquistadors for their greed, narrow-mindedness, intolerance, and cruelty, contrasting them with the Indians, "who are happier since they are free from money, laws, treacherous judges, deceiving books, and the anxiety of an uncertain future." But it was left to Montaigne, under the influence of Peter Martyr, to develop the first full-length portrait of the noble savage in his celebrated essay "On Cannibals" (c. 1580), which is also the source of the idea of cultural relativism. Deriving his rather shaky information from a plain, simple fellow, Montaigne describes some of the more gruesome customs of the Brazilian Indians and concludes, "I am not so anxious that we should note the horrible savagery of these acts as concerned that, whilst judging their faults so correctly, we should be so blind to our own. I consider it more barbarous to eat a man alive than to eat him dead; to tear by rack and torture a body still full of feeling, to roast it by degrees, and then give it to be trampled and eaten by dogs and swine—a practice which we have not only read about but seen within recent memory, not between ancient enemies, but between neighbours and fellow-citizens and, what is worse, under the cloak of piety and religion—than to roast and eat a man after he is dead."

Elsewhere in the essay, Montaigne emphasizes their inevitable simplicity, state of purity, and freedom from corruption. Even their "fighting is entirely noble." Like Peter Martyr, Montaigne's rather dubious, secondhand knowledge of these noble savages does not prevent him from criticizing and morally condemning his own culture and civilization: "[We] surpass them in every kind of barbarity."

The seventeenth century saw some truly sympathetic accounts of Islam, such as those of Jurieu and Bayle. Let us hear Mr. Jurieu: "It may be truly said that there is no comparison between the cruelty of the Saracens against the Christians, and that of Popery against the true believers. In the war against the Vaudois, or in the massacres alone on St. Bartholomew's Day, there was more blood spilt upon account of religion, than was spilt by the Saracens in all their persecutions of the Christians. It is expedient to cure men of this prejudice; that Mahometanism is a cruel sect, which was propagated by putting men to their choice of death, or the abjuration of Christianity. This is in no wise true; and the conduct of the Saracens was an evangelical meekness in comparison to that of Popery, which exceeded the cruelty of the cannibals."

The whole import of Jurieu's *Lettres Pastorales* (1686–1689) only becomes clear when we realise that Jurieu was a Huguenot pastor, the sworn enemy of Bossuet, and he was writing from Holland after the revocation of the Edict of Nantes. He is using the tolerance of the Muslims to criticize Roman Catholicism—for him the Saracens' "evangelical meekness" is a way of contrasting Catholicism's own barbarity as on St. Bartholomew's Day.

Pierre Bayle was much influenced by Jurieu and continued to sing the praises of Islamic tolerance. He contrasts the tolerance of the Turks to the persecutions of brahmins in India by the Portuguese, and the barbarities exercised by the Spaniards in America: "[The Muslims] have always had more humanity for other religions than the Christians." Bayle was a champion of toleration—was he not himself the victim of intolerance and forced to flee to Holland?

For Jurieu and Bayle in the seventeenth century, *Turk* was synonymous with *Muslim*; thus Turkish tolerance turned into Muslim tolerance in general. Later *Letters Written by a Turkish Spy*, published at the end of the seventeenth century, inaugurated the eighteenth-century vogue for the pseudo-foreign letter, such as Montesquieu's *Lettres persanes* (1721); Madame de Grafigny's *Lettres d'une peruvienne* (c. 1747); D'Argen's *Lettres chinoises* (1750); Voltaire's "Asiatic" in the *Philosophical Dictionary* (1752); Horace Walpole's *Letter from Xo Ho*, a Chinese philosopher in London, to his friend Lien-Chi, at Peking (1757); and Goldsmith's *Citizen of the World* (1762), in which Lien Chi Altangi passes philosophical and satirical comments on the manners of the English.

Count Henri de Boulainvilliers' (1658–1722) apologetic biography of Muhammad appeared posthumously in London in 1730. It is impossible to exaggerate the importance of this book in shaping Europe's view of Islam and its founder, Muhammad; it certainly much influenced Voltaire and Gibbon. Boulainvilliers was able to use Muhammad and the origins of Islam as "a vehicle of his own theological prejudices" and as a weapon against Christianity, in general, and the clergy, in particular. He found Islam reasonable; it did not require one to believe in impossibilities—no mysteries, no miracles. Muhammad, though not divine, was an incomparable statesman and a greater legislator than anyone produced by Ancient Greece.

George Sale's translation of the Qur'an (1734) is the first accurate one in English. Like Boulainvilliers, whose biography of Muhammad he had carefully read, Sale firmly believed that the Arabs "seem to have been raised up on purpose by God, to be a scourge to the Christian church, for not living answerably to that most holy religion which they had received."

The attitude of Voltaire can be seen as typical of the entire century. Voltaire seems to have regretted what he had written of Muhammad in his scurrilous, and to a Muslim blasphemous, play *Mahomet* (1742), where the Prophet is presented as an impostor who enslaved men's souls: "Assuredly, I have made him out to be more evil than he was." But Voltaire, in his *Essai sur les Moeurs* (1756) and various entries in the *Philosophical Dictionary*, shows himself to be prejudiced in Islam's favor at the expense of Christianity in general, and Catholicism in particular.

In his *Sermon of the Fifty* (1762), Voltaire attacks Christian mysteries like transubstantiation as absurd, Christian miracles as incredible, and the Bible as full of contradictions. The God of Christianity was a cruel and hateful tyrant. By contrast, Voltaire finds the dogmas of Islam to be simplicity itself: there is but one God, and Muhammad is his Prophet. For all deists, the supposed rationality of Islam was appealing: no priests, no miracles, no mysteries. To this was added other beliefs such as the absolute tolerance in Islam of other religions, in contrast to Christian intolerance.

Gibbon, like Voltaire, painted Islam in as favorable a light as possible in order to better contrast it with Christianity. He emphasized Muhammad's humanity as a means of indirectly criticizing the Christian doctrine of the divinity of Christ. His anticlericalism led Gibbon to underline Islam's supposed freedom from that accursed class, the priesthood. Gibbon's deistic view of Islam as a rational, priest-free religion, with Muhammad as a wise and tolerant lawgiver, enormously influenced the way all Europeans perceived a sister religion for years to come.

But the work that exemplifies the Enlightenment's openness to the Other and its universalism and tolerance is surely Gotthold Lessing's *Nathan the Wise*, written in 1778/1779. The two themes—"it suffices to be a man" and "be my friend"—run through the play and give it its humanity. Preaching friendship among the three monotheist religions (Saladin [1137–1193], the great Muslim leader who defeated the Christian Crusaders, is one of the three main characters), Lessing recounts the allegory of the father (God) who gives each of his three sons (representing Islam, Christianity and Judaism) a ring (representing religion):

> If each of you
> Has had a ring presented by his father,
> Let each believe his own the real ring.

'Tis possible the father chose no longer
To tolerate the one ring's tyranny;
And certainly, as he much loved you all,
And loved you all alike, it could not please him
By favouring one to be of two the oppressor.
Let each feel honoured by this free affection.
Unwarped of prejudice; let each endeavour
To vie with both his brothers in displaying
The virtue of his ring; assist its might
With gentleness, benevolence, forbearance,
With inward resignation to the godhead.[30]

I could multiply examples of Said's quite deliberate omissions, writers sympathetic to the Arabs, Turks, and Islam, writers like W. S. Blunt (1840–1922), whose travels in Egypt and Arabia "produced in him a violent reaction against British Imperialism, and the second half of his life was spent in publishing a stream of poems, books and pamphlets championing the nationalist cause in Egypt, India, Arabia and Ireland."[31] Writers like Lady Mary Wortley Montagu (1689–1762), who wrote, "Sir, these people [the Turks] are not so unpolish'd as we represent them. Tis true their magnificence is of a different taste from our, and perhaps of a better. I am allmost of opinion they have a right notion of Life, while they consume it in Music, Gardens, Wine, and delicate eating, while we are tormenting our brains with some Scheme of Politics or studying some Science to which we can never attain."[32] Or writers like Marmaduke Pickthall, who eventually converted to Islam, translated the Qur'an, wrote novels of Egypt, and edited the journal *Islamic Culture*. Or E. G. Browne (1862–1926) who wrote the monumental *Literary History of Persia* (1902–1924) and who also took up the cause of Iranian nationalism.

The important thing to emphasize here is the deliberately biased nature of Said's apparently learned and definitive selection; I could just as easily go through Western literature and illustrate the opposite point to the one he is making. Furthermore, my selection is not of some peripheral figures culled from the margins of Western culture, but the very makers of that culture, figures like Montaigne, Bayle, Voltaire, Gibbon, Lessing, and some I have not quoted, like Montesquieu (*Persian Letters*, 1721) and Diderot (*Supplément au Voyage de Bougainville*, 1772), the latter two exemplifying the European Enlightenment's appeal to reason, objective truth, and universalist values.

Most of the time we have the impression that Said is simply resentful at how thorough and scholarly—in short, scientific and successful—the Orientalists were; Said is particularly jealous of their mastery of the various languages. For example, Said grudgingly admits that D'Herbelot read Arabic, Persian, and Turkish, and then seems to resent the fact that D'Herbelot arranged his *Bibliothèque orientale* alphabetically (p. 65)! Said talks of "specific Orientalist techniques—lexicography, grammar, translation, cultural decoding" (p. 121) as though they were instruments of torture, used to violate, subjugate, and dominate the Orient. The same resentment is expressed of "regulatory codes, classifications, specimen cases, periodical reviews, dictionaries, grammars, commentaries, editions, translations," (p. 166) which can only be seen as Said's hatred of science. Western intellectual energy and curiosity, that is, "activity, judgment, will-to-truth, and knowledge" is dimissed as "all aggression" (p. 204).

MISUNDERSTANDING OF WESTERN CIVILIZATION

The golden thread running through Western civilization is rationalism. As Aristotle said, Man by nature strives to know. This striving for knowledge results in science, which is but the application of reason. Intellectual inquisitiveness is one of the hallmarks of Western civilization. As J. M. Roberts put it, "The massive indifference of some civilisations and their lack of curiosity about other worlds is a vast subject. Why, until very recently, did Islamic scholars show no wish to translate Latin or western European texts into Arabic? Why when the English poet Dryden could confidently write a play focused on the succession in Delhi after the death of the Mogul emperor Aurungzebe, is it a safe guess that no Indian writer ever thought of a play about the equally dramatic politics of the English seventeenth-century court? It is clear that an explanation of European inquisitiveness and adventurousness must lie deeper than economics, important though they may have been. It was not just greed which made Europeans feel they could go out and take the world. The love of gain is confined to no particular people or culture. It was shared in the fifteenth century by many an Arab, Gujarati, or Chinese merchant. Some Europeans wanted more. They wanted to explore."[33]

Vulgar Marxists, Freudians, and anti-imperialists, who crudely reduce all human activities to money, sex, and power, respectively, have difficulties in understanding the very notion of disinterested intellectual inquiry—knowledge for knowledge's sake. European man by nature strives to know. Science undoubtedly owed some of its impetus to finding ways of changing base metal into gold, to attempts to solve practical problems, but surely owes as much to the desire to know, to get at the truth, and is the reason why philosophers like Karl Popper have called it a spiritual achievement. Hence the desperate attempts by Said to smear every single Orientalist with the lowest of motives are not only reprehensible but fail to give due weight to this golden thread running through Western civilization.

One should remind Said that it was this desire for knowledge on the part of Europeans that led to the people of the Near East recovering and discovering their own past and their own identity. In the nineteenth and early twentieth centuries archaeological excavations in Mesopotamia, Ancient Syria, Ancient Palestine, and Iran were carried out entirely by Europeans and later Americans—the disciplines of Egyptology, Assyriology, and Iranology, which restored to mankind a large part of its heritage, were the exclusive creations of inquisitive Europeans and Americans. Whereas, for doctrinal reasons, Islam deliberately refused to look at its pre-Islamic past, which was considered a period of ignorance.[34]

It is also worth pointing out that often the motives, desires, and prejudices of a scholar have no bearing upon the scientific worth of a scholar's contribution. Again, vulgar Marxists, for example, dimiss an opponent's arguments not on any scientific or rational grounds but merely because of the social origins of the scholar concerned. Theodor Nöldeke's bigotry was well known, indeed a source of acute embarrassment to his colleagues, but no modern scholar of Islam can ignore his *Geschichte des Qorans*; similarly, Henri Lammens's hatred for the prophet Muhammad is notorious, but as Professor F. E. Peters once said, Lammens has never been refuted. Conversely, a scholar who manifests sympathy for all aspects of Islam is not necessarily a good scholar. Said, for instance, quotes with approval Norman Daniel, but as Maxime Rodinson pointed out, Daniel was not an objective historian but an apologist of Islam: "In this way the anti-colonialist left, whether Christian or not, often goes so far as to sanctify Islam and the contemporary ideologies of the Muslim world. . . . An historian like Norman Daniel has gone so far as to number among the conceptions permeated with medievalism or imperialism, any criticisms of the Prophet's moral attitudes, and to accuse of like tendencies any exposition of Islam and its characteristics by means of the normal mechanisms of human history. Understanding has given way to apologetics pure and simple."[35]

Rather surprisingly, Said also singles out Louis Massignon for lavish praise for his sympathetic understanding of Islam. Massignon's scholarship is not in doubt; his biography of Al-Hallaj, for example, is considered a masterpiece. But Massignon also exemplifies the very qualities that Said himself dismisses in others. The Frenchman is responsible for perpetuating the myth of the spiritual East as against the materialist West. Said praises him for "identifying with the 'vital forces' informing 'Eastern culture'" (p. 265), and yet earlier Said informs us that "the Orient was overvalued for its pantheism, its spirituality, its stability, its longevity, its primitivity, and so forth" (p. 150). Massignon also displays other unattractive traits that Said does not mention, namely, his antisemitism, in the sense of virulent anti-Jewish sentiments— something even Massignon's biographers acknowledge.[36] Finally, Massignon was far from the paragon of Christian spirituality that he becomes in Said's eyes since one of Massignon's interest in the East was to search its cities for male prostitutes, something he dared not do in the "decadent West"! As Mircea Eliade recounts in his journal, "This evening I dine with Massignon. We talk for several hours. Terribly voluble! He is, besides, obsessed with pederasty; again and again he brings the conversation around to 'young male prostitutes' and so on."[37] Massignon was quite ready to exploit the East when it suited him.

Maxime Rodinson has also criticized Massignon and others for taking too far the idea of seeing the Qur'an on its own terms, though their perspective represented

a necessary reaction against an understanding of a text in terms that were too often foreign to the text, and a tendency to isolate themes from the religious context to which they belong—tendencies which were characteristic of the nineteenth century. However, the historian must occasionally ask himself if the reaction has not gone too far. Some of the methods of this school of thought [Massignon and others] must be a matter of concern to historians. To study the internal logic of a faith and to show respect are very legitimate objectives. The scholar has a perfect right to attempt to reexperience within himself the "fire" and the exigencies of the religious consciousness under study. However, the elements that comprise a coherent system could indeed have derived from a variety of very different sources and might well have played an entirely different role in other systems. Respect for the faith of sincere believers cannot be allowed either to block or deflect the investigation of the historian. The result derived from examining a particular faith on a personal "mental testing bench" ought to be made the object of a very severe critical examination. One must defend the rights of elementary historical methodology.[38]

SAID'S *ORIENTALISM*

Orientalism reveals at times Said's own contempt for the non-European, negative attitudes toward the Orient far greater than that of some imperialists he constantly condemns. Said speaks of "books and journals in Arabic (and doubtless in Japanese, various Indian dialects, and other Oriental languages)" (p. 322). As Lewis says, this is indeed a contemptuous, sneering, listing with its "assumption that what Indians speak and write are not languages but dialects"; even earlier, Said talks of "innumerable Indian dialects "(p. 52), despite the fact that there are, in India, more than fifteen languages each of which is spoken by more than forty million people, and each with a long and rich literary tradition. Where Said, the anti-Orientalist taketh away, the Orientalist restoreth, for, ironically, it was during the British period in India that Sir George A. Grierson carried out *The Linguistic Survey of India* (between 1866 and 1927), which resulted in his monumental study in several thousand pages where he identified and studied 179 Indian languages. All later research is indebted to this magnificent work of scholarship, which, for Grierson, was a token of his love for India, and what is more, far from being neglected or reviled as Said would no doubt have liked, this Orientalist classic is still in print in India, nearly eighty years after its publication in 1927. This work illustrates perfectly the fact that much Orientalist research gave back to, for instance, Indians, their own rich and varied heritage of which they themselves were not aware.

Said also claims, "No Arab or Islamic scholar can afford to ignore what goes on in scholarly journals, institutes, and universities in the United States and Europe; the converse is not true. For example, there is no major journal of Arab Studies published in the Arab world today" (p. 323). Said simply chooses to ignore such distinguished journals as *Majallat al-Ahfad* (Omdurman), *Alif: Journal of Comparative Poetics* (Cairo), *Al-Majalla al-'Arabiya li-l-'Ulum al-Insaniya* (Kuwait), *Al-Tawasul al-Lisani* (Fez), *Review of the Arab Academy* (Damascus), *al-Abhath* (Beirut), the *Review of Maghribi History* (Tunis), and the Bulletins of the faculties of Arts and of Social Sciences of Cairo, Alexandria, and Baghdad, to name a few.

SAID, SEX, AND PSYCHOANALYSIS

If Said can be said to have a bête-noir, it must surely be Bernard Lewis. In a recent review of Lewis's book *What Went Wrong?* in *Harper's*,[39] Said gave vent to his loathing for Lewis, who is characterized as repetitious, having a veneer of English sophistication, and whose book is unrelieved rubbish, an intellectual and moral disaster, the terribly faded rasp of a pretentious academic voice. "One can almost hear him [Lewis] saying," continues Said, "over a gin and tonic, 'You know, old chap, those wogs never really got it right, did they?'" Then there is Said's ultimate argument against Lewis: "His jowly presence seems to delight his interlocutors and editors"!

But what struck me most was Said's sentence where he accuses Lewis of persisting "in such 'philological' tricks as deriving an aspect of the predilection in contemporary Arab Islam for revolutionary violence from Bedouin descriptions of a camel rising." Said, twenty-five years later, still has not forgotten his battle with Lewis on the issue of a camel rising, to which I will now turn. In *Orientalism*, Said quotes from Lewis's essay "Islamic Concepts of Revolution":

> In the Arabic-speaking countries a different word was used for [revolution] *thawra*. The root *th-w-r* in Classical Arabic meant to rise up (e.g., of a camel), to be stirred or excited, and hence, especially in Maghribi usage, to rebel. It is often used in the context of establishing a petty, independent sovereignty; thus, for example, the so-called party kings who ruled in eleventh-century Spain after the breakup of the Caliphate of Cordova are called *thuwwar* (sing. *tha'ir*). The noun *thawra* at first means excitement, as in the phrase, cited in the Sihah, a standard medieval Arabic dictionary, *intazir hatta taskun hadhihi 'lthawra*, wait till this excitement dies down—very apt recommendation. The verb is used by al-Iji, in the form of *thawaran* or *itharat fitna*, stirring up sedition, as one of the dangers which should discourage a man from practising the duty of resistance to bad government. *Thawra* is the term used by Arabic writers in the nineteenth century for the French Revolution, and by their successors for the approved revolutions, domestic and foreign, of our own time.

Among Said's conclusions is:

> Lewis's association of *thawra* with a camel rising and generally with excitement (and not with a struggle on behalf of values) hints much more broadly than is usual for him that the Arab is scarcely more than a neurotic sexual being. Each of the words or phrases he uses to describe revolution is tinged with sexuality: *stirred, excited, rising up*. But for the most part it is a "bad" sexuality he ascribes to the Arab. In the end, since Arabs are really not equipped for serious action, their sexual excitement is no more noble than a camel's rising up. Instead of revolution there is sedition, setting up a petty

sovereignty, and more excitement, which is as much as saying that instead of copulation the Arab can only achieve foreplay, masturbation, coitus interruptus. These, I think, are Lewis's implications.[40]

Can any rational person have drawn any conclusion which even remotely resembled that of Edward Said's from Lewis's scholarly discussion of classical Arabic etymology? Were I to indulge in some prurient psychobiography, much in fashion, I would be tempted to ask, "What guilty sexual anguish is Said trying to cover up? Just what *did* they do to him at his Cairo English prep school?" Lewis's concise and elegant reply to Said's conclusions is to quote the Duke of Wellington: "If you believe that, you can believe anything."

But that is not all. In *Orientalism*, Said seems to be obssessed with sexual imagery. He finds D. G. Hogarth's account of the exploration of Arabia "aptly titled *The Penetration of Arabia* (1904)" (p. 224). And yet, Said himself wrote, "[Sir Richard Burton] was able to penetrate to the heart of Islam and disguised as an Indian Muslim doctor accomplish the pilgrimage to Mecca" (p. 195); and also, "For Lamartine a pilgrimage to the Orient has involved not only the penetration of the Orient by an imperious consciousness" (p. 179). Or again, "The point here is that the space of weaker or underdeveloped regions like the Orient was viewed as something inviting French interest, penetration, insemination—in short, colonization. . . . French scholars, administrators, geographers, and commercial agents poured out their exuberant activity onto the fairly supine, feminine Orient." And yet again: "Before Napoleon only two efforts (both by scholars) had been made to invade the Orient by stripping it of its veils" (p. 76). Just what *did* they do to Said at prep school?

ORIENTALISTS' COMPLICITY IN IMPERIALISM

One of Said's major theses is that Orientalism was not a disinterested activity but a political one, with Orientalists preparing the ground for and colluding with imperialists: "To say simply that Orientalism was a rationalization of colonial rule is to ignore the extent to which colonial rule was justified in advance by Orientalism, rather than after the fact" (p. 39). The Orientalist provides the knowledge that keeps the Oriental under control: "Once again, knowledge of subject races or Orientals is what makes their management easy and profitable; knowledge gives power, more power requires more knowledge, and so on in an increasingly profitable dialectic of information and control" (p. 36).

This is combined with Said's thesis derived from the Coptic socialist thinker Anwar Abdel Malek that the Orient is always seen by the Orientalists as unchanging, uniform, and peculiar (p. 98), and Orientals have been reduced to racist stereotypes, and are seen as ahistorical "objects" of study "stamped with an otherness . . . of an essentialist character" (p. 97). The Orientalists have provided a false picture of Islam: "Islam has been fundamentally misrepresented in the West" (p. 272). Said adds Foucault to the heady mix;[42] the French guru convinced Said that Orientalist scholarship took place within the ideological framework he called "discourse" and that "the real issue is whether indeed there can be a true representation of anything, or whether any and all representations, because they *are* representations, are embedded first in the language and then in the culture, institutions, and political ambience of the representer. If the latter alternative is the correct one (as I believe it is), then we must be prepared to accept the fact that a representationis *eo ipso* implicated, intertwined, embedded, interwoven with a great many other things besides the 'truth,' which is itself a representation" (p. 272).

It takes little thought to see that there is a contradiction in Said's major thesis.[43] If Orientalists have produced a false picture of the Orient, Orientals, Islam, Arabs, and Arabic society—and, in any case, for Said, there is no such thing as "the truth"—then how could this false or pseudoknowledge have helped European imperialists to dominate three-quarters of the globe? "Information and control," wrote Said, but what of "false information and control"?

To argue his case, Said very conveniently leaves out German Orientalist scholarship, for their inclusion would destroy—and their exclusion does indeed totally destroy—the central thesis of *Orientalism*, that all Orientalists produced knowledge which generated power, and that they colluded and helped imperialists found empires. As we shall see, German Orientalists were the greatest of all scholars of the Orient, but, of course, Germany was never an imperial power in any of the Oriental countries of North Africa or the Middle East. Bernard Lewis wrote, "[A]t no time before or after the imperial age did [the British and French] contribution, in range, depth, or standard, match the achievement of the great centers of Oriental studies in Germany and neighbouring countries. Indeed, any history or theory of Arabic studies in Europe without the Germans makes as much sense as would a history or theory of European music or philosophy with the same omission."[44]

Those omitted are not peripheral figures but the actual creators of the field of Middle Eastern, Islamic, and Arabic Studies; scholars of the standing of Paul Kahle (1875–1964), Georg Kampffmeyer (1864–1936), Rudolf Geyer (1861–1929), F. Giese (1870–1944), Jacob Barth (1851–1914), August Fischer (1865–1949), Emil Gratzl (1877–1957), Hubert Grimme (1864–1942), Friedrich Schulthess (1868–1922), Friedrich Schwally (1863–1919), Anton Baumstark (1872–1948), and Gotthelf Bergsträsser (1886–1933); others not discussed include G. Wustenfeld, Von Kremer, J. Horovitz, A. Sprenger, and Karl Vollers. Though Nöldeke (1836–1930), Fuck, G. Weil, Becker, E. Sachau, and Carl Brockelmann are mentioned, their work and significance are not discussed in any detail; Nöldeke, whose *Geschichte des Qorâns* (1860) was to become the foundation of all later studies, is considered one of the pioneers, along with Goldziher, of Islamic Studies in the West.

But of course German scholars are not the only ones omitted; Russians (e.g., Belayev and Tolstov), Italians (Caetani), and many Jewish scholars who studied Islam with sympathy, considering it a sister religion (e.g., Abraham Geiger and Paul Kraus), do not rate a mention.

Furthermore, to argue that the French and British Orientalists somehow prepared the ground for the imperialists is to seriously distort history. The first chair of Arabic in France was founded in 1538 at the Collège de France, and yet the first French venture into an Arab country was Napoleon's in 1798. In England, the first chair of Arabic was founded in 1633, at Cambridge, and yet the first British incursion into Arab territory was not until the nineteenth century. Where is the complicity between Orientalists and imperialists here? When the first two chairs of Arabic were founded in the West, it was the Muslims who dominated the Mediterranean, the Balkans were under Turkish rule, and the Turkish Siege of Vienna was still to come.[45]

Said quotes at length speeches and essays by British statesmen like Lord Cromer, Arthur Balfour, and Lord Curzon, which do mention the work of some Orientalists. But, as Keith Windschuttle points out, "these quotations come from works written between 1908 and 1912, that is, more than twenty-five years after the peak of Britain's imperial expansion. Rather than expressing the aims and objectives of potential imperial conquests, these speeches are ex post facto justifications, sanctioned by hindsight." Said quotes Curzon as saying, "our familiarity, not merely with the languages of the people of the East but with their customs, their feelings, their traditions, their history and religion . . . is the sole basis upon which we are likely to be able to maintain in the future the position we have won" (p. 214). But here Curzon is speaking to the House of Lords in 1909 to support the funding of a new London school of Oriental Studies, and, unsurprisingly, "was painting its prospects in the best light he could."[46]

SACY DE SILVESTRE, ERNEST RENAN, AND IGNAZ GOLDZIHER

Lawrence Conrad, in a remarkable book edited by Martin Kramer, has shown with his usual superb scholarship, clarity, and analytical brilliance, how Said's account is not just flawed but fundamentally wrong:

> [I]t is difficult to credit the curious linearity that Said postulates for the development of orientalism from Silvestre de Sacy. As is amply attested by the vast Oriental collections of such centers of Orientalist learning as Leiden and Berlin, where there were no imperial considerations to stimulate interest in the Orient, or at least (in the case of the Netherlands) not in the Middle East, it is a gross error to characterize European Orientalist scholarship as dependent upon "imperial Britain and France" for access to texts. The Orientalist tradition in the Netherlands and Germany was already well-established by the eighteenth century. In Leiden the decisive impetus (if one is to think in terms of contributions of individuals) had been provided by Jacob Golius (1596–1667), and the treasures of the Warnerian Library provided materials for study by an expanding circle of scholars; in Germany a founding father figure may be identified at Leipzig in Johann Jacob Reiske (1716–74), who had been trained at Leiden."[47]

As Conrad points out in a footnote, "The Islamic holdings at the Leiden University Library roughly equal those of the British Library (ca. 23,000), and those of the Deutsche Staatsbibliothek in Berlin and the Bibliothèque Nationale in Paris are again about the same (ca. 12,000)."[48]

Said first exaggerates de Sacy's influence on Renan, and then compounds his error by further overestimating the importance of both in the history of Orientalism. Renan himself felt he was continuing the work of Bopp, and only makes "a few passing references to Silvestre de Sacy and assigns him no particular importance for his own intellectual or professional development." Renan had little esteem for de Sacy's kind of scholarship, compiling, editing, or translating.[49] As Conrad concludes, "All this speaks decisively against Said's claim (on p. 177) that Orientalists after Silvestre de Sacy simply copied and rewrote him."[50] The reception of Renan's *Langues sémitiques* in the nineteenth century also tells decisively against Said's essentialist argument that Orientalism became a static system of ideas that did not generate any new ways of conceptualizing the subject of its study and analysis.[51] Or as Said himself put it, after Silvestre de Sacy and Renan "[all that] German Oriental scholarship did was to refine and elaborate techniques whose application was to texts, myths, ideas, and languages almost literally gathered from the Orient by imperial Britain and France."

But Renan's theories were attacked by Semiticists, philologists, and Orientalists in general.[52] Scholarly criticism of Orientalist scholarship is going on all the time; academic integrity demands constant criticism of the research and results of colleagues, individual scholars, or whole groups of scholars, ensuring that their discipline is not a static archive of knowledge never to be disturbed.[53]

One of the most searching critiques of Renan was provided by Ignaz Goldziher, who was recognized as early as 1889 as the founder of a new field of scholarship—Arabic and Islamic studies. Goldziher, the most important Orientalist of all, is dismissed by Said in three lines, though Henry Kissinger merits three pages.

It is impossible to overestimate the influence of Goldziher and the new paths he opened up in the study of Islam, Islamic history, Islamic theology, the study of Hadith, and so on. As Conrad says, Goldziher's *Muhammedanische Studien* (1888–89) "encompassed the entire vast range of Arab-Islamic literary culture—historical texts, poetry, *adab*, proverb collections, Qur'anic exegesis, doctrinal works, fiqh, hadith, biographical dictionaries, and so forth—and from them laid out an incredibly rich vista of historical experience that not only had not been known before, but even had not been sought. It would be no exaggeration to say that Goldziher's colleagues were stunned by his work."[54]

Goldziher was not at all influenced by Silvestre de Sacy, or Renan, or French Orientalism but rather by Abraham Geiger of the Jewish Enlightenment, the Tübingen school led by Bauer, and by Moses Mendelssohn, and Immanuel Kant. Here is Conrad's summary of Goldziher's criticism of Renan:

> [Renan's research on matters "Semitic "] systematically demeaned and deprecated the object of its study, robbed it of historical worth, defined it almost wholly in terms of negative attributes, denied its relevance as anything more than an artifact, and even then insisted that it be judged against the standard of values and norms of another people and another time a priori privileged and protected from the same harsh scrutiny directed at other peoples. Renaniana was a slippery sphere: one could hold it or drop it, but not work with it. Having demonstrated, along with other scholars, how flawed

it was in both conception and execution, Goldziher wisely decided to drop it and urged others to do the same.[55]

Goldziher was to remain an objective but always sympathetic observer of the Islamic world.[56] He constantly criticized Westernization and Western influence in the Near East, he particularly despised Christian missionaries, and had no sympathy for Zionism. Goldziher subscribed to the Enlightenment values and felt that his insights into Islam were equally relevant to Jews since his conclusions about a kindred faith had a universal dimension to them. His spiritual empathy for Islam and Muslims resulted in this extraordianry conclusion: "I became inwardly convinced that I myself was a Muslim. [In Cairo, i]n the midst of the thousands of the pious, I rubbed my forehead against the floor of the mosque. Never in my life was I more devout, more truly devout, than on that exalted Friday."[57]

Since Said spends more time on Renan than other Orientalists despite the fact that Renan is not as important a figure as Said imagines, it is worth pointing out that Renan himself also changed his views. Those who would see Renan as a racist would do well to read his celebrated lecture of 1882, *"Qu'est-ce qu'une nation?"* where he implicitly repudiates his earlier views on racial inequality put forward in the *Dialogues*, and he explicitly rejects the attempt to rest the concept of nationhood on race, language, economics, geography, and religion. Shmuel Almog has argued that Renan was not consciously antisemitic, and points to Renan's explicit denunciation of antisemitism, his protest against Tisza-Eszlar blood libel in 1882, his efforts with Victor Hugo to organize relief committees for the Jews of Russia, and so on.[58]

Basing himself on Muslim sources, Renan drew an exceedingly favorable portrait of the Prophet,[59] while recognizing his moral failings: "On the whole, Muhammad seems to us like a gentle man, sensitive, faithful, free from rancour and hatred. His affections were sincere, his character in general was inclined to kindness. . . . Neither ambition nor religious rapture had dried up the personal feelings in him. Not at all akin to this ambitious, heartless, and machiavellian fanatic [depicted by Voltaire in his drama *Mahomet*]." Renan is at pains to defend Muhammad from possible criticisms: "As to the features of the life of Muhammad which, to our eyes, would be unpardonable blots on his morality, it would be unjust to criticize them too harshly. . . . It would also be unjust to judge severely and with our own considered ideas, the acts of Muhammad, which in our days would be called swindles." The Prophet was no imposter. "It would be to totally lack a historical sense to suppose that a revolution as profound as Islam could be accomplished merely by some clever scheming, and Muhammad is no more explicable by imposture and trickery than by illuminism and religious fervour." Being a religious humanist, Renan valued Islam, and religion in general, "because it manifested what was divine in human nature"[60] and seemed to answer the deepest instincts of human nature, and in particular it answered the needs of seventh-century Arabia, an idea taken up in modern times by Montgomery Watt.

Second, Renan concludes his essay with the following observation:

> It is superfluous to add that if ever a reformist movement manifests itself in Islam, Europe should only participate in it by the influence of a most general kind. It would be ungracious of her to wish to settle the faith of others. All the while actively pursuing the propagation of her dogma which is civilisation, she ought to leave to the peoples themselves the infinitely delicate task of adjusting their own religious traditions to their new needs; and to respect that most inalienable right of nations as much as of individuals, the right to preside oneself, in the most perfect freedom, over the revolutions of one's conscience.

These are hardly the words of a cultural imperialist. Nor does Renan believe that Islam is unchanging or essentially incapable of changing:

> Symptoms of a more serious nature are appearing, I know, in Egypt and Turkey. There contact with European science and customs has produced freethought sometimes scarcely disguised. Sincere believers who are aware of the danger do not hide their disquiet, and denounce the books of European science as containing deadly errors, and subversive of all religious faith. I nevertheless persist in believing that if the East can surmount its apathy and go beyond the limits that up to now it was unable to as far as rational speculation was concerned, Islam will not pose a serious obstacle to the progress of the modern mind. The lack of theological centralisation has always left a certain degree of religious liberty to Muslim nations.[61]

ORIENTALISTS FIGHT BACK

For a number of years now, Islamologists have been aware of the disastrous effect of Said's *Orientalism* on their discipline. Prof. Herbert Berg has complained that the latter's influence has resulted in "a fear of asking and answering potentially embarrassing questions—ones which might upset Muslim sensibilities."[62]

Prof. Montgomery Watt, now in his nineties, one of the most respected Western Islamologists alive, takes Said to task for asserting that Sir Hamilton Gibb was wrong in saying that the master science of Islam was law and not theology. This, says Watt, "shows Said's ignorance of Islam." But Watt, rather unfairly, adds, "since he is from a Christian Arab background."[63] Said is indeed ignorant of Islam, but surely not because he is a Christian, since Watt and Gibb themselves were devout Christians. Watt also decries Said's tendency to ascribe dubious motives to various writers, scholars, and stateman such as Gibb and Lane, with Said committing doctrinal blunders such as not realising that non-Muslims could not marry Muslim women.[64]

R. Stephen Humphreys found Said's book important in some ways because it showed how some Orientalists were indeed "trapped within a vision that portrayed Islam and the Middle East as in some way essentially different from 'the West.'" Nonetheless, "Edward Said's analysis of Orientalism is overdrawn and misleading in many ways, and purely as [a] piece of intellectual history, *Orientalism* is a seriously flawed book." Even more damning, Said's book actually discouraged, argues Humphreys, the very idea of modernization of Middle Eastern societies. "In an ironic way, it also emboldened the Islamic activists and militants who were then just beginning to enter the political arena. These could use Said to attack their opponents in the Middle East as slavish 'Westernists,' who were out of touch with the authentic culture and values of their own countries. Said's book has had less impact on the study of medieval Islamic history—partly because medievalists know how distorted his account of classical Western Orientalism really is."[65]

Even scholars praised by Said in *Orientalism* do not particularly like his analysis, arguments, or conclusions. Maxime Rodinson thinks "as usual, [Said's] militant stand leads him repeatedly to make excessive statements," due, no doubt, to the fact that Said was "inadequately versed in the practical work of the Orientalists."[66] Rodinson also calls Said's polemic and style "Stalinist."[67] While P. J. Vatikiotis wrote, "Said introduced McCarthyism into Middle Eastern Studies,"[68] Jacques Berque, also praised by Said, wrote that the latter had "done quite a disservice to his countrymen in allowing them to believe in a Western intelligence coalition against them."[69]

For Clive Dewey, Said's book "was, technically, so bad; in every respect, in its use of sources, in its deductions, it lacked rigour and balance. The outcome was a caricature of Western knowledge of the Orient, driven by an overtly political agenda. Yet it clearly touched a deep vein of vulgar prejudice running through American academe."[70]

The most famous modern scholar who not only replied to but who mopped the floor with Said was, of course, Bernard Lewis. Lewis points to many serious errors of history, interpretation, analysis, and omission. Lewis has never been answered, let alone refuted.

Lewis points out that even among British and French scholars on whom Said concentrates, he does not mention at all Claude Cahen, Evariste Lévi-Provençal, Henri Corbin, Marius Canard, Charles Pellat, William and George Marçais, or William Wright, and, he only mentioned in passing, usually in a long list of names, scholars like R. A. Nicholson, Guy Le Strange, Sir Thomas Arnold, and E. G. Browne. "Even for those whom he does cite, Mr. Said makes a remarkably arbitrary choice of works. His common practice indeed is to omit their major contributions to scholarship and instead fasten on minor or occasional writings." Said even fabricates lies about eminent scholars: "Thus in speaking of the late-eighteenth-/early-nineteenth-century French Orientalist Silvestre de Sacy, Mr. Said remarks that 'he ransacked the Oriental archives. . . . What texts he isolated, he then brought back; he doctored them .'"[71] If these words bear any meaning at all, it is that Sacy was somehow at fault in his access to these documents and then committed the crime of tampering with them. This outrageous libel on a great scholar is without a shred of truth.[72]

Another false accusation that Said flings out is that Orientalists never properly discussed the Orientals' economic activities until Rodinson's *Islam and Capitalism* (1966). This shows Said's total ignorance of the works of Adam Mez, J. H. Kramers, W. Björkman, V. Barthold, and Thomas Armold, all of whom dealt with the economic activities of Muslims. As Rodinson himself points out elsewhere, one of the three scholars who was a pioneer in this field was Bernard Lewis.[73]

Said also talks of Islamic Orientalism being cut off from developments in other fields in the humanities, particularly the economic and social (p. 261). But this again only reveals Said's ignorance of the works of real Orientalists rather than those of his imagination. As Rodinson says, the sociology of Islam is an ancient subject, citing the work of R. Lévy. Rodinson then points out that Émile Durkheim's celebrated journal *L'Année sociologique* listed every year starting from the first decades of the twentieth century a certain number of works on Islam.[74]

Negative Arab and Asian Reaction to Said's *Orientalism*

It must have been particularly galling for Said to see the hostile reviews of his *Orientalism* from Arab, Iranian, or Asian intellectuals, some of whom he admired and singled out for praise in many of his works. For example, Nikki Keddie, praised in *Covering Islam*, talked of the disastrous influence of *Orientalism*, even though she herself admired parts of it:

> I think that there has been a tendency in the Middle East field to adopt the word "orientalism" as a generalized swear-word essentially referring to people who take the "wrong" position on the Arab-Israeli dispute or to people who are judged too "conservative." It has nothing to do with whether they are good or not good in their disciplines. So "orientalism" for may people is a word that substitutes for thought and enables people to dismiss certain scholars and their works. I think that is too bad. It may not have been what Edward Said meant at all, but the term has become a kind of slogan.[75]

Keddie also noted that the book "could also be used in a dangerous way because it can encourage people to say, 'You Westerners, you can't do our history right, you can't study it right, you really shouldn't be studying it, we are the only ones who can study our own history properly.'"[76]

Albert Hourani, who is much admired by Said, made a similar point, "I think all this talk after Edward's book also has a certain danger. There is a certain counterattack of Muslims, who say nobody understands Islam except themselves."[77]

Hourani went further in his criticism of Said's *Orientalism*: "Orientalism has now become a dirty word. Nevertheless it should be used for a perfectly respected discipline. . . . I think [Said] carries it too far when he says that the Orientalists delivered the Orient bound to the imperial powers. . . . Edward totally ignores the German tradition and philosophy of history which was the central tradition of the Orientalists. . . . I think Edward's other books are admirable."[78] Similarly, Aijaz Ahmed thought *Orientalism* was a "deeply flawed book," and would be forgotten when the dust settled, whereas Said's books on Palestine would be remembered.[79]

Kanan Makiya, the eminent Iraqi scholar, chronicled Said's disastrous influence particularly in the Arab world:

> *Orientalism* as an intellectual project influenced a whole generation of young Arab scholars, and it shaped the discipline of modern Middle East

studies in the 1980s. The original book was never intended as a critique of contemporary Arab politics, yet it fed into a deeply rooted populist politics of resentment against the West. The distortions it analyzed came from the eighteenth and nineteenth centuries, but these were marshaled by young Arab and "pro-Arab" scholars into an intellectual-political agenda that was out of kilter with the real needs of Arabs who were living in a world characterized by rapidly escalating cruelty, not ever-increasing imperial domination. The trajectory from Said's *Orientalism* to his *Covering Islam . . .* is premised on the morally wrong idea that the West is to be blamed in the here-and-now for its long nefarious history of association with the Middle East. Thus it unwittingly deflected from the real problems of the Middle East at the same time as it contributed more bitterness to the armory of young impressionable Arabs when there was already far too much of that around.[80]

Orientalism, continues Makiya, "makes Arabs feel contented with the way they are, instead of making them rethink fundamental assumptions which so clearly haven't worked. . . . They desperately need to unlearn ideas such as that 'every European' in what he or she has to say about the world is or was a 'racist.' . . . The ironical fact is that the book was given the attention it received in the 'almost totally ethnocentric' West largely because its author was a Palestinian."[81]

Though he finds much to admire in Said's *Orientalism,* the Syrian philosopher Sadiq al-Azm finds that "the stylist and polemicist in Edward Said very often runs away with the systematic thinker."[82] Al-Azm also finds Said guilty of the very essentialism that Said ostensibly sets out to criticize, perpetuating the distinction between East and West. Said further renders a great disservice to those who wish to examine the difficult question of how one can study other cultures from a libertarian perspective. Al-Azm recognizes Said's antiscientific bent, and defends certain Orientalist theses from Said's criticism; for example, al-Azm says:

I cannot agree with Said that their "Orientalist mentality" blinded them to the realities of Muslim societies and definitively distorted their views of the East in general. For instance: isn't it true, on the whole, that the inhabitants of Damascus and Cairo today feel the presence of the transcendental in their lives more palpably and more actively than Parisians and Londoners? Isn't it tue that religion means everything to the contemporary Moroccan, Algerian, and Iranian peasant in a manner it cannot mean for the American farmer or the member of a Russian kolkhoz? And isn't it a fact that the belief in the laws of nature is more deeply rooted in the minds of university students in Moscow and New York than among the students of al-Azhar and of Teheran University.[83]

Al-Azm also criticizes Said's accounts of Karl Marx and his contradictory appraisal of Louis Massignon. What Said finds insufferable is the nineteenth-century European's feeling of superiority, but Sadiq al-Azm says that indeed "nineteenth-century Europe was superior to Asia and much of the rest of the world in terms of productive capacities, social organisation, historical ascendancy, military might, and scientific and technological development."[85]

Nadim al-Bitar, a Lebanese Muslim, finds Said's generalizations about all Orientalists hard to accept, and is very skeptical about Said having read more than a handful of Orientalist works. Al-Bitar also accuses Said of essentialism: "[Said] does to [Western] Orientalism what he accuses the latter of doing to the Orient. He dichotomizes it and essentializes it. East is East and West is West and each has its own intrinsic and permanent nature."[85] Al-Saghir, an Iraqi scholar, also takes Said to task for dismissing all Orientalists a priori. For example, al-Saghir looks at Orientalist work on the Qur'an, and finds it, on the whole, very valuable, "carefully researched and intellectually honest," their "overrall characteristic is purely scholarly."[86]

The most pernicious legacy of Said's *Orientalism* is its support for religious fundamentalism, and its insistence that "all the ills [of the Arab world] emanate from Orientalism and have nothing to do with the socioeconomic, political, and ideological makeup of the Arab lands or with the cultural historical backwardness which stands behind it."[87]

Thus ironically, Said, a Christian agnostic becomes a de facto apologist and protector of Islam, the least Christian and certainly the religion least given to self-doubt. Despite his claims that he does not know anything about Islam, and despite the fact he has never written a single scholarly work devoted to Islam, Said has always accepted the role in the West of an Islamic expert, and has never flinched from telling us what the real Islam is. One's reaction is "stop telling us what Islam is, let the Muslims do that, stop talking for the Muslims." As a secularist defending Islam, one wonders how he will be able argue for a nontheocratic state once Palestine becomes a reality. If Islam is such a wonderful religion, why not convert to it, and why not accept it as the basis for any new constitution? At some stage, Said will have to do what he has been avoiding all his adult life, criticize Islam, or at least indirectly the idea of a theocracy.

Said has much to answer for. *Orientalism*, despite the fact that it is worthless as intellectual history, has left Western scholars in fear of asking questions—in other words, has inhibited their research. Said's work, with its strident anti-Westernism, has made the goal of modernization of the Middle Eastern societies that much more difficult. His work, wherein all the ills of Middle Eastern societies are blamed on the wicked West, has made much-needed self-criticism nearly impossible. His work has encouraged Islamic fundamentalists whose impact on world affairs needs no underlining.

NOTES

1. Edward Said, "Israel-Palestine: A Third Way," *Le Monde Diplomatique* (Paris) August–September 1998.

2. Edward Said, *Orientalism* (New York: Vintage Books, 1994). Specific page references to this work are given in the text.

3. Quoted by Jon Manchip White, introduction to Edward William Lane, *Modern Egyptians* (New York: Dover, 1973), p. v.

4. F. E. Peters, *The Hajj* (Princeton, NJ: Princeton University Press, 1994); references to and quotes from Burton are to be found on pp. 72, 100, 128–29, 175–77, 187–88, 215–18, 225–26, 242, 255–56, 257–58, 265, 289, 338, 350.

5. Keith Windschuttle, "Edward Said's 'Orientalism Revisited,'" *New Criterion* 17, no. 5 (January 1999).

6. Ibid.

7. Ibid.

8. J. M. Roberts, *History of the World* (New York: Oxford University Press, 1993), p. 503.

9. Ibid., p. 504.

10. See Bertrand Russell, *In Praise of Idleness* (London: Allen and Unwin, 1935), pp. 82–108.

11. See the afterword to *Orientalism*, p. 341, where *Cahen* is misspelled *Cohen*. *Rushdie* is also misspelled, on p. 351.

12. R. W. Southern, *Western Views of Islam in the Middle Ages* (Cambridge, MA: Harvard University Press, 1962), pp. 91–92, 108–109.

13. The Jones quote comes from his *Collected Works*, vol. 3 (New York: New York University Press, 1993), pp. 34–35.

14. K. Paddaya, "Sir William Jones: An Appreciation," http://www.picatype.com/dig/da2/da2aa06.htm.

15. See Keith Windschuttle, "The Ethnocentrism of Clifford Geertz," *New Criterion* 21, no. 2 (October 2, 2002).

16. See Daniel Pipes, *The Hidden Hand: Middle East Fears of Conspiracy* (New York: St. Martin's Griffin, 1998).

17. Edward Said, *The Question of Palestine* (New York: Vintage Books, 1980), p. 29.

18. Windschuttle, "Edward Said's 'Orientalism Revisited.'"

19. Ian Buruma, review of *Out of Place: A Memoir*, by Edward Said, *New York Times Book Review*, October 3, 1999.

20. Quoted in *Courrier International*, May 28, 1998, no. 395.

21. Efraim Karsh and Inari Karsh, *Empires of the Sand: The Struggle for Mastery in the Middle East, 1789–1923* (Cambridge, MA: Harvard University Press, 2001), p. 27.

22. Ibid., p. 45.

23. Ibid., p. 2.

24. Ibid., p. 3.

25. Ibid., p. 203.

26. Howard Bloom, *The Lucifer Principle: A Scientific Expedition into the Forces of History* (New York: Atlantic Monthly Press, 1995), p. 231.

27. Windschuttle, "Edward Said's 'Orientalism Revisited.'"

28. Quoted in J. L. Myers, "Herodotus," in *The Oxford Classical Dictionary* (Oxford: Oxford University Press, 1978), pp. 507–509. For much of this paragraph I am indebted to Myers.

29. Maxime Rodinson, "The Western Image and Western Studies of Islam," in *The Legacy of Islam*, ed. Joseph Schacht and Charles Edmund Bosworth (Oxford: Oxford University Press, 1974), pp. 15–16.

30. Gotthold Lessing, *Nathan the Wise*, trans. William Taylor, 1830, http://onlinebooks.library.upenn.edu/webbin/butbook/lookup?num=3820.

31. P. J. Keating, "W. S. Blunt," in *The Penguin Companion to Literature*, vol. 1 (Harmondsworth, UK: Penguin Books, 1971), p. 55.

32. Quoted in B. Lewis, *Islam and the West* (New York: Oxford University Press, 1993), pp. 83–84.

33. J. M. Roberts, *The Triumph of the West* (London: BBC Publications, 1985), p.176.

34. B. Lewis, "La carte du Proche-Orient," in *Islam et Politique au Proche-Orient aujourd'hui* (Paris: Gallimard, 1991), pp.162–63.

35. Rodinson, "The Western Image and Western Studies of Islam," p. 59.

36. C. Destremau and Jean Moncelon, *Louis Massignon* (Paris: Plon, 1994), p. 258.

37. Mircea Eliade, *Journal I, 1945–1955*, trans. Mac Linscott Ricketts (Chicago: University of Chicago Press, 1990).

38. Maxime Rodinson, "A Critical Survey of Modern Studies on Muhammad," in *Studies on Islam*, ed. M. Swartz (New York: Oxford University Press, 1981), p. 57.

39. E. W. Said, "Impossible Histories: Why the Many Islams Cannot Be Simplified," review of *What Went Wrong? Western Impact and Middle Eastern Response*, by B. Lewis, *Harper's* (July 2002).

40. Quoted by Said, *Orientalism*, pp. 314–15, from B. Lewis, "Islamic Concepts of Revolution," in *Revolution in the Middle East, and Other Case Studies: Proceedings of a Seminar*, ed. P. J. Vatikiotis (London: G. Allen & Unwin, 1972), pp. 33, 38–39.

41. Said quoting Malek.

42. It is ironic that Said draws much of his inspiration from the French philosopher Michel Foucault, since the latter has often defended the thesis that non-Western peoples do not share the same "rationality " as Western peoples, a viewpoint that Said denounces throughout *Orientalism*. Said also inherited from Foucault the antihumanism of much postmodernist thought, where "the death of man" is announced with much glee. But this antihumanism of Foucault results in the denial of individual freedom and individual responsibility, and we see it resurfacing in Said's entire philosphical outlook where Arabs are encouraged to see themselves as helpless victims of the dark impersonal forces of imperialism, rather than free agents in charge of their own destinies, willing to take to responsibility as adults for their own acts. Reflections gathered from K. Windschuttle's very important work *The Killing of History* (New York: Free Press, 1996).

43. Windschuttle, "Edward Said's 'Orientalism Revisited.'"

44. Lewis, *Islam and the West*, p. 108.

45. Ibid., p. 126.

46. Windschuttle, "Edward Said's 'Orientalism Revisited.'"

47. Lawrence I.Conrad, "Ignaz Goldziher on Ernest Renan: From Orientalist Philology to the Study of Islam," in *The Jewish Discovery of Islam,* ed. M. Kramer (Tel Aviv: Moshe Dayan Center for Middle Eastern and African Studies, 1999), p. 140.

48. Ibid., note 18, p. 170. The rest of the footnote reads: "See Geoffrey, ed., *World Survey of Islamic Manuscripts* (London: Al-Furqân Islamic Heritage Foundation, 1992–94), 1:275–90 (Paris); 320–29 (Berlin); 2:365–76 (Leiden); 3:471–90 (London)."

49. Ibid., p. 142.

50. Ibid.

51. Ibid., p. 139.

52. See ibid., notes 30–34 for the full references.

53. Lewis, *Islam and the West*, p. 118.

54. Conrad, "Ignaz Goldziher on Ernest Renan: From Orientalist Philology to the Study of Islam," pp. 162–63.

55. Ibid., p. 161.

56. Ibid., p. 164.

57. Raphael Patai, *Ignaz Goldziher and His Oriental Diary* (Detroit: Wayne State University Press, 1987), p. 28.

58. S. Almog, "The Racial Motif in Renan's Attitude to Jews and Judaism," in *Antisemitism Through the Ages*, ed. Shmuel Almog (Oxford: Pergamon, 1988), pp. 255–78. Referred to by Conrad, "Ignaz Goldziher on Ernest Renan: From Orientalist Philology to the Study of Islam," p. 156.

59. E. Renan, "Muhammad and the Origins of Islam (1851)," in *The Quest for the Historical Muhammad*, ed. Ibn Warraq (Amherst, NY: Prometheus Books, 2000), pp. 127–66.

60. H. W. Wardman, *Ernest Renan: A Critical Biography* (London: Athlone Press, 1964), p. 89.

61. Renan, "Muhammad and the Origins of Islam (1851)," p. 163.

62. Herbert Berg, "The Methods and Theories of John Wansbrough," in *The Quest for the Historical Muhammad*, p. 502. Herbert Berg is professor at the University of North Carolina at Wilmington.

63. W. Montgonery Watt, *Muslim-Christian Encounters* (London: Routledge, 1991), p. 110.

64. Ibid.

65. R. Stephen Humphreys, "Tradition and Innovation in the Study of Islamic History: The Evolution of North American Scholarship Since 1960," lecture presented at the Institute of Oriental Culture, University of Tokyo, October 21, 1997. R. Stephen Humphreys is King Abdul Aziz Ibn Saud Professor of Islamic Studies at the University of California, Santa Barbara.

66. Maxime Rodinson, *Europe and the Mystique of Islam*, trans. Roger Veinus (Seattle: University of Washington Press, 1987), p. 131, n. 3; quoted by M. Kramer, *Ivory Towers on Sand* (Washington, DC: Washington Institute for Near East Policy, 2001), p. 30.

67. Interview with Rodinson, in *Approaches to the History of the Middle East*, ed. Nancy Elizabeth Gallagher (London: Ithaca Press, 1994), p. 124; quoted by Kramer, *Ivory Towers on Sand*, p. 38.

68. P. J. Vatikiotis, *Among Arabs and Jews: A Personal Experience*, 1936–1990 (London: Weidenfeld and Nicolson, 1991), p. 105; quoted by Kramer, *Ivory Towers on Sand*, p. 38.

69. J. Berque, "Au–delà de l'Orientalisme: Entretien avec Jacques Berque," *Qantara* 13 (October–December 1994): 27–28; quoted by Kramer, *Ivory Towers on Sand*, p. 30.

70. C. Dewey, "How the Raj Played Kim's Game," *Times Literary Supplement*, April 17, 1998, p. 10; quoted by Kramer, *Ivory Towers on Sand*, p. 31.

71. Said, *Orientalism*, p. 127.

72. B. Lewis, "The Question of Orientalism," in *Islam and the West*, p. 112.

73. Maxime Rodinson, *La Fascination de l'Islam* (Paris: Editions La Découverte, 1989), p. 97, note 132. The other two scholars are Jean Sauvaget and Claude Cahen.

74. Ibid., p. 123.

75. Interview with Nikki Keddie, in *Approaches to the History of the Middle East,* pp. 144–45; quoted by Kramer, *Ivory Towers on Sand*, p. 37.

76. Quoted by Kramer, *Ivory Towers on Sand*, p. 38.

77. Interview with Albert Hourani, in *Approaches to the History of the Middle East*, p. 41; quoted by Kramer, *Ivory Towers on Sand*, p. 38.

78. Interview with Albert Hourani in *Approaches to the History of the Middle East*, pp. 40–41; quoted by Kramer, *Ivory Towers on Sand*, p. 30.

79. A. Ahmed, *In Theory: Classes, Nations, Literatures* (London: Verso, 1992), pp. 160–61.

80. Kanan Makiya, *Cruelty and Silence* (New York: W. W. Norton, 1993), pp. 317–18.

81. Ibid., p. 319.

82. Sadiq al-Azm, "Orientalism and Orientalism in Reverse," in *Forbidden Agendas: Intolerance and Defiance in the Middle East*, ed. Jon Rothschild (London: Al Saqi Books, 1984), p. 350.

83. Sadiq al-Azm, "Orientalism and Orientalism in Reverse" [in Arabic] (Beirut, 1981), p. 18; quoted in E. Sivan, *Interpretations of Islam: Past and Present* (Princeton: Darwin Press, 1985), p. 144.

84. Sadiq al-Azm, "Orientalism and Orientalism in Reverse," in *Forbidden Agendas:Intolerance and Defiance in the Middle East*, p. 363.

85. Quoted in Sivan, *Interpretations of Islam: Past and Present*, p. 136.

86. Quoted in ibid., p. 139.

87. Al-Bitar, quoted in ibid., p. 151.

51. JIHAD AND THE PROFESSORS

Daniel Pipes

Last spring, the faculty of Harvard College selected a graduating senior named Zayed Yasin to deliver a speech at the university's commencement exercises in June. When the title of the speech—"My American Jihad"—was announced, it quite naturally aroused questions. Why, it was asked, should Harvard wish to promote the concept of jihad—or "holy war"—just months after thousands of Americans had lost their lives to a jihad carried out by nineteen suicide hijackers acting in the name of Islam? Yasin, a past president of the Harvard Islamic Society, had a ready answer. To connect jihad to warfare, he said, was to misunderstand it. Rather, "in the Muslim tradition, jihad represents a struggle to do the right thing." His own purpose, Yasin added, was to "reclaim the word for its true meaning, which is inner struggle."

In the speech itself, Yasin would elaborate on this point:

> Jihad, in its truest and purest form, the form to which all Muslims aspire, is the determination to do right, to do justice even against your own interests. It is an individual struggle for personal moral behavior. Especially today, it is a struggle that exists on many levels: self-purification and awareness, public service and social justice. On a global scale, it is a struggle involving people of all ages, colors, and creeds, for control of the Big Decisions: not only who controls what piece of land, but more importantly who gets medicine, who can eat.

Could this be right? To be sure, Yasin was not a scholar of Islam, and neither was the Harvard dean, Michael Shinagel, who enthusiastically endorsed his "thoughtful oration" and declared in his own name that jihad is a personal struggle "to promote justice and understanding in ourselves and in our society." But they both did accurately reflect the consensus of Islamic specialists at their institution. Thus, David Little, a Harvard professor of religion and international affairs, had stated after the attacks of September 11, 2001, that jihad "is not a license to kill," while to David Mitten, a professor of classical art and archaeology as well as faculty adviser to the Harvard Islamic Society, true jihad is "the constant struggle of Muslims to conquer their inner base instincts, to follow the path to God, and to do good in society." In a similar vein, history professor Roy Mottahedeh asserted that "a majority of learned Muslim thinkers, drawing on impeccable scholarship, insist that jihad must be understood as a struggle without arms."

Nor are Harvard's scholars exceptional in this regard. The truth is that anyone seeking guidance on the all-important Islamic concept of jihad would get almost identical instruction from members of the professoriate across the United States. As I discovered through an examination of media statements by such university-based specialists, they tend to portray the phenomenon of jihad in a remarkably similar fashion—only, the portrait happens to be false.

Several interlocking themes emerge from the more than two dozen experts I surveyed.[1] Only four of them admit that jihad has any military component whatsoever, and even they, with but a single exception, insist that this component is purely defensive in nature. Valerie Hoffman of the University of Illinois is unique in saying (as paraphrased by a journalist) that "no Muslim she knew would have endorsed such terrorism [as the attacks of September 11], as it goes against Islamic rules of engagement." No other scholar would go so far as even this implicit hint that jihad includes an offensive component.

Thus, John Esposito of Georgetown, perhaps the most visible academic scholar of Islam, holds that "in the struggle to be a good Muslim, there may be times where one will be called upon to defend one's faith and community. Then [jihad] can take on the meaning of armed struggle." Another specialist holding this view is Abdullahi Ahmed An-Naim of Emory, who explains that "war is forbidden by the Sharia [Islamic law] except in two cases: self-defense and the propagation of the Islamic faith." According to Blake Burleson of Baylor, what this means is that, in Islam, an act of aggression like September 11 "would not be considered a holy war."

To another half-dozen scholars in my survey, jihad may likewise include militarily defensive engagements, but this meaning is itself secondary to lofty notions of moral self-improvement. Charles Kimball, chairman of the department of religion at Wake Forest, puts it succinctly: jihad "means struggling or striving on behalf of God. The great jihad for most is a struggle against oneself. The lesser jihad is the outward, defensive jihad." Pronouncing similarly are such authorities as Mohammad Siddiqi of Western Illinois; John Iskander of Georgia State; Mark Woodard of Arizona State; Taha Jabir al-Alwani of the graduate school of Islamic and social sciences in Leesburg, Virginia, and Barbara Stowasser of Georgetown.

But an even larger contingent—nine of those surveyed—deny that jihad has any military meaning whatsoever. For Joe Elder, a professor of sociology at the University of Wisconsin, the idea that jihad means holy war is "a gross misinterpretation." Rather, he says, jihad is a "religious struggle, which more closely reflects the inner, personal struggles of the religion." For Dell DeChant, a professor of world religions at the University of South Florida, the word as "usually understood" means "a struggle to be true to the will of God and not holy war."

Concurring views have been voiced by, among others, John Kelsay of John Carroll University, Zahid Bukhari of Georgetown, and James Johnson of Rutgers. Roxanne Euben of Wellesley College, the author of *The Road to Kandahar: A Genealogy of Jihad in Modern Islamist Political Thought*, asserts that "[f]or many Muslims, jihad means to resist temptation and become a better person." John Parcels, a professor of philosophy and religious studies at Georgia Southern University, defines jihad as a struggle "over the appetites and your own will." For Ned Rinalducci, a professor of sociology at Armstrong Atlantic State University, the goals of jihad are: "Internally, to be a good Muslim. Externally, to create a just society." And Farid Eseck, professor of Islamic studies at Auburn Seminary in New York City, memorably describes jihad as "resisting apartheid or working for women's rights."

Finally, there are those academics who focus on the concept of jihad in the sense of "self-purification" and then proceed to universalize it, applying it to non-Muslims as well as Muslims. Thus, to Bruce Lawrence, a prominent professor of Islamic studies at Duke, not only is jihad itself a highly elastic term ("being a better student, a better colleague, a better business partner. Above all, to control one's anger"), but non-Muslims should also "cultivate . . . a civil virtue known as jihad":

Jihad? Yes, jihad . . . a jihad that would be a genuine struggle against our own myopia and neglect as much as it is against outside others who condemn or hate us for what we do, not for what we are. . . . For us Americans, the greater jihad would mean that we must review US domestic and foreign policies in a world that currently exhibits little signs of promoting justice for all.

Here we find ourselves returned to the sentiments expressed by the Harvard commencement speaker, who sought to convince his audience that jihad is something all Americans should admire.

The trouble with this accumulated wisdom of the scholars is simple to state. It suggests that Osama bin Laden had no idea what he was saying when he declared jihad on the United States several years ago and then repeatedly murdered Americans in Somalia, at the US embassies in East Africa, in the port of Aden, and then on September 11, 2001. It implies that organizations with the word *jihad* in their titles, including Palestinian Islamic Jihad and bin Laden's own "International Islamic Front for the Jihad against Jews and Crusade[rs]," are grossly misnamed. And what about all the Muslims waging violent and aggressive jihads, under that very name and at this very moment, in Algeria, Egypt, Sudan, Chechnya, Kashmir, Mindanao, Ambon, and other places around the world? Have they not heard that jihad is a matter of controlling one's anger?

But of course it is bin Laden, Islamic Jihad, and the jihadists worldwide who define the term, not a covey of academic apologists. More importantly, the way the jihadists understand the term is in keeping with its usage through fourteen centuries of Islamic history.

In premodern times, jihad meant mainly one thing among Sunni Muslims, then as now the Islamic majority.[2] It meant the legal, compulsory, communal effort to expand the territories ruled by Muslims (known in Arabic as *dar al-Islam*) at the expense of territories ruled by non-Muslims (*dar al-Harb*). In this prevailing conception, the purpose of jihad is political, not religious. It aims not so much to spread the Islamic faith as to extend sovereign Muslim power (though the former has often followed the latter). The goal is boldly offensive, and its ultimate intent is nothing less than to achieve Muslim dominion over the entire world.

By winning territory and diminishing the size of areas ruled by non-Muslims, jihad accomplishes two goals: it manifests Islam's claim to replace other faiths, and it brings about the benefit of a just world order. In the words of Majid Khadduri of Johns Hopkins University, writing in 1955 (before political correctness conquered the universities), jihad is "an instrument for both the universalization of [Islamic] religion and the establishment of an imperial world state."

As for the conditions under which jihad might be undertaken—when, by whom, against whom, with what sort of declaration of war, ending how, with what division of spoils, and so on—these are matters that religious scholars worked out in excruciating detail over the centuries. But about the basic meaning of jihad—warfare against unbelievers to extend Muslim domains—there was perfect consensus. For example, the most important collection of Hadith (reports about the sayings and actions of Muhammad), called *Sahih Bukhari*, contains 199 references to jihad, and every one of them refers to it in the sense of armed warfare against non-Muslims. To quote the 1885 *Dictionary of Islam*, jihad is "an incumbent religious duty, established in the Qur'an and in the traditions [Hadith] as a divine institution, and enjoined especially for the purpose of advancing Islam and of repelling evil from Muslims."

Jihad was no abstract obligation through the centuries, but a key aspect of Muslim life. According to one calculation, Muhammad himself engaged in seventy-eight battles, of which just one (the battle of the Ditch) was defensive. Within a century after the Prophet's death in 632, Muslim armies had reached as far as India in the east and Spain in the west. Though such a dramatic single expansion was never again to be repeated, important victories in subsequent centuries included the seventeen Indian campaigns of Mahmud of Ghazna (r. 998–1030), the battle of Manzikert opening Anatolia (1071), the conquest of Constantinople (1453), and the triumphs of Uthman dan Fodio in West Africa (1804–1817). In brief, jihad was part of the warp and woof not only of premodern Muslim doctrine but of premodern Muslim life.

That said, jihad also had two variant meanings over the ages, one of them more radical than the standard meaning and one quite pacific. The first, mainly associated with the thinker Ibn Taymiyya (1268–1328), holds that born Muslims who fail to live up to the requirements of their faith are themselves to be considered unbelievers, and so legitimate targets of jihad. This tended to come in handy when (as was often the case) one Muslim ruler made war against another; only by portraying the enemy as not properly Muslim could the war be dignified as a jihad.

The second variant, usually associated with Sufis, or Muslim mystics, was the doctrine customarily translated as "greater jihad" but perhaps more usefully termed "higher jihad." This Sufi variant invokes allegorical modes of interpretation to turn jihad's literal meaning of armed conflict upside down, calling instead for a withdrawal from the world to struggle against one's baser instincts in pursuit of numinous awareness and spiritual depth.

But as Rudolph Peters notes in his authoritative *Jihad in Classical and Modern Islam* (1995), this interpretation was "hardly touched upon" in premodern legal writings on jihad.

In the vast majority of premodern cases, then, jihad signified one thing only: armed action versus non-Muslims. In modern times, things have of course become somewhat more complicated, as Islam has undergone contradictory changes resulting from its contact with Western influences. Muslims having to cope with the West have tended to adopt one of three broad approaches: Islamist, reformist, or secularist. For the purposes of this discussion, we may put aside the secularists (such as Kemal Atatürk), for they reject jihad in its entirety, and instead focus on the Islamists and reformists. Both have fastened on the variant meanings of jihad to develop their own interpretations.

Islamists, besides adhering to the primary conception of jihad as armed warfare against infidels, have also adopted as their own Ibn Taymiyya's call to target impious Muslims. This approach acquired increased salience through the twentieth century as Islamist thinkers like Hassan el-Banna (1906–1949), Sayyid Qutb (1906–1966), Sayyid Abuul Ala Maududi (1903–1979), and Ayatollah Ruhollah Khomeini (1903–1989) promoted jihad against putatively Muslim rulers who failed to live up to or apply the laws of Islam. The revolutionaries who overthrew the shah of Iran in 1979 and the assassins who gunned down President Anwar el-Sadat of Egypt two years later overtly held to this doctrine. So does Osama bin Laden.

Reformists, by contrast, reinterpret Islam to make it compatible with Western ways. It is they—principally through the writings of Sir Sayyid Ahmad Khan, a nineteenth-century reformist leader in India—who have worked to transform the idea of jihad into a purely defensive undertaking compatible with the premises of international law. This approach, characterized in 1965 by the definitive *Encyclopedia of Islam* as "wholly apologetic," owes far more to Western than to Islamic thinking. In our own day, it has devolved further into what Martin Kramer has dubbed "a kind of Oriental Quakerism," and it, together with a revival of the Sufi notion of "greater jihad," is what has emboldened some to deny that jihad has any martial component whatsoever, instead redefining the idea into a purely spiritual or social activity.

For most Muslims in the world today, these moves away from the old sense of jihad are rather remote. They neither see their own rulers as targets deserving of jihad nor are they ready to become Quakers. Instead, the classic notion of jihad continues to resonate with vast numbers of them, as Alfred Morabia, a foremost French scholar of the topic, noted in 1993:

> Offensive, bellicose jihad, the one codified by the specialists and theolo-
> gians, has not ceased to awaken an echo in the Muslim consciousness, both
> individual and collective. . . . To be sure, contemporary apologists present a
> picture of this religious obligation that conforms well to the contemporary
> norms of human rights, . . . but the people are not convinced by this. . . .
> The overwhelming majority of Muslims remain under the spiritual sway of
> a law . . . whose key requirement is the demand, not to speak of the hope,
> to make the Word of God triumph everywhere in the world.

In brief, jihad in the raw remains a powerful force in the Muslim world, and
this goes far to explain the immense appeal of a figure like Osama bin Laden
in the immediate aftermath of September 11, 2001.

Contrary to the graduating Harvard senior who assured his audience that
"jihad is not something that should make someone feel uncomfortable," this
concept has caused and continues to cause not merely discomfort but untold
human suffering: in the words of the Swiss specialist Bat Ye'or, "war, dispossession, *dhimmitude* [subordination], slavery, and death." As Bat Ye'or
points out, Muslims "have the right as Muslims to say that jihad is just and
spiritual" if they so wish; but by the same token, any truly honest accounting
would have to give voice to the countless "infidels who were and are the victims of jihad" and who, no less than the victims of Nazism or communism,
have "their own opinion of the jihad that targets them."

Islamists seeking to advance their agenda within Western, non-Muslim environments—for example, as lobbyists in Washington, DC—cannot frankly
divulge their views and still remain players in the political game. So as not
to arouse fears and so as not to isolate themselves, these individuals and organizations usually cloak their true outlook in moderate language, at least when
addressing the non-Muslim public. When referring to jihad, they adopt the
terminology of reformists, presenting warfare as decidedly secondary to the
goal of inner struggle and social betterment. Thus, the Council on American-
Islamic Relations (CAIR), the most aggressive and prominent Islamist group
in the United States, insists that jihad "does not mean 'holy war'" but rather
is a "broad Islamic concept that includes struggle against evil inclinations
within oneself, struggle to improve the quality of life in society, struggle in
the battlefield for self-defense (e.g., having a standing army for national
defense), or fighting against tyranny or oppression."

This sort of talk is pure disinformation, reminiscent of the language of
Soviet front groups in decades past. A dramatic example of it was on offer at
the trial of John Walker Lindh, the Marin County teenager who went off to

wage jihad on behalf of the Taliban regime in Afghanistan. At his sentencing in early October, Lindh told the court that, in common with "mainstream Muslims around the world," he himself understood jihad as a variety of activities ranging "from striving to overcome one's own personal faults, to speaking out for the truth in adverse circumstances, to military action in defense of justice."

That a jihadist caught in the act of offensive armed warfare should unashamedly proffer so mealymouthed a definition of his actions may seem extraordinary. But it is perfectly in tune with the explaining away of jihad promoted by academic specialists, as well as by Islamist organizations engaging in public relations. For usage of the term in its plain meaning, we have to turn to Islamists not so engaged. Such Islamists speak openly of jihad in its proper, martial sense. Here is Osama bin Laden: Allah "orders us to carry out the holy struggle, jihad, to raise the word of Allah above the words of the unbelievers." And here is Mullah Muhammad Omar, the former head of the Taliban regime, exhorting Muslim youth: "Head for jihad and have your guns ready."

It is an intellectual scandal that, since September 11, 2001, scholars at American universities have repeatedly and all but unanimously issued public statements that avoid or whitewash the primary meaning of jihad in Islamic law and Muslim history. It is quite as if historians of medieval Europe were to deny that the word *crusade* ever had martial overtones, instead pointing to such terms as "crusade on hunger" or "crusade against drugs" to demonstrate that the term signifies an effort to improve society.

Among today's academic specialists who have undertaken to sanitize this key Islamic concept, many are no doubt acting out of the impulses of political correctness and the multiculturalist urge to protect a non-Western civilization from criticism by making it appear just like our own. As for Islamists among those academics, at least some have a different purpose: like CAIR and other, similar organizations, they are endeavoring to camouflage a threatening concept by rendering it in terms acceptable within university discourse. Non-Muslim colleagues who play along with this deception may be seen as having effectively assumed the role of *dhimmi*, the Islamic term for a Christian or Jew living under Muslim rule who is tolerated so long as he bends the knee and accepts Islam's superiority.

As I can attest, one who dares to dissent and utter the truth on the matter of jihad falls under enormous censure—and not just in universities. In June of this year, in a debate with an Islamist on ABC's *Nightline*, I stated: "The fact is, historically speaking—I speak as a historian—jihad has meant expanding the realm of Islam through armed warfare." More recently, on a PBS *Newshour with Jim Lehrer* program about alleged discrimination against Muslims in the United States, a clip was shown of a role-playing seminar, conducted by the Muslim Public Affairs Council, in which Muslim "activists" were practicing how to deal with "hostile" critics. As part of this exercise, my image was shown to the seminar as I spoke my sentence from the *Nightline* debate. The comment on this scene by the show's PBS narrator ran as follows: "Muslim activists have been troubled by critics who have publicly condemned Islam as a violent and evil religion." We have thus reached a point where merely to state a well-known fact about Islam earns one the status of a hostile bigot on a prestigious and publicly funded television show.

Americans struggling to make sense of the war declared on them in the name of jihad, whether they are policymakers, journalists, or citizens, have every reason to be deeply confused as to who their enemy is and what his goals are. Even people who think they know that jihad means holy war are susceptible to the combined efforts of scholars and Islamists brandishing notions like "resisting apartheid or working for women's rights." The result is to becloud reality, obstructing the possibility of achieving a clear, honest understanding of what and whom we are fighting, and why.

It is for this reason that the nearly universal falsification of jihad on the part of American academic scholars is an issue of far-reaching consequence. It should be a matter of urgent concern not only to anyone connected with or directly affected by university life—other faculty members, administrators, alumni, state and federal representatives, parents of students, and students themselves—but to us all.

Notes

1. To see what the public is told, I looked at op-ed pieces, quotations in newspaper articles, and interviews on television rather than at articles in learned journals.

2. The following analysis relies on Douglas Streusand, "What Does Jihad Mean?" *Middle East Quarterly* (September 1997).

52. THE ISLAMIC DISINFORMATION LOBBY
American Muslim Groups' Politically Motivated Distortions of Islam

Robert Spencer

Islam has an image problem, and American Muslim organizations know it.

If you ask them, this problem comes from people lying about Islam. Irresponsible, hate-filled Christian preachers and others decry Islam as a violent religion, Muslim spokesmen claim, and this bigotry gives rise to acts of violence against Muslims. The Council on American-Islamic Relations (CAIR) and other Muslim groups have dedicated themselves to heading off such attacks by setting the record straight. On its Web site CAIR says that it was established in order to "promote a positive image of Islam and Muslims in America," and declares that "we believe misrepresentations of Islam are most often the result of ignorance on the part of non-Muslims and reluctance on the part of Muslims to articulate their case."[1]

Laudable—but the cure offered by American Muslim groups may be worse than the disease. Instead of taking the post–September 11 interest in Islam as an opportunity for a thorough and searching examination of the root causes of Islamic terrorism and the hatred that fomented the terrorist attacks, all too often these groups have constructed a "positive image of Islam" out of smoke and mirrors. Instead of dealing forthrightly and constructively with the concerns and questions that non-Muslims have had since the attacks, CAIR, the International Institute of Islamic Thought (IIIT), and others seem interested in what one former Muslim termed "throwing sand in our eyes."

Sand in hand, the IIIT recently sponsored general mailing of a flyer titled

"Q & A on Islam and Arab Americans." Virtually everything about this little flyer is misleading, starting with the title itself: although it purports to be about "Arab Americans," in fact it is solely about Islam. Several times the author of the flyer does what American Muslim groups in other contexts scold non-Muslims for doing: equating Muslims and Arabs. In one place it states that American Muslims come "from a wide variety of ethnic backgrounds and national origins," yet in the very next column it poses the question "What is an appropriate way to greet an Arab American?" and explains in the answer that "some Muslims feel it is inappropriate for unrelated men and women to shake hands."[2] While it acknowledges that "most Arab Americans grew up in the USA and do not require special greetings," it makes no mention of the main reason why for most American Arabs, it's completely irrelevant what Muslims feel about shaking hands or anything else: the vast majority of Arab Americans are Christians.

This confusion is common; it even appears at the American-Arab Anti-Discrimination Committee (ADC). This organization lists boxer Muhammad Ali as a member of its advisory board. Ali is a famous American convert to Islam, but does that make him an Arab? The ADC does acknowledge that most Arab Americans aren't Muslims, but the boxer's inclusion raises an intriguing question about the group's overall agenda: it "welcomes people of all backgrounds, faiths, and ethnicities as members," but is it welcoming them into an Arab group or a Muslim group? Perhaps the blurring of the distinction between a racial group (Arabs) and a religious group (Muslims) is in the service of efforts to portray Muslims as a racial group subject to discrimination in the United States, and thus entitled to privileged victim status.

In any case, the distortions and inaccuracies of this flyer are indicative of the half-truths and untruths that American Muslim groups are propagating today.

1. *Islam means peace.* The flyer notes that "the Arabic word for 'Islam' means 'submission,' and it derives from a word meaning 'peace.'" Indeed, in Arabic, *Islam* and *salaam* ("peace") share the same linguistic root, but this in itself is virtually meaningless. All sorts of words share the same roots and can still have quite divergent meanings—such as the English word *love* and the related Sanskrit word *lubh* (lust). Noting the derivation of the word *Islam* in this brief informational flyer can only be an attempt to lend credibility to the currently fashionable idea that Islam is a religion of peace.

But that idea glosses over some troubling facts.

2. *"Jihad does not mean 'holy war,'"* says the IIIT flyer, which originally ran in *USA Today.* "Literally, jihad in Arabic means to strive, struggle, and exert effort. It is a central and broad Islamic concept that includes struggle against evil inclinations within oneself, struggle to improve the quality of life in society, struggle in the battlefield for self-defense or fighting against tyranny or oppression."

This is the prevailing notion in academic circles today. Articulating the currently accepted orthodoxy, Duke University professor of Islamic studies Bruce Lawrence agreed that jihad doesn't mean "holy war": he defines this all-important Islamic concept as "being a better student, a better colleague, a better business partner. Above all, to control one's anger." To its credit, the flyer's explanation goes further than Lawrence by mentioning the battlefield, and in this it is more accurate than the professor's preposterously innocuous farrago. Islamic theology distinguishes between the "greater jihad," which involves "struggle against evil inclinations within oneself," and the "lesser jihad," which is hinted at here as "struggle in the battlefield for self-defense or fighting against tyranny or oppression."

Still, left unmentioned is the fact that throughout history, Muslims have not stopped at self-defense or fighting against tyranny. "In premodern times," observes the noted scholar of Islam Daniel Pipes, "jihad meant mainly one thing among Sunni Muslims, then as now the Islamic majority. It meant the legal, compulsory, communal effort to expand the territories ruled by Muslims (known in Arabic as *dar al-Islam*) at the expense of territories ruled by non-Muslims (*dar al-Harb*). In this prevailing conception, the purpose of jihad is political, not religious. It aims not so much to spread the Islamic faith as to extend sovereign Muslim power (though the former has often followed the latter). The goal is boldly offensive, and its ultimate intent is nothing less than to achieve Muslim dominion over the entire world."

Pipes adds: "Jihad was no abstract obligation through the centuries, but a key aspect of Muslim life. . . . Within a century after the Prophet's death in 632, Muslim armies had reached as far as India in the east and Spain in the west. Though such a dramatic single expansion was never again to be repeated, important victories in subsequent centuries included the seventeen Indian campaigns of Mahmud of Ghazna (r. 998–1030), the battle of Manzikert opening Anatolia (1071), the conquest of Constantinople (1453), and the triumphs of Uthman dan Fodio in West Africa (1804–1817). In brief, jihad was part of the warp and woof not only of premodern Muslim doctrine but of premodern Muslim life."

Has this changed? Certainly it's quite different from the idea of jihad purveyed by Muslim groups and the major media today. But this older idea of jihad is alive and well in the Islamic world. One manual of Islamic law—said to conform "to the practice and faith of the orthodox Sunni community"[3] by Al-Azhar University of Cairo, Egypt, the oldest and most prestigious university in the Islamic world—calls jihad "a communal obligation" to "war against non-Muslims. . . . The caliph makes war upon Jews, Christians, and Zoroastrians . . . until they become Muslim or else pay the non-Muslim poll tax. . . . The caliph fights all other peoples until they become Muslim."[4]

Some Muslims assert that because there is no caliph today (the caliphate was abolished by the secular state of Turkey in 1924), there can be no jihad. That's one reason why some radical Muslims urge that the caliphate must be restored. Says Britain's Sheikh Omar Bakri: "The Muslim Ummah [worldwide Muslim community] has never before been in a position where we are divided into over 55 nations each with its own oppressive kufr [infidel] regime ruling above us. There is no doubt therefore that the vital issue for the Muslims today is to establish the Khilafah [caliphate]."[5]

Unfortunately, Osama bin Laden isn't waiting for this restoration to declare jihad, and he is by no means isolated in this perspective in the Islamic world—witness the many terrorist groups around the world that rally under the name of jihad. Pipes asks, "And what about all the Muslims waging violent and aggressive jihads, under that very name and at this very moment, in Algeria, Egypt, Sudan, Chechnya, Kashmir, Mindanao, Ambon, and other places around the world? Have they not heard that jihad is a matter of controlling one's anger?"[6]

3. *Islam condemns terrorism.* The "Q & A" asserts that "Islam does not support terrorism under any circumstances. Terrorism goes against every principle in Islam. If a Muslim engages in terrorism, he is not following Islam. He may be wrongly using the name of Islam for political or financial gain."

This assertion is closely allied to the differing explanations of the meaning of jihad. There is no necessary connection between jihad and terrorism, and indeed, many moderate Muslims declare that their extremist brethren who justify terrorism on Islamic grounds only do so by distorting the concept of jihad. "Jihad is misused," says an expert in PBS's documentary *Muhammad: Legacy of a Prophet*. "There is absolutely nothing in Islam that justifies . . . the claim of Osama bin Laden, al Qaeda, or other similar groups to kill innocent civilians. That is unequivocally a crime under Islamic law. Acts of terror violence that have occurred in the name of Islam are not only wrong, they are contrary to Islam."

Once again, this is not as much of an open-and-shut case as these authorities would like us to believe. After all, no less an authority than George W. Bush's "imam of peace," Sheikh Muhammad Sayyed Tantawi of Al-Azhar University, disagrees. Bush quoted him in late 2001 at the United Nations as saying that "terrorism is a disease, and that Islam prohibits killing innocent civilians." But evidently his definition of terrorism would differ from that of the average American: according to the Middle East Media Research Institute (MEMRI), last spring Tantawi called suicide bombing "the highest form of jihad operations," and added that "every martyrdom operation against any Israeli, including children, women, and teenagers, is a legitimate act according to [Islamic] religious law, and an Islamic commandment."[7]

Tantawi is no isolated crank. He holds his position at Al-Azhar by the grace of the Egyptian government, and he uses that position to wield enormous influence in the Islamic world: the *New York Times* called Al-Azhar the "revered mosque, the distinguished university, the leading voice of the Sunni Muslim establishment. . . . It has sought to advise Muslims around the world that those who kill in the name of Islam are nothing more than heretics. It has sought to guide, to reassure Westerners against any clash of civilizations."[8]

Nor is Tantawi singular in his opinions. Abu Bakar Bashir, suspected mastermind of the 2002 terrorist bombings in Bali as well as bombings of churches in 2000, declared that "martyrs' bombs are a noble thing, a jihad of high value if you are forced to do it. For instance, in Palestine there is no other way to defend yourself and defend Islam. All Ulamas [Muslim leaders] agree with martyrs' bombs because we are forced to do it. There is no other way to defend ourselves and to defend Islam. . . . We are obliged to defend ourselves and attack people who attack Islam. In Islam there is no word for hands up, there is no word for surrender, there are only two things, win or die . . . if infidels do want to attack Islam, fight Islam, so we are instructed to fight them."[9]

Instructed by whom? Does Abu Bakar Bashir read the same Qur'an that moderate Muslims say condemns terrorism?

After a shooting at a church in Pakistan, police detained another Muslim cleric, Mohammed Afzal, who is alleged to have told his people that "it is the duty of every good Muslim to kill Christians. . . . You should attack Christians and not even have food until you have seen their dead bodies."[10]

Presumably Afzal would not consider Christians "innocent civilians." Osama and other Muslim extremists have maintained that the people killed in the World Trade Center and the Pentagon were not innocent, but complicit in what they imagine to be the American government's worldwide oppression of Muslims. Consequently, they argue that they were fitting victims of jihad—even envisioned only as a struggle against "tyranny or oppression."

Disquieting evidence indicates that such ideas are not restricted to obscure covens of ranting radicals, shunned by decent Muslims everywhere. According to MEMRI, "Mahmoud al-Zahhar, a Hamas leader in Gaza, told the Israeli Arab weekly *Kul Al-Arab*, 'Two days ago, in Alexandria, enrolment began for volunteers for martyrdom [operations]. Two thousand students from the University of Alexandria signed up to die a martyr's death. This is the real Egyptian people.'"[11]

Two thousand students from one university? Didn't these two thousand students know that "those who kill in the name of Islam are nothing more than heretics"? Didn't they know that "terrorism goes against every principle in Islam"?

The point is not that the moderates who wrote the flyer are wrong and that these radicals are right. The point is that these radical Muslims use the Qur'an and other core Islamic sources to justify their actions, and their exegesis is compelling enough to win over large numbers of Muslims. Moderate Muslims have thus far not been remotely successful in reading the radicals out of Islam. Certainly terrorism is not universally accepted in the Islamic world, but with terrorist groups rallying under the banner of jihad in all corners of the globe today, the IIIT might have performed a valuable service by explaining how this violation of "every principle in Islam" came to be so widely accepted in the Muslim world.

4. *"Islam is a religion of peace, mercy, and forgiveness."* This assertion is made but left unsupported in the IIIT flyer; elsewhere it is often buttressed with quotations from the Qur'an. One verse in particular is often invoked to make the claim that Islam teaches peace and mercy: "That was why We laid it down for the Israelites that whoever killed a human being, except as a punishment for murder or other villainy in the land, shall be looked upon as though he had killed all mankind; and that whoever saved a human life shall be regarded as though he had saved all mankind" (sura 5:32).

There are exceptions in this verse, however—"murder *or other villainy in the land*"—and these are particularly troubling in light of other teachings of the sacred book of Islam:

Muhammad is Allah's Apostle. Those who follow him are ruthless to the unbelievers but merciful to one another." (sura 48:29)

Prophet, make war on the unbelievers and the hypocrites and deal rigorously with them. Hell shall be their home: an evil fate." (sura 9:73)

The true believers fight for the cause of Allah, but the infidels fight for the devil. Fight then against the friends of Satan." (sura 4:76)

When you meet the unbelievers in the battlefield, strike off their heads and, when you have laid them low, bind your captives firmly. (sura 47:4)

Fight for the sake of Allah those that fight against you, but do not attack them first. Allah does not love the aggressors. Slay them wherever you find them. Drive them out of the places from which they drove you. Idolatry is worse than carnage. (sura 2:190–91; the part of this passage that forbids striking first explains why Osama and other terrorists couch their self-justifications in the terminology of self-defense)

When the sacred months are over slay the idolaters wherever you find them. Arrest them, besiege them, and lie in ambush everywhere for them. If they repent and take to prayer and render the alms levy [i.e., the *jizya*, the special tax on non-Muslims], allow them to go their way. Allah is forgiving and merciful. (sura 9:5)

Fight against such of those to whom the Scriptures were given [i.e., Jews and Christians] as believe neither in Allah nor the Last Day, who do not forbid what Allah and His Apostle have forbidden, and do not embrace the true Faith, until they pay tribute out of hand and are utterly subdued." (sura 9:29)

Permission to fight (against disbelievers) is given to those (believers) who are fought against, because they have been wronged and surely, Allah is able to give them (believers) victory. (sura 22:39)

Muslim apologists today condemn virtually any quotation of such verses as quoting "out of context." One Islamic information Web site cautions against this and notes that "it should be emphasized that so many revelations in the Holy Qur'an came down to provide guidance to prophet Muhammad and the Muslims based on what they were confronting at that time. Therefore, it is important to understand and know the historic context of the revelations for a proper understanding of these verses."[12] Muslims have declared that the violent verses above were revealed to Muhammad at a time when the infant Islamic community was in danger of being exterminated altogether by powerful external enemies, and that these verses have no force unless Muslims find themselves in similar circumstances.

However, in November 2002, Dr. Sheikh Bakr Abed al-Razzaq al-Sama-raai said in a Ramadan sermon at Mother of All Battles Mosque in Iraq that "jihad has become an obligation of every individual Muslim. Anyone who does not comply, will find himself lost in [hell], side by side with Haman, Pharaoh, and their soldiers. These are not just words of a sermon delivered from the pulpit of a mosque with enthusiasm, they are religious law. Ask the jurisprudents, if you don't know that."[13]

How could the good doctor issue such a challenge if he knew that Islam was a religion of peace, mercy, and forgiveness, and that anyone who investigated his claim would find that out?

Also speaking of fighting during Ramadan was Dr. Fuad Mukheimar, whom MEMRI identifies as "an Al-Azhar University lecturer and secretary-general of the Egyptian Sharia Association." According to Mukheimar, throughout history Muslims have waged "a number of honorable battles during the month of Ramadan—to the point where this month came to be called 'the Month of Jihad.' The nation of Islam came to be called 'the jihad-fighting nation,' and its moral values came to be called 'the values of warfare.'"

Was this cleric referring merely to self-control and the like, as explained in Bruce Lawrence's concept of jihad? Unfortunately, no. He assumes that jihad involves fighting for Islamic society: "Fasting is a continuous commandment, until Judgment Day . . . and the same is true for jihad, because Muslim society needs it to defend [its] faith, honor, and homeland."[14]

Similarly, the November 2002 letter purporting to be from Osama bin Laden and offering a sweeping justification for terrorism invoked several of the verses quoted above as well as many other Quranic texts. After issuing a series of demands to America and the West, the letter warns: "If you fail to respond to all these conditions, then prepare for fight with the Islamic Nation. . . . The Nation which is addressed by its Qur'an with the words: 'Do you fear them? Allah has more right that you should fear Him if you are believers. Fight against them so that Allah will punish them by your hands and disgrace them and give you victory over them and heal the breasts of believing people. And remove the anger of their (believers') hearts. Allah accepts the repentance of whom He wills. Allah is All-Knowing, All-Wise' (sura 9:13–15)."[15]

Muslim terrorists either blithely ignore the context that moderate Muslims use to hedge the Qur'an's violent verses, or claim that the believers today face the same sort of challenge that they did at the time the verses were revealed, and so the verses are applicable to the present situation.

Again: this is not to say that the extremists are right and the moderates are wrong, but only that the extremist view is based on ample Quranic support that moderate elements have not yet effectively refuted.

What's more, the Islamic theory of abrogation (*naskh*) also cuts against the idea of Islam as a religion of peace, mercy, and forgiveness. This is the doctrine that Allah cancels certain verses of the Qur'an and replaces them with other ones. Curious as it may seem, the doctrine of abrogation is founded upon the Qur'an itself: "None of Our revelations do We abrogate or cause to be forgotten, but We substitute something better or similar: knowest thou not that Allah Hath power over all things?" (sura 2:106).

Devised by Muslim divines in order to explain away contradictions in the Qur'an, this theory holds that the canceled verses remain in the Quranic text, but without any binding force for believers. The scholars who have advanced this doctrine, which is generally accepted in the Islamic world, work from simple chronology: verses that were revealed later in Muhammad's prophetic career cancel contradictory verses from earlier.

There is no universally accepted chronology of the revelations of the Qur'an, but the broad outlines of the Prophet's life make it clear that the bellicose verses were revealed later than the peaceful ones. His more conciliatory revelations come from his early prophetic career in Mecca, when he still had high hopes of winning over Arabian Jews and Christians. Later, however, when it became abundantly clear that Jews and Christians would not accept him as a prophet, Allah's messenger became bellicose: revelations from the latter part of his career in Medina are considerably more hard-edged. Hence, according to the idea of *naskh,* the peaceful verses are abrogated but the violent ones are still in effect. Muslim extremists are fully aware of this. It is another reason why they feel free to quote the Qur'an in support of their violent actions today: they clearly believe that when they do so, they are using the book properly and "in context."

No refutation of such ideas is included in the IIIT's informational flyer or from virtually any American Islamic source. Unfortunately, this is the sort of reading of the Qur'an that they decline even to discuss.

5. *Islam is tolerant of other beliefs.* Moderate Muslims like to quote sura 2:256, "There is no compulsion in religion," in support of the idea that Islam is a broadly tolerant faith. It has become a commonplace of discussions about Islam today that the great Islamic empires of old were tolerant of Jews and Christians to an extent that non-Christians were never tolerated in medieval Christendom. "It is a function of Islamic law," says the IIIT flyer, "to protect the privileged status of minorities. Islamic law also permits non-Muslims to

set up their own courts, which implement family laws drawn up by minorities themselves."

Once again, there is some truth to this, but it is neither wholly true nor the whole truth. It is true that Islamic law, the Sharia, allows Jews and Christians to practice their religious beliefs in an Islamic state; however, other religions are not accorded the same privilege: while Islamic states can, according to the Sharia, make "a formal agreement of protection" with Jews, Christians, and Zoroastrians, "such an agreement may not be effected with those who are idol worshippers," that is, Hindus, Buddhists, and others.[16]

Also, the "tolerance" granted to Jews and Christians is severely circumscribed. Jews and Christians are termed "People of the Book" in the Qur'an—that is, communities that have received a genuine revelation from Allah. That's why they're offered this "protection" in an Islamic state. However, the Qur'an also teaches that both Jews and Christians have incurred the curse of Allah (cf. sura 5:60 and many others) for their refusal to receive Muhammad as a legitimate prophet and his Qur'an as a book from Allah. Consequently, the tolerance they enjoy is nothing like that of a modern-day secular state, although Muslim apologists often succeed in equating the two in the face of the general Western ignorance of Islamic history and theology.

In fact, the Sharia dictates that such a "protection" agreement between Muslim rulers and Jewish and Christian subjects "is only valid when the subject peoples: follow the rules of Islam . . . (those involving public behavior and dress, though in acts of worship and their private lives, the subject communities have their own laws, judges, and courts, enforcing the rules of their own religion among themselves); and pay the non-Muslim poll tax (*jizya*)."[17]

The *jizya* is a special levy on non-Muslims, whose higher tax rates contributed much to the magnificent Islamic empires of old. It is not the Sharia's only restriction on non-Muslims: according to classic Islamic law, non-Muslims in an Islamic state "are distinguished from Muslims in dress, wearing a wide cloth belt (*zunnar*); are not greeted with "as-Salamu 'alaykum" [the standard Muslim greeting, "Peace be with you"]; must keep to the side of the street; may not build higher than or as high as the Muslims' buildings, though if they acquire a tall house, it is not razed; are forbidden to openly display wine or pork, . . . recite the Torah or Evangel aloud, or make public display of their funerals and feastdays; and are forbidden to build new churches."[18]

There is indeed no "compulsion" in any of this: Jews and Christians are not forced to become Muslims. But there is also precious little dignity and respect.

Such humiliating laws are rarely enforced today even where the Sharia is the law of the land, although they have not disappeared entirely from the Islamic world. Nor have they been renounced or rejected by Islamic clerics of any sect. There is no mufti or imam in the world today apologizing for the abject status of the dhimmis, the Jews and Christians under Islamic rule, as the pope and many Protestant groups have apologized for the Crusades and other perceived enormities of Christendom. These laws could be revived by any Muslim ruler who wants to restore the pure observance of Islam—and such reformers have not been rare in Islamic history.

Even if this never happens, however, such laws should be borne in mind by anyone who wants a true and accurate picture of Islamic "tolerance."

6. *Islam respects Christianity.* The IIIT flyer correctly informs readers that "Islam teaches that Christians and Muslims are both 'people of the book.' By that it means that the two religions share the same basic beliefs articulated through the Bible and the Koran. The main difference between Christians and Muslims is that Muslims do not believe that Jesus was the Son of God."

It is debatable whether or not much is left of the "basic beliefs articulated through the Bible," or at least of the New Testament, once the idea of Jesus' divine Sonship is removed. Although the Qur'an states that "nearest among them in love to the believers wilt thou find those who say, 'We are Christians'" (sura 5:82), it also claims that Christians are under Allah's curse: "The Jews call 'Uzair [Ezra] a son of Allah, and the Christians call Christ the son of Allah. That is a saying from their mouth; (in this) they but imitate what the unbelievers of old used to say. Allah's curse be on them: how they are deluded away from the Truth!" (sura 9:30).

Once again, this is no dead letter. Anti-Christian Muslims point to the fact that the Qur'an even undercuts its own assertion that Christians will be "nearest in love" to Muslims: "O ye who believe! take not the Jews and the Christians for your friends and protectors: They are but friends and protectors to each other. And he amongst you that turns to them (for friendship) is of them. Verily Allah guideth not a people unjust" (sura 5:51).

In a recent Friday *khutba* (sermon) at a mosque in Saudi Arabia, Sheikh Abd al-Muhsin al-Qadhi, in a decidedly unecumenical mood, called Christianity "one of the distorted religions," and "a faith that deviates from the path of righteousness." He also labeled it a "false faith" and a "distorted and deformed religion." The sheikh decried the present-day situation, in which "many Muslims . . . know about Christianity only what the Christians claim about love, tolerance, devoting life to serving the needy, and other distorted slogans. . . . After all this, we still find people who promote the idea of bringing our religion and theirs closer, as if the differences were miniscule and could be eliminated by arranging all those [interreligous] conferences, whose goal is political."[19]

Another Saudi imam, Sheikh Muhammad Saleh sl-Munajjid, preached in a similar vein: "Muslims must . . . educate their children to jihad. This is the greatest benefit of the situation: educating the children to jihad and to hatred of the Jews, the Christians, and the infidels."[20]

Of course, these Wahhabi sheikhs are no more representative of Islam as a whole than are the moderates who claim that Islam respects Christianity. But they have read the Qur'an as well as the moderates, and their conclusions about Islam and Christianity are quite different. The irenic vision of the IIIT flyer is anything but a full or adequate description of the real Muslim perspective on Christianity.

7. *Islam respects Judaism*. In its treatment of Judaism, the IIIT flyer replicates its language regarding Christianity: "Islam teaches that Jews and Muslims are both 'people of the book.' By that it means that the two religions share the same basic beliefs articulated through the Torah and the Qur'an. The main difference between Jews and Muslims is that Jews do not believe in prophets after the Jewish prophets, including Muhammad and his teachings."

Jews and Muslims may share basic beliefs, but we have already seen that the Qur'an places Jews under Allah's curse. This idea recurs in the Qur'an, which also says that Allah turned the Jews into detested beasts: "Say: 'O people of the Book! Do ye disapprove of us for no other reason than that we believe in Allah, and the revelation that hath come to us and that which came before (us), and (perhaps) that most of you are rebellious and disobedient?' Say: 'Shall I point out to you something much worse than this, (as judged) by the treatment it received from Allah? Those who incurred the curse of Allah and His wrath, those of whom some He transformed into apes and swine, those who worshipped evil; these are (many times) worse in rank, and far more astray from the even path!'" (sura 5:60).

Muslim radicals today routinely echo this language. Sheikh Ibrahim Madhi of the Palestinian Authority declared recently that Jews are "the enemies of Allah, the nation accursed in Allah's book. Allah described [them] as apes and pigs."[21]

Sheikh Ibrahim Madhi was clearly referring to the Qur'an. Is it then remiss to trace at least some of the impetus for the antisemitism that is rampant in the House of Islam today to the core beliefs of Muslims? But again, the IIIT flyer gives readers no inkling that this problem even exists.

8. *Muhammad was a man of peace.* "This is his message," says the American convert to Islam Hamza Yusuf in PBS's documentary *Muhammad: Legacy of a Prophet*: "spread peace, feed people food, and do some devotional practice and you will enter paradise without any trouble."

Spread peace? Perhaps, but radical Muslims might add that this must be done by the force of arms. After all, this is the example of the Prophet himself. "According to one calculation," notes Daniel Pipes, "Muhammad himself engaged in seventy-eight battles, of which just one (the battle of the Ditch) was defensive."[22]

The Prophet was a man of principle: he not only engaged in these battles, but his teachings were consistent with them. Says a Muslim tradition about Muhammad: "A man came to Allah's Messenger and said, 'Guide me to such a deed as equals jihad (in reward).' He replied, 'I do not find such a deed.'"[23]

How would Hamza Yusuf explain this? There's no way to tell—evidently he would prefer to ignore it.

As the American people learn more and more about Islam, Islam's image problem is getting worse, not better. One principal reason for this may be the dissonance between the loud and repeated claims of Islamic spokesmen in the United States and the facts that Americans are learning about Islam. If the International Institute of Islamic Thought and other Muslim groups really want to educate the American people about Islam, they would acknowledge and deal squarely with the questions that are really in people's minds: Does Islam provide a justification for terrorism? Have the dozens of groups that preach and perpetrate violence in the name of Islam all around the world really "hijacked" the religion? If they are using the Qur'an to justify their actions, what are moderate Muslims doing to forestall this kind of interpretation of the sacred book of Islam?

It isn't enough to say, as Muslim spokesmen never tire of repeating, that there are kooks of every creed and that every creed can be used to justify violence. This still leaves unanswered the question of why there are so many more terrorist groups worldwide invoking Islam than there are terrorist Christian groups.

By ignoring such questions, Muslim advocacy groups in the United States have only made matters worse, giving non-Muslims good reason to suspect their intentions and honesty. The next time American Muslim spokesmen decry Islam's image problem, in all fairness they should point fingers not at Christian fundamentalist preachers or at scholars who raise uncomfortable questions, but at themselves.

NOTES

1. Council on American-Islamic Relations, "About CAIR," http://www.cair-net.org/asp/aboutcair.asp.

2. International Institute of Islamic Thought, "Q & A on Islam and Arab Americans," 2002.

3. Ahmed ibn Naqib al-Misri, *Reliance of the Traveller: A Classic Manual of Islamic Sacred Law*, trans. Nuh Ha Mim Keller (Beltsville, MD:Amana Publications, 1999), p. xx.

4. Ibid., o9.0, o9.1, o9.8, and o9.9.

5. Middle East Media Research Institute, "Islamist Leader in London: No Universal Jihad as Long as There Is No Caliphate,'" MEMRI Special Dispatch no. 435, October 30, 2002, www.memri.org.

6. Daniel Pipes, "Jihad and the Professors," *Commentary* (November 2002).

7. Middle East Media Research Institute, "Leading Egyptian Government Cleric Calls For: 'Martyrdom Attacks That Strike Horror into the Hearts of the Enemies of Allah,'" MEMRI Special Dispatch no. 363, April 7, 2002, www.memri.org.

8. Douglas Jehl, "Moderate Muslims Fear Their Message Ss Being Ignored," *New York Times*, October 21, 2001.

9. Stephen Gibbs and Matthew Moore, "Australia Will Be 'Destroyed Instantly' If It Strikes at Muslim Countries, Says Cleric," *Syndey Morning Herald*, December 13, 2002, www.smh.com.au.

10. "Radical Cleric Held over Church Attack," December 26, 2002, www.cnn.com.

11. MEMRI, "Leading Egyptian Government Cleric Calls For: 'Martyrdom Attacks That Strike Horror into the Hearts of the Enemies of Allah."

12. The Sabr Foundation, "The Quran on War, Peace and Justice," November 8, 2001, www.islam101.com.

13. Middle East Media Research Institute, "Ramadan Sermon from Iraq," MEMRI Special Dispatch no. 438, November 8, 2002, www.memri.org.

14. Middle East Media Research Institute, "Egyptian Cleric: Ramadan the Month of Jihad," MEMRI Special Dispatch no. 308, December 5, 2001, www.memri.org.

15. "Full text: bin Laden's 'Letter to America,'" *Guardian Unlimited Observer,* November 24, 2002, http://www.observer.co.uk/worldview/story/0,11581,845725,00.html.

16. Ibn Naqib al-Misri, *Reliance of the Traveller*, o11.1, o11.2.

17. Ibid., o11.3a, b.

18. Ibid., o11.5.

19. Middle East Media Research Institute, "Friday Sermons in Saudi Mosques: Review and Analysis," MEMRI Special Report no. 10, September 26, 2002, www.memri.org.

20. Ibid.

21. Aluma Solnick, "Based on Koranic Verses, Interpretations, and Traditions, Muslim Clerics State: The Jews Are the Descendants of Apes, Pigs, and Other Animals," MEMRI Special Report no. 11, November 1, 2002, www.memri.org.

22. Pipes, "Jihad and the Professors."

23. Muhammed ibn Ismaiel al-Bukhari, *Sahih al-Bukhari: The Translation of the Meanings*, trans. Muhammad M. Khan (Riyadh: Darussalam, 1997), vol. 5, book 56, no. 2785. Bukhari (810–870) is generally considered by Muslims to be the most reliable source for traditions about Muhammad.

53. 'ISA, THE MUSLIM JESUS

Mark Durie

The word Christian *is not a valid word, for there is no religion of Christianity according to Islam.*

— www.answering-christianity.com

Today we increasingly hear and read that Christianity and Islam "share" Jesus, that he belongs to both religions. So also with Abraham: there is talk of the West's "Abrahamic civilization" where once people spoke of "Judeo-Christian civilization." This shift of thinking reflects the growing influence of Islam.

These notes offer some information and reflections on the "Muslim Jesus," to help put this trend in its proper context.

References in brackets are to the Qur'an. Numbering systems for the Quranic verses are not standardized: be prepared to search through nearby verses for the right one.

ISLAM THE PRIMORDIAL FAITH

Islam regards itself, not as a subsequent faith to Judaism and Christianity, but as the primordial religion, the faith from which Judaism and Christianity are subsequent developments. In the Qur'an we read that Abraham "was not a Jew nor a Christian, but he was a monotheist, a Muslim" (Al-Imran 3:66). So

First published in 2002 as "'Isa, the Muslim Jesus," on the Answering Islam Web site at http://answering-islam.org/Intro/islamic_jesus.html.

it is Muslims, and not Christians or Jews, who are the true representatives of the faith of Abraham to the world today (Al-Baqarah 2:135).

The Biblical Prophets Were All Muslims

Many prophets of the past received the one religion of Islam (Ash-Shura 42:13). Who were these previous prophets? According to Al-Anam 6:85–87 they include Ibrahim (Abraham), 'Ishaq (Issac), Yaqub (Jacob), Nuh (Noah), Dawud (David), Sulaiman (Solomon), Ayyub (Job), Yusuf (Joseph), Musa (Moses), Harun (Aaron), Zakariyya (Zachariah), Yahya (John the Baptist), 'Isa (Jesus), Ilyas, Ishmael, al-Yash'a (Elisha), Yunus (Jonah), and Lut (Lot).

THE MUSLIM 'ISA (JESUS)

There are two main sources for 'Isa, the Muslim Jesus. The Qur'an gives a history of his life, while the Hadith collections—recollections of Muhammad's words and deeds—establish his place in the Muslim understanding of the future.

THE QUR'AN

'Isa Was a Prophet of Islam

Jesus' true name, according to the Qur'an, was 'Isa. His message was pure Islam, surrender to Allah (Al-Imran 3:84). Like all the Muslim prophets before him, and like Muhammad after him, 'Isa was a lawgiver, and Christians should submit to his law (Al-Imran 3:50; Al-Maidah 5:48). 'Isa's original disciples were also true Muslims, for they said, "We believe. Bear witness that we have surrendered. We are Muslims" (Al-Maidah 5:111).

"The Books"

Like other messengers of Islam before him, 'Isa received his revelation of Islam in the form of a book (Al-Anam 6:90). 'Isa's book is called the Injil or "gospel" (Al-Maidah 5:46). The Torah was Moses' book, and the Zabur (Psalms) were David's book. So Jews and Christians are "People of the Book." The one religion revealed in these books was Islam (Al-Imran 3:18).

As with previous prophets, 'Isa's revelation verified previous prophets' revelations (Al-Imran 3:49,84; Al-Maidah 5:46; As-Saff 61:6). Muhammad himself verified all previous revelations, including the revelation to 'Isa (An-Nisa 4:47), and so Muslims must believe in the revelation that 'Isa received (Al-Baqarah 2:136). However, after 'Isa the Injil was lost in its original form. Today the Qur'an is the only sure guide to 'Isa's teaching.

The Biography of 'Isa

According to the Qur'an, 'Isa was the Messiah. He was supported by the "Holy Spirit" (Al-Baqarah 2:87; Al-Maidah 5:110). He is also referred to as the "Word of Allah" (An-Nisa' 4:171).

'Isa's mother Mariam was the daughter of 'Imran (Al-Imran 3:34,35)—compare the Amram of Exodus 6:20—and the sister of Aaron (and Moses) (Maryam 19:28). She was fostered by Zachariah (father of John the Baptist) (Al-Imran 3:36). While still a virgin (Al-Anam 6:12; Maryam 19:19–21). Mariam gave birth to 'Isa alone in a desolate place under a date palm tree (Maryam 19:22ff; not in Bethlehem).

'Isa spoke while still a baby in his cradle (Al-Imran 3:46; Al-Maidah 5:110; Maryam 19:30). He performed various other miracles, including breathing life into clay birds, healing the blind and lepers, and raising the dead (Al-Imran 3:49; Al-Maidah 5:111). He also foretold the coming of Muhammad (As-Saff 61:6).

'Isa Did Not Die on a Cross

Christians and Jews have corrupted their scriptures (Al-Imran 3:74–77, 113). Although Christians believe 'Isa died on a cross, and Jews claim they killed him, in reality he was not killed or crucified, and those who said he was crucified lied (An-Nisa 4:157). 'Isa did not die, but ascended to Allah (An-Nisa 4:158). On the day of Resurrection 'Isa himself will be a witness against Jews and Christians for believing in his death (An-Nisa 4:159).

Christians Should Accept Islam, and All True Christians Will

Christians (and Jews) could not be freed from their ignorance until Muhammad came bringing the Qur'an as clear evidence (Al-Bayyinah 98:1). Muhammad was Allah's gift to Christians to correct misunderstandings. They should accept Muhammad as Allah's Messenger and the Qur'an as his final revelation (Al-Maidah 5:15; Al-Hadid 57:28; An-Nisa 4:47).

Some Christians and Jews are faithful and believe truly (Al-Imran 3:113, 114). Any such true believers will submit to Allah by accepting Muhammad as the prophet of Islam—that is, they will become Muslims (Al-Imran 3:198).

Although Jews and pagans will have the greatest enmity against Muslims, it is the Christians who will be "nearest in love to the believers," that is, to Muslims (Al-Maidah 5:82). True Christians will not love Muhammad's enemies (Al-Mujadilah 58:22). In other words, anyone who opposes Muhammad is not a true Christian.

Christians Who Accept Islam or Refuse It

Some Jews and Christians are true believers, accepting Islam: most are transgressors (Al-Imran 3:109).

Many monks and rabbis are greedy for wealth and prevent people from coming to Allah (At-Taubah 9:34,35).

Christians and Jews who disbelieve in Muhammad will go to hell (Al-Bayyinah 98:6).

Muslims should not take Christians or Jews for friends (Al-Maidah 5:51). They must fight against Christians and Jews who refuse Islam until they surrender, pay the poll tax, and are humiliated (At-Taubah 9:29). To this may be added hundreds of Quranic verses on the subject of jihad in the path of Allah, as well as the "Book of Jihad" found in all Hadith collections.

Christian Beliefs

Christians are commanded not to believe that 'Isa is the son of God: "It is far removed from his transcendent majesty that he should have a son" (An-Nisa 4:171; Al-Furqan 25:2). 'Isa was simply a created human being and a slave of Allah (An-Nisa 4:172; Al-Imran 3:59).

Christians are claimed by the Qur'an to believe in a family of gods—Father God, mother Mary, and 'Isa the son—but 'Isa rejected this teaching (Al-Maidah 5:116). The doctrine of the Trinity is disbelief and a painful doom awaits those who believe it (Al-Maidah 5:73).

'ISA (JESUS) IN THE HADITH

'Isa the Destroyer of Christianity

The prophet 'Isa will have an important role in the end times, establishing Islam and making war until he destroys all religions save Islam. He shall kill the Evil One (Dajjal), an apocalyptic anti-Christ figure.

In one tradition of Muhammad we read that no further prophets will come to earth until 'Isa returns as "a man of medium height, or reddish complexion, wearing two light garments, looking as if drops were falling down from his head although it will not be wet. He will fight for the cause of Islam. He will break the cross, kill pigs, and abolish the poll tax. Allah will destroy all religions except Islam. He ('Isa) will destroy the Evil One and will live on the earth for forty years and then he will die" (Sunan Abu Dawud, 37:4310). The Sahih Muslim has a variant of this tradition: "The son of Mary . . . will soon descend among you as a just judge. He will . . . abolish the poll tax, and the wealth will pour forth to such an extent that no one will accept charitable gifts" (Sahih Muslim 287).

What do these sayings mean? The cross is a symbol of Christianity. Breaking crosses means abolishing Christianity. Pigs are associated with Christians. Killing them is another way of speaking of the destruction of Christianity. Under Islamic law the poll tax buys the protection of the lives and property of conquered "People of the Book" (At-Taubah 9:29). The abolition of the poll tax means jihad is restarted against Christians (and Jews) living under Islam, who should convert to Islam or else be killed or enslaved. The abundance of wealth refers to booty flowing to the Muslims from this conquest. This is what the Muslim 'Isa will do when he returns in the last days.

Muslim jurists confirm these interpretations: consider, for example, the ruling of Ahmad ibn Naqib al-Misri (d. 1368),

> [T]he time and the place for [the poll tax] is before the final descent of Jesus (upon whom be peace). After his final coming, nothing but Islam will be accepted from them, for taking the poll tax is only effective until Jesus' descent (upon him and our Prophet be peace).[1]

Ibn Naqib goes on to state that when Jesus returns, he will rule "as a follower" of Muhammad.

CRITICAL COMMENTS ON THE MUSLIM 'ISA (JESUS)

'Isa Not a Historical Figure

The Qur'an's 'Isa is not a historical figure. His identity and role as a prophet of Islam is based solely on supposed revelations to Muhammad over half a millennium after the Jesus of history lived and died.

Jesus' Name Was Never 'Isa

Jesus' mother tongue was Aramaic. In his own lifetime he was called *Yeshua* in Aramaic, and *Jesu* in Greek. This is like calling the same person John when speaking English and Jean when speaking French: *Jesu*, pronounced "Yesoo," is the Greek form of Aramaic *Yeshua*. (The final-*s* in *Jesu-s* is a Greek grammatical ending.) *Yeshua* is itself a form of Hebrew *Yehoshua'*, which means "the Lord is salvation." However Yehoshua' is normally given in English as *Joshua*. So Joshua and Jesus are variants of the same name.

It is interesting that Jesus' name *Yehoshua'* contains within it the proper Hebrew name for God, the first syllable *Yeh-* being short for YHWH "the LORD."

Yeshua of Nazareth was never called *'Isa*, the name the Qur'an gives to him. Arab-speaking Christians refer to Jesus as *Yasou'* (from *Yeshua*) not *'Isa*.

Jesus Did Not Receive a "Book"

According to the Qur'an, the "book" revealed to 'Isa was the *Injil*. The word *Injil* is a corrupted form of the Greek *euanggelion* "good news" or *gospel*. What was this *euanggelion*? This was just how Jesus referred to his message: as good news. The expression *euanggelion* did not refer to a fixed revealed text, and there is absolutely no evidence that Jesus received a "book" of revelation from God.

The "Gospels" of the Bible Are Biographies

The term *euanggelion* later came to be used as a title for the four biographies of Jesus written by Matthew, Mark, Luke, and John—the "gospels." This was a secondary development of meaning. Apparently this is where Muhammad got his mistaken idea of the Injil being a "book."

Most So-Called Prophets of Islam Received No Book

Virtually all of the so-called prophets of Islam, whose names are taken from the Hebrew scriptures, received no "book" or law code. For example, the Psalms are not a book revealing Islam, as the Qur'an claims, but a collection of songs of worship, only some of which are David's. There is not a shred of evidence in the biblical history of David that he received a book of laws for the Israelites. They already had the Torah of Moses to follow. So David was not a prophet in the Qur'an's sense of this word. Likewise, most of the prophets claimed by Islam were neither lawgivers nor rulers.

Biblical Prophecy and Islamic Prophecy Are Not the Same Thing

The biblical understanding of prophecy is quite different from Muhammad's. A biblical prophecy is not regarded as a passage from a heavenly eternally preexistent text like the Qur'an, but a message from God for a specific time and place. A biblical prophet is someone to whom God reveals hidden things, and who then acts as God's verbal agent. When a Samaritan woman called Jesus a prophet (John 4:19) it was because he had spoken about things in her life that he could only have known supernaturally. Christianity teaches that Jesus was a prophet, but he brought no "book": he himself was the living "Word of God," a title used of 'Isa in the Qur'an.

All prophecies referred to in the Bible became part of the biblical text. The Bible consists of a wide variety of materials originally written for many different purposes, including letters, songs, love poetry, historical narratives, legal texts, proverbial wisdom, as well as prophetic passages. These are regarded as inspired by God, but not dictated from a timeless heavenly book.

As Prophetic History, the Qur'an Contains Many Errors and Anachronisms

The claim that Jesus was not executed by crucifixion is without any historical support. One of the things that all the early sources agree on is Jesus' crucifixion.

Mariam the mother of 'Isa is called a sister of Aaron, and also the daughter of Aaron's father, 'Imran (Hebr. Amram). Clearly Muhammad has confused Mary (Hebr. Miriam) with Miriam of the Exodus. The two lived more than a thousand years apart!

In the Bible Haman is the minister of Ahasuerus in Media and Persia (Esther 3:1–2). Yet the Qur'an places him over a thousand years earlier, as a minister of Pharoah in Egypt.

The claim that Christians believe in three Gods—Father, son Jesus, and mother Mary—is mistaken. The Qur'an is also mistaken to claim that Jews say Ezra was a son of God (At-Taubah 9:30). The charge of polytheism against Christianity and Judaism is ill informed and false (Deut. 6:4, James 2:19a).

The story of the "two-horned one" (Al-Kahf 18:82; cf also Dan. 8:3, 20–21) is derived from the Romance of Alexander. Certainly Alexander the Great was no Muslim.

The problem with the name 'Isa has already been discussed. Other biblical names are also misunderstood in the Qur'an, and their meanings lost. For example, Elisha, which means "God is salvation," is given in the Qur'an as *al-Yash'a*, turning *El* "God" into *al-* "the." (Islamic tradition did the same to Alexander the Great, calling him *al-Iskander* "the Iskander.") Abraham "Father of many" (cf. Gen. 17:5) might have been better represented as something like *Aburahim* "father of mercy" instead of *Ibrahim*, which has no meaning in Arabic at all.

The Qur'an has a Samaritan making the golden calf, which was worshipped by the Israelites in the wilderness (Ta Ha 20:85) during the Exodus. In fact, it was Aaron (Exod. 34:1–6). The Samaritans did not exist until several centuries later. They were descendants of the northern Israelites centuries after the Exodus.

Many Quranic stories can be traced to Jewish and Christian folktales and other apocryphal literature. For example, a story of Abraham destroying idols (As-Saffat 37) is found in a Jewish folktale, the Midrash Rabbah. The Quranic story of Zachariah, father of John the Baptist, is based upon a second-century Christian fable. The story of Jesus being born under a palm tree is also based on a late fable, as is the story of Jesus making clay birds come alive. Everything the Qur'an says about the life of Jesus that is not found in the Bible can be traced to fables composed more than a hundred years after Jesus' death.

Jesus' titles of Messiah and Word of God, which the Qur'an uses, find no explanation in the Qur'an. Yet in the Bible, from which they are taken, these titles are well integrated in a whole theological system.

The Qur'an mentions the Holy Spirit in connection with Jesus, using phrases that come from the gospels. Ibn Ishaq (*Life of Muhammad*) reports Muhammad as saying that this "Spirit" was the angel Gabriel (cf. also An-

Nahl 16:102, Al-Baqarah 2:97). However, the biblical phrase "Spirit of God" (Ruach Elohim) or "Holy Spirit" can only be understood in light of the Hebrew scriptures. It certainly does not refer to an angel.

Jesus' alleged foretelling of Muhammad's coming (As-Saff 61:6) appears to be based on a garbled reading of John 14:26, a passage which in fact refers to the Spirit.

The Hebrew scriptures were Jesus' Bible. He affirmed their authority and reliability and preached from them. From these same scriptures he knew God as *Adonai Elohim*, the Lord God of Israel. He did not call God *Allah*, which appears to have been the name or title of a pagan Arabian deity worshipped in Mecca before Muhammad. Muhammad's pagan father, who died before Muhammad was born, already bore the name *'Abd Allah,* "slave of Allah," and his uncle was called *Obeid Allah.*

We read that An-Najm 53:19–23 seeks to refute the pagan Arab belief that Allah had daughters named al-Uzza, al-Ilat, and Manat. (See also An-Nahl 16:57 and Al-Anam 6:100.)

The biblical narratives are rich with historical details, many confirmed by archaeology. They cover more than a thousand years and reveal a long process of technological and cultural development. In contrast, the Qur'an's sacred history is devoid of archaeological support. Its fragmentary and disjointed stories offer no authentic reflection of historical cultures. No place name from ancient Israel is mentioned, not even Jerusalem. Many of the supposed historical events reported in the Qur'an have no independent verification. For example, we are told that Abraham and Ishmael built the Kaaba in Mecca (Al-Baqarah 2:127), but this is totally without support. The biblical account, more than a thousand years older, does not place Abraham anywhere near Arabia.

The Qur'an Is Not a Credible Source for Biblical History

The Qur'an, written in the seventh century CE, cannot be regarded as having any authority whatsoever to inform us about Jesus of Nazareth. It offers no evidence for its claims about biblical history. Its numerous historical errors reflect a garbled understanding of the Bible.

ISLAM APPROPRIATES THE HISTORY OF JUDAISM AND CHRISTIANITY TO ITSELF

When Muhammad linked the name of *Allah* to the religious histories of Judaism and Christianity, this was a way to claim them for Islam. In the light of later events, the claim that Islam was the original religion, and that all preceding prophets were Muslims, can be regarded as an attempt to appropriate the histories of other religions for Islam. The effect is to rob Christianity and Judaism of their own histories.

Consider that many biblical sites, such as the tombs of the Hebrew patriarchs and the Temple Mount, are claimed by Islam as Muslim sites, not Jewish or Christian ones. After all, the Qur'an tells us that Abraham "was a Muslim." Under Islamic rule all Jews and Christians were banned from such sites.

The Place of the Jewish Scriptures in Christianity Is Completely Different from the Place of the Bible in Islam

There is a fundamental difference between Christian attitudes toward the Jewish scriptures and Islamic attitudes toward the Bible. Christians accept the Hebrew scriptures. They were the scriptures of Jesus and the apostles. They were the scriptures of the early church. The whole of Christian belief and practice rests upon them. Core Christian concepts such as "Messiah" (Greek "Christos"), "Spirit of God," "Kingdom of God," and "Salvation" are deeply rooted in the Hebrew biblical traditions.

We note also that Christian seminaries devote considerable effort to studying the Hebrew scriptures. This is an integral part of training for Christian ministry. The Hebrew scriptures are read (in translation) every Sunday in many churches all around the world.

In contrast, Islam's treatment of the Bible is one of complete disregard. Although it purports to "verify" all earlier prophetic revelation, the Qur'an is oblivious to the real contents of the Bible. The claim that Christians and Jews deliberately corrupted their scriptures is made without evidence, and this only serves to cover up the Qur'an's historical inadequacies. Muslim scholars rarely have an informed understanding of the Bible or of biblical theology and so remain ignorant of these realities.

Some Contemporary Muslim Voices on Jesus

Yasir Arafat, addressing a press conference at the United Nations in 1983, called Jesus "the first Palestinian fedayeen who carried his sword" (i.e., he was a freedom fighter for Islam).

Sheikh Ibrahim Madhi, employee of the Palestinian Authority, broadcast live in April 2002 on Palestinian Authority television: "The Jews await the false Jewish messiah, while we await, with Allah's help . . . Jesus, peace be upon him. Jesus' pure hands will murder the false Jewish messiah. Where? In the city of Lod, in Palestine."

Author Shamim A. Siddiqi of Flushing, New York, put the classical position of Islam toward Christianity clearly in a recent letter to Daniel Pipes, *New York Post* columnist:

> Abraham, Moses, Jesus, and Muhammad were all prophets of Islam. Islam is the common heritage of the Judeo-Christian-Muslim community of America, and establishing the Kingdom of God is the joint responsibility of all three Abrahamic faiths. Islam was the din (faith, way of life) of both Jews and Christians, who later lost it through human innovations. Now the Muslims want to remind their Jewish and Christian brothers and sisters of their original din [religion]. These are the facts of history.

This historical negationism—appearing to affirm Christianity and Judaism whilst in fact rejecting and supplanting them—is a linchpin of Muslim apologetics. What is being affirmed is in fact neither Christianity nor Judaism, but Jesus as a prophet of Islam, Moses as a Muslim, and so on. This is intended to lead to "reversion" of Christians and Jews to Islam, which is what Siddiqi refers to when he speaks of "the joint responsibility" of Jews and Christians to establish "the Kingdom of God." By this he means that American Christians and Jews should work to establish Sharia law and the rule of Islam in the United States.

Conclusion

'Isa (Jesus) of the Qur'an is a product of fable, imagination, and ignorance. When Muslims venerate this 'Isa, they have someone different in mind from the Yeshua or Jesus of the Bible and of history. The 'Isa of the Qur'an is based on no recognized form of historical evidence, but on fables current in seventh-century Arabia.

For most faithful Muslims 'Isa is the only Jesus they know. But if one accepts this Muslim "Jesus," then one also accepts the Qur'an: one accepts Islam. Belief in this 'Isa is won at the cost of the libel that Jews and Christians have corrupted their scriptures, a charge that is without historical support. Belief in this 'Isa implies that much of Christian and Jewish history is in fact Islamic history.

The Jesus of the gospels is the base upon which Christianity developed. By Islamicizing him, and making of him a Muslim prophet who preached the Qur'an, Islam destroys Christianity and takes over all its history. It does the same to Judaism.

In the end times as described by Muhammad, 'Isa becomes a warrior who will return with his sword and lance. He will destroy the Christian religion and make Islam the only religion in all the world. Finally, at the last judgment he will condemn Christians to hell for believing in the crucifixion and the incarnation.

This final act of the Muslim 'Isa reflects Islam's apologetic strategy in relation to Christianity, which is to deny the Yeshua of history and replace him with a facsimile of Muhammad, so that nothing remains but Islam.

> The Muslim supersessionist current claims that the whole biblical history of Israel and Christianity is Islamic history, that all the Prophets, Kings of Israel and Judea, and Jesus were Muslims. That the People of the Book should dare to challenge this statement is intolerable arrogance for an Islamic theologian. Jews and Christians are thus deprived of their Holy Scriptures and of their salvific value.[2]

APPENDIX: THE HISTORICAL EVIDENCE FOR JESUS (YESHUA) OF NAZARETH AND HIS DEATH BY CRUCIFIXION

Non-Christian Sources for Jesus

- Tacitus (55–120 CE), a renowned historical figure of ancient Rome, wrote in the latter half of the first century that "Christus . . . was put to death by Pontius Pilate, procurator of Judea in the reign of Tiberius: but the pernicious superstition, repressed for a time, broke out again, not only through Judea, where the mischief originated, but through the city of Rome also" (Annals 15:44).
- Suetonius writing around 120 CE tells of disturbances of the Jews at the "instigation of Chrestus," during the time of the emperor Claudius. This

could refer to Jesus, and appears to relate to the events of Acts 18:2, which took place in 49 CE.

- Thallus, a secular historian writing perhaps around 52 CE, refers to the death of Jesus in a discussion of the darkness over the land after his death. The original is lost, but Thallus's arguments—explaining what happened as a solar eclipse—are referred to by Julius Africanus in the early third century.
- Mara Bar-Serapion, a Syrian writing after the destruction of the Temple in 70 CE, mentions the earlier execution of Jesus, whom he calls a "King."
- The Babylonian Talmud refers to the crucifixion (calling it a hanging) of Jesus the Nazarene on the eve of the Passover. In the Talmud Jesus is also called the illegitimate son of Mary.
- The Jewish historian Josephus describes Jesus' crucifixion under Pilate in his Antiquities, written about 93/94 CE. Josephus also refers to James the brother of Jesus and his execution during the time of Ananus (or Annas) the high priest.

Paul's Epistles

- Paul's epistles were written in the interval twenty to thirty years after Jesus' death. They are valuable historical documents, not least because they contain credal confessions that undoubtedly date to the first few decades of the Christian community.

Paul became a believer in Jesus within a few years of Jesus' crucifixion. He writes in his first letter to the Corinthians, "For I delivered to you first of all that which I also received: that Christ died for our sins according to the Scriptures, and that He was buried, and that He rose again on the third day according to the Scriptures, and that he was seen by Cephas (Peter), then by the twelve." This makes clear that belief in the death of Jesus was there from the beginning of Christianity.

The Four Gospels

- The four gospels were written down in the period twenty to sixty years after Jesus' death, within living memory of the events they describe.

The events that the gospels describe for the most part took place in the full light of public scrutiny. Jesus' teaching was followed by large crowds. There were very many witnesses to the events of his life. His death was a public execution.

Manuscript Evidence for the Bible and Its Transmission

The manuscript evidence for the Greek scriptures is overwhelming, far greater than for all other ancient texts. Over twenty thousand manuscripts attest to them. Whilst there are copying errors, as might be expected from the hand of copyists, these are almost all comparatively minor and the basic integrity of the copying process is richly supported.

Futhermore, when Western Christians studied the Hebrew scriptures during the Renaissance, they found them to agree remarkably closely with their Greek and Latin translations, which had been copied again and again over a thousand years. There were copying errors and some other minor changes, but no significant fabrications of the stupendous scale that would be required to concoct the story of Jesus' death.

Likewise when the Dead Sea Scrolls were discovered, they included Hebrew biblical scrolls dating from before the time of Jesus. These too agreed very closely with the oldest Hebrew Masoretic manuscripts of more than a thousand years later. Again, no fabrications, but evidence of remarkably faithful copying.

CONCLUSION: JESUS OF NAZARETH IS A FIGURE OF HISTORY

Clearly there are events recorded in connection with Jesus' life that many non-Christians will not accept, such as the miracles, the virgin birth, and the resurrection. However what is beyond dispute is that Yeshua ("Jesus") of Nazareth was a figure of history, who lived, attracted a following in his lifetime among his fellow Jews, and was executed by crucifixion by the Roman authorities, after which his followers spread rapidly. Both secular and Christian sources of the period agree on this.

The primary sources for the history of Jesus' public life are the gospels. These were written down relatively soon after his death—within living memory—and we have every indication that these sources were accepted as reliable in the early Christian community, during a period when first- and secondhand witnesses to Jesus' life were still available.

We conclude that any statements about 'Isa (Jesus) in the Qur'an, made six centuries after Jesus' death, must be judged against the historical evidence from these first-century sources, and not vice versa.

Some useful discussions of these issues are found at:

http://www.debate.org.uk/topics/theo/islam_christ.html

http://www.debate.org.uk/topics/theo/qur-jes.htm
http://www.answering-islam.org/Intro/replacing.html
Further reading: *The Jesus I Never Knew*, by Philip Yancey (Grand Rapids, MI: Zondervan, 1995).

NOTES

1. Ahmad ibn Naqib al-Misri, *The Reliance of the Traveller: A Classic Manual of Islamic Sacred Law*, ed. and trans. Nuh Ha Mim Keller (Evanston, IL: Sunna Books, 1991), p. 603.

2. Bat Ye'or, *Islam and Dhimmitude: Where Civilizations Collide*, trans. Miriam Kochan and David Littman (Madison, NJ: Fairleigh Dickinson University Press, 2002), p. 370.

ISLAM AND THE
54. DHIMMIS

Bat Ye'or

In his article "Islam and the Jews: Myth, Counter-Myth, History,"[1] Mark Cohen inquires whether, in the Middle Ages, Jews under Islamic rule were "treated better than their brethren in Europe." He then posits two opposing theses: the "myth" of Judeo-Islamic harmony and its "counter-myth," referring to my recent book[2] as "a classic example of this revisionist trend." Cohen's article has the merit of opening a debate on factual comparative history and its validity as a basis for value judgments. I will endeavor to examine these two aspects, but will first make a few necessary corrections to some of his statements.

My book is not limited to an exclusively Jewish perspective, but rather encompasses all aspects of the dhimmi condition. Consequently, Cohen has quoted me out of context in relation to my expression: "thirteen centuries of sufferings and humiliations," since it refers to the experiences of both Jews and Christians.

The association of Jews (and Christians) with the Devil is not uncommon in Islam. Numerous Quranic verses and hadiths associate the Jews and Christians with both hell and Satan; Ibn Abdun (d. 1134), a Muslim jurist from Spain, quoted from the Qur'an (58:20) to this effect in his legal treatise.[3] The decree of Caliph al-Mutawakkil (850) illustrates this association, whereby "wooden images of devils be nailed to the doors of their homes to distinguish them from the homes of Muslims."[4] Moreover, Jewish and Christian cemeteries were considered a part of hell, to which the dhimmis were destined.

Article (Rejoinder: "Islam and the *Dhimmis*") published in *Jerusalem Quarterly* 42 (Spring 1987): 83–88. The original text was translated from the French by David G. Littman, with the author.

The notion of collective guilt is encountered in Muslim legal texts and has led to collective reprisals. As for forced conversions, it is clear from the account of Joseph ibn Aqnin (d. 1220) and al-Marrakushi (d. 1224) that Jewish converts to Islam were not only persecuted, but also their children could be abducted and entrusted to Muslim custodians.[5] Jews did become the property of Muslim rulers in Morocco, in the Saharan regions of North Africa, in Kurdistan, in Bukhara, and elsewhere.

As for the economic function of the Jews that Cohen notices in Christendom but not in Islam, it seems to me to be at the very root of the dhimmi status, as defined in the Qur'an (9:29) and in the hadith relating to the Jews of Khaybar and the Jews and Christians of Sawad (Iraq). Moreover, this is also the origin of the *jizya* (poll tax), as well as of the higher taxation paid by dhimmis and of the fiscal oppression to which they were subjected. Numerous legal texts link the dhimmis' existence to their economic utility, concerning which history has preserved several examples. The *jizya* did not only have an economic function, but the degradation attached to the tax itself was intended to debase the dhimmis.

I also disagree with Cohen's arbitrary periodization (640–1240) because this methodology is specious, despite the apparent chronological parallel. Different civilizations do not necessarily evolve along similar lines. Besides, a comparison between Christendom and Islam during any other time segment (e.g., the Age of Emancipation and Enlightenment) would provide a completely different picture. But even if one adopts Cohen's *chosen* period, the expulsions of Jews from Christian Europe to which he refers occurred after 1240 (e.g., 1290, 1306, 1394, 1492–97), while under Islam they occurred during that period (and after). It should also be recalled that the *auto-da-fé* (public burning) of the Talmud that took place in Paris under St. Louis (1240) was instigated by Nicholas Donin, a renegade Jew, and was in fact the indirect result of a Jewish controversy between rabbinical literalists opposing the rationalists of the school of Maimonides.

The first three centuries of Islam in the East overlapped the Carolingians in Christian Europe (747–987), a period recognized by Cohen as one when European Jewry "experienced a considerable degree of security and prosperity." Rare indeed are the extant documents from the first two centuries of Arab conquest. Muslim chroniclers later described the ongoing jihad, involving the destruction of whole towns, the massacre of large numbers of their populations, the enslavement of women and children, and the expropriation of vast regions. This picture of catastrophe and destruction corresponds to the period of the gradual erosion of Palestinian Jewry. According to al-Baladhuri (d. 892), forty thousand Jews lived in Caesarea alone at the Arab conquest, after which all trace of them is lost. Indeed, this period (640–1240) witnessed the total and definitive destruction of Judaism and Christianity in the Hijaz and the decline of the once flourishing Christian and Jewish communities in Palestine (particularly in Galilee for the Jews), Egypt, Syria, Mesopotamia, and Persia. In North Africa, the Christians had been virtually eliminated by 1240 and the Jews decimated by Almohad persecutions. It is perfectly true that during much of the earlier Umayyad rule in Spain the situation of Jews was, on the contrary, prosperous; similarly, in Egypt and beyond, the Shiite Fatimids reigned with tolerance. However, notwithstanding some brighter intervals, these six centuries witnessed a dramatic demographic reversal, whereby the Arab-Muslim minority developed into a dominant majority, resorting to oppression in order to reduce the numerous indigenous populations to tolerated religious minorities. The emergence of a rich class of merchants should not obfuscate the overall picture of marked deterioration.

Cohen has chosen northern Europe as his "point of comparison with Islam, so that the contrast will be sharpened with more meaningful distinctions" (instead of southern Europe, where the Jews had a long indigenous presence, as in the Islamized lands). In all fairness, he should have compared this alleged European Christian heartland to its equivalent—the Islamic heartland—Arabia, North Africa, the Sahara—rather than to the Islamized Byzantine regions, with their ethnic and religious pluralism. Jews and Christians were expelled and forbidden to reside in the Hijaz (Arabia). Christianity was eliminated and Judaism could only survive in degradation on the fringes of the Arab heartland (Yemen). This is because Islamic legislation distinguishes between Arab land and *kharaj* land (i.e., the conquered land of the dhimmis), and accordingly stipulates different regulations concerning the indigenous non-Muslim peoples. Only within dhimmi lands (i.e., conquered territory), with its Judeo-Christian cultural heritage, was pluralism tolerated for economic and political reasons. Pluralism is not indigenous to Islamic culture (a concept which needs to be defined), but an element incorporated by conquest into Muslim dominions where a Scriptuary (*ahl al-kitab*/People of the Book) population resided.

The alleged nonapplication of the Pact of Umar on the basis of its innumerable renewals is a classic argument whose logic escapes me. On the contrary, I consider its frequent renewal and the attempts to enforce its strict application as proof of the Muslim authorities' determination to reimpose it in every generation. The sources that I have consulted, including British diplomatic correspondence up to the end of the nineteenth century, confirm this situation.

Another classic argument is that the Jewish dhimmis suffered less since they shared their status with the Christians. Either it means that Jews allegedly suffered less because Christians were also oppressed—which is not only untrue but spurious; or it means that Christians suffered more than Jews—which is true, but this argument is irrelevant to the comparison between the status of the Jews in Christendom and in Islam. Besides, it does not prove that Jews did not suffer.

Referring to A. L. Udovitch's point that the stipulations concerning the Jew are "incorporated subject by subject into the conventional categories of the classical Islamic law codes," Cohen concludes: "This stands in sharp contrast to the isolation of Jewry law provisions in the law of medieval Christian states and is a reflection of the greater degree of integration of the Jew in medieval Muslim society." For my part, I find in these approaches merely a difference of method in the classification of legal matters by Christian and Muslim jurists. This disparity appears in all aspects of their respective laws and is not restricted to the subject of Jews. It is not the arrangement of laws in a book, "subject by subject," which determines the degree of social integration of the persons involved, but the very substance of the laws themselves and, even more so, the actual behavior in real life.

Cohen criticizes me for "characterizing every bleak aspect of the Judeo-Islamic experience as 'the dhimmi condition.'" Having defined the terms *dhimma* and *dhimmi* in my book, I shall not reiterate my analysis here, it being understood that dhimmis designate the Jews and Christians—and sometimes others—under Muslim rule. Just as the history of Western Jewry is studied against its Christian background, so, too, the history of the dhimmis should be understood in its Islamic environment, rather than in a vacuum.

The analytical method of comparison often masks certain snares. Thus, in view of the differing attitude of Christianity and Islam on the subject of usury, Cohen concludes that the West—but not Islam—degraded the Jews by forcing them to practice usury, which was repugnant to the Christians. Yet in Muslim countries the most degrading tasks were set aside for the Jews: executioners, grave-diggers, head-salters of rebels, cleaners of latrines, and so on. Consequently, it was not the principle of social degradation that differed from East to West, but the nature of the impositions.

This brings us to the fundamental issues. What scientific value is there in an arbitrary time division that proposes a value judgment embracing thirteen centuries while considering only a single period? Surely Jewish emancipation, equal rights, human rights, and secularization are also part of Christian societies. Human societies not being static, they must be considered as evolving entities of dynamic interactions, concerning which periodization should exclude generalizations. Besides, should one's judgment be on a short- or long-term basis?

Moreover, the historian who wants to express a value judgment must establish preliminary criteria for evaluations. What is tolerance? Should one judge the dogmas that are subject to diverse interpretations, or the historical facts based on complex elements of a circumstantial and temporary nature? Supposing the concept of tolerance can be defined, should one speak of relative tolerance—that is, toward one people (the Jews), whereas other peoples may be exterminated—or of absolute tolerance?

Cohen's analysis emanates from a specific European perspective, ignoring realities that are exclusively Islamic: for example, the devastating effect of invading nomads, and a bellicose Bedouin mentality, upon Jewish (and Christian) rural populations with sedentary cultures; the jihad rules, such as the obligatory billeting of Muslim soldiers on dhimmi peasantries; military slavery; the peculiarities of Muslim justice and government; and the repercussions for dhimmi communities of the Muslim doctrine that all children are born Muslim.

Cohen's article only quotes antisemitic features that are peculiar to Christianity, and this leads him to conclude that since Muslims did not have Christological reasons for oppressing Jews, the latter were ipso facto better treated. But reality is not so simple, nor so logical. Why should there not have been other original forms of oppression in the Islamic world that were absent in European societies? Cohen has tried to show that the West had a greater motivation to persecute the Jews; he has not proven that Jews were in fact less oppressed under Islam. These two propositions are not necessarily linked.

It would certainly be interesting to pore over the demographic statistics—comparing the percentages in absolute and proportional terms of Jewish converts and martyrs, respectively, in the East and West, according to year and country—that one presumes Cohen has used to infer that European Jewry confronted with persecutions often preferred martyrdom, while Oriental Jewry chose conversion to Islam.

Many of Cohen's assertions are subjective opinions and pure hypotheses, since it is impossible to apprehend thirteen centuries of a history spanning Europe, Asia, and Africa. In fact, the futility and inadequacy of this sort of comparison are evident. The criteria for comparative studies are inevitably chosen from among the register of Jewish sufferings in the West, and never the reverse. Thus it can be asked: what is the Christian equivalent—say, for the fifteenth century—of Jewish (and Christian) girls being abducted for Muslim harems; the *devçirme* system (enslavement and forced conversion of Christian children); the Turkish collective deportation of Jews and Christians, which followed similar earlier Arab practices; the legalization of their enslavement (including women and children) during warfare, revolts, or for economic reasons (impossibility of paying the *jizya*); the obligation for a Jew or a Christian to dismount from his donkey on sight of a Muslim; the obligation in some regions for Jews to walk barefoot outside their quarters; or the prohibition for Jews and Christians of Persia to remain indoors when it rained for fear of polluting Muslims. And when does one find in Islam a current similar to the Christian philo-semitic movement after the sixteenth-century Protestant Reformation? The list of such "disputations" is endless.

My book was not written in order to destroy a flimsy "myth." The discarding of the amorphous image of a "golden age," allegedly spanning thirteen centuries and three continents, was an indirect consequence of my research on dhimmi history, in which I distinguish historical stages and the diversity and complexity of its interdependent aspects. I voluntarily refrained from moral judgments based on fallacious comparisons, for the Christian and Islamic civilizations are coherent and systemic entities, from which one cannot arbitrarily extract one particular element without taking into account the whole historical and cultural context that makes it comprehensible. Moreover, these comparisons serve no other purpose than to prove the superiority of Islam—or of Christianity—which for a historian is pointless. For my part, I do not consider myself a referee who awards points and penalties. Students of history know full well that there is nothing more widely shared among mankind than cruelty and barbarity, but it has not been my task to determine who outdid whom.

NOTES

1. Mark Cohen, "Islam and the Jews: Myth, Counter-Myth, History," *Jerusalem Quarterly* 38 (Spring 1986): 125–37.

2. Bat Ye'or, *The Dhimmi: Jews and Christians under Islam*, preface by Jacques Ellul, trans. David Maisel, Paul Fenton, and David G. Littman (Madison, NJ: Fairleigh Dickinson University Press, 1985).

3. Ibid., document 10, p. 187.

4. Ibid., document 8, pp. 185–86.

5. Ibid., documents 12, 94, 98, 99, and others.

55. ANSWERING AL-AZHAR

Bat Ye'or

I read with interest Dr. Abdel-Moti Bayoumi's refutation of my article "Jihad and Human Rights Today"[1] in his "Wrong Zionist Perceptions of *Jihad* in Islam via the Internet."[2] Regrettably, Dr. Bayoumi has totally misunderstood my position. I am not engaged in the discussion as to whether the jihad is justified or not by the Qur'an and the Sunna. This is a matter among Muslim scholars and I am happy to see that it is being vigorously undertaken by Dr. Bayoumi himself, as the secretary of the Islamic Center of Al-Azhar University in Cairo. He described me as an "American Jewish writer." Born in Cairo, I was obliged to leave the country of my birth, stateless, in 1957; I have been a British citizen since 1959.

Indeed, I wrote that Muslim jurisconsults from the eighth and ninth centuries have based the doctrine of jihad on their interpretation of Quranic verses and on the hadiths. Dr. Bayoumi's contestation of these interpretations in the twenty-first century is very encouraging. However, Muslim opponents advance other verses and invoke the Quranic principle of abrogation, according to which some later verses abrogate the earlier ones. As one of the most prominent Islamic scholars in Cairo, Dr. Bayoumi's opinions on the correct interpretation of the Qur'an concerns Muslim scholars. Non-Muslims—and certainly not myself—have no part in this discussion. It is noteworthy that Dr. Bayoumi has recognised that a war situation between the *dar al-Islam* (the region of Islam) and the *dar al-Harb* (region of war)

Rejoinder to Dr. Abdel-Moti Bayoumi, secretary of the Al-Azhar University, Cairo. Submitted to *National Review Online* after Dr. Bayoumi replied to an initial article by Bat Ye'or ("Jihad and Human Rights Today," July 1, 2002). Neither Dr. Bayoumi's text nor Bat Ye'or's rejoinder was published in NRO. This text, published here for the first time, was translated from the French by David G. Littman, with the author.

existed in the past, but he was misled in attributing to me an opinion on jihad in fact given by the al-Muhajiroun London organization that I quoted clearly in my text.

Concerning the UN's 1948 Universal Declaration of Human Rights, Muslim scholars have explained their reservations about it by the fact that it is based on secularism and a Judeo-Christian tradition, a principle which they refute because, according to them, it is opposed to Islam, which does not separate politics and religion. This argument is repeated countless times by distinguished Muslim scholars. Hence, the need to have an Islamic Declaration of Human Rights based on Sharia regulations. Muslims consider such a charter as universal because the universality of the Islamic mission is enshrined in Islam's doctrine and in the Qur'an. However, billions of Hindus, Chinese, Christians, and others who are not Muslims will not accept the Sharia's regulations and, therefore, in our pluralistic world it cannot be described as "universal." The quotation "Reaffirming the civilization and historical role of the Islamic *Ummah* which God made the best nation that has given mankind a universal and well-balanced civilization . . . and the role that this *Ummah* should play to guide a humanity confused by competing trends and ideologies" is in the preamble of the 1990 Cairo Declaration on Human Rights in Islam. Its concluding articles state: "All the rights and freedoms stipulated in this Declaration are subject to the Islamic *Shari'ah*";[3] "The Islamic *Shari'ah* is the only source of reference for the explanation or clarification of any of the articles of this Declaration."[4]

Dr. Bayoumi has denied slavery in Islam, yet slavery in Islam is very well documented in Muslim chronicles and all legal treatises that expound the tactics of jihad and the fate of prisoners from the earliest times. Hence, Abu Yusuf Yaqub, in the eighth century, states that Khalid b. al-Walid enslaved thousand of inhabitants in Iraq and Syria in the course of his military campaigns (634–637). Not only distinguished Islamic and Western scholars have written extensively on slavery in Islam, but also countless historic chronicles exist from the countries where slaves were taken: Armenian, Greek, Serb, Hungarian, French, Italian, Spaniard, and others. Piracy for slaves existed in the Barbary States until it was ended by the naval battle of Algiers (1816) and at the 1818 Congress of Aix-La-Chapelle. The living condition of Christian slaves in Algiers was described extensively by American consul general William Shaler in his *Sketches of Algiers*.[5]

In his book on Egypt under Muhammad Ali,[6] Mohammed Sabry, an Egyptian scholar, provided details on the campaign ordered by Muhammad Ali in the Sennar region of Sudan to collect gold and to bring forty thousand slaves for his army (1820–1822). The exaction of the Egyptian soldiers provoked an insurrection among the Africans who killed the Egyptian general; this led to a retaliatory massacre of thirty thousand Africans. Muhammad Ali's son, Ibrahim, was sent to quell the Greek insurrection against the Ottoman sultan. In his campaign he enslaved thousand of Greeks, whom he sent to Cairo and Istanbul. These facts are recorded in the French consular papers because France backed Muhammad Ali's policy.

Recently, in a letter to former UN high commissioner for human rights Mary Robinson, dated March 24, 1999 (circulated then at the UN Commission on Human Rights), the former elected prime minister of Sudan, al-Sadiq al-Mahdi—referring to slavery in Sudan today—wrote: "The traditional concept of JIHAD . . . is based upon a division of the world into two zones: one the zone of Peace, the other the zone of War. It requires initiating hostilities for religious purposes. . . . It is true that the [NIF] regime has not enacted a law to realize slavery in Sudan. But the traditional concept of JIHAD does allow slavery as a by-product."[7] Prime Minister al-Sadiq al-Mahdi, a pious Muslim, is the great grandson of al-Mahdi who practiced traditional slavery abundantly in Sudan.

As for the accusation by Dr. Cornelius Hulsman against me,[8] it does not deserve an answer. Hatred is not born from truth, but by defamation.

The comment of a modern Greek historian, writing on the Islamized Christian slaves in the fourteenth century, is pertinent: "Spiritually reborn into the Islamic world, they became the state's most disciplined, zealous, and able soldiers. It was they who dealt the Byzantine Empire its final and most decisive blows. It was they who were the most merciless persecutors of their fellow countrymen and former coreligionists. It was they who contributed most signally to the organization, extension, and consolidation of the Ottoman state."[9]

Slavery is not only the bondage of the body but also of the soul.

NOTES

1. Bat Ye'or, "Jihad and Human Rights Today," *National Review Online*, July 1, 2002, http://www.nationalreview.com/comment/comment-yeor070102.asp.

2. Bayoumi, Abdel-Moti, "Wrong Zionist Perceptions of Jihad in Islam via the Internet,"*Al-Musawwar* (mainstream Egyptian Arabic weekly), August 23, 2002, p. 55.

3. "Cairo Declaration of Human Rights in Islam," adopted and issued at the Nineteenth Islamic Conference of Foreign Ministers in Cairo, August 5, 1990, article 24.

4. Ibid., article 25. It was published in the UN's *Regional Instruments*, vol. 2 of *Human Rights: A Compilation of International Instruments* (New York/Geneva: UN [Office of the High Commissioner for Human Rights], 1997).

5. William Shaler, *Sketches of Algiers: Political, Historical, and Civil, Containing an Account of the Geography, Population, Government* (Boston: Cummings & Hilliard, 1826).

6. Mohammed Sabry, *L'Empire Egyptien sous Mohamed-Ali et la Question d'Orient, 1877–1849* (Paris: Paul Geuthner, 1930).

7. Under the subheading "War Crimes," section III.

8. See the replies of Dr. Bayoumi in the Q/A of September 3, 2002, to the questions of Dr. Hulsman, editor in chief of the Religious News Service for the Arab World, Cairo.

9. Apostolos E. Vacalopoulos, *The Greek Nation, 1453–1669: The Cultural and Economic Background of Modern Greek Society*, trans. Ian and Phania Moles (New Brunswick, NJ: Rutgers University Press, 1976), p. 44.

ISLAM, TABOO, AND DIALOGUE

56. Reclaiming Historic Truths in Seeking Present-Day Solutions

Bat Ye'or

In the current political climate, it is tempting to maintain the taboos on those historical subjects that could be easily exploited by xenophobes. One such taboo is dhimmitude, which resulted when Christians and Jews (dhimmis), in addition to other non-Muslim indigenous peoples, were conquered by jihad wars, and henceforth "tolerated" and "protected" as subjects of Islam. This "tolerance" and "protection," however, was afforded only upon submission to Islamic domination by a dhimma, or pact, that imposed discriminatory and humiliating regulations. The main principles of dhimmitude are: (1) the inequality of rights in all domains between Muslims and dhimmis; (2) the social and economic discrimination against the dhimmis; and (3) the degradation and vulnerability of the dhimmis.

Dhimmitude has existed for thirteen centuries in the Muslim empire, established, primarily, on former Christian lands. Extending over three continents—Africa, Asia, and Europe—this field of history was the setting for jihad, the Crusades, the Reconquista, and the Balkan and Israeli wars of independence. Countless populations, swept along in the whirlwind of centuries, were marked in the crucible from which issued the death of civilizations and the birth of others. Dhimmitude convulsed the whole nineteenth century, and Europe—as obsessed as it was divided—floundered in endless debates on the Eastern question: how to put an end to dhimmitude.

World War I effected a 180-degree turn. Colonial imperatives; World

---

The core of this article first appeared in a French newspaper version in 1997 and then as "Islam and Taboo" in *Midstream* 44, no. 2 (February–March 1998): 7. This enlarged text appeared in *National Review Online*, August 9, 2002, with editing contributions from Dr. Andrew Bostom. The French texts were translated by David G. Littman, with the author.

War II and the cold war; oil, economic, geostrategic, and religious interests in the Muslim world—all combined to suppress this history. Today, a heightened desire for security recommends leaving this cadaver to rot in its bandages of lies and oblivion. Is amnesia not preferable, particularly during the crisis period we currently live in? Not at all. A candid discussion of this history of dhimmitude, which embraces the three-dimensional relationship of the People of the Bible—Jews and Christians—and of the Qur'an, is essential if current ideological conflicts are to be unraveled and deadlocks broken.

Let us hope we have not missed the opportunity to talk frankly and initiate that critical dialogue with the Muslim elites about dogmas and jurisdictions that were so traumatic for the People of the Book—Jews and Christians, whom Islam joined together in the same dhimmi status—"protected" and "tolerated," because subjugated and humiliated. It is imperative for Jews, Christians, and Muslims to explore together the cruel episodes in this shared history in order to alleviate, if not eliminate, the cultural conflicts in which religious fanaticism takes root.

Following the cataclysmic events of September 11 there has been a tendency to recall nebulous "golden ages" of idyllic multireligious societies, invented so effectively that today one feels defenseless and disoriented when brought face-to-face with the conflicts from another age, deliberately erased from history. We must forgo this whitewashing and opt instead for a shared, candid reflection on the past to unite us in a joint effort for peace and mutual respect. The history of dhimmitude, so long repressed by our collective cowardice, is unfolding around us, before our very eyes. It is claiming victims in Algeria, Egypt, Palestine, Lebanon, Sudan, Nigeria, Iran, Pakistan, Kashmir, the Philippines, Indonesia, and elsewhere. It even forms part of our daily lives, governed by antiterrorist measures in the United States, Europe, and now worldwide, and it wreaks havoc among the Muslim elites, responsible for having concealed it. This forbidden history, banished from memory, is casting its dark shadow over the world's future.

Dhimmitude must be discussed in academia, the media, and elsewhere, without apology. This frank discussion will allow Muslim intellectuals to rethink their whole relationship with the People of the Book—and non-Muslims in general—without renouncing their faith, and uniting all peoples in the fight against tyrannical oppression and dehumanization. In the absence of such genuine interfaith dialogue, I fear the twenty-first century will become a bloodbath in which civilizations will continue to collide.

ISRAEL, CHRISTIANITY, AND ISLAM

57. The Challenge of the Future

Bat Ye'or

U nlike most wars, solving the conflict in the Middle East does not depend only on the cession of land, since Israel is also the focus of age-old religious hatreds. The bigotries involved are so appalling that one avoids mentioning them, yet they still underlie the struggle.

From its beginnings, the Arab-Israeli conflict involved not only the region of the Middle East but also Europe and the Church. It was hardly on account of its wealth and territorial extent that the Holy Land became a land of hostilities, but rather because it was the place where theological extremisms confronted one another. Only there, in their ancient homeland, could the Jewish people be freed from the curse with which Christianity had afflicted them. This malediction, which had been transmitted through Christian channels to Islam, was henceforth combined within the context of jihad and associated Jews and Christians in the same condemnation. Thus, the principle of a divine curse against the Jews as a people, first conceived by the early Church Fathers in patristic writings, was later adopted and reinterpreted through Islamic dogma against both Jews and Christians.

Despite the Islamic persecutions of Christians, Judeophobia—common to both Christianity and Islam—has sealed the tight alliance between the Church and Islam in favor of the Palestinian cause. Thus, in the Land of Israel, the Jewish people have been confronted not only by prejudices arising from Christian ideas but also by those arising from Islamic doctrine. The suppression of these Muslim prejudices against Jews that are generated by jihad

Article published in *Midstream* 47, no. 3 (February–March 2001): 2–9. The original text was translated from the French by David G. Littman, with the author.

doctrine would also imply the abolition of these same Muslim prejudices against Christians. The restoration of Israel's rights in its biblical homeland is opposed to a concept of allegedly accursed peoples, hated by God and condemned to humiliation for eternity until they convert. Peace in the Middle East means equality among religions. Therefore, their historical zones of confrontation and interaction should be examined in order to understand their modern expressions.

CHARACTERISTICS OF THE CONFLICT

The Arab-Israeli conflict is only one regional, limited aspect of the traditional, worldwide struggle engendered by the ideology of jihad. For over a millennium, Muslims had conquered and held lands populated by Christians and Jews on three continents: Africa, Asia, and Europe. In East Asia, they also colonized and Islamized Buddhist and Hindu empires. Caliphs and sultans administered this multitude of peoples through a legal-political system based on interpretations of the Qur'an and the hadiths,[1] which integrated the pre-Islamic laws and customs of the vanquished peoples into an Islamic conceptual structure. This system of governing subjected populations, which I have called *dhimmitude*,[2] determined the demographic, religious, and ethnic changes in the countries absorbed by jihad. The term *dhimmitude* encompasses all the aspects and complexities of a political system, whereas the word *tolerance* implies a subjective opinion. The system of dhimmitude includes the notion of tolerance, but this latter term cannot express all the interactions of political, religious, and legal factors that over the centuries shaped the civilization of dhimmitude.

The jihad ideology requires that the Sharia—the law that governs the Islamic domain—be applied over all the jihad-conquered lands. In this context, the Jews formed a small minority among the non-Muslim populations, all to be targeted by the jihad ideology. Islamic law confers an identical status on Jews and Christians as the People of the Book (the Bible), while Zoroastrians and others, considered pagans, were relegated to a far worse situation and subjected to more severe oppression.

In the Muslim-Christian context, the jihad wars of Islamization, unleashed from the seventh century and sustained for over a millennium, have again—in the last decades—ignited jihad fires in Lebanon, the Balkans, the Caucasus, Armenia, Sudan, Nigeria, Kashmir, the Philippines, and Indonesia. The Arab-Israeli conflict is only a recent and small component of the age-old geographic struggle that emerged from this jihad ideology. From the Islamic point of view, the position of the Jews, as with the Christians, comprises two aspects: as Jews and as Israelis. The first concerns their legal situation as a tolerated, dhimmi religious minority in an Islamic country. The second is rooted in the complex issues involved in a dhimmi people liberating its country from the laws of jihad, a system that imposes dhimmitude.

This process of liberation was manifested in all the Christian countries, where—from Portugal to the Caucasus—the laws of dhimmitude imposed by invading jihad armies on indigenous non-Muslim populations were progressively abolished. It is this common ground that imparts to these east European states, and to Israel, certain similar factors that are superimposed over different characteristics. In fact, these similarities do not result from any European backing of Israel, but rather these links emerge from the Islamic doctrine that binds together Jews and Christians.

Common Traits

Without going into historical detail, one may recall that those European Christian lands Islamized by jihad were liberated only after centuries of bloody struggle. The process of de-Islamization began in the Middle Ages, first in Spain, Portugal, and the Mediterranean Islands; it then continued in the eighteenth century and throughout the whole of the nineteenth century in the Balkans. In central Europe, Islamized territories had reached up to southern Poland and Hungary; in the nineteenth century they still encompassed Greece, Serbia, Montenegro, Bulgaria, and the semiautonomous Romanian principalities. These wars of national liberation continued up to World War I. The recent bloody, unfinished conflicts in the Balkans are a reminder.

From the standpoint of Muslim dogma and law, Israel's situation today is not very much different from these nineteenth-century Balkan wars of liberation. Like the Israelis, those peoples also were threatened with annihilation by a jihad war that challenged their right to separate from the *dar al-Islam*. As with Palestine, the Balkan territories conquered by jihad constituted a *waqf* in Islamic law—also called a *fay* land, the booty granted by Allah to the Islamic community collectively—to be managed by the caliph.

Moreover, the *waqf* principle is not limited to territories conquered by jihad. According to this dogma, the whole world constitutes a *waqf*, promised by Allah to the Muslims; it is a religious duty to occupy it at an appropriate time and rule it by the Sharia law. It is this duty that imposes upon the Muslims the obligation of jihad, by which these lands—still illegally held by the infidels—"revert" to the Muslims. There lies the origin, the justification, and the ideological driving force behind the jihad wars of conquest. It is incorrect to assert that this injunction to achieve world conquest is a modern extremist interpretation by Islamist fanatics, as some contemporary political commentators assert. This interpretation has in fact constituted the basis of jihad since its principles were first elaborated by Muslim jurists and theologians in the eighth and ninth centuries. In this context, the principle of *waqf* land applied to Israel constitutes a tiny part of a universal, geopolitical concept. If Israel— whatever its size—is viewed as illegally established on "Arab-Muslim lands," then Spain, Portugal, the Balkan states, and so on may also be considered as occupying former "Muslim lands." And, likewise, all non-Muslim states are "illegal," since they are situated on potential Muslim *waqf* land.

The nineteenth-century wars of liberation restored national territorial sovereignty to east European peoples, in the same way as the Jewish people recovered a part of their Land of Israel (Palestine) in 1948. This process allowed the free development of their culture and their legal system. The rebirth of those Christian states led to the dramatic flight to Anatolia, Syria, and Palestine of millions of Muslims, whose laws had subjected the indigenous non-Muslims to the dehumanizing system of dhimmitude. It would be an absurdity in the twenty-first century to claim that the descendants of those populations suffered an "injustice" and had a "right of return" to Spain, Portugal, Sicily, the Balkans, and elsewhere. It would destabilize the descendants of those peoples who had suffered over the centuries under the yoke of dhimmitude.

The wars that abolished the system of dhimmitude suppressed an injustice, which any return to the previous situation would reimpose. As with these European examples, the "right of return" to the State of Israel for Palestinian Arabs—the embodiment of jihad values—would restore those same conditions leading to dhimmitude for the Jews. It should be stressed that dhimmitude implies the expropriation of indigenous people, who are relegated to dhimmi status after their land has become a Muslim *waqf* for the sole benefit of the Muslim community (*umma*). Jews and Christians are only tolerated as dhimmis, provided they submit to restrictive rules that include prohibition on land ownership in their own country.

To sum up, it may be affirmed that from an Islamic doctrinal viewpoint, Israel's situation is identical to that of those European populations from Portugal to the Crimea, passing through Sicily and the Balkans of the Ottoman Empire, who managed to free themselves from the laws of dhimmitude—

laws imposed as a result of a jihad war and the application of the Sharia. The abolition of those laws enabled these populations to restore their national independence and their rights. The clash here is between the liberation of dhimmi people against their subjugation and death in the grip of dhimmitude.

Contrasting Aspects

Geographically speaking, Israel's situation differs from that of the Balkan peoples, since Israel—like Lebanon, Georgia, and Armenia—is wedged into a wholly Muslim region. In other respects, even though the condition of the Jews and Christians as dhimmis is identical from the Islamic point of view, there are important differences on the theological and the political levels.

Theological Aspects

On the doctrinal plane, there is convergence and fusion between the Christian idea that alleges a divine condemnation of the Jews to exile and degradation and the Muslim doctrine that retains the divine condemnation of the Jews to humiliation but applies it also to the Christians. For Jews, the Islamic position represented an improvement compared to Christian theology, which isolated them from the rest of humanity in a unique, demonized category. For the Christians, to be placed on the same level as the people who aroused their hate-filled contempt was severely felt as a further deliberate humiliation imposed on them by Islam. This resentful attitude on the part of the Christians was one factor contributing for so long to the obfuscation of the history of dhimmitude, which was the common juridical and theological condition for both Jews and Christians.

Christianity developed from Judaism. The breach of this close symbiosis was accompanied by a hostile rejection of the mother religion. It is important to stress that the conflict between the early Byzantine Church and Palestinian Jewry was fought most intensely in the Holy Land itself—where Judaism had been central since the second millennium BCE. When the Roman Empire was Christianized in the early fourth century, the patriarchate could then reimpose the emperor Hadrian's ban on Jews living in Jerusalem (135 CE), which, it seems, had lapsed. In the fifth century, the alliance between a Church, strongly influenced by paganism, and the Byzantine state institutionalized in law and policy the Church Fathers' anti-Jewish statements. It was in fifthcentury North Africa that St. Augustine (d. 430), bishop of Hippo—today Bône in Algeria—most clearly formulated the view that prevailed pertaining to the Jewish people: a "deicide people" condemned to exile and to wandering in servitude and degradation.

The idea of supersession constituted the foundation of the Church's policy toward Judaism and the de-Judaization of Jerusalem. The responsibility for upholding this idea fell upon the Church in the Holy Land. It was this Church that supervised the exclusion of Jews from Jerusalem, their humiliation, and the implementation of their persecution. Only a few years before the Arab conquest, after the brief Persian occupation and at the instigation of the patriarch Sophronius, the emperor Heraclius decreed the first massacre of Jews in the Byzantine Empire. It was this same patriarch who later implored the Muslim conquerors to retain one basic principle of Christian praxis: the de-Judaization of Jerusalem. Thus, it was through local Christian channels that this policy was transmitted to Islam. Conscious of being the guardians of this idea, the churches in the Holy Land heaped humiliation and suffering on Palestinian Jewry and upon the few allowed back in Jerusalem by the Muslim authority.

In this Christian theological context, the Zionist movement and the Balfour Declaration of 1917 fed the frenetic antisemitism that provided a fertile ground in Christian Europe for the Holocaust. The Christian idea that condemned the Jews to wandering and to degradation was maintained largely unchallenged until Second Vatican Council (1962–1965). Revision of this view aroused passionate opposition, particularly within the Eastern Arab dhimmi Churches, mouthpieces of their patrons, the Arab League states.

Despite the efforts of religious and lay Christians who felt close to Jews and Judaism, the results of Second Vatican Council were rather ambiguous and marked the success of the antisemitic majority in the Catholic Church. They maintained a policy of delegitimizing and demonizing the State of Israel and supported its replacement by a State of Palestine. In other words, the principle of "wandering" remained a decisive goal. Besides, the condemnation of antisemitism was not accompanied by a total rehabilitation of the Jews. This ambiguity allowed Christians to pity the misfortunes of the Jews, allegedly brought about by their own malevolent natures.[3] Indeed, the ambiguity allowed Christians in subsequent decades to reconcile compassion for Jews with the most virulent hostility toward Israelis. The transfer of the malevolent nature of the Jews to the State of Israel was steadily sustained by a tireless activism from the Palestinian church leaders allied to the Palestine Liberation Organization (PLO).

This whole process of demonizing the State of Israel was conceived of, elaborated upon, and transmitted to Europe by these Palestinian dhimmi Arab

Churches. The reunification of Jerusalem in 1967 exacerbated that tendency; ever since, the European populations have been flooded in the media by anti-Israeli indoctrination.[4] It is true that the proclamations of national councils of bishops in Europe expressed different, more positive opinions. Yet the anti-Zionist phobia—culminating in the 1975 antisemitic UN General Assembly's resolution 3379 ("Determines that Zionism is a form of racism and racial discrimination")—only began to abate when this resolution was rescinded in December 1991, after the Gulf War. When, in December 1993, the Vatican recognized Israel, it almost simultaneously recognized the Palestinian National Authority (PNA). This step left the unpleasant impression that the belated establishment of diplomatic relations with Israel needed to be balanced by recognition of the PNA.

This situation resulted from the weight of the antisemitic and pro-Islamic tendencies representing a sizable sector of the Church. Those same currents had succeeded in imposing on Second Vatican Council in 1965 a perfectly symmetrical position on the part of the Church in regard to both Jews and Muslims. But this symmetry caught the Church in a trap, since the relation of Christianity to the Jews was totally asymmetrical to the Church's position toward Muslims—even being in contrast to it. The Christian idea of supersession concerns the Jews, but not Muslims. Conversely, Islam applied this idea to Judaism and Christianity, both of which, according to Islamic doctrine, were preceded and completed by Islam. The biblical personalities mentioned in the Qur'an, who barely resemble the originals—Abraham, Moses, David, Solomon, Jesus, and others—are considered Muslims. The absence of such reasoning in Judaism concerning Christianity creates a false symmetry between Judaism and Islam.

Likewise, on a historical plane, no Christian country was ever conquered by the Jews, but Christian lands were Islamized on three continents—Africa, Asia, and Europe—and governed by the Sharia. Moreover, from its beginning, Islamic jurisprudence established and perfected a mandatory Christian status, based on theology. Hence, there is an absolute absence of symmetry in the theological, juridical, political, and historical domains between Islam and Judaism in relation to the Christians. The Christian refusal to acknowledge the radical asymmetry between Judeo-Christian and Muslim-Christian relations creates confusion on the path to reconciliation. Moreover, this symmetry, which allegedly represents "justice," does injustice to the Jews, because it denies the obvious differences between Judaism and Islam.

Despite many high-quality works by Christian theologians and thinkers—and their tireless efforts supporting a Judeo-Christian rapprochement—anti-Judaism and anti-Zionism still remain dominant forces throughout Europe. In addition, the pro-Islamic lobbies use the Jewish tragedy of the Holocaust to invent a European guilt toward Palestinian Arabs and Muslim immigrants in Europe, as allegedly symmetrical to Europe's guilt for the Holocaust. Thus, not only has the Holocaust been taken over for the benefit of those who otherwise deny it and want to pursue a policy for Israel's demise, but the unjustified exaggeration of Christian guilt toward Islam—based on a false connection to the Jewish tragedy in Europe—reinforces antisemitism. This tactic is widespread among certain clerical groups in both the Eastern and Western "Islamized" Churches, especially in their wide support for a free Muslim immigration policy into the European Union.

Political Aspects

Generally speaking, since the 1970s, the policy of various European governments toward Israel has been manifested by hostility. This policy has combined the economic and political interests of these states with their rivalries to obtain markets in the Arab world, especially for sales of military weapons. This cynical policy has not been burdened by any scruples and has hidden its purposes under cover of "humanitarian causes"—particularly that of the Palestinian Arabs.

In this context, Israel is treated like those Christian peoples whose claims hindered the interests of the major European powers in the nineteenth century. State interests took precedence over any solidarity regarding humanitarian principles. In the nineteenth century, only public opinion obliged the powers to intervene belatedly to curtail the massacres of Christians during the course of the many rebellious struggles in the Balkans. Later in the century, the Armenians were abandoned, since no European power, even Russia, had an interest in destabilizing Turkey.

After World War I, France and Great Britain sacrificed the claims of the Armenians and the Assyro-Chaldeans (in Iraq) in favor of a pro-Muslim policy. Half a century later, the destruction of the Christian political structures in Lebanon by the Muslim-Palestinian alliance left Europe and America generally indifferent. This Christian tragedy earned no more than shameful silence from most European intellectuals and in the media—particularly from all those who showed compassion for the Arab Palestinians, day after day, for decades. This observation applies equally to the victims in East Timor and the Moluccas as well as to the Sudanese African Christians and animists, who for years have undergone a jihad war and enslavement by northern Arab Muslims without much protest from the European Union. This silence was all the more striking in that it contrasted with the massive media campaign on behalf of the Muslims in Bosnia, in Kosovo, and later in Chechnya. Today, the genocide of Christians in Indonesia is hardly mentioned in the press.

Furthermore, the various forms of discrimination suffered more and more by Christians in Muslim countries have rarely aroused a media campaign or consistent interest from major humanitarian organizations. One could therefore place Europe's anti-Zionist option in the category of general political cynicism. This raises the question of what political criteria determine the media's "selection" of information: is it criteria operating through either omission, disinformation, systematic neglect (Algeria, Sudan, Nigeria, East Timor, the Moluccas, the Philippines, etc.), and/or directly related to economic and geostrategic interests?

Hence, in its relations with the Muslim world, the West applies a similar policy to Christians and Jews alike. One should also stress—and it is of major importance—the totally different policy of the Turks from that of the Arabs toward former dhimmi populations. The Ottomans in the nineteenth century and Turkey in the twentieth century received and settled millions of Muslim refugees, and both made peace with their former subjugated peoples. With the exception of Jordan (78 percent of the former League of Nations Palestine Mandate), the other twenty states of the Arab League, despite covering immense territories—10 percent of the earth's surface—refused to welcome, settle, and grant citizenship to their Palestinian Arab kin; only Egypt and Jordan have recognized Israel's de jure existence.

THE SHORT-TERM POLICY OF ECONOMIC INTERESTS

European democracies are governed by parties whose representatives dispose of little time to apply their policies, which are based mainly on economic and social improvement. As a rule, the aims of democracies are short-term issues. This situation does not exist in third world dictatorships—like Egypt, Syria, Iraq, and Libya, for example—whose dictators-for-life plan long-term ideological policies. Experts usually claim that economic development is an essential factor toward achieving peace and the suppression of hatred and prejudice. This claim is belied by the situation in Saudi Arabia, one of the richest countries in the world, where the prejudices toward women and non-Muslims have barely changed over the centuries. Moreover, such generalizations neglect significant civilizational differences, whereby some societies bestow prestige on a religious-inspired, warlike strategy of world conquest over any current economic considerations. In the jihad civilization, peace is only an interval between a continuation of hostilities.

The overlapping of the two domains, the economic and the political, has fostered Europe's—especially France's—Arab policy; in the years ahead, this policy will develop significant political and cultural changes in Europe. In particular, one may point to wide divergences concerning the status of women, polygamy, and the integration of some Sharia rules into the European juridical system, as demanded by millions of the recent Muslims immigrants to Europe. The European Union's Arab policy is rooted in a planned political project, which aims at creating a Euro-Arab economic and geostrategic continent conceived as a counterbalance to American influence. It implies the fusion of North-South populations and the intensification of European economic interests in the Arab and Muslim world. Since the 1960s, a European immigration policy has been developed within this economic-strategic context.

This Euro-Mediterranean, North-South project had as its utopian model the "Andalusian paradise" of a perfect Muslim-Christian symbiosis. This foundation myth served to consolidate the Euro-Arab alliance and to project the responsibility for the current discrimination undergone by Christians in Muslim countries onto Israel's intransigence. The European Union refuses to denounce Islamic religious prejudices, preferring to expiate its impotent frustration on Israel. Yet it is obvious that the discrimination in question is rooted in the laws of the Sharia. This mythical Andalusian paradise would be reborn—it has often been claimed since the 1970s—if only a democratic Arab Palestine were to replace Israel. Here it is important to point out that this Andalusian multicultural paradise is a political myth. In reality, female Christian slaves taken in continuous border raids filled the Andalusian harems, and the Muslim state's power was based on armed forces made up of thousands of Islamized Christian male slaves, while all non-Muslims remained dhimmis. They were governed by rulers who enforced the rigorous Malikite Islamic rite. Andalusia—a typical example of a jihad-orientated country—was constantly agitated by Christian insurrections, while all traces of Christianity in Muslim-conquered Spain were eliminated from the thirteenth century until the Reconquista in the sixteenth century.

PALESTINIANISM: THE DHIMMI PALESTINIAN-CHRISTIAN CONTRIBUTION IN THE CONTEXT OF THE EURO-ISRAEL-ARAB RELATIONSHIP

The contribution of the Palestinian Arab Christians in this context is considerable in three areas of policy: (1) the Muslim immigration into Europe; (2) the ongoing destruction of Christianity in the Arab and the larger Muslim world; and (3) the growing European anti-Zionism.

The theme of Muslim-Christian symbiosis, a "golden age" preceding the advent of "Sin"—personified by the State of Israel—replaced history with myth. This theme, which forms one of the principles of Arab nationalism, was propagated especially after the 1920s. It embodied in the Levant, and especially in Mandatory Palestine, a policy of Muslim-Christian collaboration against Zionism. After 1948, this myth formed the weapon justifying the elimination of the Jewish state.[5] It provided a strategy absolving the Arab world of any guilt, Israel being held responsible for the sufferings of the Christians in the region. This connivance allowed trade between the West and the Arab-Muslim world without hindrance. It reinforced the anti-Zionist campaign and curbed the Judeo-Christian rapprochement.[6] However, this policy, as practiced by Palestinian Arab Christians, both lay and clergy, does not represent all Christian opinions. The success of this propaganda in Europe since the 1960s—totally disproportionate to the demographic importance of the Palestinian Arab Christians, well under 5 percent of the total Palestinian Arab population—results from alliance with antisemitic lobbies. Today, these same Christians are faced with the progress of the Hamas movement in the areas now under Yasir Arafat's administration.

Arab immigration into Europe had been planned and encouraged from the early 1960s on by European politicians and their Arabist advisors. It continued the pro-Arab, pro-Muslim policy maintained by European powers and Church hierarchies since the beginning of the century. In the 1960s, the overtures to other religions announced after the Second Vatican Council represented a generous innovation that broke with the prejudices of the past. Concerning the Jews, however, the policy of rapprochement with Judaism was counterbalanced by anti-Zionism and the defense of Palestinian interests. Thus, the condemnation of antisemitism went hand in hand with the propagation of anti-Zionism. The unilateral commitment of the Vatican and many Protestant churches to the advocacy of the Palestinian Arab cause sustained the Christian theology of supersession that had delegitimized the State of Israel.

After the Second Vatican Council, and at the instigation of the Palestinian churches, Catholic and Protestant theological bodies reinforced their dialogue with Islam.[7] Rapprochement with Judaism was overshadowed by Christian interests in the Muslim world and the adamant opposition of Arab Churches. These dhimmi churches function solely within the conceptual universe of dhimmitude, which they have perpetuated for thirteen centuries. Their survival is linked to their promotion of Muslim interests, the "service" of the dhimmis to Islam.

"Palestinianism" has sidelined the history of dhimmitude and prevented its critical examination. The knowledge of these realities would have encouraged the desacralization of the traditional Muslim prejudices concerning the People of the Book. Such a step would have led to a Muslim aggiornamento. But the Muslim-Christian symbiosis, which was to be accomplished in a future democratic Palestine—on Israel's demise—became virtually a dogmatic axiom. It prevented any knowledge of the history and of critical reflection about Muslim-Christian relations in the context of jihad and dhimmitude—the concepts that were at the very foundation of these relations. The prohibition on challenging this Muslim-Christian symbiosis imposed a taboo on the deteriorating conditions of Christian communities in Muslim countries.[8] As Israel was labeled the "Evil" in order to maintain the Euro-Muslim alliance, this general silence also contributed to a worsening of their own situation, inducing an irreversible Christian movement of conversion to Islam and a massive emigration from Arab Muslim countries to the West.[9]

For both commercial and theological motives, holding Israel guilty for the deterioration of the condition of the Christians in the Arab world is still a common practice. This response forms part of a continuing tradition of triangular relations between Jews, Christians, and Muslims in the context of dhimmitude. In the past, persecuted by Muslims and powerless to avenge themselves upon their persecutors, Christians often took out their frustration by attacking Jews. The persecution of Jews in medieval Europe was often a Christian reaction to Muslim persecutions suffered by Christians in Spain and the Levant. The modern indictment of the State of Israel forms part of this tradition. Not daring to confront the Arab world, for fear of losing their markets, European politicians take revenge on Israel for their own impotence. However, it is obvious that it is the Sharia laws, unrelated to Israel, that limit the rights of Christians in Arab countries, and the discrimination and attacks they suffer there express traditional Islamic prejudices.

The Palestinian Arab cause was an essential and fundamental element in Europe's anti-Zionism. The Christian idea of the Jews as a "deicide people" was often revitalized by the presentation of a Muslim-Christian Palestine "crucified" by the Jewish state. As recently as December 11, 2000—two weeks before the Christmas Jubilee—a new Palestinian daily, *Intifada*, displayed on half of its front page a provocative caricature showing a crucified young woman with the name "Palestine" above her head. Blood spurts from her martyred body onto a trio of caricatured Jews looking up at the crucified woman were meant to represent Jesus/Palestine. Three days later, *Intifada* provided another message in the design of a massive cross, this time without the crucifixion scene, but with a prayer addressed to "My Lord the Betrayed—betrayed by the contemptible treasonable kiss," and ending: "O Son of the Virgin, they cannot overcome you twice."[10]

Pressed by the Arab states, the Palestinian dhimmi Churches torpedoed the Judeo-Christian rapprochement in Europe. As the heirs and guardians of an age-old tradition of debasing, even of murdering, Jews in their homeland, they loudly justified the PLO's international campaign of terrorism. The political struggle against Israel prolonged and updated the theological struggle.

This phenomenon is unrelated to legitimate criticism of some aspects of Israeli policy, as is normal for any state. Rather, it derives from the compulsive urge to hate and defame. Deicidal allusions, ritual murder and world conspiracy accusations, supersessionist theology, and negationism of the Holocaust are constantly recycled in the Muslim-Christian media of the Middle East, including the Palestinian, while the European Union continues to finance the PNA's educational system, which even omits Israel's existence on maps.

Thus, as Europeans become reconciled with the Jewish communities in the EU countries—negligible populations that survived a European genocide—anti-Zionism projects all its traditional prejudices onto the State of Israel, which has come to embody the malevolent nature of Judaism itself. It is true that the religious catechisms have been expurgated, but every day the teaching of contempt echoes in another register. The more antisemitism is condemned, the more anti-Zionism is unleashed by a sort of mimicry. This recycling of old hatreds projects onto the victims the crimes of their oppressors. The more Israel's Christian friends try to modify the Churches' understanding, the more support for Palestinianism and Palestinian Arab supersessionism is reinforced. Arab-Palestine is seen as the heir to biblical Israel and the root of Christianity itself. The negation of Israel's identity and history has enhanced the purity of the replacement theology.

It is not by coincidence that anti-Zionism has grown to such proportions in Europe, in that same continent where the Holocaust was perpetrated. For decades, in some countries, Nazi collaborators and sympathizers were to be found in senior places of power within the state, high finance, and the media. Efforts to judge those responsible have often been blocked. Only Germany, under an international obligation to do so, has courageously undertaken a critical examination of its own past. By championing the Palestinian Arab cause, European antisemitism has absolved itself, removing the stain of guilt and projecting it, with a vengeance, onto the Jews by demonizing and "Nazifying" Israel.

It is not easy to estimate the strength of political European antisemitism today, bearing in mind the objections to publish pro-Zionist opinions in the mainstream media. Indeed, it is certain that the success of anti-Zionism can only be explained by the occult, or overtly political, support it receives at the highest political and religious levels. Nonetheless, the Catholic encyclical *Nostra Aetate* (1965), the tireless struggle against antisemitism by many Catholic and Protestant theologians, the Vatican's recognition of Israel, and the desire to deepen and maintain the Judeo-Christian rapprochement—as exemplified by Pope John Paul II's pilgrimage to Israel in March 2000— have created new forms of behavior. The secularization of Western societies and increasing individualism have developed the most varied range of opinions among all sectors of the population. Without a constant media pounding as in recent years—strengthened from October 2000 with the second *intifada*—it would be difficult to discern a consensus of European public opinion, although the tendencies and policies of the European Union are clear. Some indicators for the future trends may be seen in: (1) the violently hostile reactions to the 1996 election of Binyamin Netanyahu as prime minister; (2) the explicit boycott by the European Community of the third millennium Jerusalem celebration (a denial of its Jewish biblical history); (3) the refusal to recognize even West Jerusalem as the capital of the State of Israel (a symbolic reminder of the prohibition of Jewish sovereignty in Jerusalem); (4) praise for Ehud Barak so long as Palestinian demands were constantly satisfied in the "peace process"; (5) the anti-Israeli war propaganda in the media after Arafat launched Intifada II; (6) the almost universal hostility to Ariel Sharon's election; and (7) the growing tendency to root Christianity in Arab Palestinianism.

The End of Judeo-Christianity?

Is the road toward "Palestinian Liberation Theology" leading to a total divorce between the two religions? The rejection of its Jewish roots has constituted a permanent movement in the Church. This problem appears clearly at two levels. The first has led to the elimination of the Jews, justified by their demonization. As many Christians have so well understood, the Holocaust and the Nazi return to paganism sounded Christianity's death knell. In other words, the executioner perishes spiritually in the death of his victim.

The second level appears in a process of de-Christianization, through hatred of a Jewish essence and spirituality structuring and sustaining Christian thought. The total expulsion of Judaism from the Christian consciousness is taking place through the elaboration of a theology seeking to de-Judaize the Bible, including the New Testament. It has already been expressed in Europe through the "Palestinization" of the Bible—that is, in its de-Judaization.[11]

Palestinian Liberation Theology thus forms part of this historical movement to eliminate Judaism from Christianity. Jesus is no longer considered to be a Jew born in Judea but an Arab from Palestine—so, too, his mother, his family, his disciples, and the apostles. This travesty would seem childish if it did not actually express an implicit desire to expel Judaism totally from Christianity and to usurp its heritage through Muslim-Christian Palestinianism. The de-Judaization of Christianity proceeds from a self-destructive dynamic and an impossibility to reconcile the hatred for Jews with the Jewish origin of Christianity. This hatred is particularly virulent in the historic Palestinian paganized Churches—in the Land of Israel itself—and explains this new avatar of the theology of supersession. The filial relationship between Judaism and Christianity is unacceptable and scandalous for Christian Arabs steeped in anti-Judaism. It is out of this conflict between a Christianity born of Judaism and its rejection of Judaism that arise "the Bible problems" of the Palestinian Christians. The current attempts to detach the New Testament from the Old by de-Judaizing Jesus, and his disciples and apostles (through their Palestinization, Arabization, or even Islamization), fall within the scope of this controversy.

Yet the positive change in Vatican policy toward Israel, as well as the Judeo-Christian rapprochement, undermines the traditional Judeophobic stance of the Syrian-Palestinian Churches. These Churches are now confronted by a revision of theology that removes them from the role of Israel's victims, which they enjoyed and widely proclaimed throughout the world, and places them in the role of persecutors of the Jewish people in its ancient homeland for nearly two millennia. And this role—for which they have not yet atoned—excludes them from assuming the position of the arbiters of "justice" in relation to the Jews and Israel.

The de-Judaization of the gospels, and of all the biblical texts, indicates an incapacity to reconcile Judaism with Christianity in a Church that first endeavored to bring Jewish ethics to the pagan world. The pagan deviation—represented by Judeophobia as manifested in communism and Nazism—became the greatest digger of Christianity's grave. Today, this same Judeophobic tendency is reappearing in the Arabization of the gospels, and a drift toward Islamizing Christian theology. It is difficult to know whether this step results from Judeophobia itself or from the intolerance of the Islamic environment (which rejects Judaism and Christianity in the same way, hence the Islamization of the Arab dhimmi Churches in their quest for toleration). Be that as it may, this trend, which is currently being relentlessly propagated in Europe by a pro-Islamic, Judeophobic, Christian clergy, forms part of those constant surrenders arising out of the dhimmi mentality.

Making due allowance for historical differences, the situation after the Holocaust is somewhat reminiscent of that which prevailed in the Orient on the eve of Islam's rise in the seventh century and the subsequent collapse of empires. The massacres of Jews by the Byzantine emperor Heraclius at the instigation of the Palestinian clergy was followed a few years later by the Arab conquest and the Islamization of large areas of Eastern Christendom. The latter was facilitated by virulent anti-Judaism and bloody doctrinal conflicts among the Churches, an alliance between the Christians and the Muslims against the Jews and against each other, a spiritual void, and corruption among the leaders of both Church and State.

HISTORY—WHY BOTHER?

One often hears that history is superfluous. The truth is that history becomes a snare for those who forget it and for those who get bogged down in it and try to revive it today at all costs. The liberating dimension of history can only develop through the relativization of conflicting truths and through the resolve not to revive history but to invent a future. Yet a knowledge of history is essential for inventing the future. Forgetting history leads one to fall fatally into its pitfalls.

The tragic developments in Lebanon since the mid-1970s may well have been programmed by the political options that were adopted at the beginning of the twentieth century.[12] Likewise, the restoration of the State of Israel represented the outcome of a long process. Europe in twenty or thirty years will have been transformed by policies that were decided in the 1960s and 1970s. Thus history constantly projects itself into the future; it is not an insignificant element of the past but an active catalyst of our present and our future.

History ought to lead us to reflect upon the ways out of history in order to resolve conflicts through policies of peace and reconciliation. Such policies deal with strategic aspects: territories and borders—but with ideologies, too. The peace that seemed to be taking shape between Israel and its Arab neighbors, including the Palestinian Arabs, implied a total modification of mentalities. Yet the Arabization of biblical geography and history perpetuates within the Palestinian dhimmi Churches the old theology of supersession; they seem condemned either to endless hostility or to an Islamization that underlies the self-proclaimed Palestinian Arabness of their origins.

But peace also means recognizing the Other in respect of his being. Peace must put an end to negationist substitutions, perverse forms of a fundamental rejection of human diversity. For Palestinian Arabs, peace means accepting Israel's legitimacy—de jure, and not by tolerance—as well as Israel's history in its ancestral homeland. And for Israel, peace also means recognizing that Christianity and Islam are universal religions, whose contributions to civilization are fundamental. Peace means accepting and respecting their legitimacy within the State of Israel. The liberation of the Jews in the Land of Israel from the Christian theological curse and from Islamic dhimmitude would abolish for all peoples the concept of divine hatred and divine condemnation.

Ending this history of conflict means approaching one another with equal respect. Then peace among religions, peace among men and women, can radiate from Israel and the Middle East throughout the world, eliminating the darkness of fanaticism. For the restoration of the State of Israel—its acceptance by the nations with its capital Jerusalem—rejects the concept of a people, collectively cursed, excluded from divine love, and dispossessed by replacement theologies. In that way, the atonement for this greatest injustice also bears within it the reconciliation among Jews, Christians, and Muslims.

NOTES

1. Sayings or acts attributed to the prophet Muhammad that are considered normative and obligatory. Compiled in manuals of Islamic jurisprudence, they form—

with the Qur'an—the foundation of Islamic law, the Sharia. According to Muslim doctrine, the Qur'an, the Hadith, and the Sharia are expressions of the divine will, hence their character as a sacred norm that cannot be violated.

2. *Dhimmitude*: from the word *dhimmi*—the condition attributed by the Islamic conquerors to the non-Muslim populations vanquished by jihad. It means "protected," since these indigenous, non-Muslim peoples were theoretically protected from death or slavery if they submitted to Islamic rules. For a historical overview, see *The Decline of Eastern Christianity under Islam: From Jihad to Dhimmitude*, trans. Miriam Kochan and David G. Littman (Madison, NJ: Fairleigh Dickinson University Press, 1996). Dhimmitude permeates Muslim religious perceptions of Jews and Christians, and some of its rules are still applicable today, either mildly or strictly, in several Muslim countries. For an analysis of what I call the "civilizations of dhimmitude," see *Islam and Dhimmitude: Where Civilizations Collide*, trans. Miriam Kochan and David G. Littman (Cranbury, NJ: Fairleigh Dickinson University Press, 2002).

3. The late Abbé Youakim Moubarac, a Syrian Catholic priest, and secretary-general of the Council of Catholic Patriarchs of the Orient, became the most virulent protagonist of this thesis. See his, *L'Islam et le Dialogue Islamo-Chrétien*, vol. 3 of *L'Islam et le Dialogue Islamo-Chrétien. Pentalogie Islamo-Chrétienne*, 5 vols. (Beyrouth: Edition du Cénacle Libanais, 1972–1973), pp. 155–70. Father Moubarac's theses are described in *Islam and Dhimmitude*, as well as those of Canon Naim Stifan Ateek and Bishop Kenneth Cragg, a former Anglican deputy bishop of Jerusalem.

4. Within a week of the beginning of the al-Aqsa *intifada* in October 2000, under the auspices of the Jerusalem patriarch Michael Sabbah, the chancellor of the Latin Patriarchate, Fr. Raed Awad Abusahlia, seized the occasion to begin a pernicious anti-Israel campaign by the publication of twelve-page "messages" twice a week, through his Olive Branch from Jerusalem. They aimed at persuading Western churches and groups to influence their governments in favor of the Palestinian cause and to exert maximum pressure on Israel. This "service" is discussed in the conclusion to *Islam and Dhimmitude*.

5. For this symbiosis, see Robert Brenton Betts, *Christians in the Arab World: A Political Study* (London: SPCK, 1979), pp. 226–27. This "golden age" myth was regularly expressed by Arab politicians and clergymen; for example, by Abbé Moubarac, who quotes the then Syrian patriarch Sayegh in his *L'Islam et le Dialogue Islamo-Chrétien* vol. 4 (*Les Chrétiens et le monde arabe*), p. 64, and vol. 5 (*Palestine et Arabité*), p. 139.

6. The Arab League strongly opposed the movement for Jewish-Christian reconciliation by insisting—through the Eastern dhimmi churches—on maintaining the "deicide people" accusation.

7. Moubarac gives details in his *Palestine et Arabité*, p. 28.

8. Michel Hayek, a Lebanese Maronite priest, declared: "Why not admit clearly—so as to break a taboo and a political proscription—what is so resented in the flesh and in the Christian conscience: that Islam has been the most dreadful tor-

ment that ever befell the Church. Christian sensibility has remained traumatized to this day." "Nouvelles approches de l'Islam," *Les Conférences du Cénacle* (Beyrouth) 22, no. 970 (1968); English translation from *Islam and Dhimmitude*.

9. See *Middle East Quarterly* 8, no. 1 (Winter 2001). The entire issue is devoted to "Disappearing Christians of the Middle East."

10. A long spear transfixes the woman's body and the cross, its protruding point embossed with a star of David, and an American flag at the shaft end. (Palestinian Media Watch, December 13 and 15, 2000, pmw@netvision.net.il.) At Easter 1997, in a mock Passion Play, three Arab Palestinians had themselves bound to crosses at Har Homa overlooking Jerusalem, with the inscription: "The Crucifixion of the Peace Process, of Jerusalem, and of Bethlehem." The Palestinian poet Mahmoud Darwish—probably assisted by Christians—often exploits the traditional Christological anti-Jewish themes of the crucifixion.

11. Abbé Moubarac proposes to "débiblioniser" ("de-Bible-ize") the Bible, in his *L'Islam et le Dialogue Islamo-Chrétien*, pp. 124–25. This theme is discussed in *Islam and Dhimmitude*.

12. Walid Phares, *Lebanese Christian Nationalism: The Rise and Fall of an Ethnic Resistance* (Boulder, CO: Lynne Rienner, 1995).

HONEST INTELLECTUALS MUST SHED THEIR
58. SPIRITUAL TURBANS

Ibn Warraq

Aldous Huxley once defined an intellectual as someone who had found something in life more important than sex: a witty but inadequate definition, since it would make all impotent men and frigid women intellectuals. A better definition would be a freethinker, not in the narrow sense of someone who does not accept the dogmas of traditional religion, but in the wider sense of someone who has the will to find out, who exhibits rational doubt about prevailing intellectual fashions, and who is unafraid to apply critical thought to any subject. If the intellectual is really committed to the notion of truth and free inquiry, then he or she cannot stop the inquiring mind at the gates of any religion—let alone Islam. And yet, that is precisely what has happened with Islam, criticism of which in our present intellectual climate is taboo.

The reason why many intellectuals have continued to treat Islam as a taboo subject are many and various, including:

- political correctness leading to Islamic correctness;
- the fear of playing into the hands of racists or reactionaries to the detriment of the West's Muslim minorities;
- commercial or economic motives;
- feelings of postcolonial guilt (where the entire planet's problems are attributed to the West's wicked ways and intentions);
- plain physical fear;
- and the intellectual terrorism of writers such as Edward Said.

Reprinted from the *Guardian*, November 4, 2002.

Said not only taught an entire generation of Arabs the wonderful art of self-pity (if only those wicked Zionists, imperialists, and colonialists would leave us alone, we would be great, we would not have been humiliated, we would not be backward) but intimidated feeble Western academics, and even weaker, invariably leftish, intellectuals into accepting that any criticism of Islam was to be dismissed as Orientalism, and hence invalid.

But the first duty of the intellectual is to tell the truth. Truth is not much in fashion in this postmodern age when Continental charlatans have infected Anglo-American intellectuals with the thought that objective knowledge is not only undesirable but unobtainable. I believe that to abandon the idea of truth not only leads to political fascism but stops dead all intellectual inquiry. To give up the notion of truth means forsaking the goal of acquiring knowledge. But man, as Aristotle put it, by nature strives to know. Truth, science, intellectual inquiry, and rationality are inextricably bound together. Relativism, and its illegitimate offspring, multiculturalism, are not conducive to the critical examination of Islam.

Said wrote a polemical book, *Orientalism* (1978), whose pernicious influence is still felt in all departments of Islamic studies, where any critical discussion of Islam is ruled out a priori. For Said, Orientalists are involved in an evil conspiracy to denigrate Islam, to maintain its people in a state of permanent subjugation, and are a threat to Islam's future. These Orientalists are seeking knowledge of Oriental peoples only in order to dominate them; most are in the service of imperialism.

Said's thesis was swallowed whole by Western intellectuals, since it accords well with the deep anti-Westernism of many of them. This anti-Westernism resurfaces regularly in Said's prose, as it did in his comments in the *Guardian* after September 11. The studied moral evasiveness, callousness, and plain nastiness of Said's article, with its refusal to condemn outright the attacks on America or to show any sympathy for the victims or Americans, leave an unpleasant taste in the mouth of anyone whose moral sensibilities have not been blunted by political and Islamic correctness. In the face of all evidence, Said still argues that it was US foreign policy in the Middle East and elsewhere that brought about these attacks.

The unfortunate result is that academics can no longer do their work honestly. A scholar working on recently discovered Quranic manuscripts showed some of his startling conclusions to a distinguished colleague, a world expert on the Qur'an. The latter did not ask, "What is the evidence, what are your arguments, is it true?" The colleague simply warned him that his thesis was unacceptable because it would upset Muslims.

Very recently, Prof. Josef van Ess, a scholar whose works are essential to the study of Islamic theology, cut short his research, fearing it would not meet the approval of Sunni Islam. Gunter Luling was hounded out of the profession by German universities because he proposed the radical thesis that at least a third of the Qur'an was originally a pre-Islamic, Christian hymnody, and thus had nothing to do with Mohammed. One German Arabist says academics are now wearing "a turban spiritually in their mind," practicing "Islamic scholarship" rather than scholarship on Islam. Whereas biblical criticism has made important advances since the sixteenth century, when Spinoza demonstrated that the Pentateuch could not have been written by Moses, the Qur'an is virtually unknown as a human document susceptible to analysis by the instruments and techniques of biblical criticism.

Western scholars need to defend unflinchingly our right to examine Islam, to explain its rise and fall by the normal mechanisms of human history, according to the objective standards of historical methodology.

Democracy depends on freedom of thought and free discussion. The notion of infallibility is profoundly undemocratic and unscientific. It is perverse for the Western media to lament the lack of an Islamic reformation and willfully ignore books such as Anwar Shaikh's *Islam—The Arab Imperialism* or my *Why I Am Not a Muslim*. How do they think reformation will come about if not with criticism?

The proposed new legislation by the Labour government to protect Muslims, while well intentioned, is woefully misguided. It will mean publishers will be even more reluctant to take on works critical of Islam. If we stifle rational discussion of Islam, what will emerge will be the very thing that political correctness and the government seek to avoid: virulent, racist populism. If there are further terrorist acts, then irrational xenophobia will be the only means of expression available. We also cannot allow Muslims subjectively to decide what constitutes "incitement to religious hatred," since any legitimate criticism of Islam will then be shouted down as religious hatred.

Only in a democracy where freedom of inquiry is protected will science progress. Hastily conceived laws risk smothering the golden thread of rationalism running through Western civilization.

CONTRIBUTORS

BAT YE'OR is the author of four books on jihad and dhimmitude, *The Dhimmi: Jews and Christians under Islam* (1985), *The Decline of Eastern Christianity under Islam: From Jihad to Dhimmitude* (1996), *Islam and Dhimmitude: Where Civilizations Collide* (2002), and her latest study, *Eurabia: The Euro-Arab Axis* (Fairleigh Dickinson University Press, January 2005)

ROY BROWN is president of the International Humanist and Ethical Union, an NGO at the UN, and has written extensively on human rights, humanism, and population issues.

PAUL COOK is advocacy manager for the Institute for the Study of Islam and Christianity in the UK. He headed its international campaign on apostasy and was involved at the UN.

MARK DURIE holds a PhD in Linguistics from the ANU (1984). He is a senior associate of the Department of Linguistics and Applied Linguistics at the University of Melbourne and a minister at St. Hilary's Anglican Church in Kew.

LARS HEDEGAARD is a regular contributor to two Copenhagen newspapers, *Berlingske Tidende* and *Weekendavisen*.

IBN WARRAQ is the author of *Why I Am Not a Muslim* (Prometheus Books, 1995) and the editor of the essay collections *Leaving Islam* (Prometheus Books, 2003), *What the Koran Really Says* (Prometheus Books, 2002), and *The Quest for the Historical Mohammed* (Prometheus Books, 2000).

SHAFIQUE KESHAVJEE is a pastor and author of *The King, the Sage, and the Fool (Le Roi, le Sage, et le Bouffon*, Paris: Le Seuil, 1998), which was translated into fifteen languages.

DAVID G. LITTMAN is a historian, translator, and author of many articles and publications on dhimmis. Since 1986 he has been active on human rights issues for several NGOs at the UN Commission on Human Rights in Geneva. He is currently an NGO representative there for the Association for World Education and World Union for Progressive Judaism.

WALID PHARES is a professor of Middle East Studies at Florida Atlantic University and Senior Fellow with the Foundation for the Defense of Democracies.

DANIEL PIPES is director of the Middle East Forum, a member of the presidentially appointed board of the US Institute of Peace, and a prize-winning columnist for the *New York Sun* and the *Jerusalem Post*. His most recent book, *Miniatures: Views of Islamic and Middle Eastern Politics* (Transaction Publishers) appeared in late 2003.

SAMUEL SHAHID is professor of missions at Southwestern Baptist Theological Seminary in Fort Worth, Texas.

MUHAMMAD YOUNUS SHAIKH, a medical doctor, was sentenced to death for blasphemy in Pakistan in 2001 and spent two years in solitary confinement before his release following a fourth trial. He received asylum in Switzerland, where he now lives.

PATRICK SOOKHDEO holds a PhD from London University's School of Oriental and African Studies. He is director of the Institute for the Study of Islam and Christianity. His books include *A People Betrayed: The Impact of Islamization on the Christian Community of Pakistan* (Christian Focus, 2002) and *Understanding Islamic Terrorism: The Islamic Doctrine of War* (Isaac Publishing, 2004).

ROBERT SPENCER is the director of Jihad Watch. His previous books include *Onward Muslim Soldiers* (Regnery, 2003), *Islam Unveiled* (Encounter, 2002), and *Islam: A Guide for Catholics* (with Daniel Ali, Ascension, 2003).

Srdja Trifkovic is the author of *Sword of the Prophet* (Regina Orthodox Press, 2002); director of the Center for International Affairs at the Rockford Institute, a think tank in Rockford, Illinois; and foreign affairs editor of *Chronicles: A Magazine of American Culture*.

René Wadlow is currently the main representative to the United Nations in Geneva of two NGOs: the Association of World Citizens and the Association for World Education. He is editor of www.transnational-perspectives.org. and formerly professor and director of research at the Graduate Institute of Development Studies, University of Geneva.

Robert S. Wistrich is a professor of modern history at the Hebrew University of Jerusalem, director of its Vidal Sassoon International Center for the Study of Antisemitism, and editor of its journal (*Antisemitism International*). He is the author of many highly acclaimed books and has edited several documentaries for British TV (in 2003, *Blaming the Jews*).